BAMBOULA AT KOURION

The twelfth publication
in the Haney Foundation Series
University of Pennsylvania

Girl smelling a flower, from Window Krater B 1067

BAMBOULA AT KOURION

THE NECROPOLIS AND THE FINDS

Excavated by J. F. Daniel

By J. L. Benson

with contributions by

Edith Porada and J. Lawrence Angel

University of Pennsylvania Press

Philadelphia

Museum Monograph of the University Museum

Publication of this book has been made possible by a grant from
the Haney Foundation of the University of Pennsylvania

Library of Congress Catalog Card Number: 72-133204
ISBN: 0-8122-7635-3
Printed in the United States of America

In memoriam John Franklin Daniel

1910–1948

CONTENTS

PREFACE AND ACKNOWLEDGMENTS

A career of brilliant promise was cut short by the sudden death of J. F. Daniel during a reconnaissance trip in Turkey in 1948. He had just finished his terminal campaign at Bamboula and so had not had time to analyze the results. His work was not taken up again until the summer of 1951, when S. S. Weinberg, with the aid of a grant from the American Philosophical Society, went to Cyprus and made an intensive study of the architecture of the site. He was accompanied and ably assisted by Ellen Kohler, who at all times has rendered useful assistance in the preparation of this volume. The spring of 1953 saw the tragic death of George McFadden, whose interest and financial support had made possible all the excavations undertaken at Kourion by the University Museum of the University of Pennsylvania. In September 1953, G. R. Edwards went to Cyprus for a year to represent the University Museum in the settlement of McFadden's affairs. He was accompanied by J. L. Benson, who undertook to publish all phases of the site of Bamboula, apart from the architecture, and also the necropolis of Kaloriziki. Although his chief task while in Cyprus was the inventorying and studying of the material—especially the voluminous quantity of sherds—excavated by Daniel, time was also found for a brief exploratory excavation. For the academic year 1954/55 the University Museum's Curium Fund provided a fellowship for Benson to study and classify such of the excavated materials as are conserved in Philadelphia, while for the fall term of the academic year 1955/56, the Institute for Advanced Study, Princeton, granted him a membership to continue work on the project.

Other assistance was provided from the Faculty Research Fund of the University of Mississippi during the academic year 1958/59 in the preparation of several articles pertaining to Kourion. J. L. Angel kindly consented to report on the anthropological aspects of the skeletal remains from the necropolis of Bamboula. His work was carried out in Philadelphia in the years 1956–1958. Edith Porada had already made a preliminary study of the Kourion seals during Daniel's lifetime and she evinced her continuing interest in them by describing and commenting on the glyptics in the Catalogue. Sara Immerwahr gave valuable advice and suggestions on the Mycenaean pottery.

Throughout the course of work on this publication, the personnel of the Department of Antiquities of the Government of Cyprus and the staffs of Curium House in Episkopi, the Cyprus Museum and the University Museum (of the latter, G. R. Edwards in particular) have given generously and devotedly of their time and effort to further the project. It is with particular gratitude that acknowledgment is made of the great amount of complex photographic work expertly rendered by the photographer of the University Museum, Reuben Goldberg, who was completing the last stages of this almost at the very hour of his untimely death in 1960. Numerous non-professional friends of the University Museum also gave valuable assistance in the routine and uninspiring tasks which always accompany a large publication of this kind. These are too numerous to acknowledge individually, but it is a pleasure to thank—symbolically for all the others—Allen Reischstein, who gave of his time in particularly generous measure. Likewise, the staff of the Greek and Roman Department of the British Museum kindly facilitated the study and re-publication of objects from the excavations at Kourion conducted by the British Museum at the end of the nineteenth century. For permission to publish these objects I am grateful to the Trustees of the British Museum. Finally, I must acknowledge gratefully the indefatigable assistance and indispensable advice of Linda Benson in the preparation of the manuscript and the plates at all stages of the work.

Because of the division of finds among Curium House, the Cyprus Museum and the University Museum, it has not been possible to obtain uniformity in the photographs and drawings used in the plates. Thus, photographs made by Daniel, Edwards, Goldberg, Benson and the photographers of the Cyprus Museum, and drawings made by C. Polycarpou, G. R. H. Wright, Marion Welker, Leonard Woodworth, Grace Muscarella and J. L. Benson have been combined to illustrate the publication. It proved impossible out of this diversity to organize plates strictly to scale, but full information about the size of objects is, of course, given in the Catalogue. Polycarpou prepared all the drawings of house, tomb and site plans under the able supervision of J. S. Last of Episkopi, who at all times has rendered invaluable and selfless service to the excavation.

The definitive publication of the excavations of J. F. Daniel at Kourion has been completed for eight years except for one expected contribution. Owing to a continuing delay in the preparation of the section on architecture, it has been reluctantly decided to make the completed parts available separately from the architecture. This includes the necropolis and finds from the settlement at Bamboula and a separate volume on the necropolis at Kaloriziki. The report on stratification has, for economic reasons, been separated from the materials just mentioned and is now published in the *Report of the Department of Antiquities, Cyprus* 1969–1970, through the generosity of Dr. Vassos Karageorghis, Director of Antiquities, Cyprus. The report on architecture will also be published separately.

Finally, but by no means least, profound gratitude is owed to the Haney Foundation Series of the University of Pennsylvania and the University Museum itself, which have generously provided substantial financial support to make the publication of this volume possible. The increasing span of years since Daniel excavated and the increase in further exploration and interpretative publication of Cypriote and Aegean material threaten to inundate the very important finds and results which he obtained, unless they are made known. With the single thought of making the material itself available to other scholars as soon as possible, I have limited revision and incorporation of new comparisons and facts to a minimum. Professor E. Porada and Dr. J. L. Angel kindly consented to bring their respective contributions up to date. The revisions mentioned were accomplished in the years 1966 and 1967. I regret that the pressure of other commitments has made any additional revision impossible.

J. L. BENSON

ABBREVIATIONS OF BOOK AND PERIODICAL TITLES

The following list contains abbreviations used in this publication in addition to those current in *American Journal of Archaeology* (see Vol. 69, 1965, 201 ff.). As copious bibliographies for the field of Aegean and Levantine studies are available in *Swedish Cyprus Expedition* IV (2), in *Problems of the Late Cypriote Bronze Age* by E. Sjöqvist and in *The Mycenaean Pottery* by A. Furumark, it has not been thought necessary to repeat them here.

AFF	*Arkeologiska Forskningar och Fynd:* Utgiven till H. M. Gustaf VI Adolfs 70. Årsdag 11.11.1952 (Stockholm). The preliminary report on Sinda published in *AFF* by A. Furumark has been republished in English in *OpusAth* 6, 1965, 99–116: "Excavations at Sinda."
Ain Shems II	E. Grant, *Ain Shems Excavations* Pt. II (Haverford, 1932).
Alalakh	C. L. Woolley, *Alalakh* (Oxford, 1955).
ANE	*The Aegean and the Near East:* Studies presented to Hetty Goldman, ed. by S. S. Weinberg (Locust Valley, N.Y., 1956).
Bamboula SS	J. L. Benson, "Bamboula at Kourion: The Stratification of the Settlement," *Report of the Department of Antiquities, Cyprus,* 1969, 1–28, and 1970, 25–74.
Beck	H. C. Beck, "Classification and Nomenclature of Beads and Pendants," *Archaeologia* 77, 1927, 1 ff.
Beth-Pelet I	W. M. F. Petrie, *Beth-Pelet* I, British School of Archaeology in Egypt (London, 1930).
CatBMV I, II	*Catalogue of the Greek and Etruscan Vases in the British Museum,* Pt. I: Prehistoric Aegean Pottery by E. J. Forsdyke (London, 1925); Pt. II: Cypriote, Italian and Etruscan Pottery by H. B. Walters (London, 1912).
CatJBM	F. Marshall, *Catalogue of the Jewellery . . . in the . . . British Museum* (London, 1911).
CBW	H. W. Catling, *Cypriot Bronzework in the Mycenaean World* (Oxford, 1964).
CCM	J. L. Myres and M. Ohnefalsch-Richter, *A Catalogue of the Cyprus Museum* (Oxford, 1899).
CesAt	L. P. di Cesnola, *A Descriptive Atlas of the Cesnola Collection of Cypriote Antiquities in the Metropolitan Museum of Art, New York,* Vols. I–III (Boston, 1885–1903).
CesCol	J. L. Myres, *Handbook of the Cesnola Collection of Antiquities from Cyprus* (New York, 1914).

ClR	*Clara Rhodos.* Studi e materiali pubblicati a cura dell' Istituto storico-archeologico di Rodi (Rhodes, 1928–1941).
CMP	A. Furumark, *The Chronology of Mycenaean Pottery* (Stockholm, 1941).
CPP	J. G. Duncan, *Corpus of Palestinian Pottery* (London, 1930). *British School of Archaeology in Egypt*, Vol. 49.
CT	A. J. B. Wace, *Chamber Tombs at Mycenae* (Oxford, 1932)—*Archaeologia* 82 (1932).
DFCL	Judy Birmingham. "The Development of the Fibula in Cyprus and the Levant," *PEQ*, 1963, 80–112.
Dikaios, *Guide*	P. Dikaios, *A Guide to the Cyprus Museum* (Nicosia, 1961).
ECCM	E. Coche de la Ferté, *Essai de Classification de la Céramique Mycénienne d'Enkomi* (Paris, 1951). Institut Français d'Archéologie de Beyrouth. *Bibliotheque Archéologique et Historique*, Vol. 54.
Enkomi-Alasia	C. F. A. Schaeffer, *Enkomi-Alasia* (Paris, 1952).
Etudes Crétoises	*Etudes Crétoises.* Ecole française d'Athènes.
ExC	A. S. Murray, A. H. Smith and H. B. Walters, *Excavations in Cyprus* (London, 1900).
Gezer	R. A. Macalister, *The Excavation of Gezer*, I–III (London, 1912).
Hama	H. Ingholt, *Rapport Préliminaire sur Sept Campagnes de Fouilles à Hama en Syrie. Det Kgl. Danske Videnskabers Selskab, Arkeologisk Kunsthistoriske Meddelelser*, III (Copenhagen, 1940).
Kaloriziki	J. L. Benson, *The Necropolis of Kaloriziki* (forthcoming).
KBH	M. Ohnefalsch-Richter, *Kypros, The Bible and Homer* (London, 1893).
Kerameikos I	W. Kraiker and K. Kübler, *Kerameikos, Ergebnisse der Ausgrabungen.* I: Die Nekropolen des 12. bis. 10. Jahrhunderts (Berlin, 1939).
Korakou	C. Blegen, *Korakou.* A Prehistoric Settlement near Corinth. (Concord, N. H., 1921).
Kypriakai Spoudai	ΚΥΠΡΙΑΚΑΙ ΣΠΟΥΔΑΙ (Nicosia, 1946–).
Lachish II	O. Tufnell, C. Inge and L. Harding, *Lachish* II. The Fosse Temple (London, 1940).
Lachish IV	O. Tufnell, *Lachish* IV. The Bronze Age (London, 1958).
LMTS	V. R. d'A. Desborough, *The Last Mycenaeans and Their Successors* (Oxford, 1964).
MCBA	Paul Åström, *The Middle Cypriote Bronze Age* (Lund, 1957).
MCh	C. F. A. Schaeffer, *Missions en Chypre* (Paris, 1936).
Megiddo II	G. Loud, *Megiddo* II (Chicago 1948). Oriental Institute Publications, Vol. 42.

Megiddo Tombs	P. Guy and R. Engberg, *Megiddo Tombs* (Chicago, 1938). *Oriental Institute Publications*, Vol. 33.
MP	A. Furumark, *The Mycenaean Pottery*. Analysis and Classification (Stockholm, 1941).
MPL	F. Stubbings, *Mycenaean Pottery from the Levant* (Cambridge, 1951).
Mycenae	A. J. B. Wace, *Mycenae* (Princeton, 1949).
Myrtou-Pigadhes	J. du Plat Taylor and others, *Myrtou-Pigadhes* (Oxford, 1957).
Nouveaux Documents	Ecole Française d'Athènes, *Etudes Chypriotes*, III. *Nouveaux Documents pour l'Etude de Bronze Récent à Chypre* by Vassos Karageorghis (Paris, 1965).
OA	*Opuscula Archaeologica*. Skrifter Utgivna av Svenska Institutet i Rom.
OpusAth	*Opuscula Atheniensia*. Skrifter Utgivna av Svenska Institutet i Athen.
PM	A. Evans, *The Palace of Minos*, Vols. I–IV (London, 1921–1935).
Problems	E. Sjöqvist, *Problems of the Late Cypriote Bronze Age* (Stockholm, 1940).
RDAC	*Report of the Department of Antiquities, Cyprus.*
Prosymna	C. Blegen, *Prosymna* (Cambridge, Mass., 1928).
SCE	E. Gjerstad, ed., *Swedish Cyprus Expedition*, Vols. I–IV (Stockholm, 1934–continuing).
SPC	E. Gjerstad, *Studies on Prehistoric Cyprus* (Uppsala, 1926).
Tarsus I	H. Goldman, *Excavations at Gözlü Küle, Tarsus*, I: The Hellenistic and Roman Periods (Princeton, 1950).
TFKC	J. and S. Young, *Terracotta Figurines from Kourion in Cyprus* (Philadelphia, 1955).
Tiryns	*Tiryns. Die Ergebnisse der Ausgrabungen*, Vols. I–III (Berlin, 1912–1930). Deutsches Archäologisches Institut.
Toronto	D. M. Robinson, C. G. Harcum and J. H. Iliffe, *A Catalogue of the Greek Vases in the Royal Ontario Museum of Archaeology* (Toronto, 1930).
Troy	Blegen, C., ed., *Troy. Excavations conducted by the University of Cincinnati, 1932–1938*, Vols. I–IV (Princeton, 1950–1958).
Ugaritica	C. F. A. Schaeffer, *Ugaritica. Etudes relatives aux découvertes de Ras Shamra*, Vols. I–III (Paris 1939–1956).
Vounous	E. and J. Stewart, *Vounous 1937–38* (Lund, 1950). Svenska Institutet i Rom. Skrifter, Vol. 14.

PREVIOUS PUBLICATIONS OF BAMBOULA MATERIAL

Excavations and excavated material from Bamboula have been treated in special studies prior to the present volume as listed below (excluding broad studies which include objects found at Bamboula):

A. S. Murray, A. H. Smith, H. B. Walters, *Excavations in Cyprus*, 1900, 56–86.

J. F. Daniel, "Kourion—The Late Bronze Age Settlement," *UPMB* 7, no. 1, 1937, 15–18.

———. "Excavations at Kourion. The Late Bronze Age Settlement — Provisional Report," *AJA* 42 (1938) 261–275.

———. "Kourion—The Late Bronze Age Settlement," *UPMB* 7, no. 3, 1939, 14–21.

———. "The Inscribed Pithoi from Kourion," *AJA* 43, 1939, 102–103.

———. "The Achaeans at Kourion," *UPMB* 8, no. 1, 1940, 3–14.

———. "Prolegomena to the Cypro-Minoan Script," *AJA* 45, 1941, 249–282.

———. "Kourion — Past Achievements and Future Plans," *UPMB* 13, no. 3, 1948, 7–15.

See also pertinent sections of a review by Daniel: *AJA* 46, 1942, 285–293 (Sjöqvist).

J. L. Benson, "A Tomb of the Early Classical Period at Bamboula," *AJA* 60, 1956, 43–50.

———. "Aegean and Near Eastern Seal Impressions from Cyprus," *The Aegean and The Near East: Studies Presented to Hetty Goldman*, ed. by S. S. Weinberg (Locust Valley, N.Y., 1956) 59–70.

———. "A Syrian Krater from Bamboula at Kourion," *PEQ*, 1960, 64–69.

———. (with O. Masson) "Cypro-Minoan Inscriptions from Bamboula, Kourion," *AJA* 64, 1960, 145–151.

———. "Pictorial Mycenaean Fragments from Kourion, *AJA* 65, 1961, 53–54.

———. "Coarse Ware Stirrup Jars of the Aegean," *Berytus* 14, 1961, 37–51.

———. "The White Slip Sequence at Bamboula, Kourion," *PEQ*, 1961, 61–69.

———. "Bamboula at Kourion: The Stratification of the Settlement," *Report of the Department of Antiquities, Cyprus*, 1969, 1–28, and 1970, 25–74.

V. Karageorghis, "The Mycenaean 'Window-Crater' in the British Museum," *JHS* 77, 1957, 269–271.

ILLUSTRATIONS

PART 1
THE NECROPOLIS

1. THE NECROPOLIS

Extent and Topography

The present report cannot give an absolutely certain picture of the total extent and composition of the necropolis on the Bamboula hill. Obstacles to doing so are incomplete investigation of the entire site and unsatisfactory presentation of the results of the earlier British Museum excavations. With the latter problem Daniel had concerned himself in considerable detail, so that it seems best to present his views substantially as he left them. First, however, a brief orientation on the tombs is offered.

The Late Cypriote necropolis appears from the evidence of the University Museum's excavations to have been concentrated on the slope of the hill just to the northeast of Area E. The difficulties of supplementing this picture with evidence gleaned from the earlier excavation are formidable. Suffice it to say here that another small group of Late Cypriote tombs (OT 36, 106, 107, 109) was found somewhere on higher ground above the settlement; yet another group (OT 86, 88) somewhere to the south of the settlement. Tombs of earlier and later periods, which are in the minority as compared with the Late Cypriote period, will be discussed later.

Looking more closely at the main Late Cypriote necropolis, we find that it virtually surrounds the northeast arm of Area E (Pl. 1). Its tombs lie (in somewhat higgledy-piggledy fashion) to the northeast, then to the northwest in a line along the edge of the bluff on which Area E is laid out, and finally up the slope of the hill in a line roughly indicated by the street dividing Area E into two arms. It must be emphasized that no settlement remains were found over the main, i.e. northeast, part of the necropolis; also that there was no formal connection between tombs and houses of Area E. Daniel wrote:

> The edge of the bluff serves as the dividing line between the settlement, which lies above it, and the tombs below. The chambers of several tombs run under the outer rooms of the houses. These tombs were all entered from dromoi cut in the face of the cliff outside the houses and none was accessible from within the houses. They are to all intents and purposes separate. The edge of the rock has retreated since antiquity, and most of the tombs in the face of the

cliff are poorly preserved. Tomb 26 is an exception to this, Tomb 28 is nearly so. Elsewhere we must reckon with a loss of as much as two or three meters from the edge of the bluff.

As a supplement to this remark, attention is called to the fact that in the case of a number of tombs (e.g., Tomb 20) in the main area of the necropolis there was evidence which could be interpreted as a considerable, perhaps drastic, lowering of the bedrock level since ancient times.

In the Bamboula necropolis we are concerned with a region which has been disturbed by looting and robbing perhaps since antiquity (cf. Tomb 17). Of the forty tombs investigated by the University Museum expedition, relatively few were found intact. More than half a century ago, an expedition from the British Museum also found plundered tombs.[1] For the interpretation of the plan of the area published by this expedition it seems advisable to quote from Daniel's manuscript, with slightly altered terminology in a few instances:

> A special problem concerns the tombs in the area approached by the street. Our excavations indicate that this inner necropolis runs from the central part of Area E back to the rock ledge north of trench 15 (in Area B), an area of perhaps thirty meters square. The plan of the tombs excavated by the British Museum expedition, published in *Excavations in Cyprus*, however, gives a totally different picture, and suggests that the entire northern and western slopes of Bamboula were covered with tombs.
>
> Ideally it should be possible to determine the scale of the map in *Excavations in Cyprus* and reduce it to uniformity with our plans. Unfortunately this is impossible. A superficial glance suffices to show that the published map is highly inaccurate. Three long rock-girt terraces are shown on the northern slope of the hill; there are only two. The northernmost bluff is represented turning south by tombs 29 and 93, and fading into the hillside. In reality the bluff follows the Paphos road fairly closely as far as its junction with the 'road from Episkopi', which it then follows south.

1. *ExC*, 61. See O. Masson, *Inscriptions Chypriotes Syllabiques* (Paris, 1961) 189 for brief comments on the history and exploration of Kourion. The same scholar proposes at a future date to review this question in detail with full bibliographical panoply.

The turn south shown on the map may be the shallow bend which begins by the ancient street and runs to a point just north of our House V, Room 1 in Area E. Finally, seven or eight small hills are shown on the summit of Bamboula. Actually there are only two, separated by the long depression examined in our Area B. One of the actual summits is apparently where tombs 35, 36, 105–110 are placed (threshing floor?). The other would appear to be that marked by the Archaic tomb 95. The Archaic cemetery, however, is well to the south, and would not appear on this map if it were to scale. We made numerous soundings in the area most closely resembling that to which tomb 95 is attributed, and found no traces of a cemetery. Rather there was clear evidence of extensive quarrying since antiquity but prior to the British Museum excavations.

Obviously, the tombs excavated by the British Museum expedition cannot be located on the basis of their indicated relation to the natural features of the hill. The possibility remains that the natural features were added freehand from memory to a carefully drawn map showing only the tombs, which might be correctly related to each other, if not to the contours of the hill. This too we were able to check, thanks to the certain identification of the British tombs 53, 102, 50 and 104. Numerous new fragments of British Museum C 391 assure the identity of our tomb 17 with the British tomb 53, and through it, of our tomb 17A with the British tomb 102 [but see p. 20]. In our tomb 26 we found many fragments of a false-necked jar of coarse-tempered Late Helladic III ware, British Museum C 501, from the British tomb 50. This and the position of the tomb justify the equation. Finally, the well discovered in our trench 19 (main necropolis) appears to be that picturesquely labelled 'tomb 104' in the published report.[*]

On the basis of these established common points we can check the spacing of these tombs on the plan in *Excavations in Cyprus* against our own verified measurements. From the eastern end of tomb 17 (OT 53) to the western side of tomb 26 (OT 50) is 38 m. On the British plan the distance is 0.05 m.; the scale is thus 1:760. From the eastern end of tomb 17 (OT 53) to the well in trench 19 (OT 104) is 14 m.; on the plan it is 0.015 m., giving a scale of 1:933. From the western side of the same well to the western

side of tomb 26 (OT 50) is 23.25 m.; on the plan it is 0.036 m., giving a scale of 1:646. From the southern side of tomb 17A (OT 102) to the southern edge of the road, in a line perpendicular to the road, is 54 m. The plan shows 0.0315 m. or a scale of 1:1390. From the southern edge of tomb 26 (OT 50) to the road is 23.7 m. The plan, with 0.01 m., has a scale of 1:2370. From the northern side of tomb 17 (OT 53) to the center of the threshing floor on the top of the hill is 78 m. The plan shows approximately 0.085 m., giving a scale of 1:910. From the northern edge of the outcropping east of tomb 17 (OT 53) to the junction of the two roads at the western end of Bamboula is 161 m. The plan has 0.156 m.—again a scale of 1:910. From the center of the threshing floor to the road is 126 m. The plan, with 0.09 m., has a scale of 1:1400.

The scale between different points on the map in *Excavations in Cyprus* varies between 1:646 and 1:2370. Neither the natural features of the hill nor the tombs are consistent scales. That two measurements are to the same scale of 1:910 is probably due to coincidence, particularly so as one of the measurements involves the center of the threshing floor, which can only be approximated on the British Museum map. The measurements between the tombs seem more nearly accurate than those of the contours of the hill, though they too fall wide of the mark. It may be that the tombs were plotted freehand on the side, without the notation of the features of the hill, and that these were added at a later date with increased inaccuracy.

Our immediate concern with the above maligned map is to determine the extent of the cemetery south of Area E. OT 30, 31, 41, 45–48, 51, 89, 90–94, 100 and 101, which particularly concern us, occupy a rectangle 0.041 by 0.052 m. on the map. If our task were to select one of the available scales and apply it consistently to the chart, we could find an area measuring anywhere from 26.48 by 33.59 m. to 97.17 by 123.34 m. Unfortunately the chart in question is not drawn to any set scale. We can merely point out that our limitation of the necropolis to a relatively small space immediately back of the central part of Area E can be achieved by applying the scale of 1:646 to the tombs shown on the British map. Certainty will be possible only after much more extensive excavations.

History of the Site

The earliest tomb known on the Bamboula hill is Tomb 1, dating from the Early Cypriote period. It is located under a portion of the circuit wall of Area A and is the only tomb of any date whatsoever discovered in Area A. Since the settlement and necropolis of the Early Cypriote period have been found on the central coastal plain to the south of Bamboula at Phaneromeni,[2] it may be assumed that Tomb 1 is a more or less isolated phenomenon on

the outer fringe of the Early Cypriote community. The two tombs of Early Cypriote date found by the British Museum expedition (OT 97 and 98, cf. *ExC*, 73) are not specifically located, but according to the rough indications given on the chart (*ExC*, 61) lay

[*] NT 13 and OT 101 should also be considered in this context.—J. L. B.

2. S. S. Weinberg, "Exploring the Bronze Age in Cyprus," *Archaeology* 9 (1956) 112 ff.

to the south of the Late Cypriote necropolis in the direction of Phaneromeni. Somewhat more difficult to interpret are the truncated remains of two tombs found in trench 20:15b (southeast of the southernmost part of Area E; see *Bamboula SS*). These appeared to be earlier than the earliest tombs of the Late Cypriote necropolis; if so, they suggest that there may have been habitation somewhere in the general area in Middle Cypriote times. A few sherds characteristic of the Early Cypriote and Middle Cypriote periods (see B 35 to B 71) were found on the site, generally in Late Cypriote (or later) contexts, occasionally on the surface. Apparently the British Museum expedition found no objects of Middle Cypriote date anywhere in the Kourion area. On the whole, the present evidence for use of the Bamboula hill as a necropolis prior to Late Cypriote times is very slight and hardly justifies anything but a negative conclusion.

It has already been pointed out that the majority of the tombs excavated by the University Museum were found plundered. The evidence they offer is thus greatly vitiated. On the other hand, in the excavation and study of the individual tombs an attempt has been made to sift out what could be gleaned from the havoc wrought by those earlier on the scene; and there can hardly be any doubt that the picture which emerges is, in its broad general outlines, reliable. In the following paragraphs no account is taken of the tombs excavated by the British Museum expedition (except of those re-excavated by the University Museum expedition) because the publication of these is too scanty to offer any firm basis for interpretation. A re-study of the actual objects and museum records would be required to establish what evidential value these tombs have: probably little, for it appears that indifferent care was taken to distinguish the burials in the tombs.[3]

In the LC I period, use of our Tombs 9, 11, 12 and 13 in the main necropolis, and possibly one, Tomb 34, in the so-called inner necropolis (following the street of Area E) is indicated. To these tombs correspond in the settlement principally Houses I and II of Area E and some not well-defined activity in Area C. The fewness of the tombs is, therefore, in accordance with the indication of a small-sized settlement (perhaps deceptive if contemporary houses were widely scattered or obliterated by re-building). On the other hand, the richness of these tombs and their connotations of luxury and cosmopolitan relations show that the community, if small, was not necessarily poor and provincial.

In the LC II period, there was a veritable "boom" in the growth of the town, to judge from the evidence of the tombs. There was continued use of the main necropolis and the line of tombs was extended along the lower bluff of Area E and up its street. The following tombs were used (or re-used): Tombs 2, 3, 5, 6, 7, 12, 13, 17, 18, 19, 20, 21, 22, 24, 25, 26, 27, 28, 29, 33, 34, 36, 37, 38, 39, 40. Doubtless many of the tombs excavated by the British Museum expedition—with their numerous Mycenaean vases—would also fall into this period. From the point of view of both richness and numbers of tombs there can be little doubt that this period represents the high water mark of prosperity and size of Bamboula. To these tombs correspond in Area A Houses III and IV, in Area B the great well and some not clearly defined houses, in Area C continuing activity, in Area D the "cellar," and in Area E Houses III and IV together with the metal industry represented by the "furnaces" of the hearth area. The fact that there are not more material remains of this area in the settlement is owing, as stated elsewhere, to the thoroughness with which—after some kind of catastrophe—the ground was prepared for the dwellings of the following period. It is therefore with some caution that one must interpret the more complete and extensive settlement remains of the LC III period. These comprise in Area A Houses IV, V, VI, VIa, VII and VIII, in Area B some use of at least one house, in Area D a house and in Area E Houses IV, V, VI, VII and VIII. Moreover, corresponding to these, the necropolis evidence shows an appreciably reduced use of tombs, viz., of Tombs 2, 3, 5, 14, 16, 17, 18, 19, 23, 25, 27, 32, 33 and 40. In this situation, the necropolis evidence seems more decisive.[4] We may conclude that in the LC III period the settlement was at least no more flourishing and populous than it had been in the preceding period; and that in all probability it had already passed its peak in these

3. Cf. *ExC*, 86.
4. By actual count of the burials which could be controlled on the basis of more or less complete skeletons or skulls in connection with finds, there were only 31 burials in the LC II period as against 75 in the LC III period. But the latter figure is swollen by the enormous number of interments—47—in Tomb 19, which most likely indicates an epidemic of some kind, and by the generally better preservation of the later burials as against the earlier, e.g. in Tomb 40, where nine burials of LC III were preserved as against an unspecified number of earlier burials. In many of the plundered tombs where the sherd distribution indicated burials of the LC II period there were no bones whatsoever. In view of the dreadfully disturbed condition of the necropolis it seems to me therefore better to rely on the impression given by the number of tombs in use in the respective periods.

respects—at this site at least.[5] This is particularly evident for the latter part of the period (LC IIIB) when the whole settlement seems to be represented by only Houses V, VI and VIII; no more than two or three tombs (Tombs 19, 33 and possibly 27) are associated with these houses. Probably during this phase the site of the city was moved—presumably to the coastal plain at Kaloriziki where tombs of the LC IIIB and Geometric periods—but none earlier— have been found. It is therefore not justifiable to make any conclusions about the demise of importance of the community as such. This subject is treated in greater detail in the publication of the Kaloriziki necropolis.

Returning to the Bamboula hill, we find three instances in which use was made of the necropolis in the CG I period. Tomb 30 is—and Tomb 8 is likely to have been—a poor grave, perhaps of squatters in the abandoned settlement. Tomb 11 was a Late Cypriote tomb re-used, possibly for reasons of economy, no doubt by one of the inhabitants of the lower city. An awareness in later periods that ready-made tombs were to be had here is demonstrated as well by Tomb 2, which was re-used in the CG III period, and by Tomb 24, likewise re-used in Archaic times. In the cases of Tombs 17, 29, 35 and 39, the evidence for re-use is unfortunately only inferential. The Geometric burial connected with Tomb 38 is likely to be accidental destruction rather than deliberate re-use of an existing tomb. From the British Museum excavations there is some evidence for re-use of Late Cypriote tombs (OT 44 and perhaps 89 and 98) as well as continued sporadic use of the necropolis (OT 1, 52, 56 and 95), but from neither old nor new excavations has come any indication that tombs were constructed or re-used here after the Cypro-Archaic I period.[6] In connection with OT 95, Daniel (see p. 4) referred to an Archaic cemetery "well to the south" (of the Bamboula settlement?). This reference is not intelligible to me unless Daniel had in mind Tomb 4 of the early Cypro-Classical period. This could conceivably be part of a necropolis, as I speculated in the publication of that tomb.[7] If so, it would represent a new chapter in the history of Bamboula.

Tomb Types

Excavations at Bamboula yielded, with very few exceptions, nothing but the rock-cut chamber tombs one might have expected to find for the Late Cypriote period. This generalization seems valid also for the British Museum excavations, to judge from the very scanty remarks on tomb types in *Excavations in Cyprus*, pp. 58-59. The only definite exception mentioned there, viz., OT 104 as being "like a well," seems to have been rediscovered by Daniel and found actually to be a well.[8]

It is true that many of the tombs explored by Daniel were badly disturbed by previous plundering and erosion.[9] Nevertheless, in most cases, enough was preserved to reveal the ground plan and often even the location and type of dromos. The three earliest tombs of which the shape is known are Tombs 11, 12 and 13 of the LC I period. The shapes of their ground plans are quite irregular, the only common denominator being that they have no sharp corners. Tomb 11 had its dromos on the east, Tomb 13 preserved several small steps down into the chamber from the dromos which is on the south. All the remaining tombs of the Late Cypriote period of which the shape is known—except Tomb 14— appear to have had their origin in the LC II period, regardless of whether their use continued into the next period. It is not practicable to distinguish any development *within* the LC II period, so that all these are treated here as a chronological unit. Here again, it is not possible to speak of any one predominant shape, although a tendency to regularize the plan into a rectangle is perhaps the most persistent feature of the development. In any case, ground plans range from completely round (Tombs 18, 29 and 34), through the more or less oval form (Tombs 2, 5, 19, 26 and 27) and kidney bean shape (Tombs 21 and 28), to a more or less recognizable rectangle (Tombs 3, 7, 16, 32, 33, 36 and 40). Others appear to be completely irregular if not haphazard in shape (Tombs 3, 17 and 38—this latter badly destroyed). There are two examples of double chambers connected by a single dromos (Tombs 17 and 33).

There is no predominant orientation for the

---

5. There is a certain parallel for this in the situation at Ialysos, where the upper stratum (Late Helladic III) seems to show an impoverishment as compared with the middle stratum (Late Helladic II): see *ClR* X, 176.

6. Cf. *AJA* 60 (1956) 49.

7. See *AJA* 60 (1956) 50.

8. There is no formal record of this in the field notebooks but cf. p. 4.

9. A number of tombs (e.g. Tombs 20, 22, 23) were eroded almost out of existence, making difficult any conclusions at all about them. The sloping terrain of the necropolis and the exposed outcroppings of the limestone shelf in several places are responsible for this.

dromos to be observed. All the points of the compass seem to have been favored. Tombs 6, 7 and 34 had the dromos on the north, Tombs 17A and 33 on the east, Tombs 32 and 39 on the south, Tombs 2, 17 and 36 on the west. Again, Tombs 5 and 40 had dromoi on the northeast and Tomb 19 on the southeast. All of this is in perfect agreement with Sjöqvist's finding that in the Late Cypriote period "the orientation of the tombs according to the compass is not governed by any ritualistic principle."[10] There is one example of a dromos which is merely a circular break in the bedrock (Tomb 3). Other preserved dromoi, however, are more or less square, shallow depressions in the bedrock which might be characterized appropriately by the name "pan-dromoi" (Tombs 5, 7, 19, 26, 28, 32, 34 and 40). At least four of these were equipped with side niches or "cupboards." The "matched" position of the dromoi of Tombs 19 and 40, which has a parallel at Pylos, is worth noting.[11]

Only Tomb 14 appears to have been associated with the LC III period exclusively. Unfortunately there is very little information about it. If a chamber tomb, it would be unusual in this period.[12] Its small size, at least, might predispose one to think that it could have been a simple shaft grave. The absence of new tombs in the Late Cypriote III period seems somewhat surprising in view of the clear evidence for continued use of the settlement. On the other hand, it tends to corroborate my earlier conclusion that the real highpoint of the settlement, at least in size, was the LC II period. It also supports—if only with negative evidence—Sjöqvist's conclusion that there was a radical break in tomb building practices between LC IIC and LC III.[13]

Exceptional types of tombs and tomb features can now be treated. The most clear-cut case is that of Tomb 37, a triple cist grave, apparently associated with the LC II period. Unfortunately, this was very poorly documented and not much reliance can be placed on its evidence. In any case, Tomb 37 is similar to the simple shaft type, which is not totally without precedent in the period in question. Another variant type of tomb, according to the excavator's interpretation, is represented by Tombs 9 (LC IA) and 16 (LC IIA and earlier). The lower part of the tomb was a cutting in the bedrock and the upper part was constructed of mud bricks and perhaps covered with earth, like a mound. In the individual discussion of these tombs I have pointed out certain objections to this theory. However, it is worth noting that such a type would be similar to the strange Tomb 21 at Enkomi—hitherto without

parallel—that is, if one overlooks the fact that this latter tomb was constructed of undressed stone instead of mud brick.[14]

Another deviation from the norm may have occurred in Tomb 2, if the excavator's opinion that the interior was faced with masonry is correct. This does not in any other way, however, suggest a built tomb and there are certainly other possible explanations for the presence of stones in a tomb. In Tomb 40, for example, stones and mud bricks seem to have been thrown in as a layer between one set of burials and the next. The basic shape of Tomb 19 was altered by the building of a stone wall.[15] On the other hand, Tomb 29, which was only partially preserved, does offer an incontestable example of an ordinary chamber tomb with rubble masonry facing. The total extent of this facing is not known. Unfortunately, the evidence is contaminated by the possibility of a re-use in the Archaic period, so that the facing could conceivably—though it is not likely— have been added then. Another feature which occurs twice (Tombs 9 and 32) is a pit in the floor of the tomb.[16] This has been reported elsewhere in Cyprus and explained as having the purpose of keeping the chamber dry.[17] In view of the really thorough flooding which has taken place in many tombs, however, it may be questioned whether a small pit would have been thought adequate to keep the tomb dry, especially as it would soon have become clogged with silt.[18] In any case, it is not a common feature

---

10. *Problems*, 26.

11. *ILN*, April 7, 1957. For other parallels to the niches at Bamboula, cf. *RDAC*, 1963, 5.

12. *Problems*, 25.

13. *Problems*, 25.

14. *Problems*, 19. Real mound tombs are virtually unknown during the Late Cypriote period. Tomb 7 at Enkomi is stated by the excavator to have been surmounted by a low tumulus. The Middle Cypriote tumuli at Paleoskontella hardly have any connection with this. The built tomb in a mound at Hagia Katerina, considered by Murray (*ExC*, 1 f.) to have been of the Mycenaean epoch, is Cypro-Archaic or later (cf. A. Westholm, "Built Tombs in Cyprus," *OA* 2, 1939, 43.

15. Cf. the wall of stone and mud bricks found in the re-used tomb in Trench 20: 15b (*Bamboula SS*, Hearth Area).

16. Cf. also Tomb 4 of Cypro-Classic I date (*AJA* 60, 1956, 50) and Tomb 29 in the Kaloriziki necropolis (Early Geometric period). Another example of a CG IIIB tomb with a pit has been recently reported from Salamis: *AA*, 1963, 142. Cf. also *RDAC*, 1964, 53: four pits with bowls in them in a tomb at Idalion (Cypro-Archaic period).

17. *Problems*, 18.

18. Cf. *Mycenae*, 37. It is fair to point out that the principle of tomb drainage was not unknown in the period under consideration, but in the unmistakable example of it at Mycenae there is a proper drain and the tomb is a large and important one.

at Bamboula, nor is the well-built stone platform or bench along one wall of Tomb 33. The date of construction of this bench need not be that of the construction of the tomb itself. Benches are found in the LC II period[19] but also in the LC IIIB period.[20]

The only tomb exclusively associated with the Geometric period is Tomb 30. This was a cist grave for which no definite size or shape could be established. In any case, it seems to be the most modest Geometric tomb as yet reported.[21]

Burial Customs

Representative skeletal remains were preserved from the LC II, LC III and Geometric periods which can supplement the picture of Cypriote burial customs drawn from the Swedish excavations. In order to extract the most information possible from these remains, it seems advisable to discuss them under the headings of burial positions, treatment of former occupants, and incidental information about burial practices.

It may be stated at the outset that there is no evidence for any type of burial except inhumation—with a single exception in the Geometric period—from the whole necropolis of Bamboula. The oldest skeletons which can be cited are those of Tomb 36 and Tomb 40 in the LC IIA period. All these were in the dorsal position. One skeleton in Tomb 36 had its head toward the south and was stretched out opposite the door; the other was oriented east-west. The skeleton of Burial Period B in Tomb 40 also had its head to the south and was in a somewhat sprawling position opposite the door.[22] Representing the LC IIB period are Skeletons 1-II of Burial Period E in Tomb 12. These were in the dorsal position with their heads toward the east. From these few indications it seems that there was no more a canonical position or orientation for bodies within the tomb than there was a canonical orientation for the tomb itself. They were, however, as Gjerstad stated,[23] usually placed alongside a wall unless there was no room for them there. There were no assured instances of burial in a sitting position, which occurred sometimes at Enkomi (cf. ST 2, 6 and 11). From the drawings it is conceivable, although not obligatory, to suppose that burials in this position may have occurred in Bamboula Tombs 6 and 21.

The same general situation continued in the LC III period although a wider range of burial positions is recorded. Two instances of the *Hockerstellung* occurred.[24] There are, to my knowledge, no other instances of this reported for the Late Bronze Age in Cyprus.[25] There was one lateral burial with head to the door, and there were various instances of dorsal position.[26] In one case, a corpse had been laid on a platform.[27] During the Geometric period the same general tendencies continued.[28] An example of direct superimposition of burials—which was practiced in the contemporary necropolis of Kaloriziki—was recorded for the CG III burial period of Tomb 2. It is a curious fact that the only example of cremation—associated in some frequency with the contemporary chamber tombs of Kaloriziki—was provided by the very poor and makeshift surface Tomb 30.

Owing to the great amount of disturbance from flooding and plundering it is difficult to speak with real certainty about the disposition of former occupants of tombs, a vital subject in view of the widespread—almost universal—re-use of the tombs. There are a number of cases already in the LC II period (Tombs 12, 36, 40) where it appears that the bones were simply swept aside without ceremony to make room for a new occupant, and this practice continued in the following period (Tombs 2, 3, 5, 19, 33 and 40).[29] On the other hand, there are a few

19. See *Problems*, 23.
20. See *AJA* 58 (1954) 133 and Pls. 19-20.
21. Cf. *SCE* IV, 29 ff.
22. Cf. *Praktika*, 1952, 445, fig. 13, Mycenae.
23. *SPC*, 85.
24. Tomb 5, head to east, and Tomb 19 (Skeleton XXXV), head to north.
25. Cf. *SPC*, 86.
26. Respectively Tomb 40, Burial Period C and Tomb 3 (head south to door); Tomb 5 (Skeleton II, head south); Tomb 14 (orientation north-south: cf. Enkomi ST 11, dromos burial); Tomb 19 (Skeleton XLV, head southeast).
27. Tomb 33 (northeast-southwest orientation).
28. Tomb 11 in the CG IB period had a dorsal burial with north-south orientation; Tomb 2 in the CG III period had one dorsal and one lateral burial with heads to north.
29. The CG IB re-use of Tomb 11 is a special case; in view of the long lapse since the previous use of the tomb (LC IB period) and the general scarcity of skeletal remains, it cannot be certain that the early occupant(s) was merely swept aside; in the interpretation of this evidence I prefer to be guided by the contemporary necropolis of Kaloriziki where this practice was not in effect. In any case, it must remain doubtful what the attitude of Geometric people to burials as old as this would have been. A parallel case is that of Tomb 11 at Milia, where an LC IA tomb was re-used in the CG III period. The earlier burials seem simply to have been covered up to make a new floor (see *QDAP* 8, 1938, 9 ff.).

instances—notably during the LC III period in Tombs 19 and 40—when an earlier occupant was not cast aside but was covered over with debris to make a cushioning for a new occupant. In view of the general practice of pushing the remains of earlier occupants out of the way in a heap it seems doubtful that one should say that putting a layer over earlier occupants was treating them with "great respect."[30] Quite utilitarian reasons may suffice. Perhaps the corpses had not sufficiently disintegrated to be swept aside, or the layer of debris helped to smother the stench, or the floor seemed too full in any case for the new occupant to be placed in a suitable position.

Incidental information about burial customs is included in the following summary: All burials (in the Late Cypriote period) were of the inhumation type. Tombs were almost universally re-used, a fact which makes quite possible—although it certainly does not prove—that they were family vaults as has been suggested.[31] With this is connected the problem of tomb markers. There is not the slightest evidence for such at Bamboula. On the other hand, there is no evidence that previously existing tombs were damaged by those digging new tombs; thus it seems likely that the position of existing tombs was always known. I cannot suggest any plausible solution to this dilemma. In some parts of the necropolis at Bamboula it might have been practicable to leave the pan-dromoi open, but hardly in the street of

Area E, even if that "street" did not accommodate vehicular traffic.

The skeletons of (presumably) decomposed bodies and their gifts (often found in fragments) were pushed aside, apparently rather unceremoniously, to make room for new occupants. Occasionally, however, corpses (of recently interred persons) were covered over with earth and stones to make a new floor. Position of burials was usually dorsal with several examples of lateral and *Hocker* positions in the LC III period. Perhaps the most unusual position was that of a skeleton in Tomb 40 in a sprawling attitude. In Tomb 5, fragments of wood charcoal were found in the earth about and under the skeletons, and in Tomb 40 a number of pots had ashes adhering to their outer surface. In these cases one may certainly assume some sort of purification, whether or not ritual. The practical necessity for some such practice seems apparent in view of the consistent re-use of tombs. Nevertheless, one may note the lack of widespread evidence for purification of tombs by fire both at Bamboula and elsewhere.[32] Perhaps there were other means of accomplishing this purpose which have left no trace.

30. *Problems*, 27. Only one instance of a mass of bones being heaped in a side chamber is adduced; and it is difficult to see why this implies great respect.
31. *SPC*, 86.
32. *Problems*, 27.

2. THE TOMBS AND THEIR CONTENTS

Tomb 1

GENERAL REMARKS

This tomb was discovered just outside and extending partly under the Circuit Wall during the course of excavations in Area A (*Pl. 1*). With the possible exception of a nearby bothros (see *Bamboula SS*), this is the only tomb associated with Area A. It was sunk only slightly into the bedrock, which Daniel estimated must have been about a meter above its present level when the tomb was made. The original confines of the tomb could not be definitely determined, so that no plan was drawn.

STRATIFICATION

Bones and fragments of pottery were found about ten centimeters above bedrock, covered by a very hard layer of earth with much white rock. The bones and sherds were in a disturbed state and nothing could be determined concerning their original position. *Pl. 2* (upper l.) shows the objects in position as found. It appears that the tomb collapsed soon after

building, which probably accounts for its partial preservation.

FINDS

1. B 46. Red Polished I amphoriskos.
2. B 47. Red Polished I-II amphora.
3. B 49. Red Polished jug(?) base.
4. B 1608. Terracotta spindlewhorl.
5. 114 sherds of Red Polished ware, some with white-filled incisions.

CHRONOLOGY

The only firmly dateable object is No. 1. No. 2 can be dated only by inference. However, the general homogeneity of finds suggests a single burial period. Since white-filled incisions begin first in the Red Polished II category and do not become common until the Red Polished III category, one should allow the Early Cypriote II–III periods as the range of date for this tomb.

Tomb 2

LOCATION, SIZE AND SHAPE

This tomb was found in the north section of Area F. Its shape (*Pl. 5*) is irregular, roughly rectangular in the west, ovoid on the east side. A slight curvature indicating the door was visible at the top of the preserved rock at the middle of the west side. Size of the tomb is unknown since no scale was indicated in field drawings. On the basis of stones found at the lower level, Daniel entertained the possibility that the interior of the tomb may have been faced originally with masonry. Although there is no convincing evidence for this, one may nevertheless point out that Tomb 19 contained stones which had been used in constructing wall and floor.

STRATIFICATION AND BURIALS

The bedrock roof of the tomb had collapsed and its fragments went down directly on top of the latest

burial (C) at about 80 cm. from the present surface. There is no extant plan of this level but a photograph (*Pl. 3*) indicates that both Skeletons I and II were stretched out in a dorsal position, though the upper torso of one seems to be twisted somewhat to the side. Associated with Skeleton I, which was placed along the east wall, was a fibula (No. 1). On the shoulder of Skeleton II was a whetstone (No. 4) and with him an iron knife (No. 3). Two sherds of Black-on-Red ware seem also to have been found at this level. These skeletons were separated from lower burials by a thin layer of earth and numerous stones going down directly onto the burials of Period B. The more recent skeleton of Period B is III, lying beneath II, and with the same orientation. It was lying outstretched, but on its side, as indicated by the curvature of the spine and the position of the ribs. The flask No. 5 lay on its side.

There was some confusion in the excavation of the skeletons marked IV and V, which were separated by a layer of gray earth from III. In reality, these two, with which No. 6 is associated, seem to be one skeleton lying directly over and (intermingled?) with Skeleton VI, which had no associated finds.

Below these burials, at one meter from the surface, was a substantial layer of stone and brick resting on light brown earth which had silted under water and which contained the sherds of the earliest burial remains. These remains had been badly disturbed even before the stony fill was put in (if it does not represent collapsed wall masonry). In the northern half were occasional sherds and a few broken pots "surely not *in situ*." In the southern half were a group of pots, Nos. 7–11 *in situ* to the east, and a deposit of earth containing a bead, No. 6a, pottery, Nos. 12–14, and a human arm bone, which had been thrown into the corner prior to the stony fill. All this early material lay directly on bedrock.

FINDS

1. B 1272. Bronze fibula in two pieces, found lying on a stone.
2. B 1302. Bronze wire in brown soil over tomb.
3. B 1384. Iron knife.
4. B 1547. Whetstone.
5. B 1213. Foreign Polychrome pilgrim flask.
6. B 584. LC III Decorated jug.
6a. B 1448. Stone bead.
7. B 261. Base-Ring I–II jug.
8. B 262. Base-Ring I–II jug.
9. B 263. Base-Ring I–II jug.
10. B 264. Base-Ring I–II jug.
11. B 265. Base-Ring I–II jug.
12. B 302. Monochrome krater.
13. B 227. Base-Ring II bowl.
14. B 129. White Slip II bowl, with No. 13.
15. Sherds (49-12-21) from below stony fill, including B 958: see Table, a.

CHRONOLOGY

Period C is dated by the associated sherds—if these are not intrusive—to the CG III period. In any case, it is dated by the fibula to the Cypro-Geometric epoch. The more recent burial of Period B may have taken place early in the Geometric period. The earlier burial of Period B belongs to the LC IIIA period. Burial Period A may be assigned to the LC IIA period (but see p. 7).

Tomb 3

LOCATION, SIZE AND SHAPE

This tomb lies in a line with, and to the northeast of, the series of tombs which skirts the lower border of Area E (Tombs 7, 26–28: see *Pl. 1*). Roughly rectangular in shape, it measured 1.79 m. x 2.16 m. at the floor (*Pl. 5*). At the highest point, the roof of the chamber was 92 cm. from the floor.

STRATIFICATION

A roughly circular break in the bedrock, about a meter in diameter, led into the chamber. Otherwise the roof of the chamber was intact. It was cut from hard white calcareous sandstone which lies very close to the present surface. Two cut blocks of stone, but no collapsed rock, were found. The circular break may have been cut for the last burial, or if this portion had already collapsed, the debris may have been cleared out at that time. In any case, the earth of the tomb showed no signs of disturbance other than from frequent flooding. The upper stratum, beginning 50 cm. below the highest preserved part of the roof, was much silted. Below this was a gray layer with much decomposed rock going to bedrock.

BURIALS

Skulls I–III and Nos. 1–16 were in the silted earth, but not, of course, *in situ*. At the bottom of the flooded area (70 cm. from the top) was found Skeleton IIIa, to which Skull III probably belongs. This skeleton lay on the gray layer. Nos. 17–26, a few scattered bones and skull fragments (Skull IV) and some sherds were found in this stratum. Skeleton V —in greatly disturbed condition—lay on bedrock. The bones in this stratum represent an earlier burial thrown aside to make room for the later ones. The White Slip II bowls were associated with Skeleton V.

FINDS

Note: Depths given are reckoned from roof of tomb at highest point.
1. B 574. LC III Decorated krater-amphora; 60 cm.
2. B 499. LC III Decorated bowl with wishbone handle; 50 cm.

3. B 443. LC III Decorated bowl; 70 cm.
4. B 444. LC III Decorated bowl.
5. B 445. LC III Decorated bowl; 50 cm.
6. B 528. LC III Decorated bowl; 65 cm.
7. B 529. LC III Decorated bowl; 60 cm.
8. B 448. LC III Decorated bowl; 65 cm.
9. B 410. LC III Decorated bowl; 60 cm.
10. B 411. LC III Decorated bowl; 55 cm.
11. B 412. LC III Decorated bowl; 60 cm.
12. B 901. LC III Decorated bowl; 60 cm.
13. B 449. LC III Decorated bowl.
14. B 450. LC III Decorated bowl.
15. B 451. LC III Decorated bowl; 65 cm.
16. Part of No. 7.
17. B 1256. Bronze bowl; 80 cm.
18. B 1424. Bone or ivory button; 90 cm.
19. B 441. LC III Decorated bowl; 75 cm.
20. B 555. LC III Decorated bowl; 80 cm.
21. B 446. LC III Decorated bowl.
22. B 442. LC III Decorated bowl; 85 cm.
23. B 447. LC III Decorated bowl.
24. B 452. LC III Decorated bowl.
25. B 127. White Slip II bowl; 85 cm.
26. B 128. White Slip II bowl; 90 cm.
27. B 1418. Ivory rod from screening.
28. Sherds (49-12-49) in flooded area: see Table, b.
29. Sherds (49-12-50) in gray earth: see Table, c.

CHRONOLOGY

It seems necessary to regard all the finds, with the exception of Nos. 25 and 26 and possibly No. 18, as belonging to the latest burial period (B), that of Skeleton IIIa. The LC III Decorated bowls exhibit a stylistic unity and appear to come from the same atelier. In view of the confusion caused by flooding, it is not possible to depend on the sherd distribution. Nos. 25 and 26 and possibly No. 18—since it was found at bedrock—belong to an earlier burial period associated with Skeleton V (and probably also IV). In screening, a great proportion of White Slip II and Base-Ring sherds was found—remains, no doubt, of this earlier period (A).

Tomb 4

Although given a number in the sequence of tombs excavated in or near the Bronze Age settlement at Bamboula, Tomb 4 actually lies apart from this sequence both in location and in period. It is situated at the junction of two wagon roads from the village of Episkopi, in Lot 40 (Land Registry Sheet LVIII 5) about 300 meters south of Area E. Its period is approximately the first half of the fifth century B.C. A separate detailed publication of this tomb appeared in *AJA* 60 (1956) 43–50.

Tomb 5

LOCATION, SIZE AND SHAPE

This tomb is located in Area E in the so-called Street of Tombs (*Pl. 2*) between Houses V and VI. It was plundered in 1935 by villagers, and the sherds brought to Daniel. There is no record of what these sherds were. Until re-excavation by Daniel, the tomb simply remained open. The plunderers had entered by the dromos, as did Daniel, who found the chamber intact. The southern third of the tomb had completely escaped the notice of the plunderers, so that the remains of at least two burials were found *in situ*. The drawings left by Daniel (*Pl. 6*) show only the intact third. The shape of the tomb, however, is roughly circular, with a diameter of 3 meters and a height of 1.5 meters. Entered through a stomion on the northwest side, it has a rectangular, pan-shaped dromos 1.3 m. x 1.35 m. and 45 cm. deep.

There are two niches on the east: a large one, 80 cm. x 70 cm. and 60 cm. deep; a small one, 30 cm. x 17 cm. and 20 cm. deep. A niche on the west, said to have contained bones, measures 40 x 65 cm.

STRATIFICATION

No complete account of the stratification was left in Daniel's notes. The following key, however, explains the strata shown in the cross-section (*Pl. 6*):

1. Red loose earth
2. Gray gritty earth
3. Reddish clay
4. Red or gray gritty earth
5. Clay.

It will be observed that the objects belonging to the second level do not appear in the cross-section.

BURIALS

Skeletons I and II comprise the first burial level (C). Skeleton I had the *Hockerstellung:* the right shoulder up, the face down and the knees brought up towards the chest, with the legs stretching east. Find No. 1 belongs with this skeleton. The bottom of this pot had been knocked out, possibly in a libation ceremony. Skeleton II, apparently laid out flat at the east of the tomb, was represented only by part of the legs. These burials lay over stones on gritty gray earth at 30 cm. over bedrock. There were numerous fragments of wood-charcoal in the earth about and under the skeletons. Daniel thought these may have represented ceremonial fumigation before burial. In the next (second) burial level (B), Skull III and other fragments of a skeleton were found in association with No. 2 at 20 cm. over bedrock. Nos. 1a–9a were mended from sherds and come from the mass of sherds, presumably swept together, shown on the plan on the south side. Owing to confusion in the preservation of these sherds, no specific breakdown of categories is offered. The bulk of them, however, was Base-Ring ware with a thin scattering of other wares typical of the LC II period. At the third level (A), *ca.* 15 cm. over the bedrock, three piles of bones were found swept up against the wall. Associated with this level were Nos. 3 and 4. Nos. 5–7, all missing, were presumably found in the clay stratum just above bedrock.

FINDS

1. B 533. LC III Decorated bowl.
2. B 164. White Slip II bowl.
3. B 146. White Slip II bowl.
4. B 229. Base-Ring II bowl.
5. Missing. Ostrich egg.
6. Missing. Plain ivory disk.
7. Missing. Ivory button.
8. B 779. Inscribed handle from Plain White jug (not on plan); with period A or B.

Mended from sherds (see also note on White Slip II kraters):

1a. B 1185. Mycenaean III jug base.
2a. B 1186. Mycenaean III jug base.
3a. B 161. White Slip II bowl.
4a. B 152. White Slip II bowl.
5a. B 162. White Slip II bowl.
6a. B 180. Base-Ring II bowl.
7a. B 163. White Slip II bowl.
8a. B 116. White Slip II bowl.
9a. B 153. White Slip II bowl.

CHRONOLOGY

Burial period C belongs to the LC III period. Burial periods B and A belong to the time when White Slip II ware was most popular, the LC IIB period. Although these assignments are based on only a third of the area covered by the respective strata, the evidence, as it exists, is completely unequivocal.

Tomb 6

LOCATION, SIZE AND SHAPE

This tomb lay almost midway between Areas E and F, northeast of Tomb 3. Measuring 2.1 m. x 3 m., it had a roughly rectangular shape, though rounded off at the corners. Daniel's field sketch (see *Pl. 7*) did not give the orientation, though he commented that the dromos (not shown) was on the north side.

STRATIFICATION

A surface intrusion with a fair proportion of Geometric wares, and also B 807, was found over the tomb, but it did not reach the chamber, the roof of which had partly collapsed. The tomb was excavated from the top and proved to contain a mixture of red earth and fallen stone going down onto skeletal and ceramic remains (*Pl. 2*). A large piece of fallen rock lying on a still hollow, well preserved skull suggests the inference that the tomb had collapsed before the skull dried out, so that it was not crushed by the fall.

BURIALS

A great heap of bones, including two skulls, was found on the east side. No objects were found *in situ* either with the bones or below them at bedrock. Daniel suggested that the existing burials had been swept aside in preparation for a later burial which never took place, perhaps because the tomb collapsed before it could be made. It is perhaps more satisfactory to explain the chaotic condition of the burials, which appear to be more or less contemporary, by flooding of the tomb.

FINDS

1. B 1322. Faience bead.
2. B 1396. Ivory disk.

3. Missing. Spiral silver ring, broken.
4. B 1289. Bronze ring.
5. B 1260. Bronze chisel.
6. Missing. Pestle.
7. B 1063. Mycenaean III krater.
8. B 1013. Mycenaean III bowl.
9. B 1008. Mycenaean III bowl.
10. B 1169. Mycenaean III pilgrim flask fragments.
11. B 807. Plain White inscribed jug handle (over the tomb).
12. B 1089. Mycenaean III krater fragment.
13. Sherds (49-12-103) from the chamber: see Table, d.

CHRONOLOGY

In spite of the lack of stratification, there can be little doubt that the burials were roughly contemporary and occurred late in the LC IIB period or early in the LC IIC period. B 1063, however, seemed to the excavator to be dateable to the end of the LC IIC period and may have prompted his suggestion about a later interment which was never carried out (so that B 1063 could be considered to belong to that). I have pointed out certain reasons for dating B 1063, on a stylistic basis, to the second quarter of the thirteenth century B.C. (contemporary with the other objects in the tomb) in *JNES* 20 (1961) 77.

Tomb 7

LOCATION, SIZE AND SHAPE

This tomb lies in close proximity to Tomb 26 in the series of tombs along the northwest edge of Area E. Measuring 2.3 m. x 2.6 m., it is roughly square in shape with somewhat rounded corners (*Pl. 7*). The vertical shape of the chamber is approximately rectangular with the roof 1.9 m. from the floor. The dromos is on the north side, with a sharp drop from the *stomion* to the floor of the chamber. The dromos is roughly a square, 1.25 m. x 1.4 m., with a maximum depth of 1.1 m.

GENERAL REMARKS

Two small pits had been sunk into the tomb on the north but otherwise it is perfectly preserved. When investigated by Daniel, it had been thoroughly plundered. He did not discuss stratification, burials or the two finds, which were presumably not *in situ*.

FINDS

1. B 1092. Mycenaean III pyxis.
2. B 232. Base-Ring II bowl.
3. Sherds (49-12-106) found in the chamber: see Table, e.

CHRONOLOGY

The picture presented by the known finds cannot be conclusive. The distribution of wares points to the very beginning of the LC IIC period.

Tomb 8

GENERAL REMARKS

This tomb is included in a list in the field notebooks, but no description of the excavation exists. This is unfortunate for, although in a very much destroyed condition, it can be discerned immediately to the east of Tomb 30 and would have lain under the suppositional east and south walls of Room 2 of House I in Area E. This would clearly make it a very old tomb which must have been filled in before the construction of House I. On the other hand, the only objects listed from the tomb are of Early Iron Age date. If there is no mistake about this, then these doubtless have come from a shallow grave—of the type and period of nearby Tomb 30—on the site of the destroyed Bronze Age tomb.

FINDS

1. B 739. Black Slip I Bucchero amphora.
2. B 720. White Painted I bowl.
3. B 722. White Painted I bowl.

CHRONOLOGY

In view of the paucity of information and confusion about this tomb, there is nothing to add to the General Remarks.

Tomb 9

LOCATION, SIZE AND SHAPE

Tomb 9 is second in the series of tombs stretching east from Tomb 6 and ending with Tomb 22 (*Pl. 1*). Its floor, only 30–80 cm. below the present surface of the lot, is rectangular in shape and measures 2.5 m. x 2.65 m. There was a pit at the center measuring 60 cm. x 1.3 m., 30 cm. deep. In the fill were found many fragments of mud brick. Daniel interpreted this to mean, as also in the case of Tomb 16, that the tomb had a brick superstructure over a rectangular sinking in the soft limestone. He thought the whole might have been covered with a mound of earth; if true, this would be a most unusual and not very practical feature, particularly in view of the stress which would have thus been put on the brick superstructure.

BURIALS

In view of the proximity of the floor to the surface, it is not surprising that this tomb had been plundered. Apparently no human remains were found. The sherds found in the region of the tomb have not been considered in the dating as, lying near the surface, they have many intrusions among them; even many of the Bronze Age sherds may be intrusive.

FINDS

1. B 1328. Fragment of faience pot.
2. B 980. Red Lustrous III spindle-jar.
3. B 994. "White Lustrous" bottle.
4. B 1532. Steatite spindlewhorl.
5. B 196. Base-Ring I jug.

CHRONOLOGY

The existing finds suggest that the tomb was in use during the LC IA period.

Tomb 10

GENERAL REMARKS

This tomb is adjacent to Tomb 11 in the series of tombs stretching eastward from Tomb 15 along the base of an outcropping rock ledge (*Pl. 1*). Daniel described the dromos as of the usual LC II type, but built over the tumble of the chamber of a large tomb by means of a fill of river stones. No further description of the excavation and no plans exist. Although Daniel mentioned finding some LC IIIA pots in the chamber of Tomb 10, there is no record of these.

Tomb 11

LOCATION, SIZE AND SHAPE

Tomb 11 is just west of Tomb 10. It is described as being of the usual LC I or LC II type with the dromos on the east side. Roughly rectangular, with rounded corners, it measured 2.35 m. x 2.84 m. (*Pl. 7*). According to a photograph (*Pl. 3*), the floor lay relatively close to the surface, perhaps 60–70 cm. below it. Daniel does not comment on this circumstance (nor does he mention any mud bricks in the fill, in which case Tomb 11 might have been of the same type as Tombs 9 and 16). The explanation is probably that the upper part of the tomb was in bedrock of the outcropping ledge which has eroded away since the tomb was built.

BURIALS

The latest burial (Period B) appears to have been stretched out on the north-south axis of the tomb with gifts, Nos. 1–8, disposed along the east side of the body (*Pl. 7*). A few remnants of an earlier burial (Period A), Nos. 9–15, were found moved aside for the later burial in the center.

FINDS

1. B 724. White Painted I amphora.
2. B 740. Black Slip I Bucchero jug.
3. B 723. White Painted I amphora.
4. B 1211. Foreign pilgrim flask.
5. B 714. White Painted I bowl.

6. B 716. White Painted I bowl.
7. B 972. Coarse Ware bowl.
8. B 717. White Painted I bowl.
9. B 1508. Steatite button.
10. B 218. Base-Ring I–II jug fragment.
11. B 88. White Slip I bowl.
12. B 266. Base-Ring I–II jug neck.

13. Missing. Jug.
14. B 147. White Slip II bowl.
15. B 295. Monochrome bowl (not shown on plan).

CHRONOLOGY

Period B is assignable to the CG IB period. Period A is dated to the LC IB period.

Tomb 12

LOCATION, SIZE AND SHAPE

Tomb 12 lay 80 cm. to the south of Tomb 9. Measuring 2.47 m. x 2.9 m., its shape is irregular (*Pl. 7*). It began perhaps as an oval which became somewhat displaced at the north end. There is no definite indication in the field notes or on the plan as to the location of the dromos. Nor are there any indications of the nature of the roof. It seems likely from photographs, however, that this was the usual sort of chamber tomb with more or less flat roof hewn from the rock (*Pl. 2*). The floor is 80 cm. below the present surface of the bedrock.

STRATIFICATION AND BURIALS

The tomb was unplundered and offered a clear stratified sequence. The latest burial is E, to which Skeletons I and II, found stretched out in a dorsal position in the south part of the tomb, pertain (*Pl. 2*). Three pots, Nos. 11–13, a bronze chisel, No. 5, and an ivory button, No. 15, belong to these skeletons, which lay on dark sand. In the west part was found a large mass of pottery and bones, remnants of an earlier burial period, D, swept aside to make room for E. This mass, consisting of Skull III, Nos. 4, 16–19, 21–26, 70, 78 and 90, rested on and in red sandy earth heaped up along the north and northeast sides. Some of the objects of D were swept onto the top of B. The excavator chose, therefore, to regard the overlapping region, made up of objects from B and D, as a separate intermediate group C (Nos. 27, 63–69, 71, 73, 75, 79, 80, 82, 88). B consisted of Nos. 2, 3, 28–45, 49–56, 72, 74, 76, 77, 81, 83–87, 89, 91, 92). With these are associated Skulls IV, V, IX–XIII. The earliest groups of all consisted of pottery and skulls heaped along the east wall. With Skulls VII and VIII, Daniel associated No. 59; with Skulls XIV and XV, Nos. 46–48, and with Skull VI, Nos. 1, 6a–b, 7, 14, 57 and 58. These early burials, perhaps slightly earlier than B, are designated as Period A.

FINDS

1. B 1364. Gold earring.
2. B 1301. Bronze tweezers, broken.
3. B 1288. Double bronze ring, broken.
4. B 1397. Ivory disks, superimposed.
5. B 1261. Bronze chisel.
6a. B 1522. Steatite spindlewhorl.
6b. B 1523. Steatite spindlewhorl.
7. B 1247. Bone disk.
8. B 1315. Pointed bronze fragment.
9. This number not used.
10. B 1267. Bronze dagger.
11. B 100. White Slip II bowl.
12. B 233. Base-Ring II bowl.
13. B 306. Monochrome jug.
14. B 996. Syrian Bichrome jug.
15. B 1420. Ivory button; under No. 12.
16. B 1154. Mycenaean III stirrup jar.
17. B 772. Plain White jug.
18. B 1155. Mycenaean III stirrup jar.
19. B 758. Plain White bowl.
20. Missing. Bronze rod, 13.5 cm. long.
21. B 1622. Steatite cylinder seal.
22. B 1398. Ivory disk, broken.
23. B 1623. Steatite cylinder seal.
24. B 130. White Slip II bowl.
25. B 213. Base-Ring I–II jug.
26. B 131. White Slip II bowl.
27. B 165. White Slip II jug.
28. B 374. Wash Ware jug.
29. B 212. Base-Ring I–II jug.
30. B 208. Base-Ring I–II jug.
31. B 214. Base-Ring I–II jug.
32. B 197. Base-Ring I juglet.
33. B 1511. Steatite spindlewhorl.
34. B 314. Monochrome bowl.
35. B 173. Monochrome bowl.
36. B 75. White Slip I bowl.
37. B 72. White Slip I bowl.
38. B 986. Red Lustrous III bottle.
39. B 372. Monochrome jug.
40. B 1512. Steatite spindlewhorl.
41. B 76. White Slip I bowl.
42. Missing. Base-Ring bowl.
43. B 987. Red Lustrous III bottle.

44. B 1513. Steatite spindlewhorl.
45. B 211. Base-Ring I–II jug.
46. B 780. Plain Wheelmade I jug.
47. B 1226. Foreign jug.
48. Missing. White Slip I bowl.
49. B 375. Wash Ware jug.
50. B 373. Wash Ware jug.
51. B 81. White Slip I bowl.
52. B 83. White Slip I bowl.
53. B 198. Base-Ring I juglet.
54. B 1250. Fragments of bronze awl(?)
55. B 1514. Steatite spindlewhorl.
56. B 1515. Steatite spindlewhorl.
57. B 98. White Slip I jug.
58. B 370. Wash Ware jug.
59. B 1265. Bronze dagger.
60. B 1516. Steatite spindlewhorl.
61. B 1517. Stone weight. Over tomb.
62. B 1518. Steatite spindlewhorl. In earth thrown out of tomb.
63. B 132. White Slip II bowl.
64. B 133. White Slip II bowl.
65. B 134. White Slip II bowl.
66. B 135. White Slip II bowl.
67. B 136. White Slip II bowl.
68. B 137. White Slip II bowl.
69. B 138. White Slip II bowl.
70. B 139. White Slip II bowl.
71. B 140. White Slip II bowl.
72. B 96. White Slip I jug.
73. B 73. White Slip I bowl.
74. B 74. White Slip I bowl.
75. B 77. White Slip I bowl.
76. B 78. White Slip I bowl.
77. B 82. White Slip I bowl.
78. B 199. Base-Ring I(?) juglet.
79. B 209. Base-Ring I–II jug.
80. B 210. Base-Ring I–II jug.
81. B 215. Base-Ring I–II jug.
82. B 174. Base-Ring I bowl.
83. B 175. Base-Ring I bowl.
84. B 176. Base-Ring I bowl.
85. B 203. Base-Ring I jug.
86. B 287. Monochrome bowl.
87. B 288. Monochrome bowl.
88. B 289. Monochrome bowl.
89. B 291. Monochrome bowl.
90. B 303. Monochrome jug.
91. B 304. Monochrome jug.
92. B 371. Wash Ware jug.
93. B 158. White Slip II bowl fragment. Not on plan. Period unknown.
94. B 167. White Slip II jug. Not on plan. Period unknown.
95. B 305. Fragment of Monochrome jug. In screening.

In addition, the following unstratified and uncatalogued fragments are worthy of mention:

49-12-222ab. Fragment of Handmade Bucchero jug.
49-12-223ab. Fragments of White Slip I bowl.
49-12-224. Fragmentary White Shaved juglet.
49-12-225. Fragment of Base-Ring II jug.
49-12-226. Fragment of Base-Ring I jug like B 213.

CHRONOLOGY

Periods A and B belong to the LC IA:2 period, with B possibly late in that period. Period D belongs to the LC IIA period and E to the LC IIB period. Burial Period C, being intermediate between B and D, may represent the LC IB period. The problematical character of this burial period can only be understood in relation to a broad background of stylistic factors in the development of White Slip ware. I have undertaken to elucidate these factors in a special study, "The White Slip Sequence at Bamboula, Kourion," which appeared in *PEQ*, 1961, 61–69.

Tomb 13

LOCATION, SIZE AND SHAPE

This tomb lies a few meters to the southeast of Area E, and adjoins Tomb 14. Its shape is roughly oval, measuring 3 m. x 3.9 m. (*Pl. 8*). The original height of the chamber can be estimated from the cross-section as being 1.5 m. The small dromos is on the south side.

GENERAL REMARKS

This tomb and Tomb 14 had been ransacked by plunderers who, however, did not clear the tombs completely; in Tomb 13 they left several pillars of earth standing to hold up the roof. They had thrown to the side great masses of pottery and sherds, from which the finds listed below were recovered. The recognition by Daniel of a sherd found in OT 101 as a part of No. 27 identifies Tomb 13 as Tomb 101 of the British Museum excavations: see *Berytus* 14 (1961) 37.

FINDS

1. B 1376. Gold earring with grape cluster.
2. B 1363. Small circular gold bead.
3. B 1294. Bronze saw.
4. B 1345. Glass bead fragment.
5. B 1106. Mycenaean III 3-handled jar.
6. B 981. Red Lustrous III bottle.
7. B 982. Red Lustrous III bottle.
8. B 333. Burnished Slip bowl.
9. B 396. Handmade Shaved Ware juglet.
10. B 377. Wash Ware jug.
11. B 141. White Slip II bowl.
12. B 142. White Slip II bowl.
13. B 143. White Slip II bowl.
14. B 144. White Slip II bowl.
15. B 145. White Slip II bowl.
16. B 159. White Slip II bowl.
17. B 169. White Slip II krater.
18. B 84. White Slip I bowl.
19. B 85. White Slip I bowl.
20. B 86. White Slip I bowl.
21. B 87. White Slip I bowl.
22. B 255. Base-Ring II bowl.
23. B 179. Base-Ring I bowl.
24. B 187. Base-Ring I kylix.
25. B 188. Base-Ring I kylix.
26. B 186. Base-Ring I kylix.
27. B 1224. Foreign krater: "Domino Pot."
28. B 257. Base-Ring II krater.
29. B 206. Base-Ring I jug.
30. B 228. Base-Ring II bowl.
31. B 245. Base-Ring II bowl.
32. B 204. Base-Ring I–II jug.
33. B 217. Base-Ring I–II jug.
34. B 189. Base-Ring I kylix.
35. B 148. White Slip II bowl.
36. B 90. White Slip I bowl.
37. B 983. Red Lustrous III bottle.
38. B 984. Red Lustrous III bottle.
39. Missing. Fragments of ten Base-Ring II plain-mouthed jugs.

CHRONOLOGY

The objects in this tomb appear to belong to burials of the LC I–LC IIA periods. The gold objects, cylinder seals and imported vases of Tombs 12 to 17 make these early tombs the richest at Bamboula, even though all except the first-mentioned had been plundered, or at least disturbed, prior to excavation. Besides the objects listed under the tombs, one must reckon in this complex objects found scattered between Tombs 12, 13 and 17, which either may be fragments from these tombs left behind by plunderers or may be from other tombs which lay very close to the surface.

Tomb 14

GENERAL REMARKS

Tomb 14 lay adjacent to Tomb 13. It, too, had been plundered and was obviously not thoroughly excavated by Daniel. He found a skeleton stretched out in dorsal position at an unspecified depth below the surface. This burial was associated with LC III Decorated bowls (not catalogued). Below the skeleton in a layer of red earth were found some pottery (not further defined) and several objects, but nothing in situ. According to Daniel's field sketch (Pl. 8) the shape of the tomb as excavated was roughly oval and it measured 2.68 m. x 1.55 m.

FINDS

1. B 1362. Semicircular gold bead.
2. B 1404. Ivory disk.
3. B 1347. Glass fragments.

CHRONOLOGY

The skeleton apparently belongs to the LC IIIA period. There is no basis for dating earlier periods in this tomb.

Tomb 15

LOCATION, SIZE AND SHAPE

Tomb 15 lay about midway between Tombs 12 and 14. It was oval in shape and measured 2.6 m. x 2.8 m. with a depth of 1.8 m. No plan exists, nor any indication of the location of the dromos.

GENERAL REMARKS

Apparently the roof had collapsed, for Daniel dug through successive layers of fallen chavara (cf. SCE I, xvii for definition of this term) expecting to find an intact tomb. Since, on the contrary, it was found to have been thoroughly plundered, the possibility is raised that it had been plundered already in antiquity. A few bones and a skull were found on the east side in clearing the chamber to bedrock.

FINDS

1. B 1365. Gold earring (found in screening).

2. B 1377. Gold spiral ring. On floor, south.
3. B 1366. Gold earring. On floor.
4. B 1367. Gold earring. On floor.
5. B 1329. Fragment of faience pot.
6. B 1369. Thin spiral of gold (found in screening).

CHRONOLOGY

There is no certain basis for dating this tomb but the richness of the finds, even after plundering, puts it unequivocally in the same context as the early tombs 12–14 and 16–17 (which are nearby).

Tomb 16

LOCATION, SIZE AND SHAPE

This tomb lies immediately east of Tomb 12. Its shape was roughly rectangular but with very irregular ends (*Pl. 8*). Measurements are 2.42 m. x 3.14 m. Daniel found mud-brick fragments beginning 65 cm. below the present surface, and postulated from this fact a brick superstructure over the tomb. This was also the case with Tomb 9, where the explanation is made more convincing by the proximity of the tomb floor to the surface. Since the original floor of Tomb 16 lay 1.4 m. below the surface, however, one is at a loss to understand why so deep a chamber would have been dug to receive a superstructure.

STRATIFICATION AND BURIALS

The tomb was intercepted on the east by a *voupha*, or pit, perhaps in Roman times, and this area was clearly disturbed. A floor with scattered bones and objects was reached at one meter below the surface. Three skulls were found close together but there was no semblance of a skeleton. The tomb does not appear to have been plundered but the chaotic mixture of early finds (e.g., Nos. 15 and 16) with later finds (e.g., No. 12 and Nos. 29–44) suggests that this tomb, like the nearby Tomb 3, was subject to flooding. The excavator was of the opinion that nothing in the tomb was truly *in situ* and did not attempt to establish a chronological sequence. However, the following find-positions were noted. Nos. 1, 8–15, 19–22: over the one-meter floor. Nos. 2–7, 16–18: on the one-meter floor. No. 23: below the one-meter floor (notice that this is the other half of No. 21, found above the floor). Nos. 24, 27: below 1.2 meters; No. 28: above rock floor. No. 25: on rock floor (at 1.4 meters).

FINDS

1. B 1407. Ivory duck's head.
2. B 1411. Cylindrical ivory object.
3. B 1408. Head of ivory pin.
4. B 1638. Blue paste scarab.
5. B 1639. Blue paste scarab.
6. B 1419. Ivory button.
7. B 1392. Ivory button.
8. B 1635. Crystal seal.
9. B 1451. Steatite bowl.
10. B 1474. Pestle.
11. B 461. LC III Decorated bowl.
12. B 1017. Mycenaean III bowl.
13. B 1253. Bronze bowl.
14. B 1452. Steatite bowl with tripod base, broken.
15. B 1353. Fragments of glass pot.
16. B 193. Base-Ring I jug.
17. B 1047. Mycenaean III bowl.
18. B 253. Base-Ring II bowl.
19. B 1476. Pestle.
20. B 1385. Fragment of iron knife.
21. B 1393. Ivory disk with peg.
22. B 1410. Cylindrical ivory object, with No. 21.
23. Part of No. 21.
24. B 1395. Ivory disk.
25. B 1354. Cylindrical gold bead.
26. B 1355. Cylindrical gold bead (in screening).
27. B 1394. Fragment of ivory disk, with No. 24.
28. B 254. Base-Ring II bowl.

The following were mended from sherds:
29. B 462. LC III Decorated bowl.
30. B 463. LC III Decorated bowl.
31. B 464. LC III Decorated bowl.
32. B 465. LC III Decorated bowl.
33. B 466. LC III Decorated bowl.
34. B 416. LC III Decorated bowl.
35. B 417. LC III Decorated bowl.
36. B 418. LC III Decorated bowl.
37. B 419. LC III Decorated bowl.
38. B 903. LC III Plain bowl.
39. B 904. LC III Plain bowl.
40. B 905. LC III Plain bowl.
41. B 503. LC III Decorated bowl.
42. B 504. LC III Decorated bowl.
43. B 467. LC III Decorated bowl.
44. B 468. LC III Decorated bowl.
45. B 1018. Mycenaean III bowl.
46. B 1103. Mycenaean III 3-handled jar.
47. B 1104. Mycenaean III 3-handled jar.

48. B 1105. Mycenaean III 3-handled jar.
49. B 216. Base-Ring I–II jug.
50. B 79. White Slip I bowl.
51. B 1072. Fragments of Mycenaean III krater.
52. B 332. Burnished Slip bowl. In earth over tomb.

CHRONOLOGY

From the general situation it seems quite certain that an LC III burial period, probably entirely of LC IIIB date, originally lay over one or more earlier burial periods.

Tombs 17-17A

LOCATION, SIZE AND SHAPE

These two tombs, connected by an oblong dromos, form one complex (*Pl. 9*). This scheme had a certain currency at Kourion (see Tomb 33, and Kaloriziki, Tomb 36). I do not know of any exact parallels although multi-chambered tombs are known from Cyprus (*Problems*, 21, Fig. 4), and multiple tombs with one dromos occurred at Mavro Spelio in Crete (*BSA* 28, 1926–7, 244 ff.). Tombs 17–17A are located at the edge of the upper terrace above Area E, about 15 m. east of Tomb 15. They are entered from the dromos at the east and west ends respectively, and are of highly irregular shape, each having a kind of buttress approximately opposite the stomion dividing the chambers, as it were, into two (*Pl. 2*). This latter feature appears to be an early, and probably a foreign, one (cf. *Problems*, 146 ff.). The maximum dimensions of Tomb 17 were 2.2 m. x 4 m.; of Tomb 17A, 2.7 m. x 5.4 m. The chamber of Tomb 17 was 1.5 m. in height.

GENERAL REMARKS

These two tombs proved to be Tombs 53 and 102 explored by the British Museum in 1895. This fact was established beyond doubt by the finding of many fragments of the so-called "Window Krater," a Mycenaean chariot vase (British Museum C 391). Since fragments of this vase were originally found, curiously enough, in both Tombs 53 and 102, there must remain some doubt as to precisely which of the New Tomb series should be equated with which of the Old Tomb series. Since, however, Find No. 14 (NT 17) appears to be from the same pot as No. 6 (OT 102), it seems reasonable to equate NT 17 and OT 102, although Daniel stated that NT 17A was OT 102. No help on this score is to be had from the completely ambiguous and unsatisfactorily oriented map of the British excavations (*ExC*, 61): see p. 4. These tombs had already been plundered when the British found them. Daniel found Tomb 17 to be full of red earth with bones and pottery, mainly of the LC III period. He proceeded to the floor of the tomb, but, in view of the disturbed state of things, proposed abandoning the excavation. Thanks to the insistence of the foreman, Christos Grigoriou, he continued clearing the tomb and was immediately rewarded by finding two pairs of gold earrings in the shape of calf's heads (Nos. 1–4), and then other objects. Tomb 17A was found to be more thoroughly ransacked than Tomb 17. Only a few sections of the original fill of the tomb were found high on the walls, tunnelled under and devoid of finds. A mass of sherds, clearly discarded by the earlier excavators, was found in the center. Over the sherds was a well-cut block of unspecified proportions.

FINDS

Tomb 17:

1. B 1370. Gold earring with gold wire.
2. B 1371. Gold earring with gold wire.
3. B 1375. Gold earring with gold wire.
4. B 1372. Gold earring with gold wire.
5. B 1373. Gold earring with gold wire. In earth thrown out of tomb.
6. B 1374. Gold earring with gold wire. Found in screening.
7. B 1507. Steatite button.
8. Missing. Fragment of haematite cylinder. Found in screening.
9. Missing. Fragments of gold leaf.
10. B 1441. Silver earring.
11. Missing. Lantern-shaped gold bead, smashed.
12. B 1442. Silver ring. Found in screening.
13. B 1269. Bronze dagger. Found in screening.
14. B 1348. Fragments of blue glass bottle.
Mended from sherds:
15. B 1062. Mycenaean III krater.
16. B 608. LC III Decorated jug.
17. B 453. LC III Decorated bowl.
18. B 565. LC III Decorated bowl.
19. B 523. LC III Decorated bowl.
20. B 524. LC III Decorated bowl.
21. B 454. LC III Decorated bowl.
22. B 455. LC III Decorated bowl.

23. B 456. LC III Decorated bowl.
24. B 457. LC III Decorated bowl.
25. B 1454. Stone mortar.
26. B 1067. Sherds of Mycenaean III krater (BM C 391).
27. Miscellaneous sherds: see Table, f.

Tomb 17A

1. B 1453. Stone mortar.
2. B 1475. Pestle.
3. B 1388. Iron nail.
4. Miscellaneous sherds: see Table, g.

CHRONOLOGY

The distribution of sherds in Tomb 17, being quite poor in White Slip wares, though not in Base-Ring wares, and with adequate quantities of imported wares (Mycenaean and Syrian), rather parallels that of the cellar deposit in Area D. So far as one can speak with authority on the matter of a badly plundered tomb, the probable range of its use was from LC IIA to LC IIIB. It would be well also to recall the early shape of the tomb as pointed out above. The prevalence and type of LC III Decorated bowls speak definitely for a late LC III burial period, probably entirely of LC IIIB date, lying over a burial or burials of the LC II period. The Roman sherds noted in the Table, f, must be intrusive: but the Geometric sherds may well point to an actual re-use, or partial re-use, of the tomb in ancient times. This is made even more probable by the fibula (No. 8 of the OT list; on this fibula, see now Birmingham, *DFCL,* 92). The sherds of Tomb 17A likewise point to use of the tomb soon after the Bronze Age. In this case the first plundering of these rich tombs may have occurred already at that time.

Tomb 18

LOCATION, SIZE AND SHAPE

Tomb 18 lay about 22 meters southwest of Tomb 2 (in Area F). Its basic shape appears from the drawing to have been roughly square, though with rounded corners (*Pl. 8*). At the 90 cm. level it measured 2.09 m. x 2.19 m. There is no information available as to location of the dromos.

STRATIFICATION

From excavation photographs this tomb appears to have been a chamber tomb, the roof of which had collapsed or been eroded away, though this is nowhere expressly stated. Burial Period B comprised Skulls I–IV and Nos. 1–8, found 75 cm. below the surface on red earth. Below this level was very red sandy earth. Burial Period A comprised Skulls V–VIII and Nos. 10–20, found at 90 cm. below the surface on gray, gritty, sandy earth. Bedrock was reached at one meter below the surface. The position of the bones and finds suggests that the tomb had been flooded.

FINDS

1. Missing. Spiral silver ring.
2. B 534. LC III Decorated bowl.
3. B 830. Plain Wheelmade II jug.
4. B 917. LC III Plain jug.
5. B 1255. Bronze bowl.
6. B 587. LC III Decorated jug.
7. B 471. LC III Decorated bowl.
8. B 472. LC III Decorated bowl.
9. Missing. Carnelian bead. Found in screening earth from below 75 cm., therefore to be reckoned with Period A.
10. B 1519. Steatite spindlewhorl.
11. B 1402. Ivory disk.
12. B 1158. Mycenaean III stirrup jar.
13. B 973. Coarse Ware jug.
14. B 247. Base-Ring II bowl.
15. B 331. Burnished Slip bowl.
16. B 109. White Slip II bowl.
17. B 1335. Glass bead.
18. B 1270. Bronze dagger.
19. B 1297. Bronze spearhead.
20. B 1298. Bronze spearhead.
21. Missing. Pestle. Found in screening.

CHRONOLOGY

Period B belongs to the LC IIIA period. Period A may be assigned to the LC IIB period, although, owing to the small quantity of wares, a slightly wider range, particularly upward in time, must be allowed.

Tomb 19

LOCATION, SIZE AND SHAPE

This tomb is situated in the so-called "Street of Tombs" in Area E, virtually opposite Tomb 40 but with reversed orientation. It was entered on the southeast side from the usual pan-shaped, almost square, dromos measuring 1 m. x 1.3 m. with a depth of 58 cm. Hewn out of the bedrock on the east side is a niche 45 cm. x 52 cm. with a circular mouth and a depth of 33 cm.; on the south side is another measuring 36 cm. x 60 cm. with an oval mouth 35 cm. high. These were found closed with large stone slabs whereas the stomion was closed with small irregular stones (*Pl. 3*). The original shape of the tomb at the 1.9 m. level is that of an oval, somewhat displaced to the west at the upper end (cf. Tomb 12). It measured 2.13 m. x 2.39 m. with an estimated height to the roof of 1.5 m. During the LC III period, the shape was altered and the area considerably reduced by the construction of a stone wall across the southwest part of the tomb. This is shown by the plans of the 1.35 m. and the 1.80 m. levels (*Pl. 10*).

STRATIFICATION

No section exists but the stratigraphy can be recovered to some extent from the field notes. The dromos itself was filled with firm brown earth. The tomb, which presumably had collapsed, was entered not through the *stomion* but from above. The latest burial group was found at 70 cm. below the top of the bedrock (*Pl. 10*). There were various other burials down to a firm gritty layer over the 1.35 m. floor. Also over this floor in the north was a carefully laid packing of stones. These were set in a layer of gritty red earth, entirely without bones, and—according to Daniel's surmise from the pithos sherds found in it—brought in from the settlement. This layer went at places to 1.45 m., where it ended on soft sandy gray earth by the door, and to 1.8 m. (*Pl. 2*) where it ended on great masses of bones. Rather large stones were found throughout the various levels except at bedrock (1.9 m.).

BURIALS

In view of the numerous burials it is convenient to present them in tabular form:

BURIAL	LEVEL	BONES	FINDS
F	70 cm.	Skull I	Nos. 1–3, 22
	85 cm.	Skulls II–III (adults) IV–IX (babies)	No. 5 (with IV); Nos. 4, 6–10 (with VI–IX)
E	1 m.	Skulls X–XXXIV and skeletal remains of many babies	Nos. 11–17, 25
D	1.20 m.	Skulls XXXV–XLIV	Nos. 18–21; 23, 24
C	1.35 m.	Skeletons XLV–XLVI	Nos. 26–30 (on chest of XLV); 31 (on finger of XLV); 32–36
B	1.80 m.	Skulls XLVII–LI	Nos. 40–46; 58
A	1.90 m.	Skull LII	Nos. 51–53; 56, 57

In addition to the attributions given above, it may be noted that Nos. 38 and 39 were found between 1.35 and 1.45 m. depth. They must therefore be associated with Burial B. Nos. 47, 49 and 50 were found below 1.8 m. and may belong to either B or A. No. 54 was found in the east niche of the dromos and No. 55 in the dromos itself. No. 22 was found above 70 cm. It may still belong to Skull I. The large number of more or less contemporary burials, especially of babies, might seem plausibly to be the result of an epidemic. Skeleton XXXV is an instance of the *Hockerstellung*, whereas XLV is dorsal. In this tomb it is not clear to what extent bones were disturbed by other factors than re-use of the tomb.

FINDS

1. B 1273. Bronze fibula.
2. B 1520. Steatite spindlewhorl.
3. B 702. Bucchero jug.
4. B 1632. Dome-shaped seal.
5. B 1323, B 1351, B 1439. Necklace of one glass bead, one glass loop and 17 sea-snails.
6. B 1389. Bronze pin with conical ivory bead.
7. B 1321. Faience bead.
8. B 1320. Faience bead.
9. B 531. LC III Decorated bowl.
10. B 469. LC III Decorated bowl.
11. B 532. LC III Decorated bowl.
12. B 556. LC III Decorated bowl.

13. B 1590. Loomweight.
14. B 586. LC III Decorated jug.
15. B 436. LC III Decorated bowl.
16. B 1259. Bronze bracelet.
17. B 1344. Glass bead.
18. B 836. Plain Wheelmade II jug.
19. B 470. LC III Decorated bowl.
20. B 1309. Bronze rod.
21. Missing. Bronze rod with ivory bead.
22. B 1399. Ivory disk.
23. Missing. Ivory button.
24. Missing. Ivory pin head.
25. Missing. Glass bead.
26. B 1629. Cylinder seal.
27. B 1356. Paste cylinder with gold ends.
28. B 1636. Dome-shaped seal of steatite.
29. B 1631. Dome-shaped seal of steatite.
30. B 1626. Cylinder seal of steatite.
31. Missing. Bronze ring on small finger of right hand of Skeleton XLV.
32. B 1254. Bronze bowl.
33. B 866. Plain Wheelmade II jug.
34. B 867. Plain Wheelmade II jug.
35. B 283. Handmade Bucchero jug.
36. B 1334. Glass bead.
37. Missing. Small faience bead. Found in screening.
38. B 1281. Bronze needle.
39. B 1432. Handle with impressed ornament.
40. B 1563. Base-Ring female figurine with earrings.
41. B 1107. Mycenaean III 3-handled jar.
42. B 108. White Slip II bowl.
43. B 107. White Slip II bowl.
44. B 246. Base-Ring II bowl.
45. B 789. Plain White jug.
46. B 105. White Slip II bowl.
47. B 1400. Oval ivory disk.
48. Number not used.
49. B 803. Handle, inscribed, of Plain White jug.
50. B 1357. Gold bead.
51. B 280. Handmade Bucchero jug.
52. B 281. Handmade Bucchero jug.
53. Missing. Horse-shoe shaped silver bead.
54. B 1534. Steatite spindlewhorl. In east niche of dromos.
55. B 1535. Steatite spindlewhorl. Dromos.
56. B 1537. Steatite spindlewhorl.
57. B 1403. Ivory disk.
58. B 106. White Slip II bowl (with sherds of No. 43).

CHRONOLOGY

The excavator considered that Skulls I–IX represented the latest burial period (F: see *AJA* 45, 1941, 272, n. 54) from a late phase of the LC III period (LC IIIB). This view is especially supported by the presence of the fibula (No. 1) and the fact that there exist in the tomb many burials (37 in E, D and C) of the LC IIIA period, suggesting already a concentrated use of the tomb during a relatively long span of time. It is more difficult to assign a certain date to the earlier burial periods. The excavator's remarks (*loc. cit.*) make it clear that he considered Burial Period B to be late in the LC IIC period. However, the remarkable similarity of Nos. 42, 43, 46 and 58 with B 110 and B 120 from LC IIA contexts advises extreme caution in accepting this. One would expect all these to be roughly contemporary. Moreover, an earlier date would be much more appropriate also for Nos. 40, 41 and 45. It seems better to me, therefore, to assign the range LC IIA–B to Burial Period B and also to Burial Period A, with the added remark that this range is entirely appropriate on stylistic grounds to the Handmade Bucchero jugs, B 280 and B 281. On the other hand, P. Åström has advised me, after seeing the material, that he considers the Mycenaean jar, No. 41, to be probably a survival since No. 44 appeared to him to be a late form of Base-Ring II, while No. 45 could perhaps go with this. The dating of the earliest burials must apparently remain uncertain.

Tomb 20

GENERAL REMARKS

Tomb 20 lay at the base of the same outcropping of rock as Tombs 10 and 11, slightly to the east of those tombs (*Pl. 1*). Almost nothing was preserved of this tomb, for it had been cut down and largely destroyed. Daniel did not express an opinion as to whether this effect had been produced by man or by erosion (cf. the similar case of Tomb 11). In any case, the tomb had presumably been plundered for only a spearhead and some fragments of pottery were found on the rock floor in the southwest corner. No plan was made.

FINDS

1. B 1295. Bronze spearhead.
2. Sherds (49-12-441): see Table, h.

CHRONOLOGY

On the basis of the sherds the tomb may be dated to the LC IIA period.

Tomb 21

LOCATION, SIZE AND SHAPE

Tomb 21 was located about 40 cm. west of Tomb 20, at the base of the same cliff. Being deep and set farther back into the cliff, it was better preserved. It has a roughly rectangular shape, with the usual rounded corners and a kind of bilobate effect (*Pl. 11*; cf. Tomb 6) on the north side. Its dimensions and the position of the dromos are not recorded.

GENERAL REMARKS

Masses of bones and skulls were found along the south wall in a careful arrangement which appears intentional; a few pots were found in the northeast corner. Since there is no distinct evidence of plundering, a possible explanation for this state of the tomb is that it was prepared for a later burial which never took place. One may recall a similar suggestion made in the case of Tomb 6. An Iron Age pot, No. 10, associated with this tomb, may come from the surface, or it may date the contemplated re-use of the tomb.

FINDS

1. B 110. White Slip II bowl.
2. B 1159. Mycenaean III stirrup jar.
3. B 1177. Mycenaean III 2-handled jar.
4. B 784. Plain White jug.
5. B 205. Base-Ring I jug.
6. B 200. Base-Ring I juglet.
7. B 1182. Mycenaean III miniature jug.
8. B 1286. Bronze ring, on finger in southwest mass of bones.
9. B 732. White Painted jug.
10. Sherds (49-12-339): see Table, i.

CHRONOLOGY

Both the pots and the sherds suggest a date for the original use of the tomb in the LC IIA period, if one discounts the four sherds of LC III Decorated ware. These may be intrusive or may represent a later burial.

Tomb 22

GENERAL REMARKS

This tomb lay about 25 meters east of Tombs 20–21 in terrain sloping down towards Area A (*Pl. 1*). It was very close to the surface and almost completely destroyed. There is no plan nor any indication of whether it was originally a chamber tomb or had a mud-brick superstructure.

FINDS

1. B 1108. Mycenaean III 3-handled jar.
2. Missing. Base-Ring jug.
3. B 768. Plain White jug.
4. B 1330. Blue glass bead. Under No. 2.
5. B 1331. Blue glass bead.
6. B 1332. Blue glass bead.
7. B 1333. Blue glass bead.
8. B 1248. Bone rod, found with Nos. 4–7.
9. B 1536. Incised spindlewhorl, found with Nos. 4–7.
10. B 1243. Terracotta spindlewhorl, found with Nos. 4–7.
11. Sherds (49-12-350). See Table, j.

CHRONOLOGY

Existing finds and sherds suggest a date for use of the tomb in the LC IIA period.

Tomb 23

GENERAL REMARKS

Tomb 23 lay in the line of the series of tombs stretching eastward from Tomb 6, some 20 meters short of Tomb 22, the terminus of this series. Like Tomb 22, it lay very close to the surface and was largely destroyed. Bedrock was found at 30 to 50 cm. below the present surface. A field sketch (*Pl. 11*) without indication of scale shows the position of several finds.

FINDS

1. B 473. LC III Decorated bowl.
2. B 588. LC III Decorated jug.
3. B 859. Plain Wheelmade II jug fragment.
4. B 868. Plain Wheelmade II jug fragment.
5. B 249. Base-Ring II bowl.
6. Uncatalogued (49-12-365): Bronze hook diseased at both ends, 2.1 cm. in length. Apparently from this tomb but not on plan.
7. Sherds (49-12-359): see Table, k.

CHRONOLOGY

The burial represented by the pots found probably belongs to the LC IIIA period. The sherds, however, suggest that the tomb had been in use in the LC II period.

Tomb 24

GENERAL REMARKS

This tomb lay in the line of the series of tombs stretching eastward from Tomb 6 (*Pl. 1*). A *voupha* (pit) had been sunk into its north side; also a burial had taken place in it during the Archaic period while the chamber was still intact. The roof later collapsed and *chavara* blocks from it went down onto the Archaic burial. Daniel did not excavate the Archaic burial but tunneled under it to recover objects from an LC II stratum, which he described as completely disturbed. There are no drawings and no information about the size and dimensions of the tomb.

FINDS

1. B 1184. Mycenaean III jug.
2. Missing. Circular gold bead. Diam. 0.4 cm.
3. B 1380. Gold leaf fragment.
4. B 1352. Glass pomegranate.
5. B 1336. Colored glass bead.
6. B 1413. Ivory rod.
7. B 1414. Head for ivory rod.
8. B 1415. Head for ivory rod.
9. B 1405. Head for ivory rod.
10. B 1406. Ivory disk.
11. B 1422. Ivory button.
12. B 1540. Steatite spindlewhorl.
13. Uncatalogued. Head for ivory rod, completely covered with white accretion.
14. Sherds: see Table, l.

CHRONOLOGY

The sherds point to a date in the LC IIC period for the earlier stratum.

Tomb 25

GENERAL REMARKS

Tomb 25 was adjacent to Tomb 24 on the west. No information whatsoever was recorded about it, except that it had been completely disturbed by a large *voupha* (pit) in the east.

FINDS

1. Missing. Fragments of bronze bowl. ED: 16 cm.
2. Discarded. Lump of iron (later found to be stone).
3. B 1381. Iron chisel.
4. Discarded. Fragment of Roman glass. Presumably from *voupha*.
5. B 1617. Miniature terracotta shield (?)
6. B 294. Monochrome bowl.
7. Missing. Small hemispherical bowl with burnished exterior.
8. B 530. LC III Decorated bowl.
9. B 458. LC III Decorated bowl.
10. B 476. LC III Decorated bowl.
11. B 902. LC III Plain bowl.
12. B 1055. Mycenaean III kylix fragment.
13. B 1056. Mycenaean III kylix fragment.
14. B 1057. Mycenaean III kylix fragment.
15. Sherds (49-12-376): see Table, m.

CHRONOLOGY

In view of the dearth of information it is not feasible to do more than suggest a possible range for the use of this tomb: from the LC IIB to the LC IIIB periods.

Tomb 26

LOCATION, SIZE AND SHAPE

Tomb 26 is cut into the rock ledge along the southwest border of Area E. Although no drawing was made (apparently), the following description, in effect, was recorded in the field notebook: The dromos is very carefully cut and rectangular, 1.3 m. x 1.35 m. It has a niche 55 cm. x 55 cm. and 35 cm. deep with a round door 30 cm. in diameter in the west wall. The floor of the dromos slopes slightly toward the *stomion* which is 80 cm. high and 10.4 m. in width. Within the door there is an almost sheer drop of 1.15 m. to the floor of the tomb. The chamber is approximately oval in shape, measuring 3.35 m. x 4.2 m. and 2.2 m. in height. The greatest length is in the axis of the dromos.

GENERAL REMARKS

Although this tomb is still exposed, it is now largely silted up. It was found completely plundered but still contained numerous fragments of pottery. The fact that this is the same tomb as OT 50, excavated by the British Museum in 1895, was established through sherds of an octopus pot (Sh 547) which join British Museum C 501. This circumstance has been discussed in detail in *Berytus* 14 (1961) 37 f.

FINDS

1. B 1421. Ivory button.

2. Sherds (49-12-378) including B 270, B 991, B 1134 and B 1231: see Table, n.

To be added to these are the objects listed under Tomb 50 in *ExC*, 79.

CHRONOLOGY

Apart from Archaic sherds which are obviously intrusive, the sherds found suggest that this tomb was in use during the LC II period.

Tomb 27

GENERAL REMARKS

Tomb 27 is situated in the rock ledge along the southwest border of Area E. The only information recorded about it is that it was roughly circular in shape and filled with powdered *chavara* (see *SCE* I, xvii, for definition of this term); it was doubtless much caved in. Though thoroughly plundered it yielded two objects and a number of sherds.

FINDS

1. B 664. Proto-White Painted amphoriskos.
2. B 1412. Ivory rod.
3. Sherds (49-12-386): see Table, o.

CHRONOLOGY

The distribution of sherds is not very conclusive. Taken as a whole, they might suggest use in the LC IIC period; however, No. 1 indicates that the tomb was also used in the LC IIIB period.

Tomb 28

GENERAL REMARKS

Tomb 28 lies just to the southwest of Tomb 27. It is a chamber tomb, stated to be roughly rectangular in shape and with a rectangular dromos, but no dimensions are given. Although still visible, it is so silted up that its measurements could not be recovered without extensive excavation. It had been plundered but a few objects were found.

FINDS

1. B 224. Base-Ring bull.

2. B 1368. Gold earring.
3. B 1014. Mycenaean III bowl.
4. B 1015. Mycenaean III bowl.
5. Various sherds (49-12-392) including B 895 and one of same fabric as B 1203: see Table, p.

CHRONOLOGY

The distribution of the sherds suggests that this tomb was used during the LC II period. There is no definite assurance of later use since the few sherds of later date may be intrusive.

Tomb 29

LOCATION, SIZE AND SHAPE

Tomb 29 lies just west of Tombs 13 and 14. It is circular in shape with a diameter of 2.3 m. The position of the dromos could not be determined. The tomb had been cut on the west by a *voupha* (pit). The east half was found to be faced with rubble masonry (see *Pl. 4*), which is preserved to a height of one meter. The floor is 1.5 m. below the surface.

GENERAL REMARKS AND CHRONOLOGY

In view of the absence of a list of finds and any description of the excavation, one may assume that the tomb was found plundered. Some sherds (49-12-394) however, including the graffito B 883, are associated with it. Their distribution suggests use of the tomb in the LC II period and, possibly, re-use in the Geometric or Archaic period: see Table, q.

Tomb 30

LOCATION, SIZE AND SHAPE

Tomb 30 was a cist grave lying over the *chavara* floor of Room 6 in House VII of Area E in a corner of a bedrock cutting (*Pl. 11*). The eastern side was delimited by two cut stones. Two large cut stones to the north may have covered the grave (*Pl. 4*). In any case, the walls of the graves were originally higher. Daniel did not establish any definite shape or size for the grave, but it probably was not any longer than the space required for the funeral gifts.

BURIALS

The lower part of a large pot (No. 1), probably an amphora, contained the burnt bones of a child. No other bones were found.

FINDS

1. B 979. Base of Plain White I amphora (?)
2. B 738. Bichrome I jug.
3. B 715. White Painted I bowl.
4. B 712. "Pseudo-monochrome" bowl.
5. B 721. White Painted I bowl.
6. B 728. White Painted I jug fragment.
7. B 1210. Foreign pilgrim flask.
8. B 713. "Pseudo-monochrome" bowl.
9. B 718. White Painted I bowl.

CHRONOLOGY

The burial is clearly dated to the early part of the CG I period. House VII had already been abandoned for a considerable period before its ruins were thus chosen as the site of a grave.

Tomb 31

GENERAL REMARKS

The number 31 was given to an area partially under Room 1 of House VI in Area E. Actually this is part of a large underground cutting of irregular shape which extends to the southwest under House VI and to which access may have been had from the north corner of Room 3. It may have consisted originally of two (or even more) tombs pierced from one into the other, but it seems best to consider it—at least during the occupation of House VI—as a kind of cellar, on the analogy of the cellar in Area D. However, the entire extent of this cutting, which was filled with debris, was not excavated by Daniel. At some stage it may have served as a stable of sorts, for several hitching holes are cut into the rock walls. This is likely to have been after House VI had been abandoned and Room 1 had partially collapsed, thus providing sufficient access for fairly large animals. The large number of Geometric and early Archaic sherds among the deposit surely indicates, in fact, use of some sort during those periods, whereas the absence of any later sherds probably means that the entrance became silted up after that and the cave forgotten.

FINDS

1. B 777. Plain White jug fragment.
2. B 1228. Hellenistic (?) juglet.
3. B 745. Black-on-Red II plate.
4. B 974. Gray Ware jug.
5. B 731. White Painted IV jug fragment.
6. B 730. White Painted IV amphora neck.
7. B 733. White Painted amphora fragments.
8. B 1262. Bronze chisel.
9. Sherds: see Table, r.

Tomb 32

LOCATION, SIZE AND SHAPE

Tomb 32 lay five meters southeast of Tomb 33. It had a square dromos with three deep niches (*Pl. 4*). The chamber was roughly rectangular, with an oblong depression in the center and a niche to the right of the door (*Pl. 11*). Dimensions cannot be given for they are not recorded, no scale appeared in the field drawing and the tomb is no longer visible. It was recorded, however, that the east niche of the dromos was 50 cm. deep, the south niche 30 cm. deep and the west niche 45 cm. deep. The floor of the chamber was 1.1 m. from the roof, and the depression was 15 cm. below the floor.

GENERAL REMARKS

The tomb was described as plundered and full of gritty brown earth and large stones. Parts of three skulls and various objects were found.

1. B 282. Handmade Bucchero jug.
2. B 420. LC III Decorated bowl.
3. B 906. LC III Plain bowl.
4. B 474. LC III Decorated bowl.
5. B 674. Proto-White Painted jug.
6. B 824. Plain Wheelmade II jug.
7. B 475. LC III Decorated bowl.
8. B 1401. Ivory disk.

Mended from sherds:

9. B 421. LC III Decorated bowl.
10. B 422. LC III Decorated bowl.
11. B 423. LC III Decorated bowl.
12. B 285. Handmade Bucchero jug.
13. B 1387. Fragment of iron knife (with No. 8).

14. B 415. Fragment of LC III Decorated bowl from the chamber (unstratified).
15. Sherds (49-12-418) from the niches: see Table, s.

CHRONOLOGY

The pots found must have belonged to burials of the LC III period. The evidence of the sherds associated with the chamber was confused, but admits the possibility of there having been earlier (though not later) use of the chamber. Very possibly, most of the evidence of earlier burials was cleared out in preparation for the latest burial. The construction of the tomb is roughly dated by sherds from the niches to the LC 1B period.

Tomb 33

LOCATION, SIZE AND SHAPE

Tomb 33 lies at the northeast edge of Area E beyond Tombs 19 and 40. It was actually the west chamber of a double tomb served by a single dromos (cf. Tombs 17–17A). The east chamber was found collapsed and plundered. The shape of the west chamber is roughly square, though with rounded corners, measuring each way 2.4 m. Maximum height of the chamber is 1.5 m. The *stomion* was on the east side.

STRATIFICATION

The chamber was filled to the roof with dark loose earth, black above and red-brown below. This went down onto a level of pots and bones in brown clay with white grits in the west, and onto a large, well-built platform of stones set in loose green *chonnos* (cf. *SCE* I, xvii and *Problems*, 16 for definition of this term) in the east (*Pl. 4*). For a discussion of this feature, see supra, p. 8. There was clear evidence of flooding with consequent disturbance of the skeletons. The following key explains the strata shown in the cross-section (*Pl. 12*):

1. Brown earth with sand and fine white grits, hard.
2. Soft brown earth.
3. Loose earth with some brick fragments.
4. Brick.

BURIALS

The latest burial, C, was laid on the stone platform with Nos. 1–14 as gifts. Two leg bones of this skeleton still remained on the platform. Nos. 15 and 16, found in disturbed earth over the tomb, were also associated by the excavator with the latest burial. It must be admitted that the significance of "earth over the tomb" is not clear, since the chamber is still reasonably intact. Perhaps it was actually partially collapsed on the east side, so that the pots might have floated up and out of the tomb. Whatever the correct explanation may be, there can be no doubt that these two pots belong integrally in type and date with Nos. 1–14. Daniel considered their original position to be on the east platform. To make room for C, the burials with which Nos. 17–32 and 44–46 were associated (Period B) had been swept aside to the west (in Level 1 of the cross-section: (*Pl. 12*). These in turn lay over remnants of a still earlier burial (or burials) in Level 2 of the cross-section. This is Period A, with which Nos. 33–42 are associated. It is not clear whether Nos. 33, 40 and 42 were in or under the stone platform, but presumably they were on the floor under the platform.

FINDS

1. B 680. Proto-White Painted jug.
2. B 681. Proto-White Painted jug.
3. B 925. Ringed potstand.
4. B 873. Plain Wheelmade II jug.
5. B 687. Proto-White Painted jug.
6. B 655. Proto-White Painted amphora.
7. B 642. Proto-White Painted bowl.
8. B 679. Proto-White Painted jug.
9. B 644. Proto-White Painted bowl.

10. B 686. Proto-White Painted jug.
11. B 651. Proto-White Painted amphoriskos.
12. B 643. Proto-White Painted bowl.
13. B 688. Proto-White Painted jug.
14. B 435. LC III Decorated bowl.
15. B 654. Proto-White Painted krater-amphora.
16. B 645. Proto-White Painted bowl.
17. B 609. LC III Decorated jug.
18. B 822. Plain Wheelmade II jug.
19. B 344. Burnished Slip bowl.
20. B 477. LC III Decorated bowl.
21. B 500. LC III Decorated bowl.
22. B 502. LC III Decorated bowl.
23. B 501. LC III Decorated bowl.
24. B 1102. Mycenaean III 3-handled jar.
25. B 1521. Steatite spindlewhorl. In earth over burials.
25a. B 857. Plain Wheelmade II jug.
26. B 1473. Stone pestle.
26a. B 858. Plain Wheelmade II jug.
27. B 1450. Stone mortar. On platform.
27a. B 821. Plain Wheelmade II jug.
28. B 694. Black Slip Bucchero jug.
29. B 459. LC III Decorated bowl.
30. B 460. LC III Decorated bowl.
31. B 104. White Slip II bowl.
32. Fragments of No. 31.

33. B 1246. Alabaster jar.
34. B 835. Plain Wheelmade II jug.
35. B 1179. Mycenaean III juglet.
36. B 1180. Mycenaean III juglet.
37. B 1181. Mycenaean III juglet.
38. B 1443. Silver ring fragments.
39. B 1378. Loop of gold wire.
40. B 1285. Bronze spiral ring, on finger.
41. B 101. White Slip II bowl.
42. B 1358. Gold bead.
43. Missing. Bronze ring found in screening.
44. B 102. White Slip II bowl.
45. B 103. White Slip II bowl.
46. B 234. Base-Ring II bowl.
From screening: no level given
47. B 1524. Steatite spindlewhorl.
48. B 1346. Glass bead.
49. B 1308. Bronze rod.
50. Sherds: with C, see Table, t.
        with B, see Table, u.
        with A, see Table, v.

CHRONOLOGY

Burial Period C belongs to the LC IIIB period. B is dated to the LC IIIA period, possibly late within that span of time. A belongs to the LC II period, probably in its middle phase: LC IIB.

Tomb 34

LOCATION, SIZE AND SHAPE

This tomb is located in the "Street of Tombs" which cuts Area E on a northwest-southeast axis. It is a roughly circular chamber tomb, 2.5 m. in diameter and 1.3 m. from floor to roof. A pan-shaped dromos 1.3 m. square on the north side was the means of access. Presumably no plan of the tomb was made.

GENERAL REMARKS

The tomb had been opened from above in two places and thoroughly ransacked.

FINDS

1. B 1538. Steatite spindlewhorl.
2. B 1287. Bronze spiral.

3. Uncatalogued (49-12-421: M 1036): Two fragments of bronze wire.
4. B 1293. Bronze ring.
5. B 581. LC III Decorated pyxis.
6. B 837. Plain Wheelmade II jug.
7. B 825. Plain Wheelmade II jug.
8. B 220. Base-Ring I flask.
9. Sherds (49-12-427): see table, w.

CHRONOLOGY

The distribution of pots and sherds, insofar as these can be relied on, suggests at least one earlier and one later burial period. The former might be late in the LC I or early in the LC II period, the latter probably in the LC IIC period.

Tomb 35

GENERAL REMARKS

Tomb 35 lay just west of Tomb 23. There is no information whatsoever recorded other than that it was a destroyed tomb.

FINDS

1. B 775. Plain White jug.
2. B 785. Plain White jug.
3. B 607. LC III Decorated jug.

4. Uncatalogued (49-12-436): Fragmentary Black Slip Bucchero jug.
5. Sherds (49-12-435): see Table, x.

CHRONOLOGY

As in the case of Tomb 34, here also one infers an earlier burial, probably still in the LC I period, and a later use of the tomb, possibly in the LC IIIA period. Re-use of the tomb in the Geometric period seems strongly indicated by the presence of many fragments of an Iron Age Black Slip Bucchero jug.

Tomb 36

LOCATION, SIZE AND SHAPE

This is one of three tombs (36–38) discovered on the north side of the old Paphos road about 25 m. north of Area E (Pl. 1). It had the usual roughly rectangular shape with somewhat rounded corners and measured 2 m. x 2.6 m. (Pl. 12). A step on the west side showed that the dromos was located there but otherwise no trace of it could be found. The floor was 1.65 m. below the present surface.

STRATIFICATION AND BURIALS

The tomb had collapsed and was full of chonnos (see SCE I, xvii for definition of this term) and dark earth. This went right down onto pots and skeletal remains, which were badly splintered. The tomb had clearly collapsed before there was time for earth to accumulate in it. It was found completely unplundered. There were two burials in situ, the one along the south side, and the other lying on the north-south axis in the center. These are the latest. There were a few traces of bones lying east-west along the north side. In the east there was a mass of bones from at least two skeletons, which seem to represent the earliest burial period, thrown aside for the later interments. Daniel did not attempt to separate the finds by burials, and to do so now might seem temerous. However, a few general considerations may be offered. The necklace of glass beads (Nos. 5, 6; 13–26; 53–55; 61) was presumably a gift for the center burial. The objects in the northwest corner and along the east wall (Nos. 32–51) appear at first to belong mostly to the earlier burials, the parts of which must have been separated in making room for the later interments. Nevertheless, it can hardly be supposed that the latest burials were without any gifts of pottery. The presence of No. 34, in particular, suggests a terminus post quem of the LC IIC period for the final use of the tomb; some of the Base-Ring II bowls and Mycenaean ware could go with this. Speculation beyond this point would certainly be unprofitable.

FINDS

1. B 1416. Fluted top of an ivory rod.
2. B 1417. Fragments of an ivory rod.
3. Missing. Gray glass bead, in earth thrown out of tomb.
4. B 1628. Gold-plated steatite cylinder seal.
5, 6. B 1342. Glass beads; as Nos. 13–26.
7. B 1359. Gold bead.
8. B 1360. Gold bead.
9. B 1379. Gold bead.
10. Missing. Ivory button.
11. B 1350. Pear-shaped pendant of dark glass.
12. Missing. Spiral bronze earring.
13-26. B 1342. Glass beads of various colors.
27. B 1324. Faience bead.
28. B 1325. Faience bead.
29. B 1271. Bronze earring.
30. B 1271. Bronze earring.
31. B 1271. Bronze earring.
32. B 1156. Mycenaean III stirrup jar.
33. B 1093. Mycenaean III 3-handled pyxis.
34. B 580. LC III Decorated 2-handled pyxis.
35. B 235. Base-Ring II bowl.
36. B 258. Base-Ring II bowl.
37. B 236. Base-Ring II bowl.
38. B 787. Plain White jug.
39. B 237. Base-Ring II bowl.
40. B 268. Base-Ring II jug.
41. B 1016. Mycenaean III bowl.
42. B 269. Base-Ring II juglet.
43. B 788. Plain White jug.
44. B 238. Base-Ring II bowl.
45. B 239. Base-Ring II bowl.
46. B 781. Plain White jug.
47. B 1094. Mycenaean III 3-handled pyxis.
48. B 1157. Mycenaean III stirrup jar.
49. B 240. Base-Ring II bowl.
50. B 241. Base-Ring II bowl.
51. B 242. Base-Ring II bowl.
52. B 774. Plain White jug.
53-55. B 1342. Glass beads.

56. B 1337. Glass bead.
57. B 1339. Glass bead.
58. B 1341. Glass bead.
59. B 1340. Glass bead.
60. B 1338. Glass bead.
61. B 1342. Glass bead. Found in screening.
62. B 823. Plain Wheelmade II jug.
   In earth over tomb.

From sherds:
63. B 243. Base-Ring II bowl.
64. B 244. Base-Ring II bowl.

CHRONOLOGY

On the basis of the pottery, the earlier burials may be as early as the LC IIA period, while final use of the tomb appears to be in the LC IIC period.

Tomb 37

GENERAL REMARKS

Tomb 37 lay about 8 m. east of Tomb 36. It comprises two oval cists, in which only sherds were found, and a circular cist with a few bones (*Pl. 12*). There was no indication of scale on the field sketch; however, it appears from photographs (e.g., *Pl. 4*) that the cists were only a few centimeters deep in the bedrock. The oval cists, which were covered with large stone slabs, were stated to be 40 cm. below the present surface.

FINDS

1. B 1304. Bronze tool.
2. B 293. Monochrome bowl.
3. Sherds (49-12-439): see Table, y.

CHRONOLOGY

From very scanty indications, it would appear that all the cists belong to the LC II period.

Tomb 38

GENERAL REMARKS

Tomb 38 lay about 8 m. east of Tomb 37. A retrospective interpretation of the excavation of this tomb is very difficult. Daniel found a large cutting through the bedrock with a skeleton along the south side. Fragments of Geometric pottery (Table, z) were associated with it. Apparently the cutting for this burial intercepted a Bronze Age tomb which contained Nos. 1–18, between 1.55 m. and 2.45 m. below the surface; also many sherds (Table, aa). At 2.6 m. below the surface were Nos. 19–21 and various sherds (Table, bb). The plan (*Pl. 12*) apparently does not show any particular level, since there seemed to be no real stratification, but rather indicates the spatial relationship of the skeleton and the scattered pithos sherds (No. 19). The presence of Geometric sherds at all levels shows how thoroughly disturbed this tomb was, probably by two agencies: (a) the Geometric burial; (b) frequent flooding. See also my remarks in *ANE*, 68. The original tomb had its dromos on the south and appears to have been roughly circular with a diameter of approximately 2.8 m.

FINDS

1. B 221. Base-Ring bull figurine.
2. B 222. Base-Ring bull figurine.
3. B 695. Black Slip Bucchero jug.
4. B 1175. Mycenaean III 2-handled flask.
5. B 1176. Mycenaean III 2-handled flask.
6. B 296. Monochrome bowl.
7. B 307. Monochrome jug.
8. B 760. Plain White bowl.
9. B 790. Inscribed handle of Plain White jug.
10. B 881. Inscribed handle of Plain Wheelmade II jug.
11. B 1000. Fragment of Syrian Bichrome krater.
12. B 275. Incised handle of Base-Ring II jug.
13. B 1096. Fragment of Mycenaean III pyxis.
14. B 112. White Slip II bowl.
15. B 113. White Slip II bowl.
16. B 114. White Slip II bowl.
17. B 115. White Slip II bowl.
18. B 149. White Slip II bowl.
19. B 952. Fragments of pithos.
20. B 1433. Impressed rim fragment of pithos.
21. B 776. Plain White jug fragment.
22. Sherds: see Table, z-bb.

CHRONOLOGY

In view of the thoroughly disturbed condition of this tomb, nothing can be said of the chronology other than that, in the Bronze Age categories, predominantly pots and sherds of the LC II period are represented, and in proportions which suggest the later, rather than the earlier, phase of that period.

Tomb 39

GENERAL REMARKS

This tomb is located near the northwest corner of Area E. It is now in destroyed condition. There is no description in the field notebooks. It is a chamber tomb measuring 1.6 m. x 1.8 m. at its widest point, roughly rectangular in shape with dromos at the west side. Presumably it was found plundered.

FINDS

1. B 150. White Slip II bowl.
2. B 151. White Slip II bowl.
3. B 267. Base-Ring II jug.
4. Sherds: see Table, cc.

CHRONOLOGY

Pots and sherds in this tomb are predominantly of the LC II period. The possibility of re-use of the tomb in the Archaic period is not excluded.

Tomb 40

LOCATION, SIZE AND SHAPE

Tomb 40 is adjacent to Tomb 19. Their dromoi, lying 60 cm. apart, appear as two matched adjoining squares, but the chamber of Tomb 19 lies to the northwest, that of Tomb 40 to the southeast. This might recall the tendency of tholos tombs to occur in pairs at Pylos (cf. *ILN*, April 6, 1957, 540). The dromos of Tomb 40 is of the usual pan shape, approximately 1.4 m. square, varying in depth from 30 to 55 m. as the terrain rises to the south in this region. An *armoraki* (niche) directly opposite the *stomion* is approximately 55 cm. high and 45 cm. wide with a roughly circular aperture of 25 cm. diameter. Small uncut stones blocked the *stomion* (*Pl. 4*), which measured 40 cm. by 50 cm. (width). The chamber has the usual rectangular shape with rounded corners, but its center portion is displaced toward the southeast (*Pl. 13*). It measures 1.4 m. x 2.6 m. (maximal) with estimated height of chamber, 1.9 m.

STRATIFICATION

An almond tree was growing over the tomb to the southeast and had to be destroyed in the course of excavations. A definitely artificial cutting was found in the roof of the chamber. There is no obvious explanation for this since the tomb was found intact. Most of the roof from this cutting had collapsed into the tomb, but this took place after sufficient earth and silt had collected over the upper burials to protect them from being smashed. The tomb was excavated from above, through the cutting. *Chavara* (see *SCE* I, xvii for definition of this term; cf. also *RDAC*, 1964, 36 and 58, "havara"), went down to a layer of fine, rather sandy earth, between 40 cm. and 50 cm. in thickness, which was reddish brown except on the north side, where it was greenish. This stratum covered the latest burials at the 1.26–1.46 m. level (Period D). There was no real change of earth below this to the 1.62 m. level, which was a fairly hard, firmly packed floor surface (Period C). Below this level—with no essential change of earth—appeared nonetheless many stones and large mud bricks (20–30 cm. in length) embedded in the loose earth in more or less random positions; there can be little doubt that these were thrown over burials on a lower floor to serve as a cushion for later interments. Below these was a floor of hard mud (Period B). This lay 5–10 cm. above the original bedrock floor of the tomb (Period A).

BURIALS

The uppermost burial level (D) had been greatly disturbed by flooding. Pots and bones were found embedded in silt. The latest interments (Skulls I–III) are apparently represented by the bones stretched out along the northeast wall (*Pl. 13*). Nos. 1–12, and possibly others, belong with this. Nos. 13–39 may be connected with Skull IV which may have been swept aside to make room for the other interments. In any case, all the interments of this level appear to be roughly contemporary. A number of pots from Burial Period D have ashes on their surface, suggesting that some kind of ritual purification took place in the tomb. At the 1.62 m. level (C) a small heap of bones and sherds was found along the northeast side which had been covered by stones, no doubt deliberately when the floor of the latest level was being prepared. A (headless) skeleton lay along the south wall (*Pl. 14*). It had apparently been placed on its side with the right leg and arm bent. Its head is most likely Skull V (at 1.46 m.). In view of the ancient disturbance of this level, it is not possible to be certain what gifts belonged with the skeleton and what with Skulls VI–IX. Nos. 40–56 and 68–72 are associated with Period C. On the 1.82 floor (B) was found a rather well-preserved skeleton in an unusual variation of the dorsal position: the right arm bent at the elbow to bring the hand to the hip; the left arm stretched out at approximately shoulder height; the legs stretched out and apart (*Pl. 14*). Several bowls seemed to be laid between the legs. To make room for this sprawling position, earlier skeletons had been swept back, apparently unceremoniously, for broken bones were found in a confused heap at the head and foot. All these bones were much larger and more robust-looking than those in the upper strata. Nos. 58–63 and 73–78 were associated with B. A few bones and objects, Nos. 64–67 (Period A), were found below the 1.82 level and must be slightly earlier than those of B.

FINDS

1. B 603. LC III Decorated jug.
2. B 832. Plain Wheelmade II jug.
3. B 594. LC III Decorated jug.
4. B 483. LC III Decorated bowl.
5. B 619. LC III Decorated pilgrim flask; under No. 4.
6. B 843. Plain Wheelmade II jug.
7. B 593. LC III Decorated jug.
8. B 284. Handmade Bucchero jug.
9. B 919. LC III Plain jug.
10. B 595. LC III Decorated jug.
11. B 834. Plain Wheelmade II jug.
12. B 920. LC III Plain jug.
13. B 828. Plain Wheelmade II jug.
14. B 827. Plain Wheelmade II jug.
15. B 361. Pink Burnished jug.
16. B 424. LC III Decorated bowl.
17. B 831. Plain Wheelmade II jug.
18. B 536. LC III Decorated bowl.
19. B 591. LC III Decorated jug.
20. B 537. LC III Decorated bowl.
21. B 596. LC III Decorated jug.
22. B 833. Plain Wheelmade II jug.
23. B 541. LC III Decorated bowl.
24. B 907. LC III Plain bowl.
25. B 540. LC III Decorated bowl.
26. B 489. LC III Decorated bowl.
27. B 870. Plain Wheelmade II jug.
28. B 488. LC III Decorated bowl.

29. B 557. LC III Decorated bowl. In No. 28.
30. B 918. LC III Plain jug.
31. B 590. LC III Decorated jug.
32. B 841. Plain Wheelmade II jug.
33. B 869. Plain Wheelmade II jug.
34. B 592. LC III Decorated juglet.
35. B 922. LC III Plain jug.
36. B 871. Plain Wheelmade II jug.
37. B 782. Plain White jug.
38. Missing. Fragment of bronze wire.
39. B 1526. Steatite spindlewhorl.
40. B 542. LC III Decorated bowl.
41. B 842. Plain Wheelmade II jug.
42. B 840. Plain Wheelmade II jug.
43. B 610. LC III Decorated jug.
44. B 484. LC III Decorated bowl.
45. B 485. LC III Decorated bowl.
46. B 482. LC III Decorated bowl.
47. B 845. Plain Wheelmade II jug.
48. B 1257. Bronze bowl.
49. B 487. LC III Decorated bowl.
50. B 486. LC III Decorated bowl.
51. B 539. LC III Decorated bowl.
52. B 923. LC III Plain pilgrim flask.
53. B 118. White Slip II bowl.
54. B 844. Plain Wheelmade II jug.
55. B 879. Plain Wheelmade II jug.
56. B 538. LC III Decorated bowl.
57. Uncatalogued. Two sea shells.
58. B 1525. Steatite spindlewhorl.
59. B 1343. Glass bead.
60. B 250. Base-Ring II bowl.
61. B 251. Base-Ring II bowl.
62. B 97. Sherd of No. 74.
63. B 172. Base-Ring I bowl fragment.
   B 252. Base-Ring II bowl fragment.
64. B 276. Base-Ring II piriform jar.
65. B 1541. Steatite spindlewhorl.
66. B 1423. Incised ivory button.
67. B 1290. Bronze ring.

Mended from sherds:

68. B 582. LC III Decorated juglet.
69. B 583. LC III Decorated juglet.
70. B 912. LC III Plain bowl.
71. B 481. LC III Decorated bowl.
72. B 786. Plain White jug.
73. B 122. White Slip II bowl.
74. B 97. White Slip II jug fragment.
75. B 91. White Slip I bowl.
76. B 95. White Slip I bowl.
77. B 278. Handmade Bucchero jug fragment.
78. B 310. Monochrome jug.

79. Sherds (of 1.46–1.62 m. level): see Table, dd.
80. Sherds (below 1.46–1.62 m. level): see Table, ee.

CHRONOLOGY

Burial periods D and C belong to the later part of the LC IIIA period. The distribution of wares in B suggests a date in the LC IIA period (notice especially the sherds of Table, ee). A is slightly earlier than B but there is no reason to place it any earlier than the LC IIA period.

Voupha Tomb

GENERAL REMARKS

The series of tombs stretching east from Tomb 6 is broken just east of Tomb 24 by a large number of *vouphas* (pits). From the number and type of finds from this region, it seems certain that there was a tomb here, though no trace of it could be found. It has therefore been designated as the "Voupha Tomb." The sherds Nos. 1–3 were built into one of the *vouphas*.

FINDS

1. B 1076. Fragments of Mycenaean III krater.
2. B 1077. Fragments of Mycenaean III krater.
3. B 1066. Fragments of Mycenaean III krater.
4. B 635. Fragment of Proto-White Painted bowl.
5. B 1087. Fragment of Mycenaean III krater.
6. B 783. Plain White jug.
7. B 1100. Mycenaean III 3-handled jar.
8. B 1101. Mycenaean III 3-handled jar.
9. B 1258. Bronze bowl.
10. B 1296. Fragment of bronze spearhead.
11. B 1268. Fragment of bronze dagger.
12. B 99. White Slip II bowl.
13. B 988. Red Lustrous III bottle.
14. B 48. Red Polished III jug.
15. B 1111. Mycenaean III jar.
16. B 993. Red Lustrous III arm-shaped vessel (?)
17. B 763. Inscribed handle of Plain White jug.
18. Uncatalogued (54-41-18/19): Rim fragments of bronze hemispherical bowl.
19. Uncatalogued (54-41-20): Fragment of bronze knife blade.

Miscellaneous Plundered Tombs

A

The following pots and sherds, in spite of some confusion in the records, appear to have been found in a large plundered chamber tomb in the rock ledge just to the north of Room 1 of House VIII in Area E:
1. B 725. White Painted amphora fragments.
2. B 726. White Painted amphora fragments.
3. B 727. White Painted amphora fragments.
4. B 201. Base-Ring I juglet.
5. B 260. Base-Ring II jug fragment.
6. B 194. Base-Ring I juglet.
7. B 995. "White Lustrous" bottle neck.
8. B 190. Base-Ring I bowl.
9. B 334. Burnished Slip bowl.
10. B 1227. Foreign plain jug.
11. B 977. Coarse Ware pot.
12. B 80. White Slip I bowl.
13. B 89. White Slip I bowl.
14. B 111. White Slip II bowl.
15. B 160. White Slip II bowl.
16. Sherds, including various catalogued ones: see Table, ff.

B

The following pots and sherd were found in the area between Tombs 12 and 13:
1. B 1161. Mycenaean III stirrup jar.
2. B 1183. Mycenaean III juglet.
3. B 752. Fragment of incised bowl.

C

The following were found in the area between Tombs 13 and 17:
1. B 992. Red Lustrous III lentoid flask.
2. B 479. LC III Decorated bowl.
3. B 791. Inscribed handle fragment of Plain White jug.

D

The following objects were found in various unspecified plundered tombs in the east half of the cliff in Lot 270. This means presumably between Tombs 20 and 22:
1. B 1212. Foreign pilgrim flask.
2. B 978. Plain White bowl.

3. B 729. White Painted I jug.
4. B 882. Inscribed handle of Plain Wheelmade II jug.
5. B 1591. Terracotta loomweight.

E

The following objects were found in unspecified plundered tombs in the corresponding west half of the cliff in Lot 270 (see D). This would mean west of Tomb 20:
1. B 195. Base-Ring I miniature jug.
2. B 248. Base-Ring II bowl.
3. B 761. Plain White bowl.

4. B 1116. Mycenaean III stirrup jar.
5. B 759. Fragment of inscribed Plain White bowl.

F

The following objects were found in a trial pit south of Tomb 19 (this must have been in, or to the south of, the Street of Tombs):
1. B 771. Plain White jug.
2. B 762. Plain White bowl.
3. B 1559. Crucible (?) fragment.

G

In the same general area as F, but closer to Tomb 34, was found a miniature terracotta tray, B 1618.

Table of Sherds and Miscellaneous Finds from Tombs

An explanation of the format of this table appears with the similar tables in *Bamboula SS* (*RDAC*, 1970).

TOMB	CODE	% PLAIN WARES	PITHOS	H-M	PWM I	PWM II	BS	RED POL.	WS I	WS II	BR	MONO-CHROME	BUR. SLIP	MISC. BUR.	WASH
2	a	60						4	9	23	229				8
3	b	85	B958			Rep.			7	1			1		5
3	c	25							16	12	24		1 B339		11
6	d	70					2	7	11	63	631	13			72
7	e		23					10		25	44				3
17	f	75			B805(?)	Rep. B890		11	5	44	487		9		22
17A	g	67				19					6				
20	h	10						2	14	20	270	7			2
21	i	22	84	40		7		10	41	45	168	5			5
22	j	20		27				1	2	5	90+				1
23	k	48	14	56	19	32+		10	17	24	80		2		
24	l	75								11	34				
25	m	40						1		3	16			2	2
26	n	80	Most			Rep.		12		40	92 B270	21	3	13	7
27	o	60						2	2	5	12			5	4
28	p	60			B895(?)			1	1	14	55	9	2	1	4
29	q	17		14	3	29 B883(?)			7	30	86	9			2
31	r	70			4	171		1		10	87	9		4	5

Table of Sherds and Miscellaneous Finds from Tombs

An explanation of the format of this table appears with the similar tables in *Bamboula SS* (*RDAC*, 1970).

Tomb	Code	LC III Dec.	LC III BSB	H-M Shaved	Ware VII	Standard Myc. III	Coarse Myc. III	Inferior Myc. III	RL III	Foreign Painted	Syrian	CG BSB	CG PWH	WhP	Black-on-Red	Attic	Miscellaneous
2	a					11	4		10								
3	b	4							1								
3	c	2															4 WS I or II
6	d					54	3										
7	e	1				12						1					
17	f	45		2		122 B1073, B1168			49	13				7	2		6 Roman Red
17A	g		1					1					5	4			
20	h										1						
21	i	4				2					5						
22	j																
23	k	4				17		4	8								Frag. bronze fishing hook(?), frag. diorite(?) vessel
24	l	37				15				1				3	16		
25	m	36				17 B1055, B1056, B1057				1				1(III)	2		
26	n			1		50	30 B1134		18 B991	12				3	2	1	Frag. BR figurine; frag. solid figurine (leg?)
27	o	2				6			2						2		
28	p	2	1			10			1	1				1			
29	q	2										3		34	78		1 Grooved ware pestle
31	r	29				7							63	218	201		

Table of Sherds and Miscellaneous Finds from Tombs

An explanation of the format of this table appears with the similar tables in *Bamboula SS* (*RDAC*, 1970).

TOMB	CODE	% PLAIN WARES	PITHOS	H-M	PWM I	PWM II	BS	RED POL.	WS I	WS II	BR	MONO-CHROME	BUR. SLIP	MISC. BUR.	WASH
32	s	4		1				2	7	3	11				
33	t	50					1				23				10
33	u	45						1		3	15			1	
33	v	33									4				4
34	w	18	20			24		1		43	148+				2
35	x	40							10	3	27			1	1
37	y	90						2			3				
38	z	100	17												
38	aa	61	67					1		74	27				4
39	bb	40	3							2	1	2			4
39	cc	20	5						12	31	82				22
40	dd	12	8				2		1	22	29				5
40	ee	8.5							92	65	335	18	1	1	2
A	ff		131					2		196 B157, B168, B170	354 B171, B183, B184, B191, B192, B207, B219, B274	1 B292			11

Table of Sherds and Miscellaneous Finds from Tombs

An explanation of the format of this table appears with the similar tables in *Bamboula SS* (*RDAC*, 1970).

TOMB	CODE	LC III DEC.	LC III BSB	H-M SHAVED	WARE VII	STANDARD MYC. III	COARSE MYC. III	INFERIOR MYC. III	RL III	FOREIGN PAINTED SYRIAN	CG BSB	CG PWH	WHP	BLACK-ON-RED	ATTIC	MISCELLANEOUS
32	s															
33	t	4				1			1				2	3		
33	u	1														
33	v															
34	w	2				1							2	7		1 frag. faience
35	x	4											16(II–III)	21		
37	y					1										
38	z											6				
38	aa	3	15					1				4	2(I)			
39	bb											3				
39	cc	1				1							9(I)			1 Red Slip
40	dd	1														
40	ee					8	1	1		1						
A	ff	30	10		5			1 B1043				15	1 B736		2	

[39]

PART 2
THE FINDS

3. THE POTTERY OF THE
LATE CYPRIOTE III PERIOD

Introduction

Even to one who has devoted much study to this subject, its complexities remain formidable. The present publication at last gives the opportunity to see the contrasting views of Daniel and other scholars as a whole in the light of all that can be discovered about the actual situation at Kourion. Needless to say, it is unfortunate that Daniel, the actual excavator, did not live to present his own case.[1] I find myself, therefore, in the position of an arbiter whose task is to bring what order I can into the situation with justice to all concerned, including those who have since worked on the subject—all of whom have quite rightly recognized the evidence of Kourion to be peculiarly important. In view of all this it seems justifiable to give a brief review[2] of the problems involved from my specific point of vantage, before turning to the actual finds from Bamboula.

In a pioneering effort, Sjöqvist delineated an earlier and a later phase, which he called A and B,[3] of what he considered to be the LC III period. This organization of the material has been specifically accepted by Gjerstad and Furumark.[4] Daniel admitted the possibility of recognizing an early and a late phase in the period under consideration, but regarded Sjöqvist's LC IIIA–B as LC IIIA only, in the sense that one might speak of subdivisions of a phase.[5] At this point it is mandatory to point out a discrepancy which annoyingly complicates the problem. Daniel, in his outline of the Bamboula stratification,[6] assigns Area A: Levels E–G to the LC IIIB phase. Level E:1–3, however, is equivalent to period 2 which Sjöqvist *also* assigned to LC IIIB. Therefore, only Levels E:4–G (periods 3–4) represent the point where there is disagreement as to terminology. The final study of the stratification[7] shows that it is not possible to detach these, unfortunately not too vivid, levels from period 2. A further sort of discrepancy is that Daniel did not at this important

juncture evaluate the absolutely critical stratigraphical evidence of Bamboula Tomb 33 which, together with Bamboula Tomb 40 (not known to either Daniel or Sjöqvist) greatly clarifies the situation at that site.[8] In order to present that evidence fully and emphatically I have arranged special plates and given this material particular prominence (see below).

The evidence from Bamboula and Kaloriziki, with their interlocking settlement and necropoleis and interesting ramifications is, as of now, more comprehensive than evidence from other sites at the same

1. The most advanced statement of Daniel's views on the site of Kourion is contained in his review of *Problems* in *AJA* 46 (1942) 287 ff.
2. *Stand der Forschung:* cf. *Handbook to the Nicholson Museum* (Sydney, 1948) 168–173; *AJA* 58 (1954) 136; *PEQ*, 1956, 22–37.
3. *Problems,* 126–135.
4. Respectively *OA* 3 (1944) 76; *OA* 3 (1944) 232.
5. *AJA* 45 (1941) 272.
6. *Loc. cit.*
7. Presented in *Bamboula SS*; cf. also *AJA* 46 (1942) 288 (second column). The stratification of periods 3–4 as presented in the Survey of Finds by Strata does not offer any basis for separating them from period 2. Unfortunately, these levels emerged in a somewhat shadowy fashion owing to their nearness to the surface. Likewise, it is unfortunate that their excavator, who alone could have thrown light on several objects mentioned but not catalogued, did not live to present the results himself. Possibly these objects were not considered to have any indicative value. In any event, the distribution of sherds allows no other conclusion than that periods 3–4 are a late and probably poor phase of the same temporal subdivision as period 2, viz., LC IIIB. The Proto-White Painted sherds do not differ in type from those found elsewhere in the settlement. There are no White Painted sherds except in the very last accumulation which contained sherds of assorted periods so that no significance can be attached to them. The main settlement had already been moved to another site by this time and apparently only a few squatters continued to live on at Bamboula; however, before White Painted I pottery came into use, even they had presumably abandoned the place.
8. Tomb 33 is referred to briefly in *UPMB* 8 (1940) 8 ff. as proving continuity of burial customs with the 12th century (and cited in *AJA* 46, 1942, 288) but I am at a loss to understand omission of all reference to it in *AJA* 45 (1941) 272.

period (which I will review briefly below).[9] It requires a redefinition of the concept of Proto-White Painted ware (which I have undertaken in *Kaloriziki*, Ch. 4) in terms which are valid for Kourion and, presumably, at least for the general part of the island dominated by that kingdom.

Review of Pertinent Cypriote Sites

In the first place it must be stated that any attempt to compare the situation at Kourion with the other stratified sites of comparable period—Idalion, Kition and Ayia Irini (for Enkomi, see below)—is left almost completely in a theoretical stage by the absence of a publication of any sherds from these sites, especially since they yielded only a handful of complete pots. Although some statistics are presented, they have limited value for one cannot see what it is that the excavators are calling Proto-White Painted and White Painted I, the critical categories which are at stake in this matter. If these sherds really have some character, it is to be hoped they will be presented in *SCE* IV (1) so that they can be compared with our Pls. 22, 23, etc. Otherwise they cannot have much value for the problem.

At Idalion, only the western acropolis was explored and this was found to be a citadel in the Bronze Age; nothing is known about the east acropolis. LC III embraces periods 1–3 which are called LC IIIA–C (on a local basis). Comparatively few pots[10] were recovered and only a few squares offered a more or less complete stratified sequence of all periods, viz., E 8 (minus period 1), F 9, F 10 (minus period 1), G 9, G 10, H 8 (minus period 1) and L 7. All of these were poor in decorated ware. The lower part of the stratum of period 4 contained small quantities of Geometric types I and II, but there is no distinct stratum containing only these types of pottery, and no remains of architecture are combined with them. The latter part of period 4 is contemporary with CG III, when the acropolis was used as a temenos. Although it is stated that the probability of a "non-architectural, intermediate period with a poor survival of the cult" filling the gaps between the LC III and CG III periods must be reckoned with, it is quite obvious that the evidence from Idalion is essentially discontinuous and cannot as yet furnish any positive guide-line for the critical period LC IIIB–CG II.[11]

Ayia Irini, like Idalion, existed in the LC III period, but similarly the transition to the Geometric period is rather obscure. There is very little pottery from the LC III period and no sherds are listed. This is period 1. Iron Age pottery was found in periods 2–6. Period 2 began in CG-I–II, "most probably already in Cypro-Geometric I," although no layer of exclusively Type 1 sherds was found. The LC III sanctuary seems to have been purposely covered at the beginning of period 2 with a thick layer of red earth resting immediately on the debris of the sanctuary. This situation is made to justify the conclusion that the "temenos of per. 2 succeeded the Bronze Age sanctuary without a long intermediate period," even though it is admitted that the finds of period 2 are few and the culture stratum thin. Period 2 lasted until about the middle of CG III. Here again the evidence is scant and, if not absolutely discontinuous, at least not very illuminating. Gjerstad[12] himself came to approximately this conclusion.

At Kition, remains of a house in period 1 were found by the Swedish excavators. There were two phases: A, assigned to the LC III period, and B, assigned to the CG I period. Gjerstad (*loc. cit.*) pointed out the importance of the continuity at this site for it has enabled the relationship of Proto-White Painted and LC III Decorated wares to be brought into sharper focus. Unfortunately, the actual material was again very scant (Squares K 2 and J 2)[13] and is not illustrated. Fortunately, the site of Kition has recently become the object of renewed investigations by the Cyprus Antiquities Service. In excavations in 1959 a burial complex in a settlement (comparable with the necropolis within

---

9. My remarks may be taken to supplement the useful review by J. du Plat Taylor, *PEQ*, 1956, 22–37. H. W. Catling, writing in 1964, speaks of Kouklia, Lapithos and Kition as showing continuity of occupation from LC III into developed Geometric times (*CBW*, 53). On Kition see below, note 14. V. Desborough, *LMTS*, 198 f., also reviews the evidence and points out that at Nicosia and Lapithos it is insufficient "to say whether there was, or was not, immediately earlier occupation." A general study of the site of Kouklia is expected from Catling (see *Nouveaux Documents*, 157, n. 4).

10. *SCE* II, Pl. CLXIV shows most of them. They are largely plain ware.

11. Bibliography and further references on Bronze Age and Iron Age cemeteries: *RDAC*, 1964, 29 n. 1.

12. *OA* 3 (1944) 82.

13. Cf. *OA* 3 (1944) 84, n. 2, where a combined (and somewhat enlarged?) version of the original sherd lists is presented.

the Late Bronze Age city at Episkopi) revealed an LC II phase and an LC IIIA phase. The pottery of the latter is quite reminiscent of that found in tombs at Bamboula-Kourion, particularly, for example, the krater-amphora of Caveau III in comparison with B 574, while certain LC III Decorated bowls from the latest inhumation of Caveau I, dated by the excavator to the end of the LC IIIA period, exhibit the tendency toward tallness which was found to be characteristic of the LC IIIB period at our site. The contents of a well with Mycenaean IIIC:2 and Proto-White Painted attest to the existence of an LC IIIB phase at Kition, and this has been confirmed by material found more recently on house floors, which indeed seem to show continuity into the Early Iron Age at which time the population evidently moved to a new site—a phenomenon closely paralleling the course of events at Bamboula-Kourion. As yet this latest sequence has not been published in any detail.[14]

The excavations at Sinda have not as yet been fully published but it is apparent that the habitation, as at Apliki and Pigadhes, did not outlast the LC IIIA phase and cannot therefore give much assis- tance in the critical problem of defining the LC IIIB phase.[15] Only from Enkomi can illumination on this subject be expected. It does not seem worthwhile at this point to attempt any further interpretation of the site than has been undertaken by Miss Taylor, who has called attention to the appearance of "wavy line" pottery as a general criterion for the beginning of LC IIIB. One must await corroboration of this from the excavators, of course, but the generalization is valid enough for Bamboula.

In the light of this review the importance of Bamboula becomes evident, not only for its geo- graphic position in relation to Enkomi as the coun- terpole on the other side of the island, but for its considerable stratification throughout the LC IIIA and B phases.[16] Moreover, although the new site of the town, which was removed from Bamboula to another location sometime during the LC IIIB phase, has not been found, its necropolis (Kaloriziki) has, so that there is an adequate measure of continuity to be analyzed. What is important and abundantly clear in this situation is a fact which has never been doubted by any of the scholars involved, viz., that there is no hiatus at Kourion.

Proto-White Painted and Late Cypriote III Decorated Ware at Kourion

At this point it is necessary to examine the term Proto-White Painted.[17] It was Gjerstad's merit to coin a term which accurately indicates the existence of precursors to the fully developed Geometric White Painted ware. This antecedent class of ware has been the subject of considerable study on the part of both Gjerstad and Furumark, who have ex- amined its relationship to the Mycenaean fabric. The former scholar has given a list of the pottery he so far admits to this class, viz., two tombs at Lapithos and material of the LC IIIB layers at Idalion and Kition (tabulated and extended by Furumark, *OA* 3 (1944) 242. The importance of Gjerstad's definition of this class of Cypriote ware cannot be over-estimated. On the other hand, his remarks[18] calling for a finding of more wares of this "transitory stage" show that his analysis has uncov- ered a problem without entirely solving it.

The correlations between Proto-White Painted ware and LC III Decorated ware at Kourion are numerous, even though the inception of the latter fabric is certainly anterior to that of the former (for further remarks on this subject, see *Kaloriziki*, Ch. IV, Proto-White Painted Shapes). Furumark con- tributed the latter term, which is by far the most satisfactory yet suggested for the class in question. I have altered his order of words (from Decorated LC III ware) for reasons of euphony. The most characteristic shape of this class is the bowl, which can now, along with other shapes, be studied in detail in the light of ample stratification and related to the scheme suggested by Furumark, *OA* 3 (1944) 235. The general validity of this scheme is unques-

14. Cf. *OA* 6 (1950) 268. Essential bibliography: *BCH* 84 (1960) 504 f.; *BCH* 87 (1963) 364 f.; *RDAC* (1963) 9 f.; *BCH* 88 (1964) 350 f.; *BCH* 90 (1966) 362 f. Cf. also *BCH* 89 (1965) 267, fig. 55.

15. *PEQ* (1956) 37, and *passim* for further literature. The final publication of Myrtou-Pigadhes appeared in 1957. Further summaries of Enkomi evidence: V. Karageorghis in *BCH* 84 (1960) 581 and V. Desborough *LMTS*, 192 f.; cf. also the chronological chart published in *OpusAth* 6 (1965) 115 which presents the chronology from Sinda and Enkomi adopted by Furumark and Dikaios.

16. Even into the CG I period, according to the view pre- vailing among Swedish scholars till now: cf. *OA* 3 (1944) 82, n. 16. For a recent comment on the problem of continuity at Enkomi-Salamis, see V. Karageorghis, *Salamis* (New York, 1969), 20–22.

17. See also *Kaloriziki*, Ch. IV, Introduction.

18. *OA* 3 (1944) 103.

tioned; nevertheless, our material suggests certain qualifications and modifications.[19] A similar pictorial presentation[20] of stratified material from Kourion, including plain and Proto-White Painted wares—which have many interconnections with LC III Decorated ware—has been undertaken in this publication (*Pls. 55–57*). The organization of these pictorial charts is largely self-explanatory: the exact find circumstances of each piece can be easily ascertained by reference to the catalogue (below) and stratification tables (in *Bamboula SS*). The objects from tombs and those from the settlement are illustrated separately for the obvious reason that a settlement yields more reliable information than tombs.[21] It seems therefore appropriate to explain and justify in some detail my reasons for apportioning the finds from the tombs in the way this material actually appears in the charts. The clearest evidence comes from the afore-mentioned Tomb 33, excavated by Daniel, and Tomb 40, excavated by myself.

Late Cypriote III Decorated Shapes at Bamboula

The bowls of Type 1 do not change greatly in the course of the LC III period, so far as the rather sparse evidence of the settlement on this point indicates, but in the LC IIIB phase, as illustrated by B 406 in contrast to B 404 (*Pl. 55*), the fabric does become coarser, the base less finely turned and the shape, if anything, taller, fuller and more integrated. The series of bowls from Tomb 40 (*Pl. 58*) are approaching but have not as yet reached this stage, so that they should still be LC IIIA. The only indication for bowl type 3 obtainable from the settlement is from the sherd B 440, which shows that in the LC IIIA phase the shape was of moderate height, rather spreading, and with a pronounced, quite graceful carination. B 483 and its fellows of Tomb 40 exhibit the full mature stage of these characteristics with, as yet, no signs of degeneration. Bowl type 4 is not represented in Tomb 40; it is, however, in Tomb 33:b. B 501 and B 502 from a clearly LC IIIA context (*Pl. 61*) represent respectively the fully developed angular and round variations of the one-handled bowl with panel style decoration; B 502 is closely comparable with C 718 (Furumark's C 2:9), also from Bamboula.[22] Moreover, the LC IIIB version of this shape, with a tall slender handle and degenerate panel decoration, must be represented—on grounds of stylistic progression—by B 503 from Tomb 16. This new evidence involves on Furumark's chart a retrogression to the LC IIIA phase for C 718, which on any reckoning could hardly fail to be chronologically parallel with C 703 (Furumark's G:16), designated by him as LC IIIA. B 539, of Tomb 40, as a hemispherical bowl of Type 6, is comparable to B 526 of the settlement; in the LC IIIB phase the sides tend to become more spreading and flaring (B 527 and B 531).

The jugs B 582 and B 593 (*Pl. 56*), of Tomb 40, are similar to the LC IIIA examples given by Furumark, as is also B 603, which is no doubt from the same workshop, if not the same potter, as C 703 (*Pl. 62*). The one fragmentary LC IIIA example from the settlement, B 602, has a somewhat wider base. There is so far no evidence that this shape survived into the LC IIIB period in this fabric, but the shape as such continued to exist.[23] In plain ware, there are some immediate points of contact between settlement and tombs. Thus, B 843 of Tomb 40 has a very similar profile to that of B 838 in the settlement, and the same may be said of B 857 from the LC IIIA stratum of Tomb 33, in comparison with B 848 from the settlement. Likewise, there is ample correspondence between B 869 of Tomb 40 and B 865 from an LC IIIA stratum of the settlement. Moreover, B 827 (*Pl. 57*) of Tomb 40 appears to be stylistically an immediate predecessor of B 820.

On the whole, the pottery associated with the burials of Tomb 33:b and Tomb 40:c,d, seems to represent the apogee of the LC III Decorated class just before decline and degeneration set in, and hence

19. Cf. also the remarks of du Plat Taylor, *op. cit.*, 32 ff.
20. In most cases I have in the interests of accuracy used profiles rather than drawings prepared from photographs.
21. Cf. A. J. B. Wace in *ANE*, 127.
22. C 718 is illustrated on *Pl. 62* in a new photograph. Cf. especially the profile of B 502 on *Pl. 44* with the drawing of C 718 in *OA* 3 (1944) 235.
23. See K 160, of the Proto-White Painted class, illustrated on *Pl. 61*. It must be noted that this LC IIIB shape is remarkably close to that of A 882 (illustrated in juxtaposition on *Pl. 61*) which Furumark (*MP*, 609) classified as Myc. III C:le with a qualifying query. See also the LH III C jug from Perati (*Ergon*, 1958, 27, Fig. 27:553). It may well be that the shape of A 882, which flourished in Greece perhaps a little later than Furumark thought, was fresh in the minds of the LC IIIB Kourion colonists when they created the Proto-White Painted shape. Also, the possibility of an even more direct influence is suggested by a find at Sinda dated by Furumark to Myc. III C:1b (*AFF*, 62, upper left). *Enkomi-Alasia*, 22:26 (= *ECCM*, Pl. 5:6) is described as local and may belong to the same class as B 603 and C 703.

probably in the later rather than the earlier part of the LC IIIA phase. Assignment of these equivalent levels to the LC IIIA period itself is particularly supported by the generous occurrence in Tomb 33:b of wares still characteristic of the preceding LC IIC period: White Slip, Base-Ring, Handmade Bucchero and Mycenaean. The context of C 718, from OT 89, as far as recoverable, agrees admirably with that of the two tombs under discussion. The two handleless bowls, C 723 and C 724[24] (*Pl. 62*) correspond to the numerous bowls of this type in Tomb 40, as also the LC III Decorated bowl of Type 3, C 713[25] (*Pl. 62*) has numerous counterparts there (*Pl. 62*); the Mycenaean jug, C 591[26] (*Pl. 61*) and the imitation Mycenaean bowl, C 659[27] (*Pl. 63*) correspond to the Mycenaean survival, B 1102, in Tomb 33:b. C 207[28] is Handmade Bucchero very similar to B 284 of Tomb 40 (*Pl. 58*). The same combination exists in the case of C 703[29] which was found with the Mycenaean juglet, C 594[30] (*Pl. 61*).

I have pointed out the more characteristic features of the pottery of these tombs in comparison with that of the settlement so as to enable us to obtain a perceptible contrast between the LC IIIA and LC IIIB phases. Variations of the shapes discussed, from tombs where stratification is lacking but which exhibit no late features, have been included in the chart to assist in this differentiation, e.g., B 452 (*Pl. 55*), a very low shape and thus probably early, from Tomb 3. An additional reason for considering burial period B of this tomb to be early in the LC IIIA phase is that it has mostly simply decorated bowls and in general does not display evidence of contact with Philistine influences like the LC III Decorated pottery of Tombs 33 and 40 (see below). By this I intend only to point to a trend, not to establish a firm distinction between early and late in the LC IIIA phase, for which there is not sufficient evidence from the settlement. It is first of all from Tomb 33:c that we obtain a confirmation of the developmental trend in the LC IIIB phase as it was revealed by the settlement material: the Type 1 bowl B 418 (*Pl. 55*) exhibits an intensification of those features noted in B 406—a more heavily conceived base and a distinct tendency to tallness. These features occur consistently in the Type 1 and 3 bowls of Tombs 16 and 17 (e.g., B 454), carrying with them B 503 (Type 4) which already for typological reasons appeared to belong to the LC IIIB phase (see p. 46). From the same mould is the Type 3 bowl, B 469 of Tomb 19:f which we have likewise already noted as having a Type 6 bowl of advanced shape (B 531). It may

also be noted that the curiously wide-rimmed Base-Ring imitation bowl in plain ware from the LC IIIB phase of the settlement, B 899 (*Pl. 56*) is paralleled in this feature by B 903 of Tomb 16, which we have just characterized as having other LC IIIB types. To return to Tomb 33:c, however, obviously the most significant feature for our purpose is that it contains largely pottery of the Proto-White Painted class, comparable to that found in the Kaloriziki necropolis. This corresponds precisely to the situation in the settlement where numerous examples of this ware were found in the LC IIIB levels represented by periods 2–4 stratified directly over period 1, the LC IIIA level. One is, in fact, tempted to suppose that the family which introduced so much of this ware into House VI of Area A is the very one responsible for Tomb 33:c. The fact, moreover, that a few sherds of a fabric which it seems appropriate to call Proto-White Painted occur even in the LC IIIA level of the settlement, corresponds to the appearance of a complete pot of this sort, B 674, in Tomb 32. This tomb, although plundered, had a context which seems otherwise to belong to the LC IIIA phase. This will have to be discussed in more detail later.

For the moment, it will be valuable to sum up the results obtained so far in the matter of distinguishing between the A and B phases of the LC III period—results based on the harmonious evidence of settlement and tombs. In the A phase, especially in the later part, LC III Decorated ware is at the height of its popularity and its technique has not yet begun to deteriorate. It is accompanied by plain vertically grooved jugs (*Pl. 59*, lower register) and the very first scattered intimations of Proto-White Painted ware; it is also accompanied by Handmade Bucchero and other fabrics which look to the past rather than to the future: Mycenaean, White Slip and Base-Ring. In the B phase these latter virtually disappear. Proto-White Painted ware to a great extent, although not entirely, replaces LC III Decorated ware which also shows a

24. *ExC*, Fig. 129; C 724 = *CVA* BM Fs. 1 II Cc, Pl. 3:4.
25. *ExC*, Fig. 129.
26. *ExC*, Fig. 124:89 = *BMCatV* I, Pl. III.
27. *ExC*, Fig. 129 = *CVA* BM Fs. 1 II Cb, Pl. 5:15; *MPL*, Pl. 12:4. Stubbings published this along with what he considers to be Mycenaean III A-B bowls, but the difference in technique and decoration is apparent even in his photograph. From inspection of the clay and paint I would range this and C 660 (*Pl. 63*) with superior quality LC III Decorated bowls.
28. *ExC*, Fig. 125 = *BMCatV* I, Pl. I = *CVA* BM Fs. 1 II Ca, Pl. 12:6.
29. *ExC*, Fig. 134 = *CVA* BM Fs. 1 II Cc, Pl. 1:26.
30. *ExC*, Fig. 124:109.

deterioration of technique. The shapes of this latter undergo a change: for example, the Type 1 and 3 bowls grow taller, whether as a normal typological development or under the influence of the high bowls of mainland Mycenaean III C ware.[31] In both the settlement (*Pl. 63*: B 663) and the tombs (*Pls. 60, 63*), the "wavy line" style makes a most emphatic appearance.

It may be noted that the incomplete repertory of shapes in both plain and decorated wares which is characteristic of the Bamboula settlement and necropolis in the LC IIIB phase is in harmony with the assumption that most of the population moved to a new site during the course of this phase. Moreover, since it appears that LC III Decorated ware was to a great extent abruptly replaced by the new Proto-White Painted ware, as for example in Tomb 33:c, any discrepancy is removed by the realization that the early tombs of the Kaloriziki necropolis are roughly contemporary with the LC IIIB phase of the settlement: that is, the existing repertory of settlement shapes may be thought of as completed and supplemented by the repertory of early Kaloriziki shapes in such wares as the Proto-White Painted and Plain Wheelmade II. Specific examples of this kind of overlap are adduced in *Kaloriziki*, Ch. IV; obviously, it must be borne in mind that complete continuity is not to be expected since a new spirit was at work in the new ware. A few striking confirmations of this synchronism may be cited already here. The two bowls, B 643 from Bamboula Tomb 33:c and K 46 from Kaloriziki Tomb 26:a, were obviously made by the same artisan (*Pl. 63*). To the same workshop, if not potter, one may confidently assign B 821 from Bamboula Tomb 33:b and K 844, again from Kaloriziki Tomb 26:a (*Pl. 63*).

General Remarks on Late Cypriote III Decorated Shapes

On the basis of the Kourion material, Furumark's subdivision of the LC III period by shapes can now be discussed (in the order of his scheme):

A. The deep two-handled bowl does not occur at all at Bamboula, unless the sherd B 1058 represents this shape. In this case the possibility of connections with locally made Mycenaean III B ware is strengthened (see below). Du Plat Taylor[32] has pointed out that this shape properly belongs to an earlier phase.

B. Bowls were abundant at Bamboula, allowing a more detailed analysis than previously. B(1) appears to me to be closer to locally made Mycenaean ware than Furumark supposes and must be merely an imitation of the type current in this fabric (cf. B 1012 ff.). I have elsewhere stated my supposition that LC III Decorated bowls are derived from Levanto-Mycenaean bowls.[33] Faithful imitations are, however, rare and the ordinary native Cypriote bowl of Types 1 and 3 has throughout the *whole* period the small handles—which were previously said to show attrition—as a glance at Pl. 21 makes clear. In the LC IIIB phase the shape becomes somewhat taller and the technique coarser.

C. The type represented by Furumark's no. 6 occurs only in the Mycenaean fabric at Bamboula (B 1040), and attention is drawn to the early context (cf. A). Nos. 8–9 are bowls of Type 4, which it has been possible to differentiate into a more rounded and a more angular variety.

D. The handleless bowl occurs at Bamboula in three variations: Types 5–7. The impetus for Type 5 may come from native plain ware, as Furumark suggests. Type 6 looks like an adaptation of the hemispherical bowl popular in native wares (cf. B 99 ff. and B 293, 294, etc.). Type 7 is possibly a geometricized version of Type 6.

E. The variation B 620 emphasizes the close links of this shape to the Asiatic continent.

F. The original LC IIIA adaptation of this shape is perhaps provided by B 607 with Furumark's no. 15 representing an LC IIIB development under the influence of Base-Ring ware. This would be comparable to the influence of the Base-Ring tradition on plain ware: cf. B 899 ff.

G. It is important to point out that, contrary to the statement made in *AJA* 42 (1938) 271 ff., Daniel in his final organization of Area A definitely placed the material which includes B 602 in pe-

---

31. See *MP*, 53, Fig. 15:295. The occurrence of the same shape at Sinda (*AFF*, 61, lower right) early in the twelfth century makes this a distinct possibility. It remains to be seen whether this prototype affected LC III Decorated bowls in the eastern part of the island.

32. *PEQ*, 1956, 32.

33. P. 108, n. 8 and cf. Daniel's discussion of the descendance of LC III Decorated bowls: *AJA* 44 (1940) 554. It is a curious fact that the example for Submycenaean ware Bowl type 1 (*Problems*, 67) is classified as 'Levanto-Helladic' in *SCE*. Another example of direct imitation of Mycenaean proto-type in LC III Decorated ware is given by the pyxides B 580 and B 581.

riod 1. There is therefore no evidence from Bamboula that the type figured as Furumark's G continued into the LC IIIB phase without change. We have already noted that the LC IIIA dating of C 703 is confirmed by our Tomb 40. The LC IIIB development of this shape can be surmised from K 160 (*Pl. 61*), which I have taken to be a Proto-White Painted survival in Kaloriziki Tomb 26:b; in any case, K 160 gives approximately the Proto-White Painted adaptation of type G.[34]

H. This shape occurs only in LC IIIA contexts at Bamboula (and almost exclusively in tombs). Although well represented, it furnishes only one specimen with the so-called metallic handle,[35] which is therefore a sporadic feature at this site.

I. Furumark's nos. 25 and 26 are offered as typological developments of the LC IIIA shape. Their contexts reveal considerable similarity with the pottery of Bamboula Tombs 33:b and 40:c-d, but may after all be slightly more advanced, particularly in the bowl shapes. FT 6² and 13 may tentatively be accepted as belonging to the early LC IIIB phase, with the observation that they do not as yet reveal all of the features we have seen to be characteristic of the corresponding period at Bamboula. This may be accidental, a matter which cannot be decided until the full report of the Enkomi excavations is published. If these tombs should, on the contrary, be dated to the late LC IIIA phase, then the I(2) shapes may be taken as contemporary variations of I(1). In any case, the Proto-White Painted adaptation of I(1) is K 163, whereas the I(2) shapes had no future.

J. Although the example from Idalion is handmade and B 619 is wheelmade, their shapes agree well enough in the key feature: rather long handles from shoulder to rim, which is only vaguely defined.

The LC IIIB version of this shape, K 2 and K 167, shows the rim more prominent and the handles brought down to rest distinctly under it. In the CG I period, the lip of the rim vanishes, leaving a slightly flaring mouth, and the handles drop still more to about mid-neck (K 415).

K. The example cited by Furumark, B 1004, is not Cypriote. Nevertheless, this shape does occur in the native fabric in LC IIIA contexts at Bamboula. The most interesting of these examples is B 574 (*Pl. 55*) because it furnishes a strong link with the very popular Proto-White Painted krater-amphora, e.g., K 78. Daniel[36] included all the variations of the krater-amphora of the LC IIIB phase in the category of Mycenaean derivatives. This view fails to recognize the possibility that the Proto-White Painted amphora *may* be a transformation of the LC III Decorated krater-amphora, whereby the latter acquired a conical foot under the influence of the ubiquitous "wavy line" cup with conical foot. A special study should be made of this problem. For the Mycenaean and native connections of B 815, see p. 98.

L. This shape occurs only in Proto-White Painted ware at Kourion: K 62.

A few concluding remarks may be permitted on the subject of Furumark's chart. A₂, C₂(10) and H₂ are, as I understand it, from unknown contexts and have only inferential value as typological derivatives of the corresponding shapes. C₁(8,9), E₂, G and K are from Bamboula and Furumark's placement of them is satisfactory, with the exception of C 718 (see p. 46). Bamboula has shed considerable light on the development of bowl shapes. More evidence is still needed to obtain an absolutely secure picture of the development of the basket-handled spout jug and of the krater-amphora.

Late Cypriote III Decorated Repertory of Motifs

From this analysis largely on the basis of shapes, we may follow Furumark's lead and proceed to a brief discussion of decorative elements. It is already abundantly evident that considerable influence was exercised from the Syro-Palestinian quarter in shapes, so that it is not surprising that parallels to many of the decorative elements may be found there. Some of these have already been pointed out by Furumark.[37] However, with the material now at hand (summarized in *Pls. 64–65*), the fact must be

emphasized that in LC III Decorated ware there is a real Cypriote synthesis of what appear to be Syro-

---

34. See n. 23. Notice also the variation provided by K 161 and K 162.

35. *OA* 3 (1944) 238. It may at least be noted that fascicules of the type which Furumark derived from Syrian grooved ware occur on Early Bronze painted pottery in Crete: *Deltion* 4 (1918) 46, 1; 12 (1929) 112, 8.

36. *AJA* 41 (1937) 68. One might also compare the Plain Wheelmade krater-amphora, *Problems*, 56, type 4a.

37. *OA* 3 (1944) 238 ff.

Palestinian and particularly "Philistine" elements[38] in a well-defined panel style: B 501–506, B 516, B 517, B 522 and C 718. There is also experimentation with the combining of elements in an uninterrupted series: in effect, a frieze style: B 497, B 603, C 703. It is presumably from the Syro-Palestinian repertory that vertical wavy lines are borrowed (B 501, B 520) although the fact cannot be overlooked that these are a common feature of Cypriote Bronze Age White Painted ware[39] and occur also in "Rude Style" Mycenaean (cf. B 1088). From the same (Syro-Palestinian) quarter is the tree motif of B 453.[40] The individually dotted semicircles of C 703 may be regarded in the light of the decoration on B 1004, a Syrian import.[41] Most of the other elements seem to be derived from the Mycenaean repertory in the spirit of the Philistine pottery, a fact which tends to support the suggestion made by du Plat Taylor,[42] that the carriers of this pottery alighted on both sides of the strait separating Cyprus from the mainland. In this case, the strong qualification has to be added that the effect of this penetration was quite different in the two cases, ceramically at least. A few of the particularly close parallels may be emphasized here: the fringe of scallops, each with a dot in the center, of B 569,[43] the careless series of contiguous vertical zones on B 603[44] and the lozenge of C 718.[45] The stacked loops which occur on later Mycenaean pottery furnish a good test case. On the mainland they are, to my knowledge, not usually filled each with a dot;[46] yet it is precisely this variation which occurs on B 453 and on a Philistine jar.[47] In addition, the special problem presented by the panel with semicircles on C 718, which again points to exact connections between Cypriote and Philistine decorative practice, has been treated in detail below (see n. 50).

As a parenthesis, it may be mentioned that there are some designs, like the sea-anemone of B 519, which are too universal to allow their origin to be determined (it could be either Mycenaean or Cypriote: see *Pl. 41*). Likewise, the use of solid and stippled triangles and even the dotting of such triangles is attested for both Mycenaean and Syro-Palestinian ware,[48] so that this factor is of little value as evidence.

The result of this analysis confirms the general correctness of Furumark's position in minimizing direct Mycenaean influence on LC III Decorated pottery. Nevertheless, in addition to influences from the Syro-Palestinian quarter, it has become apparent that many of the motifs of the LC III Decorated panel and frieze style do derive *ultimately* from the Mycenaean repertory and that they are best explained as adaptations in a manner akin to that of the Philistine pottery.[49] It is true, of course, that the excavations of sites lying in the east of the island, especially Sinda and Enkomi, may throw more light on this relationship. Moreover, the connection of the basic LC III Decorated bowl shape with Levanto-Mycenaean prototypes has already been stressed and it would not be strange if some similar connections did eventually show up in the decoration. Daniel, in his notes, pointed out that such a situation would be typical of the breakup into local schools characteristic of the panel style period. There is no need, nor, I think, really any possibility of lifting C 718 out of

38. Cf., e.g., *Gezer* III, Pl. 167:9 with the prevailing panel decoration system of the Bamboula examples; it is true that this type of panel is well known in the Mycenaean repertory, but its occurrence with certain unusual features discussed below (see n. 43–45) calls for explanation. Notice furthermore that the Cypriote and Philistine practice is to use angular horizontal zigzag whereas the Mycenaean practice is horizontal wavy lines (see *OA* 3, 1944, 239).

39. Cf. also White Slip I ware motifs C, H, L of *Pl. 40*.

40. In the catalog entry of this pot, I discussed this motif as possibly connected with the Mycenaean repertory, but I confess that a Near Eastern derivation seems much more likely: cf. *Megiddo Tombs*, 93, Fig. 111; *Megiddo* II, Pl. 56:8 (both Syrian Bichrome) and *ibid.*, Pl. 58:2 (dated 1500–1350 B.C.); *Gezer* III, Pl. 165:1–2.

41. See *PEQ*, 1960, Pl. IV, Fig. 9a–b. It may well be objected that the element referred to is not, strictly speaking, dots; furthermore, I am aware that dotted concentric semicircles occur in the Mycenaean repertory at a late period (*MP*, 345, Fig. 58:i, k, o, s, t). But the peculiar trait of dotting every semicircle in turn might perhaps occur most easily to an artist who was used to seeing "leaves" put on every branch of the tree (see references in n. 40).

42. *PEQ*, 1956, 36.

43. For fuller discussion of this, see *PEQ*, 1960, 67.

44. This view can be particularly well tested by comparing *CVA* Copenhagen Fs. 1, Pl. 47:6, from Rhodes, with *Gezer* III, Pl. 168:1 and B 603 (*Pl. 65*). The latter two, in my opinion, are closer to each other in spirit than to the Rhodian example.

45. Cf. *Gezer* III, Pl. 166:13 with second column panel of C 718 (*Pl. 64*).

46. *MP*, 343; Mot. 42: 21 ff. Nevertheless, a krater fragment from Enkomi described as Mycenaean III B has this motif seemingly in pendant form: *ECCM*, Pl. 2:2. Thus a survival of Mycenaean influence may be the explanation of this motif in Cypriote and Philistine pottery.

47. *CPP*, Dec. Frags. 8; C9. Notice also the tendency of the Philistine painter occasionally to insert two dots: *ibid.*, C13 and compare with B 453 (*Pl. 64*).

48. Solid triangles: *MCh*, 60, Fig. 25; *OA* 3 (1944) 215, Fig. 6:7. Stippled triangles: *MCh*, 60, Fig. 25; *MP*, 343 Mot. 42:26. Dotting of triangles: *Gezer* III, Pl. 167:17; *OA* 3 (1944) 215, Fig. 6:7.

49. An LC III Decorated jug from Enkomi (*BCH* 86, 1962, 395 fig. 91) has a fish of a type directly related to Mycenaean prototypes. It may be compared closely with *Tarsus* II, no. 1330, with a stirrup jar from Langada (Kos, C 152, *ASAtene* 27/28, 1965–6, 190, fig. 196 c–d) and with Athens NM 2654 (*AJA* 72, 1968, Pl. 67, fig. 15).

this general background and assuming any special connection with the Mycenaean IIIC:1c style.[50] The class to which this bowl belongs is given its imprint by the "LC IIIA interlude" when *direct* Mycenaean influence at Bamboula was at a low ebb; we have already referred to B 503 as showing the final demise of this class. On the other hand, a brief infusion of life into LC III Decorated bowls under more direct Mycenaean influence during the LC IIIB phase is apparent in B 453: the stylization of the trees certainly presupposes the arrival of "wavy line" pottery. This would correspond to the tall shape of bowls of this ware if this feature is the result of direct Mycenaean influence (cf. p. 48). In general, however, the decorative repertory of the LC IIIB phase of LC III Decorated pottery displays not innovation but simply a more careless handling of the elements introduced earlier (*Pl. 64*).

At this point we can turn our attention to the Proto-White Painted ware which occurred at Bamboula. Although it has seemed advisable to concentrate the general discussion of this problem in the *Kaloriziki* volume, some discussion of the ware which occurred together with LC III Decorated ware cannot be dispensed with here, particularly since it can be made evident that there are many points of contact between the two. I have already touched on the question of shapes; and, although for further discussion of this as a specific problem I must refer the reader to *Kaloriziki*, Ch. IV, I should like here to insert a parenthesis about a shape not definitely reported at Kourion but occurring in the fabric, that is, the small stirrup jar.[51] It is, of course, conceivable that f, g, k and l below did actually originate from Kourion. Furumark listed the seven examples known to him in *OA* 3 (1944), 242:E, a list which can be expanded as follows:[52]

  a. Idalion: MV 14:91; *OA* 3 (1944) 91, Fig. 4:10; *OA* 3 (1944) 242:16. H: 18.5 cm.

  b. Lapithos: *KBH*, Pl. 157:2 (= 98:1) e; *CCM*, no. 435; *OA* 3 (1944) 91, Fig. 4:8; *OA* 3 (1944) 242:17. H:14 cm.

  c.-e. Lapithos, T. 503:1–3: *OA* 3 (1944) Pl. I; *OA* 3 (1944) 242:18–20. Fragmentary.

  f. Unknown provenance: *CesCol*, no. 412 (MM 74.51.769); *OA* 3 (1944) 79, Fig. 2:2, 92, Fig. 5:6; *OA* 3 (1944) 241, Fig. 11:21. *Pl. 63*. (Photo MM; purchased by subscription 1874–1876). H:16.5 cm.

  g. Unknown provenance: *CesCol.* no. 413 (74.-51.759 = CP 801); *OA* 3 (1944) 79, Fig. 2:1; *OA* 3 (1944) 241, Fig. 11:22. H:14.8 cm.

  h. Kouklia: C 695, *CatBMV* I, 132, Fig. 259.

CVA BM Fs. 2 II C.c Pl. 1:11. *Pl. 62* (courtesy, Trustees of British Museum). H:11.4 cm.

  i. Kouklia: C 696, *CatBMV* I, Pl. 4. *SPC*, 223, No. 10; *CVA* BM Fs. 2 II C.c Pl. 1:19; V. Desborough, *LMTS*, Pl. 18, c. *Pl. 62* (courtesy, Trustees of British Museum). H:12 cm.

  j. Kouklia: Ashmolean AE 321 (Cyprus Exploration Fund). *Pl. 62* (courtesy, Ashmolean Museum). H:9.2 cm.

  k. Purchased in Athens: Bryn Mawr P 68. *Pl. 62* (courtesy Bryn Mawr College Museum). H:11.5 cm.

  l. Unknown provenance: *CVA* Brussels Fs. 3 IIC Pl. 3:4a–b. H:11.5 cm.

  m. Unknown provenance: Hartford, Wadsworth Atheneum 16.26 (ex Cesnola). H: 13.3 cm. Published by J. L. Benson in "Two Cypriote Vases of Late Bronze Age Type," *Wadsworth Atheneum Bulletin,* Winter 1966, 25–32.

With the exception of the example from Idalion and m (and possibly also of c-e which are fragmentary), the vases in this list are characterized by re-

---

50. A few words may be devoted to Furumark's discussion of the panel with half circles. The type occurring on C 718 can be exactly paralleled on Philistine ware (*Gezer* III, Pls. 159:70; 160:2). The vertical wavy line is ubiquitous in Syro-Palestinian pottery. In the Mycenaean examples cited by Furumark, it is always enclosed by flanking straight lines. But the practice of interrupting a design with it (as in C 718) seems to be a Philistine specialty (cf. *Gezer* III, Pl. 165:10, Pl. 167:7). Nevertheless, it must be admitted that the basic design, a wavy line flanked by scallops in an outlined panel, does occur on a bowl from Boula in the Piraeus Museum (from Tomb 2, inv. Ab 108). The finds from this tomb are described in *Praktika*, 1954, 77 as eleven pots dated Late Helladic IIIB–C. The photograph, reproduced on *Pl. 54* by kind permission of the late Dr. I. Papadimitriou, is of a deep bowl apparently of Late Helladic IIIC shape. Although this design and that of C 718 may have a common ancestor, it is clear that C 718 has undergone Philistine influence on the basis of the similarities mentioned above (cf. also n. 43). Panels with geometricized horizontal zigzag also existed independently at a somewhat earlier time in Palestine (*QDAP* 8, 1938, Pl. XVII) as well as in Philistine ware.

51. For a survivor of this class into the CG I period, see *BCH* 85 (1961) 284, fig. 37 (from Kition).

52. In addition to the vases listed one must take into account four stirrup jars of this class from a tomb at Idalion recently published by V. Karageorghis (*Nouveaux Documents*, 192 f.). He lists additionally several others which have been published since 1960 and emphasizes the great similarity of this class with examples found in the Athenian Kerameikos. Also, the sites of Kition and Enkomi are reported to be producing examples of this shape. It appears, therefore, inappropriate at this time to go beyond the general summary which I give on the basis of the examples a-m. But it will obviously be possible at some time in the not too distant future for a renewed stylistic investigation of the entire class of Proto-White Painted ware to be made with the prospect of useful results for the chronology of mainland Greece.

markable stylistic unity. All make heavy use of matt dark paint over all of the body except the shoulder and have variations of the triangle design as shoulder decoration (*Pl. 63*). There are basically two shapes, the wide-based type, represented by g, k and l, and a type with conical base-ring. The latter type includes a, which, however, does not have its body covered with paint. The shape and decoration of g and l are sufficiently similar that we may postulate the same workshop; something of the spirit of this workshop seems to be observable in the shoulder decoration of the amphora K 129 (*Pl. 63*). Similarly, f, h, i and j come as if from one mould. The similarity of profile between f and the amphoriskos B 663 from the LC IIIB phase of the settlement is clear from the juxtaposition on Pl. 63; furthermore, the similarity in design between B 663 and K 129 which can be observed on the same plate serves to emphasize the contemporaneity of the whole group of stirrup jars in question and the wares associated with the LC IIIB strata at Bamboula and Kaloriziki. The general practice of covering the lower portion of the stirrup jars with matt paint is in accordance with the practice on Granary class, and especially Submycenaean, stirrup jars and one is inclined to attribute these features to colonists bringing it as the current mode. The similarity of k to Kerameikos stirrup jars is noteworthy;[53] it even has the wavy vertical line so characteristic in Athens, but the total shoulder design is geometricized in a manner quite at home in Cyprus.

The development of the Proto-White Painted stirrup jar into the White Painted I class can be postulated on a purely stylistic basis through another specimen from the Cesnola Collection shown on *Pl. 62* (MM 74.51.1104).[54] The shape has sagged and the decorative system has become broader and more tectonic, as well as less refined. It is difficult to be certain how to date a stirrup jar illustrated in Dikaios, *Guide*, Pl. 10:4. In the shape of the spout and the emphasis on the shoulder decoration, it seems close to the New York specimen. If the wide bands on the body are red, as one might surmise from the photograph, then the contemporaneity of the two pots seems assured.

It is appropriate at this point to consider the decorative system in more detail. The pieces which I have classified under the heading of Proto-White Painted from LC IIIA levels do not differ essentially in decoration from LC III Decorated ware. The latticed triangles of B 647, the horizontal zigzag panel of B 658 (*Pl. 66*) are examples of this. The chevrons

of B 665 (*Pl. 66*) are a universal motif, the origin of which cannot be specified. The facts, however, that B 665 seems to be part of an amphoriskos and that B 684 introduces a jug shape characteristic of Proto-White Painted ware, and that all these items stand out clearly from LC III Decorated ware in point of technique—in the sense I have defined in *Kaloriziki*, Ch. IV, Characterization of Proto-White Painted Technique—have induced me to regard them essentially as the very first manifestations of the ware which is characteristic of periods 2–4 and which prevails in the early tombs of the Kaloriziki necropolis. Granted the possibility that some of these examples could be intrusive, it does not seem possible to explain the entire group in that way. Nor can the absence of fragments with actual "wavy line" decoration be owing to anything but chance. The placement of B 674, from Tomb 32, as contemporary with these early sherds is probable but unfortunately cannot be absolutely guaranteed, as the tomb was disturbed (see *Kaloriziki*, Ch. IV, Proto-White Painted Shapes).

All in all, I think that these pieces can be regarded as a very late manifestation of the LC IIIA phase, in which the fusion of elements which is so characteristic of the LC IIIB phase appears *in statu nascendi*: both the nuclear affinity of Proto-White Painted ware to existing Cypriote wares and its new spirit can be singled out.

The most characteristic single motif of this ware at Bamboula is one which has been frequently mentioned, that is, the horizontal wavy line, generally in combinations of two or three. The second most popular feature is the triangle: latticed, solid, or stacked. This, of course, is not new but the frequency and manner of its use in zones (see below) mark a departure. Some motifs seem to be borrowed directly from the LC III Decorated repertory, as dotted panels (cf. B 629, *Pl. 66* with B 510, *Pl. 65*) and opposed semicircles (cf. B 634, *Pl. 66*, with C 718,

53. E.g., *Kerameikos* I, Pl. 8; also Pl. 11:503 (considered by Furumark, *OA* 3 (1944) 244, n. 8, to be Mycenaean III C:1c). Also very similar are the two jars published by C. Styrenius, *OpusAth* 4 (1962) Pl. 2:3610 and 3616. If the Bryn Mawr jar is indeed Cypriote, as seems to me a necessary inference from the technique, its potter may have been a recent immigrant from the mainland. On the other hand, the fact that it was purchased in Athens might suggest that it was found in Greece. It is interesting to note that Mrs. Birmingham has postulated the importation of Cypriote fibulae to the Kerameikos cemetery (*DFCL*, 90).

54. *CesCol*, no. 414 (photo MM; bought by subscription 1874–76). For other CGI specimens, see *OA* 3 (1944) 79, Fig. 2:344. These must be earlier in the sequence than the New York example.

Pl. 64). The pots from Tomb 33:c clearly tell the same story. The main motifs are those mentioned above; but the formal latticework zones of B 654 (*Pl. 60*) may be a borrowing from the Syro-Palestinian repertory (cf. B 1003 and examples cited there), while the crosshatch zone on that same pot (*Pl. 66*) may show belated influence from White Slip II ware, where crosshatched pendants are *par excellence* at home.[55]

It is certainly pertinent to mention here the correspondence between the manner of using color in the Philistine and the Proto-White Painted wares.[56] The intimate relationship between LC III Decorated ware and the Philistine milieu is thus re-confirmed from an unexpected quarter, in view of what I have already pointed out about the interconnections between LC III Decorated and Proto-White Painted ware. It would thus appear that influences from the Syro-Palestinian littoral in both technique and artistic vocabulary were, to a considerable extent, operative on the principal local Cypriote wares of the twelfth century. We see here actually a Levantine community of taste which cannot be surprising in view of the tendency of Cypriote pottery at all periods to reflect foreign influence.

To return to the question of local influence among Cypriote wares, it may be pointed out that, although Proto-White Painted ware agrees in a liberal use of encircling bands with the LC III Decorated practice, the *manner* of use is totally different. In the latter ware, individual bands or groups of bands are used at intervals, and the bands are generally of the same moderate width. There is also a tendency to cover the entire surface with close-set bands.[57] In Proto-White Painted ware there is a distinct tendency to use groups of narrow bands enclosed by wider bands, or groups of wide bands, generally below the handle and about midway to the base, in a manner thoroughly reminiscent of Mycenaean ware.[58] A close observation of this point alone makes it plain that a new spirit, which must certainly be connected with the contemporary influx of Greek settlers, is at play here in organizing the decoration. There can also be observed a rather superior restraint in the very sparing use of bands—as the only decoration—at rim, neck and base of the burnished jugs of

Type 3a, as well as of certain types of bowls (cf. B 644) and other shapes. The uniform covering bands disappear totally.[59] Tongues, both continuous (cf. especially B 669) and grouped, are introduced on the necks of pots. This is obviously another Greek feature, which flourished particularly in the LH IIIC period. The "panel" style of LC III Decorated bowls, which consisted of more or less isolated units of framed decoration placed uninterruptedly around the entire periphery of the bowl, is transferred to the necks and shoulders of krater-amphoras and to the shoulders of jugs and amphoras. Two-handled bowls also occasionally have a similar decoration but more often wavy lines. The whole manner of decoration should perhaps be designated as a "frieze" style. In any case, the tendency is to operate on an uninterrupted frieze principle whenever possible. Although the decoration is generally executed with somewhat greater discipline and restraint on the Proto-White Painted pottery than on LC III Decorated ware, there is, even in the former, practically no effort to go beyond a simple paratactic series of more or less identical decorative elements.[60] Nevertheless, there is often a rather refreshingly simple and bold dynamism to be observed in the handling of these elements, as, for example, in the use of ray-like triangles on the shoulders of the jugs K 145 and K 160 (*Pl. 63*).

---

55. It may also be noted that zones of hatching in the vertical sense are at home on the Syro-Palestinian littoral (e.g., *Megiddo* II, Pls. 56:3; 57:5) while not commonly encountered in Mycenaean ware. An interesting parallel to the decoration of B 654 is provided by a Proto-White Painted (?) krater in the Fitzwilliam Museum (*CVA* Cambridge Fs. 2, II C, Pl. 9:14), the shape of which is of immediate Mycenaean inspiration.

56. I have discussed this problem in *JNES* 20 (1961) 81 ff. To my note 27, *ibid.*, add the following reference: *Enciclop. dell' Arte Antica* III, 677, fig. 833.

57. Cf. Type 7 bowls and *OA* 3 (1944) 238.

58. Cf. especially B 679 (*Pl. 60*) and K 106 (*Pl. 61*); see also Furumark's comment on this feature (*OA* 3, 1944, 247).

59. A few partial examples of this (on neck only), not in any way derived from the LC III Decorated practice, can be observed, e.g., K 114, 117; Lapithos, Tomb 420:5, etc.

60. A few instances like the decoration on the neck of K 66 and on the shoulder of K 77 might be noted as mild exceptions to this. A beginning concern for a closed compositional effect seems evident in these.

Conclusions

From the foregoing considerations, the LC IIIB phase with its characteristic Proto-White Painted pottery emerges as a tangible transition from the Bronze Age to the Geometric Age. There is not the slightest doubt that the basic spirit of the latter age is already to a great extent present and dominant in the Proto-White Painted pottery at Bamboula from the very beginning. From a morphological point of view the Cypro-Geometric Age begins with period 2 and Tomb 33:c. It is worth recalling at this point than an even greater simplification of matters has been proposed by C. Schaeffer, who includes even Sjöqvist's LC IIIA phase under the designation *Chypriote Fer I*.[61] This is a matter of terminology and I do not intend to depart from the generally prevailing practice of designating as LC IIIB the phase which immediately follows the LC IIIA phase. What must be emphasized, however, is the fact that *there is no gap at Bamboula*. The material which immediately follows the LC IIIA phase is the new ware of period 2, Bamboula Tomb 33:c and the contemporary early tombs at Kaloriziki. The designation Proto-White Painted must apply to this ware if it is to have any meaning whatsoever for the site of Kourion. And, in fact, it will be quite evident from the closer study of it which appears in the Kaloriziki volume that the material just designated does occur in very specific and recognizable circumstances which set it off clearly from the ware about which there can be not the slightest dispute, from any point of view, as to its being Cypro-Geometric.[62] It will be seen that the material here designated as Proto-White Painted manifests, indeed, a geometricizing spirit, but as yet in a tentative, hesitant manner which still remembers freshly the old Bronze Age way of doing things. In short, the value of retaining a special term like Proto-White Painted for the pottery of the transition between Bronze Age and Geometric Age will become apparent.

Excursus on Relative Chronology

It may be useful to discuss here some Palestinian points of departure, based on bucchero ware, for the relation between the LC IIIA and B phases brought forward by du Plat Taylor.[63] The Bamboula LC IIIA examples of Black Slip Bucchero, like that of Enkomi Tomb 5 (her Fig. 2:3), lack the flaring neck and encircling horizontal grooves above the ribbing which are characteristic of the Palestinian examples; moreover, they show rather plainly an experimental spirit. There is more or less conscious effort, on the one hand, to make the vertical ribs on the pot look like those of the handmade counterpart, that is, added to the surface. On the other hand, the practice of modeling vertical grooves by cutting away the interstices also begins (B 695); the bucchero type LC III Plain jugs of Bamboula Tomb 40 seem also to be at this stage, although executed rather crudely. Judging from admittedly rather scanty evidence (B 698, B 702, K 543–545), one may conclude that this tendency simply continues during the LC IIIB phase and culminates in the rather coarse mass ware of the CG IA phase; this latter has horizontal grooves above the ribbing and a completely changed repertory of shapes.

Starting at this point I would suggest a slightly different distribution of some of the Palestinian tombs discussed by Miss Taylor than she does. To begin with, the shape of C 192, which must be regarded virtually as a sporadic find,[64] seems, by comparison with the Bamboula material, to belong to the LC IIIA phase (cf. particularly the foot), but it may well have continued in use during the next phase. In any case, it must be earlier than the Palestinian complex, Tell Fara Tomb 237, which is comparable to the CG I period. This latter equation is particularly confirmed by the pilgrim flask *CPP*, 85L:1, with its handles to mid-neck, the usual CG I position (see *Kaloriziki*, sub K 415). This flask belongs to the Foreign White Painted Pilgrim Flask category

61. *Enkomi-Alasia*, 69.
62. Such, for example, as B 714–B 728 or two pots from earlier excavations at Bamboula, C 708 and C 721, illustrated with new photographs on *Pl. 63*.
63. *PEQ*, 1956, 33 ff.
64. Classified by Walters as "Cypriote Bucchero" ware but not included with other vases of this category in *CVA BM Fs. 1, II Ca, Pl. 12*. I am not in a position at this point to say whether it is of Cypriote manufacture.

(B 1209, e.g.). The bucchero jug 59D3 from the same tomb has apparently a duplicate in 59B1 from Tell Fara Tomb 640, which, although its finds are more nondescript, must also be at least as late as Tomb 237. The two bucchero jugs just referred to have a low ring base and thus represent a new departure from the base-ring type exclusively prevalent at Bamboula (and apparently at Enkomi) during the LC III period. On the other hand, this ring base occurs as an innovation at Kourion in the CG I period (*Kaloriziki*, sub K 585 ff.). Very possibly this feature reflects influence from the Syro-Palestinian quarter upon Cyprus at this time, for such influence is certainly attested by an unusual hybrid jug in Larnaca[65] combining low base, vertical grooves and a horizontal zone of grooved zigzag triangles with White Painted designs on the shoulder. It is thus tempting to suggest that the introduction of the encircling horizontal grooves above the vertical grooves during the CG I period is another direct influence from the Syro-Palestinian littoral. There can be no doubt, of course, about the existence of direct relations between the regions at this time in view of the famous Tell Fara Tomb 506 with its imported White Painted I cup.

If C 192 is assigned to the LC III period, it is equally possible to consider *CPP*, 59F2, 59F3 and 59E2, carrying with them Tell Fara Tombs 102, 105 and 647, as contemporary with the bucchero jugs in Cyprus which they resemble, that is, those of LC III type without horizontal grooves. The pilgrim flasks associated with this group (*CPP*, 85E1, E7; 85J3, N2, S2) accord very well with the LC IIIB type with handles joining under the lip (see *Kaloriziki*, Pl. 20). Moreover, there are deep bowls in Tomb 102 which would accord with the LC IIIB tendency in Cyprus. One would then reckon Tomb 615 with its deep bowl and 'fruit stand' of the late Bamboula type in this same group,[66] which is contemporary with the LC IIIB period. A detailed re-study of the Tell Fara objects along the lines followed by Miss Taylor might assist in an exact appraisal of the equations discussed here. Nevertheless, some validity is certainly inherent in them and may prove to be a helpful factor in considerations of absolute chronology.

65. *AA*, 1934, 113, Fig. 21.
66. This ascription is further supported by the presence of a Philistine type cup assigned to Tomb 615 in *CPP* Addenda 27D3. See *Beth-Pelet* I, Pl. 31:289.

4. ABSOLUTE CHRONOLOGY

All absolute chronologies for the period involved at Bamboula are, at this stage of our knowledge, purely schematic attempts to bridge over long gaps of time for which there are no chronicles. The problematic character of early Cypriote chronology has recently been emphasized by Desborough;[1] I cannot help agreeing with the implications of his discussion that, until there is more certain evidence from the Near East, which must ultimately hold the key to the problem, there is not yet really an adequate basis for disturbing the chronological system proposed by Gjerstad. The views presented in the foregoing discussion on the relative chronology of Proto-White Painted ware do not affect the absolute dates of Gjerstad's system adversely; in fact they make it more plausible by eliminating a drastic application of the heirloom theory. Moreover, since Furumark's paper[2] it had been clear that at least approximately the relative sequences which has been demonstrated here to fit the facts at Kourion was required on general considerations. We shall therefore accept Gjerstad's date of 1050 B.C. as the starting point to determine the range of the LC III period. The comment may be inserted at this point, for absolute clarity, that the later material from the Kaloriziki tombs published by me contains no new "navigational fixes" for judging the absolute dates of the later Iron Age chronology.[3]

The suggestion has already been made that the LC IIIB transitional phase which embraces the early geometricizing type of Proto-White Painted ceramics must be a short one, say fifty years.[4] This brings us to about 1100 B.C. for the end of the LC IIIA phase. A valuable check on the validity of this is given by B 674, which we have placed at the turn between the LC IIIA and LC IIIB phases. B 674 is comparable to one of the very earliest pieces in the Submycenaean cemetery of the Kerameikos.[5] In this connection it cannot be without significance that there is a generic similarity in shape between the amphoriskoi and lekythoi of the early Kaloriziki tombs and those of the Kerameikos Submycenaean tombs.[6] These have also some decorative traits in common, especially use of the wavy line; however, it is clear that the tendency to retain only wavy lines

and a minimum of linear framework is a mainland rather than a Cypriote characteristic. Likewise the Cypriote Greeks did not develop consistently the tendency to cover part or most of the body of a pot with dark color, although they did occasionally use this technique at first. Altogether, the similarities in shape and decoration of pottery and of burial cus-

1. *JBS* 77 (1957) 218; Van Beek, however, still adheres to the high chronology: *AJA* 64 (1960) 194. Although the consequences of this seem rather unworkable for the later part of the Geometric period in Greece, as Desborough implies, it would be unreasonable to deny that *at least* a fifty year period at the upper end of the Geometric period can be disposed of *ad libitum* by anyone suggesting a chronology for the period in question. Thus the duration of the LC IIIB period could be fixed at 1150–1100 without doing violence to the material at Kourion, and indeed this would relieve the necessity for postulating a duration of 125 years for the LC IIIA period (if one accepts ca. 1225 as its beginning date) which is perhaps excessively long. On the other hand, such a solution would necessitate a duration of one of the Geometric subperiods which might seem equally excessive. Desborough in his thorough study of the mainland evidence, *LMTS*, 197, n. 2. has adopted provisionally the dating proposed here for LC IIIB. The placement of its end at 1050 is strengthened, in my opinion, by the fact that Desborough arrives on quite independent evidence at the conclusion that the break between LH IIIB and LH IIIC is possible, or even likely, at 1200 rather than 1230 (*ibid.*, 239 f.). Insofar as this may strengthen the case for dating the end of LC IIC at 1200 rather than a quarter of a century earlier (see note 12) it thereby gives us a shorter and more reasonable duration (150 instead of 175 years) for the entire LC III period.
2. *OA* 3 (1944) 194 ff.
3. Cf. *Kaloriziki*, Ch. IV, Chronology. See also *PEQ*, 1956, 37.
4. *Op. cit.* and cf. *OA* 3 (1944) 258. The chronology which I have arrived at is proposed also by du Plat Taylor and Judy Birmingham: see *AJA* 67 (1963) 39. On Mrs. Birmingham's chart of relative chronology, Kaloriziki Tombs 26A and 25 are correctly dated to the LC IIIB period. Cf. also *DFCL*, 89 for a reaffirmation of this. It appears also that V. Karageorghis accepts 1100 as the date for the transition between LC IIIA and LC IIIB (cf. *BCH* 84, 1960, 580 f.).
5. *Kerameikos* I, 56, 73 and Pl. 24: inv. 438 from Tomb 19.
6. Cf. e.g., *Kaloriziki*, Pls. 17–19 with *Kerameikos* I, Pls. 12–20. Daniel, in his latest notes, also proposed the equation Proto-White Painted Submycenaean, but du Plat Taylor (*PEQ*, 1956, 30) still refers to Proto-Geometric parallels and heirlooms. V. Karageorghis in a study of Proto-White Painted pottery from Idalion stresses the similarities with Myc. IIIC:2 (*Nouveaux Documents*, 198). Cf. also V. Desborough, *LMTS*, 27 f. A recent study of fibulae has also confirmed the contemporaneity of LC IIIB at Kourion and the Submycenaean period on the mainland (Birmingham, *DFCL*, 90, 94).

toms (see *Kaloriziki*, Ch. I) suggest that the LC IIIB period at Kourion could only be contemporary with the Submycenaean period[7] on the mainland, for after the LC IIIB period the development of Cypriote pottery and culture diverges irrevocably from that of other Greek centers.

Wace has already suggested the latest part of the twelfth and the eleventh centuries as a range for the Submycenaean ware;[8] the most recent, as yet unpublished, version of the mainland chronology would agree with this.[9] The presence of K 970 as a product of the second half of the twelfth century in a tomb dated to the first half of the eleventh century would not call for any particular application of the heirloom theory, for as few as ten or twenty years might lie between manufacture and final use of the pot. This will simply be another link in the chain of contemporary relations with Rhodes as evidenced both by the Kaloriziki necropolis and stylistic associations pointed out by Furumark.[10] The groups of Proto-White Painted ware which Furumark considered to be the earliest would on this basis fall in the second half of the twelfth century if the stylistic equations he proposed prove to be valid in a strictly chronological sense.[11]

The upper limit of the LC IIIA phase is a disputed matter, on which the site of Bamboula does not throw as much light as could be hoped. We have seen that the stylistic affiliations of the more elaborate LC III Decorated ware are to a considerable extent with Philistine pottery, and this ware apparently does not reach back even quite to the beginning of the twelfth century, let alone the end of the third quarter of the thirteenth century—the date usually accepted for the end of the LC IIC phase.[12] I must remark here that in the discussion of the Bamboula stratification (*Bamboula SS*) it is shown that a catastrophe of some sort overtook the settlement at the end of the LC IIC or beginning of the LC IIIA phase. It is not possible to say what this catastrophe was. If, however, despite elimination of actual physical remains of any specific destruction level, it could be related to one of the two catastrophes at Enkomi and Sinda[13]—particularly the latter, *ca.* 1190 B.C.—it would be possible to assume that the habitation evidence from period 1 dates from the twelfth century only. In any case, the fact must be reckoned with that there is virtually no evidence of Mycenaean III C:1 pottery from the site in a period when this occurs at Enkomi and Sinda. The only deposit which seems to bridge this gap is Area D, Stratum A. The presence in this of LC III

Decorated bowls—not of panel style, it must be noted—makes the appearance of banded bowls in the thirteenth century seem likely. Similar evidence is provided by Area A, Stratum D:1 and Area E, Stratum C:1–6. This suggests the conclusion that the LC III Decorated ware literally began as "bowl-ware" (although the feeding bottle also occurs in early contexts at Enkomi), a degraded version of Levanto-Mycenaean bowls, and developed gradually a manner of its own, coming strongly under Syro-Philistine influences in the advancing twelfth century.

The problem then, at Bamboula, concerns exactly the critical period between 1230 and 1190. Does period 1 begin at the former or the latter date—or at some time in between? Unfortunately the stratified evidence fails us here. The virtual lack of Mycenaean pottery later than the IIIB variety leaves us in the dark. In order not unduly to prolong the life-span of LC III Decorated pottery, which does not show any very marked development, I incline towards the lower date.[14] But this reason obviously does not have much cogency of an absolute nature.

7. Apparently the same conclusion has been reached by Dikaios in his study of the Enkomi material: cf. *AA*, 1962, 38, n. 46. "The end of Enkomi coincides with the prevalence of Mycenaean IIIC:2 pottery or the transition from Proto-White Painted to Cypro-Geometric I period."

8. *ANE*, 134.

9. Desborough, *LMTS*, 241, does not attempt to suggest absolute dates for sub-phases of LH IIIC, but there can be no doubt from his discussion of the relation between Argolid LH IIIC and Submycenaean wares (*ibid.*, 17 f.) that he would place Submycenaean in the fifty years or so prior to 1050.

10. *OA* 3 (1944) 243. Daniel also decidedly rejected the heirloom theory: *AJA* 44 (1940) 556.

11. For a fuller discussion on this point, cf. *Kaloriziki*, Ch. IV, Dating of Tombs.

12. Cf. *OA* 3 (1944), 260; *AJA* 45 (1941) 272. This date, however, based on 1230 B.C. as the end of the Mycenaean III B phase, has been challenged by H. Catling, *OpusAth* 2 (1955) 26, who refers to Wace's lower date for the end of LH IIIB. On this, cf. n. 8 above. Furthermore, Sir Leonard Woolley (*Alalakh*, 376) has expressed a decided preference for a date about the end of the twelfth century (or even the beginning of the eleventh) as the end of the Mycenaean IIIB period. I have noted above Desborough's acceptance of the lower date for the end of the LH IIIB period (see also his remarks on the dating of Philistine ware, *loc. cit.*). Thus we are back to the date suggested by Sjöqvist, *Problems*, 197, for the beginning of the LC IIIA period. This is, to be sure, in conflict with the date of 1230 which is still adhered to by Furumark and Dikaios (*OpusAth* 6, 1965, 115).

13. *AFF*, 67. It is important, in this connection, to notice the statement of du Plat Taylor that Pigadhes was deliberately wrecked, though not burnt, at the beginning of LC III: *PEQ*, 1956, 30.

14. Cf. also *PEQ*, 1956, 36, where on other grounds an extension upward of the LC IIC phase is advocated.

Daniel held to the date of 1225 B.C. for the beginning of the LC III period until his death; reasons seem to be accumulating to lower it, but it is obvious that we shall have to depend on the evidence of other sites in Cyprus for the elucidation of this point of absolute chronology.

For the subdivisions of the Late Cypriote period prior to LC IIIA no internal or external evidence from Bamboula has come to light to necessitate a change in the scheme proposed by Daniel; however, I have deemed it advisable to bring the opening date of this period into accordance with recent research on the subject, that is, by placing it at 1600 B.C. with LC IA:1 lasting about fifty years and LC IA:2 lasting about a century.[15] Thus, the complete system of absolute chronology adopted in this report is as follows:

LC IA:1	1600–1550
LC IA:2	1550–1450
LC IB	1450–1400
LC IIA	1400–1350
LC IIB	1350–1275
LC IIC	1275–1225
LC IIIA	1225–1100
LC IIIB	1100–1050

15. Daniel's chronology: *AJA* 45 (1941) 271 ff. See also my discussion of the LC IA period in connection with White Slip ware in *PEQ*, 1961, 69 with further references. It must be noted, however, that J. B. Hennessy rejects 1600 for the beginning of LC I and argues for 1560/50 at the very earliest (*Stephania*, London, 1964, 52 f.).

CATALOGUE OF FINDS

OUTLINE OF CONTENTS

Part I: Cypriote Pottery

Part III: Miscellaneous Finds

ABBREVIATIONS

Words used repeatedly in the Catalogue have been arbitrarily abbreviated. The list is as follows:

B	Bamboula	ls.	lustrous
BR	Base-Ring	lt.	light
bur.	burnished, burnish	m.	matt
C	clay	MPT	Miscellaneous Plundered Tombs
c-c	concentric circles	n.	narrow
C-ch	complete but chipped	N-c	nearly complete
CG	Cypro-Geometric	N-c-m	nearly complete and mended
C-i	complete and intact	P	paint
C-m	complete and mended	pres.	preserved
c-s	concentric spiral	PD	preserved diameter
C-sp	complete but sprung	PH	preserved height
Cw	Circuit wall	PL	preserved length
d-o	double outlined	PW	preserved width
dec.	decorated, decoration	PWM	Plain Wheelmade
dk.	dark	res.	reserved
ED	estimated diameter	resp.	respectively
ext.	exterior	RP	Red Polished
g.	gritty	RS	Red Slip
I-m	incomplete and mended	S	slip
inc.	including	sl.	slightly
int.	interior	s-o	single-outlined
frag.	fragment	Th	thickness
H	height	t-o	triple-outlined
H-m	handmade	unbur.	unburnished
h-z	handle zone	Unstrat.	unstratified
hor.	horizontal	vert.	vertical
K	Kaloriziki (but in the case of inscribed objects refers to the numbers established by Daniel in *AJA* XLV, 1941, 273 ff.)	VT	Voupha Tomb
		W	width
		w.	wavy
		wfs	with fine sand
		wfds	with fine dark sand
L	length	w-l	wavy line
lat-loz.	latticed lozenges	W-m	wheelmade
lat-tr.	latticed triangles	WS	White Slip
LC	Late Cypriote		

NOTES EXPLANATORY TO THE CATALOGUE

Information given in the entries: The number in parentheses immediately following the B number is the field catalogue number of the object; if the object is in the University Museum, Philadelphia, the accession number of that museum is given immediately after the field catalogue number. Absence of an accession number indicates that the object is in Cyprus, either in the Cyprus Museum, Nicosia or at Curium House, Episkopi. Following this entry, the find-spot of the object is indicated: if from the settlement, by area (e.g., A=), level (e.g., D:3) and house (e.g., V); if from the necropolis, by tomb number and find number, thus T.1:5, the fifth find removed from Tomb 1. Immediately following the find spot is given *the general date of the context*, if any can be determined, e.g., LC IIIA. It must be emphasized that this is *not necessarily a final or absolute date for the object*, although in many or perhaps most instances it will be. In any case, it is recommended that reference be had to the appropriate section of the text dealing with the level or tomb in question for verification of the relation of the object to the general context. Reference to illustrations of the object *in this publication* is given next, followed by a description of present condition, shape, remarks on material and decoration (where applicable) and dimensions (in centimeters unless otherwise indicated). Following this is a notation of any previous publication of the object and any suggested comparisons from archaeological literature or miscellaneous comment. Objects in the British Museum published in the Catalogue of Terracottas or the Catalogue of Vases of that museum are referred to only by their designations in those publications, e.g., A 501 or C 72.

PART I: CYPRIOTE POTTERY

Decorated Wares

"NEOLITHIC"

For an explanation of the presence of these sherds, which occur only in Area A, see *Bamboula SS*. The material is far too fragmentary to serve as the basis for a real stylistic analysis. The condition of most of the pieces is poor; all appear to have been slipped and on many there is evidence of burnishing. Otherwise there is no decoration. Only a few sherds can be assigned to a definite shape (and then only to bowls). Their chief interest lies in the indication that—if they are truly Neolithic—there may be a settlement of that date quite near to Bamboula, as yet undiscovered. In any case, the term Neolithic is used here loosely to define a fabric which, though similar to, is distinguishable from Red Polished ware: in general, this fabric is thicker and coarser and appears more primitive. No specific analogies from Neolithic sites, however, can be offered here.

Bowls

B 1 (Sh 152) A-D:3(V) LC IIIA. Rim frag. joining B 4; see also B 31. C: g. coarse lt. orange-brown. S: hor. bur. red-orange to dk. gray. H: 8. W: 5.2. **B 2** (Sh 167) A-D:3(V) etc. LC IIIA. Rim frag. of large bowl; probably from this same pot are B 3, B 5 and B 7. C: g. coarse gray-tan. S: like the foregoing. H: 4.7. L: 7. **B 3** (Sh 168) A-D:3(V) etc. LC IIIA. *Pl. 15.* See the foregoing. Fired dk. gray in places. L: 6.6. W: 6.6. **B 4** (Sh 195) A-E:3(V) etc. LC IIIB. See B 1. Fired dk. gray in places. L: 3.6. W: 3. **B 5** (Sh 219) A-D:2(V) LC IIIA. *Pl. 15.* See B 2. Fired dk. gray in places. L: 5.1. W: 3.2. **B 6** (Sh 224) A-B:5 LC IIB. C: g. red-brown to gray. S: m. red to mottled gray. L: 2.6. W: 1.6. **B 7** (Sh 256) A-D:3(IV) LC IIIA. See B 2. L: 2.2. W: 1.6. **B 8** (Sh 266) A-A:5 LC IIA. Flat base of bowl. C: coarse, pebbly; red-brown to gray. S: yellow-brown to red (ext.); probably not bur., much worn. Int. certainly not bur. H: 2.3. L: 5.5. **B 9** (Sh 465) A-A:5 LC IIA. Wall frags. of deep bowl. C: g. gray at core to lt. orange-brown, soft. Imperfect stroke bur. S: if any, entirely gone. H: 8. W: 4.3. **B 10** (Sh 473) A-C:2a LC IIB. *Pl. 15.* Rim frag. C: lt. gray-tan, hard. S: ls. red-orange, almost gone. H: 2.6. W: 2.5.

Undetermined shapes

B 11 (Sh 117) A-D:3(VI) LC IIIA. C: dk. gray to lt. brown. S: red-orange. Possibly RP ware. L: 3.2.

W: 3. **B 12** (Sh 174) A-B:5 LC IIB. *Pl. 15.* C: g. yellow. S: dk. red-brown, crackly, mostly off; once ls. L: 3.3. W: 3. **B 13** (Sh 202) A-C:3 LC IIB. C,S: like the foregoing and perhaps from the same pot. L: 6.5. W: 7. **B 14** (Sh 203) A-E:2(St.2a) LC IIIB. *Pl. 15.* C: dk. gray at core to lt. red-brown. S: if any, now entirely gone. L: 5.6. W: 4.8. **B 15** (Sh 207) A-D:2(St.1) LC IIIA. C: g. gray at core to red. S: red (int.); mottled brown to gray (ext.), bur. L: 4.3. W: 2.5. **B 16** (Sh 210) A-E:2(St.2a) LC IIIB. *Pl. 15.* C: g. dk. gray to dk. red-brown. S: mottled brown (int.); red to black (ext.), peeling. L: 3.6. W: 3.3. **B 17** (Sh 213) A-E:3(V) LC IIIB. *Pl. 15.* C: g. gray to lt. gray-brown. S: red-brown, partly gone. L: 4.2. W: 4. **B 18** (Sh 217) A-E:3(V) LC IIIB. C: like B 13. S: ls. red-brown. L: 6. W: 4.5. **B 19** (Sh 222) A-B:5 LC IIB. C: g. lt. brown. S: thin ls. red-brown to dk. gray. L: 3.8. W: 1.8. **B 20** (Sh 226) A-B:5 LC IIB. C: g. gray core to brick-red; hard. S: mottled black to red, peeling. L: 6. W: 4.5. **B 21** (Sh 255) A-D:3(IV) LC IIIA. C: g. red-brown. S: red to black, not bur. L: 8.5. W: 8.2. **B 22** (Sh 260) A-E:4 LC IIIB. C,S: like B 18. L: 4. W: 3.2. **B 23** (Sh 265) A-A:5 LC IIA. C: hard black. S: brown to black (int.); red and black (ext.), highly bur. L: 4.8. W: 3.5. **B 24** (Sh 267) A-A:5 LC IIA. *Pl. 15.* C: g. gray at core to yellow-orange, soft. P: traces of ls. dk. red bur. visible. L: 5. W: 2.5. **B 25** (Sh 271) A-D:3(IV) LC IIIA. C,S: like B 2. L: 4.5. W: 1.5. **B 26** (Sh 286) A-D:1(IV.1) LC IIC. C,S: like B 2. L: 2.7. W: 2. **B 27** (Sh 289) A-D:1(IV.1) LC IIC. C,S: like B 2. L: 2. W: 1.4. **B 28** (Sh 378) Cw Vb CA II. *Pl. 15.* C: g. dk. gray to dull red. S: coal-black, bur. (ext.), int. unbur. L: 3.7. W: 3.5. **B 29** (Sh 381) A-F:1 LC IIIB. *Pl. 15.* C,S: like B 2. L: 5.3. W: 2. **B 30** (Sh 382) A-F:1, etc. LC IIIB. C,S: like B 2. L: 3.5. W: 1.5. **B 31** (Sh 399) A-D:3(V) LC IIIA. Like B 1. Part of same pot? L: 2.6. W: 1.9. **B 32** (Sh 443) A-E:3(V) LC IIIB. C,S: like B 2. L: 2.9. W: 2.2. **B 33** (Sh 444) A-D:3(V) LC IIIA. C,S: like B 2. L: 3.1. W: 3.1. **B 34** (Sh 488) A-E:2(VI) LC IIIA. C: lt. g. gray-brown. S: hor. bur. red-orange. L: 6.5. W: 3.2.

RED POLISHED WARE

All of the specimens recovered were either very fragmentary or merely sherds.

Bowls: all the following are plain rim fragments.

B 35 (Sh 121) A-E:3(VI) LC IIIB. *Pl. 15.* With lug. C: slate-gray to lt. orange. S: bur. orange-brown.

H: 4. W: 3. **B 36** (Sh 150) A-E:3(V) LC IIIB. Punched. C: soft lt. gray-tan. S: like the foregoing. H: 2.5. W: 1.8. **B 37** (Sh 169) A-E:3(V) LC IIIB. Pinched lip. C: lt. gray-brown. S: bur. red-brown. H: 2.8. W: 1.5. **B 38** (Sh 216) A-E:3(V) LC IIIB. *Pl. 15.* C: gray-buff. S: like B 35 but darker, fired black in places. H: 2.3. L: 3. **B 39** (Sh 264) A-A:5 LC IIA. *Pl. 15.* C: hard lt. gray-tan. S: bur. lt. red-brown to dk. gray. H: 1.8. W: 4.5. **B 40** (Sh 376) Cw Vb CA II. *Pl. 15.* Incised triangle(?). C: hard gray-green to gray-brown. S: like B 38. H: 2.7. W: 1.7. **B 41** (Sh 395) A-E:3(VIII) LC IIIB. *Pl. 15.* C: like B 39. S: vermilion (int.); streaked yellow-orange to yellow-brown (ext.); bur. H: 1.8. L: 3.6. **B 42** (Sh 634) E:A:7 LC IIA. *Pl. 15.* Incised. C: very hard lt. gray-brick color. S: bur. dk. red-brown. Incisions white-filled. H: 1.8. L: 2.4.

Basins

B 43 (Sh 379) Cw VIII Roman context. Frag. of wall and spout. C: g. lt. gray at core to orange-brown. S: brown, bur. (int. unfinished). H: 5.2. L: 8.5. **B 44** (Sh 583) D-A. *Pl. 39.* About ¼ of large, shallow basin with rounded base. Long hor. triangular lug at rim; below rim a hor. relief band with incised notches. C: gray-brown at core to brick-red, with lt. sand. S: bur. red to gray. H: 13. ED: 26. Probably RS III (or later): cf. *SCE I* Pl. XCIX:3 and *Vounous* Pl. XIX:37.

Cup

B 45 (Sh 416) A-Surface. *Pl. 15.* Vert. handle to rim, probably same type as *Vounous* Pl. LXXVII:e. C: dk. g. gray, fired reddish brown to yellow-brown; once bur. H: 5.1. W: 2.2.

Amphoriskos

B 46 (P 932; 49-12-2) T.1:1. *Pls. 16, 39.* About half pres. Very badly weathered. Flat base, biconical belly with no articulation to concave neck and wide flaring round mouth. Vert. lug handle(s?) on shoulder. C: soft g. brown. S: bur. dk. pink (partially covering). H: 8.5. D: 7.3. This is a smaller version of the RP I amphora type 1 (*SPC*, 92). Vertical lug handles are not particularly common and when occurring are likely to be horned (cf. *Vounous* Pl. LXIX:e).

Amphora

B 47 (P 933; 49-12-3) T.1:2. *Pl. 16.* About ⅔ pres. with full profile. Wide flat base. Squat rounded belly with short vert. neck not set off from body. Traces of vert. handle. C: hard g. gray at core to red, with chaff temper. S: red to dk. gray-brown, ext. only; crudely bur. H: 15. D: 15.4. Probably a cooking pot of the type illustrated in *SCE I* Pl. XCVIII:12-13. The shape as far as I can see is not attested until later (cf. *SPC*, 178 No. 3) but it is likely to have existed in the repertory of coarse ware from perhaps quite early times.

Jugs: cf. also C 84 (*ExC*, Fig. 125:98 = *CVA BM* Fs.1 Pl. 3:14), which is very similar to the RP II examples given in *SPC*, 107.

B 48 (P 2741; 54-41-14) VT:14. About half, including much of lower body, pres. Small flat base with

elongated spherical body. C: gray at core to lt. reddish brown, soft and thick. S: sl. ls. dk. red-brown to red-gray; incisions filled with a white chalky substance. Belly divided into two zones by groups of hor. incisions, dotted above. Below: zigzag. Above: disconnected zigzag or chevrons. PH: 11.8. ED: 12.5. For complete shape cf. *Vounous* Pl. LXV: e-g. Date is suggested by *SPC*, 112 Nos. 3 and 17 (RP III). **B 49** (P 2841; 49-12-4) T.1:3. Base and small portion of adjoining wall; probably from a jug. C: like the foregoing. S: ls. dk. reddish brown. PH: 4. D (of base): 8. **B 50** (Sh 76) A-E:3(St) LC IIIB. *Pl. 15.* Frag. of neck of jug with incised line at top. C: g. lt. red-brown, sandy. S: bur. lt. red-brown. H: 6.2. ED (at base): 4.7. **B 51** (Sh 144) A-E:4 LC IIIB. *Pl. 15.* Frag. of wall. C,S: like B 49. Incised multiple zigzags. H: 2.3. L: 3.7. **B 52** (Sh 377) Cw Vb CA II. Several sherds of beaker-mouthed jug, incl. frag. of handle. C: gray at core to lt. gray-buff, soft. S: like B 35. L: 6.5. W: 3.7. **B 53** (Sh 403) Cw Vb CA II. Flaring rim of jug, with hor. incisions. C: grayish brick-red, very coarse and hard. H-m. Apparently never bur. May be a crude imitation of RP ware. PH: 2.3. ED: 5. **B 54** (Sh 428) Cw VIII Roman context. *Pl. 15.* Neck with 4(?) pierced string holes. C: hard slate-gray. S: thin red-orange(?), mostly off. H: 5.1. D (at base): 3.7.

Miscellaneous sherds

B 55 (Sh 212) A-C:3 LC IIB. Frag. from near handle of large pot. C: g. lt. gray-brown. S: bur. red-brown, ext. only. L: 5.3. W: 6.2. **B 56** (Sh 221) A-D:1(V) LC IIIA. C: lt. gray at core to lt. gray-brown. S: bur. pinkish brown (int. and ext.). L: 5.2. W: 4.5. **B 57** (Sh 272) A-D:3(IV) LC IIIA. C: hard sandy red-brown. S: bur. dk. red-brown (one face) and dk. gray-brown (other). L: 3.6. W: 2.2. **B 58** (Sh 274) A-C:2b LC IIB. *Pl. 15.* Incised and punched. C: lt. gray to dk. gray-brown. S: dk. red-brown. L: 2. W: 1.9.

BLACK SLIP WARE

Bowls

B 59 (Sh 63) A-C:1b LC IIB. *Pl. 15.* Sherd from rim with filled incisions: circle over part of irregular dotted area. C: hard slate-gray. S: ls. orange-brown, nearly gone. H: 2.5. L: 3. **B 60** (Sh 323) A-D:3(VII) LC IIIA. Incurved rim, sl. flattened. C: hard dk. gray. S: ls. thick orange-brown to dk. gray. The similarity of this frag. to BR ware illustrates the close connection of the wares. H: 2.1. L: 4.

Jugs

B 61 (Sh 101) A-G LC IIIB. Neck of jug; tall and narrow. Handle came to mid-neck. C: lt. slate-gray, hard. S: traces of black paint as well as drip marks on inside of mouth; very much worn. H: 5.9. D (at mouth): 2.3. **B 62** (Sh 312) A-D:2(VII,2) LC IIIA. *Pl. 15.* Sherd from neck. Rough incisions. C: hard slate-gray. S: m. dk. gray, probably much worn. H: 3.1. W: 1.8. **B 63** (Sh 500) Cw Vb CA II. *Pl. 15.* Sherd from neck(?) with incised and punched patterns. C: gray at core to lt. brown, soft. S: ls. red-gray to mahogany color. L: 5. W: 3.3.

Undetermined shapes

B 64 (Sh 94) A-E:1(VIII) LC IIIB. *Pl. 15*. C: gray at core to red-brown. S: hard ls. black int., brick-red to gray-brown ext. L: 3.3. W: 3. **B 65** (Sh 178) A-Surface. *Pl. 15*. Frag. with 3 filled incisions and protuberance ("breast"). C: like B 61. S: dk. gray, nearly gone. L: 2.3. W: 2.6. **B 66** (Sh 329) A-D:2(VII,2) LC IIIA. *Pl. 15*. Incised. C: like B 63. S: like the foregoing, sl. ls. H: 2.5. W: 2.5. **B 67** (Sh 339) A-Unstrat. *Pl. 15*. Incised. C: like B 61. S: entirely gone. L: 3. W: 2.5. **B 68** (Sh 452) Cw Vb CA II. Incised and punched. C: like B 63. S: like B 66, much worn off and crackled. H: 3.5. W: 3.5.

WHITE PAINTED WARE

The almost complete absence of this ware underscores the dearth of Middle Cypriote fabrics at Bamboula. However, several specimens not listed here were found on the surface.

B 69 (Sh 372) Cw Vb CA II. *Pl. 15*. Jug handle, top part. C: lt. gray at core to pinkish brown, not well smoothed. P: traces of m. dk. gray-brown. Stripe down center of handle? L: 6.6. H: 2.5.

RED-ON-BLACK WARE

B 70 (Sh 476) A-A:2b LC IIA. *Pl. 15*. Sherd from rim and handle of deep bowl. C: lt. brown, fine. S: ls. red-black. P: m. red. Vert. red lines int. and ext. and lines around handle. H: 5.1. W: 4.5. **B 71** (Sh 489) A-A:2a LC IIA. *Pl. 15*. From pot with closed shape. C: orange-brown. S,P: like the foregoing. L: 3.6. W: 2.1.

WHITE SLIP I

The classification used here follows *Problems*, 43 ff., with exceptions noted. The italicised letters in parentheses refer to decorative schemes on Pls. 40 and 41. For a detailed discussion of this fabric see "The White Slip Sequence at Bamboula, Kourion" in *PEQ*, 1961, 61 ff. Remarks on recent finds in this fabric in *Nouveaux Documents*, 133 ff. Its origins discussed *ibid.*, 49 and 106, and by M. R. Popham, "The Proto-White Slip Pottery of Cyprus," *OpusAth* 4 (1962) 277–297.

Bowls

Type 1: **B 72** (P 1230; 49-12-166) T.12:37 (B) LC IA:2 N-c-m. C: lt. gray-brown. S: pale gray to yellow, bur. P: orange to deep brown. (*i*). Opposite handle: vert. x's bordered by dots and flanked by x's between lines; crossed by dots between hor. lines. H: 11.5. D: 20.4. *PEQ*, 1961, 64 Pl. 7:3. **B 73** (P 1231; 49-12-200) T.12:73 (C) LC IB. N-c-m. C,S: like the foregoing. P: gray to rust. (*i*). Opposite handle: vert. w. lines and dots crossed by 3 hor. lines.

H: 11.6. D: 21.9. *PEQ*, 1961, Pl. 8:2. **B 74** (P 1232; 49-12-201) T.12:74 (B) LC IA:2. N-c-m. C,S: like the foregoing. P: lt. to dk. orange. (*h*). Opposite handle: like the foregoing. H: 10. D: 19.8. *PEQ*, 1961, 64 Pl. 7:4. **B 75** (P 1233; 49-12-165) T.12:36 (B) LC IA:2. N-c-m. C: dk. gray. S: pale gray, bur. P: rust to dk. gray. (*k*). Opposite handle: like B 72. H: 10.6. D: 20.3. *PEQ*, 1961, 64 Pl. 7:5. **B 76** (P 1234; 49-12-170) T.12:41 (B) LC IA:2. C-m. Sl. warped. C: brick-red. S,P: like B 72. (*c*). Opposite handle: vert. w. lines bordered by dots and flanked by x's between lines: crossed by dots between hor. lines. H: 11.5. D: 21.4. *PEQ*, 1961, 64 Pl. 7:1. **B 77** (P 1235; 49-12-202) T.12:75 (C) LC IB. *Pl. 16*. C,S: like B 75. P: olive to gray. (*c*). Opposite handle: like B 76. H: 11.4. D: 21.5. *PEQ*, 1961, Pl. 8:1. **B 78** (P 1236; 49-12-203) T.12:76 (B) LC IA:2. N-c-m. C: gray to brick-red. S: like B 75 with yellow areas. P: like B 75. (*c*) without crossbar on group of 3 vert. fasicules. Opposite handle: like B 76. H: 11.2. D: 20.6. *PEQ*, 1961, Pl. 7:2. **B 79** (P 1370) T.16:50. I-m. C: reddish gray with white sand. S: lt. pinkish gray. No dec. H: 7.3. D: 14.4. **B 80** (P 2723) MPT-A:12. I-m. C: dk. pink, well cleaned. S: buff int. and bottom ext.; upper ext. cream-colored. P: m. lt. orange to m. dk. gray-brown. (*c*). H: 10.9. D: 20.

Type 2: With horizontal round handles unless otherwise noted. B 83 is approximately like Type 1a of White Slip II ware (*Problems*, 45). **B 81** (P 1237; 49-12-178) T.12:51 (B) LC IA:2. *Pl. 16*. C-i. Wishbone handle and sidespout. C: brick-red. S: yellow to lt. brown, bur. P: red to dk. gray. (*l*). Opposite handle: 2 vert. w. lines from under spout to vert. hatched lozenges—all outlined with dots and flanked by vert. lines. Spout and handle: groups of three bars. H: 9.5. D: 19.5. *PEQ*, 1961, 64 Pl. 7:7. **B 82** (P 1238; 49-12-204) T.12:77 (B) LC IA:2. N-c-m. Sidespout. C,P: like the foregoing. S: pink to lt. gray, bur. (*j*). Base outlined by w. line and has cross of joined x's. Spout: 3 groups of 2 lines. Handle: bars and w. line. H: 8.3. D: 18. *PEQ*, 1961, 64 Pl. 7:6. **B 83** (P 1239; 49-12-179) T.12:52 (B) LC IA:2. *Pl. 39*. C-m. With vert. lug handle, pierced; shallow. S: yellow-gray, unbur. P: like the foregoing, quite matt. (*m*). Inside rim: 4 vert. groups of double dot rows, outlined. H: 5.9. D: 17. *PEQ*, 1961, 63 Pl. 7:8. **B 84** (P 1385) T.13:18 LC I—LC IIA. *Pl. 39*. I-m. With sidespout and concave flaring rim. C: brick-red wfs. S: buff with hor. bur. P: like B 81. (*a*). H: 10. D: 20.9. **B 85** (P 1386) T.13:19 LC I—LC IIA. *Pl. 39*. I-m, lime-encrusted. With sidespout and inturned rim. C: brick-red to purplish wfs. S: pinkish gray, bur. P: like the foregoing. (*b*). H: 9.3. D: 20. **B 86** (P 1387) T.13:20 LC I—LC IIA. *Pl. 16*. Shape like foregoing, about one-half missing; may have had sidespout. C: like B 84. S,P: like the foregoing. (*g*). H: 9.4. D: 18.1. **B 87** (P 1388) T.13:21 LC I—LC IIA. I-m. Shape like B 85 but no sidespout; 4 small equidistant hor. lugs on outside of rim. C: like B 85. S: pale gray, bur. No dec. H: 9.2. D: 19.3. **B 88** (P 2650; 49-12-126) T.11:11 LC IB. Shape apparently like B 84 but only about 1/5 pres. C: gray to brown, with mica.

S: buff, now matt. P: reddish brown to dk. m. brown. (*f*). H: 11. PD: 17.4. **B 89** (P 2724) MPT-A:13. I-m. Handle missing. With sidespout. C: hard pinkish gray. S: buff to white. P: m. red-brown to dk. gray-brown. Rim pattern as (*a*) with body dec. approximately like (*f*). H: 10. D: 21. **B 90** (P 2734) T.13:36. I-m. About ¼ pres. with sidespout. C: gray at core to dk. brick-red. S: gray-green to orange-cream, with hand bur. P: sl. ls. orange to red-brown. Rim: (*a*); under rim border vert. fasicules alternating 3 groups of 2 lines and one of 3 lines. PH: 9.2. ED: 19. **B 91** (P 2892) T.40:75 LC IIA. *Pl. 58*. About 1/3 pres. Type of handle not known. C: like the foregoing. S: chalky white. P: sl. glossy red-brown. (*d*). H: 8.3. PD: 15.6.

Bowl sherds

B 92 (Sh 118) A-D:3(VI) LC IIIA. Rim frag. C: dk. gray-brown. S: sl. ls. white to buff. P: m. red to red-brown. W. line on rim; crosshatch and lat-loz. below. H: 2. W: 1.8. **B 93** (Sh 529 a-d) C-A:5 LC IB. *Pl. 15*. 5 rim frags., one very large. C: red-brown to dk. gray wfs. S: white, bur. P: like B 81. (*e*). L (of *a*): 9.8. W: 9. *PEQ*, 1961, 66 Pl. 9:5. **B 94** (Sh 713) C-A:6 LC IIA. Frag. from bottom. C: g. brick-red. S: sl. ls. pinkish. P: m. red-brown. Cross design consisting of tangent x's bordered by dots and framing lines. At 45° to this, a secondary cross with same elements minus framing lines. L: 6.5. W: 6. Cf. *Problems*, 48:1. **B 95** (Sh 760) T.40:76 LC IIA. *Pl. 58*. 2 rim frags. C: lt. reddish gray with white particles. S: silvery white. P: sl. ls. orange to red-brown. (*n*). L (of larger frag.): 6.9. W (of same): 5.9.

Jugs

Type 2: **B 96** (P 1228; 49-12-199) T.12:72(B) LC IA:2. *Pl. 39*. N-c-m. Neck rather more slender than the example in *Problems*, 45. C: brick-red. S: lt. bluish gray, bur. P: m. dk. gray-brown. Rim: w. line. Neck: bands. Belly: like example in *Problems*, 45. H: 24. D: 15.1. *PEQ*, 1961, 64 Pl. 7:9. **B 97** (Sh 763) T.40:74(B) LC IIA. *Pls. 16, 58*. Large frag. giving profile of belly. C: g. gray-brown to reddish-brown. S: dead white. P: m. dk. brown. Dec. of belly like example in *Problems*, 45. H: 12.5.

Round-bodied: **B 98** (P 1229; 49-12-184) T.12:57(A) LC IA:2. *Pl. 39*. Small flat concave base, off center, making pot lopsided; elongated spherical body; long sl. concave neck to round mouth with beveled rim. Rounded strap handle from shoulder to mid-neck. C: g. lt. gray-brown. S: lt. buff to yellow, hor. bur. P: m. reddish brown to dk. gray, firm. Inside neck and extending onto rim: 4 groups of 3 outlined dots. On neck and body: zones of dotted vert. stripes and vert. w. lines marked off by dotted hor. stripes and lat-loz. Lower belly: 9 groups of triple vert. lines. On base: cross of triple w. lines. H: 26.5. D: 19. *PEQ*, 1961, 63 Pl. 7:10.

WHITE SLIP II

Bowls: the classification of *Problems*, 45 is used to distinguish in general between deeper bowls (2b) and shallower bowls (2a) though the distinction is not so important as in the White Slip I category, where the shallower type usually exhibited a flat bottom and a sidespout. Here both types are round-bottomed. There are groups of bars on handles unless otherwise stated. The italicised letters in parentheses refer to decorative schemes on Pl. 41.

Type 2a: **B 99** (P 1214; 54-41-12) VT:3. *Pl. 16*. I-m. C: brick-red with lt. and dk. sand. S: chalky white, smooth. P: m. dk. gray. (*pp*). H: 10. D: 20.5. *PEQ*, 1961, 66. **B 100** (P 1215; 49-12-141) T.12:11(E) LC IIB. C-m. C: gray core to reddish brown near surface. S: dk. buff. P: m. purple-brown. (*jj*). Without dots on rim edge. H: 8.5. D: 19.3. *PEQ*, 1961, 67 Pl. 9:4. **B 101** (P 1310) T.33:41(A) LC IIB. *Pl. 60*. C-i. Sl. warped. C: dk. gray wfs. S: lt. gray-brown. P: dk. m. gray-brown. (*jj*). H: 8.1. D: 15.7. **B 102** (P 1311) T.33:44(B) LC IIIA. *Pl. 61*. N-c-m. C: lt. gray wfs. S: yellow-brown. P: m. dk. brown. (*ii*). H: 10.2. D: 20.4. **B 103** (P 1312) T.33:45(B) LC IIIA. *Pl. 61*. N-c-m. C: like B 99. S: buff-gray. P: like B 101. (*ii*). H: 9.6. D: 21. **B 104** (P 1313) T.33:31-2(B) LC IIIA. *Pl. 61*. N-c-m. C: like B 100. S: lt. brownish gray. P: like B 101. (*ii*). H: 10.2. D: 20.4. **B 105** (P 1414; 49-12-311) T.19:46(B) LC IIA-B. N-c-m. C: like B 100. S: grayish yellow to orange. P: m. dk. gray-brown. (*ii*). H: 8.6. D: 19.2. **B 106** (P 1415; 49-12-321) T.19:58(B) LC IIA-B. I-m. Handle missing. C,S,P: like B 105. (*ii*). H:9. D: 19.8. **B 107** (P 1416; 49-12-308) T.19:43(B) LC IIA-B. C-m. C,S,P: like B 105. (*ii*). H: 9.5. D: 19.6. **B 108** (P 1417; 49-12-307) T.19:42(B) LC IIA-B. N-c-m. C,P: like B 105. S: lt. bluish gray. (*ii*). H: 9.5. D: 20.8. **B 109** (P 2664; 49-12-250) T.18:16(A) LC IIB. *Pl. 16*. I-m. Over half missing. C: dk. g. gray. S: sl. ls. chalky white. P: firm m. brown. (*nn*). PH: 8.6. PD: 19.5. *PEQ*, 1961, 66. **B 110** (P 2665; 49-12-331) T.21:1 LC IIA. I-m. Handle missing. C,S,P: like B 105. (*ii*). H: 9.1. D: 19.1. **B 111** (P 2725) MPT-A:14. N-c-m. C: dk. g. gray to dk. red. S: buff to white, powdery. P: lt. to dk. m. brown. (*ll*). H: 10.9. D: 17.5. **B 112** (P 2748) T.38:14. I-m. C: gray core to dk. brown, white grits. S: m. chalky white. P: like B 105. (*rr*). Handle: lattice design. H: 9.1. D: 21.5. *PEQ*, 1961, 66. **B 113** (P 2749) T.38:15. I-m. C,S,P: like B 105. (*ii*). PH: 8. D: 20. **B 114** (P 2750) T.38:16. I-m. Over half missing; very shallow. C: g. gray to pink. S: yellow gray. P: like B 105. (*ff*). H: 8.1. D: 16.8. **B 115** (P 2751) T.38:17. I-m. About 2/3 pres., handle missing. C: like B 114. S,P: like B 105. (*ii*). PH: 7.3. D: 15. **B 116** (P 2788; 49-12-65) T.5:8a(B) LC IIB. *Pl. 16*. I-m. Surface very much damaged by water or soil action. Very shallow. C: g. gray-brown. S: m. brownish white. P: m. gray-brown. (*ee*). H: 7.2. D: 14.6. **B 117** (P 2844) E-B:2 LC IIB. I-m. C: g. brick-red. S: like B 112. P: m. reddish brown. (*oo*). H: 10. D: 19. *PEQ*, 1961, 66. **B 118** (P 2902) T.40:53(C) LC IIIA. *Pl. 58*. I-m. Over half missing; very shallow. C: gray at core to gray-brown at surface. S,P: like B 114. (*dd*). H: 9.4. D: 19.7.

Type 2a sherds: **B 119** (Sh 461) Found in dump at Bamboula. *Pl. 15*. Frag. of rim. C: g. gray-brown.

S: dead white. P: m. dk. purple-brown. Tree and vert. crosshatch. (*nn*). H: 3.5. W: 4. *PEQ*, 1961, 66. **B 120** (Sh 481) A-A:3 LC IIA. Frag. of rim and side. C: dk. gray to gray-brown. S: m. lt. brownish buff. P: m. chocolate brown. (*ii*). H: 6.2. W: 6. **B 121** (Sh 662) Exact provenance uncertain. Frag. of base and side. C: g. gray-brown. S,P: like B 112. Tree and vert. crosshatch. Greatest length: 12. *PEQ*, 1961, 66. **B 122** (Sh 761) T.40:73(B) LC IIA. *Pl. 58.* Frag. of rim and base. C: like B 117. S: glossy pinkish to chalky white. P: m. dk. gray. (*qq*). PH: 6.5. PD: 15. *PEQ*, 1961, 66.

Type 2b: **B 123** (P 748) A-B:6 LC IIA. About ⅛ pres., giving profile. C: blue-gray. S: chalky white. P: m. black. (*cc*). PH: 11.5. PD: 12. **B 124** (P 749) A-B:6 LC IIA. About half, including most of handles, missing. C: g. blue-gray to red-brown. S: grayish white. P: like B 123. (*cc*). PH: 10.7. ED: 18.7. **B 125** (P 761) A-B:6 LC IIA. I-m. C: like B 124. S: lt. brown. P: m. dk. brown. (*jj*). H: 10.5. D: 19.2. **B 126** (P 763) A-B:6 LC IIA. About half missing. C,P: like the foregoing. S: lt. pinkish brown to gray. (*hh*). PH: 10.3. ED: 18.8. **B 127** (P 955; 49-12-46) T.3:25(A). About half pres. in two frags. C: g. slate-gray. S: m. brownish buff. P: m. dk. gray-brown. (*ii*). With cross bar on pendant dots in center panel. PH: 9.5. D: 17.5. **B 128** (P 956; 49-12-47) T.3:26(A). Less than half pres. C: g. lt. gray. S: m. grayish white. P: m. dk. gray-brown. (*ii*) like B 127. PH: 11.2. ED: 21. **B 129** (P 968; 49-12-20) T.2:14(A) LC IIA. *Pl. 16.* N-c-m. C: g. slate-gray to reddish brown. S: m. chalky white to bluish white below stack line. P: m. chocolate brown to dk. gray-brown. (*gg*). H: 10.6. D: 19.3. **B 130** (P 1216; 49-12-153) T.12:24(D) LC IIA. About ¼ missing. C,P: like B 124. S: grayish yellow. (*ll*). H: 11.4. D: 18.7. *PEQ*, 1961, Pl. 9:1. **B 131** (P 1217; 49-12-155) T.12:26(D) LC IIA. C-ch. C: dk. gray. S: chalky gray to brown; stacking line visible. P: like B 125. (*cc*) without vert. dots. H: 10.6. D: 17.4. *PEQ*, 1961, Pl. 9:3. **B 132** (P 1218; 49-12-190) T.12:63(C) LC IB. About ⅓ missing. C: lt. gray. S: grayish white. P: m. dk. gray-brown. (*cc*) without vert. dots. H: 11.2. D: 18. *PEQ*, 1961, 65 Pl. 8:5. **B 133** (P 1219; 49-12-191) T.12:64(C) LC IB. About ⅓ missing. C,S: like B 130. P: m. brown. (*cc*). H: 10.6. D: 18.4. *PEQ*, 1961, Pl. 8:9. **B 134** (P 1220; 49-12-192) T.12:65(C) LC IB. N-c-m. Handle missing. C,S,P: like B 125. (*cc*). H: 11.1. D: 18.8. *PEQ*, 1961, Pl. 8:10. **B 135** (P 1221; 49-12-193) T.12:66(C) LC IB. N-c-m. C,S,P: like the foregoing. (*cc*). H: 11. D: 19.3. *PEQ*, 1961, Pl. 8:6. **B 136** (P 1222; 49-12-194) T.12:67(C) LC IB. N-c-m. C,S,P: like the foregoing. (*cc*). H: 11. D: 18.7. *PEQ*, 1961, Pl. 8:4. **B 137** (P 1223; 49-12-195) T.12:68(C) LC IB. I-m. C: brick-red. S: blue-gray to lt. brown. P: m. dk. gray-brown. (*hh*). H: 10.7. D: 19.7. *PEQ*, 1961, 65 Pl. 8:3. **B 138** (P 1224; 49-12-196) T.12:69(C) LC IB. I-m. C,P: like B 132. S: like B 130. (*ll*). H: 11.6. D: 19.6. *PEQ*, 1961, Pl. 8:7. **B 139** (P 1225; 49-12-197) T.12:70(D) LC IIA. N-c-m. C: like B 124. S: like B 130. P: like B 137. (*ll*). H: 10.1. D: 16.6. *PEQ*, 1961, Pl. 9:2. **B 140** (P 1226; 49-12-

198) T.12:71(C) LC IB. N-c-m. C,P,S: like the foregoing. (*ll*) but lozenges only in front panel, otherwise ladders. H: 11.6. D: 18.5. *PEQ*, 1961, Pl. 8:8. **B 141** (P 1378) T.13:11. I-m. C: gray with lt. sand. S,P: like B 103. (*cc*). H: 11. D: 17.4. **B 142** (P 1379) T.13:12. N-c-m. C,S,P: like B 132, bur. (*cc*). H: 11.2. D: 18.7. **B 143** (P 1380) T.13:13. Less than half pres. C,S,P: like B 141. (*cc*). EH: 12. D: 20. **B 144** (P 1381) T.13:14. About ⅔ pres. C: gray core to brick red surface. S: lt. gray-green. P: like B 132. (*hh*). H: 10.7. D: 18.3. **B 145** (P 1382) T.13:15. About half missing. C: like the foregoing. S: pinkish brown. P: m. gray-brown. (*ii*). H: 10. D: 19.3. **B 146** (P 2637; 49-12-53) T.5:3(A) LC IIB. C-i (except for part of handle). Midway between shallow and deep. C: dk. g. red-brown. S: thin, chalky white, bur. inside and out. P: m. dk. brown. (*ii*). H: 10. D: 18.9. **B 147** (P 2653; 49-12-128) T.11:14(A) LC IB. I-m. C: dk. gray. S: chalky white. P: m. gray-brown. (*aa*). H: 11.1. D: 17.3. **B 148** (P 2733) T.13:35. I-m. About ¼ pres. C: gray at core to lt. brick red. S: lt. reddish brown. P: m. gray-brown. (*hh*). PH: 7.5. D: 16.9. **B 149** (P 2752) T.38:18. About half pres. in two non-joining frags. C: g. gray at core to pink at surface. S: discolored. P: m. gray-brown. (*hh*). H (of larger frag.): 9.8. **B 150** (P 2753) T.39:1. I-m. C: like the foregoing. S: chalky bluish white. P: m. dk. brown. (*ll*). H: 10.4. D: 16.5. **B 151** (P 2754) T.39:2. About ⅓ pres. C: like the foregoing. S: lt. buff, upper part discolored blue. P: lt. to dk. m. brown. (*bb*). PH: 10.2. **B 152** (P 2782; 49-12-59) T.5:4a(B) LC IIB. *Pl. 16.* About half missing. Probably owing to the striking size of this bowl the top of the rim was flattened and sl. profiled. C: g. gray (core) to brown (surface). S: yellowish white, streaky. P: like B 149. (*bb*). H: 19.1. ED: 28.4. **B 153** (P 2789; 49-12-66) T.5:9a(B) LC IIB. About half missing. C: like the foregoing. S: m. streaky chalk with stacking ring visible. P: like B 145. (*aa*). H: 10.5. PD: 17.9. **B 154** (P 2842) E-B:2 LC IIB. About ⅓ pres. C: g. gray. S: like the foregoing. P: m. reddish brown. (*hh*). PH: 10.2. PD: 18.

Type 2b sherds: B 157 may be from a Type 1 bowl. **B 155** (Sh 291) A-D:1(IV.1) LC IIC. *Pl. 17.* About ⅛ pres. C: g. lt. gray. S: m. lt. yellow-brown. P: m. chocolate brown. (*cc*). H (of largest frag.): 8. L: 6.1. **B 156** (Sh 480) A-A:3 LC IIA. Frag. of rim and side. C: g. gray-blue to gray-brown. S: m. chalky white, with stack mark. P: m. dk. gray-brown. (*cc*). H: 6. W: 7.5. **B 157** (Sh 629) MPT-A:16. Frag. with handle. C: lt. gray. S: buff to white. P: m. brown-black. (*ll*). PH: 6.5. **B 158** (Sh 765; 49-12-220) T.12: stratum unknown. About ⅛ pres. C: lt. g. gray. S: dead white to yellow-gray, with stacking ring visible. P: m. dk. gray-brown. (*mm*). H: 10.2. PD: 9.5.

Type 3: all the following have, in addition to horizontal round handles, sidespouts. This combination carries on the tradition of White Slip I, Type 2, which, however, was flat-bottomed. **B 159** (P 1383) T.13:16. N-c-m. C: like B 144. S: blue-gray. (*ii*). H: 10.4. D: 17.9. **B 160** (P 2726) MPT-A:15. I-m. About ⅓ pres. Handle missing. C,S,P: like B 111. (*bb*).

PH: 9.8. **B 161** (P 2781; 49-12-58) T.5:3a(B) LC IIB. About half missing. C: lt. g. gray. S,P: like B 147. (*bb*) without dots. PH: 9. PD: 18. **B 162** (P 2783; 49-12-60) T.5:5a(B) LC IIB. About half pres. in 2 large frags. C,S,P: like B 161. (*bb*) without dots. PH (of larger frag.): 9.5. PD (of same): 17.2. **B 163** (P 2786; 49-12-63) T.5:7a(B) LC IIB. *Pl. 16.* About half missing. C: g. dk. gray. S,P: like B 147. (*bb*). PH: 9.2. D: 17.2.

Miscellaneous: the following tripod bowl is at least unusual although not unique. Athens National Museum inv. 12290 is a WS II milk bowl with an inner and an outer ring of tripod legs (outer tripod legs broken off). The decoration, consisting of a wavy line around the rim and hanging lozenges, is carelessly executed. Cf. also *SPC,* 195:25. **B 164** (P 2636; 49-12-52) T.5:2(B) LC IIB. *Pl. 16.* About ¼ missing. Hemispherical bowl with sl. flattened rim and three short feet. One stringhole and part of another pres.; also a small non-joining frag. of spout. C: like B 152. S,P: like B 150. (*kk*). H: 9.5. D: 15.1.

Jugs

Type 1: this category, though not listed in *Problems,* appears to be a continuation of the White Slip I, Type 2, though with more squat proportions and high arched handle. **B 165** (P 1227; 49-12-156) T.12:27(C) LC IB. *Pl. 39.* Flat, sl. concave base, squat globular body and wide concave neck. Flaring trefoil mouth. Strap handle from shoulder to mouth. C: lt. yellow-brown. S: lt. blue-gray. P: m. dk. gray-brown. On neck and handle groups of hor. parallel lines. Belly dec: (*bb*). H: 15.5. D: 10. *PEQ,* 1961, 65 Pl. 8:11. **B 166** (Sh 712) C-A:5 LC IB. *Pl. 17.* Frag. showing transition from neck to shoulder. C: like B 144. S: chalky white. P: m. brown. Neck: like B 165. Belly: (*ll*). PH:7.6. PL: 9.

Type 2: this continues, in a general way, the type of B 98, though unfortunately the kind of base is not known. It has also some affinity to White Slip I, Type 1. **B 167** (P 2937; 49-12-221) T.12:94. *Pl. 39.* Level not known, but cannot be later than LC IIB. About half of shoulder, a non-joining neck frag. and handle frag. pres. Body ovoid (or spheroid) with small flat shoulder; concave, rather tall neck; strap handle to neck. C: coarse brick-red. S: ls. lt. gray. P: m. brown. Neck: groups of hor. parallel lines. Handle: 3 vert. w. lines. Shoulder: vert. lat-loz. (double and single between bands of crosshatch). PH: 15. D: 18.

Type 3a: this is a class assigned in *Problems,* 45 to White Slip I. On this matter, see Daniel's remark, *AJA* 46 (1942) 287. The present example, at least, is technically White Slip II. Cf. *AA* 1934, p. 111, Fig. 20 (left). Another example from Kourion which looks like White Slip II is C 249 (*ExC* Fig. 125:54 = *CVA BM* Fs.1 IICa Pl. 7:17). **B 168** (Sh 638) MPT-A:16. *Pl. 17.* Frag. of neck with transition to shoulder. C: lt. gray-blue. S: m. bluish white. P: m. dk. gray-brown. On neck: vert. band with 2 rows of lat-loz. Body: hor. crosshatch zone with pendant vert. zones: alternating

crosshatch and lat-loz. Plain lozenges pendent between these. H: 8.6. W: 5.8.

Kraters: the following kraters are not paralleled in *Problems.* B 169 is obviously a later form of *Problems,* 45 Type 3 (there called "bowl") with much higher neck and an additional handle. B 170 and some unlisted fragments (P 2787) from Tomb 5 may, strictly speaking, be tankards, but clay and technique are distinctly of the White Slip II variety. Cf. *AJA* 46 (1942) 287. See also *PEQ,* 1961, Pl. 6:4.

B 169 (P 1384) T.13:17. *Pl. 17.* I-m. Small flat base; fat, squat ovoid body with short shoulder; long tapering neck; undercut beveled lip. Two raised horizontal round handles (one horned). C: blue-gray with lt. sand. S: sl. ls. lt. gray. P: dk. m. gray-brown. Rim: w. line on inner and outer edge, interrupted by 4 groups of dots and bars. Neck: vert. double lat-loz rows and single dotted lozenges. Shoulder: hor. crosshatch and hatched lozenges. Belly: pendent crosshatch, double and single hatched lozenges and fill ornament No. 1. H: 33.8. D: 35.4. **B 170** (Sh 658) MPT-A:16. *Pl. 17.* Large frag. of neck and belly, giving a shape like that of B 169 except that the neck is shorter. C: dk. gray with red grits. S: thin bluish white, stained yellow in places. P: m. dk. brown. Rim: dec. like B 169. Neck: vert. double lat-loz rows alternating with vert. double plain lozenge rows (cf. fill ornament No. 4); also fill ornament No. 2. Belly: apparently like B 169 with substitution of fill ornament No. 3 for No. 1. PH: 24. ED (at mouth): 24.

BASE-RING I

The repertory presented in *Problems,* 34 ff. is considerably enlarged by types found at Bamboula. Several pieces of what might be called a "luxury" fabric of unusually fine workmanship, B 178 and B 202, are paralleled in conception by a krater from Atchana, ATP 38/228 (*Alalakh,* Pl. 125:c).

Bowls

Type 3: the following fragments with vertical ribbing appear to have belonged to the Type 3 variety. **B 171** (Sh 627) MPT-A:16. Base ring (center missing) and several joining body frags. C: dk. gray with lime particles. S: pink to black. D (of base): 6.5. **B 172** (Sh 764a) T.40:63(B) LC IIA. *Pl. 58.* Frag. of carinated rim (with profiled lip) and portion of wall with 2 pairs of plastic ribs to rim. C: fine and thin gray. S: ls. jet black (int.), reddish brown to dk. gray-brown (ext.). PH: 7. PD: 11.5.

Type 5: this is virtually Sjöqvist's Base-Ring II Type 1 (cf. *AJA* 46, 1942, 288). The true forerunner of the ubiquitous Base-Ring II bowls is not the Base-Ring I Type 3, which has a concave profile, but rather the following types with concave-convex profiles represented at Bamboula. Distinctly the earlier typologically is Type 5a, the base of which is similar to, and provides a link with, Type 3 (cf. also relief lines on B 176). This occurs only in small format. A rather flamboyant variation, with high profiled rim and flaring base ring—both features perhaps imitated from Base-Ring I jugs—

is Type 5b. Generally executed in large format, its technique is distinctly that of Base-Ring I. The contexts in which it occurs are early, but not definitely dated. B 180 is surely already a Base-Ring II descendant, but technically it belongs with Type 5b.

Type 5a: small base ring, steep flaring wall with convex profile and prominent bulge at transition to low carinated rim. Uplifted forked handle on shoulder; thin ware, occasionally with relief decoration. **B 173** (P 1241; 49-12-164) T.12:35(B) LC IA:2. *Pl. 16.* N-c-m. C: hard, gray wfs. S: semi-ls. dk. olive to brown and black. H: 7.2. D: 13. **B 174** (P 1242; 49-12-209) T.12:82(C) LC IB. *Pl. 16.* I-m. C,S: like B 173. H: 7. D: 13. **B 175** (P 1243; 49-12-210) T.12:83(B) LC IA:2. I-m. C: red-brown to gray wfs. S: like B 173. H: 8.8. D: 16.2. **B 176** (P 1244; 49-12-211) T.12:84(B) LC IA:2. *Pl. 16.* C,S: like B 175. 3 groups of 2 vert. relief lines on body. H: 8.2. D: 16.3.

Type 5b: rather prominent base ring, steep flaring wall with convex profile and prominent bulge at transition to high tapering rim with profiled lip. Uplifted forked handle on shoulder; thin ware. Sometimes with relief decoration. Restored base too small on B 177 and B 178; see B 179 for proper size. **B 177** (P 989) E-Intrusion: note sub C: 5. About ⅓ pres., mended and restored. C: lt. gray. S: ls. black (int.), ls. gray to brown (ext.). H (as restored): 11.6. D: 20. **B 178** (P 990) E-Intrusion: note sub C: 5. *Pl. 42.* I-m. Base restored. C: like B 173. S: ls. coal black (int. and lower ext.), leather brown (rim); small pock marks on surface. Deeply incised chevrons on each wing of handle flare; opposite each handle and at middle of each side 3 vert. relief bands on body. H (as restored): 18.8. D: 30.2. **B 179** (P 1390) T.13:23. I-m, restored. C: gray at core to brick-red. S: purple to dk. gray with 2 flame-red patches. Three groups of 2 vert. relief bands on body. H: 14.1. D: 22.3. **B 180** (P 2785; 49-12-62) T.5:6a(B) LC IIB. *Pl. 16.* About ⅓ missing, including base. C: like B 177. S: semi-ls. dk. gray to rust. H: 8.5. D: 17.4. *AJA* 64 (1960) 146, Ill. 1.

Bowl sherds

B 181 (Sh 173) A-B:5 LC IIB. *Pl. 15.* Frag. of wall with incised band. C: slate-gray to lt. brown. S: dk. ls. red-brown (int.); and dk. gray (ext.). H: 2.3. W: 2.5. **B 182** (Sh 482) A-A:3 LC IIA. Rim frag. C: like B 177. S: ls. gray-brown to dk. gray. H: 2.4. L: 2.6. **B 183** (Sh 626) MPT-A:16. Frag. of forked handle. C: dk. gray, fine. S: dull black on handle but ls. inside of bowl. L: 9. **B 184** (Sh 628) MPT-A:16. 3 frags. of rim. C: like B 177. S: semi-ls. red to brown, black. H (of largest frag.): 4.

Squat bowl: for the type see *SPC*, 186, No. 6 (imitation of a Mycenaean pyxis?) **B 185** (Sh 83) A-E:2(VI) LC IIIB. *Pl. 15.* Frag. of shoulder with pierced vert. lug. C: fine hard slate-gray. S: apparently none. P: m. red and dk. brown, in semi-circular bands, nearly gone. H: 2.8. W: 3.5.

Kylikes

Type 1: wide flaring base ring and short thick stem; wide shallow bowl with semi-carinated rim and beveled lip. Small vertical loop handle just below rim. **B 186** (P 1393) T.13:26. *Pl. 42.* C-m. S: orange-brown to dk. gray, bur. H: 7.2. D: 22.5.

Type 2: wide flaring base ring with very short stem; moderately deep bowl with straight flaring sides to semi-carinated rim and flattened lip, undercut on the inside. Gently raised horizontal ribbon handle on shoulder. **B 187** (P 1391) T.13:24. *Pl. 42.* I-m. Most of handle missing; warped. C: gray with dk. and lt. sand. S: sl. ls. orange to dk. gray. H: 7.8. D: 19.9. **B 188** (P 1392) T.13:25. I-m, restored. C: gray core to brick-red, wfds. S: red-brown to dk. gray, bur. H: 10.5. D: 24. **B 189** (P 1401) T.13:34. About half missing. C,S: like B 187. H: 7. D: 18.2. **B 190** (P 2719) MPT-A:8. About half missing; base completely sheared off (cf. B 191). C: lt. gray core to pink. S: like B 184. PH: 2.5. ED: 21.

Type 2 sherds: **B 191** (Sh 624) MPT-A:16. *Pl. 42.* Kylix base, perhaps of B 190. C,S: like B 190. D: 7.3. **B 192** (Sh 631) MPT-A:16. Kylix base frag. C: like B 183. S: semi-ls. black, applied with brush. ED (of base): 9.

Jugs

Type 2a: the bodies of all the examples listed below are ovoid rather than spherical. The first two have two horizontal relief bands where handle joins neck. **B 193** (P 1368) T.16:16. I-m. Most of handle missing. C: gray. S: ls. grayish red. H: 11.6. D: 4.7. **B 194** (P 2717) MPT-A:6. I-m. Most of handle missing. C: gray core to pink near surface. S: sl. ls. gray to black, unevenly fired and mouth chipped off. H: 13.1. **B 195** (P 2765; 54-41-63) MPT-E:1. *Pl. 16.* N-c. Miniature format. Most of mouth missing. C: fine slate gray. S: sl. ls. reddish brown. PH: 7.8. D: 3.2.

Type 2b: B 196 has a rather fuller, heavier body than is usual with this type, and also two horizontal relief rings where handle joins shoulder. **B 196** (P 971; 49-12-114) T.9:6 LC IA. *Pl. 16.* I-m. C: like B 195, eroded very thin in places. S: semi-ls. gray-brown, mostly gone. H: 17.5. D: 10.6. **B 197** (P 1245; 49-12-161) T.12:32(B) LC IA:2. *Pl. 16.* C-i. Surface somewhat pocked. C: reddish brown (with lime?). S: semi-ls. orange-brown to dk. gray-brown. H: 14.2. D: 7.1. **B 198** (P 1248; 49-12-180) T.12:53(B) LC IA:2. I-m. Surface somewhat pocked. C: gray (with lime?). S: ls. dk. gray. H: 14.7. D: 7.5.

Type 2c: the body of the following jug shows a very angular transition from shoulder to belly. It may already be Base-Ring II. It has no relief scroll. **B 199** (P 1247; 49-12-205) T.12:78(D) LC IIA. *Pls. 16, 42.* I-m. Handle entirely missing. C: gray wfs. S: bur. brown to black. H: 15.1. D: 8.6.

Miscellaneous: the following jugs have the neck and handle of Type 2 but not enough of them is preserved to determine to what subdivisions (a, b or c) they belonged. **B 200** (P 2670; 49-12-336) T.21:6 LC IIA. Neck and handle only pres. C: gray core to reddish brown at surface. S: ls. orange-brown to dk. brown. PH: 10.7. D (of mouth): 3.6. **B 201** (P 2715) MPT-

A:4. Neck, handle and about half of upper body pres. C: like B 194. S: semi-ls. brown-black. PH: 19. D (of mouth): 6.5.

Type 3: B 203 and B 205 are closely in accord with the types in *Problems.* Likewise, B 204 which differs from E.3.280 (*Problems,* 36) only in having a round mouth. B 202 has distinctive variations but still seems to belong to this category, perhaps late in the series.

Type 3a: **B 202** (P 991) E-Intrusion: note sub C: 5. *Pl. 42.* I-m. Restored. Small base ring. Full ovoid body with gently sloping shoulder. Long neck flaring to pinched raised spout. Curved strap handle from shoulder to upper neck has 3 relief ridges. C: gray with small white particles. S: ls. red-brown to olive, somewhat pocked. H: 50.3. D: 23.8. **B 203** (P 1257; 49-12-212) T.12:85(B) LC IA:2. *Pl. 16.* I-m. Much of body and top of spout missing. C: gray. S: surface too badly flaked to allow definition of slip. H: 14.2. D: 8.1. **B 204** (P 1399) T.13:32. I-m. C: gray wfs. S: bur. thick gray. H: 42. D: 20.5.

Type 3b: **B 205** (P 2669; 49-12-335) T.21:5 LC IIA. C-i. Surface much chipped and eroded. Body ovoid. C: fine gray-brown. S: m. mahogany-brown. H: 11.1. D: 6.

Type 5b: the following pot has a taller neck than the example in *Problems.* **B 206** (P 1398) T.13:29. *Pl. 52.* I-m. Restored. C: gray wfds. S: yellowish to gray-brown and dk. gray, somewhat flaked. Incised relief: w. line on neck bordered by 2 hor. lines above and one below; vert. w. line on handle between ridges; double spirals on sides, connected with handle by hor. bands and joined to neck ridge by vert. bands. H: 24.8. (with horn, 29). D: 19.1. **B 207** (Sh 625) MPT-A:16. Frag. of handle and horn of a Type 5a or 5b jug. C: fine gray. S: ls. red to black. PH: 6.7.

Type 7: this type appears to be the forerunner of the Base-Ring II Type 1 jug (cf. also *AJA* 46, 1942, 287). Low base ring, rather fat ovoid body tending toward a spherical shape. Tall, relatively slender neck flaring to a plain round mouth. Curved strap handle from shoulder to neck. All examples have horizontal relief lines where the handle joins the neck. Relief spirals on shoulder unless otherwise noted. **B 208** (P 1249; 49-12-159) T.12:30(B) LC IA:2. I-m. Restored. C: brick-red. S: semi-ls. orange-brown to dk. gray; surface pocked. No spirals but 2 vert. bands on front. PH: 23.5. D: 14. **B 209** (P 1250; 49-12-206) T.12:79(C) LC IB. I-m. Mouth entirely missing. C: lt. gray at core to lt. brown. S: smoothly bur. orange-brown to gray. No spirals. PH: 21.2. D: 12.7. **B 210** (P 1251; 49-12-207) T.12:80(C) LC IB. About half pres. Mouth entirely missing. C: like B 208. S: semi-ls. rust to dk. mahogany. Relief incised: 3 low ridges on handles. PH: 23. D: 13.6. **B 211** (P 1252; 49-12-173) T.12:45(B) LC IA:2. *Pl. 16.* C-i. Warped. C: gray. S: lt. brown to dk. gray. H: 29.1. D: 16.4. **B 212** (P 1253; 49-12-158) T.12:29(B) LC IA:2(late). Base missing and surface pocked. C,S: like B 208. Handle grooved. PH: 28. D: 15.5. **B 213** (P 1254; 49-12-154) T.12:25(D) LC IIA. N-c. Surface badly

pitted on one side. C,S: like B 212. Ridge on handle. H: 27. D: 15.4. **B 214** (P 1255; 49-12-160) T.12:31(B) LC IA:2. I-m. C: lt. gray wfs. S: lt. orange brown to gray brown. H: 30.8. D: 16.9. **B 215** (P 1256; 49-12-208) T.12:81(B) LC IA:2. *Pl. 42.* N-c-m. C: like B 214. S: like B 208. Double relief spirals. H: 28.4. D: 16.2. **B 216** (P 1369) T.16:49. I-m. Base ring and much of side and mouth missing. C: gray at core to brick-red, wfds. S: like B 209. PH: 24. D: 14.4. **B 217** (P 1400) T.13:33. *Pl. 42.* I-m. Base ring and parts of side and mouth missing. C: gray at core to brick-red, wfs. S: well-bur. reddish brown to dk. reddish gray. PH: 25.6. D: 15.3.

Miscellaneous jug fragments

B 218 (P 2649; 49-12-125) T.11:10(A) LC IB. Base and lower part of body pres. C: slate gray. S: m. metallic gray, much weathered. 2 vert. w. relief lines on body. PH: 10.4. D: 14. **B 219** (Sh 623) MPT-A:16. *Pl. 42.* Frag. of flaring mouth. C: like B 218. S: black, badly worn. D (of mouth): 9.2.

Bottle

Type 3: **B 220** (P 2934; 49-12-426) T.34:8. Handle and about half of body missing. Does not have shoulder lugs. C: reddish brown wfs. S: sl. ls. dk. red-brown to gray and black. Most of surface completely eroded. H: 13. D (of body): 8.

Bull-shaped Vases: these are listed here though the evidence from Bamboula does not unequivocally warrant their inclusion with Base-Ring I Wares. But B 224 and B 225 have certain characteristics, especially incisions, which suggest a quite early date. They are not strictly vases, but are included here because of obvious similarity to the bull vases. In any case, these latter were probably made during the LC I and II periods. Cf. also B 1565, B 1566 and B 1572, figurines in a technique similar to that of Base-Ring Ware. Other bull vases from Kourion: A 6 (*ExC* Fig. 109 = *CVA* BM Fs. 1 IICa Pl. 9:1); A 7.

B 221 (P 1712) T.38:1. *Pl. 17.* I-m. Restored. C: slate-gray with white grits; extremely hard fabric. S: none. P: m. white. Dec: four bars over head, on horns, on each shoulder, each flank, each leg, and tail. H (inc. horns): 14. L: 16. **B 222** (P 1713) T.38:2. Large portions of trunk missing but restored. C: gray at core, buff near surface. S: none (?). P: traces of m. white. Dec: apparently like B 221. PH: 9.2. **B 223** (P 2710; 54-41-106) E-A:7 LC IIA. *Pl. 17.* N-c. Horns restored. C: gray. S: sl. ls. orange-red to gray. P: m. white. Dec: groups of bars as on B 221 but only 2 stripes on forehead. H (to handle): 11. L: 15.5. **B 224** (F 62; 49-12-387) T.28:1. *Pl. 17.* Ears, tail and part of 3 legs missing. Vent hole under belly and under muzzle. No handle and no hole in top of back. Very large head and slender body. C: slate-gray. S: lt. orange-brown to dk. gray, almost entirely matt. Several lateral incisions above and below eyes; ∧ incised on the nose. H: 10.3. PL: 12.3. Cf. *SCE II*, Pl. 224. **B 225** (F 66) D-A. *Pl. 17.* All extremities missing. C: gray. S: m. dk. gray. Lateral incisions above and below eyes. Incisions above eyes crossed by an oblique series. PL: 13.5. **B 226** (Sh 307) A-D:2(VII,2) LC IIIA. Leg of bull figurine. C: lt. gray to lt. red-brown. S: traces of dk. brown. P: traces of m. white. Stripes on leg. H: 5.

BASE-RING II

Bowls: heights are given to rim.

Type 1: see Base-Ring I, Type 5.

Type 2a: **B 227** (P 967; 49-12-19) T.2:13(A) LC IIA. *Pl. 18.* I-m. Restored. C: gray. S: semi-ls. dk. brown to black. H: 7.2. D: 14.8. **B 228** (P 1394) T.13:30. Less than half pres. C: like B 227. S: sl. bur. orange to dk. gray. H: 7. D: 18.1. **B 229** (P 2638; 49-12-54) T.5:4(A) LC IIB. *Pl. 18.* N-c-m. Base sharply profiled. C: like B 200. S: semi-ls. rust-red to dk. gray. H: 7. D: 15.

Type 2b: B 230 has vertical ribs on body. B 244 is much smaller than normal. **B 230** (P 750) A-B:6 LC IIA. Part of base and lower wall pres. C: gray at core to brown. S: brick-red to black. PH: 6.8. D (of base): 6.3. **B 231** (P 988) E-Intrusion(V), see *Bamboula SS* under C: 5. N-c-m. C: gray wfs. S: m. gray wash, uneven, red-brown on ext. H: 7.3. D: 16.3. **B 232** (P 993; 49-12-105) T.7:2 LC IIA(?). *Pl. 18.* N-c-m. C: dk. blue-gray with lt. grits. P: m. thin gray. H: 7. D: 17. **B 233** (P 1240; 49-12-142) T.12:12(E) LC IIB. C-m. C: gray. S: like B 229. H: 7.9. D: 17.7. **B 234** (P 1314) T.33:46(B) LC IIIA. I-m. C: gray wfds. S: pinkish brown to dk. gray. H: 7.9. D: 16.8. **B 235** (P 1333) T.36:35. *Pl. 42.* C-i. Surface worn. C: gray wfs. S: m. red to dk. violet gray. H: 7.1. D: 17.7. **B 236** (P 1334) T.36:37. N-c-m. Badly pitted and chipped. C,S: like B 235. H: 7.2. D: 16.2. **B 237** (P 1335) T.36:39. N-c-m. C: gray at core to lt. brick-red wfds and air-holes. S: m. orange-brown to dk. gray-brown. H: 7.1. D: 16.3. **B 238** (P 1336) T.36:44. C-i. Chipped and pitted. C: like B 237. S: m. vermilion to gray-brown. H: 6.3. D: 15.8. **B 239** (P 1337) T.36:45. N-c-m. Base damaged in manufacture. Body warped. C: slate-gray. S: dk. g. gray. H: 7. D: 15.4. **B 240** (P 1338) T.36:49. C-m. C: dk. brick-red. S: like B 235. H: 6.7. D: 17. **B 241** (P 1339) T.36:50. C-m. C: gray at core to brick-red. S: m. orange-brown to gray. H: 6.9. D: 17. **B 242** (P 1340) T.36:51. N-c-m. C: gray at core to dk. violet wfs. S: m. violet-brown to dk. gray. H: 7.1. D: 16.4. **B 243** (P 1341) T.36:63. N-c-m. C: orange with lt. particles. S: m. brick-red to dk. gray. H: 6.5. D: 17.4. **B 244** (P 1342) T.36:64. I-m. Base and half of handle missing. C: like B 234. S: m. lavender to dk. gray. PH: 4.2. D: 10.3. **B 245** (P 1395) T.13:31. I-m. About half missing, inc. handle. C: gray wfs. S: m. thin gray. H: 7.3. D: 18.3. **B 246** (P 1418; 49-12-309) T.19:44(B). *Pl. 52.* LC IIA-B. N-c. C: blue-gray. S: g. m. brick-red to dk. gray. H: 9.5. D: 16.7. **B 247** (P 2662; 49-12-248) T.18:14(A) LC IIB. *Pl. 18.* N-c-m. C: lt. gray. S: gray-brown to dk. gray, probably originally ls. H: 7.1. D: 16.9. **B 248** (P 2766; 54-41-64) MPT-E:2. N-c. End of handle missing. Contours greatly simplified. C: lt. gray core to lt. pinkish orange. S: m. sparse self-slip, apparently

not fired; rubbed off in places. H: 4.3. D: 9. **B 249** (P 2790; 49-12-358) T.23:5 LC IIIA. About ⅓, giving profile, pres. C: like B 230. S: m. reddish brown to gray-brown. H: 8. PD: 16.2. **B 250** (P 2903) T.40:60(B) LC IIA. *Pl. 58.* I-m. C: g. gray at core to reddish near surface with fine lt. particles. S: m. purple-black to gray-black. H: 7.5. D: 17.8. **B 251** (P 2904) T.40:61(B) LC IIA. *Pl. 58.* N-c-m. C: like B 250. S: m. orange to gray-black. H: 7.6. D: 16.7. **B 252** (Sh 764b) T.40:63(B) LC IIA. *Pl. 58.* Frag. of rim and wall. C: lt. gray. S: sl. ls. orange-brown to dk. gray. PH: 6.6. PD: 11.5.

Type 3: B 253 is exactly like the example given in *Problems.* The others vary slightly in proportion and details. **B 253** (P 1366) T.16:18. N-c-m. C: like B 241, wfs. S: like B 243. P: m. pale buff. Bars on rim and groups of hor. strokes around base. H: 6.3. D: 11.8. **B 254** (P 1367) T.16:28. N-c. Rim chipped. Plain rim. C: m. brick-red. S: ls. red-brown to gray. H: 5.7. D: 12.2. **B 255** (P 1389) T.13:22. *Pl. 42.* N-c-m. Rather straight sides and very low ring base. C: gray at core to brick-red wfs. S: like B 243. H: 6.3. D: 11.1. **B 256** (Sh 535) A-B:3 LC IIB. Frag. of rim and handle. Rim rolled out. C: like B 230. S: sl. ls. red (int.); ext. apparently unslipped. H: 2. W: 3.3.

Type 4: **B 257** (P 1397) T.13:28. I-m. Missing one handle and much of body. Sides of handles sl. raised, ending in lines on body: a groove down the center of each. C: gray wfs. S: red-brown to lt. gray. H: 23.1. D: 33.9.

Type 5: low base ring, high flaring walls to slightly inturned rim; lifted plain horizontal handle at rim. Very similar: C 174 (*ExC* Fig. 125:101 = *CVA* BM Fs. 1 IICa Pl. 9:8). Cf. also B 292. **B 258** (P 1332) T.36:36. *Pl. 42.* N-c-m. Warped. Badly pitted and worn. C: like B 257. S: m. red-brown. H: 9.9. D: 18.

Jugs

Type 2: **B 259** (Sh 508) C-C:2 LC IIIA. 3 sherds from neck, probably of a Type 2 jug. C: like B 230. S: sl. ls. dk. gray. P: m. cream. Hor. bands alternating with dashes. H (of largest frag.): 6.9. W: 2.7.

Type 2a: **B 260** (P 2716) MPT-A:5. Handle, frag. of neck and shoulder showing neck ridge. C: like B 241. S: gray-black, badly weathered. PH: 18. D (of mouth): 10.

Type 2c: cf. C 155 (*ExC* Fig. 125:107 = *CVA* BM Fs. 1 IICa Pl. 10:19).

Type 2e: a clear link between Base-Ring I, Type 3a (cf. especially B 204) and Base-Ring II, Type 2 jugs is furnished by a series of jugs found in Tomb 2. Thus, strictly considered, these are transitional between Base-Ring I and II. They have a high base ring, tall ovoid body and tall straight neck with flaring round mouth. They also have a concave profiled lip, double relief rings where the curved handle joins the neck (well below mouth), neck ridge, and relief scrolls, sometimes incised. The handle is usually incised. Cf. P. Baur,

73

Catalogue of the Rebecca Darlington Stoddard Collection (New Haven, 1922), 137, Fig. 51: No. 9. **B 261** (P 961; 49-12-13) T.2:7(A) LC IIA. *Pls. 18, 42.* C: gray. S: semi-ls. mottled mahogany to dk. gray. Handle incised with double zigzag. H: 35. D: 17. **B 262** (P 962; 49-12-14) T.2:8(A) LC IIA. *Pl. 18.* I-m. C,S: like B 261. 3 vert. incised lines on handle. H: 35.7. D: 17.2. **B 263** (P 963; 49-12-15) T.2:9(A) LC IIA. *Pl. 18.* I-m. C: grayish red. S: sl. ls. black. Relief elements incised; handle plain. H: 37.3. D: 18.2. **B 264** (P 964; 49-12-16) T.2:10(A) LC IIA. *Pl. 18.* I-m. C,S: like B 263 but slip barely ls. Relief elements incised; incised diagonal bands on handle. H: 38. D: 18.5. **B 265** (P 965; 49-12-17) T.2:11(A) LC IIA. I-m. C,S: like B 263. Relief elements incised and handle incised with triple zigzag. H: 36.4. D: 18.5. **B 266** (P 2651; 49-12-127) T.11:12(A) LC IB. Neck only, without handle; flares considerably. C: hard gray with mica, reddish brown near surface. S: semi-ls. mahogany-brown. H: 16.8. D (at mouth): 9.1.

Type 4: **B 267** (P 2755) T.39:3. Considerable frag. of body and neck of a jug probably of Type 4. C: dk. gray at core to dk. rose at surface with fine lt. particles. S: ls. orange-brown to dk. gray-brown. PH: 15.8. PD: 14.2. The following jug has all the elements of Type 4 though proportions are somewhat different and the axis is vertical, not tilted. It has a low base ring, squat ovoid body; long, slightly tapering slender neck with round profiled mouth; handle from shoulder to just below mouth. **B 268** (P 1330) T.36:40. *Pl. 42.* N-c-m. C: like B 241. S: like B 243. P: m. white groups of vert. bands on body with diagonal bands on lower body. H: 15.5. D: 11.

Type 6: see B 279.

Type 7a: **B 269** (P 1331) T.36:42 LC IIA. *Pl. 18.* C-i. C: brick-red. S: m. orange-brown. H: 7.3. D: 6.1.

Type 7b: the following fragment appears closely related to this type. **B 270** (Sh 548; 49-12-380) T.26:2. *Pl. 18.* Neck, handle and part of shoulder. Neck flares up to a pinched mouth. C: like B 230. S: lt. to dk. red-brown. 3 vert. incised lines (of varying length) on handle. PH: 8.5. PD: 10.5.

Miscellaneous jug fragments

B 271 (G 65: K 48) E-D:2c LC IIIA. Frag. from middle of jug handle. C: gray at core to reddish near surface. L: 3.6. W: 2.2. *AJA* 60 (1960) 146, Ill. 1. **B 272** (Sh 89) A-E:4 LC IIIB. *Pl. 15.* Frag. from wall with incised relief band. C: lt. gray-green to gray. S: ls. lt. red-brown, worn. H: 3.3. L: 3.8. **B 273** (Sh 620) E-13 Unstrat. Frag. of wall with 2 parallel ridges 0.8 cm. apart. C: brick-red, fairly fine with some gray residue. S: ls. thin red-brown. L: 3.5. W: 2.5. **B 274** (Sh 632) MPT-A:16. Lower part of handle with 2 vert. incised lines. C: gray at core to pink. S: m. red to purple-brown. PW: 4. PL: 9.5. **B 275** (Sh 652) T.38:12. *Pl. 18.* Most of handle with adjoining frag. of shoulder. C: g. brick-red. S: ls. red-brown to red-gray, much worn. Incised chevrons on back of

handle, 2 pellets at its base (cf. Types 4-5). PW: 2.3. PL: 7.9.

Three-handled Jar

B 276 (P 2878) T.40:64(A) LC IIA. *Pls. 18, 58.* Neck, all of one and part of another handle missing. Small hole in shoulder. Prominent rolled ring base, well-proportioned ovoid body with rather accentuated break to shoulder. Above this break 3 vert. lug handles, pierced. C: gray at core, reddish brown near surface; well cleaned but surface now crumbly. S: sl. ls. orange to dk. brown. P: m. white. More or less hor. white lines engirdle lower part of body crossed by a few random vert. or oblique lines. H: 7.6. D: 6.5. **B 277** (Sh 581) D-A. *Pls. 17, 42.* One handle, part of rim and body of jar (apparently with 3 handles). Short everted rim. Body shape probably pithoid. Vert. hole at top of handle. C: like B 234. S: orange-brown to dk. gray. Hor. incised ridge (scroll?) in h-z. Shoulder incised with vert. bands enclosing dashes. PH: 10. ED: 12.

HANDMADE BUCCHERO WARE

The intimate connection of this ware with Base-Ring is demonstrated not only by their technical similarities but by the fact that even the shapes are occasionally interchangeable: B 279 has the shape of the Base-Ring II, Type 6 jug. An unstratified fragment from Tomb 12 (49-12-222) cannot have occurred later than LC IIB and B 278 is from what seems to be an LC IIA context, which gives a provisional upper range for the introduction of this ware. Cf. also B 280 and B 281.

Jugs

B 278 (P 2880) T.40:77(B) LC IIA. *Pls. 18, 59.* Entire neck, most of shoulder with stump of vert. handle and one joining belly frag. (others non-joining) pres. Plain round mouth with squared lip. Neck tapers down to low neck-ridge. Body spherical (?); vert. ribbing on body to level of base of handle where it breaks off indeterminately. C: hard gray at core to lt. red-brown. S: red-brown to dk. gray-brown. H: 11.2. ED: 13.7. **B 279** (P 1430:K 8) D-A. I-m. Mouth, handle and much of body missing. C: brick-red wfs. S: lt. gray-brown to dk. gray. Low vert. ribs from base to neck-ring. As a point of technique it appears that the grooved effect was always obtained—on Bamboula examples at least—by laying strips of clay over the plain surface of the body. H: 14.6. D: 12. *AJA* 64 (1960) 146, Ill. 1.

Type 1b: **B 280** (P 1421; 49-12-315) T.19:51(A) LC IIA-B. *Pl. 18.* C-ch. C: gray at core to brick-red. S: thick sl. ls. dk. gray, somewhat flaked. H: 8.1. D: 6.1. **B 281** (P 1422; 49-12-316) LC IIA-B. C-ch. *Pl. 43.* C: like the foregoing. S: orange to gray-brown, somewhat flaked. H: 8.5. D: 6.3.

Type 2: **B 282** (P 2688; 49-12-405) T.32:1 LC IIIA. *Pl. 18.* C-m. Chipped and flaked. Beveled lip; tilted axis.

C: like B 230. S: m. gray to dk. gray-brown. H: 13.6. D: 8.3.

Type 3: several vases occurred at Bamboula of a shape very close to Type 3 of *Problems;* but in contrast to the latter, which is stated to be wheelmade, these are handmade and have all the other characteristics of genuine Handmade Bucchero fabric. **B 283** (P 1413; 49-12-302) T.19:35(C) LC IIIA. *Pl. 18.* C-i. Flaring base ring with beveled foot. C: hard, with some airholes. S: almost ls. orange-brown. H: 12.9. D: 8.2. **B 284** (P 2909) T.40:8 LC IIIA. *Pls. 18, 58.* N-c-m. Most of handle missing. Chipped and flaked. C: grayish brown. Straw-bound(?). S: sl. ls.(?) red-brown. H: 21.8. D: 13.8. **B 285** (P 2933; 49-12-416) T.32:12 LC IIIA. *Pl. 43.* I-m. Chipped and flaked. C: dk. brick-red wfds. S: bur. (or shaved?) gray (in traces); very much weathered. H: 14.2. D: 8.5.

Miscellaneous: **B 286** (Sh 494) A-D:2(VII,1). LC IIC. Frag. from wall. C: slate-gray. S: firm lt. gray-brown to reddish brown. L: 4. W: 3.4.

MONOCHROME WARE

Although this fabric is represented at Bamboula by a wide repertory of shapes, none of them correspond exactly with types in *Problems.* A few show closer similarities to shapes given in *SPC,* and this is mentioned where applicable. In general, the classification of *Problems* has been continued and extended. Some of the new types are not strictly speaking Monochrome Ware since they are unslipped. These may correspond to "Apliki ware": cf. *AntJ* 32 (1952) 159. On this ware see now H. W. Catling in *Myrtou-Pigadhes,* 32. Recently also V. Karageorghis, *BCH* 84 (1960) 531 and *RDAC,* 1964, 20. It is said not to be rare at Angastina.

Bowls

Type 4: low ring base distinctly set off from body, which has gently curving sides to a semi-carinated rim with concave flattened lip. Side spout opposite lifted horizontal ribbon handle. Technique similar to that of Base-Ring Ware. **B 287** (P 1259; 49-12-213) T.12:87(B) LC IA:2. *Pl. 18.* N-c-m. C: hard, gray wfs. S: hor. bur. orange-brown to gray. H: 7.9. D: 16. **B 288** (P 1260; 49-12-214) T.12:87(B) LC IA:2. *Pl. 18.* N-c-m. Spout lost since cataloguing. C: like B 287. S: bur. mottled lt. orange-brown to dk. wine-red. H: 6.8. D: 15.3. **B 289** (P 1261; 49-12-215) T.12:88(C) LC IB. *Pls. 18, 43.* I-m. C,S: like B 287 but fabric somewhat thinner. H: 7.4. D: 15.8. **B 290** (Sh 644) E-A:8 LC IIA. Frag. of wall of semi-carinated bowl with profiled lip. C: slate-gray at core to pinkish, with much mica. S: lavender-red to dk. gray, liberally applied inside and on rim with brush, none on lower part of outside which is fired brick-red. H: 5. L: 12.2.

Type 5: hemispherical bowl with flat concave base. Forked side-spout opposite horizontal ribbon handle.

Apparently same as *SPC,* 183, No. 4 except for handle. This is virtually the shape of White Slip I, Type 2. **B 291** (P 1262; 49-12-216) T.12:89(B) LC IA:2 (late). *Pl. 18.* N-c-m. C: hard gray at core to brown, sandy. S: bur. mahogany color to yellowish gray. H: 8. D: 17.

Miscellaneous: the bowl from which the following sherd originates was probably much like Type 4 or 5, but a close connection with B 258 may also be indicated. **B 292** (Sh 630) MPT-A:16. Lifted hor. ribbon handle with adjoining portion of body. C: dk. g. gray, with mica. S: m. red to red-brown. Technique much like that of Base-Ring. L: 6.

Type 6: deep hemispherical bowl with concave rim and plain lip. Slightly lifted horizontal wishbone handle with a single central spur. Cf. *SPC,* 183, No. 5. **B 293** (P 2699; 49-12-438) T.37:2. I-m. *Pl. 18.* C: like B 291. S: sl. ls. gray-brown to dk. gray; white accretion in int. H: 7.8. D: 12.5.

Type 7: this is basically a handmade shallow hemispherical bowl supplied with a variety of handle types and with the general appearance of monochrome ware but rather coarser in fabric and unslipped (though generally burnished). **B 294** (P 997; 49-12-368) T.25:6. *Pl. 18.* C-i. Small pinched vert. ribbon handle. C: g. lt. red-brown to dk. purple-brown, roughly bur. H: 5.2. D: 12.5. **B 295** (P 2930; 49-12-129) T.11:15 LC IB. I-m. Base largely missing. Incurving rim, hor. wish-bone handle below rim (with horn?). C: dk. g. brick-red, hand bur. PH: 6.3. D: 15. **B 296** (P 2745) T.38:6. About half pres. Pierced hor. lug handle with deep central depression. C: like B 295 with m. red to blue-gray surface. H: 4.9. PD: 12.8. **B 297** (Sh 525) B-D:2 LC IIIA. *Pl. 20.* Frags. of rim and wall including handle; all apparently like B 296. C: like B 291, with reddish brown surface, roughly bur. PH: 7.4. W: 5.6. **B 298** (Sh 704) D-A. Like B 297. Rim flattened on top and sl. inverted. C: g. gray-brown to brick-red, with low bur. int. and ext. PH: 6.5. PD: 8. **B 299** (P 2826) D-A. About half of rim and much of wall pres. C: dk. gray to brick-red. Ext. probably had a low bur. PH: 7. D: 18. **B 300** (Sh 702) D-A. Frag. of sl. inverted, plain rim; just below rim the ends of a greatly elongated raised hor. loop handle. C: g. brick-red, bur. ext. PL (of handle): 9.8. PD: 8.9. **B 301** (Sh 703) D-A. *Pl. 20.* Entire elongated handle like B 300 with a small adjoining section of wall on one prong. C: like B 299. L: 12.2. W: 5.7.

Krater: again the technique of this piece is very similar to that of Base-Ring, but there is no slip. Ring base well set off from full rounded body with concave rim and wide mouth. One lifted horizontal wide ribbon handle. Cf. *SPC,* 183, No. 1 and *Problems,* 33.

B 302 (P 966; 49-12-18) T.2:12(A) LC IIA. *Pl. 19.* N-c-m. C: dk. g. gray with dk. gray to pink surface, rough; int. pared. H: 24.7. D: 29.

Jugs

Type 3: flat base, elongated spherical body, wide concave neck with round mouth and squared rim; vertical relief line on belly opposite handle, which goes from shoulder to rim. Cf. *SPC,* 183, No. 5. **B 303** (P 1264;

49-12-217) T.12:90(D) LC IIA. *Pl. 19*. Handle missing. C: gray at core to m. brick-red, with lt. and dk. sand. S: mottled lt. gray to brick-red, bur. hor. in narrow scratchy strokes, dipping to vert. relief line in front. Definitely superior technique. H: 23.3. D: 16.5. **B 304** (P 1266; 49-12-218) T.12:91(B) LC IA:2. *Pls. 19, 43*. I-m. Looped-up ribbon handle with 2 lines incised at top. C: like B 303. Though unslipped, this piece exhibits the same scratch bur. as B 303. H: 28.5. D: 20.1. **B 305** (Sh 768; group number: 49-12-227) T.12:95 (screening). Sl. concave irregularly shaped frag. perhaps from near mouth of jug. C: gray at core in a well-defined layer to lt. brick-red at surface; hard, compact. Sl. ls. dk. red slip on both surfaces with scratch bur. L: 2.6. Th: 0.3.

Type 4: the following jugs have essentially round, gourd-like baseless bodies from which wide necks rise without articulation. They have pinched lips, roll rims (usually) and handles from shoulder to rim. Of rather coarse fabric and generally burnished without slip, they correspond to the Type 7 bowls. Cf. *SPC*, 183, No. 4. **B 306** (P 1265; 49-12-143) T.12:13(E) LC IIB. *Pl. 43*. N-c-m. Thick roll lip. Handle sl. looped up. C: hard brick-red wfs, scratch bur. H: 19.8. D: 14.5. **B 307** (P 2746) T.38:7. *Pl. 19*. Most of handle, which sloped rakishly from rim, missing. Plain lip. C: m. g. pink with much mica, very coarse. On neck: m. lavender-pink to dk. blue slip; brush marks plainly visible. Rest of jug unslipped. H: 14.7. D: 10.3. **B 308** (P 2824) D-A. All of neck and a frag. of belly, giving profile, pres. Roll rim and sl. arched handle. Fire-blackened on one side of neck. C: dk. g. gray at core to brick-red. Neck vert. shaved. PH: 15.3. ED: 16.2. **B 309** (P 2825) D-A. Part of neck and shoulder and all of handle pres. Probably made on slow wheel. C: g. dk. reddish brown. Ext. of neck shaved and vert. bur. Body apparently hor. bur. PH: 12. D (of mouth): 9. **B 310** (P 2906) T.40:78(B) LC IIA. *Pls. 20, 59*. Most of neck—with handle—and part of shoulder pres. Handle like B 307 with metallic-type center ridge; rolled rim. C: g. slate-gray to brick-red. Neck (at least) vert. shaved. PH: 15.6. ED: 17.6. **B 311** (G 75) E-Hearth:C upper part of handle and adjoining portion of rim. C: dk. g. gray-brown. Ext. scratch bur. H: 3.2. L: 4.8. *AJA* 64 (1960) Pl. 35 and p. 146, Ill. 1.

Miscellaneous: **B 312** (P 1432) C-A:5 LC IB. *Pl. 20*. Neck and most of handle, including "spur" of a jug which evidently closely resembled in shape and Base-Ring I Type 5. Small hole at base of spur, which was probably two-pronged. Coarse relief ridge at mid-neck. C: gray at core to brick-red; surface roughly bur. PH: 10. D: 8.5. **B 313** (Sh 711) C-Unstrat. *Pl. 52*. Frag. of rim with upper portion of handle, made with flaps which have been turned up as pointed flanges. Deep incision down mid-handle and along edges of flange. C: like B 312, with small dk. grits. H: 5.6. W: 6.6.

FUSED TEMPER

A fabric very much akin to Monochrome (and Base-Ring) received this designation from Daniel. Its technical characteristic is a very hard metallic clay, slate-gray to darker gray in color, with a denser consistency than is the case with any other Cypriote fabric. Coupled with this is usually a brownish red slip which has been burnished. However, the ware is not invariably slipped. Occasionally it has a black wash. Unfortunately, very little is known of the vase shapes. Occurrence is usually in late contexts but, since this refers only to isolated sherds whereas one whole pot (B 314) occurs in an early context, there is no cogent reason to suppose it a late ware. Most of the sherds appear to be from handmade vessels, though one cannot always be certain about this.

Bowls

Type 1: hemispherical bowl with truncated flat bottom and horizontal ribbon handle below rim; four narrow flaring lugs (equidistant) at rim. **B 314** (P 1258; 49-12-163) T.12:34(B) LC IA:2. *Pls. 19, 43*. N-c-m. Considerably warped. C: g. gray. S: brownish red, vert. and diagonally bur. H: 6.2. D: 16.2. **B 315** (Sh 263) A-Unstrat. *Pl. 20*. Frag. of handle of bowl apparently like B 314. C,S: like B 314. L: 15.5. W: 2.4.

Various bowl fragments

a. With (small) flaring rim: **B 316** (Sh 72) A-D:3(IV) LC IIIA. *Pls. 20, 53*. C: like B 314. S: dk. gray-brown to dk. gray, bur. H: 2.9. L: 3.2. **B 317** (Sh 143) A-E:4 LC IIIB. *Pl. 53*. C,S: like B 314. H: 2.5. W: 5.1. **B 318** (Sh 351) A-surface. *Pl. 53*. C: g. black. S: lt. gray to gray-brown (over-fired?). H: 2.8. L: 4.3. **B 319** (Sh 352) A-surface. *Pls. 20, 53*. C: lt. gray at core to olive-brown. S: like B 314. H: 2.9. L: 3.2. **B 320** (Sh 405) Cw Vb CA I. *Pls. 20, 53*. C: lt. blue-gray to reddish brown. S: ext. possibly self-slipped. Bur. ext. and int. H: 2.9. L: 3.2.

b. With (large) flaring rim: **B 321** (Sh 183) A-Unstrat. *Pl. 53*. C: blue-gray, mottled. S: dk. gray-brown to gray-olive; int. bur. H: 2.9. **B 322** (Sh 404) Cw Vb CA I. *Pl. 53*. C,S: like B 320. H: 2.8. L: 5.7. **B 323** (Sh 438) A-surface. *Pl. 53*. C,S: like B 321, but ext. brick-red. H: 3.2. L: 5.7.

c. With (large) thickened rim: **B 324** (Sh 353) A-surface. *Pl. 53*. C,S: like B 314. H: 2.1. L: 3.1. **B 325** (Sh 391) A-E:3(VIII) LC IIIB. *Pl. 53*. C: like B 321. S: mottled orange-brown to dk. gray. H: 3.2. L: 4.2. **B 326** (Sh 440) A-surface. *Pl. 53*. C,S: like B 325. H: 3.4. L: 8.5.

d. With (small) squared rim: **B 327** (Sh 147) A-E:3(V) LC IIIB. *Pls. 20, 53*. C,S: like B 314. H: 2.7. L: 5.7. **B 328** (Sh 439) A-surface. *Pl. 53*. Rim grooved. C: slate-gray. S: traces of brown to black. H: 3.8. L: 4.2. **B 329** (Sh 441) A-surface. *Pls. 20, 53*. Rim grooved. C,S: like B 328. H: 2.2. L: 4.2.

Jug fragment

B 330 (Sh 415) Cw Vb CA I. Frag. from base of neck. H-m. C,S: similar to B 325. H: 4. L: 4.2.

BURNISHED SLIP WARE

This fabric may, at least tentatively, be considered unique to Bamboula, where it occurs in considerable quantity. It might indeed be termed "Bamboula ware" in the same spirit that coarse monochrome has been termed "Apliki ware." A careful comparison with sherds and pots from Enkomi and other sites represented in the Cyprus Museum has failed to reveal anything of this type, although, of course, burnished wares of various other sorts exist. And it need hardly be pointed out how prevalent burnished wares are on the Syro-Palestinian littoral both in the Bronze Age and later. Burnished Slip Ware is confined almost entirely to bowls and related shapes and generally manifests itself as plain ware fabric—both handmade and wheelmade—with a pinkish or orangeish burnished slip, on the interior only of large bowls, on both sides of small bowls. Occurring both in tombs and the settlement, it might at first sight seem to be a *de luxe* ware, perhaps that reserved for special occasions. On the other hand, Sir Leonard Woolley has suggested to me that the sole purpose of the slip can have been to reduce porosity of the bowls. In any case, the handsome appearance of a carefully burnished large bowl such as B 348 reveals that the craftsman must have taken a certain pride in producing an aesthetically pleasing article.

Bowls

Type 1a: small to medium-sized shallow bowls with low, rather heavy ring base and vertical lug at rim pierced horizontally. Carinated rim and slightly profiled lip. Very similar to but less shallow than Type 2c of *Problems,* 56 (Plain Wheelmade I ware). **B 331** (P 2663; 49-12-249) T.18(E) LC IIC. *Pl. 19.* C-i. Made by hand or slow wheel. C: lt. grayish buff, very sandy. S: firm pinkish orange, over entire surface except underside of base, bur. to a full luster; int. peeling, ext. rather dull, probably from soil action. H: 5.1. D: 13.8.

Type 1b: small to medium-sized shallow bowls with low ring base and vertical lug at rim pierced horizontally. Swelling sides and slightly incurving rim to plain lip. **B 332** (P 1371) T.16:52. *Pl. 43.* N-c. Rim badly chipped. C: green-gray wfds. S: violet-gray, bur. int. and ext. H: 4. D: 9.3. **B 333** (P 1375) T.13:8. *Pl. 43.* C-ch. C,S: like B 332. Slip almost entirely gone. H: 4.7. D: 11.3. **B 334** (P 2720) MPT-A:9. *Pl. 19.* Over half pres. Handle missing. Rim profiled. C: dk. gray to pink. S: pinkish to black. H: 5.4. D: 14.8.

Miscellaneous sherds with ring base: **B 335** (Sh 119) A-B:6 LC IIA. *Pl. 53.* Frag. of base. H-m? C: g. lt. gray-brown wfds. S: dk. violet-gray (ext.), orange-buff (int.). H: 4.7. W: 8.7. **B 336** (Sh 483) A-A:3 LC IIA. *Pls. 20, 53.* Frag. of base. W-m. C: g. lt. pinkish gray. S: pinkish brown to pinkish orange, beautifully bur. H: 1.8. W: 6.5.

Miscellaneous sherds from small bowls: **B 337** (Sh 567) E-B:1 LC IIB. *Pl. 53.* Rim. C: sandy gray-brown. S: traces of orange. H: 2.7. W: 2.9. **B 338** (Sh 645) E-Unstrat. *Pl. 20.* Frag. of wall and rim. W-m. C: hard brick-orange with lime. S: medium orange, bur. int. and ext. (from 1.5 cm. below lip). H: 2.6. W: 4. **B 339** (Sh 659) T.3:29. Rim and wall frag. W-m? C: g. dk. buff wfds. S: pink to reddish brown (int. and ext.). P: m. dk. brown. Radiating spokes (?) int. under rim. H: 3. W: 1.2. **B 340** (Sh 670) B-LC IIC context. *Pls. 20, 53.* Rim and wall frag. C: like B 339. S: pinkish orange, bur. (ext. and int.). H: 5.3. W: 4.5. **B 341** (Sh 741) E-LC IIC context. Frag. from wall. Probably w-m. C: g. greenish gray. S: pink to reddish brown (int. only). H: 4.8. W: 4.2. **B 342** (Sh 747) C-LC IIA (or earlier) context. *Pls. 20, 53.* Rim and wall frag. Probably w-m. C: g. gray-buff with red sand. S: lt. smooth pink, flaked (all surfaces, though ext. rim may have been reserved); apparently not bur. H: 4.6. W: 4.4. **B 343** (Sh 753) E-A:7 LC IIA. *Pl. 53.* Considerable frag. of rim and floor. W-m. C: g. lt. gray-brown. S: pink to reddish brown (int. bur. by wheel, then cross-bur. by hand?; ext. apparently unbur.). H: 5. D: 16.8.

Type 2: rather large, relatively shallow bowls with flat base, semi-carinated rim and vertical lug handle, pierced longitudinally. The fabric suggests coarse plain ware, and indeed the shape is roughly similar to B 762 and to Type 1c of *Problems,* 56 (Plain Wheelmade I ware). **B 344** (P 1308) T.33:19 LC IIIA. *Pls. 43, 61.* N-c. Rim considerably chipped. Made by hand or on slow wheel. C: g. greenish with much lt. and dk. sand. S: thin dk. reddish brown, bur. (int.). H: 7.5. D: 20. **B 345** (P 2812) D-A. *Pl. 43.* About half pres., giving complete profile. Rather deeper than B 344. C: g. reddish brown (cinnamon) wfds. S: dk. reddish brown, bur. (int. and possibly rim ext.). H: 9.5. ED: 24. **B 346** (Sh 64) A-Unstrat. *Pl. 53.* Lug handle and adjoining wall frag. H-m? C: lt. gray-peach color wfds. S: ls. pink to orange-brown. H: 4.6. W: 4.4. **B 347** (Sh 172) A-B:5 LC IIB. Frag. of base and adjoining wall. H-m? C: lt. gray-buff to gray-green, wfds. S: ls. dk. reddish brown, almost purple. L: 7.9. W: 7.2.

Type 3: very large bowls or basins with flat base, semi-carinated rim and squared, profiled lip; probably no handles. **B 348** (P 762) A-B:6 LC IIA. *Pls. 19, 43.* About ¼ pres. giving complete profile. Made by hand or on slow wheel. C: sandy orange-brown at core to yellow-gray wfs. and lime. Ext. well smoothed, base set on sand. S: rich pinkish orange to silver-gray, bur. in long thin strokes diagonally. H: 13.5. ED: 20.5. **B 349** (Sh 120) A-B:6 LC IIA. *Pl. 53.* Frag. of rim. W-m. C: like B 347 but sl. darker. S: ls. orange-brown to dk. gray-brown, almost olive. Most of ext. apparently res. L: 4.7. W: 4.1. **B 350** (Sh 220) A-D:1(V) LC IIC. *Pls. 20, 53.* Rim frag. W-m? C: sandy lt. orange-buff. S: ls. dk. orange, int. and ext. H: 4.3. W: 5. **B 351** (Sh 640) E-Hearth:E LC IIA. *Pl. 53.* Base of bowl with portions of sides. Made by hand or on slow wheel. C: pinkish brown with lt. and dk. sand. Ext. wet-smoothed. S: dk. reddish brown, bur. D (of base): 9. PL (of frag.): 14.5.

Krater-amphora

B 352 (P 2731) E-LC IIC context. *Pl. 19.* Base and part of body missing. Piriform body with short flaring neck and wide mouth. Flat vert. handles from shoulder to rim. C: g. buff to dk. orange-buff. S: reddish brown, wheel bur. (upper half of ext. and small portion of inner surface below rim). PH: 21.7. D (of mouth): 28.2.

Pithos ware: the following fragments show that even pithoi were treated with this technique.

B 353 (Sh 436) A-Unstrat. Frag. from base of flaring mouth with neck ridge. C: g. orange-buff to gray-green. S: traces of ls. pink. Mouth slipped int. and ext. L: 4.7. W: 4.7. Th: 2.2. **B 354** (Sh 442) A-surface. Frag. of neck? C: g. lt. brown-buff wfds. S: hor. bur. pinkish violet (ext. only). H: 6. W: 12.2. Th: 2.5. **B 355** (Sh 710) C-B LC IIB. *Pl. 20.* Frag. of wall with 2 relief ridges perhaps from rope design. Probably w-m. C: g. pinkish gray. S: bur. orange-brown (ext.). H: 7.5. W: 9. Th: 2.

Jugs: the following fragments are from the wall of closed vessels which appear to be basically Plain Wheelmade II ware. Only the exterior surface is slipped.

B 356 (Sh 725) A-B:5 LC IIB. C: g. buff, not well sifted. S: thick pinkish brown with cross (?) bur.; flaked. H: 5.2. W: 5.3. **B 357** (Sh 754) E (Tr.20:15a sub Hearth E) LC IIIA context. *Pl. 20.* C: g. dk. buff wfds. S: bur. dk. thick red-orange, flaked. H: 3.4. W: 4.3.

MISCELLANEOUS BURNISHED WARES

Handmade Stroke-Burnished Ware: this ware has a characteristically brown appearance; the clay is hard in the examples known from Bamboula.

B 358 (Sh 333) A-D:2(VII,2) LC IIIA. *Pl. 20.* Various sherds of a jug. Wide neck, round mouth with sl. set-off rim. C: lt. gray-tan. S: dk. chocolate. Upper rim not bur.; rest imperfectly bur. Int. bur. H (of rim frag.): 3.6. W: 6.6. **B 359** (Sh 528) C-A:5 LC IB. *Pl. 20.* Four joins from neck and shoulder of pot with wide neck, flaring rim and handle at neck base. C: g. red-brown. S: stroke-bur. dk. red-brown ext. and int. of neck. H: 9.8. W: 12.

Pink Burnished Ware: this fabric is also represented at Kaloriziki (K 972).

Jugs

B 360 (P 2850) See E-4 LC IIB; see also E-D:1a and D:2a. *Pl. 43.* I-m. Upper part missing. W-m.

Low ring base distinctly set off from squat fat ovoid, almost spherical body. Non-joining neck frags. show neck was rather wide and sl. concave. C: lt. pink; hard, firm, compact, smooth wfds. S: thin self-slip, sl. ls. hor. bur. PH: 11.5. PD: 11.7. **B 361** (P 2905) T.40:15(D) LC IIIA. *Pls. 43, 58.* Upper part of body only pres.; undoubtedly to be restored with the shape of the Type 1b jug of PWM II ware; cf. K 972. W-m. C: lt. pinkish orange, well sifted, wfs. and lt. and dk. grits. Finer fabric than B 360. Though most of the surface has been completely eroded, traces of a vert. bur. self-slip remain. PH: 21.8. D: 14.8. **B 362** (Sh 373) Cw Vb CA I. *Pl. 20.* Base of lifted handle, oval in section. C: lt. pinkish brown, well cleaned, highly bur. L: 5.5.

Indeterminate Burnished Ware

B 363 (Sh 319) A-D:3(VII) LC IIIA. Frag. of bowl(?) with stump of thick cylindrical handle. H-m. C: fine hard slate-gray to buff at surface. S: bur. self-slip. Resembles BR. H: 6. W: 3.8. **B 364** (Sh 398) A-G. Frag. of rim and (upper) stump of handle of a large jug. C: heavy compact gray-black to gray-brown with micaceous(?) temper. Surface now much worn but appears to have been scratch-bur. L: 9.1. W: 4.9. **B 365** (Sh 491) A-D:2(VII,1). Rim frag. of deep bowl. Chain design in relief on ext. below rim. C: dk. gray to lt. brown with lime grits. S: gray-red to dk. gray, bur. int. and ext. H: 3.2. L: 3.4.

WASH WARE

Daniel's terminology (see *AJA* 45, 1941, 271 n. 52) seems preferable for this fabric. The difficulty of the Swedish terminology is illustrated by B 370. The ware is wheelmade except where noted.

Bowls: unfortunately no complete examples of this rather rare shape were recovered.

B 366 (Sh 170) A-B:5 LC IIB. *Pl. 53.* Frag. of base with prominent heavy ring foot. C: very sandy lt. peach to gray-green heavy fabric. Wash: m. thick black. H: 3. L: 8.5. **B 367** (Sh 345) A-surface. *Pl. 53.* Like B 366. C: g. lavender-gray, sandy. Wash: m. dk. gray. H: 3.3. L: 7.2. **B 368** (Sh 249) A-surface. *Pl. 53.* Bowl rim with 2 lines deeply incised before applying wash, possibly intended as signs. H-m. C: g. gray at core to orange-brown. Wash: m. red-brown to red-gray. H: 3.5. L: 4.7. **B 369** (Sh 474) A-D:3(VIa) LC IIIA. *Pl. 53.* Rim with groove (to receive lid?). Probably h-m. C: g. lt. orange-brown. S: like B 368. H: 3.5. L: 5.4.

Jugs

Type A: this is apparently identical with the Black Slip III jug No. 7 of *SPC*, 146. Handmade, it has a small flat base, biconical body, wide slightly tapering neck and round mouth with flattened rim. Strap handle from neck to rim, arched high above rim. From appearance and technique the Bamboula piece must be considered as Wash Ware. **B 370** (P 1270; 49-12-185) T.12:58(A) LC IA:2. *Pl. 19.* N-c-m. C: lt. orange-brown wfs. Wash: m. dk. gray with a few wine-red patches, much flaked. H: 20.3. D: 12.5.

Type B: this is quite similar to, though not identical with, *Problems*, 60, Type 1 (Red Slip Wheelmade Ware). Its descent from the so-called Black Slip Ware of Gjerstad will be evident if one compares *SPC*, 146, No. 3 and the earlier No. 4 of p. 135. It is wheelmade, has a flat base and elongated spherical (gourd-like) body with tall narrow neck and flaring round mouth. Vertical handle to mid-neck. **B 371** (P 1267; 49-12-219) T.12:92(B) LC IA:2. *Pl. 19.* N-c-m. C: like B 370. Wash: thick, barely ls. dk. gray with red patches, somewhat flaked. H: 34.8. D: 21.7.

Type C: to this class belong jugs with flat base, biconical (or globular) bodies, straight necks and flaring trefoil mouths, with more or less vertical handle from shoulder to rim. In many respects this recalls Type 2b of *Problems*, 63, without being identical. It is essentially the shape of B 96 adapted to the heavier fabric of Wash Ware. Cf. also *SPC*, 203: "Black Slip Ware," which Gjerstad classified as foreign. **B 372** (P 1263; 49-12-168) T.12:39(B) LC IA:2. *Pl. 19.* N-c-m. H-m. Quite tall neck; handle has broad concave groove imitating metal technique. Clearly related in shape to *SPC*, 183, No. 3. C: hard g. gray-brown. Wash: m. dk. gray to lt. brick-red. H: 20.6. D: 14. The fabric of B 372 and B 373 has a superficial resemblance to Monochrome Ware. **B 373** (P 1268; 49-12-177) T.12:50(B) LC IA:2. *Pls. 19, 43.* N-c-m. C: hard lt. g. gray-brown. Wash: thin wine-red and rust to dk. gray. H: 15. D: 11.3. **B 374** (P 1269; K 21; 49-12-157) T.12:28(B) LC IA:2. *Pl. 19.* N-c-m. Body globular. Base not entirely flat so that pot rocks. Handle incised. C: sandy, greenish gray. Wash: m. dk. lavender-gray. H: 19. D: 15. *AJA* 64 (1960) Pl. 35. **B 375** (P 1277; 49-12-176) T.12:49(B) LC IA:2. *Pl. 19.* N-c-m. C: m. brick-red with much lt. sand. Very heavy fabric. Wash: like B 374, much worn. H: 21. D: 14.5.

Type D: this class is something of a monumental version of Type 1 of *Problems*, 63, but must certainly have had its origin in large Plain Ware jugs (cf. B 772). It is wheelmade, with flat base and nearly biconical shape, very short neck and thickened flaring rim, flattened on top. Vertical handle from shoulder to just below rim. **B 376** (P 751) A-B:6 LC IIA. *Pl. 19.* Handle, with part of neck and shoulder. Has a rough neck ring. C: sandy pinkish brown. Wash: m. mahogany to violet-gray. H: 22.7. ED: 32. **B 377** (P 1377) T.13:10. *Pl. 43.* I-m. Parts of handle, neck and body missing. C: hard sandy yellow-brown to orange-brown. Wash: thick dk. wine-red with black patches. H: 44.6. D: 33.8.

Miscellaneous jug fragments: **B 378** (Sh 77) A-E:3(St) LC IIIB. Wall frag. H-m. C: sandy lt. gray-buff; heavy fabric. Wash: m. red-brown to purple-gray. L: 9.7. W: 5.4. **B 379** (Sh 171) A-B:5 LC IIB. Base of neck, with neck ring. H-m. C: g. gray-brown to red-brown. Wash: like B 368. H: 3.2. L: 4.5. **B 380** (Sh 281) A-D:3(IV) LC IIIA. *Pl. 20.* Wall frag. C: g. dk. gray-brown with lime. Wash: m. dk. gray

with applied white (or blue). L: 3.3. W: 1.9. **B 381** (Sh 282) A-D:3(IV) LC IIIA. Base of neck with neck ring. H-m? C: sandy lt. gray-buff to gray-green. Wash: m. dk. gray-purple. H: 4.2. L: 8.5. **B 382** (Sh 253) A-D:3(IV) LC IIIA. *Pl. 20.* Rim frag. C: lt. gray to gray-green. Wash: m. lavender to brown. H: 2.8. L: 3.1. **B 383** (Sh 315) A-D:2(VII,2) LC IIIA. *Pl. 20.* Frag. of semi-cylindrical rim. C: soft sandy orange-brown. Wash: thick m. red-brown. H: 2.9. L: 3.3. **B 384** (Sh 388) A-E:3(VIII) LC IIIA. *Pl. 20.* Wall frag. C: g. reddish-brown. Wash: like B 378 with a small res. band (?) over which a dk. gray zigzag has been painted. L: 5.1. W: 3.4. **B 385** (Sh 450) Cw Vb CA I. Wall frag. C: like B 381. Wash: like B 384, but underfired to red in patches. Band of applied white, now much faded, around belly. L: 6.3. W: 3.5. **B 386** (Sh 512) C-A:2 LC IA:2. Wall frag. C: like B 383. Wash: like B 378. Dec: like B 385. L: 11.8. W: 5.7. **B 387** (Sh 641) E-Hearth:E. Wall frag. C: lt. tan-buff, very sandy. Wash: like B 378 but firm and sl. ls. L: 5. W: 3.3.

Inscribed handle fragments: **B 388** (G 5:K 31) A-Unstrat. Probably h-m. Handle inserted. Cut after applying wash, and probably after baking. C: sandy, lt. orange-brown. Wash: like B 382. L: 8.6. *AJA* 42 (1938) 273 Fig. 13:j. *AJA* 64 (1960) Pl. 35. **B 389** (G 16:K 27) A-D:3(VII) LC IIIA. C: g. gray at core to orange-brown. Traces of ls. dk. gray wash (according to Daniel; none now observable). L: 5.5. *AJA* 64 (1960) Pl. 35. **B 390** (G 30:K 49) C-A:5 LC IB. C: sandy lt. gray-green. Wash: dk. gray. L: 7.7. *UPMB 13* (1948) Pl. III; *AJA* 64 (1960) Pl. 35. **B 391** (G 31:K 12) C-A:5 LC IB. C, Wash: like B 390. L: 10. *AJA* 64 (1960) Pl. 35. **B 392** (G 33:K 54) C-A:5 LC IB. C: g. lt. gray-brown. Wash: dk. gray, flaked. L: 7. *AJA* 64 (1960) Pl. 35. **B 393** (G 36:K 34) C-B LC IIB. C, Wash: like B 392. L: 9.3. *AJA* 64 (1960) Pl. 35. **B 394** (G 53:K 14) E-Unstrat. C: g. pinkish to gray-brown. Wash: firm, almost ls. dk. gray. L: 6.3. *AJA* 64 (1960) Pl. 35. **B 395** (G 57:K 55) Stray. C: lt. gray-buff, well cleaned. Wash: m. dk. gray, crackled. L: 10.3. *AJA* 64 (1960) Pl. 35.

WHITE SHAVED WARE

Handmade

Juglets: these have slightly flattened, curved bottoms, thus differing from examples in *Problems*, 32. Besides those listed below, an (unstratified) fragment (49-12-222) occurred in Tomb 12.

B 396 (P 1376) T.13:9. *Pl. 52.* I-m. Handle arched above rim. C: soft lt. brown wfs. Vert. paring. H: 6.8. D: 3.9. **B 397** (P 2739) Stray. *Pl. 20.* I-m. Most of handle missing. C: lt. buff wfs. H: 5.4. D: 3.

Jugs

B 398 (Sh 148) A-E:3(V) LC IIIB. *Pl. 20.* Frag. of wall with transition to shoulder. C: lt. gray-green; surface now stained dk. yellow. H: 6.5. PD: 4.8. **B 399** (Sh 227) A-B:6 LC IIA. Considerable frag. of wall with transition to neck. C: lt. gray-brown to gray-green, well cleaned. H: 7.6. PD: 6.3. **B 400** (G 25:K 17) C-A:6 LC IIA. Frag. of shoulder, neck and handle, which was inserted. Inscribed near base of handle. C: buff to lt. creamy green, beautifully cleaned. H: 7.3. W: 5.1. *AJA* 64 (1960) Pl. 35.

Wheelmade

Jugs: the following appear to be wheelmade imitations of *Problems,* 32, Type 1a.

B 401 (P 986) E-D:1f LC IIIA. *Pl. 20.* I-m. Handle and base missing. C: gray at core to pinkish surface, well sifted. PH: 11.5. D: 6.7. **B 402** (Sh 250) A-surface. *Pl. 20.* Base only pres. C: g. lt. brown-buff to gray-green, wfds. H: 8.6. ED: 8.

PAINTED SHAVED WARE

Jug

B 403 (Sh 699) D-A. *Pl. 20.* Neck and adjoining frag. of body pres. H-m. Pinched mouth, narrow neck widening gradually to rather steeply sloping shoulder. Handle from rim to shoulder. C: g. gray-brown, thick fabric, surface shaved and after this apparently covered with lt. yellowish slip, ls. in places. P: m. dk. gray-brown, washy. Stripes on inside of rim and outside of handle. Stripe around base of neck. 2 narrower stripes around body below handle. PH: 6.9. ED: 10.

LATE CYPRIOTE III DECORATED WARE

The clay of this category is in general rather porous and gritty, the paint often thin and washy and, of course, matt. The proportion of better-made examples is small (they are indicated in the catalogue by the comment, "superior fabric") and these provide virtually a link between the technique of some of the off-shade Mycenaean bowls and the average LC III Decorated ware technique, which may therefore be, as I have suggested (p. 110), ultimately inspired by the Mycenaean ware. In this sense Gjerstad's term "Debased Levanto-Helladic" would be descriptive. However, for other reasons Furumark is right in rejecting it. A more detailed discussion of terminology is given on p. 110.

Bowls: this shape comprises by far the majority of the specimens of this ware represented at Bamboula. So prevalent is it that Daniel and, I believe, others, have referred to it as "Bowl Ware", but its inclusion in the present category is more convenient for the purposes of style history: the shapes found at Bamboula considerably enrich the repertory as presented in *Problems,* 67, of which Type 1 (Painted "Submycenaean" ware) is used in this catalogue. No examples of Type 2 occurred.

Type 1: the bases vary slightly from low base-ring type if commented on. Diameters given do not include handles. **B 404** (P 725) A-D:2(VII,2) LC IIIA. *Pls. 21, 55.* N-c-m. C: brown to gray-green at surface, sandy, hard. P: m. gray-violet. Bands at rim, below handles and about halfway down (int.); c-s int. center.

H: 6. D: 16. **B 405** (P 726) A-D:2(VII,2) LC IIIA. About half pres. including profile. Handle sl. raised. C: orange-brown, sandy, hard. P: m. red-brown. Int. center: 3 narrow c-c around a small solid circle. H: 6. ED: 16. **B 406** (P 742) A-E:2(V) LC IIIB. *Pls. 21, 55.* I-m. Much of rim missing. C: lt. brown, sandy. P: m. gray-brown. Dec: like B 405 plus a wide stripe about ⅔ down ext. H: 6. D: 15.8. **B 407** (P 791) A-Unstrat. Sturdy double-rolled ring base and part of adjoining walls, sl. burnt. C: brown to gray-green, well-cleaned. P: m. streaky brown. Dec: like B 405 plus a stripe about halfway up int. and ext. PH: 5.2. PD: 14. **B 408** (P 795) A-D:2(VI) LC IIIA. Sturdy rolled ring base and part of adjoining curving walls. C: g. gray-brown, sandy, hard, rough. P: m. brown to gray, mostly thin. Int. center: c-s with solid circle center. Farther up, a stripe. PH: 3.5. PD: 15. **B 409** (P 805) A-D:2(IV) LC IIIA. Most of rim missing but profile pres. C: brick-red, sandy, hard. P: m. red. Int. center: 3 c-c around a small circle. Stripe about halfway up; stripe on lip and below handle. H: 7. ED: 16. **B 410** (P 947; 49-12-30) T.3:9(B) LC IIIA. *Pl. 21.* N-c-m. Sl. profiled flaring ring base. Signs of burning on rim. C: dk. brown wfds. P: m. orange-brown, worn. Dec: like B 404 plus paint on rim and band halfway down int. H: 5.2. D: 15.6. **B 411** (P 948; 49-12-31) T.3:10(B) LC IIIA. *Pls. 21, 55.* C-ch. C: lt. orange-brown to gray-green. P. and dec: like B 410. H: 5.6. D: 16. **B 412** (P 949; 49-12-32) T.3:11(B) LC IIIA. *Pl. 21.* C-i. C: g. dk. pink-brown to red-brown wfs. P: m. dk. red. Int. center: c-s. Band about ⅓ down (int. and ext.); paint on rim. H: 5. D: 13.8. **B 413** (P 982) E-D:1h LC IIIA. More than half pres. including profile. C: like B 411, wfds, well-smoothed. P: m. firm red-brown. Superior fabric. Paint on rim and near base ext. H: 5.6. D: 15.7. **B 414** (P 984) E-D:1f LC IIIA. *Pl. 44.* I-m. C: lt. gray-brown to red-brown wfs, rather soft; rough surface. P: m. firm red. Int. center: c-c. Paint on rim and halfway down ext. H: 5.5. D: 16. **B 415** (Sh 766; group number: 49-12-418) T.32:14. Frag. of rim. C: lt. to medium dk. tan with scattered impurities. P: m. reddish purple to grayish purple; washy. Two bands ext., one int. L: 5.3. **B 416** (P 1351) T.16:34. *Pl. 44.* I-m. Ring base. Existence of handles uncertain. C: like B 414. P: m. gray. Int. center: c-s. 3 bands halfway up and 3 at rim int.; one band halfway up ext. Paint on base. H: 5.8. D: 15.1. **B 417** (P 1353) T.16:35. C-m. Sturdy ring base; "omphalos" at int. center. C: lt. greenish brown, sandy. P: like B 406. Dec: like B 406 (but dot outlined) plus a stripe below handles int. and on rim. H: 5.7. D: 15.3. **B 418** (P 1354) T.16:36. *Pls. 44, 55.* I-m. C: like B 413. P: m. purple to gray. Dec: like B 417. H: 6.4. D: 15.2. **B 149** (P 1355) T.16:37. N-c-m. C: like B 413. P: m. red-brown to purple-brown. Int. center: d-o small circle. Stripe about ⅔ up int. and ext. H: 4.9. D: 15.3. **B 420** (P 2689; 49-12-406) T.32:2 LC IIIA. *Pl. 21.* N-c-m. Ring base. C: lt. gray-brown to gray-green, with black sand; well smoothed. P: m. firm gray-brown. Int. center: c-s. Two bands ⅓ down int. Paint on rim and base, narrow band about halfway down ext. H: 5.5. D: 15.1. **B 421** (P 2792; 49-12-

413) T.32:9 LC IIIA. *Pl. 44.* I-m. Most of rim missing. Profiled base ring. C: g. m. reddish brown. P: like B 420. Int. center: c-s. 3 bands halfway up and 2 bands on rim int. Band on rim and 2 about halfway down ext. H: 5.3. ED: 16. **B 422** (P 2793; 49-12-414) T.32:10 LC IIIA. *Pl. 21.* N-c-m. Handles small and poorly made. C: g. lt. gray-pink to gray-green. P: m. washy gray-pink. Dec: like B 412. H: 6.1. D: 15.7. **B 423** (P 2794; 49-12-415) T.32:11 LC IIIA. I-m. Base like B 410. C: g. gray-brown, coarse fabric. P: m. washy purple-brown. Int. center: large c-s. Band about ⅔ up and just below rim. 2 bands ext. H: 5.4. D: 14.6. **B 424** (P 2883) T.40:16(D) LC IIIA. *Pl. 21, 55, 58.* C-i. C: g. cinnamon-colored, coarse. P: m. dk. gray-brown. Dec: like B 412 but ext. band about halfway down. H: 6. D: 15.2.

Miscellaneous fragments of Type 1: **B 425** (Sh 154) A-D:2(V) LC IIIA. Wall frags. C: coarse gray-brown. C,P: burnt and smoked. W: 4.6. L: 7.7. **B 426** (Sh 155) A-D:2(V) LC IIIA. Base and part of wall. C: g. red-brown, coarse. P: m. red-brown, crackled. Int. center: c-s. Band farther up. H: 2.7. PD: 12.2. **B 427** (Sh 327) A-D:2(VII,2) LC IIIA. *Pl. 20.* Frag. of floor and small raised ring base; bowl shape not completely certain. C: lt. gray to orange-buff, well cleaned. P: m. orange-brown to dk. gray-brown. Superior fabric. Int. center: c-s. H: 1.2. L: 2.9. **B 428** (Sh 335) A-D:3(VII) LC IIIA. Base with low raised ring. C: soft lt. gray-brown with lime grits; powdery. P: m. lt. gray-brown. Paint on base ext.; traces of paint on int. floor. H: 2. PD: 6. **B 429** (Sh 383) A-F:1 LC IIIB. Rim frag. C: lt. brown wfs, soft. P: traces on rim(?). H: 2.6. L: 4. **B 430** (Sh 394) A-E:2(VIII) LC IIIB. Rim and wall frag. C: gray-green wfs. P: sl. ls. dk. gray, lighter where thin. W: 4.5. L: 10.3. **B 431** (Sh 466) Cw IV CA I. Rim frag. with handle. C: lt. brown-buff, well cleaned. P: m. red-brown to dk. gray. Superior fabric. H: 2.3. L: 3.5. **B 432** (Sh 467) Cw IIIa LC IIIB. Two joins from same bowl as B 431. H: 3.5. L: 6.8. **B 433** (Sh 513) C-C:2 LC IIC. *Pl. 20.* Half of base and adjoining wall frag. pres. Base profiled. C: lt. brown-buff wfs. P: ls. gray-brown. Superior fabric. Int. center: c-s. 2 bands farther up. Ext: paint on base and band farther up. H: 2.7. PD: 8.3.

The following specimens appear to represent variations of Type 1: **B 434** (P 983) E-D:1d LC IIIA. About half pres. including profile. Low ring base; semi-carinated rim (handles entirely missing). C: g. gray-brown, sandy, poorly smoothed. P: m. purple-gray. Paint on rim? H: 5.6. D: 15. **B 435** (P 1293) T.33:14(C) LC IIIB. *Pls. 44, 60.* N-c-m. Rather tall base ring; 2 small hor. ribbon handles sl. raised, below rim. C: g. gray-green, coarse. P: m. firm thin greenish gray. Int. center: c-s and 2 bands. 1 band halfway down ext. H: 7.1. D: 15.9. **B 436** (P 1408; 49-12-287) T.19:15(D) LC IIIA. *Pl. 44.* C-sp. Low ring base; unperforated tripartite hor. lug at rim (cf. B 1044); also 4 shallow grooves around rim. C: gray-purple to green-gray with a pink spot; lime and sherd temper. P: firm m. mahogany to dk. gray. Int. center: d-o c-s. Paint on rim and lug and halfway down, int.

and ext. H: 8.3. D: 19.5. **B 437** (Sh 532) A-E:2(St.2b) LC IIIB. Frags. of base, wall and rim. Rim somewhat angular; 2-pointed long handle. C: lt. gray-brown wfs. P: m. pink, much worn. Apparently all of int. and part of ext. covered with wide bands. W (of largest frag.): 5. L: 8.1. **B 438** (G 50:K 9) D-A. Part of base and walls pres. Raised flat base. C: sandy orange-brown. P: m. firm dk. red-brown. Stripe around base and 2 around middle of body ext. 2 bands int. H: 3.5. D: 14.4. *UPMB* 13 (1948) pl. 3. *AJA* 64 (1960) Pl. 35.

Type 3: low ring base (variations noted, as for Type 1), flaring walls to carinated, usually concave, rims with two small horizontal ribbon handles. The height of the bowls is proportionally about that of Type 1 bowls, but in a few instances (cf. especially B 452 and B 458) they are very squat and shallow. A similar shape occurs in Plain Wheelmade II ware (cf. *Problems*, 60, Fig. 16: type 1). **B 439** (P 785) A-D:2(VI) LC IIIA. *Pl. 53.* Rim and wall frags. C: g. brown to red-brown, very coarse. P: m. chocolate color. Probably c-s at int. center. 2 bands on upper wall int., 2 ext. Paint on rim. PH: 5. PD: 3.5. **B 440** (P 792) A-D:2(V) LC IIIA. *Pls. 53, 55.* Like B 439. C: lt. gray-green wfs, well cleaned. P: firm m. brown to dk. gray. Bands at rim below handles and halfway down, int. and ext.; int. double bands. PD: 10. **B 441** (P 934; 49-12-40) T.3:19(B) LC IIIA. *Pl. 21.* N-c-m. C: g. lt. gray-green to pink wfs, well smoothed. P: m. firm gray-brown, olive-green where thin. Int. center: c-s. 3 c-c and broad band resp. ⅓ and ⅔ of way up; paint on rim, tops of handles, below carination and above base. H: 5.5. D: 16.3. **B 442** (P 935; 49-12-43) T.3:22(B) LC IIIA. *Pl. 21.* N-c. Roll rim. C: lt. gray-green with orange patches. P: m. orange-brown. Dec: like B 441. H: 5.5. D: 17. **B 443** (P 936; 49-12-24) T.3:3(B) LC IIIA. N-c-m. Metallic-like base ring. C: mottled gray to brown, coarse. P: m. gray-brown. Large discoloration on int. from burning (?) Int. center: c-s with solid dot at center. Ring under carination int. and halfway down ext. Paint on rim. H: 5.3. D: 16.3. **B 444** (P 937; 49-12-25) T.3:4(B) LC IIIA. N-c-m. Rather shallow; carination not pronounced. C: orange-brown to gray-green. P: like B 443. Dec: like B 441 but no ring above base ext. H: 4.6. D: 16.8. **B 445** (P 938:K 29; 49-12-26) T.3:5(B) LC IIIA. *Pl. 21.* C-i. Signs of burning on rim. Sturdy double roll base. C: g. lt. brown to pinkish brown. P: firm sl. ls. red-brown. Dec: like B 444. H: 5.5. D: 15.5. *AJA* 64 (1960) Pl. 35. **B 446** (P 939; 49-12-42) T.3:21(B) LC IIIA. N-c. One handle missing. "Omphalos" at center. C: orange-brown. P: m. orange-brown. Dec: like B 441. H: 5.1. D: 15.8. **B 447** (P 940; 49-12-44) T.3:23(B) LC IIIA. N-c-m. C,P: like B 446 but clay coarser; paint much worn. Dec: like B 444. H: 5.5. D: 16.5. **B 448** (P 941; 49-12-29) T.3:8(B) LC IIIA. N-c-m. C: gray at core to red-brown. P: like B 443, badly worn; int. surface eroded. Dec: like B 443 but int. center has c-s, with 2 bands ⅔ up. H: 4.7. D: 14.7. **B 449** (P 942; 49-12-34) T.3:13(B) LC IIIA. *Pl. 21.* C-i. Base ring. C: lt. gray-brown to red-brown. P: like

B 443 with drip spot on center design. Dec: like B 448. H: 5. D: 14. **B 450** (P 943; 49-12-35) T.3:14(B) LC IIIA. Complete but warped and cracked. C,P and dec.: like B 449. H: 5.1. D: 15. **B 451** (P 944; 49-12-36) T.3:15(B) LC IIIA. C-i. Shows soil discoloration. C: gray-green wfds. P: m. gray-lavender. Dec: like B 441 but 2 bands instead of 3 around spiral. H: 5.4. D: 15.5. **B 452** (P 945; 49-12-45) T.3:24(B) LC IIIA. *Pls. 21, 44, 55.* C-i. Very squat and shallow. C: g. gray with sand; pitted surface. P: like B 443 with m. red-brown patches. Int. center: c-s. 2 n. bands below rim. Paint on rim. H: 4.2. D: 17.5. **B 453** (P 974) T.17:17. *Pls. 44, 52, 64.* Much of rim and part of wall missing. Roll base. C: g. brown. P: firm m. gray-brown. Int. center: c-s. D-o in central zone: 4 triangular net patches of small dotted semi-circles (cf. *MP*, 343, Fig. 57, Mot. 42). These alternate with a palm motif (or cuttlefish?) in a variation not represented in *MP*. For further remarks, see p. 50. Paint on rim, handles, with a band halfway down ext. H: 6. D: 15.5. *UPMB* 8 (1940) Pl. IV:c. **B 454** (P 978) T.17:21 LC IIIA. *Pls. 44, 55.* About ⅔ pres. C: orange-brown wfs. C: m. brick-red to dk. yellowish gray. Int. center: c-s. Band ⅓ up int. and ext. Paint on rim and base. H: 6.7. D: 15. **B 455** (P 979) T.17:22. N-c-m. C: lt. yellowish gray with small lt. grits. P: lt. m. purple-brown. Int. surface badly worn. Dec: like B 454 but band ⅔ up ext. H: 7.1. D: 15.8. **B 456** (P 980) T.17:23. Less than half (but including profile) pres. C: brown, well smoothed. P: m. sienna to dk. gray. Dec: like B 454 plus wide ring ⅔ up int. H: 6.6. D: 17. **B 457** (P 981) T.17:24. N-c-m. C: lt. orange-buff with greenish patches on surface wfs; well smoothed. P: ls. mahogany. Superior fabric, imitating Mycenaean appearance (cf. B 479). Dec: like B 456. H: 6.2. D: 16. **B 458** (P 999; 49-12-370) T.25:9. *Pl. 44.* N-c-m. Rather shallow with disproportionately high (and flaring) carinated rim. C: orange-brown, sandy. P: firm m. thin pink to reddish. Dec: like B 454 but ext. band is just below rim. H: 4.6. D: 15.4. **B 459** (P 1302) T.33:29(B) LC IIIA. *Pls. 44, 61.* I-m. C: lt. brick-red wfs. P: m. firm red-brown. Dec: like B 455 but base unpainted. H: 4.9. D: 15. **B 460** (P 1303) T.33:30(B) LC IIIA. *Pls. 44, 61.* N-c-m. Sl. convex sides. "Omphalos" at int. center. C: like B 459 with a lt. brown and a greenish patch. P: like B 459. Int. center: c-s. 2 bands ⅔ way up int. 2 n. bands halfway down ext. Rim painted. H: 5.2. D: 15.9. **B 461** (P 1343) T.16:11. C-m. C: firm dk. red-brown wfs, rough surface. P: m. purple-brown. Dec: like B 460. H: 4.8. D: 14.7. **B 462** (P 1344) T.16:29. I-m. C: like B 461. P: firm m. dk. gray. Dec: like B 461. H: 5.4. D: 15.4. **B 463** (P 1345) T.16:30. N-c-m. C,P and dec: like B 462. H: 5. D: 16.7. **B 464** (P 1346) T.16:31. *Pl. 44.* I-m. C: lt. brown, sandy; surface pitted. P: m. gray. Int. center: t-o c-s. Another band just under rim, int. and ext. Rim painted. H: 5.1. D: 15. **B 465** (P 1347) T.16:32. I-m. Much of rim missing. C,P and dec: like B 462. H: 5.8. D: 15.9. **B 466** (P 1348) T.16:33. Base and adjoining frag. of wall giving complete profile. C,P: like B 462. Int. center: c-s. Thick band ¾ way up; paint on rim; band ⅔ way down ext. H: 5.4. PD: 11. **B 467** (P 1349) T.16:43. N-c-m. C,P and dec: like B 462. H: 5.4. D: 16. **B 468** (P 1350) T.16:44. *Pl. 44.* I-m. Handles missing. Base ring, rather tall, convex walls. C: lt. orange-brown to gray-green wfs; well smoothed. P: firm m. pink to gray-green. Int. center: c-s. Band halfway up int. and ext. Paint on rim and base. H: 6.5. D: 15.5. **B 469** (P 1404; 49-12-282) T.19:10(F) LC IIIB. *Pl. 21.* N-c-m. Shape like B 468, sl. warped. C: g. lt. orange-brown, wet-smoothed. P: m. red-brown to dk. gray-brown. Int. center: c-s. 4 narrow bands with spiral tendency ⅓ and one broad band ⅔ way up int. (latter with corresponding band ext.). Paint on rim. H: 6.1. D: 16.5. **B 470** (P 1410; 49-12-291) T.19:19(D) LC IIIA. N-c. C: g. brick-red with m. gray-green patch. P: m. brick-red. Int. center: d-o c-s. Paint on rim and halfway down ext. H: 5.8. D: 16.4. **B 471** (P 2658; 49-12-242) T.18:7(B) LC IIIA. C-i. C: like B 468. P: firm m. orange to red-brown. Dec: like B 470 but t-o c-s with ext. band repeated int. H: 5.8. D: 16.3. **B 472** (P 2659; 49-12-243) T.18:8(B) LC IIIA. C-ch. Roll base. C: g. gray-brown, sandy; very coarse. P: m. dk. pink, much worn. Int. center: c-s. 2 rings halfway up. Paint on rim, handles; band just below rim ext. H: 6.3. D: 16.3. **B 473** (P 2675; 49-12-354) T.23:1 LC IIIA. C-m. C: like P 472. Signs of burning in several places. P: m. red-brown, worn. Int. center: c-s. 3 rings ⅓ way up and stripe ⅔ way up, int. and ext. Paint on rim, handles and base. H: 6.2. D: 15.5. **B 474** (P 2691; 49-12-408) T.32:4 LC IIIA. *Pl. 21.* About ⅓ (mostly rim section) missing. C: g. grayish purple to gray-green. P: m. purple-brown. Int. center: c-s. 2 rings about ⅔ way up (ext. one band). Paint on rim. H: 5.9. ED: 15. **B 475** (P 2694; 49-12-411) T.32:7 LC IIIA. C-ch. C,P and dec: like B 474. H: 5.6. D: 15. **B 476** (P 2791; 49-12-371) T.25:10. About half pres. including profile. C: lt. gray-buff to gray-green wfds, well smoothed. P: thin m. olive-gray. Dec: like B 473 but ext. band halfway down. H: 6.6. ED: 16. **B 477** (P 1304) T.33:20(B) LC IIIA. *Pl. 44.* C-m. Ring base. C: lt. brick-red to lt. gray-green at surface wfs; poorly smoothed. P: m. thin firm gray. Int. center: c-s plus 3 n. bands and one broad band. Paint on rim and below handles ext. H: 5.3. D: 15.5. **B 478** (P 2818) D-A. I-m. Handles missing. Convex walls. C: g. brown. P: like B 474. Int. center: s-o c-s. Stripe halfway up int. and ext. Rim, base painted. H: 6. D: 15. **B 479** (P 2846; 54-41-55) MPT-C:2. *Pl. 53.* Frag. of floor and non-joining rim frag. with handle. C: powdery pinkish brown, well cleaned, soft. P: like B 477. Superior fabric imitating Mycenaean appearance (cf. B 457). Int: stripe near base and about halfway up; rim painted. PW: 7. PD: 13.7. **B 480** (P 2849) E-D:1d LC IIIA. N-c-m. Base ring. Sl. concave walls. C: g. gray-brown, coarse. P: like B 474. Dec: like B 474 but single stripe int. and paint on base. H: 5.1. D: 14.4. **B 481** (P 2881) T.40:71(C) LC IIIA. *Pl. 58.* N-c-m. Sl. convex walls, signs of burning on rim. C: g. lt. orange-brown. P: m. red-brown to purple-brown. Dec: like B 472 plus outline for c-s and stripe on base. H: 6.6. D: 16.3. **B 482** (P 2882) T.40:46(C) LC IIIA. *Pl. 58.* N-c-m. One handle missing. Sl. convex walls. Signs of burning on rim. C: g. lt. orange-brown to gray-green, coarse. P: like B 474. Int. center: c-s. Stripe halfway up, int. and ext. Top of handle and rim painted. H: 6.8. D: 15.5. **B 483** (P 2884) T.40:4(D) LC IIIA. *Pls. 55, 58.* N-c-m. One handle missing. Base ring somewhat shallow. C: lt. g. gray-brown. P: m. lt. orange to dk. gray-brown. Int. center: c-s. Ring ⅔ way up int. and ext. Paint on rim and handle. H: 6. D: 18.6. **B 484** (P 2885) T.40:44(C) LC IIIA. *Pl. 58.* N-c-m. One handle missing. Sl. concave walls. C: g. lt. reddish brown. P: m. lt. orange, faded. Dec: like B 472 but ext. stripe ⅔ way down and base painted. H: 5. D: 20. **B 485** (P 2886) T.40:45(C) LC IIIA. *Pl. 58.* I-m. Signs of burning over half of bowl ext. C,P: like B 484. Dec: like B 484 plus paint on base. H: 5.6. D: 15.8. **B 486** (P 2887) T.40:50(C) LC IIIA. *Pls. 52, 58.* C-m. Base ring. C: g. dk. gray-green. P: m. dk. gray-purple. Dec: like B 476 but 2 instead of 3 rings int. H: 7. D: 16.7. **B 487** (P 2888) T.40:49(C) LC IIIA. *Pls. 21, 58.* I-m. C: lt. gray-green, almost olive, well cleaned. P: m. dk. gray-brown. Superior fabric. Int. center: outlined (hand-drawn) c-s. Ring halfway up int. and ext. Paint on rim and handles. H: 5. D: 15.5. **B 488** (P 2890) T.40:28(D) LC IIIA. *Pl. 58.* C-i. C: g. lt. reddish brown. P: m. orange-brown, worn. Int. center: c-s(?) with 2 rings ⅔ way up. One ring ext. Paint on handles and rim. H: 6. D: 16.3. **B 489** (P 2891) T.40:26(D) LC IIIA. *Pl. 58.* C-i. Roll base and convex walls. C: lt. g. gray-green. P: m. lt. purple-gray, streaky. Int. center: c-s. One ring about halfway up; ext. one ring about ⅓ way down. Paint on rim. H: 5.3. D: 15.7.

Miscellaneous fragments of Type 3: **B 490** (Sh 87) A-E:4 LC IIIB. *Pl. 20.* C: lt. pink to lt. greenish yellow at surface. P: m. orange-brown. W: 3.7. L: 3.6. **B 491** (Sh 111) A-G LC IIIB. Rim frag. C: hard dk. cinnamon-brown. Signs of burning. P: m. dk. orange-brown. W: 2.3. L: 3.3. **B 492** (Sh 153) A-D:2(V) LC IIIA. Frag. of wall and rim. C: lt. brown to gray-green with lime grits. P: m. thin brown. Wide band int. and ext. about halfway down. W: 7.2. PD: 13. **B 493** (Sh 288) A-D:1(IV,1) LC IIC. Wall fragment. C: g. brick-red to gray-green. P: m. purple to dk. gray. Band int. and ext. L: 4.2. **B 494** (Sh 290) A-D:1(IV.1) LC IIC. Frag. of wall just below carination. C: hard compact lt. brick-red to gray-pink with fine lime particles. Superior fabric. P: m. dk. gray. Bands int. and ext. L: 3. **B 495** (Sh 317) A-D:3(VII) LC IIIA. Rim frag. C: lt. orange-buff, soft and well cleaned. P: m. red-brown. Superior fabric. W: 5. L: 2.8. **B 496** (Sh 676) D-A. (Ring) base frag. (bowl type not certain). C: g. gray-green, hard. P: m. purple-brown. Int. center: c-s outlined(?) H: 1.6. D (of base): 5.2.

Type 4: very low, usually also small ring base with wide spreading floor, nearly straight or slightly convex sides. One uplifted horizontal round handle, usually(?) provided with a spur to suggest the wishbone type. A variation to this in the form of a lug handle occurs in B 500. This shape is pre-eminently suited to panel-style decoration and very often has it. It was often executed in a superior technique, probably as a luxury ware. **B 497** (P 746) A-D:2(VI) LC IIIA. *Pls. 21, 44, 55, 64.* I-m, restored. Spurred handle. C: gray at core to brown; lt. brick-red at surface, with sand and lime. P: m. black. Frieze on rim with motifs at irregular intervals. Left to right from handle: (1) triangle; (2) 2 parallel rows of vert. chevrons; (3) dotted(?) triangles; (4) crosshatch; (5) palm tree(?) with dotted trunk; (6) solid triangle; (7) chevrons (as No. 2); (8) dotted triangle; (9) 2 rows of vert. crisscross; (10) solid triangle. Under handle, 4 vert. lines. Handle dotted front, solid back. Stripe on inside of rim. H: 8. D: 15.8. *AJA 42* (1938) 268, Fig. 6. **B 498** (P 788) A-E:2(St.2a) LC IIIB. *Pls. 53, 55.* Base and body frag. giving profile. C: g. lt. gray-green. P: firm m. gray-green. Int. center: c-s. Bands below handle and on base ext. L: 11.4. **B 499** (P 952; 49-12-23) T.3:2(B) LC IIIA. *Pls. 21, 44, 55.* I-m. According to an old photograph, handle seems to have had spur. Base wider than B 497. C: brick-red wfs and some lime grits. P: m. dk. gray. Ext: band at rim, 4 n. bands below handle, c-s on base. Dashes on handle. H: 7.4. D: 17.1. **B 500** (P 1305) T.33:21(B) LC IIIA. *Pls. 44, 61.* C-m. Very low ring base; unpierced hor. lug handle. C: yellow-brown wfs. P: thin m. pinkish brown. Int: broad and n. bands. H: 4.6. D: 15.9. **B 501** (P 1306) T.33:23(B) LC IIIA. *Pls. 44, 55, 61, 64.* N-c-m. According to catalogue description, handle (now missing) once had spur. C: red-brown to gray-brown wfs. P: firm m. gray-brown. 4 t-o panels with (a) hor. zigzag; (b) vert. chevrons-dots; (c) circles (honeycomb?); (d) dotted vert. w. lines. Hor. band under panels. On bottom (ext.): c-s. H: 5.3. D: 15.3. **B 502** (P 1307) T.33:22(B) LC IIIA. *Pls. 44, 61, 64.* I-m. Handle missing. C,P: like B 499. 4 t-o panels with (a) hor. zigzags; (b) vert. chevrons-dots; (c) 2 free-standing d-o and t-o lozenges; (d) hor. zigzags. Hor. band under panels. On bottom, ext: c-s. H: 6.6. D: 18. **B 503** (P 1359) T.16:41. *Pls. 21, 45, 55, 64.* I-m. C: g. orange-brown wfs. P: like B 499. 4 t-o panels with (a) chevrons; (b) chevrons and dots; (c) central panel missing; (d) zigzags. Panels vary in size. No hor. border under panels; base plain. Handle barred. H: 6. D: 15.4. **B 504** (P 1360) T.16:42. *Pl. 45.* I-m. Much of wall and most of rim missing. Stumps of handle pres. Very small ring base. C: like B 503. P: m. red-brown. Dec: like B 499. H: 5.9. D: 18.8.

Miscellaneous fragments of Type 4 (including a selection of unstratifed sherds): **B 505** (Sh 67) A-E:2(St.2a) etc. LC IIIB. *Pls. 20, 64.* Frags. of rim and wall. See B 512. C: lt. brown to lt. buff at surface wfs. P: m. dk. brown. Superior fabric. Quadruple outlined panels with hor. zigzag and with outlined lozenge which has a dot in the center. H (of larger frag.): 4.4. L: 3.6. **B 506** (Sh 165) A-E:3(V) LC IIIB. *Pls. 20, 64.* Wall frag. C: like B 494 but gray-buff at surface. P: like B 494. Superior fabric. Bands int. and ext. and rough zigzag(?). L: 3.4. **B 507** (Sh 257) A-surface. Frag. of handle with spur broken off. C: lt. gray-green wfs. P: m. dk. gray. Dashes. D: 0.7. L: 5.7. **B 508** (Sh 311) A-D:2(VII,2) LC IIIA. *Pl. 20.* Handle with spur. C: lt. gray-brown wfs. P: m. dk. gray. Dashes. D: 1. L (incl. spur): 6. **B 509** (Sh 341) A-Unstrat. *Pl. 65.* Frags. of wall and rim. C: lt. brown to pinkish buff; hard, well smoothed. P: firm m. brick-red. Superior fabric. Vert. outlined panel with zigzags. L (of largest frag.): 5.4. **B 510** (Sh 344) A-surface. *Pls. 20, 65.* Frag. of wall and floor. C: lt. gray-brown to gray-green wfs. P: m. dk. gray to brown. Vert. outlined panel with dots. Lowest band appears to be red paint, suggesting the influence of Proto-White Painted ware. L: 2.8. **B 511** (Sh 449) Cw Vb CA I. *Pls. 20, 65.* Frag. of wall. C: lt. gray-green wfs, powdery but well smoothed. P: m. rust-colored. Dec: like B 509. H: 2.3. W: 2.4. **B 512** (Sh 464) A-D:2(IV) LC IIIA. Frag. of wall apparently from same pot as B 505. Lozenge(?) L: 1.8. **B 513** (Sh 493) A-D:2(VII,1) LC IIIA. *Pls. 20, 64.* Frag. of floor. C: lt. brownish buff, powdery; wet-smoothed. P: very sl. ls. lt. brown to dk. gray. Superior fabric. Bands int. and ext. Lat-loz. int. and possibly ext. L: 3.5. **B 514** (Sh 526) A-D:2(St.2b) LC IIIA. *Pl. 64.* Frag. of rim. C: like B 508. P: m. dk. olive-brown. Quadruple outlined panel; motif indeterminable: outlined dots? L: 2.4. **B 515** (Sh 531) A-D:2(St.2b) and Cw IV LC IIIA. *Pls. 20, 64.* Various frags. from floor and wall. C: lt. greenish-buff wfs, wet-smoothed. P: m. orange-brown to gray-brown. Superior fabric. Large zigzag on floor ext. Rings at base of wall; panels(?). W (of largest frag.): 4.4. L: 3.7. **B 516** (Sh 553) Cw IIIa LC IIIA. *Pls. 20, 64.* Rim frag. C: lt. orange-brown to gray-green wfs. P: like B 514. Quadruple outlined panel with vert. zigzag and chevrons(?). H: 3.6. **B 517** (Sh 556) E-D:2f LC IIIA. *Pl. 64.* Rim frag. C: lt. orange-brown to gray-buff wfs. P: m. lt. red-brown. Panel of opposed semi-circles? H: 1.9. L: 3.2. **B 518** (Sh 557) E-9 LC IIIA. Rim frag. *Pls. 20, 64.* C: lt. orange-brown wfs. P: like B 517. Outlined lozenges with solid core. H: 3.1. L: 5.5. **B 519** (Sh 584) A-Unstrat. *Pls. 20, 45, 65.* About half pres. giving profile. Very small ring base (cf. B 504). Stump of small handle pres. C: lt. gray-buff to buff at surface wfds; wet-smoothed and bur(?). P: firm orange-brown. Superior fabric. Paint on rim; 4 bands where wall meets floor. Underside of base: c-s. Base of handle outlined with sea anemone under handle; cf. B 1178. H: 6. ED: 18. **B 520** (Sh 560) E-Unstrat. *Pls. 20, 65.* Rim frag. C: gray, well cleaned; very hard. P: firm m. gray-violet. Harder and technically better than others of this class. Vert. w. lines. H: 2.4. D: 2. **B 521** (Sh 729) Cw IIIa LC IIIB. Frag. of wall and floor. C,P: virtually identical with B 519. Superior fabric. 4 n. rings where floor meets wall ext. PH: 4.5. PL: 5.8. **B 522** (Sh 730) A-D:2(St.2b) LC IIIA. *Pls. 20, 64.* Rim frag. C: g. gray-brown to gray-green. P: m. purple-brown. Quadruple outlined vert. panel with a rudimentary running spiral design. Cf. *MP* 357 No. 58. H: 2.7. W: 3.7.

Type 5: handleless bowl; ring base or base ring; concave sides; thickened and flattened rim. **B 523** (P 976) T.17:19. *Pl. 21.* I-m. Low base ring. C: gray to brown at surface, sandy. P: m. red. Int. center: c-s. Ring halfway down ext.; paint on base. H: 6.7. D: 17.2. **B 524** (P 977) T.17:20. *Pl. 21.* I-m. Low ring base. C: gray-brown to gray-green. P: gray-lavender to gray-brown. Dec: like B 523 plus paint on rim. H: 6.2. D: 18. **B 525** (P 1429) D-A. *Pl. 21.* I-m. Low ring base. C: lt. yellow-brown wfs, soft. P: m. pinkish brown. Int. center: circle. Wide stripe halfway up int. and ext. Paint on rim. H: 4.8. D: 13.5.

Type 6: handleless bowl; flat, slightly recessed base, with sometimes a corresponding omphalos on the interior floor; deep bowl with rather flat floor and concave flaring sides; plain rim. **B 526** (P 727) A-D:2(VII,2) LC IIIA. *Pls. 45, 55.* About ⅓ pres. with profile. C: orange-brown, sandy. P: m. red-brown. Band halfway down and 3 near center int. H: 5. ED: 13. **B 527** (P 730) A-G LC IIIB. *Pls. 45, 55.* Less than half pres. with profile. Omphalos. C: m. gray-green, sandy. P: firm m. dk. gray-green. Int. center: c-s. Bands halfway up int. and ext. Paint on rim. H: 4.8. ED: 13. **B 528** (P 950; 49-12-27) T.3:6(B) LC IIIA. *Pls. 21, 55.* N-c. Int. eroded. Discoloration on underside of base, possibly from burning. C: gray-brown wfs. P: m. olive-brown to dk. gray-brown. Dec: like B 527 but no c-s. H: 5.2. D: 13.5. **B 529** (P 951; 49-12-28) T.3:7(B) LC IIIA. N-c-m. C: like B 528. P: m. lavender-brown. Dec: like B 527, with drip mark on rim. H: 5.2. D: 13.1. **B 530** (P 998; 49-12-369) T.25:8. *Pls. 21, 45.* About ⅛ missing. C: like B 528. P: m. gray-green to walnut brown. All dark with res. band halfway up int. and ext. Base and center floor also res. Cf. dec. of Mycenaean Type 3 bowl. H: 5.5. D: 12.5. For shape and type, cf. *Nouveaux Documents*, 159, No. 15. **B 531** (P 1403; 49-12-281) T.19:9(F) LC IIIB. *Pls. 21, 55.* C-ch. C: brown wfs. P: m. gray-brown. Paint on rim; band about ⅛ way down int. and ext. H: 6. D: 12.9. **B 532** (P 1405; 49-12-283) T.19:11(E) LC IIIA. *Pl. 21.* I-m. C: gray-brown to pink wfds. P: m. orange to dk. brown. Dec: like B 531 plus c-s at int. center. H: 6.5. D: 14.8. **B 533** (P 2635; 49-12-51) T.5:1 LC IIIA. *Pl. 21.* C-ch. Has a small hole in base. C: g. dk. gray-brown, rough surface. P: m. purple-brown. Paint on rim; 2 rings (int? and ext.) where floor meets wall. C-s int.(?) H: 8.5. D: 18.4. **B 534** (P 2654; 49-12-237) T.18:2(B) LC IIIA. C-ch. Sprung near rim. C: g. lt. gray-green; surface of base very rough. P: m. lavender-gray. Dec: like B 533, plus c-s and ring ⅔ way up int. Large blob of paint on floor. H: 6.2. D: 14.1. **B 535** (P 2707) E-11c LC IIIA. *Pl. 45.* About ⅛ pres. with profile. C: g. gray to lt. brown, coarse. P: m. purple. Dec: like B 533 but only one (wide) stripe int. H: 6. ED: 14. **B 536** (P 2893) T.40:18(D) LC IIIA. *Pls. 21, 58.* N-c-m. Omphalos. C: g. lt. gray-brown. P: like B 533. Int. center: very large c-s. A ring just below rim; paint on rim; 2 stripes about midway ext. H: 5.4. D: 14.2. **B 537** (P 2894) T.40:20(D) LC IIIA. *Pl. 58.* C-ch. C: g. lt. brownish buff to pink and gray-green, surface pocked. P: m. orange-brown. Int. center: t-o c-s. 2 rings halfway up int. and one stripe below midway ext. Paint on rim. H: 6.3. D: 14. **B 538** (P 2895) T.40:56(C) LC IIIA. *Pl. 58.* C-m. Almost hemispherical. C: neutral brown to brown-buff, well cleaned and smoothed. P: m. gray-brown to purple-brown. Dec: like B 537 but only one ring int. and stripe near base ext. H: 5.7. D: 12.5.

B 539 (P 2896) T.40:51(C) LC IIIA. *Pls. 21, 55, 58.* C-i. C: g. buff to pinkish lt. green; well smoothed; int. perhaps has self slip. P: m. orange-brown to red-brown. Superior fabric. Dec: like B 537 but s-o c-s. H: 6.3. D: 14. **B 540** (P 2897) T.40:25(D) LC IIIA. *Pls. 21, 58.* C-sp. C: g. reddish brown to dk. gray-brown, coarse. P: like B 533. Dec: like B 537 but d-o c-s and 2 rings halfway down ext. H: 5.3. D: 11.5. **B 541** (P 2898) T.40:23(D) LC IIIA. *Pl. 58.* C-i. C: lt. brown-buff to pink, very well cleaned. P: m. orange-brown to dk. brown. Dec: like B 540 but 2 rings under rim ext. H: 5.8. D: 12.5. **B 542** (P 2899) T.40:40(C) LC IIIA. *Pl. 58.* C-i. C: lt. gray-green, well cleaned and smooth. P: m. lt. to dk. brown. Int. center: d-o c-s. Wide stripe about halfway up int. and ext. H: 5.8. D: 11.9.

Miscellaneous fragments of Type 6: **B 543** (Sh 141) A-E:4 LC IIIB. *Pl. 20.* Rim frag. See B 544. C: lt. gray-brown; sandy, hard. P: m. gray-brown. Bands int. and ext. H: 3.3. **B 544** (Sh 215) A-E:3(V) LC IIIB. *Pl. 20.* Wall frag. Apparently from same pot as B 543. H: 3.8. W: 3.7. **B 545** (Sh 314) A-D:2(VII,2) LC IIIA. *Pl. 20.* Rim frag. C,P: like B 543, paint partly very thin and underfired(?) Band on and below rim int. and ext. H: 3.4. L: 3.5. **B 546** (Sh 384) A-F:1 LC IIIB. *Pl. 20.* Rim frag. C: like B 545. P: m. dk. gray. Paint on rim. H: 2.9. **B 547** (Sh 386) A-E:3(VIII) LC IIIB. *Pl. 20.* Base frag. C,P: like B 543. Apparently had c-s at int. center. L: 3.5. **B 548** (Sh 387) A-E:3(VIII) LC IIIA. *Pl. 20.* Rim frag. possibly from same pot as B 547. Bands continuous ext.; 3 bands below rim int. H: 3. **B 549** (Sh 469) Cw IIIa LC IIIA. Rim and wall frag. C: gray-green to yellow-green wfs. P: m. dk. lavender. Band int. well toward center. H: 5.1. PD: 6.2. **B 550** (Sh 492) A-D:2(VII,1) LC IIC. Rim frag. C: lt. orange-buff to creamy green; well cleaned and smoothed. P: m. dk. orange to dk. gray, crackled. H: 4.2. W: 3.8.

Type 7: handleless bowl; plain flat wide base with straight, slightly flaring sides and plain rim. The decoration—unless otherwise noted—consists of a closed spiral covering the interior floor and closely spaced parallel horizontal bands over the interior and exterior walls. **B 551** (P 728) A-D:2(VII,2) LC IIIA. *Pl. 45.* About ⅓ pres. with profile. C: brown wfs. P: m. gray to rust. H: 3. D: 9.5. **B 552** (P 757) A-E:2(V) LC IIIB. Most of base and part of side pres.; burnt. C: like B 551; very coarse. P: m. dk. brown. H: 4.2. ED: 10.4. **B 553** (P 758) A-D:2(IV) LC IIIA. *Pls. 21, 55.* I-m. C: lt. orange-brown to gray-green, sandy and fairly soft. P: m. brown to red. H: 3.4. ED: 11. **B 554** (P 816) Cw IIIa LC IIIA. Most of base and frags. of side. C: like B 552. P: m. gray-brown. H: 3.8. ED: 11. **B 555** (P 953; 49-12-41) T.3:20(B) LC IIIA. *Pls. 21, 55.* C-m. Int. eroded. Underside of base discolored from burning(?) C: lt. brown, soft. P: m. olive-brown to reddish brown. H: 3.1. D: 9.8. **B 556** (P 1406; 49-12-284) T.19:12(E) LC IIIA. *Pl. 21.* C-i. Signs of burning, int. C: gray-brown, sandy. P: m. rust-brown. H: 2.9. D: 9.2. **B 557** (P 2900) T.40:29(D) LC IIIA. *Pl. 58.* C-i. C: like B 556; well cleaned. P: m. orange-red. H: 3.8.

D: 10.4. **B 558** (Sh 133) A-E:3(V) LC IIIB. Frag. of base and wall. C: lt. pinkish brown to gray-green with fine lime particles. P: m. firm orange. H: 3.4. PD: 7.8. **B 559** (Sh 134) A-E:3(V) LC IIIB. *Pl. 23.* Most of base. C: lt. gray-brown wfds. P: m. lt. pinkish brown to dk. gray. Crackled. PD: 7.9. **B 560** (Sh 137) A-D:2(V) LC IIIA. Rim frag. Sl. flaring rim. C: lt. powdery gray to pink-brown. P: m. orange-brown. H: 3.4. **B 561** (Sh 140) A-E:4 LC IIIB. *Pl. 20.* Wall frags. C: red-brown, soft. P: m. dk. gray. Panel zone suggested by groups of 4 vert. bands; hor. bands below this. H (of larger frag.): 3.2. **B 562** (Sh 276) A-D:3(IV) LC IIIA. *Pls. 20, 65.* Wall frags. C,P: like B 558. Large crosshatch pattern ext. H: 2.8. PD: 5.2. **B 563** (Sh 280) A-D:3(IV) LC IIIA. Frag. of base and wall. Signs of burning. C: lt. pea-green, sandy. P: m. purple-brown. H: 2.8. PH: 7.2. **B 564** (Sh 542) A-Unstrat. Frag. of base and wall. C,P, dec: like B 562. H: 3.3. W: 2.9.

Miscellaneous bowl shapes: **B 565** (P 975) T.17:18. *Pl. 45.* N-c-m. LC III Plain Ware Type 3 bowl completely covered with paint: cf. B 608. C: lt. gray-brown wfs. P: sl. ls. brick-red to dk. gray. H: 8.5. D: 17. **B 566** (Sh 214) A-E:3(V) LC IIIA. *Pl. 20.* Rim frag. of bowl with wide vert. ribbon handle which is crudely attached. C: sandy lt. gray-brown. P: m. orange to dk. red-brown. Two vert. stripes on handle. H: 4. L: 5. **B 567** (Sh 731) A-D:2(VII,1) LC IIIA. *Pl. 20.* Considerable frag. of rim mended from sherds. Thin curving wall, incurving sl. at rim. The gentle gradient of the curve sets this off from all known bowl types. C: g. lt. gray-brown to gray-green. P: m. purple-brown to dk. gray. Band int. and ext. below rim, which is also painted. PH: 5.2. PD: 12.8. **B 568** (Sh 759) A-D:3(VIa) LC IIIB. *Pl. 20.* Stump of handle with adjoining frag. of rim. This is definitely a local imitation of Bamboula Type 2 Mycenaean bowl. C: g. gray-brown to gray-green at surface. P: m. black, peeling. Rim painted; handle with stripes(?) H: 3.5. W: 3.

Krater: unfortunately no complete representative of this shape was found. It has antecedents, of course, in the Mycenaean repertory and even in the Syro-Palestinian "Painted Wheel-made Ware" (*Problems*, 63, Type 1a). Indeed, it is apparent from a comparison of descriptions that B 570–B 572 have a not distant relationship to this latter ware. There is no reason, however, to separate them from the main body of LC III Decorated Ware of which they comprise a somewhat coarse variation. On the other hand, B 569 which, on the basis of technique, seems to belong also in this category, differs strongly on the point of decoration and suggests influence from the Syro-Palestinian quarter. Its very fragmentary condition makes impossible a detailed comparison in shape with B 1003 (*q.v.*) which I have taken to be actually an import to Cyprus. The similarity of decoration of B 569 and B 1003 can be explained if Cypriote potters occasionally copied an import from the Syro-Palestinian littoral.

B 569 (P 787) A-D:2(VII,2) LC IIIA. *Pls. 23, 65.* In addition to the frags. in the illustration, various non-joining frags. including Sh 530 were found in the topsoil. Stumps exist apparently for 3(?) raised hor. roll handles. C: g. gray at core to dull brown. P: dk. m. brown. Barred bands, zigzag panels. Dotted semicircle design in common with B 1003. L (of largest frag.): 8. W: 7. Cf. E. MacDonald, J. Starkey, L. Harding *Beth-Pelet* II, (London, 1932) Pl. LXIV:372. **B 570** (Sh 477) A-Unstrat., but in association with a sherd of Ware VII. *Pl. 23*. Large shoulder frag. with stump of handle. C: g. dk. red-brown to gray-brown. P: m. dk. brown. Band at neck and above handle apparently defining shoulder metopes. H: 11.8. W: 11. **B 571** (Sh 515) C-Unstrat. Frag. from lower part of body. C: lt. g. gray-brown wfds. P: like B 570. Traces of metope(?) design on belly. H: 12. PD: 18. **B 572** (Sh 756) E-Hearth:F. *Pl. 23*. 2 rim frags. and 2 non-joining handle frags. Broad squared handle to rim which is thickened and flares out; flattened on top. W-m, though rim and handles suggest h-m technique. C: g. lt. gray-buff wfds, hard. P: m. streaky orange-brown. Paint on rim and 2 vert. stripes on handle. Under rim, pendent inverted triangles(?) filled with lattice design. H (rim frag.): 5.3. W: 5. H (of larger handle frag.): 6.3.

Krater-amphora: a well defined type at Bamboula, with ring base, wide, more or less depressed, ovoid body, wide short neck, overhanging squared rim and handle from shoulder to rim. Again, as in the case of the krater, one finds a general parallel in Syro-Palestinian "Painted Wheel-made Ware" (*Problems*, 63, Type 1b). However, besides being decorated differently, this does not have handles to the rim and is altogether of broader and squatter proportions than the examples encountered at Bamboula. The amphoroid kraters of Cypriote Plain Wheelmade Ware (*Problems*, 56 and 58) likewise differ widely in conception. On the other hand, a very closely related shape with the same type of decoration occurs in Syria in roughly contemporary levels (*Hama*, Pl. XXI:5). B 1004 (*q.v.*) may actually be the imported prototype of which the examples listed below are free adaptations. Cf. also *PEQ*, 1960, 66 n. 3; 69.

B 573 (P 729) A-D:2(VII,2) LC IIIA. *Pls. 45, 55*. One handle and much of neck missing. Base relatively small. C: lt. brown, sandy; rather hard. P: firm m. yellow-brown to gray, much worn. Wide band on rim and base of neck; 2 n. bands below handles and 2 on lower belly. Handles barred. H: 15.2. D: 16.3. **B 574** (P 954; 49-12-22) T.3:1(B) LC IIIA. *Pls. 22, 45, 55*. N-c-m. Relatively small roll-base; handles come down almost to mid-body. C: lt. orange-brown to gray-green wfs. P: firm m. dk. red-brown to brown. Paint on rim, handles, neck-base and base; 3 bands on body below handles. H: 13.2. D: 13. **B 575** (P 985) E-D:1f LC IIIA. *Pl. 52*. I-m. Partly rotted. Handles, most of neck and much of body missing. Base relatively small. C: gray-brown with chaff temper and fine sand, fairly well smoothed. P: thin firm m. red-brown to gray-brown, badly worn. Paint on rim, neck-base and base; 2 bands on lower belly. H: 17. D: 16.6.

Miscellaneous fragments apparently from kraters or krater-amphoras: **B 576** (Sh 495) A-D:2(VII,1) LC IIIA. *Pl. 23*. Wall frag. C: g. orange-brown to brown-

ish buff at surface wfs. P: firm m. dk. red-brown. Belly(?) bands: legs of animal(?) in frieze (or panel). L (diagonal): 7.5. **B 577** (Sh 522) B-D:2 LC IIIA. *Pl. 23*. Shoulder frag. C: g. dull gray-green with lime particles; poorly smoothed, coarse fabric. P: thin m. lavender-gray. Part of metope(?) with rough cross-hatch pres. H: 5.5. W: 5.2. **B 578** (Sh 537) Cw IV CA I. *Pls. 23, 65*. Rim frag. Ledge rim with elliptical profile. C: firm g. red-brown, sandy. P: m. dk. brown. Paint on rim. Solid triangles on body. H: 3.1. L: 6. **B 579** (Sh 551) E-D:2f LC IIIA. *Pls. 23, 65*. Rim and body frags. Thickened squared rim. C: lt. orange-brown wfs. P: firm m. dk. orange. Inverted triangles with latticework. H (of rim frag.): 5.2. L: 6.8.

Two-handled pyxides: bichrome local imitations of Mycenaean pyxis, Type *MP* 44, Fig. 12, No. 96 (IIIB-IIIC:1) with pierced raised lug handles.

B 580 (P 1329) T.36:34. *Pl. 45*. N-c-m. One handle missing; surface badly worn. C: firm lt. yellow-brown wfs; wet-smoothed. P: m. chocolate color and dk. gray. Bands of alternating color. H: 5.6. D: 6.9. **B 581** (P 2695; 49-12-423) T.34:5 LC IIC(?). *Pl. 22*. Bottom warped. C: dull buff wfds, well smoothed. P: m. streaky brown and lavender. Bands of alternating color, but shoulder res. Underside: alternating c-c with 3 res. rings, one of which is dotted. H: 6.4. D: 7.3.

Jugs

Type 1a: the Bamboula examples have straight or slightly convex sides in contrast to the concavity of the example shown in *Problems*, 67. **B 582** (P 2870) T.40:68(C) LC IIIA. *Pls. 22, 56, 59*. I-m. Mouth missing. Rectangular handle; sl. concave neck. C: g. gray-brown to gray-green, coarse. P: m. purple-brown. Paint on lip inside with drip marks down neck outside. Thick w. line down handle with thick bow tied around its base. 4 hor. stripes with connecting dashes on spout, the base of which is encircled. Wide stripe around neck-base. 5 fasicules of 2 vert. stripes spaced around body. H: 16.4. D: 11.9. **B 583** (P 2871) T.40:69(C) LC IIIA. *Pls. 22, 59*. I-m. Mouth missing. Large sloping handle; more squat than B 582. C,P: like B 582 plus orange-brown patches on surface. Dec: like B 582 except (a) only 4 fasicules; (b) 5 hor. stripes and no dashes on spout. H: 12.2. D: 9.3.

Type 1b: B 584 and B 587, which are rather smartly drawn up into an ovoid shape and have trim base rings, stand out from the majority of examples of this type which have an elongated spherical or even baggy shape. It is impossible to be certain whether this has a chronological significance in the relative sequence. In any case, it should be noted that only B 596 has the so-called metallic handle which Furumark (*OA* III, 1944, 234) postulated as an LC III feature; in other words, its occurrence at Bamboula is rare. **B 584** (P 931; 49-12-11) T.2:6(B) LC IIIA. *Pls. 22, 56*. N-c-m. Most of mouth missing. C: lt. brown to gray wfs. P: m. olive-brown to gray. Stripe down handle and continuing to base. Ring at base of neck: 8 groups of 2 parallel vert. stripes on body. 3 hor. stripes on spout. H: 15.8. D: 10.6. **B 585** (P 1205) E-D:1h.

Pl. 22. Rim spout and handle missing. Elongated spherical body, neck-ring. C: g. gray-green wfds; surface pocked. P: thin me. gray. Band on neck-ring. Groups of 3 vert. stripes on body. PH: 16.4. D: 10.4. **B 586** (P 1407; 49-12-286) T.19:14(E) LC IIIA. *Pls. 22, 45.* Mouth, spout and base chipped. Wide ovoid body, rectangular handle, neck-ring. C: g. orange-brown wfs. P: firm m. dk. red-brown. Paint on int. and ext. of rim. Stripe at base of neck and around foot. Small loop around base of handle. 4 fasicules of 3 stripes on body. Bars on handle. H: 14.9. D: 11. **B 587** (P 2657; 49-12-241) T.18:6(B) LC IIIA. *Pl. 22.* Mouth and part of neck missing. Elongated oval body. Neck-ring. C: g. gray-green to brown, rather well smoothed. P: firm m. purple-brown. Dec: like B 584 plus paint on rim; w. line down handle and 3 hor. stripes on spout. H: 17.9. D: 10.9. **B 588** (P 2676; 49-12-355) T.23:2 LC IIIA. *Pl. 22.* A great section of lower body, all of mouth and much of handle missing. Baggy, elongated spherical body, ring base. C: g. reddish brown, close-textured. P: m. gray-brown. Dec: like B 587, plus ring around base of handle and spout. Body stripes continued on base. PH: 16.4. D: 11.3. **B 589** (P 2706) E-Unstrat. Restored. Lower portion only pres. Ring foot. C: g. orange-brown. P: m. purple. 4 fasicules of 3 vert. lines on body. PH: 7.5. D (of foot): 5. **B 590** (P 2867) T.40:31(D) LC IIIA. *Pl. 59.* Mouth mostly missing. Full ovoid body, rectangular handle, short spout near neck. C: g. dk. buff to lt. gray-green, sandy. P: like B 587. Dec: like B 588 but base of handle not ringed. H: 16.6. D: 11.4. **B 591** (P 2868) T.40:19(D) LC IIIA. *Pl. 59.* N-c. Mouth and spout chipped. Body like B 588 with neck-ring and rounded lip. C,P: like B 590 but clay coarser and fired pink in patches (identical with PWM II technique). Dec: like B 588 but spout plain. H: 17. D: 11.3. **B 592** (P 2869) T.40:34(D) LC IIIA. *Pls. 22, 59.* C-ch. Nearly spherical body; neck-ring. C: like B 590 but coarser. P: m. streaky chocolate-brown. Dec: like B 590 except (a) handle barred; (b) 4 hor. stripes on spout. H: 15.3. D: 10.5. **B 593** (P 2872) T.40:7(D) LC IIIA. *Pls. 56, 59.* C-ch. Shape identical to *Problems,* 67, Type 1b. C,P: like B 590, but most of surface pinkish brown. Dec: like B 590 except (a) straight line on handle; (b) spout plain. Careless execution. H: 18.2. D: 10.9. **B 594** (P 2873) T.40:3(D) LC IIIA. *Pl. 59.* N-c. Most of mouth and lip of spout missing. Wide disc base barely set off from rather baggy ovoid body. Neck-ring. Rectangular handle, stubby spout. C: g. lt. red-brown to greenish brown. P: like B 587. Dec: like B 590 except (a) w. line on handle continues to base; (b) spout has 5 hor. stripes; (c) base painted solid. Very summary execution. H: 16.9. D: 10.8. **B 595** (P 2874) T.40:10(D) LC IIIA. *Pl. 59.* C-ch. Roll-base. Shape as *Problems,* 67, Type 1b, but squared lip and sl. longer spout. C: g. lt. gray-brown. P: lt. m. orange-brown. Dec: like B 590 except (a) handle barred; (b) base of spout not ringed. H: 17.6. D: 11. **B 596** (P 2875) T.40:21(D) LC IIIA. *Pls. 22, 59.* N-c. Mouth missing and spout chipped. Wide base ring. Squat depressed globular body with rather tall neck. Neck-ring. "Question-mark" handle. C: g.

lt. reddish brown wfds, coarse. P: firm m. reddish brown. Dec: like B 590 except (a) straight vert. line on handle; (b) base of handle and spout not looped. H: 14. D: 10.

Miscellaneous fragments of Type 1b: **B 597** (Sh 374) Cw Vb CA I. Side-spout. C: dk. to lt. gray-brown wfs; hard. P: m. lavender-gray. Faint traces of hor. stripes. L: 4.6. D (at mouth): 1.6. **B 598** (Sh 448) Cw Vb CA I. Frags. of wall with stump of handle. C: reddish brown to gray-green wfs. P: firm m. dk. gray. Fasicules of 3 vert. stripes. PD (of largest frag.): 9. **B 599** (Sh 691) D-A. Frag. of shoulder with neck-ring. C: gray-green, coarse. P: m. thin lavender-gray. Paint on neck ring. 4 vert. stripes in a fasicule on body. H: 5. W: 5. **B 600** (G 12:K 64) Cw VIII Roman context. Frag. of handle to rim, very much worn. C: very lt. gray-green wfds. P: traces of dk. gray paint. Stripe down handle? L: 5.2. D: 1.5. *AJA 64* (1960) Pl. 35.

Type 2a: **B 601** (Sh 230) A-E:4 LC IIIB. *Pl. 23.* Frag. from base of basket-handle. C: pinkish brown to lt. gray-pink at surface. P: m. red-brown. L: 4.7.

Type 3: this is Furumark's Type G (*OA* 3, 1944, 235): ring base, graceful ovoid body, tall, slender, tapering neck to round mouth and squared lip. Rectangular handle from shoulder to rim. Cutaway strainer spout on shoulder at right angles to handle. **B 602** (P 734) A-D:2(VII,2) LC IIIA. *Pls. 22, 56.* Most of body with spout and non-joining rectangular handle pres. C: gray at core to brown; fired gray-green and brick-red wfs; hard. P: m. lavender-brown. Band on rim, neck-base and outlining spout. 2 bands below handle and 2 on lower body. Handle barred; base painted. EH: 26. D: 16.2. **B 603** (P 2866) T.40:1(D) LC IIIA. *Pls. 22, 45, 56, 59, 62, 65.* N-c-m. Part of neck missing. C: g. gray-buff to gray-green wfs; air pocks. P: m. purple-brown. Dec: like B 602 plus in shoulder zone: panels divided by vert. lines. From spout to left: hor. zigzag; chevrons; vert. tangent flattened circles; vert. w. line; solid triangle outlined by dots. Carelessly executed but gives lively effect. H: 23.9. D: 15.6. **B 604** (Sh 306) A-D:3(VII) LC IIIA. Frag. of spout (with strainer perforations) and shoulder. C: red-brown to gray-green wfs; hard. P: m. reddish brown. Spout outlined; 2 bands defining shoulder. H: 9.4. W: 5.2. **B 605** (Sh 321) A-D:2(VII,2) LC IIIA. Frag. from base of spout. C: g. orange-brown, with lime grits. P: firm m. dk. orange-red. L: 6.5. **B 606** (Sh 533) A-D:2(St.1a) LC IIC. Frag. from just below neck, incl. stump of spout. C: brick-red to blue-gray; rough surface, hard. P: m. dk. gray. H: 3.4. W: 2.7.

Type 4: low base ring, biconical globular body, straight neck, slightly bowed(?) handle. Type of mouth unknown, probably round on an analogy with Type 3, of which this may be a variation. No other clearly comparable specimens are known to me but the shape has something in common with *MCh,* 80, Fig. 33:2. Cf. also B 674 (trefoil mouth). **B 607** (P 2698; 49-12-434) T.35:3. *Pls. 22, 45.* Mouth, part of neck and handle missing. C: pinkish buff to pink and gray-buff wfds; wet-smoothed. P: firm m. orange to gray-brown. Ring around base of neck and handle. Irregular line down handle. 3 n. hor. bands under handle, 2 more on lower body, another wider round base. PH: 15.3. D: 12.

Miscellaneous jugs and fragments: see also B 684.
B 608 (P 973) T.17:16. *Pls. 22, 56.* Most of neck and handle missing. Shape, as far as preserved, identical with Type 4 except that body is depressed globular. Cf. B 566 for type of decoration. C: sl. g. orange-brown to reddish brown wfds. P: sl. ls. chocolate-brown, flaked. PH: 8.5. D: 9.2. **B 609** (P 1300) T.33:17(B) LC IIIA. *Pls. 45, 61.* Handle missing. Surface much worn. Decorated version of PWM II Type 8 jug. Nearly bobbin-shaped. C: g. lt. gray-green wfs; soft, wet-smoothed(?) P: m. gray. One band on shoulder. 3(?) bands each above and below belly zone. H: 11.5. D: 6.4. **B 610** (P 2925) T.40:43(C) LC IIIA. *Pls. 22, 59, 65.* I-m. Neck, handle and base with enough of body to give profile pres. Decorated version of PWM II Type 6 jug. Squared lip. C: g. dk. reddish brown to gray and gray-green, well smoothed. P: m. dk. reddish brown. Beginning at lower part of neck near handle and extending down over shoulder, floral design(?): 2 inverted leaves(?) These may have continued as a frieze around shoulder. H: 15.8. ED: 12.2. **B 611** (Sh 116) A-D:3(VI) LC IIIA. *Pl. 23.* Handle and frag. of neck apparently from same shape as B 610. C: lt. orange-gray to gray-green with lime grits. P: m. dk. gray. Paint on rim and handle. Daubs on neck. H: 6. **B 612** (Sh 228) A-Unstrat. Frag. from base of neck. C: lt. gray-brown. P: m. dk. gray. Vert. bands. H: 2.2. **B 613** (Sh 252) A-D:3(IV) LC IIIA. *Pl. 23.* Frag. from neck and rim of large jug(?) Rim flaring and lip beveled. C: pinkish brown to dk. buff, sandy; coarse ware. P: m. red-brown. Wide stripe just under lip ext. H: 7.2. W: 5.7. **B 614** (Sh 328) A-D:2(VII,2) LC IIIA. *Pl. 23.* Neck frag. Assignment to this category uncertain, particularly since ware is bichrome, but it looks Cypriote. C: lt. gray-brown. P: m. dk. red and gray. Hor. bands. W: 4.3. **B 615** (Sh 390) A-E:1(VIII) LC IIIB. *Pl. 23.* Frag. of shoulder with transition to neck. C,P: like B 614; same comment applies. Paint at base of neck. Vert. stripes for panels(?) on shoulder. W: 3.2. **B 616** (Sh 509) C-C:2 LC IIC. Frag. preserving part of shoulder and body with stump of handle. Spiral relief bands with punches. 2 incised vert. lines on handle. Imitation BR. C: lt. gray to lt. brown near surface, rather soft. S: m. streaky lt. chestnut to dk. gray. Technique like that of BSB. PH: 18. D: 20.

Pilgrim Flasks: almost symmetrically elliptical round body with short narrow neck flaring to round mouth. Vertical handles slope slightly near top to join mouth just below rim. Decoration consists of a closed concentric spiral (around a solid dot) on each side plus a ring around the base of the neck and bars on the handles. The following examples are all Type 1, with plain rim. Some Kaloriziki examples (Type 2) have a boxed rim.

B 617 (P 1202) E-D:1h LC IIIA. *Pl. 22.* Neck, handles and part of body missing. Body restored with plaster. C: g. yellowish gray to orange-brown at surface wfs. P: firm m. lt. brown. Bars on front connect 2 c-s. D: 10.5. W: 6.5. **B 618** (P 2705) E-13 (see also E-D:1d. *Pl. 56.* Neck, part of one handle and large frag. of upper body. C: g. lt. brown to gray-green. P: m. lt. orange to reddish brown. C-c inside mouth. PH: 10. D (of mouth): 3.5. **B 619** (P 2879) T.40:5(D) LC IIIA. *Pls. 22, 45, 56, 59.* C-sp. C: g. lt. gray-brown to gray-green. P: lt. to dk. orange-brown and reddish brown. H: 14.1. W: 6.3.

"Fruit Bowls": cf. *Troy III,* Pls. 295, 433. Similar (early) pottery stands as braziers: E. Mackay, *Report on the Excavation of the "A" Cemetery at Kish, Mesopotamia* (Chicago, 1925) 24 ff. Other references given in *OA III* (1944) 236, n. 4.

B 620 (P 740; 54-28-110) A-E:2(V) LC IIIB. *Pl. 22.* C-m. Stem vert. pared. W-m in 2 pieces and joined. Profile "lip" at base, tall hollow concave stem flaring to shallow bowl with convex (or carinated) sides and rolled lip. C: gray at core to lt. dull buff wfs but well cleaned. P: m. brown to red-brown and dk. gray-brown. Paint on lip, base of bowl and base of stem. 4 rather uneven hor. bands on stem. H: 18.1. D: 12.3. *AJA 42* (1938) 268, Fig. 7. **B 621** (P 741) A-E:2(VIII) LC IIIB. N-c-m. Technique like B 620. Large base ring, hollow stem flaring to shallow curved bowl with beveled lip. C: brick-red wfs, sherd temper; surface rough. P: m. firm mahogany red; crackled. 5 hor. stripes on stem. Vert. bands, partly overlapping the hor. stripes on base and bowl. H: 12.8. D: 12.3. *AJA 42* (1938) 268, Fig. 7.

PROTO-WHITE PAINTED WARE

For a complete explanation of shapes and types as well as a discussion of this category in general, the reader is referred to *Kaloriziki,* Ch. IV. The types presented below are based on the Kaloriziki system.

Bowls: the categorization into Types 1a and 1b is undertaken largely on the basis of decoration since practically no handle fragments are preserved. In a few cases, the possibility is not excluded that sherds classified as Type 1b might be Type 2.

Type 1a: **B 622** (P 790) A-E:2(VI) LC IIIB. *Pl. 46.* Foot and frag. of floor to wall. Signs of burning. C: brown, sandy, soft. P: m. chocolate-brown, crackled. Technique very similar to that of LC III Decorated Ware by which the potter was obviously influenced. This is a good example of the interplay of influence among the various fabrics of the LC III period. Int: 2 broad bands near center. Ext: hor. w. line. PH: 4.8. **B 623** (Sh 70) A-D:3(VI) etc. LC IIIA. *Pls. 22, 66.* Frag. of rim and wall. C: lt. gray-brown to gray-green wfds; thin fabric. P: m. firm dk. brown. Superior fabric. Paint on rim and band below rim int. Ext: 3 w. lines. H: 6.3. PD: 8.4. **B 624** (Sh 107) A-F:1 LC IIIB. *Pls. 22, 66.* Frag. of wall; may possibly belong to same pot as B 623. H: 4.3. **B 625** (Sh 138) A-E:4

LC IIIB. *Pls. 22, 66.* Frag. of rim and wall. C: lt. gray-green wfds. P: m. purple-brown. Int. dec: like B 623. Ext: 2 thick w. lines (at least). H: 4.5. **B 626** (Sh 186) A-E:2(VI) LC IIIB. *Pls. 22, 66.* Frag. of wall. C: lt. gray-buff wfds. P: like B 625. Int: band below rim and where floor joins wall. Ext: like B 625. L (diagonal): 4.5. **B 627** (Sh 459) A-E:2(VI) LC IIIB. *Pl. 23.* Rim and wall frag. C: dull gray-brown wfs; thin fabric. P: m. purple-brown. Paint where floor meets wall and on rim int. W. line ext. H: 5. PD: 9.

Type 1b: **B 628** (P 815) A-E:2(VI) LC IIIB. *Pl. 23.* Lower body pres. C: dull gray-brown wfs. P: m. dk. gray-brown. 2 bands where floor meets wall int. and ext. Paint on base. PH: 7.5. PD: 16. **B 629** (Sh 139) A-E:4 LC IIIB. *Pls. 22, 66.* Rim frag. C,P: like B 628. Overall stipple pattern (cf. *MP,* 422, Fig. 73: Variegated Stone Patterns No. 1). H: 3. W: 3. **B 630** (Sh 191) A-E:2(VI) LC IIIB. *Pl. 22.* Rim frag. and non-joining handles. C: g. lt. orange-brown. P: m. streaky gray-brown. Paint on handle and on rim int. and ext. H (of rim frag.): 2.7. **B 631** (Sh 197) A-F:2 LC IIIB. *Pl. 23.* Stump of handle and adjoining wall. C: lt. gray-green wfs, rather powdery. P: m. olive to gray-brown, crackled. Paint on handle. H: 3.2. **B 632** (Sh 229) A-E:4 LC IIIB. Wall frag. C: like B 624. P: m. firm black and dk. red. Outlines of panel pres. but design not distinguishable. H: 2. **B 633** (Sh 242) A-Surface. *Pl. 23.* Rim frag. C: lt. orange-brown to buff at surface. P: m. dk. gray and red. Butterfly pattern filled with dk. gray; all other lines red: cf. K 29. Band inside rim. H: 2.9. W: 3.5. **B 634** (Sh 268 and Sh 411) A-Unstrat. *Pls. 22, 66.* Two wall frags. not found together and not joining but probably from same pot. C: lt. orange-brown to gray-brown and buff. P: m. gray and red. Opposing but not tangent outlined semicircles in red, with field between them in gray; set in vert. outlined panels: cf. *MP,* 345, Fig. 58:25 (IIIC:1). H (of Sh 411): 3.7. W: 3. **B 635** (Sh 576; 54-41-4) VT:4. *Pls. 23, 66.* Frag. of rim and wall. C: lt. gray-green wfs, soft; fine wheelmarks on surface. P: m. gray, flaked. Int: solid. Ext: thick band on rim. In panel: stemmed spiral (or conceivably even antithetic spiral) pattern. H: 9.2. ED: 15.

The following sherds come from Type 1a or Type 1b bowls: **B 636** (Sh 187) A-E:3(VI) LC IIIB. *Pl. 23.* Part of foot and lower body. Low flaring conical base. C: like B 631. P: m. dk. gray. Band on lower body ext. and base. H: 2.4. PD: 4.7. **B 637** (Sh 238) A-Surface. *Pl. 23.* Foot and part of floor to wall. Low conical base. C,P: like B 630 but coarser fabric. Int. center: band. Corresponding band ext. Paint on base. H: 3.5. PD: 7.6. The following sherds, bell-shaped bowl rims, are executed in a hard fabric of superior technique, with no preserved decoration. Two unpublished, unstratified sherds from Tarsus seem to be exactly the same ware. **B 638** (Sh 73) A-D:3(IV) LC IIIA. *Pl. 22.* C: hard firm compact dk. gray-green; rich texture; int. sl. ls. Probably has ground sherd temper. H: 3.2. **B 639** (Sh 81) A-Unstrat. *Pl. 22.* C: like B 638 but color lighter and almost pinkish in places. H: 1.5.

Type 2: **B 640** (Sh 487) A-E:2(VI) LC IIIB. *Pl. 46.* Foot and small portions of adjoining wall. C: dull red-brown, coarse. P: m. dk. brown. Paint on base. H: 4.5. PD: 7. **B 641** (Sh 160) A-Unstrat. *Pl. 23.* Frag. of rim and floor. C: gray at core to neutral brown, soft. P: m. red. Below carination: very wide solid strip with 4 n. res. rings. Paint on rim. L (diagonal): 11.

Type 4b: **B 642** (P 1289) T.33:7(C) LC IIIB. *Pls. 46, 60.* C-m. Instead of the usual hor. roll handles, this specimen has hor. lug handles with vert. string holes. C: lt. gray-green to orange-brown, sandy; low diagonal bur. P: m. dk. gray. Dec: base ext. like K 46: 2 wide enclosing 2 n. bands; band at center and halfway up int. On underside of base: Maltese cross. Paint on rim and handles. H: 8.5. D: 20. **B 643** (P 1290) T.33:12(C) LC IIIB. *Pls. 46, 60, 63.* C-i. C: like B 642. P: m. streaky dk. violet-gray and purple. Int. center: outlined c-s. Ext: like B 642. On underside of base: Maltese cross, purple. H: 7.7. D: 19.7.

Type 6: **B 644** (P 1291) T.33:9(C) LC IIIB. *Pls. 46, 60, 66.* C-m. Two handles. C: gray-brown to gray-green wfs; sl. bur. surface. P: firm m. violet-gray. Int. center: solid circle. Ext: paint on rim and handles; on underside of base: plain cross within 3 c-c. Careless workmanship. H: 6.1. D: 11.3. **B 645** (P 1292) T.33:16(C) LC IIIB. *Pls. 46, 60.* C-ch. One handle. Sl. shallower than B 644. C: lt. gray wfs, hard; not well smoothed. P: firm m. dk. gray. Technique similar to that of LC III Dec. Ware. Paint on rim and handle. Solid circles at center int. and ext. H: 5.1. D: 10.5.

Type 7: **B 646** (Sh 71) A-D:3(VI) and Cw Vb LC IIIA. *Pl. 23.* Frag. of rim and wall with stump of handle. Signs of burning. C: dull gray-brown to gray-green, coarse. P: m. dk. gray. Paint on rim: band int. below rim. Paint on handle ext. and band below handle. H: 9.3. PD: 12.

Indeterminate: the following sherds appear to be in Proto-White Painted technique but they do not seem to belong to known bowl types: **B 647** (Sh 123) A-D:2(VI) LC IIIA. *Pl. 23.* Frag. of floor. C: lt. gray to gray-green wfds, powdery. P: m. dk. gray, much worn. Int: lat-tr with points toward center. Decoration too worn at time of control to permit of a satisfactory drawing. Ext: band. L: 5.3. **B 648** (Sh 218) A-E:3(V) LC IIIB. *Pls. 23, 66.* Wall(?) frag. with beginning of handle(?) Has some resemblance to LC III Dec. Type 7; however, there is some doubt that the sherd comes from a bowl at all. C: lt. gray-green, poorly smoothed. P: m. dk. gray. Lines crossing at right angles. L: 3.2.

Kalathiskoi: cf. *Nouveaux Documents,* 194, c, for examples of kalathoi from Idalion.

B 649 (Sh 78) A-E:2(VI) LC IIIB. *Pls. 22, 66.* Frag. of wall with edge of handle. C: dk. gray-green wfds, rather powdery. P: firm m. black. Lat-tr. Paint on base of handle and bands on int. H: 2.7. PD: 7.5. **B 650** (Sh 240) A-Surface. *Pls. 23, 66.* Fragment of wall. C: like B 649 but lighter. P: like B 649. T-o lat-loz. Bands on int. H: 2.8. L: 4.5.

Krater-Amphoras

Type 1a: **B 651** (P 1288) T.33:11(C) LC IIIB. *Pls. 46, 60.* C-m. Neck-ring, sloping handles. C: g. lt. pinkish buff wfds; possibly wet-smoothed. P: m. umber. 4 groups of bars on rim; handle barred. Band on neck base and on base. 3 n. bands below handle, a wide stripe on lower body. 4 lat-tr on shoulder (each side). H: 11.4. D: 10. **B 652** (Sh 209) A-E:2(St.2a) LC IIIB. *Pl. 23.* Frag. of neck with neck-ring and transition to shoulder (cf. B 653). C: gray-green wfds. P: m. black. Paint on neck-ring. Solid triangle(s) on shoulder(?) H: 4.5. **B 653** (Sh 211) A-E:2(St.2a) LC IIIB. *Pl. 23.* Frag. of squared overhanging rim. Probably from same pot as B 652. H: 2.5. L: 3.2.

Type 1b: **B 654** (P 1286) T.33:15(C) LC IIIB. *Pls. 46, 60, 66.* N-c-m. Short stem gives an elevated effect. C: g. lt. greenish brown wfs; well smoothed; low diagonal bur. P: m. dk. violet-gray. 7 groups of bars on rim and 2 bands inside rim; handles barred with vert. line in center; bow around base of handle. Paint on rim and on neck-base; two stripes on lower body, another on stem and another at edge of base. Neck: 8 d-o vert. zones of crosshatch, chevrons, lattice-work and in one case interlocking triangles shaded in alternating directions. H: 27.6. D: 26.9. Mention is made of this pot by J. Deshayes, *La Nécropole de Ktima* (Paris, 1963) 218, n. 2; 219, n. 1. **B 655** (P 1287) T.33:6(C) LC IIIB. *Pls. 46, 60.* C-i. High conical foot; neck short but not particularly wide. Handles sl. concave. C: orange-brown to gray-green wfds; hor. bur. P: m. dk. gray. 6 groups of bars on rim. 2 rings inside rim. Handles like B 654 but without bow. Band at and below rim, at neck-base, 3 below handles, 3 on lower body and 3 on base. H: 20.4. D: 19.

Type 3: **B 656** (Sh 540) A-Unstrat. *Pls. 23, 66.* Two sherds from neck and shoulder. C: gray to lt. gray-green wfs; firm rich texture. P: firm m. dk. gray. Inverted stacked triangles. H: 4.5. W: 5.4.

Miscellaneous sherds: the following are from rather large-sized pots of this fabric. A comparison with K 80 is suggested for the type, although, of course, there can be no certainty about shapes except in the case of B 657, which is certainly from a krater-amphora. **B 657** (Sh 149) A-E:3(V) LC IIIB. *Pl. 23.* Rim frag. Ledge rim profiled int. and ext. C: lt. pinkish gray to yellow-green at surface; somewhat powdery. P: lt. rust, worn. 2 vert. stripes below rim. H: 2.2. L:3.4. **B 658** (Sh 332) A-D:3(VII) LC IIIA. *Pls. 23, 66.* Frag. from shoulder with neck-ring (or rim?). C: buff to lt. greenish-gray, powdery. Ext. apparently bur. before painting. P: firm m. violet-brown. Hor. zigzag in panels. H: 4.7. W: 4.2. **B 659** (Sh 393) A-E:3(VIII) LC IIIB. Wall frag. (cf. B 660). C: orange-brown at core to lt. gray-green wfs; hard but powdery. P: m. lavender. Design cannot be made out. L (diagonal): 4.4. **B 660** (Sh 400) A-E:3(VIII) LC IIIB. *Pl. 23.* Wall frag. Probably from same pot as B 659. H: 5.6. **B 661** (Sh 460) A-E:2(VI) LC IIIB. Frag. of belly with stump of hor. handle. C: g. yellow-brown to lt. gray-blue at surface; very coarse fabric. P: m. lavender-brown. Two bands. H: 12. PD: 11.5. **B 662** (Sh 552) E-D:2f LC IIIA. *Pls. 23, 66.* Frag. from shoulder of closed pot(?) C: dk. gray-green; hard firm texture (cf. B 638-639): sl. ls. surface. P: m. dk. gray and dk. red. Lattice design(?) H: 2.8. L: 4.3.

Amphoriskoi

Type 1: **B 663** (P 764; 54-28-100) A-E:2(VI) LC IIIB. *Pls. 24, 63.* Lower body with profile to shoulder. Signs of burning. C: gray-green to gray-yellow, well cleaned and smoothed. P: firm m. olive black. On shoulder: s-o lat-tr; in h-z 2 w. hor. parallel lines. Below handle 2 wide enclosing 2 n. bands. Paint on foot. PH: 12.2. D: 12.4.

Type 3: **B 664** (P 2932; 49-12-384) T.27:1. *Pls. 24, 46.* One handle and part of mouth missing. Very small handles. Surface badly eroded. C: lt. grayish red-brown to brown wfds. P: m. chocolate-brown. Neck dark with 5 n. res. lines at center. 2 n. bands above, 3 below h-z. Paint on handles and base. H: 10.3. D: 7.2.

The following probably comes from an amphoriskos: **B 665** (Sh 334) A-D:3(VII) LC IIIA. *Pls. 23, 66.* Frag. from shoulder(?) C: very lt. gray-green wfs; sl. powdery; ext. perhaps bur. P: firm m. dk. gray, sl. crackled. Hor. chevrons between a series of bands. L (diagonal): 4.5.

Amphoras

Type 1: **B 666** (Sh 74) A-E:2(VI) etc. LC IIIB. *Pls. 22, 66.* Frag. of h-z and stump of handle joins with B 668. C: lt. gray-green wfds, powdery. P: m. lt. pinkish gray to dk. gray, flaking. Triple w. hor. line in h-z. H: 11. PD (with B 668): 20. **B 667** (Sh 131) Cw Vb CA I. *Pls. 23, 66.* Large shoulder frag. with "nipple". C: red-brown wfds, soft. P: m. dk. gray. Shoulder: d-o triangles subdivided into d-o lat-loz. and lat-tr. Delineating shoulder zone: one thick band and at least one n. band. H: 9. W: 11.5. **B 668** (Sh 503) A-F:2 LC IIIB. Frag. of amphora handle and h-z joining B 666, *q.v.*

Type 2b: **B 669** (P 754) A-E:2(VI) LC IIIB. *Pl. 24.* Part of both handles, sizeable frag. of neck and body pres. C: lt. orange-brown, sandy. P: m. dk. brown to gray. Vert. w. lines on handles terminating in loops on body below handles. Hor. w. line(s) on neck. Band at neck base with tongues. 3 wide and 2 n. bands at widest part of body. PH: 19.4. ED: 22. **B 670** (Sh 190) A-E:2(VI) LC IIIB. *Pls. 23, 66.* Frag. of neck. C: lt. pinkish to gray-green, powdery. P: dk. gray, crackled. Triple hor. w. line. H: 6.8. PD: 5.5. **B 671** (Sh 193) A-E:2(VI) LC IIIB. *Pls. 22, 66.* Frag. of shoulder (cf. B 672). C: g. lt. gray-green wfds. P: m. olive-green where thin to brown, crackled. Tongues. L: 3.3. **B 672** (Sh 243) A-Surface. *Pl. 23.* Frag. of neck and shoulder. C,P: like B 671; very possibly from same pot. Neck band and tongues. H: 3. **B 673** (Sh 739) C-Unstrat. *Pl. 23.* Frag. of neck and roll rim has been sl. angularized underneath to give a metallic effect. C: g. lt. gray-buff, powdery; sherd temper. P: m. gray-black. Paint on rim. Hor. w. line on neck. H: 4.8. PD: 6.2.

Jugs: Group A

Type 1a: **B 674** (P 2692; 49-12-409) T.32:5 LC IIIA. *Pls. 24, 46.* C-i. C: g. gray-green. P: firm m. purple-black, somewhat thin. Paint on rim, at base of neck and on base. Handle barred; loop around its base. 2 n. bands under handle; 2 wider at widest point of body. H: 19.5. D: 12.9. *Kaloriziki*, Pl. 59. **B 675** (Sh 192) A-E:2(VI) LC IIIB. *Pl. 23.* Handle. C: g. dk. blue-gray. P: firm m. dk. gray. Bars. H: 6.8. W: 1.8.

Type 1b: **B 676** (Sh 115) A-E:2(VI) LC IIIB. *Pl. 23.* Frag. of rim with stump of handle. C: pinkish to lt. buff wfds. P: m. violet-brown. Paint on rim. Vert. w. line on handle. L (diagonal): 7. **B 677** (Sh 127) A-E:2(VI) LC IIIB. *Pl. 23.* Frag. of body at widest point. C: lt. gray-green wfds, sl. powdery. P: m. gray, faded. Outlined wide band around belly. PD: 9.4. **B 678** (Sh 539) A-Unstrat. *Pl. 23.* Frag. of shoulder to belly and non-joining handle frag. C,P: dec: like B 677 plus groups(?) of 6 pendent lines from neck-base. But probably not from same pot. H: 8.

Type 2: **B 679** (P 1284) T.33:8(C) LC IIIB. *Pls. 46, 60.* C-i. Rather small base. C: lt. gray-green wfds, possibly wet-smoothed. P: m. violet-gray. Paint on rim, neck-base, handle, base. Scalloped fringe (like tongues) around base of neck. Wide band with 3 n. res. bands below handle, 2 wide bands on lower body. 3 hor. w. lines on neck. Handle-rib barred. H: 20. D: 14.3.

Type 3a: **B 680** (P 1280) T.33:1(C) LC IIIB. *Pls. 46, 60.* C-ch. C: lt. gray-brown wfs, lt. vert. bur. P: m. dk. gray-brown. Paint on rim, neck-ring, handle sides. Handle barred. H: 2.4. D: 16.3. *Kaloriziki*, Pl. 59. **B 681** (P 1281) T.33:2(C) LC IIIB. *Pls. 46, 60, 66.* C-i. C: lt. gray-brown to red-brown wfs. Very lt. vert. bur. P: like B 680. Dec: like B 680 but vert. w. line on handle ending in loop on body. H: 23.2. D: 15.8. **B 682** (Sh 126) A-E:2(VI) LC IIIB. *Pl. 23.* Most of neck and rim with stump of handle. C: lt. red-brown to dk. buff with lime grits. Ext: vert. bur. P: m. dk. brown. Paint on rim, handle, neck base. H: 7. D (at handle): 4. **B 683** (Sh 300) A-Unstrat. Part of shoulder and base of neck. C: g. lt. gray-brown wfds. Ext: vert. bur., now worn. P: m. dk. gray. Neck-ring painted. H: 6.6. PD: 14. **B 684** (Sh 538) A-D:2(St.2b) LC IIIA. (Shape and general appearance of this frag. suggests Proto-White Painted Ware; the clay is more like that of LC III Decorated Ware). Large frag. of shoulder and belly; neck-ring. C: dull red-brown to gray-green wfs and lime grits; not bur. P: firm but thin m. gray. Paint on neck-ring; 3 bands at widest part of body. PH: 13. PD: 6.4.

Type 3b: **B 685** (Sh 188) A-E:3(VI) LC IIIB. *Pl. 22.* Upper part of neck and mouth; handle to neck. C: very lt. gray-green, powdery. P: m. dk. gray (in traces under rim). H: 3. D (of mouth): 3.

Type 4: This is now represented by a series of rather elaborately decorated examples from a tomb at Idalion (*Nouveaux Documents*, 191: 9-13). **B 686** (P 1282) T.33:10(C) LC IIIB. *Pls. 46, 60.* C-i. C: lt. gray-brown to orange-brown wfs, well smoothed. P: m. firm umber. 2 thin bands int. rim. Paint on rim, handle sides, neck base, on base and 2 wide bands under handle, which is barred. 2 w. lines on neck, brought together in an upward stroke. 3 d-o lat-tr on shoulder. H: 11.2. D: 8.4. *Kaloriziki*, Pl. 59. **B 687** (P 1283) T.33:5(C) LC IIIB. *Pls. 46, 60.* N-c-m. Strainer holes in base. Depressed biconical shape. C: lt. orange-brown wfds, well smoothed. P: like B 686. Paint on mouth and neck-base. 2 w. lines on neck. Handle like B 686. Inverted solid triangles on shoulder. 2 n. stripes below handle. Lower part of body solid color. H: 13.1. D: 11.3.

Type 5d: small conical flaring base, wide heavy conical-ovoid body, small tapering tubular spout; otherwise like Type 5c, of which it appears to be an adaptation under the inspiration of the Type 3a jug shape. **B 688** (P 1285) T.33:13(C) LC IIIB. *Pls. 46, 60.* C-ch. C: g. gray-green wfs, well smoothed. P: m. dk. gray-purple. Neck and base dk. Paint on base of spout. Top of shoulder and widest part of body: thick band with 2 n. res. rings. Careless stripes on spout. Handle barred. H: 2.4. D: 16.4. *Kaloriziki*, Pl. 59.

Miscellaneous jug fragments: **B 689** (Sh 185) A-E:2(VI) LC IIIB. *Pl. 22.* Large rectangular handle with attached frags. of body. C: very lt. powdery gray-green wfds. P: m. olive-green to dk. gray, crackled. Vert. w. line down back of handle. H: 15. W: 3.5. **B 690** (Sh 198) A-F:2 LC IIIB. Frag. from neck-base of jug. C: lt. gray-brown wfds. Traces of purple-brown paint. L (diagonal): 3.3. **B 691** (Sh 518) A-D:2(VII,1) LC IIIA. *Pls. 22, 66.* Frag. from neck of small jug(?) C,P: like B 656. Panel design(?) L (diagonal): 2.2. **B 692** (Sh 521) B-D:2 LC IIIA. *Pl. 23.* Sherds from lower shoulder of jug(?) C: g. lt. brick-red to dull gray-green at surface. P: m. purple-gray. 3 vert. lines bordered by hor. bands. L: 7.

LATE CYPRIOTE III BLACK SLIP BUCCHERO WARE

This is the wheelmade counterpart of Handmade Bucchero ware (of which Types 2 and 3 jug have been adapted to the wheel). Being also the parent of the Iron Age ware designated in the *Swedish Cyprus Expedition* as Black Slip Bucchero (I, II, etc.), it may appropriately retain the related designation given it here (LC III Black Slip Bucchero). If an infallible distinction cannot always be drawn between parent and offspring, this is no more confusing than the similar situation with Proto-White Painted and White Painted ware. No other shape than the jug is represented. Only B 693 appears to have plastic ribs added over the body, in literal imitation of the Handmade Bucchero technique. In all other instances, the ridges appear to have been created by shaving out wide indentations. This is often done carefully enough to create the illusion of widely spaced, plastically added ribs. Occasionally, however, only narrow grooves, more or less square in section, were gouged out (e.g. B 894 and B 700). At first these tended to be widely spaced. In the Iron Age they were often close-set. For further remarks on this category, see p. 54 and *Kaloriziki*, under Black Slip Bucchero I ware.

Type 2 (of *Problems,* 53, Fig. 13): **B 693** (P 1206) E-D:1f LC IIIA. *Pl. 24.* Handle missing. Taut ovoid body; concave lip. C: g. lt. gray-brown. S: m. reddish brown to dk. gray. H: 16.9. D: 9.5. **B 694** (P 1301) T.33:28(B) LC IIIA. *Pls. 24, 47, 61.* C-i. Almost spherical body; beveled lip. C: lt. gray-brown wfs (red). S: dk. chocolate-gray with rust-colored patch. H: 15.1. D: 8.5. **B 695** (P 2742) T.38:3. *Pl. 24.* Handle and neck missing. Base has beveled "lip"; rather wide stem. Fluting of sides very restrained. C: dk. gray at core to lt. gray; well cleaned, hard. S: sl. ls. red-brown to dk. gray, much worn. PH: 6.5. D: 6.5. **B 696** (Sh 524) B-D:2 LC IIIA. Non-joining frags. of neck, shoulder and handle. C: g. lt. gray at core to brown-buff. S: gray, crackled, thin. L (diagonal): 6.

Type 3 (of *Problems,* 53, Fig. 13): **B 697** (P 745) A-D:2(VII,2) LC IIIA. *Pl. 24.* Mouth, handle and much of body missing. Globular body. Base has beveled "lip." Shape almost identical with that of B 285. C: gray-green, sandy. S: dk. gray. PH: 13.3. D: 8. **B 698** (P 2843) A-E:2(VIII) LC IIIB. Frags. of base and body, apparently very similar to B 697, but with grooves much like the Iron Age type. C: lt. brownish buff, well cleaned; rather soft. S: m. purple-brown. H (of largest frag.): 9. D (of base): 7.1. **B 699** (Sh 262) A-Unstrat. Base and frag. of adjoining wall. C: g. lt. gray-brown, sandy. S: gray with rust-colored patches. H: 3.1. PD: 8.

Type 4: this appears from incomplete samples to be a slipped and more metallic version of the type represented by B 919. It has a metallic, rather wide base ring with beveled "lip," a full ovoid body, tall narrow tapering neck and vertical handle. **B 700** (P 755) A-D:2(VI) LC IIIA. *Pl. 29.* I-m. Mouth, most of handle and part of body missing. Widely spaced indentations. C: dull brown wfs, hard. S: sl. ls. metallic gray, hard; flaked. PH: 19.7. D: 13. **B 701** (P 958) D-B:2a LC IIIA. *Pl. 29.* Shoulder, neck and handle missing. Widely spaced raised ribs. C: g. gray-buff. S: firm orange to red and dk. gray. PH: 16.6. D: 15.2.

Type 5: small high base ring, almost spherical body. Tall narrow straight neck with round mouth and profiled lip; neck-ring, rectangular handle from shoulder to mid-neck; rather close-set ribbing. Cf. K 542. **B 702** (P 1402; 49-12-275) T.19:3(F) LC IIIB. *Pls. 24, 47.* N-c-m. Part of handle missing. C: lt. gray-buff wfds. S: m. heavy red-brown, flaked. H: 10.4. D: 6.4.

Miscellaneous body fragments (various unstratified sherds not listed): **B 703** (Sh 163) A-D:3(V) etc. LC IIIA. Large wall frag. Widely spaced ribs. C: pinkish brown wfs. S: red-brown to lavender. H: 13. **B 704** (Sh 305) A-D:3(VII) LC IIIA. Shoul-

der frag. with fairly wide neck (Type 3?) and neck-ring. C: firm lt. greenish buff; smooth texture. S: m. dk. lavender-gray. PD: 8. **B 705** (Sh 324) A-D:3(VII) LC IIIA. Body frag. Widely spaced ribs. C: lt. gray-brown wfs, powdery. S: dk. gray with a brown patch, crackled; hard. L (diagonal): 5.3.

WARE VII

The following sherds are from bowls, of which not enough is preserved to make certain an ascription to exact types. For a technical description of this ware, which is quite uniform, see *AJA* 41 (1937) 72 ff. Cf. also K 976 ff.

B 706 (Sh 65) A-E:1(VI) LC IIIB. Frag. of rim with stump of handle. Incised zigzag. H: 6.3. W: 7.3. **B 707** (Sh 66) A-E:1(VI) LC IIIB. *Pl. 29.* Frag. of wall. Incised zigzag. L (diagonal): 5. **B 708** (Sh 79) A-E:2(VI) etc. LC IIIB. *Pl. 29.* Frag. of wall and profiled rim. H: 7. W: 5. **B 709** (Sh 112) A-E:1(VI) LC IIIB. *Pl. 29.* Frag. of rim and side. Plain rim, sl. flattened. H: 5.8. **B 710** (Sh 113) A-E:1(VI) LC IIIB. Frag. of wall. 3 incised lines, possibly part of zigzag. L (diagonal): 2.5. **B 711** (Sh 200) A-E:2(St.2a) LC IIIB. Rim frag. Plain rim, tapering and sl. rounded. H: 2.2.

"PSEUDO-MONOCHROME" WARE

The following bowls are a coarse ware having somewhat the appearance of coarse Monochrome Ware, but being wheelmade they have received a name to distinguish them from their earlier counterpart. These bowls may be merely examples of a potter's temporary interest in an earlier technique of which he accidentally became aware. The shape is essentially that of the Proto-White Painted Bowl Type 3a.

B 712 (P 2682; 49-12-398) T.30:4 CG IA. *Pl. 24.* I-m. Much of rim missing. C: dk. gray-brown to purplish black over part of ext; sandy. H: 6. ED: 13.5. **B 713** (P 2686; 49-12-402) T.30:8 CG IA. *Pl. 24.* I-m. About ⅔ incl. one handle pres. C: like B 712 though somewhat lighter and finer. H: 5.7. D: 14.9.

WHITE PAINTED I WARE

For a discussion of this ceramic category, see *Kaloriziki,* Ch. IV. The classification of shapes used below follows that established for this category in *Kaloriziki.*

Bowls

Type 1a (early): **B 714** (P 2645; 49-12-120) T.11:5(B). *Pl. 24.* I-m. About ⅛ of wall missing. C: g. lt. gray-brown wfs. P: m. purple-brown. Int. band at base of wall. Ext: paint on rim, handle, base. Double broadly curved line around wall. H: 10. D: 12.8.

Type 1b: Decoration with bands only. *Earlier period:* **B 715** (P 2681; 49-12-397) T.30:3 CG IA.

Pl. 47. I-m. One handle missing. Surface eroded. C: lt. gray-brown wfds. P: m. purple-brown. H: 7.9. D: 8.9. *Later period:* **B 716** (P 2646; 49-12-121) T.11:6(B) CG IA. *Pl. 24.* C-ch. Very wide foot and noticeably convex floor. C: g. reddish brown to gray-green. P: m. purple-brown. Res. band on base. H: 20. D: 24.2. **B 717** (P 2648; 49-12-123) T.11:8(B) CG IA. *Pl. 24.* I-m. Small foot with "squared" edge. C,P: like B 716. H: 14.9. D: 16.4.

Type 1b: Decoration with bands plus additional elements. *Later period*(?): **B 718** (P 2687; 49-12-403) T.30:9 CG IA. *Pl. 24.* About half missing. Small base, convex floor. Short walls. This unusual shape together with rather degenerate decoration suggests a date as late as possible but it may, of course, be CG IA. C,P: like B 714. Sides: 4(?) groups of 3 vert. lines unified by carelessly drawn oblique parallel lines. H: 12.8. D: 17.7.

Type 3: the following fragment corresponds in general to this type but was apparently somewhat shallower, on the analogy of K 256. Another example of this from Bamboula is OT 56:2 (*ExC*, Fig. 129 = *CVA* BM Fs. 1 IICc Pl. 3:10). **B 719** (Sh 613) Cw IIIb:2 LC IIIB (?) Base and part of floor pres. C: lt. gray-pink to gray-green. P: m. dk. gray. Int. center: heavily outlined c-s around solid circle. Ext: around base, thick band with 3 n. res. lines. PH: 3.2. PD: 18.5.

Type 5a: **B 720** (P 2640; 49-12-108) T.8:2. *Pl. 24.* I-m. One handle missing; the other is almost a roll handle and sl. lifted. Cf. K 266. In any case, this is a miniature and very shallow version, like a plate. C: like B 714. P: m. gray-brown. Int. center: 2 c-c, 2 bands about halfway up. Ext: paint on handle and rim. 2 bands under handles, wide band with 3 n. res. bands (one broken) above base. Underside of base: small "x" at center outlined by 2 bands of bars. H: 2. D: 10.9.

Type 5c: **B 721** (P 2683; 49-12-399) T.30:5 CG IA. *Pls. 24, 47.* C-m. C: g. pinkish buff to yellow-gray wfds. P: m. dk. gray. Paint on rim, handle barred. T-o body frieze: 4 vert. n. crosshatch zones. Underside of base: Maltese cross radiating from circle. H: 4.2. D: 17.7.

Three-handled bowl: see K 290. The Bamboula example has slightly lifted ribbon handles. **B 722** (P 2641; 49-12-109) T.8:3. *Pl. 24; Kaloriziki,* Pl. 63. I-m. One handle missing. Very shallow and plate-like. C: dk. gray-buff wfds. P: m. dk. gray-brown. Int. center: numerous c-c. Wall dk. except for 3 n. res. rings. Rim barred. Ext: handles barred. H-z: dotted hor. lozenges in a band. Underside of base: outer part has c-c, some barred; inner part has 6-pointed star inscribed in a circle; res. ring near its center. H: 2.6. D (without handles): 12:1.

Amphoras: Later period

Type 1a: **B 723** (P 2644; 49-12-118) T.11:3 CG IB. I-m. Most of body pres. with non-joining neck. Rolled ring base. C: g. lt. gray-brown to gray-green. P: m. purple-brown. Band on int. rim. Rim barred. Neck

dk. with 2 res. zones of n. bands (one at neck-base). Wide band with 3 n. res. bands above h-z, 2 bands below handles and 2 more in lower body. H-z: 2 hor. w. lines. Paint on base and handles. Shoulder zone has traces of n. vert. s-o latticed zones. EH: 37. D: 26.

Type 1b: very wide heavy neck with very low base ring. **B 724** (P 2642; 49-12-116) T.11:1 CG IB. *Pl. 24.* C-m. C,P: like B 723. 4 groups of 6 bars on rim. Neck dk. with res. zone of 6 n. bands. H-z (bordered above and below by 2 bands): hor. w. line. Paint on handles. Shoulder: on each side 2 s-o triangles filled with solid lozenges. H: 28.7. D: 23.1.

The following fragmentary pots appear to belong to Type 1, but since they lack stratification a fairly wide range (White Painted I-II) should perhaps be allowed in dating: **B 725** (P 2712) MPT-A:1. *Pl. 25.* Portion of belly with hor. loop handle pres. C: g. brick-red to buff, coarse fabric. P: m. dk. brown. Paint on handle. H-z (bordered above and below by 2 thick bands): 3 hor. w. lines. PH: 20. **B 726** (P 2713) MPT-A:2. Neck, frag. of hor. loop handle and a few non-joining body frags. pres. C: like B 725. P: m. purple-brown. Neck painted solid except for lip, which has close-set spokes and 2 res. zones with multiple fine lines. H (of neck): 10. D (of mouth): 17. **B 727** (P 2714) MPT-A:3. Frag. of belly and shoulder with stump of handle pres. C: lt. brown to greenish buff, with lime grits. P: like B 726. Shoulder has 4 t-o latticed zones. H-z: like B 725 but only 2 w. lines. PH: 20.

Jug: Group A

Type 1b: **B 728** (P 2684; 49-12-400) T.30:6 CG IA. Part of belly and neck and a non-joining frag. of lower body. Apparently identical to K 386 in shape. C: g. lt. gray-green wfds. P: m. purple-brown. Dec: paint on neck base. D-o wide band below handles. PH: 10. D: 14.5.

Group B

Type 6a: cf. C 775 (*ExC*, Fig. 129, 56:1 = *CVA* BM Fs. 1 IICc Pl. 1:8).

WHITE PAINTED II WARE

The following jug is comparable in shape to *SCE* IV(2), Fig. XIII:19 (White Painted II) and *ibid.* Fig. XVI:6 (Bichrome II).

B 729 (P 2771; 54-41-60) MPT-D:3. *Pl. 25.* I-m. Low flaring ring base, ovoid body, neck-ring, rather wide sl. tapering neck; flaring round mouth with rolled rim; rectangular handle from shoulder to rim. C: orange to pinkish brown wfds. P: m. purple-brown. Ring inside mouth under rim. Paint on rim, neck-base and base. W. line high up on neck. D-o thick band at widest part of body. Zigzag on handle. H: 18.5. D: 12.

WHITE PAINTED IV WARE

Amphora

Type 2 (see *Kaloriziki,* under WP I, Type 2a): **B 730** (P 2809) T.31:4. 4 joining frags. of neck and rim pres. Straight wide neck. Greatly thickened, everted rim with beveled and undercut overhang. C: gray-green wfds. P: m. blue-black. Band on inside of rim; hor. zigzag on outside of rim. On top and bottom of neck zone: multiple brush lines bordered by thick stripes. In neck zone: d-o lat-loz. Between metopes: 3 widely spaced "trees" (for similar design, cf. *SCE* IV, 2, Fig. XXX:2). PH: 18.8. PD: 16.2.

Jug

Type 2 (see *Kaloriziki*, under WP IV, Type 2): **B 731** (P 2807) T.31:3. Body below shoulder missing. C: gray-pink to gray-green. P: m. purple-brown. Ring inside mouth and on lip. Sl. w. hor. line just below trefoil. Paint on neck-base, sides of handle and zigzag down middle. At level of base of handle: a small c-c on each of 3 sides. PH: 16.2. PD: 24.8. The following jug may be compared for shape to *SCE* IV(2), Fig. XXIX:3 (WP IV) and *ibid.* Fig. XXXIX:3 (B-on-R II): **B 732** (P 2931; 49-12-340) T.21:19. *Pl. 25.* I-m. Much of neck, mouth and lower body missing. Flat base, well proportioned ovoid body, small neck-ring; medium neck to flaring mouth. Flaring handle from shoulder to rim. C: g. lt. gray-green wfds. P: m. dk. gray-brown. Paint on rim, mid-neck and at neck-base. Sides of handles painted and handle barred. 3 small swastikas on shoulder. H: 14.2. D: 9.

MISCELLANEOUS WHITE PAINTED FRAGMENTS OF INDETERMINATE DATE

B 733 (P 2811) T.31:5. Various frags. of neck and handle of an amphora, too abraded for mending. Rim thickened and everted. C: powdery pinkish brown wfds. P: m. charcoal, much worn. S-o subdivided running lozenges; vert. zigzags flanking neck zone. EH (of neck): 15. **B 734** (Sh 468) Cw IIIa LC IIIB(?). Wall frag. C: g. orange-brown wfds; has a straw-plait impression. P: m. dk. gray. Bands. L (diagonal): 6. **B 735** (Sh 621) E-13. Wall frag. C: g. gray-green with sherd temper. P: m. purple. Band and multiple fine lines. H: 3.5. **B 736** (Sh 622) MPT-A:16. Low ring base and large section of tapering shoulder. C: lt. gray-green, coarse. P: m. purple. Stripe at base of neck. 2 heavily outlined n. stripes at base of shoulder. Paint on base. D (of base): 6.5. ED (of belly): 14. **B 737** (Sh 762a-d) B-Well:4 CA I(?). *Pl. 29.* Many non-joining frags. of a large hydria with sl. tapering neck. Flat sturdy strap handle. C: g. reddish brown to gray. P: m. purple-brown, worn. Stripe around neck-base; 2 vert. stripes near edge of handle; s-o broad stripe around widest(?) part of belly. Traces of a tail around base of handle and flourishing down over belly. H (of neck frag.): 8.6.

BICHROME I WARE

Jug

Type 6: the following pot has a slightly flattened spherical body. Handle and neck are lost so that it cannot be specifically classified. **B 738** (P 2680; 49-12-396) T.30:2 CG IA. *Pl. 29.* Surface much eroded. C: g. gray-purple to lt. gray-green; very coarse and heavy like cement. P: m. purple-brown and dull blood-red. S-o wide red band at center and edge. On front lat-loz. with upper sides drawn down in strokes and lower sides extended like kite-tail. Cf. K 508. D: 12.5. W: 11.8.

BLACK SLIP BUCCHERO I WARE

Jugs (see *Kaloriziki*, sub K 575 f.)

Type 2a: **B 739** (P 2639; 49-12-107) T.8:1. *Pl. 25.* Almost half of mouth missing. Neck-ring. C: g. lt. gray-brown. S: practically gone. Surface eroded and partly covered with a lime-like accretion. H (without handle): 21.6. D: 17.1.

Type 2b: **B 740** (P 2643; 49-12-117) T.11:2 CG IB. *Pl. 25.* Mouth, handle and part of base missing. Base small. Depressed globular shape. C: g. greenish brown. S: m. gray-blue. H: 13.6. D: 10.9.

BURNISHED GROOVED WARE

For a discussion of this category, see *Kaloriziki*, sub K 1001 f.

Bowls

B 741 (P 2800) B-Well:2, etc. CG II-III. *Pl. 29.* Three mended frags. with base, part of rim and both handles. 5 hor. grooves ext. below rim. Apparently a duplicate of K 1008 (*q.v.*). C: g. reddish brown, sandy; vert. hand bur. EH: 15. D (of base): 7.4. **B 742** (Sh 421) A-Unstrat. *Pl. 25.* Frag. of base with low ring base. C: dk. gray-buff; compact rich texture. Ls. bur. self slip int. and ext. fired pinkish in patches. L (diagonal): 4.4. **B 743** (Sh 422) A-Unstrat. Frag. of base(?) C: hor. dk. gray-pink, hard. S: ls. bur. very dk. buff int. and ext. L: 2.4. W: 2.2.

Jug

B 744 (Sh 420) A-Unstrat. *Pl. 25.* Wall frag. with raised ridge, like bucchero fluting. C: very dk. gray-buff, hard. S: ls. bur. self-slip. L (diagonal): 3.1.

BLACK-ON-RED WARE

Plate

B 745 (P 2806) T.31:1. *Pl. 53.* Most of base pres. Sturdy ring base. Cf. *SCE* IV(2), Fig. XL:9 for shape. C: dk. buff wfs. S: sl. ls. brick-red. P: m. sooty black. On bottom of base, 3 small c-c at center, stripe around int. and ext. of foot. Band and fine multiple lines on ext. Int: 3 c-c then wide zone of fine lines heavily outlined. PH: 3.3. D (of base): 9.2.

Jug

B 746 (Sh 612) Cw IIIb:2. 2 frags. of small barrel jug (neck and handle). C: lt. brick-red, hard and clean, sl. bur. ext. P: m. dk. gray. Heavily outlined multiple c-c on belly. Handle(s) barred. H (of neck frag.): 2.5.

MISCELLANEOUS DECORATED FABRICS

B 747 (Sh 194) A-E:3(V) LC IIIB. *Pl. 29.* Frag. showing transition from shoulder to neck. H-m. C:

hard, well-cleaned slate gray. P: m. dk. brown and dk. red. Outlined red band. Fabric like BR but not slipped. H: 3.1. **B 748** (Sh 478) A-A:3 LC IIA. *Pl.* 29. Wall frag. of large jug or krater. W-m. C: lt. brown-buff wfs. P: walnut to gray-brown. Hor. band. H: 3.5. **B 749** (Sh 635) E-A:7 LC IIA. *Pl.* 29. Wall frag. of jug(?) C: dk. reddish brown to gray-blue with lime grits. P: m. dk. red-brown in 3 bands. L: 5. H: 3.3. **B 750** (Sh 602) E-Hearth:A LC II? *Pl.* 29. Wall frag. of heavy jug or krater. W-m. C: lt. reddish brown to gray-green with large lime grits. P: m. gray-brown. Panel(?) design of interlocking, crosshatched triangles. Cross-hatch partially dotted. L: 7.5. W: 6. **B 751** (Sh 320) A-D:3(VII) LC IIIA. Wall frag. of jug(?) Has some resemblance to Pink Burnished Ware. C: lt. brick-red with fine lime grits. S: ls. bur. pinkish orange ext. only. L: 2.9. Th: 0.5. **B 752** (Sh 663; 54-41-53) MPT-B:2. *Pl.* 25. Thickened rim frag. of bowl. W-m. C: sl. ls. hard micaceous gray-green. Lip has incised zigzag. Under rim incised stacked triangle. L: 3. H: 1.5. **B 753** (Sh 184) A-D:2(VI) LC IIIA. *Pl.* 25. Wall frag. of jug. This and B 754-755 belong

to the same category. They have a superficial resemblance to Black-on-Red but are coarser and rougher in appearance and occur in a Bronze Age context. Apparently w-m. Signs of burning. C: g. lt. brick-red. S: dull dk. red. P: m. dk. gray. Rough c-c(?) L (diagonal): 4. **B 754** (Sh 196) A-F:2 LC IIIB. Wall frag. C, S, P, dec: like B 753, but fabric thinner. L (diagonal): 3. **B 755** (Sh 294) A-D:2(St.2b) LC IIIA. Wall frag. with beginning of handle or knob(?) C,S,P: like B 753, plus applied white. Dec. cannot be made out. L: 4.7. W: 3.5. **B 756** (Sh 647) Cw IV CA. *Pl.* 29. Semi-carinated rim frag. with a groove below carination ext. C: pinkish buff, clean and hard. S: lt. orange-red fired dk. gray in one place. Possibly Hellenistic. Crackled. W: 3. PD: 5. **B 757** (P 1739) E-8. *Pl.* 25. Body and stump of vert. handle of miniscule jug. Base merely flattened, body wide ovoid, neck moderately wide. C: dk. gray with large white grits; very sl. ls. surface. H: 1.6. D: 1.7. This vase is not, strictly speaking, decorated, but is included here because it suggests a playful(?) imitation of Base Ring or Monochrome jugs (cf. esp. *Problems*, 39, Type 1b).

Undecorated Wares

PLAIN WHITE WARE

This term is used generically for the usual coarse undecorated ware found at Bamboula, other than that classified in certain specific categories such as Plain Wheelmade II Ware, e.g. The Plain Wheelmade I Ware of *Problems* was presented as a definite class of pottery; however, it has not been treated as such here because the pots in question represent a transitional stage from handmade to wheelmade technique and it is sometimes difficult, just as in the case of Wash Ware and Burnished Slip Ware, to be certain whether a pot was actually handmade or made on the slow wheel. Moreover, both techniques are sometimes employed on the same pot, so that the body may be handmade and the neck wheelmade. This is not an isolated ceramic phenomenon: for other examples, see H. Goldman, *Excavations at Eutresis in Boeotia* (Cambridge, Mass., 1931) 115; *Lachish IV*, 166–167, 190; and E. Dohan, *Italic Tomb Groups* (Philadelphia, 1942) 3. As will be seen from the contexts of the pots catalogued here, the handmade technique continued in use side by side with wheelmade technique, even after the latter had become completely standardized in Plain Wheelmade II Ware.

Bowls: the relative scarcity of bowls in this category may be contrasted with their more frequent occurrence in the related Burnished Slip category. The increased serviceability of burnished bowls may account for this preference.

B 758 (P 1279; 49-12-149) T.12:19(D) LC IIA. *Pl.* 25. C-m. W-m. Low base ring; sl. concave flaring sides to plain rim with semi-cylindrical lip. Comparable to, but not identical with *Problems*, 56, Type 1a. An almost exactly similar bowl occurs at Troy (W. Dörpfeld, *Troja und Ilion*, Athens, 1902, 292; *Troy* III, Pl. 309). C: lt. gray-green with dk. sand; heavy fabric. H: 6.7. D: 21.1. **B 759** (Sh 656; 54-41-67) MPT-E:5. *Pl.* 25. From ⅓ to half pres. giving complete profile. W-m. Base inscribed before firing. Low ring base; sl. concave flaring sides to plain rim and lip. Essentially a simplification of the preceding form but impossible to date on this basis alone. C: pinkish gray to dk. pink near surface; much white accretion on ext. H: 5. ED: 20.6. *AJA* 64 (1960) Pl. 36 and p. 146, Ill. 1. **B 760** (P 2747) T.38:8. *Pl.* 25. I-m. Restored. Flat bottom, sl. convex flaring sides to carinated rim and plain lip. Pierced hor. lug handle. Shape not parallel in *Problems* but apparently PWM I. C: lt. g. gray with much dk. sand; well smoothed surface. H: 4.9. D: 12.1. **B 761** (P 2767; 54-41-65) MPT-E:3. *Pl.* 25. C-ch. W-m. Sturdy ring base; concave flaring sides to semi-carinated rim with plain lip. One pierced hor. lug handle. Comparable to, but not identical with *Problems*, 56, Type 2b; however, virtually identical with Burnished Slip, Type 1b. C: g. pinkish buff to pinkish white with dk. sand; well smoothed. H: 4.9. D: 11.2. **B 762** (P 2836; 54-41-69) MPT-F:2. *Pl.* 25. C-ch. Probably w-m. Plain flat base; sl. convex flaring walls to inverted plain rim. Shape ·very close to Burnished Slip, Type 2. C: dk. g. buff with a striking amount of black sand; very thick heavy fabric almost suggesting stone; surface wet-smoothed. H: 7.2. D: 21.1. **B 763** (G 69:K 47; 54-41-17) VT:17. Wide strap handle from rim to body of a heavy but apparently fairly shallow bowl. Squared rim. H-m? Signs of burning. C: dull gray-brown wfds. L: 8.9. W: 9.1. *UPMB* 13 (1948) Pl. 3; *AJA* 64 (1960) Pl. 36.

Krater-amphoras

B 764 (P 2801) D-A. *Pl. 47.* Base and part of one side missing. Made by hand or on slow wheel. Body full ovoid and perhaps piriform; short wide convex neck set off by neck-ring. Squared ledge rim. Strap handle(s) from rim to shoulder. C: dk. buff to lt. buff at surface with dk. sand. PH: 26. PD: 32.2. **B 765** (P 2815) D-A. *Pl. 47.* Large frag. of body and rim plus various non-joining shoulder and rim frags. pres. Rim inscribed before firing. Body handmade; rim appears to have been finished on wheel. Shape probably biconical. Small neck ring. Sl. concave, short flaring neck with flat rim. On upper part of body, stumps of hor. (raised?) roll handle. C: g. gray-brown and red to gray-green on surface. General appearance suggests PWM I Ware. PH: 26. PD (approx.): 36. *AJA* 64 (1960) Pl. 36 and p. 146, Ill. 1. **B 766** (G 23:K 19) A-B:3 (given as B:4 in *AJA* 45, 1941, 275) LC IIB. Lower part of handle. Probably PWM I. C: powdery lt. pinkish brown to dk. buff wfds. H: 7. L (diagonal): 10.7. *AJA* 64 (1960) Pl. 36.

Jugs: these are classified first on the basis of technique and second on the basis of shape. As might be expected, a close correspondence exists between these two criteria.

A: this category includes various types of handmade large jugs.

Type A 1: flat wide base; the only example with complete profile has a full ovoid body, neck-ring, small concave neck, roll rim and handle from neck to rim. **B 767** (P 760) A-E:2(V) LC IIIB. *Pl. 25.* I-m. Handle and much of one side missing. C: g. pinkish brown to mottled gray surface with lime and sherd temper. H: 41.9. D: 29.7. **B 768** (P 2674; 49-12-342) T.22:3 LC IIA. *Pl. 29.* Lower half of body pres. C: g. pinkish to brown, sandy. Around upper part are fossilized remains of small worms. PH: 24. D: 27.7. **B 769** (P 2847) A-D:2(VII,2) LC IIIA. Lower half of body pres. C: g. red and cinnamon at core to grayish green at surface. PH: 29. D: 33.5. **B 770** (G 11:K 22) A-E:2(VI) LC IIIB (termed a "stray" by Daniel). Wall frag. possibly from this shape. C: dk. pinkish buff wfds. L (diagonal): 6.6. *AJA* 64 (1960) Pl. 36.

Type A 2: flat wide base; biconical body, neck and rim as Type A 1, heavy flattened handle from shoulder to just below rim. A possibility exists that these were made on the slow wheel. **B 771** (P 1208; 54-41-68) MPT-F:1. Neck, handle and part of shoulder pres. Mouth completely sealed with white chavara plaster. C: g. pinkish clay with dk. sand plus red and white particles. On handle: 3 blobs of m. wine-red paint, perhaps dipinti. PH: 21. D (of mouth): 11. **B 772** (P 1276; 49-12-147) T.12:17(D) LC IIA. *Pl. 47.* C-i. C: orange-brown with much dk. sand; heavy fabric. H: 27. D: 20.8.

Type A 3: shape identical with A 2 except that the two fully preserved examples have ovoid rather than biconical body. The peculiarity of this class is that

while the bodies are handmade, the necks are made on the wheel. (For absolute confirmation of this, see B 776.) These have been classified in the Tables (*Bamboula* SS) as Plain Wheelmade I Ware for convenience, although, of course, technically they do not entirely belong to that category. **B 773** (P 753) A-B:6 LC IIB. *Pl. 25.* Neck only with frag. of handle pres. C: lt. brick-red, sandy. PH: 9.3. D (of rim): 11.8. **B 774** (P 1320) T.36:52. *Pl. 47.* C-i. C: surface lt. pink to greenish gray wfds; base set in sand; very heavy fabric. H: 36.7. D: 26.1. **B 775** (P 2696; 49-12-432) T.35:1 LC I? C-i. C: gray-green to pink with dk. sand and some large lime grits. H: 33. D: 24.4. **B 776** (P 2803) T.38:21. Handle, most of neck and part of shoulder pres. Neck joined to body with additional clay inside body. C: g. cinnamon at core to greenish gray at surface wfds. PH: 19. D (of rim): 9.5. **B 777** (P 2804) T.31:1. Neck, handle and adjoining part of shoulder pres. Neck smoothly joined to body. C: g. gray-brown at core to pinkish gray at surface. PH: 17.8. D (of rim): 11. **B 778** (G 49:K 62) D-A. Frag. of handle to neck. PWM I? C: pinkish brown wfds. H: 8.5. ED (of mouth): 10. *AJA* 64 (1960) Pl. 36. **B 779** (G 71:K 50; 49-12-55) T.5:39(A or B) LC IIB. Frag. of handle to neck. PWM I? C: like B 778. L: 9. *AJA* 64 (1960) Pl. 36.

B: this category includes small jugs, both handmade and wheelmade. Type B 1 is the counterpart of Type A 2. Types B 2 and B 3 are respectively handmade and wheelmade trefoil jugs.

Type B 1: small wheelmade jugs of the same shape as those of Type A 2. **B 780** (P 1278; 49-12-174) T.12:46(A 2) LC IA:2. *Pl. 25.* Handle and upper neck missing. PWM I, close to *Problems*, 58, Type 3a, but almost certainly not trefoil. C: lt. brown, sandy. PH: 17. D: 13. **B 781** (P 1321) T.36:46. *Pl. 47.* N-c-m. Surface pitted. PWM I. C: brown at core to yellow-green, sandy. H: 21.2. D: 16.7. **B 782** (P 2913) T.40:37(D) LC IIIA. Missing most of mouth and neck. PWM I or early PWM II. C: g. reddish gray at core to gray-green (with pink patches) at surface. Heavy fabric. H: 29.7. D: 20.6.

Type B 2: small handmade jugs with flat base, biconical body, short neck and trefoil mouth; very low neck-ring. **B 783** (P 1213; 54-41-6) VT:6. Part of handle and neck missing, otherwise intact. C: lt. gray-brown at core to greenish gray and pinkish gray at surface. H: 17. D: 13.9. Cf. *Problems*, 58, Type 3b. **B 784** (P 2668; 49-12-334) T.21:4 LC IIA. *Pl. 25.* Part of neck, all of mouth, all but stump of handle missing. C: g. grayish brick-red wfds. PH: 24.1. D: 18.6. **B 785** (P 2697; 49-12-433) T.35:2 LC I(?). *Pl. 25.* Part of mouth and neck and all of handle missing. C: reddish brown at core to gray-pink and gray-green at surface wfds; heavy fabric. H: 26.5. D: 30. **B 786** (P 2907) T.40:72(C) LC IIIA. *Pl. 59.* Handle, most of neck and about half of upper body pres. Body may have been ovoid. C: g. lt. pinkish brown. Coarse heavy fabric; well smoothed surface. PH: 23.6. D: 20.

Type B 3: small trefoil jugs probably made on the slow wheel. Handles from shoulder to rim. **B 787**

(P 1322) T.36:39. *Pl. 47*. C-i. Biconical body and rolled rim, quite similar in shape to *Problems*, 58, Type 3d. C: brick-red with dk. and lt. sand. H: 19.9. D: 15.3. **B 788** (P 1323) T.36:43. *Pl. 47*. C-i, surface worn. Rather heavy ovoid body and rolled rim. C: like B 787. H: 21.3. D: 14.8. **B 789** (P 1420; 49-12-310) T.19:45(B) LC IIA-B. *Pl. 25*. Mouth broken, otherwise intact. Biconical body. C: lt. greenish gray wfds. H: 19.2. D: 16.3.

Inscribed jug handles: from the point of view of technique it is impossible to tell from the handle alone whether it is from a handmade or wheelmade jug of this variety. Many of the fragments listed below may be from Plain Wheelmade I jugs, even when not so designated.
B 790 (Sh 647a) T.38:9. Frag. from top of handle. Inscribed before baking. C: pinkish gray at core to greenish gray at surface, worn; coarse fabric. H: 5.3. L: 9. *AJA* 64 (1960) Pl. 36 and p. 146, Ill. 1. **B 791** (Sh 736; 54-41-57) MPT-C:3. Frag. from middle of handle. Inscribed before baking. C: g. slate-gray at core to gray-green at surface, worn. H: 4.9. W: 3.2. *AJA* 64 (1960) Pl. 36 and p. 146, Ill. 1. **B 792** (G 6:K 36) A-Unstrat. Frag. from center of handle. C: lt. orange-brown wfds. PH: 12.3. *AJA* 42 (1938) 273, Fig. 13:F; *AJA* 64 (1960) Pl. 36. **B 793** (G 8:K 43) A-Unstrat. Frag. from bottom of handle(?) C: gray at core to orange at surface; soft. PH: 8.8. *AJA* 64 (1960) Pl. 36. **B 794** (G 9:K 7) Stray. Frag. from top of handle. PWM I(?) C: lt. buff with multicolored sand. L: 7.5. *AJA* 64 (1960) Pl. 36. **B 795** (G 14:K 41) A-E:4 LC IIIB (called a "stray" by Daniel). Frag. from near base of handle(?) C: like B 793. H: 7.7. *AJA* 64 (1960) Pl. 36. **B 796** (G 17:K 39) A-Unstrat. Frag. from top of handle. Probably PWM I. C: g. gray-brown, fired lt. gray-green; very heavy fabric. L: 6.7. *AJA* 64 (1960) Pl. 36. **B 797** (G 21:K 33) A-B:5 LC IIB. Frag. from near neck of a very small jug. C: powdery lt. gray-brown wfds. L: 4. *AJA* 64 (1960) Pl. 36. **B 798** (G 27:K 18) C-A:5 LC IB. W-m. Frag. from base of handle with adjoining wall. C: powdery lt. gray-green wfds. W: 5. *AJA* 64 (1960) Pl. 36. **B 799** (G 29:K 35) C-C:2 LC IIC. Frag. from base of handle with some adjoining wall. Probably PWM I. C: lt. pinkish brown to gray-brown wfds; very heavy fabric. H: 12.1. *AJA* 64 (1960) Pl. 36. **B 800** (G 32:K 13) C-A:5 LC IB. Frag. like B 799 but from a smaller pot. C: lt. pinkish brown to gray-green wfds. H: 7.7. *AJA* 64 (1960) Pl. 36. **B 801** (G 34:K 30) C-Unstrat. Frag. from center. C: g. lt. pinkish brown; powdery. L: 9.4. *AJA* 64 (1960) Pl. 36. **B 802** (G 35:K 56) Stray according to *AJA* 45 (1941) 276 but listed as from T.2 (disturbed) on catalogue card. Frag. from near neck. C: lt. pink at core to buff at surface. L: 5.2. *AJA* 64 (1960) Pl. 36. **B 803** (G 39:K 11; 49-12-313) T.19:49(A-B) LC IIA-B. Rectangular handle to rolled rim. PWM I. C: orange-brown clay with vari-colored grits and sherd temper. H: 16.5. *AJA* 64 (1960) Pl. 36. **B 804** (G 40:K 1) D-A. Frag. to rolled rim. PWM I. C: very lt. gray-brown wfds. L: 9. *AJA* 64 (1960) Pl. 36. **B 805** (G 44:K 57) T.17:27. Frag. from center of handle. C: like B 792. L: 8. *AJA* 64

(1960) Pl. 36. **B 806** (G 54:K 24) D-A. Frag. of handle to rolled rim. C: pink to gray-buff with lime grits and sherd temper. L: 8. *AJA* 64 (1960) Pl. 36. **B 807** (G 59:K 59; 49-12-37) T.6:11. Frag. to rolled rim. C: like B 792. H: 6. *AJA* 64 (1960) Pl. 36. **B 808** (G 62:K 15) A-Unstrat. Frag. to rolled rim. PWM I. C: powdery dk. buff with grits and sherd temper. L: 9.6. *AJA* 64 (1960) Pl. 36. **B 809** (G 63:K 66) Stray. Frag. to rolled rim. C: lt. pinkish brown wfds. L: 6.5. *AJA* 64 (1960) Pl. 36. **B 810** (G 73) E-Unstrat. Frag. from top of handle. Probably w-m. Inscribed while leather hard. C: very lt. gray-green wfds, powdery. L: 8.3. *AJA* 64 (1960) Pl. 36.

PLAIN WHEELMADE II WARE

The repertory of this class as presented in *Problems* is considerably enriched by the finds from Bamboula.

Bowl (for other types, see *Kaloriziki*, sub Plain Wheelmade II Ware).

Type 2: flat base, deep bowl with convex flaring sides to rounded overhanging rim; small vertical strap handle(s) to rim. **B 811** (P 756) A-E:2(V) LC IIIB. *Pl. 25*. I-m. Part of one side including (probably) a handle missing. C: hard g. red-brown to greenish gray. H: 18.1. D: 38.3.

Krater-amphoras: owing to the incomplete condition of most of the examples no attempt is made here to classify variations of this shape. Differences are noted in the catalogue entries. Flat or ring or roll bases (this latter type is the torus-disc in the terminology of *MP*, 91); ovoid bodies; short vertical or tapering taller necks. All have vertical strap handles from shoulder to rim and overhanging squared ledge rims.
B 812 (P 752) A-B:6 LC IIB. *Pl. 25*. Most of neck and shoulder, with one handle, pres. Short steep shoulder, neck-ring, short vert. neck. C: lt. brick-red, sandy to greenish brown. H: 8.8 (without belly frag. which was missing at time of control). D: 27.7. B 812 is the earliest form of w-m krater-amphora from the site but more closely related to later Bamboula examples than to the PWM I example in *Problems*, 58. **B 813** (P 770) A-E:2(V) LC IIIB. *Pls. 25, 57*. N-c-m. Plain flat base, tall ovoid body, neck-ring, high tapering neck. C: gray-brown with greenish gray surface; rather heavy fabric. H: 44.1. D: 39.1. **B 814** (P 783) A-E:2(VIII) LC IIIB. *Pl. 25*. Almost half missing but complete profile pres. Ring base, wide ovoid body, neck-ring. Handles have vert. central rib. C: g. red-brown to greenish gray. H: 36.9. D: 37.5. **B 815** (P 809) A-D:2(IV) LC IIIA. Base and much of neck, with rim and one handle missing. Shape, as far as pres., like B 812. C: g. gray-brown to reddish gray, with poorly smoothed surface. PH: 40.5. PD: 47.1. **B 816** (P 2709) Cw IIIb LC IIIB. *Pls. 26, 57*. N-c-m. Roll foot. Short n. stem from which flare convex sides to short steep shoulder, rather tall tapering neck. Angular handles have central rib and wide flaring bases with an imitation rivet in relief; three of same inside neck on each side. C: lt. brick-red, well sifted but with many lime particles and air holes, fired gray-

green at surface. H: 42.7. D (of mouth): 29.5. Other examples of this shape are from Kaloriziki: T.19:23; T.26:87 and T.40:9. Daniel classed the shape with vases derived from the Mycenaean tradition. It seems rather to be an adaptation of the ordinary Plain Wheel-made II krater-amphora in the Mycenaean spirit. Virtually all the elements are already present in the Plain Wheelmade tradition (cf. *Problems*, p. 58 for shape and p. 59 for metallic elements; cf. B 818 for foot, other vases of this series for general shape and appearance. **B 817** (P 2834) A-D:3(IV) LC IIIA. Large frag. giving profile of upper body pres. No neck-ring, otherwise shape appears to be that of B 814. C: dk. gray-brown at core to gray-green at surface; huge rough grits. PH: 28.5. PD: 28.2. **B 818** (P 2837) E-D:1f LC IIIA. *Pl. 57*. Most of neck and belly and most of base and lower body pres. in 2 non-joining frags. Sturdy ring base. Body apparently tall ovoid. Upper body like B 813. C: like B 813. H (of upper frag.): 24. H (of lower frag.): 20.4. D (of mouth): 29.

Jugs: as in the case of Plain White Ware, this shape is by far the most common.

Type 1b: this category of *Problems*, 60 is used here to classify jugs which, although not having the specific profile of the example, exhibit base ring (or ring base, which seems interchangeable with the former in this group), ovoid bodies and neck-ring, handle from shoulder to upper neck, and round mouth with moulded lip. A *Fehlbrand* (P 2730: unfortunately without exactly known provenance) seems to indicate that there was a kiln at or near Bamboula. **B 819** (P 747) A-E:2(VIII) LC IIIB. *Pl. 26*. I-m. Restored. Low base ring. C: gray at core to lt. orange-brown, well sifted. H: 24.2. D: 14.4. **B 820** (P 803) A-E:2(VIII) LC IIIB. *Pl. 57*. I-m. Restored. Low base ring. C: lt. g. green, soft. H: 31.6. D: 17. **B 821** (P 1298) T.33:27a(B) LC IIIA. *Pls. 48, 61, 63*. N-c. Mouth missing. Low base ring. C: gray at core to greenish and lavender at surface wfs. H: 27. D: 16. **B 822** (P 1299) T.33:18(B) LC IIIA. *Pls. 48, 61*. N-c-m. Restored. Low ring base. 2 pellets on neck by handle. C: lt. brick-red wfs; surface wet-smoothed. A blob of dk. m. brown paint on handle (cf. B 771). H: 28.2. D: 17. **B 823** (P 1319) T.36:62. *Pl. 48*. I-m. Handle and much of neck and body missing. Low base ring. C: orange-brown at core to buff and gray-green surface, sandy. H: 27.5. D: 15.7. **B 824** (P 2693; 49-12-410) T.32:6 LC IIIA. *Pl. 26*. ⅓ of rim missing. Low ring base; heavy ovoid body. Inscribed handle. C: g. gray-lavender, fired lt. gray-green with a few orange patches at surface. H: 28.2. D: 20.3. *AJA* 64 (1960) Pl. 37; p. 146, Ill. 1; cf. *OA* 3, 1944, Pl. 1:22. **B 825** (P 2796; 49-12-425) T.34:7. *Pl. 26*. Rim missing, base chipped. Very low base ring. C: g. dk. red-brown at core to pink and yellow-gray. PH: 24.6. D: 16.2. **B 826** (P 2851) E-D:1f LC IIIA. An upper frag. with handle and much of neck and shoulder plus a non-joining lower frag. with base. Base ring. C: g. red-brown at core to gray at surface, hard. PH (upper body): 15.8. ED: 14. D (of base): 8.4. **B 827** (P 2914) T.40:14(D) LC IIIA. *Pls. 57, 59*. ⅓ of rim

missing. Low base ring. C: g. gray-green; well smoothed surface. 2 pellets on upper neck near handle. H: 29.5. D: 17.6. **B 828** (P 2915) T.40:13(D) LC IIIA. *Pl. 59*. N-c-m. Low base ring. C: g. red-brown at core to gray-green at surface; well smoothed. H: 26.8. D: 16.4. **B 829** (G 26:K 65) A-D:2(VIa) LC IIIA. Upper handle to neck with 2 pellets at either side of top. C: orange-brown wfds. L: 5. *AJA* 64 (1960) Pl. 37.

Type 1c: this category is added to those of *Problems*, 60 to classify jugs which exhibit base ring (or the interchangeable ring base and disc base), ovoid body, handle from shoulder to rim (or immediately under rim) and round mouth with moulded lip. **B 830** (P 2655; 49-12-238) T.18:3(B) LC IIIA. *Pls. 26, 57*. C-i. Small hole in neck probably represents flaw in manufacture. Low but distinctly flaring base ring; neck-ring. Metallically profiled rim. C: g. dull gray-brown wfs. Upper part of pot better smoothed than lower part. H: 19.2. D: 12.8. **B 831** (P 2908) T.40:17(D) LC IIIA. *Pl. 59*. I-m. Nearly all of neck missing. Low base ring. Neck-ring. 2 pellets on neck by handle. C: g. reddish brown; much of ext. surface badly eroded. H: 25. D: 15.4. **B 832** (P 2916) T.40:2(D) LC IIIA. *Pls. 57, 59*. C-i. Low base ring. Body dented in manufacture. Neck-ring. Junction of handle with pot not smoothed. C: gray-green to pink-ish wfs; heavy fabric. H: 23.5. D: 15.5. **B 833** (P 2920) T.40:22(D) LC IIIA. *Pls. 26, 59*. N-c-m. Low ring base. Body almost elongated biconical. Neck-ring. C: like B 827. Traces of ash on surface. H: 23.4. D: 14.6. **B 834** (P 2921) T.40:11(D) LC IIIA. *Pl. 59*. Sections of rim missing. Hollowed disc base. Heavy squarish body, almost biconical: 2 incised rings on base of wide neck. C: g. brick-red to gray-red at surface, white particles; well smoothed. H: 19.2. D: 13.6.

Type 1d: hollowed disc base, elongated spherical body with incised ring around base of narrow concave neck with flaring mouth. The shape appears to be an adaptation of native Cypriote types (cf. *SPC*, 146, No. 2; 169, No. 2; and 178, No. 2). **B 835** (P 1309) T.33:34(A) LC IIB. *Pls. 48, 60*. C-i. C: pinkish yellow wfds. H: 15.8. D: 12.

Type 3: this category of *Problems*, 60 is used here to classify jugs which have, if not the specific shape of the example, in any case a plain flat base (or disc base set off from body), ovoid body, neck-grooves, tapering neck, trefoil mouth and handle from shoulder to rim. **B 836** (P 1409; 49-12-290) T.19:18(D) LC IIIA. *Pls. 26, 48, 57*. C-i. Truncated ovoid body with rather flat shoulder. C: g. gray-green wfs, not well smoothed. H: 24. D: 15.2. **B 837** (P 2795; 49-12-424) T.34:6. N-c. Mouth mostly missing. C: like B 825. H: 28.1. D: 18. **B 838** (P 2831) E-D:1f LC IIIA. *Pl. 57*. I-m. About half of mouth and much of body missing. Elongated ovoid body. C: g. pinkish buff to dk. buff at surface wfs. H: 33.4. D: 17.8. **B 839** (P 2832) E-D:1f LC IIIA. *Pl. 48*. Portion of neck and shoulder and non-joining base pres. Apparently a duplicate of B 838 in shape. C: g. brick-red to gray-green at surface. PH (of upper frag.): 25. D: 18.4. **B 840**

(P 2917) T.40:42(C) LC IIIA. *Pls. 26, 59.* C-m. Disc base set off from body by 3 incised rings; full graceful ovoid body; beveled lip. C: like B 827, fired pinkish around mouth. H: 19.9. D: 12. **B 841** (P 2918) T.40:32(D) LC IIIA. *Pls. 26, 59.* C-i. Full graceful ovoid body. C: like B 828 with pink areas on surface. H: 25.4. D: 15. **B 842** (P 2926) T.40:41(C) LC IIIA. *Pl. 59.* I-m. Shape nearly identical with that of B 841. 5 incised lines around base. C: g. lt. gray-brown, well smoothed. Fine ashes(?) on ext. H: 29.8. D: 17.4. **B 843** (P 2927) T.40:6(D) LC IIIA. *Pls. 26, 57, 59.* N-c-m. Elongated ovoid body with wide neck. C: dk. g. brick-red at core to blue-gray and pink at surface; heavy fabric, well smoothed. H: 35.4. D: 17.7. **B 844** (P 2928) T.40:54(C) LC IIIA. *Pl. 59.* N-c-m. Shape very similar to that of B 842; sl. more swelling body and shorter neck. 5 incised lines around base. C: like B 842 but more reddish and sandy. H: 31.8. D: 19.1. *AJA* 64 (1960) Pl. 37 and p. 146, Ill. 1. **B 845** (P 2929) T.40:47(C) LC IIIA. *Pl. 59.* N-c-m. Shape very similar to that of B 842: neck shorter. 3 incised lines round base. H: 31.8. D: 17.8.

Type 4: this category of *Problems,* 60 is used here to classify jugs which have, if not the specific shape of the example, in any case a plain flat base, ovoid body, neck-ring(s), short tapering neck, strap handle from shoulder to neck, and round mouth with moulded lip. **B 846** (P 732:K 16) A-D:2(VII,2) LC IIIA. I-m. Base and mouth entirely missing. 2 prominent, well separated neck-rings. Handle inscribed. C: pink at core, gray-green to pinkish brown at surface; sandy, hard, fine. PH: 26.4. D: 18.1. *AJA* 42 (1938) 273, Fig. 13:d; *AJA* 64 (1960) Pl. 37. **B 847** (P 737) A-D:2(VII,2) LC IIIA. I-m. Base and most of neck missing. 2 neck-rings. C: m. brick-red, sandy to gray-green at surface. PH: 46. D: 28.1. **B 848** (P 765) A-D:2(V) LC IIIA. *Pl. 57.* C-sp. Shape identical to *Problems,* 60, Type 4. 2 neck-rings. C: gray to red-brown wfs; hard. H: 48.6. D: 28.8. **B 849** (P 779) A-E:2(VIII) LC IIIB. I-m. Lower body and base missing. Shape identical with B 848. C: gray-green to red-brown. PH: 41.7. D: 28. **B 850** (P 780) A-E:2(VIII) LC IIIB. *Pl. 26.* N-c-m. Shape identical with B 848. C: greenish brown with a yellow-gray patch. H: 52. D: 28.8. **B 851** (P 781) A-D:2(VI) LC IIIA. *Pl. 29.* Lower half of jug; upper part cut off in antiquity so that lower part could be sunk in floor. Shape apparently like B 848. C: orange-brown, sandy. PH: 31.3. D: 30.7. **B 852** (P 789:K 42) A-D:2(IV) LC IIIA. N-c-m. Mouth and much of neck missing. Handle inscribed. Single neck-ring. Shape like B 848. C: gray-green to red; hard, with much fine lime. PH: 49.6. D: 29.9. *AJA* 64 (1960) 147. **B 853** (P 793) A-E:2(VIII) LC IIIB. N-c-m. Shape like B 848. Double neck-rings. C: red at core to gray-green at surface; hard, sandy. H: 38.2. D: 23.5. **B 854** (P 806) A-E:2(V) LC IIIB. About half of neck and body pres. Double neck-rings. C: dk. brown, sandy. PH: 38.5. D: 28. **B 855** (P 808) A-D:2(V) LC IIIA. Mouth, base and most of handle missing. 4 neck-rings. Burnt on one side. C: gray-brown wfs and many small lime particles. PH: 43. D: 31.5.

B 856 (P 959) D-B:2a LC IIIA. N-c-m. Shape like B 848. Double neck-rings. C: brick-red to lt. greenish brown wfs and lime particles. H: 53.2. D: 33.3. **B 857** (P 1296) T.33:25a(B) LC IIIA. *Pls. 48, 57, 61.* N-c-m. Shape like B 848. C: g. lt. brown wfs. H: 49.4. D: 27.6. **B 858** (P 1297) T.33:26a(B) LC IIIA. *Pls. 48, 61.* N-c-m. Handle entirely missing. Shape like B 848. C: brown at core to gray-green and pink at surface wfds and lime. H: 33.1. D: 19.3. **B 859** (P 2677; 49-12-356) T.23:3 LC IIIA. Base and small adjoining section of wall plus a few semi-joining frags. Base has small round hole in bottom which can be neither erosion nor a modern break. Neatly made, it is perhaps a hole for sacrificial purposes. C: gray-brown wfs. PH: 12. D (of base): 14.4. **B 860** (P 2704) Cw IIIb:1 LC III(?). Portion of base, shoulder, neck and handle pres., non-joining. A frag. of the body has a sign inscribed before baking. C: brick-red to gray-green with numerous lime particles. D (of base): 14.5. *AJA* 64 (1960) Pl. 37 and p. 146, Ill. 1. **B 861** (P 2840) A-D:2(VI) LC IIIA. About half of neck and shoulder, with handle, pres. Single neck-ring. C: g. orange-brown, coarse. PH: 25.8. D: 25.8. **B 862** (P 2852) E-D:1h. About half of body pres. in a vertical cut, with a small part of neck. Proportions like B 848. C: g. reddish brown to gray-green; coarse. PH: 47. D: 31.2.

Type 5: flat base, rather fat, ovoid body, neck-ring, wide tapering neck, moulded lip and handle from shoulder to rim. **B 863** (P 814) A-E:2(VIII) LC IIIB. *Pl. 57.* About half pres. giving profile. Restored. C: lt. brown-buff wfs. H: 27.1. D: 20.7. **B 864** (P 2708) E-11c. *Pl. 48.* I-m. C: g. buff, well sifted with some lime particles. H: 29.3. D: 22.

Type 6: small flat base, spherical or flattened spherical body passing with little or no articulation into wide tapering neck with slightly flaring round mouth and moulded lip. Cf. B 610. Rounded handle from shoulder to rim. Undoubtedly derivative from the Monochrome Type 5 jug. **B 865** (P 736) A-D:2(VII,2) LC IIIA. *Pls. 29, 57.* Base and most of body missing but profile pres. Sl. elongated spherical body. C: g. brick-red at core to gray-green and pinkish at surface. PH: 23. ED: 13.4. **B 866** (P 1411; 49-12-300) T.19:33(C) LC IIIA. *Pls. 26, 48, 57.* N-c-m. Spherical body. Handle has center rib; lip beveled. C: orange-brown to lt. gray-green at surface, with much lime. H: 23. D: 16.5. **B 867** (P 1412; 49-12-301) T.19:34(C) LC IIIA. *Pl. 26.* C-i. Flattened spherical body. C: g. gray-brown with sand; coarse appearance. H: 13.8. D: 11.2. **B 868** (P 2678; 49-12-357) T.23:4 LC IIIA. About ¼ pres. giving profile to neck. Sack-like body with a kind of angulation at shoulder and near base. C: lt. gray-brown wfs; lt. lime grits. PH: 14.3. D: 11.4. **B 869** (P 2922) T.40:33(D) LC IIIA. *Pls. 26, 57, 59.* C-i. Spherical body with neck set off by a sl. indentation in contour. Center rib on handle. C: g. reddish brown to gray-green, with large lime particles: coarse texture. H: 23.3. D: 15. **B 870** (P 2923) T.40:27(D) LC IIIA. *Pls. 26, 59.* C-i. Somewhat more squat than B 869. C: like B 869. Signs of ashes on surface. H: 22.1. D: 15.5. **B 871**

(P 2924) T.40:36(D) LC IIIA. *Pl. 59.* C-i. Shape like B 866 though with a slight angulation. Center rib on handle. C: g. lt. gray-green; sandy coarse texture. H: 16.3. D: 11.3.

Type 7: low ring base, ovoid body, neck-ring, tapering neck, rectangular handle to neck(?) In the case of both examples given below the mouth is missing, but it was undoubtedly round. This is apparently a variation of Type 4. **B 872** (P 799) A-D:2(VII,2) LC IIIA. *Pl. 57.* I-m. Part of base and body and most of neck missing. C: g. red at core to gray-pink and blue at surface; hard and sandy. PH: 21.5. D: 14.5. **B 873** (P 1295) T.33:4(C) LC IIIB. *Pls. 48, 57, 60.* Most of neck missing. C: orange-brown to gray-green, with sand and lime; well smoothed. PH: 34.3. D: 27.

Type 8: tubular jug with pointed base and trefoil mouth; handle from shoulder to rim. K 846 also belongs to this class. Cf. B 609. **B 874** (P 1204) E-D:1h LC IIIA. Neck and handle missing, surface pitted. C: brick-red wfs and large dk. and lt. grits. PH: 16.5. D: 7.8. **B 875** (P 1207) E-D:1f LC IIIA. *Pls. 26, 48, 57.* N-c-m. Beveled lip. C: reddish brown to green-gray at surface wfds. H: 17.7. D: 7.2. **B 876** (Sh 313) A-D:2(VII,2) LC IIIA. About ⅓ of body and neck; base entirely missing. C: red-brown at core to gray-brown at surface; coarse appearance. PH: 7.9. ED: 6.

Type 9: small flat base, spherical body with wide short flaring neck. Vertical strap handle from shoulder to rim. The shape seems more appropriate for coarse ware but the technique and appearance are that of Plain Wheelmade II Ware. **B 877** (P 2727) E-11c. *Pl. 26.* C-sp. Lip partly fire-blackened. C: g. pink at core to gray-green at surface, with large lime particles; coarse texture. H: 14.8. D: 15.8. **B 878** (P 2728) E-11c. N-c-sp. Interior partly fire-blackened. C: like B 877, except finer fabric. H: 12.9. D: 12.7. **B 879** (P 2919) T.40:55(C) LC IIIA. *Pls. 26, 59.* C-sp. Traces of ashes int. and ext. Beveled lip. C: g. gray-brown to gray-green, almost khaki-colored. H: 12.5. D: 12.6.

Miscellaneous jug fragments

B 880 (Sh 389) A-E:3(VIII) LC IIIB. *Pl. 29.* Frag. from shoulder of jug(?) with neck-ring and twisted handle. C: lt. gray-pink to gray-buff wfds. H: 7.3. W: 5.4. **B 881** (Sh 648) T.38:10. Base of handle inscribed before baking. C: g. gray-brown core to dk. buff at surface wfs. L: 11.2. *AJA* 64 (1960) Pl. 37 and p. 146, Ill. 1. **B 882** (Sh 657; 54-41-61) MPT-D:4. Base of handle inscribed before baking. C: g. pinkish buff wfds. L: 6. *AJA* 64 (1960) Pl. 37 and p. 146, Ill. 1. **B 883** (Sh 664; 49-12-393) T.29. Frag. of upper handle to rim. Inscribed with a fairly sharp instrument while clay was leather hard. C: lt. gray-buff wfds; powdery. L: 7.2. *AJA* 64 (1960) Pl. 37 and p. 146, Ill. 1. **B 884** (G 2:K 25) A-Unstrat. Frag. of upper handle to rim. C: lt. gray-pink to gray-green wfds. L: 7.2. *AJA* 42 (1938) 273, Fig. 13:m; *AJA* 64 (1960) Pl. 37. **B 885** (G 4:K 63) A-D:2(St.2a) LC IIIA. Base of handle. C: lt. pinkish brown wfds.

H: 9. *AJA* 42 (1938) 273, Fig. 13:g; *AJA* 64 (1960) Pl. 37. **B 886** (G 7:K 37) A-Unstrat. Top of handle. C: lt. gray-pink wfds. L: 6.3. *AJA* 42 (1938) 273, Fig. 13:e; *AJA* 64 (1960) Pl. 37. **B 887** (G 10:K 51) A-D:2(VII,2) LC IIIA. Frag. from base of handle. C: lt. red-brown to gray-green at surface wfds. H: 8.2. *AJA* 64 (1960) Pl. 37. **B 888** (G 15:K 53) A-D:3(VII) LC IIIA. Frag. of upper handle and neck. C: lt. gray-brown wfds; sl. powdery. L: 5.2. *AJA* 64 (1960) Pl. 37. **B 889** (G 22:K 26) A-D:2(St.2b) LC IIIA. Frag. of upper handle to rim. C: lt. gray-brown at core to green-gray at surface wfs. L: 8.2. *AJA* 64 (1960) Pl. 37. **B 890** (G 45:K 20) T.17:27. Frag. of upper handle to rim. C: like B 886. L: 5.3. *AJA* 64 (1960) Pl. 37. **B 891** (G 56:K 28) D-A. Frag. from middle of handle. C: like B 886. L: 6.4. *UPMB* 13 (1948) Pl. 3; *AJA* 64 (1960) Pl. 37. **B 892** (G 61:K 46) E-Unstrat. Frag. from middle of handle. C: g. lt. yellowish gray to pinkish gray. L: 5. *AJA* 64 (1960) Pl. 37. **B 893** (G 64:K 61) E-D:2a LC IIIA. Frag. from middle of handle. C: g. reddish brown to lt. gray-green at surface, wfs. L: 6.7. *AJA* 64 (1960) Pl. 37. **B 894** (G 66:K 52) E-Unstrat. Frag. from middle of handle. C: very lt. gray-brown at core to lt. gray-green wfds. L: 5.3. *AJA* 64 (1960) Pl. 37. **B 895** (G 67:K 60; 49-12-391) T.28:5. Frag. from top of handle. C: g. dk. gray-brown at core to orange and dk. buff wfs. L: 3.5. *AJA* 64 (1960) Pl. 37. **B 896** (G 72) E-Unstrat. Upper part of handle joining rim. Possibly from a Type 1c jug—apparently inscribed while leather hard. C: lt. greenish brown to gray-green at surface, with a few grits. H: 4.1. L: 7.6. *AJA* 64 (1960) Pl. 37 and p. 146, Ill. 1.

LATE CYPRIOTE III PLAIN WARE

This category is related to Plain Wheelmade II Ware, in that it is plain ware and it is wheelmade. On the other hand, its occurrence seems to be almost exclusively confined to the LC III period and it is generally buff-colored and of rather finer texture than Plain Wheelmade II Ware. Also included in this class are pots which have the shapes of Base-Ring Ware or the shapes and clay of LC III Decorated Ware and Black Slip Bucchero Ware without the corresponding decoration.

Bowls

Type 1: hemispherical, with very small recessed base, barely interrupting rounded contour of bowl. Plain rim. Very much like LC III Decorated Type 6 bowl. **B 897** (P 960) D-B:1b LC IIIA. *Pls. 48, 56.* About ⅓ pres. giving complete profile. C: red-brown to lt. gray-green wfs and lime. H: 8. ED: 20.

Type 2: disc base set off slightly from body; slightly convex walls to tall, semi-carinated rim with rolled lip. **B 898** (P 2817) D-A. *Pl. 48.* About half pres. giving profile. 2 small string-holes near rim on each side. C: lt. g. gray-buff, powdery. H: 4.5. D: 11.5.

Type 3: wheelmade imitations of Base-Ring II bowls, being a somewhat angular adaptation of *Problems,*

Type 2. Most have the profiled foot of Type 2a (e.g. B 899, B 904) but some (B 905, B 907) have a simplified form of the Type 2b foot. Handles are generally raised to an almost vertical position. Heights given do not include handles. **B 899** (P 733) A-E:2(VIII) LC IIIB. *Pls. 26, 56.* I-m. Handle missing. C: gray at core to gray-green and buff, with some sand and sherd temper; fine, hard. H: 10.5. D: 26. **B 900** (P 744) A-E:2(V) LC IIIB. Base and most of lower body missing. C: brick-red, sandy, rather soft. D: 16.4. **B 901** (P 946; 49-12-33) T.3:12(B) LC IIIA. *Pl. 26.* C-m. C: blue-gray wfs and lime particles. H: 7. D: 16.2. **B 902** (P 1201; 49-12-372) T.25:11. *Pl. 26.* N-c-m. Handle missing. C: lt. orange-brown to lt. gray-green wfs; hard, rather coarse texture. H: 7.6. D: 16.5. **B 903** (P 1356) T.16:38. *Pl. 56.* N-c-m. Wide rim. C: g. lt. orange-brown at core to lt. brick-red and dk. buff at surface wfs. H: 6.8. D: 17.2. **B 904** (P 1357) T.16:39. I-m. Handle, most of rim, much of body missing. Shape very similar to B 903. C: g. gray-brown wfs. H: 7. D: 15.2. **B 905** (P 1358) T.16:40. *Pl. 48.* I-m. Handle and part of body missing. Crudely made. C: gray at core to lt. orange-brown at surface, which is rough. Int. center may have had paint. H: 4.6. D: 11.6. **B 906** (P 2690; 49-12-407) T.32:3 LC IIIA. *Pl. 26.* I-m. C: gray-red to brown with lime grits. H: 6.2. D: 14.2. **B 907** (P 2901) T.40:24(D) LC IIIA. *Pls. 56, 58.* C-i. Rim beveled. C: g. lt. pinkish brown to buff, coarse ext., better smoothed int. H: 7. D: 13.8. **B 908** (Sh 132) A-E:3(V) LC IIIB. Handle with spur. C: lt. gray-buff to lt. reddish brown wfds. H: 5.1. **B 909** (Sh 330) A-D:3(VII) LC IIIA. Part of handle and small wall frag. C: very lt. gray-brown wfs. H: 6.5. **B 910** (Sh 523) B-D:2 LC IIC. Part of base and walls. C: g. brick-red at core to lt. gray-green at surface wfs; not well smoothed. H: 3.5. D (of base): 5.2.

Miscellaneous bowl sherd: **B 911** (Sh 136) A-D:2(V) LC IIIA. *Pl. 29.* Piece apparently cut out of side of a plain rimmed bowl. Baked after cutting. C: lt. gray-brown wfds, rather rich texture. H: 3.5. W: 2.2.

The following is an unpainted specimen of LC III Decorated bowl, Type 3: **B 912** (P 2889) T.40:70(C) LC IIIA. *Pl. 58.* I-m. One handle and much of rim missing. C: g. lt. reddish brown to pink. H: 5.7. D: 14.2.

The following is an unpainted specimen of LC III Decorated bowl, Type 4: **B 913** (P 794) A-D:2(V) LC IIIA. About half pres. including profile. Stumps of raised hor. handle pres. Extremely low ring base. C: red-brown, sandy; rough surface. H: 5.7. D: 14.6.

Amphoras

Type 1: only the upper body is preserved in the one example extant. Full, probably biconical belly to neck-ring and slightly tapering neck with overhanging ledge rim. Two curved handles with horns near top from shoulder to mid-neck. Somewhat the same shape occurs in *handmade*(?) bucchero ware (*CVA* BM.Fs. 1 IICa Pl. 12:10,13) suggesting that the body was biconical and on a base ring. **B 914** (P 802) A-E:2(VIII) LC IIIB. *Pls. 26, 56.* I-m. C: lt. orange-brown clay at core to buff at surface wfs. PH: 41.4. D: 38.7.

Type 2: flat base, rather tall ovoid body, small short neck. Vertical loop handles at widest part of body. **B 915** (P 812) A-D:2(IV) LC IIIA. I-m. Lower part of body missing. Neck quite short and sl. flaring. C: gray-brown wfs; lime and dk. grits. PH: 30. D: 25. **B 916** (P 813) A-D:2(IV) LC IIIA. *Pls. 26, 56.* About half pres. giving complete profile. Sl. tapering neck, taller than that of B 915; beveled lip. Pour-hole just above base, indicating that this was a kind of "water cooler." C: like B 915. H: 39.2. ED: 25.7.

Jugs: wheelmade unpainted jugs with base ring (or ring base), ovoid or spheroid body, tapering neck, round mouth with moulded lip and handle from shoulder to rim. Vertical ribs produced by gouging out more or less parallel grooves from shoulder to base.

B 917 (P 2656; 49-12-39) T.18:4(B) LC IIIA. *Pls. 27, 56.* N-c. Rim missing. Wide base and tall narrow neck. Cf. *Problems*, 53, Fig. 13, Type 3. C: lt. brick-red to gray-buff. H: 18.1. D: 10.8. **B 918** (P 2910) T.40:30(D) LC IIIA. *Pls. 27, 59.* N-c-m. N. base, graceful ovoid body, tall concave neck. Cf. LC III Decorated jugs, Bamboula Type 3. C: lt. brownish buff, well sifted and smoothed but a few white grits visible. H: 23. D: 14.7. **B 919** (P 2911) T.40:9(D) LC IIIA. *Pl. 59.* N-c-m. Quite similar to B 918 but base sl. wider and body baggier. C: lt. g. greenish buff, well smoothed. H: 21.7. D: 13.3. **B 920** (P 2912) T.40:12(D) LC IIIA. *Pls. 27, 56, 59.* C-i. Low ring base, elongated spherical body, wide neck. Cf. *Problems*, 53, Fig. 13, Type 1b. C: g. red-brown to pinkish brown, coarse texture but well smoothed. H: 13.8. D: 10. **B 921** (Sh 667) North of Area E-Unstrat. Frag. of wall with rills. C: brick-red wfs. H: 4.7. D: 6.3.

The following is an undecorated specimen of LC III Decorated jug Type 1b: **B 922** (P 2876) T.40:35(D) LC IIIA. *Pl. 59.* N-c. Much of mouth missing; chipped. Small base ring, elongated spherical body. Neck-ring. Flaring handle. Short spout, scarcely canted. H: 15.8. D: 9.4.

Pilgrim Flask: undecorated specimen of the LC III Decorated type.
B 923 (P 2877) T.40:52(C) LC IIIA. *Pls. 49, 59.* Neck and handles missing. Back nearly flat, front lenticular. C: g. lt. orange-brown to gray-green; surface pitted, heavy ware. D: 11.4. W: 7.

"Candlestick"

B 924 (Sh 135) A-D:3(V) LC IIIA. *Pl. 29.* Frag. of center piece and base of shallow bowl with center cup, which in this case has a squared rim. C: coarse brown. H: 6.6. D (at mouth of inset bowl): 6.7.

Potstand: tapering cylindrical stand with three concave horizontal grooves. Four equidistant round holes in central groove.

B 925 (P 1294) T.33:3(C) LC IIIB. *Pls. 49, 60.* C-i. C: dk. buff wfs; hard. H: 7.6. D: 11.8.

PITHOS WARE

Owing to the highly fragmentary state of many of the examples it is not possible to be perfectly certain about their classification; however, a few definite types emerge from the mass of material at Bamboula. In all cases these jars exhibit prominent profiled lips. It is often difficult to be certain whether they are handmade or wheelmade.

Storage jars without handles

Type 1a: torus foot, ovoid body, short, rather wide, neck. **B 926** (P 777) A-D:2(VII,2) LC IIIA. *Pl. 27.* N-c-m. H-m. Sl. tapering neck; neck-ring. C: g. red-brown wfs, soft. H: 77. D: 60. **B 927** (P 797) A-B:5 LC IIA. About half of neck and large body frag. pres. W-m? Flaring neck; neck-ring. C: brown at core to gray-green at surface, sandy. PH: 40.

Type 1b: rather small flat base, tapering ovoid body and tall, slightly concave neck. Sometimes with relief decoration and very occasionally painted. The technique of relief decoration seems to have consisted in running the blunt end of a stick, or perhaps the thumb, over the clay before baking, thus creating two roughly parallel ridges with a flat track between them. In places these ridges are flanked by outer tracks which are just discernible. The execution of the design was not precise, nor the loops entirely uniform. This general type of decoration is known from other Cypriote sites, e.g. Apliki (*AntJ* XXXII, 1952, 143, Fig. 8:9). **B 928** (P 738) A-D:2(VII,2) LC IIIA. *Pl. 27.* Neck only. H-m. C: g. gray core to cinnamon-brown; brick-red at surface with dk. sand; surface worn. PH: 33.3. D: 38.7. W (of wall): 2.1. **B 929** (P 739) A-D:2(VII,2) LC IIIA. *Pl. 27.* Only neck pres., almost vert. W-m? C: lt. brick-red to gray-green at surface with chaff temper; surface worn. PH: 28. D: 34.8. W (of wall): 1.3. **B 930** (P 766) A-D:2(V) LC IIIA. *Pl. 27.* C-m. W-m. 4 parallel hor. ridges just above widest part of body. C: brick-red to gray-green, sandy. H: 107. D: 67. **B 931** (P 769) A-D:2(IV) LC IIIA. *Pl. 27.* N-c-m. Mouth and part of neck missing. H-m. C: lt. g. gray-red with gray-green patches; lime particles. PH: 92. D: 70. **B 932** (P 771) A-D:2(IV) LC IIIA. *Pl. 27.* N-c-m. Mouth and most of neck missing. H-m? Neck-ring. Ridges like those of B 930. C: brick-red to gray-green with dk. sand and some straw; very coarse. PH: 110. D: 85. **B 933** (P 784) A-D:2(VII,2) LC IIIA. About ⅛ pres. giving profile of upper half. W-m. Neck-ring. C: orange-brown, surface pitted. PH: 47. ED: 50. **B 934** (P 796) A-D:2(VI) LC IIIA. Large frag. of belly and shoulder plus other non-joining frags. pres. W-m? 3 w. relief lines (ridges) around shoulder and belly; above and below this 3 parallel hor. ridges. PD: 70. ED: 95. **B 935** (P 798) A-B:5 LC IIA. Frag. of neck. W-m. Neck-ring; undercut rolled rim. C: g. red-brown. H: 26.7. **B 936** (P 1842) D-B:2a LC IIIA. Neck only, flaring. W-m. C: g. rosy-buff to gray-buff, pocked. PH: 31. PD: 33.5. **B 937** (P 2702) Cw IIIb:1 LC IIIB. About ⅓ of neck and a large body frag. pres. W-m. Neck-ring.

C: g. brick-red to orange. PH: 37. W (of wall): 1.4. **B 938** (P 2813) D-A. About ⅔ of neck and large joining portion of shoulder to widest part of belly pres. W-m. Neck flaring; neck-ring. At base of shoulder zone a continuous w. line (ridge), bordered above and below by a hor. ridge. C: g. gray-brown at core to gray-pink at surface, coarse. Body and lower part of neck covered with m. reddish brown wash (not fired). PH: 46. ED: 75.

Storage jars with handles

Type 2a: has the basic shape of Type 1b. On the one partially preserved example are stumps of wide heavy strap handles with spurs at point of joining neck; from body to mid-neck. **B 939** (P 2711) E-A:7 LC IIA. *Pl. 27.* Most of concave neck pres. C: g. pinkish gray at core to pink and gray-green at surface. PH: 27. D (at mouth): 34.

Type 2b: flat base, tapering ovoid body with a tendency to be angular; wide, short neck and heavily profiled rim. Normally with vertical roll handles on shoulder but one variation has lifted horizontal handles (also painted relief decoration). A similar type occurred at Apliki (*AntJ* XXXII, 1952, 139, Fig. 6:6). **B 940** (P 773) A-D:2(VII,2) LC IIIA. *Pl. 27.* N-c-m. One handle missing. H-m. Angular profile. C: g. lt. orange-brown to lt. gray-green at surface. H: 55. D: 50.5. **B 941** (P 774:K 3) A-D:2(VI) LC IIIA. *Pl. 27.* N-c-m. One handle missing. W-m (slow wheel?) C: lt. brown to gray-green at surface, sandy and soft. H: 59. D: 56. *AJA* 42 (1938) 273, Fig. 13:b; *AJA* 64 (1960) Pl. 37. **B 942** (P 775:K 4) A-D:2(IV) LC IIIA. *Pl. 27.* N-c-m. Rather high neck. H-m? Handles have center ridge. C: g. gray at core to gray-green and orange with dk. sand. H: 62. D: 54. *UMPB* VII, 1 (1937) Pl. VII; *AJA* 42 (1938) 273 Fig. 13:a; *AJA* 43 (1939) 102 Fig. 2a; *AJA* 64 (1960) Pl. 37. **B 943** (P 776:K 5) A-D:3(VI) LC IIIA. Neck and part of shoulder pres. W-m. C: yellow-gray to orange at surface, sandy. H: 12.7. D: 33.8. *AJA* 42 (1938) 273, Fig. 13:c; *AJA* 64 (1960) Pl. 37. **B 944** (P 2814) D-A. One handle, neck and part of shoulder pres. H-m? C: g. gray-brown to reddish brown at surface. PH: 28.5. ED: 73. **B 945** (P 2835) E-D:1d LC IIIA. *Pl. 27.* Neck and most of shoulder pres. W-m. Short neck widens downward and is set off from shoulder by a prominent ridge, repeated below at handle level. In h-z, defined below by yet another ridge, is a w. relief line. All relief lines painted. Lifted hor. roll handles (largely missing). C: like B 944, with some straw binding. P: m. buff. PH: 23.5. PD: 55.5.

Type 2c: torus base, ovoid body; wide, fairly tall neck, neck-ring; moulded, overhanging lip; strap handles from shoulder to rim. **B 946** (P 768) A-D:2(IV) LC IIIA. *Pl. 27.* H-m. Center ridge on each handle. C: like B 930. H: 67. D: 51.

Type 2d: flat base, handles to rim or just under rim; otherwise like Type 2c. **B 947** (P 767) A-E:2(VIII) LC IIIB. *Pl. 27.* C-m. W-m. 4 vert. ridges on each handle. C: like B 930. H: 63. D: 59. **B 948** (P 778) A-E:2(VIII) LC IIIB. *Pl. 27.* Upper half pres.; lower part completely rotted. W-m. Grooved handles to just below rim. Raised ring with incised twilling pattern at base of neck. Incised w. line on shoulder. C: red-brown to gray-green at surface, well sifted. H: 26.5. D: 40. **B 949** (P 804) A-E:2(VIII) LC IIIB. I-m. About half pres. Restored. H-m? C: red-brown wfs. H: 55. D: 52.5. **B 950** (P 2839) E-D:1f LC IIIA. *Pl. 28.* I-m. About ⅔ pres. By exception, has no neck-ring. C: g. gray-brown to reddish brown and orange at surface, strawbound. H: 56. D (of mouth): 37.2.

Miscellaneous pithos sherds

B 951 (Sh 636) Cw IIIb:1 LC III. Rim frag. beveled and somewhat undercut; inscribed(?) C: g. lt. gray-pink to gray-green. H: 13.3. Th (of wall): 2.8. *AJA* 64 (1960) Pl. 37 and p. 146, Ill. 1. **B 952** (Sh 660) T.38:19. *Pl. 29.* Many frags. from body. Around belly was a band of 4 parallel ridges. Vert. w. lines in relief on shoulder. C: lt. gray-brown to gray-green, coarse. L (of largest frag.): 30. Th: 2.2. **B 953** (Sh 717) Cf. B-4. Rim frag. like B 951 inscribed before baking. W-m. C: g. gray-pink to greenish gray surface. H: 11.6. D: 7.8. *AJA* 64 (1960) Pl. 37 and p. 146, Ill. 1 **B 954** (G 1:K 38) A-Unstrat. Upper handle and rim frag. of large krater-amphora(?) W-m. C: orange-brown to lt. gray-green at surface, sandy. H: 5.1. *AJA* 42 (1938) 273, Fig. 13:k; *AJA* 64 (1960) Pl. 37. **B 955** (G 13:K 6) A-E:2(VI) LC IIIB. Rim frag. flaring and beveled and deeply undercut. W-m. C: g. orange-brown to gray-green at surface, with straw. H: 8.7. Th (of body wall): 2.2. *AJA* 64 (1960) Pl. 37. **B 956** (G 19:K 44) F-B. Rim frag. beveled and undercut, but not so deeply as B 955. W-m. C: gray-brown core to gray-green surface with sand and lime grits. H: 10.5. Th (of body wall): 2. *AJA* 64 (1960) Pl. 38. **B 957** (G 20:K 32) C-Unstrat. *Pl. 49.* Rim frag. very similar to B 956 but sl. smaller. W-m. C: lt. gray-green wfds; wet smoothed. H: 4.5. Th (of wall): 1.5. *AJA* 64 (1960) Pl. 38. **B 958** (G 28:K 45; 49-12-21) T.2:15(A) LC IIA. Rim frag. similar to B 956 but sl. smaller. W-m. C: pinkish brown to gray-green at surface, sandy. H: 7.7. Th (of wall): 1.9. *AJA* 64 (1960) Pl. 38. **B 959** (G 41:K 40) D-A. Wall or neck frag. W-m. C: orange-brown wfds, hard. H: 9.3. Th: 1.5. *AJA* 64 (1960) Pl. 38. **B 960** (G 52:K 2) D-A. Rim frag. beveled and very sl. undercut. W-m. C: g. gray-pink to gray-green surface wfds. H: 22. PD: 21. Th (of wall): 2. *AJA* 64 (1960) Pl. 38. **B 961** (G 55:K 58) D-A. Rim frag. similar to B 960 but larger. W-m? C: g. gray-brown to burnt dk. gray at surface in patches; very coarse and heavy fabric. H: 10.7. PD: 14. Th (of wall): 2.6. *AJA* 64 (1960) Pl. 38. **B 962** (G 74) Cw IIIb:2. Rim frag. like B 958. C: like B 951 but less coarse. H: 4.2. Th (of wall): 2. *AJA* 64 (1960) Pl. 38 and p. 146, Ill. 1.

Vats: flat bottom, flaring sides, from slightly concave to slightly convex; heavy profiled overhanging rim. This shape is also represented at Apliki (*AntJ* XXXII, 1952, 145 Fig. 10:11). Only one example, B 967, has a handle.

B 963 (P 772) A-D:2(VII,2) LC IIIA. *Pl. 28.* N-c-m. W-m. Drain-hole(?) 2 cm. in diameter just above base. C: like B 930. H: 51. D: 82. **B 964** (P 810) A-E:2(V) LC IIIB. *Pl. 28.* N-c-m. H-m. Convex sides. C: orange-brown wfs. H: 45. D: 71. **B 965** (P 811) A-D:2(VII,2) LC IIIA. *Pl. 28.* I-m. Restored. W-m? Convex sides. C: lt. gray-green at core to lt. pink at surface, well smoothed. H: 58.5. D: 80. **B 966** (P 2829) E-D:1f LC IIIA. Rim and body frag. H-m. Convex sides. C: g. gray-brown to cinnamon-brown on surface, strawbound. PH: 44. PW: 43. **B 967** (P 2833) E-D:1c LC IIIA. *Pl. 49.* Rim and body frag. H-m. Straight sides; vert. strap handle from body to rim, just large enough for hand to grasp. C: g. gray-brown to gray-green at surface, strawbound. PH: 36. PD: 29.5. **B 968** (Sh 604) E-Hearth A LC IIA-B. Body frag. H-m. Straight sides. C: hard reddish, sandy. H: 12. **B 969** (Sh 616) E-Hearth C LC II. Body frag. H-m. Straight sides. C: hard yellowish, sandy. H: 10. **B 970** (Sh 719) A-D:2(IV) LC IIIA. *Pl. 28.* Rim frag. H-m. Straight sides. C: g. pinkish brown to gray-green at surface, coarse. H: 14.2. L: 17.

MISCELLANEOUS COARSE WARE

Round-bottomed krater-amphoras: wheelmade, slightly flattened bottom, wide short neck. Rectangular strap handles from shoulder to rim.

B 971 (P 782) A-D:2(V) LC IIIA. *Pl. 28.* N-c-m. W-m. Very squat ovoid body with flattened shoulders. Overhanging squared lip. C: m. red-brown, coarse; surface smoothed. Lower part burnt. H: 25. D: 29.6. **B 972** (P 2647; 49-12-122) T.11:7(B) CG IB. *Pl. 28.* N-c-m. W-m. Depressed globular body with short shoulder; plain rim. C: g. gray-brown to blue-brown in patches. H: 13.2. D: 21.8. Cf. *SCE* IV(2), Fig. LXXI:3.

Jugs

B 973 (P 2661; 49-12-247) T.18:13(A) LC IIB. *Pl. 28.* N-c-m. H-m. Plain flat base, squat globular body with wide short concave neck. Plain rim and sl. arching handle from rim to shoulder. Fire-blackened on bottom and sides. C: g. grayish red, coarse. Vert. shaved (or bur?). Has some resemblance to Monochrome Ware but is coarser. H: 22.7. D: 20.4. **B 974** (P 2808) T.31:4. *Pl. 28.* C-ch. W-m. Side-spout jug with basket handle. Biconical globular body, neck-ring, flaring mouth. Shape quite similar to K 536. C: very dk. gray with white particles (mica?); hard. Appearance might suggest Gray and Black Polished Ware but surface was apparently never treated. H: 14. D: 8.2. **B 975** (P 800) A-D:2(VII,2) LC IIIA. About half of upper body including one handle pres. H-m. Jug or amphora. Fat biconical(?) body with wide, not clearly articulated neck and plain rim. Rounded vert. handle from shoulder to rim. C: gray at core to brick-red and black wfs; hard, coarse. PH: 20.2. ED: 18.9. **B 976** (P 1841) A-D:2(IV) LC IIIA. *Pl. 28.* I-m. Part of neck and body missing. H-m. Signs of burning ext. lower body. Flat-based jug with roughly ovoid body and wide, not strongly articulated neck with round mouth(?) and plain rim. Vert. handle from shoulder to rim. C: g. buff at core to black at surface; hard. H: 25.2. D: 20.1. **B 977** (P 2722) MPT-A:11. Base with adjoining frag. of body, non-joining shoulder and neck frags. W-m. Fire-blackened ext. Jug or amphora. Sl. raised flat base, globular(?) body, wide splaying neck. C: g. red. to black, very coarse. PH: 11. D (of base): 7.3. ED (of mouth): 11.3.

PLAIN WHITE WARE (CYPRO-GEOMETRIC)

Stemmed bowl

B 978 (P 2769; 54-41-59) MPT-D:2. *Pl. 29.* I-m. Handles and part of base missing. Flaring ring base; gently rising floor to angular break to nearly vert. wall with flaring rim. Ridge between wall and rim. Sturdy hor. loop handles. C: sl. gritty grayish core to lt. brick-red at surface. Coarse brick-like texture. H: 14.5. D: 22.5. Professor Gjerstad is of the opinion, on the basis of a photograph, that this piece should be of the CG III period (cf. *SCE* IV, 2, Fig. XVIII:10; XXV:3) although the shape occurs earlier in imported ware (cf. *SCE* I, Pl. CXXXIX:18, which is CG II).

Jug(?)

B 979 (P 2679; 49-12-395) T.30:1 CG IA. Base and lower part of body walls plus a few non-joining body sherds pres. Sturdy rolled ring base. Flaring conical walls. Cf. *SCE* IV(2), Fig. XI:8 for possible restoration. C: g. gray-purple to lt. gray-green with pinkish spots. PH: 17.1. ED: 32.

PART II: NON-CYPRIOTE POTTERY

RED LUSTROUS III WARE

Shapes and techniques follow *Problems*, 51 ff. For a comment on the inscriptions and origins of this ware, see O. Masson in *Ugaritica* III, 234, n. 4, and a recent study by R. S. Merrillees, "Bronze Age Spindle Bottles from the Levant," *OpusAth* 4 (1962) 187–196.

Bottles

Type 1a: **B 980** (P 969; 49-12-111) T.9:2 LC IA. *Pl. 28*. C-i. Inscribed while clay was wet. H: 27. D: 8.8. *AJA* 64 (1960) Pl. 38 and p. 146, Ill. 1. **B 981** (P 1373:K 86) T.13:6. I-m. Part of neck missing. H: 24.6. D: 9.4. *AJA* 64 (1960) Pl. 38. **B 982** (P 1374) T.13:7. *Pl. 49*. I-m. Base entirely missing. PH: 21.5. D: 9.5. **B 983** (P 2735) T.13:37. Handle, most of shoulder and neck and a frag. of lower body pres. PH: 22. **B 984** (P 2736) T.13:38. Part of neck and (non-joining) frag. of shoulder and belly. PH (of larger frag.): 17. **B 985** (Sh 510) C-A:6 LC IIA. About half of base and lower body. PH: 16.1. PD: 7.1.

Type 1b: **B 986** (P 1274:K 85; 49-12-167) T.12.38(B) LC IA:2. C-ch. Has sl. plastic ridge where handle joins neck; otherwise conforms to Type 1b. H: 31.4. D: 7.8. *AJA* 64 (1960) Pl. 38. **B 987** (P 1275; 49-12-171) T.12:43(B) LC IA:2. *Pl. 28*. C-ch. H: 30.1. D: 7.4. **B 988** (P 1431; 54-41-13) VT:13. I-m. Base restored. Extraordinarily elongated. PH: 53.2. D: 9.1.

Miscellaneous Type 1 sherds: **B 989** (Sh 326) A-D:3(VII) LC IIIA. Frag. from wall. L: 4.1. **B 990** (Sh 661) Stray. Handle, somewhat twisted in manufacture. Inscribed near base, somewhat awkwardly with a sharp instrument, before baking. L: 9.7. *AJA* 64 (1960) Pl. 38 and p. 146, Ill. 1. **B 991** (G 60:K 84) T.26:2. Frag. of handle from near base. L: 4.8. W (at base): 1.8. *AJA* 64 (1960) Pl. 38; *Berytus* 14 (1961) 40.

Type 2b: **B 992** (P 2845; 54-41-54) MPT-C:1. *Pl. 28*. I-m. Mouth and part of body missing. Handle vert. bur., body and neck vert. and circularly bur. Neck inserted through hole pierced in body. Clay somewhat softer than usual in this ware. PH: 25.1. D (of body): 19.

Miscellaneous: the following probably belonged to an arm-shaped vessel.

B 993 (Sh 651; 54-41-16) VT: 16. *Pl. 28*. Frag. of lower part of tubular vessel, tapering sl. towards base, which has the shape of a low truncated cone. C: slate-gray to grayish red, hard and thick. S: brick-red with vert. bur; much worn. PL: 9.6. D (at break): 4.1. Th (of wall): 1.

"WHITE LUSTROUS" WARE

A fabric obviously very closely related to Red Lustrous Ware and doubtless of the same provenance. Another example is C 175.

Bottles

B 994 (P 970; 49-12-112) T.9:3 LC IA. *Pl. 28*. N-c-m. Low flaring base ring; slender elongated ovoid-conical body; neck-ring; long slender tapering neck with flat flaring rim. Sl. rounded vert. handle to neck. A refined version of Red Lustrous III Type 1a bottles. C: lt. orange-brown wfs. S: cream-colored, bur. egg-shell smooth. H: 23.2. D: 7.6. **B 995** (P 2718) MPT-A:7. Neck, handle and part of shoulder pres. Neck-ring; slender tapering neck to sl. flaring mouth and sloping lip. Vert. handle flares out, then becomes hor. Plastic ridge where handle joins neck. C: lt. pink to gray at surface, fine. S: ls. lt. blue-gray. PH: 9.7. D (of mouth): 3.

SYRIAN BICHROME WARE

C. Schaeffer has discussed this fabric in detail in *MCh*, 49–58; cf. also *Problems*, 91.

Jugs

B 996 (P 1273; 49-12-144) T.12:14(A) LC IA:2. *Pls. 28, 54*. N-c-m. Part of mouth missing. Flat base, ovoid body. Sl. concave neck to flaring round mouth with rolled rim. Thick round handle from shoulder to mid-neck. C: gray-buff with lt. and dk. sand. P: m. wine-red and dk. gray-brown to black. Neck bordered under rim and above base by 3 stripes: black-red-black. On neck groups of triple oblique lines (alternating directions). Bars on handle. In shoulder zone, bordered below by stripes (black-red-black-red-black) there are 2 panels separated and bordered by 3 zones of latticework flanked by vert. stripes: black-red-black. In one panel, a standing bird in res. technique, with extended tail; in the other, a fish in res. technique, with both fins represented. Cf. *MCh*, 50, Fig. 21. H: 21.3. D: 14.8. **B 997** (Sh 454) Stray. *Pl. 29*. Frag. from mid-belly of a pot like B 996. C: pinkish brown with fine lime bits. P: m. firm dk. gray and dk. red. 3 black bands alternating with 2 red bands hor. on upper body: triple vert. metope containing a red band in outside zones, black zigzag in center zone. L (diagonal): 12. **B 998** (Sh 758) A-A:2b LC IIA. *Pl. 29*. Frag. from join of neck and shoulder with low neck-ring. From jug or small krater. C: orange-buff wfds and lime particles. P: m. gray-black and m. dk.

crimson. Outlined red band at base of neck. H: 3.5. L: 4.5.

Kraters: although no complete or even nearly complete specimen was recovered at Bamboula, all the fragments described below appear to come from kraters of the same general type as *MCh*, 54, Fig. 23; however, on none of our sherds was there a trace of pictorial decoration.

B 999 (Sh 550) E-3 LC IIA? *Pls. 28, 49.* Large frag. of rim and shoulder with vert. circular handle, overhanging squared ledge rim. C: lt. pinkish brown to gray-buff wfds. P: m. dk. gray and red-violet. Paint on rim, 2 bands above handle. Red band under rim and s-o vert. red stripes at intervals(?) on shoulder. PH: 10.7. PD: 19.5. **B 1000** (Sh 649) T.38:11. *Pls. 29, 49.* Frag. of neck with almost straight walls to flat rim with overhanging but unprofiled lip. Just below this is a small groove before the wall begins to swell out. Classification as Syrian not assured but probable. C: gray at core to lt. orange-red and tan with mica and black sand. P: m. crimson and black. Red band just below rim and black band well below this. Traces of vert. black and red lines on shoulder. H: 7.3. W: 7. *PEQ* (1961) 66 Pl. 10:1. **B 1001** (Sh 705) C-A:5 LC IB. *Pls. 29, 49.* Frag. of short neck and overhanging rim. C: g. lt. gray-brown to lt. orange at surface. P: m. gray-brown and dk. red. On rim 2 black stripes bordering red stripe. Below rim outside, red stripe and wider black stripe. H: 4.5. L: 10.2. **B 1002** (Sh 752) Cw IIIb:1 LC IIIB. *Pl. 29.* Frag. of rim and neck very similar to B 999. C: lt. gray-buff wfds; rather powdery. P: m. dk. gray and gray-crimson. Res. band on lip. Below rim outlined red band. H: 4.2. L: 6.3.

MISCELLANEOUS SYRIAN WARES

The following pots have close connections with wares found on the Syro-Palestinian littoral and this is doubtless their place of origin. See also B 1188 and B 1236 ff.

Krater

B 1003 (P 957) D-B:2a LC IIIA. Over half pres. giving profile; restored. Wide squared foot with sturdy hollow stem. Truncated biconical body with no neck and wide mouth. Overhanging squared rim. Lifted hor. roll handles at widest part of body. C: brown wfds and some lt. grits. P: m. brown to dk. gray-brown. Solid paint on rim. Main frieze immediately below rim: 4 t-o panels on front. Left two are separated by intervening plain ground; right two are contiguous. Left to right: (1) dotted circles in vert. tangent lozenges (at very top, concentric lozenges?); (2) lattice design with random lozenges filled solid; (3) at top, vert. bars; under these an interlocking triangle design; under this 3 rather crudely painted barred fishes placed hor.; (4) center, hor. chevrons flanked by opposing half-circles; outer 3 vert. bordering lines barred. Entire frieze bordered below by 3 stripes with 3 more halfway to base and 3 again on stem. Handles barred. Reverse side also had frieze now almost entirely missing. One remaining panel has

a tree design flanked by scallops each with a dot in the center (cf. B 569). H: 31.5. D: 33.1. *UPMB* 7, No. 3 (1939) Pl. X; *PEQ*, 1960, 64 ff., where I have published this krater with a detailed discussion of its stylistic affinities.

Krater-amphora

B 1004 (P 731) A-D:2(VII,2) LC IIIA. *Pl. 28.* Badly rotted, about half pres., restored. Base relatively wide. C: g. gray at core to dull brown wfs. P: firm m. lt. brown to gray. Paint below rim, at base of neck and below handles. Side A: neck has checkerboard design; shoulder has dotted concentric semicircles in a divided inverted triangle which is flush with a lattice design. Side B: right side of neck has part of an animal figure (stag?); shoulder has another similar figure under the handle next to a fragment of a triangular design like the one described above. H: 24. D: 21.7. *AJA* 42 (1938) 271, Fig. 11a-b; *PEQ* (1960) Pl. 4, Figs. 9a-b; see p. 68 for a discussion of the stylistic affinities of B 1004.

MINOAN WARE

Of the fragments listed here, B 1005 and 1006 are certainly Minoan, while B 1007 is probably of that fabric. In addition to these, the coarse ware stirrup jar B 1130 seems to be of Cretan provenance although I have preferred to catalogue it with the other coarse-ware stirrup jars, which are presumably of mainland provenance. Daniel at one time considered B 1130 Minoan, but later changed his mind and called it Mycenaean. I have discussed the provenance of these coarse-ware pots at some length in *Berytus* 14 (1961) 37 ff.

Sherd from a closed shape

B 1005 (Sh 511) C-A:6 LC IIA. *Pls. 28, 54.* Small body frag. W-m. C: pinkish brown with fine lime grits; rather hard. S: ls. cream. P: ls. orange, partly flaked off. The design was reconstructed with certainty as a nautilus pattern by Daniel. L: 2.5: Cf. R. B. Seager, *Excavations on the Island of Pseira, Crete* (Philadelphia, 1910) 32, Fig. 13.

Krater(?)

B 1006 (Sh 617) E-11 (notice that another sherd belonging to this pot was found in a disturbed deposit in House II of Area E. *Pls. 31, 49.* Many body frags. among which are only a few joins. C: dull gray-brown with sherd or other coarse temper; well smoothed but not ls. surface. Quality of clay not to my knowledge paralleled on the mainland of Greece. P: sl. ls. orange-brown. Belly frieze consists of a kind of outlined hor. zigzag, the angles of which are filled by parallel lines alternately curving upward and downward. The frieze is bordered by thick bands. H (of largest frag.): 5.8. PD: 13.7. This scheme is close to *MP*, 383, Mot. 61:8 but I do not know of any mainland examples with curved connecting lines. See *BSA* 9 (1902/3) 319, Figs. 18–19 for examples from Crete with curved lines used in a similar way.

Minoan(?) sherd from a closed shape

B 1007 (Sh 499) C-A:7 LC IIA. *Pl. 34.* Frag. from shoulder of a large pot. W-m. C: cinnamon-brown to gray-buff wfs; surface bur. P: ls. dk. gray mostly flaked off. A portion of papyrus design similar to *MP*, 265, Fig. 34:51 can be made out. L: 6.6. Daniel rather hesitantly classified this piece as Late Minoan III. If this should be correct one might compare *PM* IV, Pt. 2, 1017, Fig. 965h for its design. In any case an Aegean origin is assured by the design but I have not been able to identify with absolute certainty the rather unusual fabric.

Stirrup jar (coarse ware): see B 1130.

MYCENAEAN WARE

I

The organization of pottery of Mycenaean type adopted in this publication (see especially categories employed in the Tables) undertakes to differentiate the finds according to quality of technique. In view of the prevailing differences of opinion about the place of manufacture of Mycenaean wares found in the Levant, I must stress that such descriptive terms as are employed here in this differentiation are not intended to convey a fixed and final judgment on the subject of origins. Thus, 'Standard Mycenaean' simply means pottery suggesting in appearance and technique the better wares customarily found at Mycenae and other important Helladic sites. 'Coarse Ware Mycenaean' refers to a type of rather gritty heavy ware with Mycenaean designs which has been found all over the Aegean world.[1] 'Inferior Mycenaean' refers to those pieces executed in a technique inferior to 'Standard Mycenaean' but, like the latter, found all over the Aegean. This class is presented in the sense suggested by Furumark in his comment on the Mycenaean pottery found at Apliki.[2] The question of the exact provenance of these pieces seems even more difficult to determine. It seems to me quite possible that native Cypriote imitative efforts, particularly in bowls, reach out and perhaps overlap with this class; more will be said of this later.[3]

The attempt at the differentiation described above may prove to have no real value. At the least it serves as noncommittal nomenclature and thus does not endanger objectivity in assessing the phenomenon. An adequate treatment of the problem of origins is not possible within the framework of this publication. In all fairness, however, the subject cannot be entirely avoided.

Bamboula is a small link in the great chain of sites in the Eastern Mediterranean at which Mycenaean pottery has been found. The question as to whether this pottery was entirely, or partly, or not at all imported from the mainland, and if the latter is the case, where and by whom it was made, has long engaged the attention of scholars.[4] Unfortunately, the one type of concrete evidence which might prove the second and third possibilities mentioned above has not been found, viz., Mycenaean pottery kilns in the Near East. It is, therefore, the duty of each scholar dealing with this question to re-examine it from any point of view which may be suggested by his own material and experience.

At Bamboula the vast bulk of pottery found, both in settlement and tombs, is native Cypriote. The percentage of Mycenaean (of all categories) is never greater than ±1% in relation to its context (level) in this settlement. In quantity, therefore, as well as in clay, paint and design, the Mycenaean vases in everyday use at Bamboula stand out as a small foreign body. Since most of the tombs were disturbed and little can be known about individual burials, it is difficult to make a comparison with the settlement. In any case, a perusal of the list of finds of each tomb will leave the impression that Mycenaean vases form a small minority; as for sherds considered alone, only in the case of Tomb 25 does the proportion rise to as much as 13% of the total. This is considerably lower than the high percentage worked out for Enkomi, 63.7% at the peak period, LC IIC,[5] but Sjöqvist repeatedly points out the possibility that the data available were few and very possibly one-sided. Certainly the overwhelming impression from Bamboula is that Mycenaean pottery was a small factor—a situation that may·be difficult to explain if one supposes it to have been made on the very island of Cyprus, for it should then have been as available as local wares. On the other hand, this situation would be appropriate if Mycenaean pottery was largely an imported luxury ware.

1. I have discussed the problem of the origin of this class at some length in *Berytus* 14 (1961) 40 f.
2. *AntJ* 32, 1952, 157.
3. See note 8.
4. A concise summary is given by E. Coche de la Ferté, *ECCM*, 43–46.
5. *Problems*, 124; at Myrtou-Pigadhes relatively little Mycenaean pottery was found, but according to H. W. Catling the reason for this was the obscurity and unimportance of the site (*Myrtou-Pigadhes*, 46 ff.). V. Karageorhis found that Mycenaean vases comprised 25% of the pottery from a tomb at Angastina and states that this is the "normal percentage of Mycenaean wares usually found in Late Cypriote II tombs" (*RDAC*, 1964, 13). An LC IIB tomb at Tamassos had 16.2% Mycenaean ware. An exceptionally high percentage may have occurred in several tombs at Kition, but it must be noted that these had been badly disturbed already in antiquity (*RDAC*, 1963, 3).

This leads, I think, quite naturally to a consideration of the factor which seems to weigh most heavily in the minds of those who propose Levantine manufacture of much of the Mycenaean pottery found in the Levantine area, especially pottery with pictorial decoration. This factor is the heavy concentration of finds of such pottery in the Near East.[6] Various episodes in the history of ancient ceramics warn that find-places in themselves can never be a conclusive factor. Already in the Early Bronze Age occurs a type of Syrian ware with four loop handles found mostly in Egypt and Palestine.[7] In later times one may point to the export of Corinthian kraters as a close parallel to the export of chariot kraters with pictorial decoration. The great bulk of Corinthian kraters decorated with scenes has been found in Etruria, relatively fewer in Corinth and Greece. No one supposes for this reason that a group of imaginative Corinthian painters went to Etruria and did their work on the spot; or that, on the same analogy, Attic vase painters emigrated to Kertch. The preference of Etrurians for kraters with scenes is in itself no more inscrutable than the same preference in Cypriotes. In both cases it must have been called forth by an interest in the great prototypes in free painting which ultimately lay behind both Corinthian and Mycenaean krater scenes. In both cases the inhabitants of the mainland could satisfy themselves with the originals, whereas distant peoples had to content their avid appetites for the same with artisans' reproductions on pottery.[8]

On general grounds the most serious objection to Levantine origin and largely exclusive practice of the pictorial style is that it removes the most original and imaginative vase-decorators *en bloc* from the mainland.[9] First of all, it removes them from their admitted prototypes in free painting. Two hypotheses have been put forward to obviate this objection: (a) they were perhaps copying from free paintings in Mycenaean palaces as yet undiscovered in the Levant;[10] (b) they were copying textile reproductions of the prototypes.[11] Both hypotheses are interesting although indemonstrable. But neither meets the real point of the objection. Why should exactly the most original group leave their homeland in the first place, presumably attracting all other like-minded artists to themselves over a period of several generations, and settle abroad? And above all, how could they have preserved their cultural integrity so well and so long in the face of the age-old, deep-rooted foreign culture all about them? I do not see how anything less than the assumption of a Mycenaean community of at least the cultural vigor

and economic scope of, say, Rhodes, could account for the complicated phenomenon of long-continued Mycenaean ceramic manufacture and the flourishing

6. Cf. Furumark, *OA* 6, 1950, 269, n. 3.
7. R. Ehrich, *Relative Chronologies in Old World Archeology* (Chicago, 1954) 8; *idem, Chronologies in Old World Archeology* (Chicago, 1965) 15.
8. The argument to distribution based on the paucity of certain shapes, e.g. kylikes, is very inconclusive, cf. *MPL*, 36. The usefulness of kylikes is limited in a practical way: en route they cannot be made to contain anything, as more closed types can, nor can they even be stacked. This should be sufficient reason that Mycenaean exporters did not care to fill their ships with them. Nevertheless, a surprisingly large number of stemmed kylikes has been reported recently from two tombs in Kition (*RDAC*, 1963, 3). This does not affect the conclusion that export of this shape was relatively limited. Kraters were presumably valuable for their pictorial decoration and could also be stacked to some extent. Finally, there is the matter of bowls, which are found in relatively large numbers in the Levant. Although not suited to carry anything en route, they could have been stacked so as not to be too wasteful of space. However, since they were presumably not valuable for their decoration, it may be seriously questioned whether space would have been taken up to transport them. Cypriote potters could have imitated the Mycenaean clay and paint (see below) to produce a local luxury product. The shapes are simple and well within their scope. Further, if there is influence on bowl and cup shapes from local coarse ware (cf. *MP*, 66 for remarks that seem to imply this) this is most easily explained by the assumption that local potters were adapting shapes they knew. The simple and usually monotonous ornamentation would suit the theory that these are Cypriote imitations. This would also account for the occasional hybrid forms of pots found in Cyprus (*e.g.*, C 623, 660, 729) which are notable for their infrequency. Similar reasoning about bowls seems to be at the base of J. du Plat Taylor's discussion of the pottery found at Pigadhes (*Myrtou-Pigadhes*, 47: B. Fabric). I should not like to suggest that *all* the bowls in Cyprus must be accounted for in this way nor to take the responsibility of selecting which ones are and which are not. I have noted in the catalogue instances where the dividing line between the 'Mycenaean' technique and the 'LC III Decorated' technique is hard to recognize (see for example, B 457). I have made further comments on the subject of locally made bowls of Mycenaean technique in *AJA* 65 (1961) 337 f. and in regard to the related problem of 'Rude Style' vases, *ibid.*, 343. It is generally agreed that these are Cypriote categories: cf. the remarks and references by H. W. Catling, *CBW*, 43 f. V. Karageorghis has recently presented a valuable study of bowls from Kouklia (*Nouveaux Documents*, 157). He calls them Mycenaean IIIB and dates them to the last quarter of the thirteenth century. His implication is presumably that these were made by Mycenaean potters in Cyprus, for he resists wherever possible the view that local influences operated on these bowls (e.g., 176, 177); it must be the other way around. Yet elsewhere (201 f.) he argues that it is exactly the influence of local pottery shapes which proves that Mycenaean potters were settled in the Levant.
9. Cf. Daniel's remarks in *AJA* 43 (1939) 355. S. Immerwahr has already expressed this idea briefly (*AJA* 49, 1945, 555).
10. *MP*, 463.
11. *AJA* 60 (1956) 147 ff. As Mrs. Immerwahr points out to me, this could apply only to the thirteenth century and at that time frescoes on the mainland (e.g. later Tiryns hunt) develop abstract geometrical markings that agree with the "textile style."

development of the pictorial style in the Levant.[12] A mercantile "quarter" within Enkomi or Ras Shamra is hardly an adequate setting or explanation for the phenomenon. But perhaps there is some as yet undiscovered large and important Mycenaean colony that would deserve the name?

In this respect it does not seem useless to point out that when (the same) Achaean Greeks did assuredly go in large numbers to Cyprus from the twelfth century onward, their culture was quickly, in fact almost immediately, drawn into a real fusion with Cypriote elements. Even relatively pure Mycenaean pottery such as that from Sinda can be recognized as distinct from mainland work, and Proto-White Painted ware is an obvious and unmistakeable blend of Greek and Cypriote motifs and technique. This is what one would expect also to have happened to smaller groups of Mycenaean settlers in Cyprus during the late Helladic III A-B periods, if there were any.[13]

At this point, the question of clay and paint can be raised. At the beginning of the Late Minoan period (ca. 1650 B.C.) Cretan potters invented the technique of applying a reddish brown lustrous paint to a smooth buff-colored clay. A variation (at first not very usual) was the application of dark olive to brown-black lustrous paint to a light olive-green clay. This description is not prejudiced by the fact that the two schemes must have been produced (accidentally or not) by variations in firing, since there are modifications combining the two types or approaching one or the other. There seems no reason to doubt that the Cretan potters eventually desired and obtained one effect or the other; in any case, they created a norm, a convention, which was to prevail many hundreds of years over the entire Greek world. When the Mycenaeans obtained these vases and began imitating them, they took over the type of clay and paint along with other things; foreshadowing of this technique can indeed be found on the mainland, including the Argolid,[14] but the crystallization of the two schemes must have had its impetus from Crete. Moreover, mainland potters succeeded in producing vessels which in regard to technique of clay and paint are, in numerous instances, not readily distinguishable from Cretan pots. The same may be said of the clay and paint of Mycenaean pottery produced in Attica and Rhodes. In the latter place, for example, a kind of rich chocolate-brown paint seems to have been the preferred hue and yet the perfectly standard types also occur. In distinguishing provenance of Mycenaean pots one is obliged to depend heavily—if not entirely

—on stylistic and other factors.[15] Such considerations lend great probability to the observation of Casson that vases indistinguishable in clay and paint from mainland Mycenaean wares could have been produced in Cyprus.[16] As he points out, it is the people who manipulate the clay (within this general geographical unit of the Eastern Mediterranean) as much as the clay itself which can be a dominating factor. Nevertheless, there is a fundamental consideration which makes it seem probable that there were no Mycenaean potters in Cyprus (or for that matter elsewhere in the Levant) manipulating native clay—at least on a considerable scale. That is the following: in Crete, in Argolis, in Corinth, in Attica, in Rhodes, the two fundamental basic types of clay—the lustrous smooth buff and the olive—continued to be used in more or less recognizable continuity right

12. Dikaios seems to suggest local manufacture of Mycenaean vases in Cyprus "from the end of the fourteenth century B.C." (Guide, 29; cf. also Coche de la Ferté, op. cit., 43). This is a not unreasonable compromise between two extreme positions; yet it does not really obviate the main objection to Levantine manufacture suggested above.

13. Sjöqvist (Problems, 183 ff.) takes the point of view that mercantile colonies did produce the artistic phenomena under discussion. But his (correct) rejection of real Mycenaean colonization in the Levant and his admission that mercantilists were "isolated" argue against such a view, for which no definite evidence is produced, anyway. The picture I have attempted to sketch out of Aegean-Cypriote relationships is in essential agreement with the much more detailed study by H. W. Catling in Chapter II of CBW (1964) who covered many of the same points in BSA 60 (1965) 212 f. and in his summation for the Cambridge Ancient History (1966): "Cyprus in the Late Bronze Age," II, chapter XXII (b), 56 f. A different interpretation of the evidence is the discussion by V. Karageorghis in Dikaios, Guide,³ 34. Cf. also my review of Nouveaux Documents in AJA 71 (1967) 316 f.

14. Korakou, 9 and 37; inspection of the public galleries of the National Museum in Athens or the Nauplia Museum will amply confirm the presence of similar schemes in pottery before the Late Helladic period, e.g., Middle Helladic pots from the new shaft graves at Mycenae.

15. Cf. Coche de la Ferté's remarks on fabric, op. cit., 45. See also Dikaios, Guide, 30. Since I wrote these remarks the science of archaeometry has entirely changed the degree of certainty which can be obtained through chemical analysis: see H. W. Catling, E. E. Richards and A. Blin-Stoyle, "Compositions and Provenance of Mycenaean and Minoan Pottery" in BSA 58 (1963) 94–115; also BSA 60 (1965) 212 f. and note 1 for further references. This is a welcome advance and in essence almost certainly settles the question of provenance of the main bulk of Mycenaean pottery in Cyprus. Nevertheless, the archaeometrists would probably acknowledge that within this framework, strange and unexpected exceptions may possibly have occurred. The possibility cannot be excluded that in particular instances—but almost certainly not on a large scale—clay could have been imported or an occasional artisan could have emigrated. There is some likelihood that this occurred in the Late Geometric and Early Archaic period at Cumae, as Dr. G. Buchner has convinced me in conversation.

16. S. Casson, Ancient Cyprus (London, 1937) 48 ff.

on through the Late Bronze, Sub-Mycenaean, Proto-Geometric, Geometric and even Classical periods. Variations, of course, such as the Attic reddish mixture may have developed. But the technical heritage of the Mycenaean potters was never really lost. In Cyprus, however, this technique ends rather abruptly some time near the close of the LC IIC period, coincidentally when Mycenae ceased to function as a world economic power (end of Late Helladic IIIB). If there was a flourishing colony of Mycenaean potters in the Levant, more especially in Cyprus, why, after so tenaciously holding the Mycenaean ceramic tradition in the face of alien cultures, did they suddenly abandon it completely? What happened to them? There is no more lustrous smooth buff and olive ware in the Levant after this point.[17] If my supposition that local Cypriote potters produced some or many of the bowls in this technique during the LC II period be correct, the explanation for the above phenomenon will be that they thought of the Mycenaean technique as alien and exotic and abandoned it as soon as the external stimulation of Mycenaean imports ceased. On the other hand, it may well be that the color variety which existed in LC III Decorated ware, especially in bowls, namely a reddish brown and a greenish gray hue, is a pale reflection, a pale survival of the Mycenaean color tradition through the above-mentioned Cypriote potters. Of course, the quality of the clay and paint is totally different. The clay is always coarse and the paint matt, and they remain so in the succeeding Cypriote White Painted ware. It is noteworthy that this local Cypriote tradition was so entrenched that it prevailed against the influx of Greeks caused by the break-up of various Mycenaean political units. Although shapes and motifs from the mainland exercised an influence in the new pottery of the Cypro-Greeks, the local type of clay and paint held undisputed sway and was never challenged by the introduction of the standard mainland technique.

A final consideration suggested by study of the material from Bamboula is that, since the same off-shades of color and clay occur at sites in the known Mycenaean world, there is no reason to suppose that the Mycenaeans hesitated to export pots of less attractive and excellent finish along with those of the absolutely "Standard" variety. One might be misled into considering these 'off-shade' ceramic products—in which the clay is pinker or darker than usual, and sometimes chalky, while the paint tends to be dull—as Cypriote imitations (of course, some of them may be), if the same variations did not occur side by side with the standard repertory at Mycenaean sites.

II

Close dating of Mycenaean pieces can be attempted on the basis of the sequence proposed by A. Furumark. For the convenience of the reader I bring together here those finds to which I venture, on the basis of either context or shape and decoration (both, of course, where applicable) to assign a chronological classification. It is necessary to stress, however, that from the point of view of these excavations such a classification is purely an approximation; in many cases Furumark's system can only assist one in making an intelligent guess. On the basis of the Bamboula stratification I have not noticed any major discrepancies that cannot be reasonably accounted for; however, minor ones (e.g., B 1029, B 1185-6) do occur and have been noted in the appropriate entries. In Group B I have placed those pots which I felt must belong to the earlier importations to Bamboula without being able to decide whether they are early or late in the Mycenaean IIIA:2 period. Nor are the other groups free of ambiguities: e.g., Groups B-D and D-E obviously overlap.

Group A: Mycenaean IIIA:2 (early)

B 1029 (bowl); B 1067, B 1071, B 1083 (kraters); B 1101, B 1106, B 1108 (three-handled jars); B 1117, B 1119-20, B 1137, B 1150, B 1154-5, B 1159, B 1164-5 (stirrup jars); B 1177 (two-handled flask); B 1196 (jug?).

Group B: Mycenaean IIIA:2

B 1066, B 1070, B 1076-7 (kraters); B 1102-05, B 1107 (three-handled jars); B 1156-8, B 1161-2 (stirrup jars); B 1169-70, B 1174 (pilgrim flasks); B 1175-6 (two-handled flasks); B 1185-6 (juglets).

Group C: Mycenaean IIIA:2 (late)

B 1068-9, B 1072-3, B 1081-4 (kraters); B 1100 (three-handled jar); B 1134 (stirrup jar).

Group D: Mycenaean IIIA:2—LH IIIB

B 1008-54 (bowls); B 1055-61 (stemmed cups); B 1078-9 (kraters); B 1093-4, B 1097 (pyxides); B 1121, B 1148, B 1152 (stirrup jars); B 1179-83 (juglets).

Group E: Mycenaean IIIB

B 1063, B 1064-5, B 1085-90 (kraters; notice that B 1088 is "Rude Style"); B 1091 (amphora); B 1092,

17. The exception to this which proves the rule is the 'local Mycenaean' pottery found at Sinda and Enkomi during LC IIIA times. Not only is this ephemeral but it is admittedly a new introduction and in no way a real continuation of the Mycenaean pottery previously found in Cyprus.

B 1095-6, B 1098-9 (pyxides); B 1112-4 (three-handled jars); B 1116, B 1118, B 1127-9 (stirrup jars); B 1184 (juglet).

Even discounting possible overlappings it is clear that the frequency of Mycenaean pottery is greatest in the late fourteenth and thirteenth centuries, just as one would expect it to be. No doubt also the greater proportion of the more nondescript sherds not taken into account here would fall in the thirteenth century. It must be pointed out, however, that much of this numerical preponderance of later wares is accounted for by bowls which may well be of Levantine manufacture.

In the following catalogue mention of Mycenaean pottery found by the British Museum Expedition at Bamboula and published in detail in *Catalogue of Greek and Etruscan Vases in the British Museum*, Vol. I, Pt. II has been incorporated in the appropriate categories under the "C" numbers used in that publication. It is hoped that this will assist in providing a complete picture of the finds. A few pieces of Mycenaean pottery from Bamboula mentioned but not described or illustrated in *CCM*, 181, are not included here.

Bowls

Type 1a: small ring base completely set off from body, gently flaring convex walls to flattened, everted, sl. profiled rim. Horizontal ribbon handles at rim. This corresponds apparently to Furumark's type 295 (*MP*, Fig. 15 and p. 636). The fabric is standard. B 1011 varies from the above norm by having a disk base. A rim fragment, Sh 189, not included in this catalogue because it was missing at the time of my control, was classified by Daniel as Late Helladic III and no doubt belonged to the above-described type. It was found in A-E:3(VI). For a recent study of Mycenaean and LC III Decorated bowls from Kouklia, of which some are comparable to our type 1a-b, see *Nouveaux Documents*, 177 f., types 7–10, and especially 180 f. on the chronology. **B 1008** (P 996:K 76; 49-12-102) T.6:9 LC IIB. *Pls. 32, 49.* N-c-m. C: yellow-gray wfs; hard. Breaks clean and sharp; wet-smoothed. P: ls. violet-gray, much flaked. Wide band int. center with a running zigzag in m. buff paint; paint on and below rim int. and ext., on handles and base. H: 7.3. D: 20.5. *AJA* 45 (1941) 266, Figs. 10, 15; *MPL*, 48; *AJA* 64 (1960) 148. **B 1009** (Sh 97) A-Unstrat. *Pl. 30.* Rim frag. with stump of hor. ribbon handle. C: orange-buff, fine and sl. powdery. P: ls. red-brown, flaking. L (diagonal): 3.6. **B 1010** (Sh 370) A-Surface. *Pl. 30.* Frag. with profiled rim. C,P: like B 1009 but clay lighter. H: 2.8. **B 1011** (Sh 669) E-Surface. *Pl. 29.* Flat disk base. C: buff to pink; well cleaned, hard. P: sl. ls. orange-red. Int. center: multiple-brush c-c. Ext: red stripe. D (of base): 4.5.

Type 1b: the profile is quite similar to that of Type 1a but differs chiefly in being more squat and fluctuat-

ing as to type of foot and rim; it may even reveal a slight carination. The examples included here seem to correspond to Furumark's type 296, which is "principally Levanto-Mycenaean" (*MP*, Fig. 15 and p. 636). The quite early context of B 1029 is noteworthy. See also Daniel's comment (*AJA* 44, 1940, 554) in regard to the similarity of this shape to the LC III Decorated bowl Type 1. It should be noted that Furumark includes C 659 and C 660 from Kourion in this category (cf. also *MPL*, Pl. XII). The clay of the bowls catalogued below shows a wide range from standard to "off-shade." Many sherds of this type were found unstratified near the surface. A selection of these has been included here with the stratified sherds. **B 1012** (P 743) A-D:2(VII,2) LC IIIA. About ⅓ pres. giving complete profile. Very low base-ring, plain rim. C: pinkish brown wfs and sherd temper; greenish buff patches on surface. P: sl. ls. streaky gray-red (int.) to red (ext.). H: 6. D: 15. **B 1013** (P 995; 49-12-101) T.6:8 LC IIB. *Pls. 32, 49.* C-m. Raised, nearly flat base. C: buff to grayish buff; clean texture with a few mica particles; wet-smoothed. P: m. to sl. ls. orange-brown. Int. center: c-s outlined by thick band. Another halfway up and n. res. band on rim. Paint on handles, rim, upper body and base ext. H: 5.3. D: 17.5. **B 1014** (P 1209; 49-12-389) T.28:3 LC II. *Pls. 32, 49.* N-c-m. One handle missing. Low ring base. C: hard g. buff wfs; wet-smoothed. P: m. orange-brown to dk. gray-brown. Int. center: large outlined solid circle. Band about halfway down int. and ext. Paint on handles, rim and base. H: 6.3. D: 18.9. **B 1015** (P 1210; 49-12-390) T.28:4 LC II. *Pl. 32.* About half pres. Low torus base, almost straight sides. C: dk. gray-orange wfs, wet-smoothed and sl. polished. P: sl. ls. dk. orange. Dec: like B 1013. H: 6.2. D: 22. **B 1016** (P 1324) T.36:41. *Pl. 49.* N-c-m. Shape like B 1013. C: buff with lt. particles, hard; wet-smoothed. P: thick ls. red. Dec: like B 1013 but rim not res. Spiral faint. H: 5.4. D: 19. **B 1017** (P 1352) T.16:12. *Pl. 32.* N-c-m. Torus foot. Very small handles sl. lifted. C: like B 1014. P: firm m. brown. Int. center: small t-o c-s. Wider band ⅔ up int. Paint on rim, handles and near base ext. H: 5.5. D: 14.6. **B 1018** (P 1382) T.16:45. *Pl. 32.* I-m. Restored. Low ring base; handles droop. C: lt. gray-brown to lt. brick-red; wet-smoothed; surface flaked. P: m. red-brown to dk. gray. Dec: like B 1016. H: 6.5. D: 19.1. **B 1019** (P 2816) D-A. *Pl. 49.* I-m. Two frags. pres. giving complete profile. Concave disk base; plain rim. Has a sl. carination. C: g. pinkish buff to gray and pinkish brown at surface. P: m. orange to brown-black. Int. center: 2 c-c. Thick stripes int. and ext. ⅓ down. Paint on rim, handles and base ext. H: 5.2. ED: 19. **B 1020** (Sh 96) A-Unstrat. *Pl. 29.* Frag. of base and wall. Low ring base. C: lt. powdery buff wfs. P: m. dk. brown; worn. Int. center: circle. Paint on base ext. PH: 2. **B 1021** (Sh 99) A-1 LC II. *Pl. 30.* Frag. from near handle. C: lt. powdery orange-buff. P: m. streaky brown. Wide band int. and ext. L: 3.1. **B 1022** (Sh 106) F-1 LC IIIB. *Pl. 30.* Plain rim frag. Cf. B 1012. C: lt. orange-buff wfs. P: m. gray-brown. Paint on rim; band lower down int. H: 3. **B 1023** (Sh 161) A-Unstrat. *Pl. 30.* Rim frag. with rolled lip. C: fine gray-buff. P: dk. red-brown, once ls? Paint on rim. H: 2.6. **B 1024** (Sh 269) A-D:3(IV) LC IIIA. *Pl. 30.* Very sl. profiled rim frag. C: well cleaned buff, sl. powdery. P: m. firm rust. Paint on rim. L: 2.6. **B 1025** (Sh 331) A-D:3(VII) LC IIIA. *Pl. 30.* (Plain) rim frag. C: lt. gray-buff; hard, well cleaned. P: m. orange-brown. Paint on rim. H: 2.8. **B 1026** (Sh 337) A-D:3(VII) LC IIIA. Base frag. Small low ring base similar to B 1020. C: gray to lt. orange; fairly hard. P: m. dk. to red-brown. Wide band at center int. L: 3. **B 1027** (Sh 430) A-Surface. *Pl. 30.* Base frag. with beveled ring base. C: like B 1026. P: lt. m. gray. Dotted s-o semicircles on int. base. PH: 1.3. **B 1028** (Sh 462) A-B:4 LC IIB. *Pl. 29.* Frag. with flattened profiled rim. C: lt. orange-brown, hard; poorly smoothed. P: ls. orange-brown. Paint on rim. Wide band int. and ext. H: 3.7. **B 1029** (Sh 479) A-A:3 LC IIA. *Pl. 30.* Base frag. with low ring base. C: like B 1020. P: nearly m. thin brown to dk. gray-brown. Spiral(?) on int. floor. L: 3.5. **B 1030** (Sh 519) A-B:3 LC IIB. *Pl. 29.* Curved sides and plain rim. Cf. B 1035. C: lt. orange-brown to greenish gray; fairly hard, wet-smoothed. P: sl. ls. olive to walnut-brown, crackled. Stripe on rim and about ⅔ down ext. PH: 4. **B 1031** (Sh 527) D-B:2b LC IIIA. *Pl. 29.* Rim frag. similar to B 1028. C: g. buff, ls. surface. P: ls. thick dk. orange. Paint on rim. Wide stripes below this int. and ext. H: 4.1. **B 1032** (Sh 677) D-A. *Pl. 29.* Base and wall frag. Low ring base. C: g. buff to lt. pink; well-cleaned, hard. P: m. orange-brown to dk. gray-brown. Int. center: d-o thick stripe. Ext. base: thick stripe. W: 5. ED (of base): 5. **B 1033** (Sh 678) D-A. *Pl. 29.* Like B 1032. Signs of burning. C: gray-green; well cleaned, hard. P: m. purple to sooty black. 2 small c-c int. center and side stripe further up int. and ext. Thick stripe around base ext. W: 8.8. ED (of base): 3.5. **B 1034** (Sh 679) D-A. Wall frag. C: g. gray to pink, hard. P: m. reddish brown. Int: 4 n. c-c and wide stripe. Ext: 2 n. c-c and wide stripe. H: 5. W: 4.3. **B 1035** (Sh 680) D-A. *Pl. 29.* Curved wall and (plain) rim frags. C: pinkish brown; well cleaned, hard. P: m. red-brown to purple-brown. Paint on rim and wide band about ⅓ down int. and ext. H: 4.2. W: 7. **B 1036** (Sh 681) D-A. Base and wall frag. Shape like B 1020. C: pinkish buff to buff; wet-smoothed but still sl. powdery. P: m. orange to brown. Int. center: thick stripe. Ext. base: stripe. W: 9.7. D (of base): 6.5. **B 1037** (Sh 682) D-A. Like B 1020. C: g. pinkish brown, hard. P: m. orange. Dec: like B 1032 with addition of small circle at int. center. L: 6. ED (of base): 7. **B 1038** (Sh 683) D-A. *Pl. 29.* Base and wall frag. Disk base. C: like B 1037. P: m. dk. gray-brown. Int. center: thick circle. Ext: stripe above base. L: 7.2. D (of base): 5. **B 1039** (Sh 684) D-A. Like B 1038. C,P: like B 1032. Int. center: circle. About halfway up thick stripe int. and ext. Stripe around base ext. W: 9.7. D (of base): 9.7.

Type 2: one-handled bowl. The one relatively complete example distinctly has only one handle; it cannot be positively determined whether the others had one or two handles. It has considerable similarity to Furumark's Type 283 (*MP*, Fig. 13 and p. 634) which

may exhibit one or two handles placed somewhat below the rim. Only a single sherd, B 1042, of those listed below is of standard fabric. Nevertheless, in commenting on Broneer's Shape 8 (*Hesperia* VIII, 1939, 378) Daniel—obviously referring to B 1040—specifically suggests the possibility of importation from Greece. Another slightly more angular version of this shape is C 722 (*Pl. 54*). This pot, not from regular excavations, is a true Cypriote adaptation. One-handled bowls with an obliquely raised handle have been found at Kouklia: cf. *Nouveaux Documents*, 175, type 4. **B 1040** (P 1425) D-A. *Pl. 32.* Complete profile pres. C: lt. brown to greenish buff wfs. well smoothed. P: ls. gray-brown. Int. center: circle. Broad stripe halfway up int. and ext. Paint on rim and base. H: 8.5. D: 16.3. **B 1041** (Sh 105) A-F:1 LC IIIB. Frag. of handle and rim. C: very lt. orange-buff, wet smoothed. No painted dec. pres. L: 4.8. **B 1042** (Sh 124) A-Unstrat. *Pl. 29.* Frag. of handle and rim. C: lt. gray-pink to ls. creamy green surface, hard. P: ls. dk. red-brown, flaked. Paint on rim. L: 4.4. **B 1043** (Sh 633) MPT-A:16. *Pl. 30.* Frag. of handle and rim. C: pinkish buff to lt. gray-green at surface; fine-textured and fairly hard. P: m. red-brown to dk. gray, crackly. Paint on rim and a patch on handle. H: 3.

Type 3: deep bowl with low ring base and convex sides to plain rim which has pierced vertical lug handle; covered with a streaky chocolate wash. The total effect is remarkably like that of Granary Style. However, the find place of B 1044–B 1046 suggests a date of not later than LC IIC which is somewhat inconsistent with the Granary Style technique. P 15081 (Agora Museum, from Well, S 27:7), a bowl of Late Helladic IIIC shape, is closely comparable in effect of decoration. Cf. for general type, *Nouveaux Documents*, 161 no. 18 which is thought to be still Myc. IIIB. **B 1044** (P 1426) D-A. *Pls. 32, 49.* N-c-m. C: lt. orange-brown wfs; well smoothed. Entirely covered by a streaky m. orange-brown to dk. gray-brown wash. H: 8.2. D: 19.5. **B 1045** (P 1427) D-A. *Pl. 49.* I-m. Handle and much of side missing. C,S: like B 1044. H: 6. D: 14.1. **B 1046** (P 2819) D-A. *Pl. 49.* About ¼ pres. giving complete profile. C: lt. gray-brown, well cleaned, hard. P: m. gray to dk. chocolate color, streaky. H: 7.8. ED: 19.

Type 4: flat, rather wide base, double curved sides to profiled rim; slightly lifted horizontal roll handles well below rim. The shape is Furumark's Form 87 (cf. *MP*, 53, Fig. 15, No. 300) but no spout is preserved. B 1047 is of standard fabric. **B 1047** (P 1361) T.16:17. *Pls. 49, 54.* About half pres. giving complete profile. C: yellow-gray at core to orange-buff, sl. ls; wet-smoothed, hard, well cleaned. P: ls. red-brown. Int. center: thick circle. 2 thin stripes halfway up int. and ext. Paint on rim, handle and base ext. In shoulder zone, flower on long bending stem adapted to narrow frieze (rather similar to *MP*, 293, Fig. 45:82, etc.). H: 7.5. D: 15.7.

Miscellaneous Bowl Fragments

A: *Rim fragments with moulded lip from deep bowls: inferior technique.* **B 1048** (Sh 69) A-G LC IIIB.

Pl. 29. C: lt. gray-yellow to pink; soft, stained. P: m. ocher to black. Paint on rim and band below rim ext. H: 4.9. **B 1049** (Sh 82) A-E:2(VIII) LC IIIB. *Pl. 30.* C: lt. gray to lt. orange, fairly hard. P: m. red-brown to dk. gray. Paint on rim. L: 3.1. **B 1050** (Sh 86) A-E:4 LC IIIB. *Pl. 30.* C: lt. orange-buff to cream; hard. P and dec: like B 1049 but very sl. ls. H: 3.6. **B 1051** (Sh 151) A-D:3(V) LC IIIA. C: orange-brown to greenish-gray; hard. P and dec: like B 1050. H: 3.4. L: 2.8.

B: Body fragments of standard fabric. **B 1052** (Sh 145) A-E:3(V) LC IIIB. *Pl. 30.* Sherd of bowl with angular profile, probably of much the same shape as *MP*, 53, Fig. 15:231 or 252. C: gray-green to lt. olive color at surface. P: ls. dk. olive-brown, flaked. Bands ext. H: 2.5. **B 1053** (Sh 514) C-C:2 LC IIC. *Pl. 30.* C: firm orange to ls. cream at surface. P: ls. mahogany color. Ext: spiral. Int: painted solid. H: 2.4. **B 1054** (Sh 520) A-B:3 LC IIB. *Pl. 30.* C: gray-brown at core to buff. P: ls. brown, thin in places. Parts of four vertical bars defining a panel. L: 3.5.

Stemmed Cups: in the case of this category, attention is also called to C 608 (*ExC*, 72, Fig. 125) found in OT 28 at Bamboula. All examples are of standard fabric except B 1058. **B 1055** (Sh 570; 49-12-373) T.25:12. *Pl. 29.* Rim frag. with flattened overhanging lip. C: yellow-gray core to ls. orange-buff surface, wet-smoothed; hard with sharp clean breaks. P: ls. red-brown. Paint on int. and ext. of rim with 2 n. res. bands on top. Remains of a floral design. H: 2.8. ED: 16. *AJA* 65 (1961) Pl. 29: Figs. 10, 11. **B 1056** (Sh 571; 49-12-374) T.25:13. *Pl. 30.* Rim frag. with profiled lip. C: ls. pinkish buff; wet-smoothed, hard. P: like B 1055. Paint on rim. Head of woman(?) in outline with hair and body solid; upraised arm(?) in silhouette; eye given as circled dot; long beak-like nose. H: 3.7. W: 3.5. *AJA* 65 (1961) Pl. 29:6-7; Pl. 109:44. Daniel compared with *BSA* 37 (1936/7) 213–215, Figs. 1–3 (*Ugaritica* II, 217, Fig. 90) which he considered "very close . . . and very likely by the same hand," as well as British Museum C 352 from Enkomi, OT 51. **B 1057** (Sh 572; 49-12-375) T.25:14. *Pl. 29.* Wide base with part of stem; also 2 non-joining sherds probably from sides of same pot. C: firm lt. brown-buff with a few grits and sherd temper; wet-smoothed. P: sl. ls. red-brown to dk. gray-red. 4 bands on base. On body, lozenge and 3 pairs of attenuated human legs. PH (of base): 4.5. D (of same): 10.1. *AJA* 65 (1961) Pl. 29:13; Pl. 109:42-43. **B 1058** (Sh 687) D-A. *Pl. 29.* Frag. of double convex wall and floor of a deep, well-shaped, probably stemmed, bowl with flattened sl. everted lip. Inferior technique. C: g. pinkish brown with much sand, suggesting almost the appearance of coarse-tempered ware. P: m. red-brown. Rim painted. Thick stripe under rim and where floor joins wall. H: 8. W: 10. **B 1059** (Sh 688) D-A. *Pl. 30.* Rim frag. with sl. everted plain lip. C: pinkish brown, well cleaned, not extremely hard. P: ls. red-brown. Paint on rim. Tangent to this, upper termination of a murex most similar to IIIB types (cf. *MP*, 311, Fig. 51, Whorl Shell No. 8). H: 3.7. **B 1060** (Sh 689) D-A. *Pl. 30.* Rim frag. with sl. rolled lip and non-joining body frag. C: sl. ls. dk. buff to lt.

olive-buff, well cleaned. P: lt. delicate brown with patches of coal black. Upper termination of murex as on B 1059 (cf. *MP*, 311, Fig. 51, Whorl Shell Nos. 7 and 9) but not from same kylix. L (of rim frag.): 5.8. H: 3. **B 1061** (Sh 690) D-A. *Pl. 30.* About ⅔ of base and most of stem pres. Base flares broadly. Stem sl. convex. C: pinkish gray to sl. ls. buff surface. P: sl. ls. dk. gray-brown, streaky. Stripes around base and stem. H: 5.4. D: 6.9.

Kraters: Standard fabric

Bell-kraters (*MP*, Form 80:281, p. 48, Fig. 13; designation as *AJA* 60, 1956, 143, etc.). **B 1062** (P 972) T.17:15. *Pls. 32, 50.* N-c-m. Ring base. C: g. orange-brown to buff, wet-smoothed; sl. ls., hard. P: sl. ls. red-brown to dk. gray. Paint on rim, below rim, on handles, on base, and 2 stripes at widest part of body. H: 22.3. D: 24.8. Cf. *MP*, 48, Fig. 13:281 (IIIB). **B 1063** (P 994: K 74; 49-12-100) T.6:7 LC IIB. *Pl. 32.* N-c-m. Shape like B 1062. C: dk. buff, clean and firm; wet-smoothed. P: sl. ls. orange-brown. Band on rim, another sl. below rim int. and 2 halfway down int. On each handle a blotch of paint starting at the right and covering about ⅔ of handle. Ext: band below rim, 3 below handle, on and just above base. Hz divided into 2 panels on each side by vert. chain patterns between n. bands (A); and by vert. plait ornament between n. bands of which the central member is scalloped (B). In each panel: a bird with spread tail and long-beaked head turned back, its body divided by a line longitudinally and filled with small crosses or x's. Legs (A), both have v.w. lines; (B), left bird has x's, right has dots. Necks (A), both have zigzags; (B), left bird has dots, right has hor. w. lines. H: 29.3. D: 31.3. *UPMB* 8 (1940) Pl. IV:b; *AJA* 60 (1960) Pl. 38. The firm, careful rendering of these birds, their graceful contours and decorative though restrained setting, place their painter among the better Mycenaean vase-painters of the Late Helladic III period. The originality and grace of his work do not readily allow exact parallels to be found; particularly his use of the fish-tail termination goes beyond that of most contemporary applications (cf. *MP*, 253, Fig. 30:35) and reminds one in its elegance of the best Cretan Archaic painting (cf. *Hesperia* XIV, 1945, Pl. XXIX:1). I have discussed B 1063 and the subject of birds with reverted heads at some length in *JNES* 20 (1961) 76 ff. **B 1064** (P 2827) D-A. Part of lower body only pres. Flat base. C: gray-green and pink to buff at surface; well cleaned, hard, smooth. P: glossy orange-brown to black. Thick band just above base; at uppermost part of pres. portion traces of another band. PH: 12. D (of base): 9. **B 1065** (Sh 129) A-D:3(VIa) LC IIIA. *Pl. 29.* Frag. of a large lifted hor. handle. C: gray-buff at core to sl. ls. orange-buff. P: sl. ls. dk. red. Paint on mid-handle and band around base of handle. L: 9.

Deep kraters with two vertical handles (*MP*, Form 3:7, p. 23, Fig. 4). Notice that B 1067 is C 391. **B 1066** (Sh 575; 54-41-3) VT:3. *Pl. 31.* 5 frags. from various parts of body (neck to lower body). C: pinkish to buff at surface wfs. P: ls. lt. to dk. red-brown. Double semicircles (or festoon pattern) in at least

2 hor. rows connected by parallel hor. strokes. Between festoon rows is a roughly hor. row of short vert. lines. Paint on rim and 2 contiguous bands below body design. H (of rim frag.): 12.3. W: 11.8. The design is probably an adaptation of the U pattern (*MP*, 345, Fig. 58). I do not know of any specific parallel but it is not difficult to see how the combinations of B 1066 might have been invented. **B 1067** (Sh 637a-y) T.17:26. Various frags. of C 391 (*ExC*, 73, Fig. 127) showing principally a girl contemplating a flower (Frontispiece), two horses' heads and parts of horses' legs. These were reunited with C 391 which was republished in *JHS* 77 (1957) 269–271 (they have since, however, been returned to the Cyprus Museum). See also *UPMB* 8 (1940) Pl. IV: d.

Amphoroid kraters (*MP*, Form 8:53, etc., p. 23, Fig. 4). Attention is called to C 338 and C 353 (illustrated, *AJA* 65, 1961, Pl. 29: Fig. 2) as being from Bamboula. **B 1068** (Sh 273) A-D:3(IV) LC IIIA. Frag. of vert. handle with raised ridge like B 1072. C: gray to pale greenish buff, hard. P: olive to gray, nearly worn off. H: 3. **B 1069** (Sh 338) A-D:3(VII) LC IIIA. Sherd from just below neck. C: lt. gray at core to ls. buff surface; clean, hard. P: ls. brown to black, olive where thin; crackled. Neck apparently painted solid; no other design discernible. L: 5.4. **B 1070** (Sh 497) C-Unstrat. *Pl. 30.* Shoulder and neck frag. C: g. lt. buff to lt. yellow-brown wfs; sl. ls. surface. P: ls. olive-brown to black, crackled. Portion of reins, harness and horse's neck from a chariot scene. H: 5.6. W: 8.5. *AJA* 65 (1961) Pl. 29: Fig. 8. The small piece of drawing preserved allows the inference that this was an unusually fine scene. The harness is rendered in a large graceful spiral. For similar renderings, see *CVA* Brit. Mus. 1, II Cb, Pl. 9: 6 and also, as T. E. Small points out to me, *CVA* Sèvres (France 13) Pl. 13: 1,2. **B 1071** (Sh 546) E—prior to B:2 (see *Bamboula SS*). *Pl. 30.* Shoulder and neck frag. C: dk. buff, hard; wet-smoothed. P: ls. red-brown to dk. gray. Excellent technique. Neck painted solid. Part of a row of at least 3 men with angular heads in outline and solid bodies. They may be carrying spears held horizontally. H: 9.8. W: 11.5. *AJA* 65 (1961) Pl. 29: Fig. 14. **B 1072** (Sh 578a-h) T.16:51. *Pl. 31.* Frag. of neck, shoulder and one handle; 7 small non-joining frags. from body. Overhanging lip sl. inverted. Short neck. Vert. handle with central rib from shoulder to rim: 2 small holes at top, 1 near base, rounded raised lower termination and 2 pellets (inside rim) are imitative of metal prototypes. C: lt. olive-green, well cleaned, wet-smoothed. P: dk. gray almost black, crackled and mostly worn off. Neck painted int. and ext. Lip decorated with chevrons. Handle painted solid. Virtually worn-off remnants of a chariot scene visible to right of handle: 2 figures standing in a chariot, one with stippled garment, the other with chevron design on the garment; about half of wheel pres. with dots on both sides of single upright spoke. The lower part of a wheel is pres. on (c); the upper quarter of a wheel, chariot, frag. of driver in stippled garment, tail of horse on (b); to the left of handle on (a) are the neck and part of head of a horse, and part of what may be the figure of a groom standing before

the horse. Above and just under the rim is a row of hor. chevrons. H: 11. ED: 36. *AJA* 65 (1961) Pl. 29: Figs. 1, 3, 4. Shape and technique similar to, but less fine than, *AJA* 49 (1945) 535, Fig. 1. **B 1073** (G 46:K 77) T.17:27. About half of base with small portion of lower body. C: gray at core to greenish buff. P: ls. dk. brown, flaked. Dipinto in thin m. red paint. H: 5. D (of base): 11.3. *MPL*, 48; *AJA* 64 (1960) Pl. 38.

Fragments of standard fabric from kraters not certainly distinguished as to type. Several additional fragments from the University Museum's excavations have not been formally catalogued: Sh 743 (from body, with bands) from Area B, Well-1; Sh 360 (from near neck) and Sh 247 (from body), both unstratified from Area A. **B 1074** (Sh 270) A-D:3(IV) etc. LC IIIA. Frag. of profiled rim. C: lt. gray-buff, firm. P: ls. black. Spiral(?) on rim. H: 1.9. W: 0.9. **B 1075** (Sh 310) A-D:2(VII,2) LC IIIA. Frag. of handle. C: pinkish to pale gray, clean. P: ls. dk. gray, mostly flaked off. L: 3.5. D: 2.4. **B 1076** (Sh 573a-b; 54-41-1) VT:1. *Pl. 31.* 2 large body frags. C: yellow-gray; sl. ls. wet-smoothed surface. P: sl. ls. gray-brown, considerably flaked. Murex design similar to *MP*, 311, Fig. 51:1-2 in frieze which is bordered below by 3 thick stripes. H (of 573a): 17. W: 12. Shape of pot was Form 3 or 8. **B 1077** (Sh 574a-c; 54-41-2) VT:2. *Pl. 30.* 3 body frags. C: pink to buff wfs; hard, wet-smoothed. P: ls. red-brown to dk. gray-brown. Quadruped in outline technique with rows of dashes on body; much of hindlegs visible. Very fine drawing. Parallel chevrons like *MP*, 383, Fig. 67:15 (IIIA:2) and floral patterns similar to *MP*, 293, Fig. 45:63 (IIIA:2). H (of 574a): 7. W: 12. *AJA* 65 (1961) Pl. 29: Fig. 12. I take the animal of B 1077 to be a bull, but a suggestion by Mrs. Sara Immerwahr that it may be a goat deserves consideration. However, it must be noted that goat representations on the whole tend to show longer, more tenuous legs (cf. *MP*, 248, Fig. 28:6; also C 370–371 and *Kypriakai Spoudai* 10, 1956, Pl. IV: 44). **B 1078** (Sh 693) D-A. *Pl. 30.* Body frag. C: dk. buff and pink to ls. lt. buff on surface. P: sl. ls. dk. gray, flaking. Front part of body and forelegs of a horse in solid color. H: 4. L: 3. *AJA* 65 (1961) Pl. 29: Fig. 5. **B 1079** (Sh 694) D-A. *Pl. 30.* Body frag. C: like B 1078. P: ls. reddish brown, flaky. Hind portion of horse (cf. C 342) or bull (on analogy with *AJA* 60, 1956, Pl. 56: Fig. 5) in solid color. Hind leg res. H: 4. W: 4.3. *AJA* 65 (1961) Pl. 29: Fig. 9. B 1078 and B 1079 are very possibly from the same vase and may be part of a chariot scene. **B 1080** (Sh 750) E-Unstrat. *Pl. 30.* Body frag. Color unusual, perhaps owing to firing conditions or treatment of clay. C: slate-gray to glossy silvery gray surface; hard, well cleaned. P: firm m. black, crackled. H: 2.8. W: 4.5.

The following fragments of standard fabric are probably from kraters, and in any case from large pots: **B 1081** (Sh 325) A-D:3(VII) LC IIIA. Wall frag. C: fine dk. buff with glossy surface. P: ls. red-brown to dk. brown. W: 3.1. **B 1082** (Sh 471) A-C:1b LC IIB. *Pl. 30.* Wall frag. C: gray-buff with glossy pale greenish cream surface. P: ls. brown, nearly gone.

Floral(?) pattern. L (diagonal): 2.7. **B 1083** (Sh 486) A-A:3 LC IIA. *Pl. 30.* Wall frag. C: lt. gray-brown, now deteriorated with a laminated effect; surface glossy buff. P: ls. mahogany to dk. gray. W: 2.5. **B 1084** (Sh 534) A-B:3 LC IIB. *Pl. 30.* Wall frag. C: lt. gray-buff with glossy surface. P: ls. dk. gray. Frag. of papyrus design. W: 4. General type is that of *MP,* 293, Fig. 45:55–79, esp. 76.

Kraters: Inferior technique

The following are fragments from kraters or large open pots: **B 1085** (Sh 336) A-D:3(VII) LC IIIA. *Pl. 31.* Frag. of shoulder with stub of handle(?) C: g. pinkish to sl. ls. yellow-green at surface with sand; hard. P: sl. ls. olive to dk. gray, crackled. Portion of outlined zigzag pres.: 7.4. **B 1086** (Sh 426) Cw VIII. *Pl. 30.* Frag. of (profiled) overhanging rim. C: lt. gray-green wfs, rather sandy. P: ls. olive to dk. gray, much worn. Paint on rim and all ext. pres. H: 2.1. L: 5. **B 1087** (Sh 577; 54-41-5) VT:5. *Pl. 31.* Frag. of rim with overhanging ledge. C: pinkish brown to lt. gray-green wfds; m. surface. P: m. gray-brown. Band under rim as upper termination to scale pattern (or hanging grape design). H: 4.8. W: 6.7. **B 1088** (Sh 582) D-A. *Pl. 31.* Frags. from rim and body. C: g. orange-brown at core to lt. greenish gray; very sl. ls. surface. P: sl. ls. olive to dk. brown. Paint on rim and above frieze; 3 broad bands below frieze; 2 more a little below this. In frieze: a series of vert. w. lines alternating with straight vert. lines; central design is one bordered vert. w. line from which spring 3 spiral hooks on each side. Interstices filled with rows of dots or short straight lines made with brush full of paint. H (of largest frag.): 19. PD: 13. Cf. *Enkomi-Alasia,* 144, Fig. 62:8 for the motif. The general appearance and lax execution of this pot place it in the so-called "Rude Style" (cf. e.g., *Ugaritica* II, 157, Fig. 60:22, C 420 and Furumark's remarks on the spiral 'tree' in *MP,* 467). For a recent discussion of Rude Style, see *Nouveaux Documents,* 231 f., esp. 255 (4) which is the closest comparison; and my comments in a review of this book in *AJA* 71 (1967) 316f. **B 1089** (Sh 767; 49-12-103 group no.) T.6:12. Frag. from body. C: lt. tannish buff on inside wall to buff near surface. Sl. ls. buff slip. P: sl. ls. dk. brown. Three bands. L: 6.8. **B 1090** (Sh 740) E-Unstrat. *Pl. 31.* Neck frag. with stump of rim. C: g. pinkish buff to sl. ls. greenish buff at surface; powdery but surface sl. ls. P: sl. ls. olive-brown to dk. gray, crackly. Below rim a wide stripe from which depends a panel style(?) unit of design consisting of: (a) lattice work between vert. guide lines; (b) adjoining this a similar area divided by an oblique line, with parallel vert. lines in upper triangle thus formed. H: 5. W: 7.5.

Amphora

B 1091 (P 2822) D-A. Frag. of side giving profile from base to shoulder. Inferior technique. Low sl. flaring ring base. Rather fat ovoid body. The shape of the body is something like *MP,* 35, Fig. 7:69, although of course nothing can be deduced about the handles. C: g. dk. pink and gray-brown to sl. ls. gray-green at surface; hard. P: m. washy purple-brown. 2 wide

stripes at base of shoulder; 2 more above base. PH: 15. ED: 14.

Pyxides

Two-handled: see also B 580 and B 581. **B 1092** (P 992; 49-12-104) T.7:1. *Pl. 50.* N-c. Mouth chipped. Bottom sl. rounded; body has concave profile with flattened shoulder, wide neck and profiled lip. Vert. ribbon handles. C: orange-buff, well cleaned, wet-smoothed. P: ls. orange. 2 bands on body at shoulder and at base; 2 bands on neck. Paint on rim and handles. H: 4.1. D: 5.5. Cf. *MPL,* Pl. XIII:4–5 (Myc. IIIB).

Three-handled: it is difficult to date these rather nondescript shapes precisely. They are in general Furumark's Form 16:85 (Mycenaean IIIA:2 and IIIB): see *MP,* 41, Fig. 11. **B 1093** (P 1327) T.36:33. *Pl. 50.* N-c. One handle missing. Bottom flat; squat sack-shaped body with wide short concave neck and profiled lip. Lifted hor. ribbon handles on shoulder. C: lt. green wfs; wet-smoothed, hard. P: ls. lt. orange-brown to dk. gray, much flaked. Neck painted solid inside and out. Shoulder has 1 n. and 2 wide stripes. Handles painted. Belly: 2 wide stripes above and below 3 n. ones. Base: c-c. H: 7. D: 9.4. **B 1094** (P 1328) T.36:47. *Pl. 50.* C-i. Shape like B 1093 but squat globular body. C: lt. pink to lt. greenish brown; well smoothed, hard. P: ls. lt. to dk. olive-green and reddish brown. Neck, handle and base like B 1093. Stripe on shoulder, 2 on belly and 2 more near base. H: 6.8. D: 7.9.

Miscellaneous pyxis fragments: since all the following are body sherds it is impossible to be sure how many handles were on the (square) pyxides from which they came. All are wall fragments showing angular transition to shoulder and/or base. **B 1095** (Sh 254) A-D:3(IV) LC IIIA. *Pl. 30.* C: orange-buff, very lt. at surface. P: ls. orange-brown. 3 n. bands at center of belly. Lower and upper angulation have thick stripe. H: 2.2. **B 1096** (Sh 653) T.38:13. *Pl. 31.* C: g. orange-brown, soft; wet-smoothed. P: ls. orange. Shoulder angle: thick and thin stripe. Same apparently at base angle. H: 4.3. L: 7.6. **B 1097** (Sh 666) Outer necropolis—Unstrat. *Pl. 31.* C: g. lt. gray-green with apparently some ferrous content to account for rust(?) stains; sl. ls. surface. P: ls. orange-brown, fired pale and much worn. More or less evenly and closely spaced parallel lines over whole body. H: 5. W: 4.5. **B 1098** (Sh 686) D-A. C: g. gray-buff to dk. orange-brown; hard. P: m. dk. orange. 2 wide bands on shoulder. W: 5.6. L: 8.2. **B 1099** (Sh 696a-b) D-A. *Pl. 31.* 2 frags: from shoulder to neck; angular shoulder to body. C: pinkish buff to ls. cream at surface; well cleaned, flaky. P: sl. ls. orange-brown to dk. red-brown, flaky. 2 rings around base of neck; on neck close-set vert. lines bordered above and below by rings. Shoulder: like B 1096. H: 3.7. L: 6.1. For decorative system, cf. *MPL,* Pl. XVI:8–9 (Myc. IIIB).

Three-handled Jars: piriform jars with plain flat base (unless otherwise stated), 3 lifted horizontal ribbon handles (unless otherwise stated) on shoulder, and wide short concave neck with flaring rolled rim. They correspond largely to *MP*, Form 7: 44–45: see *MP*, 23, Fig. 4; C 437–439 and C 462–463 are also from Bamboula.

B 1100 (P 1211; 54-41-7) VT:7. *Pl. 32.* N-c. Part of rim and one handle missing. Base sl. concave. C: buff to pinkish buff; wet-smoothed; hard. P: ls. red-brown to mahogany color, crackled. Neck, base and handles painted solid. 2 n. lines below neck and above base; 3 at widest part of belly. In hz 7 rather crudely executed (simple line) running spirals like *MP*, 357, Fig. 60:52 (IIIA:1-B) varying in size. H: 10. D: 8.6. Shape much like *Gezer* III, T.7, Pl. 66:44 if drawing of the latter is accurate. **B 1101** (P 1212; 54-41-8) VT:8. *Pl. 32.* Most of upper body and frag. of lower body pres. C: lt. pinkish brown to ls. buff surface; hard. P: ls. red-brown to dk. gray-brown, crackled. Neck and handles like B 1100. Below widest part of body, 2 thick outlined stripes. In frieze 3 curved stemmed spirals like *MP*, 363, Fig. 62: Motif 49, No. 14 (IIIA:2, early). Under each handle 3 w. multiple stem patterns like *MP*, 299, Fig. 47:2, 34. PH: 12.4. D: 13.5. Very similar in shape to C 462 (*MPL*, Pl. VIII:1). **B 1102** (P 1315) T.33:24(B) LC IIIA. *Pls. 50, 61.* N-c-m. Shape much like B 1101. Notice also similarity in shape and decoration to other typical Myc. IIIA vases found in Cyprus (*MPL*, Pl. VIII:9–11). Context is considerably later, so that resort to the heirloom theory may have to be had. C: sl. ls. lt. green wfs. P: sl. ls. gray-green to dk. gray, much flaked. Neck, base and handles like B 1101. 3 stripes above base. N. band on shoulder, another at upper level of handles; 3 wider bands below handles. Shoulder zone: uneven serpentine line. H: 10.9. D: 9.2. **B 1103** (P 1363) T.16:46. *Pl. 50.* About ⅔ pres. including complete profile. Shape much like B 1102 but sl. more squat. C: lt. gray-brown to gray-buff wfs; ls. wet-smoothed surface. P: ls. olive to dk. gray with red streaks. Neck, base and handles like B 1100. Paint blobs accentuate ends of handles. 3 heavy rings around widest part of body. Scale pattern in frieze. H: 15.4. D: 13.6. Cf. C 452 and *MPL*, Pl. VIII:8 for shape and decoration. **B 1104** (P 1364) T.16:47. *Pls. 32, 54.* More than half of upper body pres. Shape like B 1101. C: lt. gray-brown; well smoothed ls. surface; hard. P: ls. olive to dk. gray, crackled. Neck and handles like B 1100. 3 bands just below widest part of belly. Frieze: under one handle a spiral hook, the tail of which undulates around the pot and back to starting point. In large interstices, a stemmed flower grows out of the undulating line; one pres. under a handle is a papyrus pattern similar to *MP*, 265, Fig. 34:66. No. 52 of the same Fig. illustrates the general idea of the decoration but B 1104 is undoubtedly later (IIIA:2). PH: 10. D: 13.5. **B 1105** (P 1365) T.16:48. *Pl. 50.* About half pres. giving part of profile. Shape probably much like B 1104. C: pinkish brown to buff wfs; hard. P: ls. red-brown to dk. red-brown. Handles painted solid; wide stripe with 3 n. rings at center around widest part of belly. In frieze: fasicules of from 3 to 9 vert. lines. PH: 13. D: 13.3. **B 1106** (P 1372) T.13:5. *Pl. 50.* About ⅔ pres. giving complete profile. Shape much like B 1103 but sl. more tapering. C: lt.

green-brown, soft; wet-smoothed. P: nearly m. dk. gray; very much worn. Dec. like B 1103 but additional (heavy) stripe above base and outlined heavy stripe just below widest part of belly. H: 15.5. D: 12.4. Cf. C 438 from same tomb (nowhere illustrated, to my knowledge). **B 1107** (P 1419; 49-12-306) T.19:41(B) LC IIA-B. *Pl 32.* N-c-m. Half of mouth and 2 handles missing. Chipped. *MP*, Form 7:45, p. 23, Fig. 4. C: pink to buff wfs, hard; wet-smoothed ls. surface with flaky fractures. P: ls. orange-brown to dk. mahogany color. Neck and handles solid color with 3 res. rings at base of neck; base solid color with 4 res. rings near top. Wide band around widest part of body with 5 n. res. rings. Frieze: continuous closely spaced (vert.) curved bars. H: 13.9. D: 11.8. Close to Mycenae T.525:7 in shape and decoration (see *Archaeologia* 82, 1932, Pl. XLV). **B 1108** (P 2672; 49-12-341) T.22:1 LC IIA. *Pls. 32, 50.* About half pres. in longitudinal section. *MP*, 22, Fig. 3, Form 7:31 (cf. esp. C 478 and *Toronto*, No. 79, but the absolutely flat base from which the sides rise almost perpendicularly is unusual (cf. W. Taylour, *Mycenean Pottery in Italy*, Cambridge 1958, Pl. 9:6). Mrs. Sara Immerwahr calls my attention to a somewhat similar shape from Rhodes (*MPL*, Pl. I:9). Vert. strap handles with center rib and round metallic-looking tab for attaching to body. C: pink to buff and lt. green at surface; well cleaned, ls. surface. P: m. to ls. (in patches) lt. reddish brown to black, crackled. Band inside neck; top of rim res. with continuous w. line. Paint on handle. Frieze: scale pattern closed off above by a stripe and below by 2 wide outlined bands. Base solid color with n. res. band near top. H: 23.1. D: 17.8.

Miscellaneous Piriform Sherds

B 1109 (Sh 156) F-Unstrat. Frag. of rim of piriform jar(?). C: hard pink to sl. ls. cream surface. P: ls. red-brown, flaked. 2 res. bands on rim. Paint inside rim. H: 1. PD: 3.7. **B 1110** (Sh 318) A-D:3(VII) LC IIIA. Frag. of neck of piriform jar(?). C: orange-buff, hard. P: ls. black; brown where thin. Ext. surface painted solid. H: 4.5. **B 1111** (Sh 650; 54-41-15) VT:15. *Pl. 31.* Frag. of (angular) shoulder and belly with one handle. Shape probably to be restored as a variation of the piriform jar. C: pinkish buff; wet-smoothed but powdery. P: sl. ls. orange to red-brown, crackled. Handle painted, vert. parallel lines in hz, 3 stripes at join of neck and belly. H: 4. W: 5.7.

Inscribed vertical ribbon handles of 3-handled(?) jars

B 1112 (G 37:K 71) C-C:1 LC IIC. Top of handle. C: gray-pink to sl. ls. cream at surface. P: m. olive-green to dk. gray. Res. triangle at top of handle. H: 3.6. *AJA* 64 (1960) Pl. 38. **B 1113** (G 38:K 72) D-A. Handle and frag. of shoulder pres. C,P: like B 1112. Handle encircled with a band. Res. triangle like B 1112. Scale design on body. H: 8. W: 7.3. *AJA* 64 (1960) Pl. 38. **B 1114** (G 48:K 73) D-A. Shape, C: like B 1113. P: ls. olive-green to dk. metallic gray. Res. triangle like B 1112. H: 7.3. **B 1115** (G 70:K 75) D-A. Upper part of handle and frag. of shoulder. C: buff to greenish buff. Ext. wet-smoothed but not (now) ls. P: ls. chocolate-brown, much flaked and worn. Res. triangle like B 1112. PH: 4.6. W: 5.5. *AJA* 64 (1960) Pl. 38.

Stirrup Jars

Type 1: piriform shape. To be reckoned here are also C 504–505. This shape occurs at Bamboula in the standard fabric (Group A) and in a coarse-tempered fabric (Group B).

Group A: standard fabric. **B 1116** (P 2770; 54-41-66) MPT-E:4. *Pl. 32.* More than half of upper body pres. Flat shoulder, shape possibly like *MP*, 44, Fig. 12:182 (Myc. IIIB), otherwise depressed globular. C: buff to pinkish buff, wet-smoothed. P: lt. red-brown, spread thin in patches. Hand-painted c-c on disk; on handles solid color except for res. triangles on top. Stripe at bottom of false neck, around mouth and base of spout. Outside rim of shoulder and below shoulder stripes and n. res. rings. On shoulder: 2 (and probably 4) unvoluted flower designs like *MP*, 293, Fig. 45:126–7 (Myc. IIIB). PH: 9.2. ED: 13. **B 1117** (P 2828; 54-41-105) E-A:7 LC IIA. *Pls. 32, 54.* N-c-m. Advanced piriform shape, cf. *MPL*, Pl. XV:5. Disk top flat. C: pinkish buff to buff, well cleaned, hard; sl. ls. surface. P: ls. orange to mahogany color, crackled. Top of handle and disk decorated like B 1116. Ring at base of false neck joining similar ring at spout base. Top of spout painted. In shoulder zone a design resembling parallel chevrons, closed on one side. Wide stripe with n. res. rings at edge of shoulder, just below widest part of body and near base, which is painted solid. H: 19.5. D: 14.4. C 504 from OT 30 is almost a duplicate of B 1117. **B 1118** (Sh 697) D-A. *Pl. 31.* False neck with stumps of handles, non-joining frags. from shoulder and one frag. of low ring base. For comment on shape, see B 1116. C: gray-buff to olive; hard, well cleaned, smooth. P: lt. olive-green to black. Res. ring on disk and res. triangles on handles, otherwise solid. Paint around base of false neck. On edge of shoulder, res. c-c with wide band; 2 wide stripes where shoulder joins body. Stripe around base and c-c on bottom. H (of false neck): 3.7. D (of disk): 2.2. **B 1119** (Sh 505) C-A:6 etc. LC IIA. Large frag. of base and various non-joining frags. of body and shoulder. Shape probably like B 1117. C: lt. brown to lt. buff, hard; well smoothed, ls. surface. P: lt. red-brown. On body and base wide stripes with n. res. rings. On shoulder: chevrons dotted(?) on one side. H (of largest frag.): 10.6. **B 1120** (Sh 745) C-Unstrat. *Pl. 30.* Shoulder frag. C,P: like B 1119, possibly a frag. of same pot. Chevrons and fill ornament(?). L: 3.8. *Miscellaneous fragments from stirrup jars or pots of piriform shape:* **B 1121** (P 759) A-C:1b LC IIB. *Pl. 32.* Frag. of base of piriform pot with rolled ring base. C: g. lt. orange-brown to orange-buff; smooth surface, hard. P: ls. red-brown to dk. red-black, flaked. Base solid color with 4 n. res. rings near bottom. PH: 8.3. D (of base): 5.7. **B 1122** (Sh 68) Cw IV CA. *Pl. 30.* Neck frag. Tapers upward. C: lt. olive-green, rich texture; ls. self-slip. P: ls. dk. gray; olive-brown where thin. Crackled. H: 3.7. **B 1123** (Sh 206) A-D:2(St.2a) LC IIIA.

Frag. of spout. C: pinkish to gray buff; surface worn. P: sl. ls. brownish red. Band around base. H: 2.9. **B 1124** (Sh 445) A-Surface. *Pl. 30.* Base frag. with squared moulding. C: lt. gray-buff; sl. ls. surface. P: ls. red-brown, crackled. Botton res. H: 2.3. **B 1125** (Sh 496) A-D:1(VII) LC IIC. Base frag. C: orange-brown to dk. buff; rich texture. Sl. ls. creamy surface. P: ls. red-brown. Wide and n. band. Bottom res. H: 1.7. ED (of base): 7. **B 1126** (Sh 643) E-11b. Frag. of base. Ring moulding similar to *MP*, 91, Fig. 24, lower left corner. C: buff, soft and abrasive. P: sl. ls. red-brown, flaked; apparently applied with jar on wheel. Bottom res. PH: 2.7. ED (of base): 10.3. **B 1127** (Sh 695) D-A. *Pl. 31.* Spout and adjoining shoulder frag. Convex with flaring rolled rim; shoulder almost flat. C: gray-buff to pinkish buff, powdery. P: sl. ls. orange. Paint on rim. Thick band at base of rim tangent to band encircling shoulder. H: 4.1. L: 5.5. **B 1128** (Sh 698) D-A. Most of false neck with stumps of ribbed handles. Disk flat. C: gray-buff with occasional pink streaks; surface sl. ls. pale green. P: ls. brown-black, crackled and badly weathered. Res. circle on top of disk; res. triangles at top of handles. Band at base of neck. H: 5.7. D (of disk): 7.7.

Group B: coarse-tempered ware. The chief characteristic of this ware is a rough gritty fabric with much lime, sand and generally a temper of ground sherds or stones. The paint is crumbly and the ware itself is not of really hard consistency, though it is, of course, rather thick and coarse-looking. It occurs at this site almost exclusively in large piriform stirrup jars, and the cephalopod or its derivative, octopus tentacles alone, is almost exclusively the decorative motif. I have discussed this class at some length in *Berytus* 14 (1961) 37 ff., where I have designated B 1130 as Minoan. Cf. also B 1006. **B 1129** (P 1423:K 82; 54-12-99) D-A. *Pl. 33.* I-m. Most of upper body pres. Depressed disk. Full tapering ovoid-biconical body. Foot restoration conjectural. C: lt. bluish gray to lt. yellow-orange at surface, which is sl. bur. P: m. orange-brown to lt. orange, interlocking "question marks" on handles and disk. Paint around base of false neck with U-design connecting handles and spout to neck. U-design also on spout. Body design: a double register of tentacles (cf. *MP*, 373, Fig. 65: 4–5 etc.) bordered above by 3 rings and below by 2 thick rings. H (restored): 33.8. D: 25.7. *AJA* 45 (1941) 267, Fig. 11. *AJA* 64 (1960) 148; *Berytus* 14 (1961) Pl. 18:2 and Fig. 3. **B 1130** (P 1424) D-A. *Pl. 33.* I-m. About half of body including profile to neck pres. Sl. arched base with sl. flaring and contoured base rim and tapering stem from which rises elongated ovoid-biconical body. C: gray and lt. brick-red to lt. orange-brown at surface; hard, with angular lt. grits and sea-sand. P: sl. ls. brick-red to dk. gray-brown. Loops around handle base have upper continuation. Lower body divided off by 2 n. lines within 2 thick stripes (repeated, midway lower body). Upper body has frieze: straight long stem with upright pod-like top and 3 flowing symmetrically arranged leaves on either side. An adaptation of the end of this design is used to fill interstices above plants. Daniel considered this design to be lilies, but it appears rather to be a combination of the two types of palm motif discussed by Furumark (cf. *MP*, 277, Fig. 38 and 279, Fig. 39). Bands below and ring painted around base. PH: 44.2. D: 30. *BSA* 55 (1960) 119, Pl. 29:C; *Berytus* 14 (1961) Pl. 18:1 and Fig. 4. **B 1131** (Sh 164) A-D:3(V) LC IIIA. *Pl. 31.* Frag. of flat base and sl. concave foot. C: lt. greenish with much sharp gray grit. P: ls. gray-green, much flaked. Bands on base. H: 3.5. **B 1132** (Sh 427) Cw VIII. Frag. from base of neck. C: g. orange-brown to lt. orange-buff at surface. P: m. rust, very much worn. Band around base of neck. L: 3.8. **B 1133** (Sh 498) B-Unstrat. (Flat) disk and stumps of handles of a very large jar. C: orange-buff to lt. greenish buff at surface—which is sl. bur.—with temper of sharp-edged dk. brown stones(?). P: ls. red-brown to dk. olive-gray. Disk outlined; in its center a cross. H: 4. D (of disk): 8.6. *AJA* 64 (1960) Pl. 38. **B 1134** (Sh 547) T.26:2. Various sherds of C 501. C: grayish red-brown to dk. buff surface, with sharp-edged lt. and dk. grits. P: sl. ls. mahogany color to dk. gray. These sherds have been rejoined to C 501 (see *Berytus* 14 (1961) 37 f.). **B 1135** (Sh 715) E-2. Frag. from shoulder or body; it is not possible to be absolutely certain that the frag. belongs to this class or shape. C: gray-buff to lt. buff at surface, with red and dk. grits. P: m. streaky orange-brown. One hor. stripe around pot. H: 9.6. L: 14.3. **B 1136** (Sh 742) B-Well:7. *Pl. 31.* Frag. of base like B 1131. C: dk. olive-gray with lt. olive-gray sl. ls. surface; numerous dk. grits. P: sl. ls. gray-red to dk. gray-olive. Stripe around base and another a little above this. H: 3. D: 5.6. **B 1137** (G 24:K 83) A-A:3 LC IIA. Frag. of handle near top broken off from false neck. C: lt. green with large sharp-edged dk. sand temper. No dec. L: 6.8. *AJA* 64 (1960) Pl. 38. **B 1138** (G 43:K 79) B-Well:Stray in Iron Age deposit. Disk and stump of handle. Disk sl. depressed. C: like B 1133. P: ls. dk. red to dk. gray-brown, crackled. Dec. like B 1133. Res. triangle at top of painted handle. H: 3. D (of disk): 6.4. *AJA* 64 (1960) Pl. 38. **B 1139** (G 51:K 80) E-Unstrat. Neck and one handle with connecting frag. of shoulder. C: dk. gray-buff with large, mostly brown, grits. P: m. lt. brown to black, nearly gone. Part of outline of disk and traces of paint on shoulder pres. PH: 9. D (of disk): 6.3. *AJA* 64 (1960) Pl. 38. **B 1140** (G 58:K 81) D-A. Disk and stump of handle. P: gray-buff to orange with gray-brown grits. Traces of dk. red paint on disk. L (diagonal): 8.4. *AJA* 64 (1960) Pl. 38. All the following sherds are body fragments with traces of degenerate octopus design on them (unless noted). Eight more surface or unstratified sherds are not listed: **B 1141** (Sh 146) A-E:3(V) LC IIIA. C: pinkish to sl. ls. lt. green at surface, with many large coarse grits. P: olive-brown, much worn. L (diagonal): 4.2. **B 1142** (Sh 199) A-F:2 LC IIIB. C: g. lt. gray-pink to gray-green No dec. L: 3.3. **B 1143** (Sh 204) A-D:2(St.1a) LC IIIA. C,P: like B 1141. L: 6. **B 1144** (Sh 205) A-D:2(St.1a) LC IIIA. C: like B 1135. No dec. L: 3.8. **B 1145** (Sh 223) A-B:5 LC IIB. *Pl. 31.* C: like B 1130. P: sl. ls. black. L (diagonal): 5.7. **B 1146** (Sh 232) A-E:4 LC IIIB. C,P: like B 1141. L: 4.5. **B 1147** (Sh 463) A-D:1(VI) LC IIC. C: g. dk. buff.

P: ls. brown to dk. gray, worn; very heavy fabric. W: 8.7. **B 1148** (Sh 472) A-B:4 LC IIB. C,P: like B 1141. L: 4.5. **B 1149** (Sh 475) A-D:3(VIa) LC IIIA. *Pl. 31.* C: lt. orange-brown with black and red grits; wet-smoothed. P: ls. black, worn. W: 5.8. **B 1150** (Sh 490) A-A:3 LC IIA. C: g. gray to m. orange. P: red-orange, very much worn. L: (diagonal): 5.5. **B 1151** (Sh 674) D-A. Various frags. C: dk. buff to orange-buff with large grits; soft and crumbly. P: m. orange-red. L (of largest sherd): 11. W (of same): 6.5. **B 1152** (Sh 726) A-C:3 LC IIB. C: like B 1141. P: entirely gone but its position is still traceable. L: 4. **B 1153** (Sh 732) A-D:2(St.2b) LC IIIA. *Pl. 30.* C,P: like B 1141. L: 4.2.

Type 2: globular, with low ring base. Occurs only in standard fabric. Most of the following specimens appear to be *MP*, Form 46:171 (see pp. 30–31, Figs. 5–6) and, occurring relatively early in the LC II period, are classifiable as Mycenaean IIIA:2. Other specimens from Bamboula are C 520–522.

B 1154 (P 1271; 49-12-146) T.12:16(D) LC IIA. *Pl. 33.* N-c-m. Spout missing. Dented in manufacture. C: yellowish to dk. buff; well smoothed ls. surface. P: ls. red-brown with a few red-black patches. Disk and handles like B 1116. Ring at base of neck and of spout. Vert. lines on shoulder. On body: 3 equidistant wide zones with 5, 4 and 4 n. res. lines resp. H: 9.4. D: 9.1. **B 1155** (P 1272; 49-12-148) T.12:18(D) LC IIA. *Pl. 33.* C-m. Like B 1154. C: lt. greenish buff; wet-smoothed. P: ls. dk. gray-brown, olive where thin; flaked. Dec. like B 1154, but on body 4, 4 and 5 n. res. lines. H: 9.7. D: 9.6. **B 1156** (P 1325) T.36:32. *Pl. 50.* C-ch. Disk sl. peaked. C: lt. orange-brown to lt. brownish buff at surface; wet-smoothed. P: ls. red-brown to dk. red-gray. Res. circles in disk, res. triangles in handles. Paint on lip and at base of spout. 5 filling ornaments on shoulder: circles dotted on int. Thick stripes on shoulder, belly and base with res. lines. 3 c-c on base. H: 12.7. D: 11.8. **B 1157** (P 1326) T.36:48. C-ch. Shape like B 1154. C: green and orange-brown to orange-buff at surface; wet-smoothed. P: ls. red-brown. C-s with solid center on disk; no shoulder ornament; 3 c-c around solid circle on base; other dec. like B 1156. H: 12. D: 11. **B 1158** (P 2660; 49-12-246) T.18:12(A) LC IIB. *Pl. 33.* N-c-m. Shape somewhat depressed. C: pinkish buff to buff and yellow on surface, which is sl. ls. P: semi-ls. red-brown to mahogany-brown, crackled. Neck, handles, spout: like B 1156. On shoulder: unconnected reversed N's. Body: like B 1154 but 4, 5 and 5 n. res. lines. H: 9.7. D: 10.6. **B 1159** (P 2666; 49-12-232) T.21:2 LC IIA. *Pl. 33.* C-ch. Shape very similar to B 1154. C: orange-buff to sl. ls. dk. buff at surface, well cleaned. P: sl. ls. lt. red-brown to dk. gray-brown. Dot and res. ring on disk. Handles painted. Band around base of neck continuing to spout and enveloping much of spout. Paint on lip. Body: like B 1154 but with 4, 4 and 3 n. res. lines, rather heavily executed. H: 9.1. D: 7.7. **B 1160** (P 2820) D-A. *Pl. 33.* Spout, false neck, handles and adjoining sections of shoulder pres. Shoulder rather flat. C: lt. grayish buff, well cleaned, hard. P: sl. ls. brownish buff, crackled. Disk:

res. circle. Paint on handles, spout rim (int.). Stripe unites bases of neck and spout and is tangent to a stripe around shoulder at base of handles. Beyond this n. multiple lines and another thicker stripe. PH: 4.5. PD: 10. **B 1161** (P 2823; 54-41-51) MPT-B:1. *Pl. 33.* Most of body pres. giving profile; also spout and most of neck and one handle (non-joining). Shape like B 1154. C: olive to gray-green; wet-smoothed. P: lt. greenish brown to black but fired lt. or crackled off. Dec: like B 1154 with addition of 2 n. lines between shoulders and belly zone and 4, 4 and 4 n. res. lines. PH: 15. D: 17.1. **B 1162** (Sh 225) A-B:5 LC IIB. *Pl. 30.* Sherd from outer shoulder. C: like B 1119. P: lt. to dk. olive-brown. Outlined multiple lines. L (diagonal): 3.2. **B 1163** (Sh 322) A-D:2(VII,2) LC IIIA. *Pl. 31.* Frag. from near neck or base. C: buff at core to lt. orange-buff at surface. P: ls. dk. orange. Dec: like B 1162. L: 4.5. **B 1164** (Sh 484) A-A:3 LC IIA. *Pl. 31.* Spout. Convex with rolled rim. C,P, dec: like B 1123 plus paint on rim. H: 3. **B 1165** (Sh 485) A-A:3 LC IIA. *Pl. 31.* Frag. of ring base. C,P: like B 1164. Probably from same pot. H: 0.9. **B 1166** (Sh 700) D-A. *Pl. 31.* Most of base with very low ring pres. plus a shoulder frag. probably belonging to this pot. C: pinkish to buff; sl. ls. creamy surface. P: ls. red-brown to black, crackled. At center of bottom: 5 c-c. Paint on ring base. Outlined multiple lines on shoulder. D (of base): 5.6. **B 1167** (Sh 701) D-A. Base and lower wall frag. like B 1165. Flat sl. set-off base and gradually curving walls. C: g. gray to dk. pinkish buff; hard, wet-smoothed. P: m. firm orange-brown. 2 stripes above base, another somewhat above these. H: 2.6. D (of base): 4.5. **B 1168** (G 47:K 78) T.17:27. 2 frags. of wide flat base sl. profiled. C: very lt. pink to pale gray-green; sl. powdery. P: ls. olive-green to dk. gray. Dipinto in thin red m. paint. H (of lower frag.): 2.5. ED (of base): 12. *MPL*, 48; *AJA* 64 (1960) Pl. 38.

Pilgrim Flasks: one well preserved specimen and fragments of others were found at Bamboula. Raised small disk base, perfect spherical shape, short narrow neck, flaring mouth with profiled lip. Slightly arched vertical handles from shoulder to mid-neck. This is *MP*, Form 48.

B 1169 (P 2938; 49-12-103 group no.) T.6:11. Numerous frags. from one side. C: rich pinkish buff, well levigated. P: sl. ls. dk. chocolate-brown. Fine multiple bands between wider bands, twice repeated. Front: hor. w-l. EH: 25. **B 1170** (P 987) E-Intrusion(V) and Megaron. See *Bamboula SS*: Area E-C:5. *Pl. 33.* I-m. C: dk. gray-buff to sl. ls. lt. olive at surface; wet-smoothed. P: ls. olive-brown to dk. gray, flaked. Front and back: bull's eye and multiple c-c. Vert. zigzag in hz. Paint on neck and handles, applied rather unsystematically. H: 14.2. D: 11.4. *MPL*, Pl. XVII:2 (Myc. IIIB) has nearly identical decoration but the shape of B 1170 seems closer to *MPL*, Pl. XIV:4-5, which are earlier. **B 1171** (Sh 231) A-E:4 LC IIIB. *Pl. 30.* Body frag. C,P: like B 1163. Dec: like B 1170. L: 2.6. **B 1172** (Sh 251) A-Surface. *Pl. 31.* Most of small ring base and adjoining wall frag. C: lt. buff with ls. surface; hard but sl. powdery.

P: sl. ls. dk. lavender-red. Evidence for c-c of varying thickness on one side of body. D (of base): 3.4. **B 1173** (Sh 283) A-D:3(IV) LC IIIA. Body frag. C: sl. powdery pale gray-green with sl. ls. surface. P: like B 1162. Dec: like B 1170. L: 4.2. **B 1174** (Sh 506) C-B LC IIB. *Pl. 31.* Neck and top of shoulder. C: like B 1173 but lighter and not bur. P: ls. olive-brown to dk. gray, crackled. H: 3.9.

Two-handled Flasks: very closely related to the foregoing type are the following, which have depressed globular instead of spherical shape. They are *MP*, Form 49:190, cf. p. 30, Fig. 5. Notice also the related C 571 from Bamboula.

B 1175 (P 2743) T.38:4. *Pl. 33.* I-m. Part of shoulder and body on both sides missing. C: pinkish buff to sl. ls. buff at surface; well cleaned, hard. P. ls. red. Mouth painted int. and ext. with n. res. band on top of rim. Stripe around base of neck. Handles painted ext. with stroke of brush continuing downward on neck. On body 3 equidistant dk. zones with n. res. lines. H: 12. D: 10. **B 1176** (P 2744) T.38:5. *Pl. 33.* I-m. Handles and much of body missing. Neck rather long. C: like B 1175. P: sl. ls. orange to dk. red-brown. Rim painted outside. Thick stripe under rim and at base of neck. In shoulder zone carelessly made concentric semicircles. On shoulder and at base dk. zones with n. res. lines. Between these zones 2 n. lines. H: 8.9. D: 7.3. **B 1177** (P 2667; 49-12-333) T.21:3 LC IIA. *Pls. 33, 50.* I-m. One handle missing. C: gray-buff to sl. ls. buff at surface; well cleaned. P: sl. ls. reddish brown to chocolate-brown, crackled. Neck like B 1175 but 3 res. lines on lip; small res. triangle on handles. Shoulder and body dec. like B 1154 except 6, 5 and 5 res. lines; also 3 n. bands between upper wide bands. H: 10.4. D: 9.6.

One-handled Flask: the following fragment appears to be from a shape something like *MP*, 67, Fig. 20:186.

B 1178 (Sh 536) Cw IV CA. *Pl. 31.* Neck with sl. flaring round mouth nearly closed by flat disk with small hole in center. C: buff, well smoothed; fine and rather soft. P: m.(?) red. Near handle stump a sea anemone like *MP*, 315, Mot. 27:16. Cf. B 519. H: 4.2. D (of disk): 4.

Juglets

B 1179 (P 1316) T.33:35(A) LC IIB. *Pls. 33, 50, 60.* C-i. Low ring base, baggy globular body, wide short concave neck with flaring round mouth and vert. handle to rim. C: buff wfs; wet-smoothed. P: ls. lt. to dk. orange-brown. Rim, handle and base of neck painted. Wide dk. zone with 4 n. res. lines below handle; 3 n. bands on lower belly; 2 thick bands at base. H: 9.5. D: 9. This and the following two pots are *MP*, Form 25 and from their contexts belong to the LH IIIA or early LH IIIB period. C 591 must also be reckoned with this group. **B 1180** (P 1317) T.33:36(A) LC IIB. *Pls. 50, 60.* C-i. Very small flat base set off from squat globular body. Shape like B 1179 but handle more vert. C: pinkish to buff at surface wfs; hard, wet-smoothed. P: ls. lt. to dk. red-brown, crackled. Dec: neck and handle like B 1179 but handle has res.

triangle near top. 4 n. bands below handle and 3 on lower belly. Wide zone with 4 n. res. lines near base. H: 6. D: 5.6. **B 1181** (P 1318) T.33:37(A) LC IIB. *Pls. 50, 60.* C-ch. Shape like B 1179 but handle more arched. C: orange-brown; hard, wet-smoothed. P: ls. red-brown. Dec: like B 1179 minus 3 bands on lower belly. H: 6.9. D: 6.5. **B 1182** (P 2671; 49-12-337) T.21:7 LC IIA. *Pl. 33.* Part of neck and mouth missing. Flat base, depressed globular body. Neck and handle like B 1181. C: orange-buff, well cleaned; m. surface, eroded on one side. P: sl. ls. orange-brown. Dec: neck and handle like B 1180. 3 n. bands just below shoulder. Base: 3 n. bands outlined by wider bands. H: 6. D: 5.6. **B 1183** (P 2821; 54-41-52) MPT-B:2. *Pl. 33.* N-c-m. Small raised disk base; very squat globular body with n. concave neck to flaring cutaway-type mouth; vert. handle to rim. C: dk. buff, hard; wet-smoothed. P: ls. orange-brown to dk. gray-brown. Dec: neck and handle like B 1179. Upper and lower body have 3 n. bands between wide stripes. Stripe around base. H: 7. D: 6.3. This is *MP*, Form 41:149 under which C 594 is listed (C 598 also belongs in this category). All these are, no doubt, contemporaneous with B 1179–1182. A variant shape is C 598. **B 1184** (P 2732) T.24:1 LC IIC(?). *Pls. 33, 54.* I-m. Restored. Low profiled ring base, rather squat ovoid body with concave n. neck to plain round mouth with flattened rim (mouth somewhat warped in firing); handle perpendicular from shoulder to rim. Very similar to *Problems,* 67, Shape 9 (*MP,* Form 26: IIIB). C: dk. buff to sl. ls. yellow-buff and orange at surface. P: m. dk. red-brown to sl. ls. gray-brown. Rim painted. Thick w. line on back of handle. Band at base of neck. In shoulder zone, a band of linked (not running) simple line spirals (comparable to *MP,* 357, Fig. 60:54 except that the direction of the spirals alternates). 3 thick bands below handle and below widest part of belly. 2 bands at base. H: 27.7. D: 16. **B 1185** (P 2779; 49-12-56) T.5:1a(B) LC IIB. Plain flat base and about ⅓(?) of belly wall pres. Shape probably similar to B 1186. C: orange-buff to dk. buff, well cleaned; close rich texture; beautifully smoothed. No dec. PH: 12.3. D (of base): 9.4. ED: 18–20. **B 1186** (P 2780; 49-12-57) T.5:2a(B) LC IIB. *Pl. 33.* Plain flat base with steeply rising walls curving gently to shoulder. Body about ⅓ pres. Non-joining frags. indicate a steep shoulder, sl. arched handle to rim, and trefoil mouth. A large lump of clay is left like a hub on the inside of the base. All this seems to point to *MP,* 44, Fig. 12:139 (Form 39), as the probable shape of this pot (cf. also *MPL,* Pl. XIII:9-10 and see comment below). C: like B 1185 but sl. more pinkish in hue. No dec. PH: 14.6. D (of base): 9.3. ED: 18. The occurrence of this shape, which has been considered specifically Levanto-Mycenaean, in this relatively early context and undecorated, is of interest. Attention is called to the fact that B 1185 and 1186 are in the most excellent standard fabric.

Miscellaneous Jug Fragments: B 1188, and B 1189 are of inferior technique. **B 1187** (Sh 246) A-Surface. *Pl. 31.* Frag. of flaring rim with sl. rolled lip. C: sl. powdery pinkish buff. P: ls. red-brown, flaked. Ext. painted solid. H: 4. **B 1188** (Sh 562 and Sh 723)

E-Unstrat. *Pls. 31, 50.* Sh 562: shoulder frag. with ridge at base of neck. Sh 723 is from same pot: frag. of sl. concave neck with flattened, everted lip. Adjoining shoulder frag. is steep. C: pinkish buff to dk. gray-green at surface (not ls.); well cleaned. P: like B 1162. Paint inside mouth and on top of rim. In neck zone inverted tall n. solid triangles, roughly painted; rows of hor. zigzag on shoulder, probably in a panel; non-joining sherd has panel with corner filled with dotted arcs. H (of Sh 723): 8.3. Solid triangles as decorative elements are easiest to associate with Syro-Palestine (although, of course, not confined to that region): cf. H. Bossert, *Altsyrien* (Tübingen, 1951) Figs. 640, 729 (left); *Lachish* IV, Pl. 84:963; *Ugaritica* II, 137: 8-9, 147:16, etc. In the same region, though derived from Greece, horizontal zigzag panels are ultimately at home (cf. *Gezer* III, Pl. CLXVII:9). Daniel compared the design of Sh 562 to that on a sherd from Athens: *Hesperia* 8 (1939) 404, Fig. 85, m. One might also consider its similarity to the shoulder design of B 1004 (see *PEQ,* 1960, Pl. IV: Fig. 9). This curious combination of features suggests, if it does not prove, that B 1188 is a Syro-Palestinian adaptation of Mycenaean IIIB-C ware. It is not, however, at all similar to Philistine ware from the point of view of technique. Here, again, it rather resembles Mycenaean ware. **B 1189** (Sh 675) D-A. *Pl. 50.* Frag. showing profile of concave neck with round flaring mouth and beveled profiled lip; probably from a jug similar in shape to B 1184. C: pinkish buff, well cleaned and fine but with a few small grits; surface ls. pale pink, possibly slipped. P: streaky m. red-brown to gray-brown, flaked. Paint on rim and at base of neck. H: 8.9. ED (of base of neck): 6. **B 1190** (Sh 692) D-A. *Pl. 31.* Frag. of flaring rim with plain lip from mouth of sizeable jug. C: pinkish at core to gray-buff at surface; well smoothed. P: sl. ls. streaky orange to dk. gray-brown. 2 thick bands enclosing 3 n. bands. H: 4.8. W: 5.4.

Miscellaneous sherds from jugs and other closed shapes: all are standard fabric except B 1193 and B 1198–1200.

B 1191 (Sh 93) A-Surface. Frag. of flat base, sl. profiled at edge, and thick flaring wall. C: sl. pinkish buff with a ls. cream surface. H: 2.8. ED (of base): 11. **B 1192** (Sh 98) A-E:3(VIII) LC IIIB. *Pl. 30.* Wall or shoulder frag. C: clean buff; ls. cream surface. P: ls. orange-brown. Fringe(?) and band. L (diagonal): 2.7. **B 1193** (Sh 128) A-D:3(VIa) LC IIIA. *Pl. 31.* Frag. of very low ring base and adjoining flaring wall. C: lt. gray to buff; ls. surface. P: m. gray-brown to dk. gray. Band on ring base. H: 3.2. ED (of base): 11. **B 1194** (Sh 364) A-Unstrat. *Pl. 31.* Like B 1191. C: orange-buff, well cleaned; rather powdery. Small piece of lead(?) embedded in bottom. Traces of ls. red-brown paint. H: 2.4. ED (of base): 12. **B 1195** (Sh 385) A-F:1 LC IIIB. *Pl. 30.* Wall frag. C: gray to lt. buff. P: ls. red-brown, crackled. Loop of degenerate octopus(?) L (diagonal): 2.2. **B 1196** (Sh 501) A-A:2b LC IIA. *Pl. 31.* Frag. from flat base with rounded transition to flaring wall. Small jug or alabastron(?) C: like B 1191. P: like B 1162. Large outlined dot on underside of base. 2 n. lines where base joins wall. H: 1.5. ED (of base): 5. **B 1197** (Sh 502) Cw IIa LC IIB? Shoulder frag. C: pinkish buff wfs and one large pebble; cream surface. P: like B 1162. Band at base of neck. L (diagonal): 4. **B 1198** (Sh 718) E-D:2d LC IIIA. *Pl. 30.* Wall frag. of jug or bowl. Possibly local but not typically Cypriote in technique. C: dk. gray to lt. gray, well cleaned, very hard and compact; surface glossy. P: m. dk. brown. Part of latticed triangle and tangent hor. border. H: 3.6. W: 2.5. **B 1199** (Sh 108) A-E:3(VIII) etc. LC IIIB. *Pl. 31.* Various belly(?) sherds. C: pinkish to ls. pale green at surface wfs; well cleaned. P: like B 1162. 3 hor. stripes. H (of largest frag.): 5.3. **B 1200** (Sh 208) A-E:2(St.2a) etc. LC IIIB. Frag. of beveled rim of jug or hollow base of a closed pot. Fabric uncertain but has a vague resemblance to Mycenaean. C: lt. gray to lt. pinkish brown; sl. powdery. P: m. red-brown covering all int. and ext. surfaces. H: 2.1. ED (of base and mouth): 6.

DIAGONAL PAINTED WARE

This name is suggested for a group of sherds which appear to come from angular deep bowls or pyxides, with a preferred decoration of oblique lines, either single or crossed (as in a lattice pattern). The use of wavy lines is not, however, excluded. The ware is wheelmade and matt painted. The technique is not decidedly different from ordinary Cypriote painted wares, particularly of the LC III Decorated variety. The use of diagonals and the reminiscence of a "framed caduceus" (in B 1205) vaguely recall the earlier White Painted ware (cf. *MCBA*, Fig. IX) which is, of course, handmade (but cf. *ibid.*, 129). However, the almost exclusive occurrence of our ware in Area C, with a range from the LC IA:2 to the LC IIC period, might suggest the possibility that it was imported. The appearance particularly of the specimens decorated with lattice-work recalls Palestinian "band-slip" ware; but this appears to be handmade and to occur at the latest in the Early Bronze II period (*AASOR* XXV-XXVIII, Pt. 2, p. 458 and Pls. 43, 55, 58). B 1201 is somewhat hesitantly classed with this category because it is a comparatively heavier fabric. See also Tomb 28:5.

B 1201 (Sh 292) A-A:4 LC IIA. *Pl. 34.* Wall frag. C: sandy lt. gray-buff, almost gray-green at surface. Rather thick fabric. P: m. lt. to dk. gray-brown. Diagonally crossing lines; 2 more lines apparently not related to main framework. L (diagonal): 5.5. **B 1202** (Sh 507) C-B etc. LC IIB. *Pl. 34.* Wall frag. with angulation. C: red-brown to lt. brown-buff wfds and fine lime grits. P: m. dk. gray-brown and m. dk. purple-brown. Overall lattice decoration. H: 4.4. **B 1203** (Sh 706) C-A:5 LC IB. *Pl. 34.* Frags. of wall thickening towards angular transition to another plane. Small groove ext. at thinner end. C: g. lt. brown-buff wfds and fine lime grits. P: m. purple. Hor. stripe on thinner end and below bend in wall. 4 oblique stripes

connecting them. H: 6. L: 8.5. **B 1204** (Sh 707) C-A:6 LC IIA. *Pl. 34.* Frag. of nearly straight wall beginning to curve at one end. C: g. lt. pinkish gray, wfds and lime. P: m. purple-brown. Wide hor. stripe at one end; just above this traces of another stripe, perhaps in red. Another hor. stripe where wall bends. Frag. of vert. stripe suggests a panel. Opposite this: a small blob and the lower termination of an irregular curved stroke ending in 2 root-like lines. H: 8.5. W: 6.5. **B 1205** (Sh 708) C-A:3 LC IA:2. *Pl. 34.* Wall or base frag. with more or less angular transition to another plane. C,P: like B 1203 plus m. dk. red paint. W. line flanked by a heavily outlined red stripe. H: 8.3. W: 9. *PEQ* (1961) 63 Pl. 6:1. **B 1206** (Sh 716) C-C:1 LC IIC. *Pl. 34.* Shape, C, P and dec: identical with B 1202; undoubtedly part of same pot. H: 5. **B 1207** (Sh 746) C-Unstrat. *Pl. 34.* Small frag. of wall. Same comment as for B 1206. H: 2. **B 1208** (Sh 748) C-Unstrat. *Pl. 34.* Frag. of sl. convex wall with trace of relief ridge near top(?) C: g. pinkish gray to green-gray at surface wfds. P: m. gray-black, much worn. Relief ridge painted; from this depend wide oblique stripes. H: 5. W: 5.

FOREIGN WHITE PAINTED PILGRIM FLASKS

This fabric has a context-range at Bamboula of LC IIIA to CG IB, although at Kaloriziki only one example has been noted (K 971). There appear to be at least two published examples of this ware from Cyprus: Amathus Tomb 22: nos. 39 and 44 (*SCE* II, Pl. CXXXVIII), apparently unstratified, in burials dated CG I-II. One cannot, however, be absolutely sure that this is the same fabric, as there is no description of the clay. However, the fabric and shape of B 1209–1212 definitely occur on the Syro-Palestinian coast, e.g., Tell Fara Tomb 237 (*CPP* 85L:1) and their origin is undoubtedly to be sought in that region. It seems quite possible that they may have furnished the inspiration for the LC III Decorated pilgrim flask. In any case, it will be noted that the same morphological process was at work, for B 1209, the earliest example, has a short mouth, whereas the later examples have tall mouths.

B 1209 (P 1203) E-D:1h LC IIIA. *Pl. 51.* C-i, but surface badly worn. Sloping handles joining neck directly under rim. Body made in 2 sections. C: lt. orange-brown with many air-holes on surface; heavy fabric. Sl. traces of red paint. H: 13.9. D: 10.2. W: 7. **B 1210** (P 2685; 49-12-401) T.30:7 CG IA. *Pls. 34, 51.* C-sp. Surface badly worn. Rather tall flaring mouth. C: g. gray-orange, hand bur. Traces of m. purple-brown paint. Rim dotted. 3 c-c on outer edge of body. H: 13.1. D: 8.7. W: 6.6. **B 1211** (P 2737; 49-12-119) T.11:4(B) CG IB. *Pls. 34, 51.* C-sp. Somewhat wider mouth than the foregoing and more compact handles. C: g. lt. orange-pink with some airholes; soil discoloration on most of surface. Hand bur? P: m. purple-brown. Blot of paint on rim. Handles barred. 3 c-cs at center, 3 more at edge of body.

H: 13.6. D: 8.5. W: 7.4. **B 1212** (P 2768; 54-41-58)
MPT-D:1. C-ch. Shape identical with B 1210. C: lt.
orange-pink; well cleaned, rather soft. Self-slipped and
bur. P: thin m. dk. gray-brown. Dec: like B 1211.
H: 13.1. D: 6.2. W: 6.2.

FOREIGN POLYCHROME PILGRIM FLASK

Polychrome counterpart of Foreign White Painted
Pilgrim Flasks.

B 1213 (P 930; 49-12-10) T.2:5(B) Probably CG
IA (by shape). *Pls. 34, 51.* C-i. Rudimentary conical
boxed rim. Handles sloping to mid-neck. C: yellowish
brown to orange-brown; self-slipped and bur. P: m.
white, dk. gray-brown, dk. red. Outlined red dot at
center, then white band, s-o red band, white band,
n. black border. At edge: s-o zone consisting of white-
red-white bands. Other side washed off. Long red
vert. line on handles terminated above by arrowhead(?)
Base of handle looped, with trailing "ribbons." H: 14.3.
D: 9.6. W: 7.9.

ATTIC WARE

For a comment on this fabric at Kourion, see *AJA*
60 (1956) 49, esp. n. 37. Cf. also L. Cesnola, *A Descriptive Atlas of the Cesnola Collection . . . New
York, II* (New York, 1894) pl. CXLVIII.

B 1214 (Sh 130) Cw Vb CA I. *Pl. 33.* Wall frag.
of large open shape decorated in black-figure technique. Portion of human figure(?) plus 2 thin straight
lines. H: 3.2. Th (of wall): *ca.* .07. **B 1215** (Sh 180)
A-Unstrat. *Pl. 33.* Wall frag. of cup(?) Black glaze:
int. and also below legs of delicately drawn lion(?)
Fine incisions. L: 2.5. **B 1216** (Sh 375) Cw Vb CA I.
Pl. 33. Sherd from lower body of cup in black-figure
technique, very possibly belonging to same pot as
B 1215. Res. circle at int. center(?) L (diagonal): 2.3.
B 1217 (Sh 402) Cw Vb CA I. *Pl. 33.* Wall frag. of
open shape decorated in black-figure technique. No
figures pres. L: 3.5.

MISCELLANEOUS BLACK GLAZE WARE

The glaze on the following pieces is poor and I hesi-
tate to suggest any provenance.

B 1218 (Sh 371) Cw Vb CA I. *Pl. 33.* Small portion of rim and handle of a kotyle(?). C: buff. Reddish brown to black glaze of very low lustre. Pot was
picked up before firing so that finger prints are clearly
discernible on the handle. L: 3.8. **B 1219** (G 18)
A-Topsoil. Frag. of base of bowl with heavy ring foot
(Classical Period?). Graffito incised while clay was
leather-hard on res. base. C: sl. powdery pinkish
brown to buff at surface. Barely ls. black glaze thinly
applied in places. ED (of base): 7. *AJA* 64 (1960)
Pl. 38.

MISCELLANEOUS FOREIGN AND UNIDENTIFIED FABRICS

Bowls

B 1220 (Sh 166) A-E:3(V) LC IIIB. *Pl. 33.* Frag.
from wall. C: lt. brick-red; hard, rather thin fabric.

S: thick soft cream-colored, applied int. and ext. P: m.
gray-brown, almost entirely worn off since original
cataloguing, when parallel bands were discernible.
L: 3.9. **B 1221** (Sh 685) D-A. *Pl. 33.* Profiled rim
frag. C: g. lt. yellow-gray, almost chalky color; ext.
has a ls. almost buff-colored self-slip. P: thick ls.
orange-brown. Paint on and below rim, to which the
apex of a triangle is tangent. General appearance suggests better quality LC III Decorated bowl but clay
looks entirely non-Cypriote. H: 2.4. **B 1222** (Sh 709)
C-A:3 LC IA:2. *Pl. 34.* Frag. of floor of bowl. C: g.
gray at core to gray-brown; surface well smoothed.
P: m. dk. gray-brown and purple-red. C-c on int. floor
and at least partially ext. in irregularly alternating
color. Vaguely like Syrian Bichrome ware. L: 4.5.
B 1223 (G 3:K 23) A-Unstrat. Incised base of bowl.
Called "Red Wash" ware by Daniel but not definitely
ascribable to any fabric known to me. Sl. curving(?)
base; apparently h-m. C: g. hard lt. red-brown. P: sl.
ls. dk. brownish red. L (diagonal): 3. *AJA* 42 (1938)
272 Fig. 13:h. *AJA* 64 (1960) Pl. 38.

Kraters

B 1224 (P 1396) T.13:27. *Pl. 33.* Base largely
missing (a base ring was postulated by Daniel). One
handle missing. Parts of neck and body restored.
Flaring walls with rounded transition to short steep
shoulders and wide tapering neck. Overhanging
squared ledge rim with relief line at its base (ext.).
Semicircular strap-handles from shoulder to mid-neck.
C: gray at core to brick-red; rather soft. S: thick ls.
black. P: m. lt. buff. Neck has 2 rows of festoons
separated by a band. Body has 2 tiers of hor. zigzag
and a lower tier of upside-down festoons, all separated
by outlined dotted bands. H: 27. D: 28.4. Minimum
Th: 0.15. *UPMB* 8 (1940) Pl. IV:f. A sherd found in
Kourion OT 101 (*ExC* 81, no. 2) which joins the belly
of this pot was published in *BMCatV* I, 94 (A 568)
as Middle Minoan II; cf. also *JHS* 51 (1911) III, Fig.
1:1 (where it is classified as Kamares ware). The
Minoan classification was generally accepted in archaeological literature, e.g., *ClR* 10, 165, n. 11. Daniel
considered the pot to be Base-Ring Ware: however,
the clay seems to me somewhat lighter and softer than
normal for this fabric. The shape and decoration would
certainly be unusual for Cyprus, although a Monochrome (Apliki) vase which Gjerstad calls a copy of
the Plain White Syrian krater (*SPC*, 183, 1) perhaps some similarity; cf. also *Nouveaux Documents*,
Pl. 9,1 and the discussion of this class, p. 135. I am
inclined to think that a clue to the inspiration and
probably the origin of our vase lies in the so-called
Black Impressed pottery from Atchana, which provides
a parallel—in somewhat general terms—in both shape
and decoration (*Alalakh*, Pl. C:ATP/39/14). This
ware occurs in Level 5 at Atchana dated to the six-
teenth and fifteenth centuries, B.C. In the same level
occurs local painted pottery with a scheme of decoration similar to B 1224 (cf. *ibid.*, Pl. XCVI:a) and there
is, of course, the omnipresent example of light on dark
decoration in the Atchana and Nuzi pottery (*ibid.*,
Pl. CII ff.). Even more important, however, is the fact
that an almost exact parallel to the shape of B 1224

exists in Base-Ring Ware as found at Atchana (cf. Woolley's comment on this shape, p. 358): *ibid.*, Pl. CXXV:c. All of these circumstances can be harmonized if B 1224 is a Syrian adaptation of Base-Ring combined with the light on dark tradition of decoration. **B 1225** (Sh 714) C-A:6 LC IIA. *Pls. 34, 51.* Several frags. of rim and wall. Wall virtually vert. to flaring overhanging squared ledge rim. C: slate clay at core to reddish brown; fairly well cleaned, compact. Surface covered with m. creamy slip ext. and reddish brown sl. ls. paint int. P: m. dk. gray. Band below rim ext. Clay and to some extent even slip (on int.) are reminiscent of BR Ware. However, this piece is wheelmade and does not seem to correspond to known shapes in that fabric. H: 5.7. ED: 31.

Jugs

B 1226 (P 1246; 49-12-175) T.12:47(A2) LC IA:2. *Pls. 33, 51.* N-c-m. Wide flat base, truncated bulbous body; long n. neck with flaring round mouth and rounded lip. Arched vert. handle from shoulder to just under mouth. C: lt. gray wfs. Surface badly eroded; perhaps not slipped but hor. bur. H: 14. D: 8.2. Considered Base-Ring I by Daniel, but has neither typical shape nor appearance of that fabric. **B 1227** (P 2721) MPT-A:10. I-m. Mouth and parts of body missing. Globular (round-based) body; neck ring. N. concave neck with bulge where handle joins neck. Rectangular handle consisting of 2 n. handles joined together. Shape somewhat similar to early CG I jugs, e.g. K 505, but clay does not look Cypriote. C: dk. orange to buff (weathering effect?), well cleaned but with lime particles. PH: 18.8. D: 14. **B 1228** (P 2805) T.31:2. *Pl. 51.* Body and stump of handle of juglet. Wide flat base, squat biconical body with n. neck and vert. handle. C: buff and soft, crumbly. P: m. redbrown to dk. gray. Bands at base of neck, near widest part of upper body, and 3, equally spaced, over lower body. PH: 3.9. D: 5.7. Looks Hellenistic although there are no sherds this late in deposit (see Table of Sherds and Miscellaneous Finds from Tombs). Dr. G. R. Edwards kindly informs me that this shape exists from the early third to the mid-second century B.C. in the Athenian Agora series. He is inclined to place B 1228 early in the series when the shape is relatively low and squat. **B 1229** (Sh 85) A-Unstrat. *Pl. 34.* Frag. of neck and shoulder with prominent incised neck-ring. Neck and shoulder made separately and joined together. H-m. C: dense hard slate gray; sturdy fabric. P: ls. dk. gray, nearly worn off. H: 2.5. ED (of lower neck): 2.5. Daniel designated it as True Bucchero, foreign. **B 1230** (Sh 451) Cw Vb CA I. *Pl. 34.* Wall frag. probably of jug. Probably w-m. C: gray-orange to gray-green, sandy. Fabric moderately to very thick. P: m. washy purple-brown. 3 more or less vert. bands. L: 4. Technique, but not shape, suggests LC III Dec. ware. **B 1231** (Sh 549) T.26:2. *Pl. 33.* Upper part of elongated jug with concave neck. Sloping handle from shoulder to mid-neck with plastic ring at point of joining. Round mouth with rolled rim. Shape similar to, and undoubtedly derived from, Red Lustrous III Type 1 bottles. C: lt. gray-brown to orange-brown at surface wfds, soft and

smooth. Surface vert. bur. PH: 18. ED: 10 **B 1232** (Sh 672) D-A. *Pls. 34, 51.* Joining frags. giving profile of lip, neck and shoulder. Other non-joining body frags. H-m. Tall neck flaring upward to rolled lip. Shoulder slopes from neck very gradually. C: g. orange-brown to gray-brown at surface, sandy; coarse thick ware. P: m. dk. brown. Paint on lip. On neck 3 carelessly executed hor. w. lines from which (vert.) drip lines extend as far as the shoulder. PH: 14.5. ED: 10. Both this and B 1233 could be local ware although I do not know anything comparable. **B 1233** (Sh 673) D-A. *Pl. 34.* Neck frag. and several non-joining body frags. H-m. C: g. brownish buff to gray-buff at surface, coarse thick ware. P: m. purple-brown. On neck: carelessly painted hor. stripes. Remaining body frags. show great swathes of paint but nothing can be deduced about the design. H (of neck frag.): 6.2. W (of same): 4.6. **B 1234** (Sh 749) B-A LC IIA. *Pl. 33.* Frag. with transition from neck to shoulder of juglet(?) C: g. lt. greenish gray with vari-colored particles. P: m. black and saffron. D-o vert. panel on neck, filled with saffron. Where neck joins shoulder, s-o hor. saffron band. H: 2.3. Does not look Cypriote. **B 1235** (SH 222) A-Topsail. *Pl. 34.* Frag. of a stamped amphora handle. C: slate-gray at core to red-brown. Contains a small amount of mica. Surface pinkish yellow, smooth. Complete, though worn, stamp with crab and ΡΙΔΟΥ preserved. L: 6. H: 3.3. Dr. Virginia Grace of the American School of Classical Studies, Athens, writes as follows: "The reading . . . ought to be restorable as follows:

[ΔΙΟΣΚΟΥ]

lyre

ΡΙΔΟΥ

. . . according to a similar, though not identical, stamp we have on file. . . . The handle seems to belong to a known class, of which however the provenance is not known, nor the shape of the jar. The near-duplicate is SS 12974, a handle found in the building filling of the Middle Stoa in the Athenian Agora; the context of this parallel, together with some other associations of the class, suggests a date of about 200 B.C."

Storage Jars

The following sherds are all of one fabric, almost certainly from the same pot, apparently handmade. The clay is light gray-brown to reddish brown, very coarse and gritty. Paint is a rather faded dark gray, completely matt. The fabric has a kind of generic resemblance to Syrian Bichrome ware, although it is not bichrome, has no preserved pictorial decoration and is not comparable in size. The heaviness of the fabric is such that it must really be reckoned with pithos ware, but it has no resemblance to local pithos ware. **B 1236** (Sh 88) A-E:4 LC IIIB. *Pl. 34.* Frag. with transition from shoulder to neck. Joins B 1238. **B 1237** (Sh 142) A-E:4 LC IIIB. Small wall frag. L (diagonal): 3.3. **B 1238** (Sh 287) A-D:1(IV.1) etc. LC IIC. *Pl. 34.* Frag. of neck and shoulder with ridge where these join. At base of neck: outlined band containing a hor. w. line. On shoulder: inverted chevrons with dividing line down center. H: 5.3. L (diagonal, with B 1236): 19. **B 1239** (Sh 727) A-D:3(IV) etc. LC IIIA. Several joining shoulder frags. Same shoulder design as B 1238. L (diagonal): 15.9.

Miscellaneous Closed Shapes

B 1240 (Sh 284) A-D:3(IV) LC IIIA. *Pl. 34.* Wall frag. W-m. C: sandy reddish brown; soft. S: bur. red. L (diagonal): 4.1. Resembles Wash Ware but has a thinner fabric and bur. **B 1241** (Sh 414) Cw Vb CA I. *Pl. 34.* Wall frag. W-m. C: g. gray at core to lt. red-brown; rather heavy. P: m. cream, much worn. 2 carelessly painted hor. bands around body. L (diagonal): 13.6. **B 1242** (Sh 738) E-B:1 LC IIB. *Pl. 34.* Frag. of wall or neck. W-m. C: g. lt. pinkish gray, hard; surface possibly bur. P: m. washy red-brown and lt. gray (or blue). Red band demarks zone with hor. zigzag. H: 3.5.

PART III: MISCELLANEOUS FINDS

Many of the objects in the following catalogue have been included in the lists of Lena Åström, *Studies on the Arts and Crafts of the Late Cypriote Bronze Age* (Lund, 1967), which should be consulted (using Appendix C) for further parallels.

ALABASTER

Alabaster objects, particularly vases, are a not uncommon feature of Late Bronze Age Cyprus. On the difficulties of distinguishing Egyptian imports from local products, see *CesCol*, 274 ff. The only nearly completely preserved vase, B 1246, is, in its present form, very similar to a surface find at Enkomi (*ExC*, 25:1315). Cf. also *Lachish IV*, Pl. 26:36 (calcite) and *Ugaritica* II, Fig. 52:3, 6.

Spindle Whorl

B 1243 (Mi 191; 49-12-349) T.22:7 LC IIA. *Pl. 36.* C-ch. Much discolored. Biconical-truncated. H: 2.3. D: 2.3. An object like this illustrates the tendency to imitate in alabaster forms which normally occur in other materials (cf. *CesCol*, 275 ff.).

Vases

B 1244 (St 65) A-D:2(VII,2) LC IIIA. Frag. from neck with base of handle. Very pronounced overhanging ridge at base of handle going around entire neck. H: 6. **B 1245** (St 71) C-Unstrat. Frag. from rim of jug(?) with overhanging squared lip similar to that of B 1246. ED (of mouth): 3. **B 1246** (St 72) T.33:33(A) LC IIB. *Pls. 51, 60.* Frag. missing from neck; base badly chipped but probably terminated as a low flaring ring base. Fat ovoid, almost spherical body; wide tall sl. concave neck with flaring profiled rim. H: 8.9. D: 6.

BONE

The following pieces are differentiated from ivory on the basis of their coarse, porous texture and lack of lustre.

Disk

B 1247 (Mi 178; 49-12-138) T.12:7(A) LC IA:2. *Pl. 36.* One face fairly smooth, depressed at center. Back: unworked core of bone. D: 1.7. Th: 0.3.

Rod

B 1248 (Mi 189; 49-12-349) T.22:8 LC IIA. *Pl. 36.* Considerably eroded and scratched frag. Tapering end of a cylinder. L: 2. D: 1.2.

BRONZE

Awls or similar tools, such as scrapers: cf. *SCE* I, Pl. CXLIII:12-16.

B 1249 (M 239) D-Surface. Section of bronze rod, square in section in center and at tapered blunt end. Round section toward sharp end, which is bent at a 45° angle. PL: 8.8. W: 0.3. **B 1250** (M 1041; 49-12-181) T.12:54(B) LC IA:2. *Pl. 34.* Badly diseased. Square in section; flat at one end, pointed at the other. Condition too poor for purpose to be absolutely certain. L: 6.3. D: 0.4. **B 1251** (M 1051) E-D:2d LC IIIA. Shape like B 1249 but blunt end less tapered. Now bent at a 45° angle but probably originally straight. Point broken off at sharp end. Point of bending corroded; entire piece somewhat diseased. PL: 8.6. W: 0.3.

Bowls (no handle unless indicated)

a. Hemispherical: a common type in Cyprus. Cf. *SCE* I, Pl. CLIV:12,14,16 (all late); also K 1013 ff. **B 1252** (M 25) A-E:3(V) LC IIIB. *Pl. 34.* Frag. of wishbone handle, possibly from a bowl of BR or WS shape (such as the examples immediately following). Has green patina but is not diseased. End shows clot of pocked consistency where handle was soldered to bowl. L: 4.5. D: 0.6. For a discussion of the problem of metal prototypes, see *Problems*, 41 ff. There is, of course, no way of knowing whether B 1252 is local or imported, or when it first came to Bamboula. However, the occurrence of what is undoubtedly an exact parallel, K 1018, in a contemporary context, is strong evidence that the heirloom theory cannot be invoked in either case. Indeed, the consistently late occurrence of all the examples of bronze bowls at Bamboula leads to the conclusion that they may be imitations of pottery shapes rather than *vice versa*. Wishbone-type handles on metal vases occur elsewhere in the Aegean: cf., e.g., *Prosymna*, Fig. 610. **B 1253** (M 223) T.16:13. *Pl. 51.* N-c-m. Diseased. Rim sl. thickened. H: 6.9. D: 16.4. **B 1254** (M 224; 49-12-299) T.19:32(C) LC IIIA. *Pl. 36.* N-c-m. Considerably diseased. H: 5.7. D: 13. **B 1255** (M 1030; 49-12-240) T.18:5(B) LC IIIA. *Pl. 36.* N-c-m. Badly diseased. H: 6. D: 15.9. **B 1256** (M 1049; 49-12-38) T.3:17(B) LC IIIA. Unmendable frags. only. ED: 13. **B 1257** (M 1055) T.40:48(C) LC IIIA. *Pl. 58.* Complete but dented. Badly diseased. H: 5.6. D: 14.

b. Shallow: **B 1258** (M 220; 54-41-9) VT:9. Much of sides eaten away by disease. Wide, flat bottom; low, gently curving sides. Thin walls. H: 1.9. D: 13.

Bracelet

B 1259 (M 1046; 49-12-288) T.19:16(E) LC IIIA. *Pl. 36.* N-c-m. Very badly diseased. Plain circular bracelet with non-joining ends. 2 small holes near each end. W: 0.8. D: 4.1. Cf. Enkomi, SwT 6A.15-17; 6B.1; *Myrtou-Pigadhes*, 86:72, 278.

Chisel: cf. *CesCol* no. 4648–4649. The following examples are of somewhat more elaborate design than the ones in New York or those found at Apliki (*AntJ* XXXII, 1952, 163).

B 1260 (M 215; 49-12-98) T.6:5 LC IIB. *Pl. 34.* Pitted and considerably damaged by disease. Also distorted in manufacture. Outline like that of an elongated bell with narrow extension, now partly broken off, at haft end. L: 5.6. W: 1.8. Th: 0.2. **B 1261** (M 216; 49-12-135) T.12:5(E) LC IIB. *Pl. 34.* Diseased, especially haft end. Shape like B 1261 but proportions sl. stubbier. L: 5.5. W: 2. **B 1262** (M 1025) T.31:8. C-ch. Badly diseased. Plain flaring blade with rounded (broken) cutting edge at n. end and rounded socket at opposite end to receive haft. Rounded section has a long (deliberate) split, perhaps to allow for expansion of handle. L: 12. EW (of cutting edge): 1.7. D (of rounded section): 2.

Daggers: Enkomi SwT 8.52 (not illustrated) appears, from the description, similar to the type represented at Bamboula. The following (except B 1267) do not have pronounced midriffs, which relates them to Types 20 and 21 of the series proposed by K. R. Maxwell Hyslop (*Iraq* 8, 1946, 22 ff.), although the occurrence of these types is in general earlier than the Bamboula specimens. Cf. also *CesCol*, nos. 4601–15 for a discussion of technique of manufacture. Published by Catling, *CBW*, 98, no. 1.

B 1263 (M 24) A-D:2(V) LC IIIA. Diseased. Tapering end of blade only. Blunt-ended. Missing at time of control; no dimensions available. **B 1264** (M 30) E-C:1 LC IIC. Sl. diseased. Frag. of haft and of blade with evidence for 3 nail holes; bent upward at end which would be in handle. L: 3.7. W: 1.2. **B 1265** (M 217; 49-12-186) T.12:59(A) LC IA:2. *Pl. 34.* C-m. Split and diseased. Tapering blade of triangular shape with a triangular counter-extension which has 5 (pres.) rivets, for attachment to haft. L: 20. W: 3.3. L (rivet): 1.2. **B 1266** (M 218) South of T.13—Surface. Tips of both ends broken. Shape like foregoing but 3 rivets (2 pres.) instead of 5. PL: 11.3. W: 1.7. **B 1267** (M 222; 49-12-140) T.12:10(unstrat?). *Pl. 34.* I-m. Tip of blade missing. Shape essentially like B 1266; all 3 rivets pres. but not one completely centered in its hole. Blade has raised ridge running entire length. L: 14.5. W: 2.1. Th: 0.7. L (rivet): 1.1. Cf. Mrs. Hyslop's type 8 (see reference above). **B 1268** (M 225; 54-41-11) VT:11. 3 frags. (2 now extant, non-joining) pres. Complete blade. Considerably diseased. Shape like B 1266 but triangles both appear to have blunted ends. PL: 20. Max W: 4.4. **B 1269** (M 1024) T.17:13. *Pl. 34.* N-c-m. Badly diseased. Point of blade missing. Shape like B 1266. PL: 9.8. W: 2.5. Rivets vary from 0.4 to 0.6 in length. Published by Catling, *CBW*, 127, no. 1. **B 1270** (M 1031) T.18:18(A) LC IIIA. Missing. No description available.

Earrings

B 1271 (M 893a-c) T.36:29-31. *Pl. 36.* All diseased. 3 of identical manufacture but sl. different size: thick leech-shaped bodies with tapering half-moon horns. L (a): 2. L (b): 1.9. L (c): 1.9. The type also occurs in lead and gold (*q.v.*).

Fibulae

B 1272 (M 210-duplicate field number: see K 1065; 49-12-6) T.2:1 CG. *Pl. 36.* Part of pin missing. Outlined beads to either side of sl. swollen arch. L: 5.5. H: 3. This is apparently Type II of Myres' classification (*CesCol*, 484) and find circumstances accord with the date suggested for that type. Cf. also P. Jacobsthal, *Greek Pins* (Oxford 1956) 2 and Fig. 3. **B 1273** (M 1045; 49-12-273) T.19:1(F) LC IIIB. *Pl. 36.* Complete but somewhat diseased. Triangular-shaped with broad straight swelling back, ending on one side in a 1½ coil to pin; on other in a straight sl. tapering arm to broad clasp. L: 5.6. H: 3. This appears to be a duplicate of Enkomi OT 74: no. 1511 (C. Blinkenberg, *Fibules Grècques et Orientales*, Copenhagen 1926, 54, Type 10a) which Blinkenberg dates tentatively as transition from Mycenaean to Submycenaean (cf. *Kaloriziki*, Ch. IV, Proto-White Painted Shapes). The close relationship of this to his contemporary type 8 is obvious (cf. another example of this, *Kerameikos* I, 84 and Pl. 28, 3rd row right, from a Submycenaean tomb). Mrs. Judy Birmingham informs me that the drawing of Enkomi no. 1511 in *ExC*, Fig. 27, is incorrect since the bow has a slight swelling (nodule) near either extremity. See her remarks on this and B 1273 in *DFCL*, 84 f.

Needles: two types occur, represented by B 1275 and B 1276; cf. remarks on *CesCol*, nos. 4663–73.

B 1274 (M 13) A-D:2(VII,2) LC IIIA. Point chipped, otherwise complete. Upper end flattened; oval eye. L: 5.5. W (at eye): 0.25. **B 1275** (M 22) Cw Vb CA. *Pl. 34.* Not diseased, point broken off. Like B 1274. PL: 7.9. D: 0.4. W (at eye): 0.6. **B 1276** (M 26) A-D:3(IV) LC IIIA. *Pl. 36.* Central portion eaten by disease. Eye formed by looping blunt end. L: 5.5. W (at eye): 0.7. **B 1277** (M 37) A-D:3(V) LC IIIA. Originally complete in 3 frags. Now only 2 small corroded frags. extant. Type probably like the foregoing. L: 5.6. **B 1278** (M 233) A-found in cleaning Unit 8. Piece of wire, one end sharpened. The other looped around to form very small eye. Piece now bent. PL: 4.8. D: 0.15. **B 1279** (M 241) B-B LC IIB. Diseased. Type like B 1276, now bent. PL: 5.4. D: 0.2. **B 1280** (M 250) E-Tr.20:15b(unstrat). Diseased at center. Type like B 1274. L: 16.9 D: 0.5. **B 1281** (M 1079; 49-12-322) T.19:38(B) LC IIA-B. *Pl. 34.* C-m. Badly diseased. Plain wire pointed at one end with eye at other—probably made by bending wire back over itself. L: 7.8. D: 0.3.

Pins

B 1282 (M 230) A-D:2(VII,1) LC IIIA. Now incomplete. A straight piece of round bronze; according to original catalogue card it tapered to a point at one end. PL: 6.2. **B 1283** (M 1028) Over T.36 Unstrat. C-i. Has sharp point on one end and bent back section like a crook at other. Just below bent back section appear to be 3 or 4 threadings. L: 8.9. D: 0.3.

Rings

Coil type: cf. Enkomi SwT 8.51; 18.47. See also gold rings. **B 1284** (M 35 Cw Vb CA. Originally 4 frags. of wire with overlapping ends. Now 3 very small corroded frags. extant. D: 1.8. Th: 0.2. **B 1285** (M 1026) T.33:40(A) LC IIB. *Pl. 60.* N-c-m. Badly diseased. Spiral ring of 2½ or 3 full turns. PD: 3. PH: 1.6. **B 1286** (M 1034; 49-12-338) T.21:8. *Pl. 36.* Considerably diseased. Nearly round coil sl. overlapping. One end appears to be broken off. Said to have been found on a finger. D: ca. 3. Th: 0.5. **B 1287** (M 1035; 49-12-420) T.34:2. Missing at time of control. Bronze spiral. No description available. **B 1288** (M 1044; 49-12-133) T.12:3(B) LC IA:2. *Pl. 36.* I-m. Badly diseased. Coiling end broken off at point of contact with other end so that number of spirals is unknown. PH: 2.3. Th: 0.4. **B 1289** (M 1048; 49-12-97) T.6:4 LC IIB. *Pl. 36.* Diseased. About ⅓ pres. Frag. appearing to be part of a plain or spiral ring. L: 2.4. D: 0.4. **B 1290** (M 1054) T.40:67(A) LC IIA. *Pl. 58.* C-m. Badly diseased. Sl. flattened on one side. Coiled back over its end for about ⅓ of the length. D: 3.1. Th: 0.4.

Miscellaneous

B 1291 (M 36) A-2 LC IIIA/B. *Pl. 36.* C-m. Circle of wire bent sl. out of true, so that ends do not quite meet. D: 2.5. Th: 0.15. **B 1292** (M 226) E-Unstrat (east of dromos of T. 26). C-i. Circle (not closed) of wire, ends of which hook back. Hooks are in a position to engage each other. D: 3. Th: 0.1. **B 1293** (M 1037; 49-12-422) T.34:4. *Pl. 36.* Several frags. probably of a plain ring. Badly diseased. ED: 2.2.

Saw

B 1294 (M 213) T.13:3. *Pl. 34.* C-i, but surface considerably pitted by bronze disease. Sl. tapering blade with rounded end. 6 rivet holes in handle end. L: 34. W: 4.1. Th: 0.15. Another example of a sl. different kind from Cyprus is illustrated in *SPC*, 237. Cf. also *Prosymna* Fig. 244:1 (Tomb XXXIII): two holes at upper edge, one with a wire coil. Published by Catling, *CBW*, 94, no. 1.

Spearheads

a. "Cypriote poniard": see *MCh*, 41 ff. **B 1295** (M 214; 49-12-440) T.20:1 LC IIA(?). *Pl. 34.* C-i, but surface somewhat pitted and frayed from bronze disease. Attenuated leaf design with long curved (hooked) tang. Sharply raised midriff, on both sides, with point flattened in plane of midriff on anvil, after casting. L: 22.6. W: 2.4. Th: 1.4. Another example from Kourion is *CCM*, 53, no. 558. Cf. also Ayios Jakovos, SwT 14.24.

b. The following examples have a tapering circular socket (above the blade) into which the wooden han-

dle was thrust. Cf. Enkomi SwT 18.17 and 66; Ayios Jakovos SwT 14.42. **B 1296** (M 221; 54-41-10) VT:10. *Pl. 34.* Point missing; remaining surface diseased. Blade apparently elongated triangle. PL: 9.4. W: 1.9. **B 1297** (M 1032; 49-12-252) T.18:19(A) LC IIB. N-c but bent and considerably diseased. Long leaf-shaped blade with traces of center ridge. Tip of blade broken off. Sides of circular section beaten thin and consequently much weathered. PL: 21. W (of blade): 2.7. D (of upper section): 1.7. **B 1298** (M 1033; 49-12-253) T.18:20(A) LC IIB. Same condition as, and of identical manufacture with, B 1297. PL: 21.7. W (of blade): 2.6. D (of upper section): 1.7.

Tweezers: on this class of object in general, see *Prosymna*, 349.

B 1299 (M 21) A-E:2(VIII) LC IIIA. *Pl. 34.* Pitted by disease. One long thin bronze strip, rounded at ends, bent into a shape resembling that of a modern hairpin. L: 6.7. W: 0.5. Cf. Ayios Jakovos, SwT 10A.2,14; SwT 12.39. Cf. also K 1089. **B 1300** (M 227) A-Surface. *Pl. 36.* C-i. Cut from sturdy sheet, folded in half and put through a ring of copper wire, so that the cut piece is made to spring. Cut into moulded pattern near ring. L: 4.1. W: 1.1. Presumably Cypro-Geometric. Cf. Amathus, SwT 7.47. **B 1301** (M 1042; 49-12-132) T.12:2(B) LC IA:2. *Pl. 36.* I-m. Badly diseased. Shape probably similar to that of B 1299. L (of longer frag.): 4.2. W: 0.5.

Objects of uncertain use

Hook? **B 1302** (M 1039; 49-12-7) T.22:2 (topsoil). *Pl. 36.* 3 frags. mended. Diseased. Hairpin-shaped piece of wire, broken off on one side and tapering as if to a point—which is missing—on the other. L: 2.1. W: 1.4.

Tools? Some apparently similar objects from Enkomi FT 6 are called "spatules" by Schaeffer (*MCh*, 100). **B 1303** (M 19) A-D:2(V) LC IIIA. *Pl. 34.* C-i but pitted by disease. Rectangular strip with flaring, sharp, axe-like ends. Groove down middle of each face. L: 8.8. W: 1.8. Th: 0.2. **B 1304** (M 1038; 49-12-437) T.37:1. *Pl. 34.* C-i but somewhat diseased. Tubular shape with deep socket, tapering to solid, blunt rounded end. Made by rolling up a flat piece of bronze and joining edges. L: 13.8. D (at socket): 13.8; (at dull end): 1.

Rods

B 1305 (M 20) A-D:2(V) LC IIIA. *Pl. 34.* C-ch but pitted by disease. Octagonal shaft, swelling in middle. Blunt end chipped; other end flattened and sharp. L: 15.5. Th: 0.6. **B 1306** (M 23) A-2 LC IIIA/B. *Pl. 34.* C-i. Square in section. Pointed end sl. blunt, may be broken. Other end flat. L: 10.1. W: 0.4. **B 1307** (M 237) A-D:2 (St.1:a) LC IIIA. One point(?) broken off. Square in section; ends taper rather bluntly. PL: 6.5. Th: 0.6. **B 1308** (M 1027) T.33:49. *Pl. 60.* 2 frags. badly diseased. Nail-shaped but lower part ends not in point but in a flattened straight edge, like a chisel. PL (of both frags.): 4.9. W: 0.5. **B 1309** (M 1040; 49-12-292) T.19:20(D) LC IIIA. Badly diseased. 2 non-joining frags. which probably belonged together. Long slender rod of which one end seems to have been square in section, then becoming round. L (of longer frag.): 13.6. D: 0.6.

Wire

B 1310 (M 240) A-A:3 LC IIA. Diseased. A length of wire, twisted and pointed a little more sharply at one end than at the other. PL: 5.1. Th: 0.3.

Disk

B 1311 (M 246) E-C:6 LC IIC. Missing. The following data are from original catalogue card: flat coin-like disk cut in one place with flat ribbon-like ring. L (incl. ring): 2.5. D: 1.9.

Fragments

B 1312 (M 33) A-D:1(VIa) LC IIIA. Missing. From original catalogue card: roughly in the shape of a T with arms brought around in a circle to meet. PL: 2.5. W: 1. Th: 0.15. **B 1313** (M 234) A-D:2(VII,2) LC IIIA. Frag. of rod(?) PL: 3.9. Th: 0.5. **B 1314** (M 235) A-E:2(VIII) LC IIIB. Ribbon-like piece of which one end is curled. L: 1.8. W: 0.7. **B 1315** (M 1043; 49-12-139) T.12:8 (unstrat?). Somewhat diseased. Broken-off pointed end of a tapering tubular object, possibly a large nail. L: 5. D: 0.5. **B 1316** (Sh 606) E-Hearth:B. Small irregular frag. of bronze similar to that coating B 1550 and doubtless from a crucible. L: 2.5.

COPPER

Chisel or celt (?)

B 1317 (M 892) E-A:7 LC IIA. *Pl. 34.* C-m. Badly diseased and split. Apparently double blade with rounded end tapering back to circular sl. flaring socket for haft. Two small holes near upper end of socket for securing haft. L: 12. W (of blade): 2.6. D (of socket): 2.3. Cf. *ExC*, Fig. 25:1477 and *Ugaritica* III, Fig. 227 (larger specimens designated as hoes; B 1317 seems hardly of sufficient size for this purpose).

Objects of uncertain use

B 1318 (M 12) A-E:3(V) LC IIIA. *Pl. 34.* One end probably broken off. Approximately round shaft, pointed at one end, squared and blunt (or broken?) at other. L: 13.9. Th: 0.3. **B 1319** (M 211) E-D:1h LC IIIA. Amorphous frag. of dark gray slag. Shows impressions of wood. L: 4.5.

FAIENCE

Beads: these, as well as beads of other materials, are classified as far as possible according to the system of H. C. Beck, "Classification and Nomenclature of Beads and Pendants" in *Archaeologia* 77 (1927) 1 ff. (hereafter referred to as Beck).

B 1320 (Gl 94; 49-12-280) T.19:8(F) LC IIIB. *Pl. 36.* One bead complete except for chips, and a frag. of the same type. Each bead consists of a series of joined cylinders (resp. 6 and 3). Multiple beads or spacers. Dead white fine ceramic substance with traces of green glaze. L (of complete bead): 2.3. W (of

same): 1.2. For the type, see Beck, 14:A2a; cf. also *SCE* II, Pl. LXXVIII:2; *Lachish* IV, Pl. 27:3. **B 1321** (Gl 98; 49-12-279) T.19:7(F) LC IIIB. *Pl. 36.* C-i. Surface worn in places. Tire-shaped, with small perforation. Lt. buff fine ceramic substance with a fine glaze of same color. D: 1.8. Th: 1. See Beck, Pl. II:I.B.l.b; cf. B 1330 ff. **B 1322** (Mi 149; 49-12-95) T.6:1 LC IIB. *Pl. 36.* C-i. Cylindrical piece with flat ends and large longitudinal perforation. Band at each end delimiting lattice-work on body, all incised.. Lt. yellow-green fine ceramic substance with considerable remains of a blue-green glaze. L: 1. D: 0.8. See Beck, Pl. II:I.D.2.b; cf. *Enkomi-Alasia*, Fig. 82 (left) and *CatJBM*, No. 287. **B 1323** (Mi 198a; 49-12-277) T.19:5(F) LC IIIB. *Pl. 35.* C-i. Spherical. Lt. buff ceramic substance with a lt. greenish glaze (?). 3 inset "eyes" of plain buff ceramic substance, apparently without glaze. D: 1. See Beck, Pl. II:I.C.1a and 63, Fig. 57 (although the materials involved are different). Cf. B 1351 ff. **B 1324** (Mi 557a) T.36:27 LC IIA. C-i. Like B 1322. Blue-green to dk. blue glaze. L: 0.9. D: 0.5. **B 1325** (Mi 557b) T.36:28 LC IIA. *Pl. 36.* C-i. Identical with B 1324. L: 0.8. D: 0.5.

Vases: Schaeffer (*Enkomi-Alasia*, 214) has proposed Syrian manufacture of the glass, paste and faience products found in Cyprus. For a general description of this class of ware, see *CesCol*, 272 ff. See also *Myrtou-Pigadhes*, 77.

B 1326 (P 807) A-Surface. *Pl. 54.* Frag. of wall. Paste: gray to lt. brown at surface. P: brown, crackled, worn. Lattice design and fringed disk with pendant hook(?) L: 3.3. Th: 0.3. **B 1327** (P 2740; 54-28-87) Context uncertain; possibly a stray in Area F. *Pl. 36.* Frag. of bowl with gently curving sides and plain rim. White to blue-green g. ceramic material; air holes. Glaze: lt. yellow-green to blue-green (int.); dk. blue-green (ext). P: gray-brown to dk. purple. Both paint and clay much eroded. Rim stippled with regularly spaced dots. Under rim int. a d-o row of six-spoked wheels. Under this 4 parallel lines obliquely across bowl int. L: 8.7. W: 5.3. **B 1328** (Sh 543; 49-12-110) T.9:1 LC IA. *Pl. 51.* Frag. of squat biconical(?) jug with stump of hor. ribbon(?) handle: cf. *SPC*, 251: no. 2. Lt. brown-buff ceramic material wfs. Sky-blue to lt. Prussian blue glaze. P: dk. gray. Rosette petals with papyrus design(?) inside on shoulder; same on belly in reversed orientation. Rosette under handle may not have had int. design. H: 6.7. L: 7.7. **B 1329** (Gl 99; 49-12-235) T.15:5. *Pl. 36.* Frag. of glazed base of a jar(?) with inset unglazed conical section, rounded at bottom, for insertion into another unit. Lt. buff fine ceramic substance throughout with glaze int. and ext. ranging from pearl-green and blue-green to dk. buff. H: 8.4. PD: 5.3.

GLASS

Beads: flattened globular shape with center perforation unless otherwise noted. For reference see B 1321.

B 1330 (Gl 90; 49-12-343) T.22:4 LC IIA. *Pl. 36.* C-ch. Ls. dk. blue-green glass. D: 2. Th: 1.5. Cf. *QDAP* 4 (1935) Pl. 25. **B 1331** (Gl 91; 49-12-344)

T.22:5 LC IIA. I-m. About ¾ pres. Like B 1330. D: 1.8. Th: 1.2. **B 1332** (Gl 92; 49-12-345) T.22:6 LC IIA. I-m. Over ½ pres. Like B 1330. D: 1.8. Th: 1.2. **B 1333** (Gl 93; 49-12-346) T.22:7 LC IIA. *Pl. 36.* I-m. About ¾ pres. Like B 1330. D: 1.9. Th: 1.3. **B 1334** (Gl 95; 49-12-303) T.19:36(C) LC IIIA. About ⅖ pres. Pearl-green. PD: 1. PTh: 0.9. **B 1335** (Gl 97; 49-12-251) T.18:17(A) LC IIB. *Pl. 36.* C-m. Much eroded, causing shriveled, grainy appearance. Pearl to buff in hue. D: 1.4. Th: 1. **B 1336** (Gl 182) T.24:5 LC IIC. C-ch. On four sides are respectively 3 insets of 2 connected ovals and one single oval, all in solid blue, and also t-o in solid blue, the whole decorated area being reserved in white. D: 0.9. Th: 0.55. Cf. B 1323. **B 1337** (Gl 183) T.36:56 LC IIA. C-i. Lt. yellow-green to green. D: 0.45. **B 1338** (Gl 184) T.36:60 LC IIA. C-i. Dk. blue. D: 0.5. **B 1339** (Gl 185) T.36:57 LC IIA. C-i. Pearl-gray to blue. D: 0.55. **B 1340** (Gl 186) T.36:59 LC IIA. C-i. Pearl-gray. D: 0.52. **B 1341** (Gl 187) T.36:58 LC IIA. C-i. Dk. yellow. D: 0.45. **B 1342** (Gl 190) T.36:5,6, etc. LC IIA. A series of 20 beads (of which those noted as item 61 were found in screening) which are of the same description as B 1337 to B 1341. Of the 20, the colors are as follows: 1 green, 2 gray, 8 yellow, 8 red, 1 black. They probably belonged to the same necklace which would have included the pendant B 1350. **B 1343** (Gl 334) T.40:59(B) LC IIA. *Pl. 58.* N-c-m. Pearl-gray. D: 1.9. Th: 1.5. **B 1344** (Mi 165; 49-12-289) T.19:17(E) LC IIIA. Missing. Mottled gray and white. D: 1. **B 1345** (Mi 182) T.13:4. *Pl. 36.* I-m. One side missing. Biconical shape longitudinally perforated. Gray. L: 2. D: 0.9. See Beck, Pl. III; IX,D.3.e. **B 1346** (Mi 185) T.33:48. Missing. From catalogue card: "Flattened globular. Very pale gray." H: 0.7. D: 1.1.

Bottles: see comment on faience vases.

B 1347 (Gl 96; 49-12-230) T.14:3. *Pl. 36.* 3 nonjoining larger (mended) frags. and various smaller frags. From a small bottle or jar. Pearl-gray to tan-buff with a white inlaid indeterminable pattern on the surface. L (of largest frag.): 2.8. W (of same): 2. **B 1348** (Gl 181) T.17:14. *Pl. 51.* Pres: rounded base of tapering bottle and frag. of 3-ribbed vert. handle. Blue-green glass with a chalky overlay. Traces of inlaid(?) dec. include circumcurrent interlocked leaf design; under this a blue w. line separated from base by a ring. H: 8.1. Similar designs occur on glass vases from Enkomi: cf. *ExC*, 35, Fig. 63: 1052-53; *Enkomi-Alasia*, 190, Fig. 75:214. See also *BMBeyrouth* 3 (1939) Pl. 10C. A very similar pattern in Egypt: F. Petrie, *Ilahun, Kahun and Gurob* (London 1891) Pl. XVII, Group of Tutankhamen: 35; Pl. XVIII, Ramessu II:13.

Handle

B 1349 (S 77) F-A. *Pl. 35.* Frag. of roll handle of dk. blue glass with twisted lines of applied white (one line) and red (two lines). PL: 6.5. D: 0.6.

Pendants

B 1350 (Gl 188) T.36:11 LC IIA. *Pl. 36.* C-i. Pear-shaped; flat in section but thickened at top to accommodate large string-hole made laterally. L: 1.2. W: 0.9. Th: 0.4. A similarly shaped pendant in gold: *CatJBM*, No. 649. **B 1351** (Mi 198b; 49-12-277) T.19:5(F) LC IIIB. *Pl. 35.* Together with B 1323 and B 1439 (*q.v.*). Chipped. Loop with turned-up ends. Probably part of a necklace. L: 1.4. W: 0.9.

Vases: see comment on faience vases.

B 1352 (Gl 189) T.24:4 LC IIC. *Pl. 52.* I-m. Badly damaged by workman. Aryballos imitating shape of pomegranate. Globular belly, sl. concave, short neck flaring into 6 petals at mouth. Pearl to gray-blue with 5 hor. bands of white glass spaced at intervals over body. H: 8. D: 7.2. For the type cf. *ExC*, 35, Fig. 63:1052, 1053, 1056; *Enkomi-Alasia*, 190, Fig. 75:238, 251; Enkomi SwT 3.87, etc. **B 1353** (Mi 120) T.16:15. *Pl. 51.* I-m. Lower half only pres. Flat wide base with wide tapering stem; egg-shaped body. Glass at pres. mottled gray, perhaps originally dk. blue, with 3 irregular hor. white bands. PH: 5.2. D: 5.8.

GOLD

Beads

a. Cylindrical: exact parallels for B 1354 and B 1355 are the two beads from Ayios Jakovos SwT 13.12, but the type does not appear to be well represented in Cyprus. **B 1354** (Mi 119) T.16:25. *Pl. 36.* C—somewhat crushed. Hollow with raised rings at ends. L: 1.4. D: 0.4. **B 1355** (Mi 148) T.16:26. *Pl. 36.* C—partly crushed. One ring loose. Like B 1354 in shape and dimensions. **B 1356** (Mi 202; 49-12-295) T.19:27(C) LC IIIA. *Pl. 36.* Perforated cylinder of bone or ivory, quite soft and now weathered on the surface to cork color. Capped at both ends by gold nubs, each with a raised ring around perforation. L: 1.5. D: 0.9. H (of caps): 0.4. The idea may have been adapted from gold-capped seals: cf. B 1628 and *JHS* 77 (1957) "Archaeology in Greece," Pl. IId.

b. Lantern-shaped: the following beads have convex sides like lanterns, are hollow and have rings on the ends, being thus a variation on the cylindrical type. The origin of this type of bead, which occurs not infrequently in Cyprus, is probably to be sought on the Syro-Palestinian coast: cf. *Klio* 32 (1939) 142; Wace, *Mycenae*, 108; Wace, *CT*, 205 ff. Examples from Cyprus: Enkomi SwT 3.233.234. **B 1357** (Mi 164; 49-12-314) T.19:50(A-B) LC IIA-B. *Pl. 36.* C—badly crushed. Longitudinal grooves. L: 0.8. W: 0.7. **B 1358** (Mi 168) T.33:42(A) LC IIB. *Pl. 60.* C-i. Somewhat irregular grooves on sides. L: 0.8. W: 0.6. **B 1359** (Mi 170) T.36:7 LC IIA. One ring missing. Sl. crushed. L: 0.7. W: 0.7. **B 1360** (Mi 171) T.36:8 LC IIA. One ring missing. Somewhat crushed. Like B 1358. L: 0.8. W: 0.6. **B 1361** (Mi 179) South of T.13—Surface. *Pl. 36.* Sl. crushed. Punched longitudinal grooves. L: 1.3. W: 0.6.

c. Miscellaneous: **B 1362** (Mi 152; 49-12-228) T.14:1. *Pl. 36.* C-i. Semicircular closed bead made of 2 pieces of hammered gold fastened together. 2 raised bands along edge of semicircle, separated by rows of dots. 2 holes at each end. 24 carat gold. Weight: 2 gr.

L: 1.2. W: 0.9. Th: 0.5. Apparently like *CatJBM* No. 669. Cf. the wallet bead: *Archaeologia* 77 (1927) 33:A7. **B 1363** (Mi 183) T.13:2. Missing. Similar in shape to B 1330 but with a larger perforation. H: 0.2. D: 0.3.

Earrings

a. Leech-shaped. Cf. *CatJBM* Nos. 323-346 for Enkomi parallels (also SwT 18.11.12 etc.). See *AntJ* 32 (1952) Pl. 29a:2 from Apliki. **B 1364** (Mi 151; 49-12-131) T.12:1(A) LC IA:2. *Pl. 36.* C-i. Wire with fine pointed bent and overlapping ends. The middle section is arched and greatly thickened. 24 carat gold. Weight: 20.5 gr. L: 2.5. W: 2.5. Th: 0.3. Cf. Enkomi SwT 3.48,112. **B 1365** (Mi 154; 49-12-231) T.15:1. *Pl. 36.* C-i. Arched solid back with fine pointed sl. overlapping ends. 13 carat gold. Weight: 29.5 gr. L: 2. W: 1.9. Th: 0.5. **B 1366** (Mi 155; 49-12-233) T.15:3. *Pl. 36.* C-i. Like B 1365. 14 carat gold. Weight: 26.5 gr. L: 1.6. W: 1.8. Th: 0.5. **B 1367** (Mi 156; 49-12-234) T.15:4. *Pl. 36.* C-i. Like B 1365. 16 carat gold. Weight: 29.5 gr. L: 1.9. W: 1.8. Th: 0.5. **B 1368** (Mi 166; 49-12-388) T.28:2. *Pl. 36.* C-i. Like B 1365 but one end bent down in spiral fashion. L: 1.8. W: 1.8. Th: 0.5.

b. Calf's head type: the following consist of an overlapping wire loop, from which is suspended a hollow calf's head. Made in 2 identical pieces (both showing front of head), apparently hammered over a mould, with details etched afterwards. Holes at top of head (through which wire is inserted) are surrounded by raised ring simulating cut horns. All features are indicated. The majority of the following are illustrated in *UPMB* 8 (1940) Pl. IV (as from T.13, *sic*). Numerous examples have been found in Cyprus, particularly Enkomi: *CatJBM* No. 488 ff.; SwT 19.51, 75–76, *MCh* Pl. XXXVI:1,3. For a similar pendant in steatite, cf. *BSA* 25 (1921–1923) 55, Fig. 13 from granary at Mycenae; in gold from Perati, *Praktika* (1950) 95, and from Crete, *Études Crétoises* 8 (1948) Pl. XLVII: 0 120. **B 1369** (Mi 157; 49-12-236) T.15:6. Missing, 1956. C-i. Loop only, of type associated with calf's head earrings. 24 carat gold. Weight: 2.5. gr. L: 1.6. W: 1.5. Th: 0.1. **B 1370** (Mi 158) T.17:1. *Pl. 36.* C-i. 24 carat gold. Weight: 7.5 gr. L (of head): 1.8. W (of same): 1.4. Th (of same): 0.8. **B 1371** (Mi 159) T.17:2. *Pl. 36.* C—sl. crushed. Carats and weight: like B 1370. L (of head): 1.7. W (of same): 1.4. Th (of same): 0.7. **B 1372** (Mi 160) T.17:4. C—considerably crushed. 24 carat gold. Weight: 6.5 gr. L (of head): 1.6. W: 1.3. Th: 0.7. **B 1373** (Mi 161) T.17:5. *Pl. 36.* C—sl. crushed. Carats and weight: like B 1372. L (of head): 1.8. W: 1.4. Th: 0.7. **B 1374** (Mi 162) T.17:6. *Pl. 36.* C—one face depressed. 24 carat gold. Weight: 7 gr. Dimensions: like B 1373. **B 1375** (Mi 163) T.17:3. *Pl. 36.* C-i. Nostrils pierced. 24 carat gold. Weight: 9.5 gr. L (of head): 1.5. W: 1.5. Th: 0.7.

c. Miscellaneous: **B 1376** (Mi 181) T.13:1. *Pl. 36.* C—sl. crushed. Grape cluster type. Rather thick overlapping wire loop, to which is attached a long inverted conical pendant, the surface of which is granulated.

A double groove separates pendant from loop although granulation continues onto lower part of loop. 24 carat gold. Weight: 11 gr. L (including loop): 2.6. W (of loop): 1.3. Th (of pendant): 0.4. Cf. *CatJBM* No. 536.

Ring: see *CaJtBM* Nos. 380–469 for numerous parallels from Enkomi, Marion, etc. and *SCE* I, Pl. CXLV: 7-8. Cf. also *EphArch* (1888) Pl. IX:14. **B 1377** (Mi 153; 49-12-232) T.15:2. *Pl. 36.* C-i. Spiral ring with 1½ coils, sl. thickened about midway. 14 carat gold. Weight: 15 gr. D: 2.3. Th: 0.3 **B 1378** (Mi 167) T.33:39(A) LC IIB. *Pl 60.* C-i. Plain wire with sl. overlapping ends. Wire twisted. Daniel suggested this might be child's bracelet. L: 4.2. W: 3.2. Th: 0.2. **B 1379** (Mi 172) T.36:9 LC IIA. C-i. Spiral ring with about 1½ coils. D: 1.9. Th: 1.4.

Fragment

B 1380 (M 1052) T.24:3 LC IIC. Small roughly square frag. of corrugated gold leaf. 2 edges are jagged indicating tearing away from matrix. Other 2 edges are more cleanly cut. L: 0.9. W: 0.8.

IRON

The number of iron objects found in Late Cypriote IIIA/B contexts provides additional support for Schaeffer's suggestion to call this period *Chypriote Fer I* (cf. *Enkomi-Alasia*, 69 and our p. 54). Iron objects found at Myrtou-Pigadhes seem to be post-Bronze Age.

Chisel

B 1381 (M 212; 49-12-366) T.25:3. *Pl. 35.* Roughly rectangular blade probably with squared end, suggesting a chisel. The metal is, however, too diseased for one to be absolutely certain that the end is squared and not simply broken off—in which case the object could be a knife. At opposite end is a small rectangular tab—possibly also broken off—for insertion into the haft. L: 8. W: 1.7. Th: 0.5.

Knives

B 1382 (M 15) A-2 LC IIIA/B. I-m. Curved blade of knife. Point broken off. One bronze rivet pres. at haft end. Traces of bone handle. PL: 14.1. W: 2.5. Th: 0.3. *AJA* 42 (1938) 268, Fig. 9 with reference to *SPC*, 285 (n. 3). **B 1383** (M 15a) A-E:2(VIII) LC IIIB. Frag. of apparently curved blade, from about the middle. L: 5.6. W: 2.7. **B 1384** (M 207; 49-12-8) T.2:3 CG. *Pl. 35.* N-c-m. Diseased. Long thin curved blade with cutting edge on int. Blade flattened and thickened on exterior. 2 bronze rivets. Traces of haft, which was apparently of bone, clinging to rivets. L: 15.3. W: 1.8. Very similar to Lapithos SwT 411.27 which should be roughly contemporary. **B 1385** (M 219) T.16:20. Frag. from haft end, which was triangular with 2 bronze rivets. Both ends missing. Diseased. PL: 7.7. W: 2.5. **B 1386** (M 229) A-D:2(VII,2) LC IIIA. 4 frags. and some crumbs, probably from a knife blade. L (of largest piece): 3.3. **B 1387** (M 1050; 49-12-417) T.32:13. *Pl. 35.* Diseased. Frag. of curved blade, from about middle.

Cutting edge clearly distinguishable from blunt side. PL: 4. PW: 1.8.

Nail

B 1388 (Mi 553) T.17A:3. Badly diseased. Shaft of what appears to be a long thick iron nail, head completely missing. PL: 6.2. D: 0.7.

Pin with ivory head: I am indebted to V. R. d'A. Desborough for the following parallel from an Early Geometric tomb in Greece: *Tiryns* I, 128: T.2 Bronze pins with heads of gold (SwT 417.5) and of bronze (SwT 406.15,17,101) occur at Lapithos in contemporary levels. Cf. also K 1062.

B 1389 (M 1056; 49-12-278) T.19:6(F) LC IIIB. *Pl. 35.* About ¼ of head and an undetermined portion of pin missing. Iron badly diseased, ivory split and eroded. Biconical head: convex above and concave below. Below the head, at a slight remove, is another small oblong piece of ivory. The iron pin, apparently of an even diameter, is inserted through both pieces of ivory. L:11. D (of head): 1.4. PD: *ca.* 0.4.

Miscellaneous fragments

B 1390 (M 32) A-E:2(VIII) LC IIIB. Amorphous frag. which may be the head and approximately 0.7 cm. of the shaft of some implement. D: 2. **B 1391** (M 34) A-D:3(IV) LC IIIA. Amorphous object consisting of copper and iron, in 3 frags. L (of largest frag.): 2.1. W (of same): 1.7.

IVORY

Bead: Beck, Pl. II, IX.A.1.b. (see Faience Beads for reference).

B 1392 (Mi 113) T.16:7. C-i, worn. Square tab pierced in center. Apparently undecorated. L, W: 1.5. Th:0.4.

Disks: these occur with considerable frequency at Enkomi (e.g. SwT 6, 18, FT 5, etc.) and are for the most part lids or other parts of pyxides. Similar, though not really identical, disks have been found in Syria (Minet-el-Beida, *Syria* 13, 1932, Pl. VIII:2; *Alalakh*, Pl. LXXVIII:g). Furthermore there is no evidence of the incrustation reported from Syrian sites (*Syria* 13, 1932, 6). The difficult question of the exact provenance of these products cannot be entered into here.

B 1393 (Mi 110) T.16:21,23. *Pl. 35.* N-c-m. Ivory pegs on back, going through to face (8 in outer circle, 4 in inner circle). Incised double wheel design. D-o inner wheel has 6 spokes; outer wheel 18 spokes. D-o band of curved lines as border on outer edge. D: 11.5. Th: 0.5. Pegs: 0.9 beyond back of disk. Equally rich though different decoration occurs on a lid from FT 5 (*Enkomi-Alasia*, Suppl. Pl. B). **B 1394** (Mi 114) T.16:27. Wedge-shaped frag. D-o plain band as border on outer edge. PL: 6.3. Th: 0.3. **B 1395** (Mi 115) T.16:24. *Pl. 52.* Large frag. badly chipped and weathered. S-o rosette pattern in center. S-o pattern of joined dotted circles—suggesting guilloche—as border on outer edge. ED: *ca.* 7. Th: 0.2. **B 1396** (Mi 150; 49-12-96) T.6:2 LC IIB. I-m. About ½ pres.

Surface badly rotted. Design, if any, completely gone. 2 incised bands around circumference. D: 5.8. Th: 0.5. **B 1397** (Mi 173; 49-12-134) T.12:4(D) LC IIA. *Pl. 35.* N-c-m. 2 disks, a larger and smaller, separated by a deep n. groove and carved from one piece. Larger disk plain but beautifully smoothed. Smaller has 2 compass-drawn incised circles and a center dot. 3 small drilled holes are disposed about the circumference of the smaller disk. D (resp.): 5.8 and 4.4. Th (total): 0.8. Th (of larger): 0.3. **B 1398** (Mi 175; 49-12-151) T.12:22(D) LC IIA. *Pl. 51.* I-m. About ½ pres. Incised wheel design with probably 12 spokes. Border like B 1393. ED: 6. Th: 0.4. **B 1399** (Mi 192; 49-12-293) T.19:22(F) LC IIIB. *Pl. 35.* I-m. Both surfaces badly eroded but apparently devoid of all design. 2 incised bands around circumference. Oval-shaped center perforation with a maximum length of 1.4. D: 4.4. Th: 0.8. **B 1400** (Mi 197; 49-12-312) T.19:47(A-B) LC IIA-B. *Pl. 35.* About ¼ missing. Oval-shaped; one face flat, the other sl. depressed at center. 2 incised bands around circumference. EL: 4.1. W: 3.4. Th: 0.5. **B 1401** (Mi 200; 49-12-412) T.32:8. *Pl. 35.* I-m. About ⅔ pres. Surfaces completely eroded and in places splitting apart in layers. Small circular perforation at center. Apparently undecorated. D: 6.8. Th: 0.3. **B 1402** (Mi 201; 49-12-245) T.18:11(A) LC IIB. *Pl. 35.* About ⅔ pres. Double disk like B 1397 but with neither holes nor incisions in smaller disk. Face of larger disk has a small d-o hole at center. Around this 13 s-o rosette petals, the whole bordered by 4 incised bands at outer edge. PD (of larger): 5.6. D (of smaller): 3.8. Th (total): 0.8. Th (of larger): 0.2. **B 1403** (Mi 205; 49-12-320) T.19:57(A) LC IIA-B. *Pl. 35.* I-m. Surface much eroded; without decoration. Small oval perforation at center. D: 5.4. Th: 0.2. Cf. Lapithos SwT 403.126. **B 1406** (Mi 207; 49-12-229) T.14:2. *Pl. 35.* Over half pres. Surface pitted from erosion, undecorated. 2 incised bands around circumference. D: 3.6. Th: 0.6. Cf. Enkomi SwT 18.12,38. **B 1405** (Mi 211) T.24:9 LC IIC. *Pl. 35.* I-m. About ¾ pres. Short tapering socket on underside with circular shaft pierced completely through disk: apparently for attachment of disk as head on a rod. On face: 8-petalled rosette inscribed within 2 circles. D (of disk): 3.6. D (of base): 1.1. H: 0.9. Cf. *Enkomi-Alasia*, 215 and Fig. 82 (right): extremity of a spindle. **B 1406** (Mi 212) T.24:10 LC IIC. N-c-m. Shape and dec. like B 1402 but only 12 petals. D (of larger): 4.9. D (of smaller): 2.5. Th (total): 0.5. Cf. Enkomi SwT 17.76b and *Enkomi-Alasia*, Fig. 75:249.

Handle

B 1407 (Mi 107) T.16:1. *Pl. 36.* I-m. Considerably worn; tip of duck's bill broken off. Duck's head turned back over neck. Eyes apparently compass-drawn. Open mouth. Support piece between neck and mouth. L: 5.7. H: 3.2. Th: 0.7. Cf. *Ugaritica* I, Fig. 23: technique of eyes is particularly close to B 1407. *Lachish* II, Pl. 17:10; *Alalakh*, Pl. LXXV:a, etc.

Pins

B 1408 (Mi 109) T.16:3. Frag. of upper part of hollow stem preserving a flaring flattened mushroom-type pinhead. PL: 0.15. D (of head): 0.14. Cf. B 1389. **B 1409** (S 89) C-B LC IIB. Lower part of pin with tapering but blunt end. Stained lt. gray-blue. Ls. surface. PL: 4.5. D: 0.5. Cf. Enkomi SwT 6.101.

Rods or Spindles: for a discussion of these, see *Lachish IV*, 87. Complete spindles were found at Enkomi SwT 3.240-241.

B 1410 (Mi 111) T.16:22. *Pl. 36.* C-ch. Upper termination or handle of rod? Torus base defined above by 3 incised bands, below by 4. Flaring head, flat with sl. depression at center. Hollow stem. L: 3.8. D (of head): 2.5. **B 1411** (Mi 112) T.16:2. *Pl. 52.* C—worn. Lower termination of a rod? Cylinder with one end tapering but blunt; decorated by broad and n. incised rings. Wider end hollowed out to a depth of 0.8. L: 2.5. D: 0.9. **B 1412** (Mi 199; 49-12-385) T.27:2. *Pl. 36.* Split at one end; eroded. Tapering rod hollow at both ends but not in center. Sl. swelling ring near wider end defined above and below by 3 grooves. L: 4.8. D: 1.5. **B 1413** (Mi 208) T.24:6 LC IIC. N-c-m. Several large chips and slivers missing. Flaring cylinder with small peg at top for inserting into a socket. Top of peg broken off. At wider end 3 rather widely spaced groups of 2 incised lines. L (without peg): 16.8. PL (of peg): 0.8. **B 1414** (Mi 209) T.24:7 LC IIC. *Pl. 52.* C-sp. Shape like B 1410 but head entirely flat. 3 bands above and below torus. L: 3.2. D (of head): 2.3. **B 1415** (Mi 210) T.24:8 LC IIC. *Pl. 52.* C-sp. Shape like B 1414 but shaft tapers above torus to a moulded ring emphasizing top. Completely pierced by circular shaft sl. larger at bottom than at top. L: 3.5. D (of head): 1.6. Cf. *Enkomi-Alasia*, Fig. 75:335. **B 1416** (Mi 556a) T.36:1 LC IIA. *Pl. 36.* C-i. Shape like B 1414 but no moulded ring. On side of tapering section 8 flutings. Rod hollowed out, but boring tapered. L: 3.9. D (at top): 1.3. D (at bottom): 1.1. **B 1417** (Mi 556b) T.36:2 LC IIA. I-m. Rod flaring to flattened bottom. May belong with B 1416, but the two do not join in their present condition. PL: 18. D: 0.8-1.4. **B 1418** (S 80; 49-12-48) T.3:27. *Pl. 36.* Decayed frag. of solid cylinder with a conical depression hollowed out at one end. Two deep grooves around better pres. end. PL: 1.2. D: 0.9.

Roundels: cf. *CesCol*, Nos. 5902-22.

B 1419 (Mi 108) T.16:6. *Pl. 35.* C-ch. Somewhat weathered. Incised dec: 6-petalled rosette, tips connected by concave arcs. Around outer edge on border: d-o band of curved lines. D: 3.4. H: 0.8. **B 1420** (Mi 174; 49-12-145) T.12:15(E) LC IIB. *Pl. 36.* C-ch. 2 incised rings around outer edge as border. PD: 2.3. H: 0.7. **B 1421** (Mi 196; 49-12-377) T.26:1 LC II? *Pl. 36.* Badly chipped. 3 incised rings around outer edge on border. PD: 2.9. H: 0.6. *Berytus* 14 (1961) 39 Pl. 19:6. **B 1422** (Mi 213) T.24:11 LC IIC. *Pl. 35.* C-ch. Considerably weathered. 4 incised rings around outer edge as border. D: 2.9. H: 0.9. **B 1423** (Mi 214) T.40:66(A) LC IIA. *Pl. 58.* C-i. Dec: like B 1421. D: 2.8. H: 1. **B 1424** (S 79; 49-12-39) T.3:18(A) LC II? *Pl. 35.* C-ch. Considerably weathered. D-o band of joining curves. D: 3.1. H: 0.7.

Earrings

B 1425 (M 27) A-D:3(IV) LC IIIA. *Pl. 36.* Complete(?) U-shaped piece, greatly thickened at base, with a tapering extension bent away (accidentally?) from one arm. Probably made in a mould. L: 3.2. W: 1. See *CatJBM* No. 323 for probable original shape. **B 1426** (M 244) Cw IIIa LC IIIA. C-i. Leech-shaped. Ends bent to meet and overlap about 0.2. W: 1.8. Th: 0.5. For the type, cf. B 1367. **B 1427** (M 245) E-D:1h LC IIIA. Rather rectangular U-shape. Central part a little thicker than ends. Ends overlap but do not meet. L: 2.6. Th: 0.5.

Spindle whorl: for the type, see B 1509 ff.

B 1428 (M 16) A-E:4 LC IIIB. *Pl. 36.* C-ch. Double conical with concave sides. H: 1.7. D: 1.8.

Miscellaneous

B 1429 (M 18) Cw Vb CA II. *Pl. 36.* Roughly cylindrical frag. of lead, oval in section, tapering sl. Surface quite rough, as if chipped. L: 5.3. W: 1.7. **B 1430** (M 29) A-D:3(IV) LC IIIA. Long n. flattened frag. L: 8. W: 0.7.

SEAL IMPRESSIONS ON SHERDS

This unusual class of find has been treated in detail in "Aegean and Near Eastern Seal Impressions from Cyprus" (*ANE*, 59–77) where the objects listed below are described and discussed.

B 1431 (S 102) A-B:5 LC IIB. Neck frag. of pithos. W-m. Impressed with a Babylonian seal dated to the end of the First Dynasty. *AJA* 42 (1938) 266, Fig. 5; *ANE*, Pl. VIII:1. **B 1432** (Sh 545; 49-12-304) T.19:39(B) LC IIA-B. *Pl. 36.* Complete handle of a PWM II Type 1b jug. Impressed with a foliate leaf pattern. *ANE*, Pl. VIII:12; Fig. 13. **B 1433** (Sh 579a-b; 54-28-102) T.38:20. Two rim frags. from a vat. Cf. esp. B 967. Impressed with flying birds heraldically disposed around a plant. *ANE*, Pl. VII:9; VIII:7 and Fig. 8. **B 1434** (Sh 580) E-Topsoil. Frag. from shoulder or belly of a pithos. W-m. Impressed with griffins (not amphibian animals as I thought possible previously). *ANE*, Pl. VII:6 and Fig. 10; *U. of London Inst. Class. Stud. Bull.* 10 (1963) 8, no. 14: interpreted by M. A. V. Gill as a Minoan 'dragon.' The wave design occurs earlier and oftener than I realized. A re-study of the dating is needed. **B 1435** (Sh 615) See E-11. Profiled rim frag. of pithos or vat. W-m. Impressed with a design consisting of c-c interrupted by T or I. *ANE*, Pl. VIII:16 and Figs. 17–18. **B 1436** (Sh 720; 54-28-7) Near D—surface. Frag. from wall of pithos. W-m? Impressed with bull-fighting scene. *ANE*, Pl. VII:2 and Fig. 3. The detailed drawing in *ASAtene* 6/7 (1923/4) 169 of a fragmentary Minoan parallel seems to obviate the suggestion I made in *ANE*, 66 as to its interpretation. However, Levi's suggestion that the bulls are walking on a vast altar supported by a pillar seems extravagant.

SEALS

See Appendix A: Glyptics, by E. Porada.

SHELL

In addition to the objects listed below, 2 sea shells (uncatalogued) were found in Tomb 40.

B 1437 (S 45) A-A:2b LC IIA. Small flat object with a bottle-shaped profile and 2 perforations: a large one at the center, a smaller one below this. Cut from white shell. L: 1.3. W: 1. Undoubtedly a pendant or an amulet. A similar-looking object is illustrated in *'Ain Shems* II, Pl. 49:45 but I have not succeeded in finding the least reference to it in the text. For the general type, cf. Beck, 49:A.6. **B 1438** (S 46) A-A:2a LC IIA. *Pl. 52*. Like B 1437 but smaller and cut from gray-blue shell. L: 0.9. W: 0.6. **B 1439** (Mi 198c; 49-12-277) T.19:5(F) LC IIIB. *Pl. 35*. See also B 1323 and B 1351. 17 small buff sea shells, all of one variety. Pierced for stringing. Typical dimensions: L: 1.8. W: 1.5. H: 1.

SILVER

Silver jewelry was rare at Enkomi (cf. *CatJBM*, Nos. 1–682) and is relatively infrequent at Bamboula also.

Bead: Beck, Pl. III:I.C.3.f. (see Faience Beads for reference).

B 1440 (S 47) A-D:2(VII,2) LC IIIA. *Pl. 52*. An alloy of silver and lead(?) Double-conical shape with extra large perforation; shallow fluting. L: 1. D: 1.3.

Earring

B 1441 (M 894) T.17:10. *Pl. 36*. I-m. One horn broken off. Shape like B 1263. There is an inner core of silvery particles coated with a ls. dk. blue substance. Overall is a silvery thin sheath. L: 1.6.

Rings: see Gold Rings for type.

B 1442 (Mi 552) T.17:12. Coil overlapping about half of its circumference. Both ends broken off. Badly pitted and discolored to blue-gray. Published by Catling, *CBW*, 234, no. 2. D: 1.6. **B 1443** (Mi 554) T.33:38(A) LC IIB. *Pl. 60*. 2 non-joining frags. of a thin plain finger ring. D: 1.7.

STONE

Beads

B 1444 (S 4) A-D:3(VII) LC IIIA. Broken. Missing at time of control. Carnelian. Described as flat conical, pierced longitudinally at n. end. PL. 1. **B 1445** (S 7) A-D:2(VII,2) LC IIIA. C-i. Flat, pebble-shaped with a worn hole at wide end. Lt. robin's egg blue, very smooth, with white veining. L: 3.2. W: 1.6. **B 1446** (S 13) A-E:3(VI) LC IIIB. *Pl. 36*. C-i. Cylindrical. Dk. blue-gray steatite. L: 1.6. D: 1. Shape: as B 1332 (but no decoration). **B 1447** (S 29) A-A:2b LC IIA. C-i. Missing at time of control. Cylindrical, pierced. Dk. red stone. D: 0.2. **B 1448** (S 78; 49-12-12) T.2:6a(A) LC IIA. *Pl. 36*. C-i. Tire-shaped, vert. pierced. Hard blue-gray stone. H: 1.2. D: 1.9. Type: as B 1321.

Bowls (most or all mortars) in several types: with flat bases (B 1450, 1451, 1453, 1454) like Enkomi

SwT 14.3; tripod legs (B 1452) which is more numerously represented at Enkomi (*SCE* I, Pl. CLI:9-12; cf. also Apliki, *AntJ* 32, 1952, 163); and round base (B 1449).

B 1449 (St 44) A-E:1(VIII) LC IIIB. Missing at time of control. Described as roughly hemispherical with hole worn deep. Black volcanic stone. L: 26. W: 23.2. H: 12.7. **B 1450** (St 74) T.33:27(B) LC IIIA. *Pls. 51, 61*. C-ch. Low wide ring base; low curved sides. Bowl is shallow. Blue-gray coarse-grained stone, possibly granite. H: 3. D: 16.2. **B 1451** (St 75) T.16:9. *Pl. 51*. N-c-m. Shape like B 1450 but still shallower. Flattened rim. Well smoothed gray steatite. H: 2.8. D: 17.2. **B 1452** (St 76) T.16:14. *Pl. 51*. About ⅔ pres. Tripod: flat-bottomed bowl with rounded sides on thick triangular lug-like feet. Gray steatite. Cf. *CesAt* III Pt. 4, Pl. CXV; *Etudes Crétoises* 9 (1953) Pl. XXIX. **B 1453** (St 519) T.17A:1. *Pl. 37*. N-c-m. Wide raised base, hollowed underneath. Low curved sides. Blue-gray coarse-grained stone. H: 5.5. D: 19.2. **B 1454** (St 520) T.17:25. *Pl. 51*. C-ch. Sl. raised base, low curved sides, int. partially hollowed out. Fine-grained gray stone with reddish hue on under side. H: 3.3. D: 13.5.

Figurine

B 1455 (St 952) D-A. Intrusive(?) *Pl. 37*. Trunk of male figurine (genitalia missing) with 2 pelt-ends, one over each shoulder, fastened on at chest. Legs apparently spread apart, although there is no other indication of hipshot position. Modeling—such as there is—is very crude, but the piece appears to be of the Classical period. Dull brown to gray sandstone(?) with fine black particles and some ferrous content. H: 6.1.

Lid

B 1456 (St 524; 54-41-85) Provenance unknown; possibly from a plundered tomb. *Pl. 37*. Shape like B 1397 but without groove. Dk. blue-green, sl. rough-grained stone, polished on upper surface; tool marks visible on lower. Upper surface has 10 incised compass-made, inexactly integrated rosettes inscribed within 3 compass-made circles. Center of disk has a small perforation. On rim are continuous incised oblique barred lines. D: 7.3. Th: 1.5.

Macehead

B 1457 (St 899) E-A:7 LC IIA. *Pl. 37*. Thick tire-shape with well-made inner hole. Rather fine-grained blue-gray river stone. Ext. surface somewhat rough; inner surface perfectly smooth. D: 12. D (of perforation): 2.8. Th: 7. Cf. *SCE* II, Pl. CLXXXIII:25.

Pendant

B 1458 (G 68; K 68) Stray. Long, roughly oval, flat; one end perforated conically from both sides. Lt. blue-gray stone, sandy to the touch. L: 6.5. W: 2. *AJA* 64 (1960) Pl. 38.

Pestles: these are organized, as far as possible, according to the types presented in *SCE* II, Pl. CLXXXIII:29-33. It will be seen, however, that several other types occurred at Bamboula (B 1478 to B 1493). All are of fine-grained blue-gray river stone unless otherwise indicated.

Type 1: although there is no absolute conformity among the following, all may be subsumed under the roughly globular shape. **B 1459** (St 26) A-F:1 LC IIIB. Missing at time of control; described as "roughly circular." D: ca. 8. **B 1460** (St. 37) A-D:3(VII) LC IIIA. C-ch. Sl. flattened. Blue-gray granite(?) with very coarse surface. D: 7.5. **B 1461** (St 38) A-E:2(VIII) LC IIIB. Missing at time of control; described as a "Somewhat flattened circle." D: 7.2. H: 5.7. **B 1462** (St 49) A-D:3(VI) LC IIIA. Missing at time of control. Circular. D: 7. **B 1463** (St 50) A-E:3(VI) LC IIIB. *Pl. 37.* Somewhat flattened ball. D: 7.3. H: 6.6. **B 1464** (St 51) A-E:3(VI) LC IIIB. Missing at time of control; described as "flattened circular." Apparently approached the shape of Type 6. Dk. gray granite. D: 7. H: 5.7. **B 1465** (St 57) A-D:3(VI) LC IIIA. Sl. flattened. D: ca. 7. **B 1466** (St 67) A-D:2(VII,2) LC IIIA. Missing at time of control; described as "depressed globular." Gray granite(?) D: 6.5. **B 1467** (St 68) A-D:2(VII,2) LC IIIA. Flattened on one side. Finer-grained and lighter gray stone than B 1466. D: 6.1. **B 1468** (St. 540) A-D:2(VII,1) LC IIIA. Some of surface flattened. Quite smooth on handling surfaces, pitted elsewhere. D: 6.5.

Types 3-4: truncated conical shape. **B 1469** (St 25) A-D:3(VII) LC IIIA. Flattened conical. Pounding end worn and fractured; other end chipped. H: 13. W: 6. **B 1470** (St 32) A-E:1(VIII) LC IIIB. Rounded top. Flat end and sides fractured. Lt. gray stone. H: 19. W: 7.5. **B 1471** (St 47) A-E:2(VIII) LC IIIB. C-i. Shape rather irregular. Fine-grained black stone. H: 5.5. D: 2.8. **B 1472** (St 63) A-D:3(IV) LC IIIA. Round top. Badly chipped. Fine-grained dk. gray stone. H: 14.6. D: 5.9. **B 1473** (St 73) T.33:26(C) LC IIIB. *Pl. 61.* C-i. Well-worked. H: 6.3. D: 3.7. **B 1474** (St 77) T.16:10. C-i. Hard dk. gray granite(?) H: 6.9. D: 4.9. **B 1475** (St 521) T.17A:2 C-ch. Sl. flattened conical. Has finger and palm stains. H: 4.2. W: 3.4. **B 1476** (St 522) T.16:19. C-i. Sl. rounded top. Toolmarks visible. H: 6.7. D: 3.1. **B 1477** (St 539) A-Unstrat. Smooth on bottom, pitted on sides. H: 5.5. D: 5.5.

Type 6: flat circular shape, something like a solid cylindrical section. A few have indentations, no doubt to assist in grasping the pestle. **B 1478** (St 31) A-D:2(VII,2) LC IIIA. C-ch. D: 9. H: 3.7. **B 1479** (St 39) A-D:2(VII,2) LC IIIA. C-ch. D: 10. H: 5.5. **B 1480** (St 52) A-E:1(VIII) LC IIIB. One side pitted. D: 13. H: 6.2. **B 1481** (St 53) A-D:3(VII) LC IIIA. *Pl. 37.* C-i. Very rough and pitted surface. Center indentations on either side. D: ca. 7. H: 4.4. **B 1482** (St 54) A-D:2(IV) LC IIIA. *Pl. 37.* C-i. Very precisely worked. D: 9.9. H: 5.1. **B 1483** (St 56) A-D:3(VI) LC IIIA. C-i. Center indentation on either side. Pitted gray stone. D: ca. 10. H: 5.2. **B 1484** (St 58) A-D:3(VI) LC IIIA. About half pres. D: 10.7. H: 7. **B 1485** (St 64) A-D:3(IV) LC IIIA. C-ch. Carefully worked. D: 6.6. H: 3.8. **B 1486** (St

541) B-B LC IIB. *Pl. 37.* C-ch. Center indentations on either side. D: 4.5. H: 3.5. **B 1487** (St 542) B-B LC IIB. C-i. Smooth on handling surfaces, pitted elsewhere. D: 6.5. H: 4.

Type 7: elongated ovular. **B 1488** (St 28) A-Unstrat. C-i. L: 9. D: 5. **B 1489** (St 45) A-Unstrat. *Pl. 37.* C-i. Truncated but sl. rounded ends. L: 9.2. D: 5.5. **B 1490** (St 543) B-Surface. C-i. Very much elongated. L: 7. D: 3.3.

Miscellaneous shapes

B 1491 (St 30) A-G LC IIIB. *Pl. 37.* C-i. Roughly rectangular shape, with rounded ends and flat sides. One end thickened. L: 13. W: 5.8. Th: 2.7. **B 1492** (St 55) A-D:2(IV) LC IIIB. Missing at time of control. Truncated pyramidal, rectangular in section. H: 9.2. L: 8. W: 5.8. **B 1493** (St 90) E-A:7. *Pl. 37.* LC IIA. Originally a somewhat globular stone, of which 3 sides were flattened to give a grasping surface for the fingers. D: ca. 6.

Pithos Covers: both the following objects were missing at time of control.

B 1494 (St 36) A-D:2(VII,2) LC IIIA. Thin circular slab of limestone with 2 holes drilled near the center. D: 40. Th: 1.8. **B 1495** (St 62) A-D:2(VI) LC IIIA. Sl. oblate slab of limestone. L: 37. W: 34. Th: 7.5.

Quern: all the following are saddle querns, with much the same shape apparently as *SCE* II, Pl. CLXXXIII:28. The material is fine-grained blue-gray river stone unless otherwise indicated.

B 1496 (St 29) A-Surface intrusion. C-i. Blue-gray granite. L: 31. W: 21.5. Th: 6. **B 1497** (St 33) A-D:2(VII,2) LC IIIA. About half pres. Rather soft, almost chalky limestone with a sl. brownish gray patina. L: 25. W: 16.5. Th: 6.5. **B 1498** (St 40) A-D:2(VII,2) LC IIIA. *Pl. 51.* About half pres. Stone like B 1497, but apparently not from same quern. L: 27.5. W: 14. Th: 6.5. **B 1499** (St 41) A-D:2(VII,2) LC IIIA. Missing at time of control. Apparently a frag. L: 17.3. W: 15.2. Th: 8. **B 1500** (St. 42) A-D:2(VII,2) LC IIIA. *Pl. 51.* About half(?) pres. Stone like B 1497. L: 23.1. W: 14. Th: 5. **B 1501** (St 43) A-D:2(VII,2) LC IIIA. Missing at time of control. Apparently a frag. Limestone. L: 27.5. W: 15.7. Th: 7.8. **B 1502** (St 60) A-F:2 LC IIIB. Missing at time of control. One end broken off. L: 26.7. W: 19. Th: 5. **B 1503** (St 61) A-E:1(VIII) LC IIIB. Missing at time of control. Frag. of center. PL: 21.6. W: 17.7. Th: 4.

Roundel: button-shaped spindlewhorl, according to *SCE* II, Pl. CLXXXIV:5 (Type 4).

B 1504 (S 48) A-D:2(VII,2). *Pl. 37.* C-ch. Black steatite. Band of 8 outlined compass-drawn concentric semicircles inscribed in an incised zone. D :3.4. H: 0.8. Cf. K 1130. **B 1505** (St 79) E-D:2a LC IIIA. *Pl. 37.* C-ch. Gray haematite with high polish. Design like B 1504 but upper border of zone not indicated. D: 2.9. **B 1506** (Mi 105) Topsoil east of T.12.

C-i. Gray steatite. Rather irregularly executed circle of punched dots around base of cone. D: 2.4. H: 0.8. **B 1507** (Mi 555) T.16:7. C-ch. Dk. blue-gray, lightweight stone, perhaps diorite or andesite. Around base of cone, a row of incised crescents. D: 3.1. H: 0.9. **B 1508** (Mi 559; 49-12-124) T.11:9(A) LC IB. *Pl* 37. C-ch. Worn on one side. Blue-green steatite(?) 2 incised rings around perforation and 2 around base. D: 3.1. H: 1.4.

Spindlewhorls: all the following are like *SCE* II, Pl. CLXXXIV: Type 3, and are of polished steatite unless otherwise indicated.

a. Undecorated. **B 1509** (Mi 101) D-A. C-i. Dk. green. H: 2. D: 2. **B 1510** (Mi 103) D-A. C-ch. Blue-gray. Rather rounded. H: 2.1. D: 2. **B 1511** (Mi 123; 49-12-162) T.12:33(B) LC IA:2. Blue-gray. H: 3. D: 2.9. **B 1512** (Mi 124; 49-12-169) T.12:40(B) LC IA:2. Greenish blue. H: 3.6. D: 3.3. **B 1513** (Mi 125; 49-12-172) T.12:44(B) LC IA:2. *Pl.* 37. Dk. gray-green. H: 2.5. D: 2.5. **B 1514** (Mi 126; 49-12-182) T.12:55(B) LC IA:2. *Pl.* 37. Like B 1511. H: 2.2. D: 1.8. **B 1515** (Mi 127; 49-12-183) T.12:56(B) LC IA:2. *Pl.* 37. Like B 1514. H: 1.7. D: 1.7. **B 1516** (Mi 128; 49-12-187) T.12:60(A) LC IA:2. *Pl.* 37. Gray-green; very dense texture. H: 1.8. D: 1.6. **B 1517** (Mi 129; 49-12-188) T.12:61 (over tomb). *Pl.* 37. C-ch. Possibly not a whorl in view of large size. Blue-gray; dense texture. River stone. H: 6.1. D: 5.9. **B 1518** (Mi 130; 49-12-189) T.12:62(unstrat). C-ch. Very dk. gray-blue. H: 2.2. D: 1.9. **B 1519** (Mi 131; 49-12-244) T.18:10(A) LC IIB. *Pl.* 37. C-i. Polished blue-green. H: 2.2. D: 2.2. **B 1520** (Mi 132; 49-12-274) T.19:2(F) LC IIIB. *Pl.* 37. C-i. Like B 1518. H: 1.8. D: 2. **B 1521** (Mi 133) T.33:25 (in earth over burials). C-i. Lt. grayish blue-green. H: 2.5. D: 2. **B 1522** (Mi 176; 49-12-136) T.12:6a(A) LC IA:2. C-i. Gray-green. H: 1.4. D: 1.6. **B 1523** (Mi 177; 49-12-137) T.12:6b(A) LC IA:2. C-ch. Like B 1522. H: 1.9. D: 1.8. **B 1524** (Mi 184) T.33:47(unstrat). *Pl.* 60. C-ch. Like B 1522. H: 1.8. D: 1.9. **B 1525** (St 545) T.40:58(B) LC IIA. *Pl.* 58. C-i. Dk. blue-gray. H: 2.4. D: 2. **B 1526** (St 546) T.40:39(D) LC IIIA. *Pl.* 58. C-i. Dk. leather-gray stone with dull streaky surface. H: 2.3. D: 1.9. **B 1527** (S 11) A-E:2(VIII) LC IIIA. C-i. Lt. blue-gray. H: 2.9. D: 2.7. **B 1528** (S 12) A-D:2(VI) LC IIIA. C-i. Gray-green river stone. H: 2.7. D: 2.8. **B 1529** (S 83) C-A:6 LC IIA. *Pl.* 52. C-i. Blue-gray river stone. H: 2.4. D: 2. **B 1530** (S 85) A-B:3 LC IIB. C-i. Lt. blue-gray river stone(?) H: 3.3. D: 3.

b. Decorated. Circles referred to are dotted and incised and occur in equidistant correlated position on both cones unless otherwise indicated. A few unstratified specimens with standard decoration have not been catalogued. **B 1531** (Mi 104) D-A. C-i. Grayish blue-green. 4 circles. H: 2.1. D: 2. **B 1532** (Mi 106; 49-12-113) T.9:4 LC IA. C-i. Worn. Gray-green. 5 circles. H: 2.5. D: 2.1. *ANE,* Pl. VIII:19. **B 1533** (Mi 136) E-D:1h LC IIIA. C-i like B 1532. 3 circles (not equally spaced in one cone). H: 2.4. D: 2.5. **B 1534** (Mi 138; 49-12-317) T.19:54 (east niche).

Pl. 37. C-i. Dull blue-gray. 3 circles (staggered). H: 2.3. D: 2.1. **B 1535** (Mi 139; 49-12-318) T.19:55(dromos). *Pl.* 37. C-ch. Dull gray-brown to nearly black. 4 circles (2 rows on one cone). H: 2.1. D: 2.4. **B 1536** (Mi 190; 49-12-348) T.22:9. *Pl.* 37. C-i. Dull blue-gray stone. Around each end of longitudinal perforation and where cones meet, an incised band. On each cone 3 stacked hand-drawn triangles not coordinated with those of opposite cone. H: 2.2. D: 2.5. **B 1537** (Mi 206; 49-12-319) T.19:56(A) LC IIA-B. *Pl.* 37. C-i. Like B 1534. Toolmarks visible. 3 circles (not equally spaced in one cone). H: 2.2. D: 2.2. **B 1538** (St 85; 49-12-419) T.34:1. C-i. Dk. gray to black; dull perhaps from soil action or improper cleaning. 3 circles. H: 1.7. D: 1.5. **B 1539** (St 86) Trial pit 2 m. SE of T.36. Like B 1538. 5 circles irregularly spaced. H: 1.3. D: 1.5. **B 1540** (St 544) T.24:12. C-i. Dk. olive-green. 3 circles (staggered). H: 1.8. D: 1.8. **B 1541** (St 547) T.40:65(A) LC IIA. *Pl.* 58. C-i. Dull dk. blue-gray stone. Short vert. incision across angle of join of 2 cones and another corresponding at 180°. H: 1.9. D: 1.8. **B 1542** (S 27) A-E:2(VIII) LC IIIB. C-i. Gray. 3 circles. H: 2.2. D: 2. **B 1543** (S 94) B-Surface. C-i. Dull leather-black stone. Vert. rows of circles at 90°. H: 2.3. D: 2.3. **B 1544** (S 95) C-Unstrat. C-i. Dk. blue-gray. 3 circles. Cones divided by 2 hor. bands. H: 2.5. D: 2.2. *AJA* 64 (1960) Pl. 38. **B 1545** (S 96) B-C:2 LC IIC. C-i. Worn. Blue-gray. 4(?) circles (2 staggered rows in each cone). H: 2. D: 2.4.

Miscellaneous Stone Objects

B 1546 (St 34) A-D:2(VII,2) LC IIIA. Fine-grained, smooth gray(?) stone, roughly oval in shape, flat and pierced at narrower end. Catalogued by Daniel as a whetstone. L: 8.2. W: 3.9. Th: 0.8. **B 1547** (St 70; 49-12-9) T.2:4(C) CG III(?). *Pl.* 37. Lt. gray slate-like stone, trapezoidal in shape, flat and pierced at narrower end. Whetstone or palette. L: 5.2. W: 2.9. Th: 0.5. Cf. *SCE* II, Pl. CLXXXIII:34. **B 1548** (Mi 122) E-Đ:1f LC IIIA. Flat circular object with a sizeable center perforation. Limestone. D: 4.8. Th: 0.7. **B 1549** (S 76:K 67) A-E:2(St.2b) LC IIIB. Rectangular piece of steatite. Clear oblique toolmarks. L: 2.2. W: 1.2. Th: 0.5. *AJA* 64 (1960) Pl. 38.

TERRACOTTA

Crucibles: several fragments not listed below (Sh 564 and Sh 751), from the same type of vessel as B 1550 and with the same metallic coating, were found in a deposit just east of House VIII, Area E, near the site of the hearths. For an analysis of the metallic coating on these pieces, see B 1558-1559. Cf. also B 1595 ff. For an illustration of ancient clay crucibles, see R. J. Forbes, *Metallurgy in Antiquity* (Leiden, 1950) 126.

B 1550 (Sh 554) E-D:2f LC IIIA. *Pl.* 35. Various frags. of a coarse-ware vessel. Most of the frags. are of pithos-ware thickness, but a rim fragment narrows markedly to a plain round lip, suggesting that the vessel may have had the shape of a great vat or cauldron. H-m. C: g. dk. gray and gray-brown to dull brick-red; straw-bound. Very coarse and brittle from much use over fire. On the interior is a thick metallic coating, considerably charred, with numerous spots of bronze disease. L (of largest frag.): 9. Max. Th: 3. **B 1551** (Sh 559) E-D:2e LC IIIA. *Pl. 35*. 2 frags. from same or identical vessel as B 1550 with similar metallic coating. A large section of rim shows a relatively vert. wall and has a semicircular cutting on the lip for pouring. H (of rim frag.): 8.3. The following statement was submitted by Mr. A. E. Parkinson, chemist at the University Museum, Philadelphia: "The sample chosen had a green spot on the surface, apparently copper corrosion. Qualitative analysis showed the presence of copper, lead, iron, aluminum, calcium, magnesium and silica. There was only a very small amount of lead. The silica comprised about one third of the sample and was evidently combined with at least part of the metallic constituents in the form of a silicate or silicates. In order to make certain that the copper was not present merely as an isolated spot possibly from an extraneous source, another sample not showing any visible evidence of copper was partially analyzed, and again copper was found to be present. No lead was found in this sample. The analysis was not extended to include the other constituents, which, however, were not questioned." **B 1552** (Sh 563) E-LC II deposit with B 352. 2 frags. (one a rim frag.) from same or identical vessel as B 1550, with similar metallic coating. H (of rim frag.): 4.6. **B 1553** (Sh 566) E-D:2f LC IIIA. Frag. of rim of same or identical vessel as B 1550 with same metallic coating. H (of base frag.): 3.5. **B 1554** (Sh 603) E-Hearth:A. *Pl. 35*. Wall(?) frag. of the same vessel as B 1550 or, more likely, a similar one. The deposit of metal is much thicker and heavier and betrays evidence of bronze disease. L: 9. Max. Th: (without metal): 3.5. **B 1555** (Sh 607) E-Unstrat. 2 small frags. from wall of B 1550 or identical vessel; with metallic coating. L (of larger frag.): 3.5. Th: 2.3. **B 1556** (Sh 608) E-Unstrat. Frag. from rim of vessel similar to B 1550. Much of wall has disintegrated but it was probably less thick than B 1550. C: very gritty brownish red; thick coating of metal with bronze disease int. H: 9. **B 1557** (Sh 609) E-Hearth:A. Missing at time of control. Referred to in inventory as a crucible frag. **B 1558** (Sh 665) D-A. Frag. of base of a jug of PWM II fabric. C: gray-brown to red-brown, fired gray-green at surface. Has many fine lime grits. Int. coated with a carbonized layer of metallic substance. PH: 6. Chemical analysis (by A. E. Parkinson) of the carbonized layer yielded the following results: silica 45%; iron and aluminum, large amount; lesser amount of calcium and magnesium. **B 1559** (Sh 721; 54-28-71) MPT-F:3. *Pl. 35*. Frag. of vert. wall of heavy vessel, probably of the shape of B 1550. C: pinkish brown with lt. and dk. grits, straw-bound. Int. is coated with a layer of a hard dk. gray substance which is dk. gray-green, glossy and almost vitreous at the surface, showing deep fissures at irregular intervals. L (diagonal): 10. Th: 1.8. Th (of metallic layer): 0.8. Chemical analysis (by E. A. Parkinson) of the glaze-like coating yielded the following results: silica 53%; otherwise like B 1558. The material was fused.

Figurines: Human. A selection of the post-Bronze Age figurines from Bamboula, unstratified, of course, has been published in *TFKC*, 47: nos. 967, 968 and 970. Cf. also *ExC*, Fig. 105 = A 5; Fig. 106 = A 2; Fig. 107 = A 3; Fig. 108 = A 4.

B 1560 (F 41) A-D:2(VII,2) LC IIIA. *Pl. 52*. Head and torso of male figure. H-m. Nose is only facial feature indicated. Wears flat hat. C: cinnamon-brown wfs and lime. H: 4.5. **B 1561** (F 58:K 69) C-Unstrat. Torso of a female figure; small pellet breasts. C: gray at core to orange-brown wfs; firm consistency. H: 6.5. *AJA* 64 (1960) Pl. 38. **B 1562** (F 60) B-B LC IIB. *Pl. 35*. Head and upper torso of male(?) figure. Flat head, prominent pinched nose and chin. Outline of eyes punched. Applied arms. C: gray at core to red-brown with small white grits and a little mica. P: m. dk. gray and red. Hair, eyes, necklace painted gray with traces of red on necklace. H: 5.2. W: 3.1. Th: 1. *Berytus* 14 (1961) 38. **B 1563** (F 63; 49-12-305) T.19:40(B) LC IIA-B. *Pl. 35*. C-i save for earrings in left ear. Missing at time of control. C: gray at core to orange-brown surface, smoothed in strokes; like BR. S: none. Beak-shaped face, pellet eyes, enormous ears, each pierced for 2 earrings. One hand to right breast, the other to navel. Full wide hips, tapering legs and small feet. 3 incised hor. lines at base of neck and 2 under breasts: "x" between breasts. Elaborate indication of pelvic hair outlined above on belly and below on legs. H: 19.3. W: 6.6. Th: 3.8. *UPMB* 8, (1940) Pl. IV:e. Cf. A 2 and *CesCol*, 335 ff. for a discussion of the type. **B 1564** (F 64) D-A. *Pl. 35*. Torso of body of female figure with raised arms and column body: Ψ type. Breasts sl. modeled. C: pale cream, well cleaned; rich texture. Standard Mycenaean technique. P: ls. olive, flaked. Sl. wavering vert. lines. H: 5.5. Cf. *CMP* 87, Fig. 1. **B 1565** (F 67) D-A. *Pl. 35*. Frag. of upper body and head of female figure. Hollow. Beak-like nose(?) now broken off, pellet eyes, incised mouth, breasts sl. modeled. Hor. incisions below breasts. C: gray at core to gray-brown wfs; hard, close-textured. P: firm m. brown, chocolate-red and dk. brown. Vari-colored bands on neck; mouth red; pupils and brows brown. H: 9. Cf. A 3 and *CesCol*, 336 (Fabric IX) for a discussion of the type. *Berytus* 14 (1961) 38. **B 1566** (F 68) D-A. *Pl. 35*. Frag. of head of female figure. Identical to B 1565. Nose also broken off. H: 4. *Berytus* 14 (1961) 38. **B 1567** (Sh 95) A-F:1 LC IIIB. *Pl. 35*. Sl. curved frag. possibly part of a figurine. C: orange-brown, hard. Resembles BR but not slipped. Shaved. Has band of dk. brown paint. H: 2.3.

Figurines: Animal

B 1568 (F 57) A-D:2(VII,2) LC IIIA. Part of body of bull or horse(?) of same sort perhaps as B 1569. Fashioned by joining several independent pieces. C: g. orange-brown to greenish at surface, firm. P: dk. gray, crackled. Rectangular system of applied lines may represent trappings. L: 8. **B 1569** (F 59) C-Unstrat. *Pl. 35*. Head of horse(?) as part of rhyton. Small pour-hole in mouth. Hollow. C: gray-brown to gray-yellow wfs and a few larger white grits. P: firm dk.

gray to olive-brown where thin. Relief lines, representing trappings, painted; also eyes and ears. H: 7. *UPMB* 7, (1939) 20, Fig. 3. Local work? **B 1570** (F 61) C-B LC IIB. *Pl. 35.* Trunk of quadruped(?) C: yellow-gray to buff-cream surface. P: ls. redbrown. Standard Mycenaean technique. L: 5.3. **B 1571** (F 65) D-A. *Pl. 35.* Frag. of quadruped: apparently left leg and neck. C: dk. buff to dk. orangebrown. P: like B 1570. Standard Mycenaean technique. L: 5.8. For the type, cf. *Prosymna*, Fig. 616. **B 1572** (F 69) D-A. *Pl. 35.* Frag. of bull's head with horns broken off. Traces of pellet eye. C: like B 1565, but somewhat coarser. P: dk. gray-brown. Reminiscent of BR bull figurines. L: 6.8. **B 1573** (F 70) D-A. *Pl. 35.* Frag. of animal's mouth and neck. Photograph shows beginning of left foreleg; head was turned to left. Hollow. Made in 2 pieces and joined in line of middle of neck. Join covered with softer clay and painted. C: gray-brown to orange-brown wfs. P: m. wine-red. Incised details (mouth indicated by a slit). H: 6.5. Local work?

Hanging Lamp: see *AntJ* 32 (1952) Pl. XXVI:e for a specimen more graceful than the Bamboula examples; for a recent discussion of the type, see *Myrtou-Pigadhes*, 77.

B 1574 (P 735) A-D:2(VII,2) LC IIIA. *Pl. 37.* Base only, trough entirely missing. Low ridge completely outlines base. Serpentine line from trough end to hole end incised while clay still damp. No signs of burning. C: sandy orange-brown; underside of base laid on sand. L: 33.1. W: 10.2. H: 2.8. **B 1575** (P 786) A-D:2(IV) LC IIIA. *Pl. 37.* Upper part of base missing. Ridge and w. line as on B 1575. Trough was originally a w-m deep cup, cut in two and fitted to the base. Signs of burning. C: g. reddish gray at core to pink and gray-green at surface. L (of base): 27.2. L (of trough): 13.3. **B 1576** (Sh 755) E—see *Bamboula* SS sub Hearth Area. Pl. 37. Frag. of base. Smaller and cruder than B 1574 and B 1575. Base has 2 holes for attaching to wall; trough almost entirely missing but its former position is clear. C: g. brownish buff wfs; coarse. P: m. streaky black and crimson. 2 broad stripes on stub of trough ext; int. bordered by 2 black stripes crossed at right angles by a stripe between the holes of the base. Black stripes outlined by thinner red ones. PL: 11. W: 8. PH: 5.5.

Larnax

B 1577 (Mi 207a-b) D-A. *Pl. 37.* 2 frags. showing transition from base to nearly vert. wall, and rim which is thickened and grooved. C: gray-brown to graygreen; coarse with many large grits and air holes; of pithos consistency. H (of larger frag.): 24.5. Th: 2.

Loomweights: the classification below follows Miss Taylor's system, *AntJ* 32 (1952) 161.

a. Truncated pyramidal: **B 1578** (S 14) A-E:3(VIII) LC IIIA. C-ch. C: gray-red wfs. H: 7.6. W: 5. **B 1579** (S 15) A-D:2(VII,2) LC IIIA. C-ch. Very roughly made. C: sandy lt. reddish brown. H: 7.9. W: 3.6. L: 4.4. **B 1580** (S 16) A-B:6 LC IIB. C-i. Lopsided. C: sandy orange-brown. H: 8.6. W: ca. 4.

B 1581 (S 17) A-B:6 LC IIB. C-i. Carefully finished. C: like S 16. H: 7.9. L: 5. W: 4.2. **B 1582** (S 20) A-B:6 LC IIB. C-i. Little more than a crudely made rectangle with smooth rounded edges. H: 8.3. L: 3.7. W: 3.5. **B 1583** (S 21) A-B:6 LC IIB. C-i. Carelessly made. C: lt. gray-brown wfds. H: 9. W: 4.9. **B 1584** (S 22) A-E:1(VIII) LC IIIB. Base badly chipped; sides well squared. C: sandy gray-green. H: 7.6. W: 4.7. **B 1585** (S 28) Cw IV CA. Shape like B 1582 but shallow hole bored in top. L: 7.3. W: 3.5. **B 1586** (S 84) A-E:2(St.2b) LC IIIB. C-ch. Crudely made. C: g. gray-green wfds. H: 9.5. D: 4.3. **B 1587** (S 99) C-B LC IIB. C-ch. Rounded edges. C: like B 1586. H: 9.7. W: 6.4. **B 1588** (S 100) C-A:5 LC IB. C-ch. Rounded edges. At the top the beginning of a hole pierced with a reed(?), the core still remaining. C: lt. brown wfds. H: 7.2. W: 4.3. **B 1589** (S 101) B-B LC IIB. C-ch. Edges rounded. C: lt. gray wfds. H: 7.9. W: 4.8. **B 1590** (Mi 186; 49-12-285) T.19:13(E) LC IIIA. *Pl. 35.* Base badly broken; crudely made. C: lt. brick-red with sand and chaff temper. H: 6.9. W (at top): 3.3. **B 1591** (Mi 205a; 54-41-62) MPT-D:5. C-i. C: lt. pinkish to gray-brown; straw-bound, coarse texture. H: 9. W: 6.

b. Flattened spheres, pierced in center: **B 1592** (S 1) A-D:2(VII,2) LC IIIA. C-i. C: brick-red, coarse. D: 5.5. H: 3.3. **B 1593** (S 86) A-B:3 LC IIB. Badly chipped. More or less pill-shaped and not baked. Of lt. gray-brown mud with many frags. of limestone. D: 8.2. H: 4.3. **B 1594** (G 42:K 10) D—in an LC IIIA level, according to Daniel's publication of this piece. C-i. C: sandy orange-brown. D: 5.2. *UPMB* 13 (1948) Pl. 3 (upper right) *AJA* 64 (1960) Pl. 38 (erroneously identified as B 1544).

Pipes: all the following pieces appear to be part of tubes or vent pipes used in connection with casting metal. They may have been parts of actual moulds. Although no metal coating was found in connection with any of them, they were found in the Hearth Area and the clay is very similar to that of the crucibles (B 1550 ff.). Moreover, they are brittle from much contact with heat.

B 1595 (Sh 561a-b) E-D:1h LC IIIA. Part of an object square or rectangular in section (and tapering). C: dk. brick-red to cinnamon with chaff temper; soft. Signs of burning ext. Vent hole runs length in center (D: 1.1). L (of larger frag.): 8. **B 1596** (Sh 565) E—in a deposit just east of House VIII near site of hearths (cf. introductory note on crucibles). Two joins of an object like B 1595 but apparently not tapering. C: like B 1595. Signs of burning ext. D (of vent): 1.7. L: 9.5. **B 1597** (Sh 610) E. *Pl. 35.* Occurred in an LC IIIA context which I cannot relate to any known level but which may perhaps have been debris over the furnace area. Fairly well pres. end. Square in section and tapering to a small vent hole. The inner tube is 2.5 cm. in diameter at upper part of fragment and 0.8 cm. in diameter at tapered end. C: like B 1595. Fire-blackened ext. PH: 6.5. W (at upper end): 5. **B 1598** (Sh 611) E-Hearth:A. *Pl. 37.* Large frag. of a curved tube bent at nearly right angles and tapering noticeably at the bend. Square with rounded edges in section. C: like B 1595. L: 14.6. W (at widest point): 7.2. D (of hole at tapered end): 2.5. **B 1599** (Sh 614) E-Unstrat. *Pl.* 35. Frag. of an object like B 1597 but tapering less pronouncedly. C: like B 1597; partly charred ext. H: 6.3. W (at widest part): 5.3. D (of vent): ca. 2. **B 1600** (Sh 757) E: see *Bamboula SS: Suppl.* Remarks on Stratification (the Hearth Area). One large frag. and many smaller, of a thick horn-like, sl. curving and markedly tapering tube. C: hrd dk. brown; has no grits, but apparently some metallic content which gives the illusion, on cursory examination, that the piece is actually made of metal. L (of largest frag.): 14.5. W (at widest point): 8.5. D (of hole at large end): 2.3. D (at small end): 1.

Seal Stamp: see B 1640.

Spindlewhorls

a. Truncated double conical (basic type like B 1509 ff.): **B 1601** (Mi 141) Trial pit 2 m. SE of T. 36. *Pl.* 37. C-i. C: lt. yellow-gray to pink; rich texture, bur. surface. Incised band outlining each end of perforation. 3 t-o vert. zones with 3 vert. zigzag lines in each. H: 2.5. D: 2.4. **B 1602** (Mi 142) A-Unstrat. C-ch. C: orange-brown. S: ls. red, shading to gray. RP technique. Indistinct patterns lightly incised before baking. H: 3.1. D: 3.4. **B 1603** (Mi 143) E-D:1f LC IIIA. *Pl.* 37. C-ch. C: sandy gray-brown, firm. Coarsely incised vert. gores. H: 2.2. D: 2.6. **B 1604** (Mi 146) E-A:5 LC IB. C-i. Rather elongated; coarse modeling. C: gray-brown; rich texture. H: 4.3. D: 2.8. **B 1605** (S 10) A-E:3(V) LC IIIA. *Pl.* 37. C-i. C: gray at core to lt. reddish brown. S: thin sl. ls. brown. BR technique. Incised frieze on each cone of a band of 3 vert. lines alternating with an oblique shaded band. H: 2.7. D: 2.8. **B 1606** (S 18) A-Unstrat. *Pl.* 37. C-i. Flattened double conical. C: brown; fine and soft in texture. H: 2.5. D: 4.3.

b. Spherical (sometimes depressed): **B 1607** (S 26) Stray. C-i. C: gray at core to brown, hard. Groups of 2 and 3 incised lines resp., at right angles around one end of perforation. H: 2.9. D: 3.7. **B 1608** (S 49; 49-12-1) T.1 EC II-III. *Pl.* 37. C-ch. D: dk. gray; bur. surface. 4 deeply incised hor. bands filled with a white chalky substance. D: 2.7. **B 1609** (S 90) C-B LC IIB. *Pl.* 37. About half pres. C: dk. gray wfs, firm. Similar to BR clay but coarser. Incised and punched design based on triangles. D: 3.6. **B 1610** (S 91) C-B LC IIB. *Pl.* 37. About half pres. C: dk. gray to gray-brown wfs. S: ls. brown. BR technique. Incised and punched designs. H: 2.8. ED: 3.5. **B 1611** (S 92) B-Unstrat. About half pres. C: gray to orange-brown with white grits. P: ls. dk. gray to dk. brown. Incised and punched designs based on triangles, on one side only. Incisions filled with white matter. H: 3.2. D: 3.9. **B 1612** (Mi 121) E-D:1f LC IIIA. C-i. C: gray to gray-brown. Deeply incised hor. band around middle; lighter vert. grooves. H: 2.4. D: 2.2. **B 1613** (Mi 145) E-A:5 LC IB. C-m. C: gray-brown. Groups of 3 incised vert. bands at 90°. Some lines crooked. H: 3.5. D: 4.

c. Truncated conical (cf. *SCE* II, Pl. CLXXXI:11): **B 1614** (S 2) A-E:2(VIII) LC IIIB. C-i. C: brick-red. P: thin red-brown, once ls.(?) Groups of 3 diagonal incisions at base, and of perpendicular incisions on bottom. H: 3. D: 3.7. **B 1615** (Mi 100) D-A. *Pl.* 37. C-i. C: gray. P: ls. dk. brown. On sides: triple hor. zigzag with hatched lozenges in the interstices. Bottom: 4 concentric semicircles facing toward perforation, on either side of which is a zigzag. H: 3.4. D: 4.5.

Miscellaneous Terracotta Objects

B 1616 (S 19) A-B:5 LC IIB. *Pl.* 37. Small pill-shaped object, possibly a gaming piece. C: burnt gray with some sand and coarser temper. Only one side decorated with an incised "x" in the center and dots punched coarsely around the edge. D: 3.3. Th: 0.9. **B 1617** (F 71; 49-12-367) T.25:5. C-i. Disk with a groove around the circumference; on one side at center a lug with string-hole. Called a votive shield by Daniel but possibly a lid. H-m. C: sandy red-brown; hard. D: 4.9. Th: 1.8. **B 1618** (Mi 206a; 54-28-72) MPT:G. *Pl.* 37. I-m. Roughly rectangular object with flat bottom and low walls on 3 sides. Resembles a tray. C: reddish brown with white grits. P: m. dk. gray-brown. Paint on all edges and around floor int., with bars on int. back wall; short strokes like dashes around floor. 4 small c-c on floor. L: 10. EW: 9.5. H: 4. Cf. *SCE* IV (2), Fig. XII:6; *Hesperia* 34 (1965) Pl. 11, f; also R. C. Bosanquet and R. M. Dawkins, *The Unpublished Objects from the Palaikastro Excavations* (London 1923) 45, Fig. 34. **B 1619** (Sh 558) E-D:2d LC IIIA. 8 sherds joined to form a frag. of a roof-tile(?) in the shape of a flat slab, sl. thicker near edges. C: lt. brown to orange-brown, sandy with chaff temper; soft. PL: 33. PW: 22.5. Th: 2.6.

UNIDENTIFIED MATTER

B 1620 and B 1621 are indeterminate pieces of mineral substance on which the following very brief report was rendered by D. Bradwell, Government Analyst of Cyprus: "... they are not metallic, they contain large amounts of iron oxide and a trace of copper, and appear to be some form of slag, possibly from copper smelting." No quantitative analysis was made.

B 1620 (M 10) A-D:2(VII,2) LC IIIA. Irregularly-shaped piece with airholes and small adhering deposits of bronze. Bottom flat with one squared corner. L: 7.7. W: 5.5. Th: 1.7. **B 1621** (M 11) A-D:2(VII,2) LC IIIA. Roughly square shape, though somewhat twisted and with airholes. L: 5.3. W: 4.5. Th: 2.5.

APPENDICES

GLYPTICS

by Edith Porada*

Cylinder Seals

At the suggestion of the late J. F. Daniel, nine cylinder seals found in the Late Bronze Age settlement of Bamboula were included by the present writer more than two decades ago in an article dealing with the characteristic groups of Cypriote cylinder seals.[1] Of necessity they were summarily treated at that time; they will therefore be discussed in detail in the report below, to which commentaries on the stamp seals and scarabs found at Bamboula are appended. (Objects from Kaloriziki will be discussed in the separate volume dealing with that site.) J. L. Benson's dates for the cylinder seals are accepted here; in a few cases they vary from those of the excavator.

In the finest, though badly worn, cylinder found at Bamboula, B 1622, two rampant lions flanking a "sacred tree" are easily recognized, but a small human or divine figure at the lions' backs is difficult to discern. The broad-shouldered figure seems to resemble one on a lentoid from Enkomi[2] that has one leg raised, the other bent in an exaggerated *Knielauf* posture. On the cylinder from Bamboula only the lines indicating the borders of the short garment suggest the position of the figure's legs. Moreover, it is impossible to be certain of the figure's sex. While two lions are often associated with a goddess in Aegean art,[3] there is no clearly identifiable female figure wearing a short kilt seen in any indubitably Cypriote cylinder seal. No precise interpretation of the meaning of the lions, the tree, and the small figure can therefore be given, although the coherent axial composition of lions and tree, with the small figure apparently echoing the curves of the lions' bodies, suggests that the scene was conceived as a meaningful whole.

The seal is carved with remarkable assurance: parts of the animals' bodies are hollowed out at varying depths, producing plain yet subtly curving surfaces. Details are indicated by decorative rows of small granule-like drillings or by lines which repeat and complement one another. Enough remains to show that the cylinder was made in one of the best workshops on Cyprus. The Cypriote character of the seal is indicated especially by the "sacred tree"— a motif rendered frequently in the glyptic art of the eastern Mediterranean and western Asiatic regions in the latter half of the second millennium B.C., and distinguished from an ordinary plant by volutes and other decorative devices which varied from region to region. In Cypriote designs the crown of the tree is often shown as a curving form marked by short radial lines.[4] The representation of two such forms, one above the other as in the Bamboula cylinder, is rare.

The stratigraphic date for cylinder B 1622 is LC IIA, in absolute dates about 1400–1350 B.C. In view of the worn state of the seal it should be placed at the very beginning of that period if not before, in LC IB, about 1450–1400 B.C., even though the relatively soft stone from which the cylinder was made was probably easily rubbed if fingered in the manner of "worry beads"—a likely occurrence since no other

---

* The cylinder seals are reproduced on Pl. 38 with the writer's photographs of the impressions enlarged about 1:2. B 1628, however, was not available for a new impression and is therefore reproduced with an old photograph, c. 1:1.

The stamp seal impressions were photographed c. 1:1, except for B 1635 which is slightly enlarged from an old negative. In a few cases photographs of the seal shapes have been added. No photograph of the stamp B 1640 was available.

1. "The Cylinder Seals of the Late Cypriote Bronze Age," *AJA* 52 (1948) 178–198 and Pls. VIII–XI.
2. Cf. *RDAC*, 1965, Pl. II:1, 3. Perhaps that figure is female.
3. Examples were cited by M. P. Nilsson, *The Minoan-Mycenaean Religion* (second edition, 1950), pp. 358–359. Cf. also comments by R. D. Barnett, "The Mistress of Animals," in *A Catalogue of the Nimrud Ivories* (London, 1957) 82–83 and B. Segal's interpretation of a pendant from Dodona showing lions flanking a sacred tree as a tree of life which stands for the goddess of the nether world in "The Earring with Winged Charioteer in the Classical Department," *BMFA* 40, No. 239 (1942) 51, and 53, Fig. 9. Cf. also the lentoid mentioned in note 2 above.
4. This form of the crown of the tree seems to have a remarkable similarity to designs of trees and flowers in Late Minoan IIIA and IIIB pottery. For easy reference, cf. the "Chart of Mycenaean and Late Minoan Pottery" by S. Symeonoglou, *AJA* 74 (1970) xxx: 19, 21, 22.

use would account for equally extensive wear. A date about or before 1400 B.C. for this Bamboula cylinder is also indicated by the series of granules which can be related to those in the robe of a figure preserved on a fragmentary impression of a cylinder seal found in Knossos that must have reached Crete shortly before the destruction of the palace.[5]

While the single occurrence of a cylinder of the quality of B 1622 at Bamboula makes it seem unlikely that it was made at the site, such an origin seems more probable for the three pieces B 1623 to B 1625. All three cylinders contain a distinctively rendered griffin in their designs. The monster has a plume hanging down in front almost like a beard. Usually such a plume curves from the top of the head to the nape of the neck. The crest of the griffin's head is indicated by three thin lines: slightly fan-shaped in B 1624, almost parallel in B 1625, and short and difficult to discern in B 1623. In all three cylinders, furthermore, the artist seems to have hollowed out the curving form of the griffin's body, crossing it with the form which indicates the solid part of the monster's wing. In the two cylinders B 1624 and B 1625 the seal cutter transformed the continuation of the wing into the upper part of the forelegs, a treatment resulting in a curiously incongruous body for the monster. In the cylinder B 1623 the seal cutter used the same device of crossing the body with the form of the wing and extending it in front of the body, but used it more logically by adding a row of feathers, thus suggesting the presence of a lowered second wing. Here, however, the griffin's legs are drawn incongruously: two hind legs seem to extend parallel under the body of the seated monster, in a typically Cypriote manner;[6] one leg, raised obliquely, looks more like a third hind leg than a foreleg, and the foreleg, which is very slightly engraved, is not visibly connected with the body. In view of our lack of knowledge of the working methods of seal cutters, the similarities and divergences in the designs of these three examples, all obviously from the same mediocre hand, would merit even more thorough treatment than can be accommodated within the framework of this appendix.

For the interpretation of these seal designs, attention can be drawn only to the griffin which looms so large on all three cylinders and seems to obtrude itself upon the viewer's consideration. Perhaps the monster was meant to protect the seal-owner against the powers of death and destruction which it is thought to have impersonated.[7] The long-robed figure appearing in two of the cylinders, B 1623 and

B 1624, might then be a restraining and appeasing priestess or goddess (perhaps so characterized in B 1623 by a wing,[8] which may be indicated by the otherwise inexplicable lines behind her head), while the sacred tree in the same two cylinders, as well as the ibex in B 1625, could well represent symbols of life. Admittedly, all this is most tenuous, and no explanation at all can be given for the small motif of an ibex and the bucrania and rosette which appear in the fields of B 1623 and B 1624 beyond stating that they, too, are probably symbols of divine powers, even though their obvious purpose in the seal design is that of filling the space.

The rendering of the face of the human or divine figure in B 1624 merits some comment because it shows clearly those features which distinguish the human face in many Cypriote cylinders from those of Syrian or Mitannian style. In B 1624 the tall thick neck supports a head in which an angle is formed by the slightly oblique line of the cranium and the strongly oblique one of the nose. This angle forms the eyesocket, the lower part of which is indicated by a thin line. The eye is shown by a small dot, the lips by two short lines placed before the drilling indicating the lower part of the face. This stylization of the human face is not too far removed in character from human faces on chariot kraters, a number of which were found in Cyprus. While the renderings which seem closest to that of cylinder B 1624 belong to vases of Benson's Bamboula painter,[9] which he tentatively placed in the late fourteenth or early thirteenth centuries B.C. and which would be later than the stratigraphic date for B 1623 and B 1624 (obtained from the find spot for B 1623 together with B 1622 in the LC IIA stratum of Tomb 12, c. 1400–1350 B.C.), the possibility that this type of stylization of the face was influenced by the conventions of Mycenaean figure painting may not be ruled out.

The body of the figure on cylinders B 1623 and B 1624, however, conforms to earlier Cypriote prototypes in the stress on the broad shoulders of the

5. *PM* IV, p. 598, Fig. 593. For the date of the find spot and a bibliographical note for references by various authors to this impression cf. J. Boardman, *On the Knossos Tablets* (1963) 72 (note 2).

6. For a description of this posture cf. *AJA* 52 (1948) 189 s.v. Group V *Characteristics*.

7. H. Frankfort, "Notes on the Cretan Griffin," *BSA* 37 (1936–37) especially pp. 120–121.

8. Short wings, close to the head, are seen on the Cypriote cylinders *AJA* 52 (1948) Pl. VIII:10, 12.

9. J. L. Benson, "Observations on Mycenaean Vase-Painters," *AJA* 65 (1961) text p. 344, good illustrations, Pl. 109: Figs. 44–46.

frontally posed thorax,[10] whereas in Mycenaean vase paintings a thorax in profile with exaggeratedly backward curving line is common, a feature for which Cypriote glyptic art has not yet provided a parallel.

We might conclude not only that the engraver of B 1623 to B 1625, probably a man who had his workshop in Bamboula, was influenced by designs for cylinder seals which he imitated rather unsuccessfully, if his models were earlier examples like B 1622, but that he may have also tried to incorporate striking features seen in figured vase paintings.

A noticeable feature of the cylinder B 1625 is the cross crudely cut over a recumbent ibex and a rosette, defacing part of the design. Strangely enough, a seal from Enkomi,[11] excavated by P. Dikaios, shows a similar cross-shaped design produced by cutting a horizontal line across the vertical staff of a mace held by a deity. The Enkomi seal was found in a looter's pit, the one from Bamboula in an LC IIIA context—later by one or two generations than the date attributed to the three Bamboula cylinders. This interval between creation and burial suggests that both the Bamboula cylinder and the one from Enkomi were in secondary use, perhaps worn by people who no longer appreciated the intricate designs of earlier generations and who did not shrink from damaging the engraving of a seal stone in order to put their personal mark upon it.

A cylinder that was equally long in use, to judge by its badly worn condition, is B 1626; it belongs to a different stylistic group, distinguished from B 1623 to B 1625 by more clearly defined, assured, and rounded forms and by the appearance of a series of small globules in the field. Two examples of this group were found at Aghia Paraskevi,[12] but one cylinder which may have come from the same workshop was found as far afield as Tell el Ajjul (Petrie's Gaza).[13] A great variety of figures and presumably of themes characterizes the group. The theme of B 1626 is probably that of a goddess in some relation to a bull which she faces over a stand placed between the two figures.[14] A bucranium suggestively placed above the hand of the deity may have some meaning with reference to her, whereas the bird with spread wings and the rows of globules are not so obviously connected with the seated figure. Beyond the observation of such visual facts, no interpretation can be made of the scene.

The date of B 1626 may be established by comparison with a cylinder found by P. Dikaios at Enkomi in an LC IIB context.[15] That cylinder is carved in a related, deeply cut, yet rounded and

very assured manner but with somewhat larger forms than B 1626. In view of the general tendency toward deterioration of craftsmanship in the Aegean areas toward the end of Late Helladic IIIB, in the latter part of the thirteenth century B.C.[16] the cylinder from Enkomi may be assumed to have been made somewhat later than the more carefully and delicately carved cylinders like B 1626. In turn, the date of the latter cylinder may be placed before the LC IIB period, in the late fourteenth century B.C.

Another cylinder from Bamboula, however, B 1627, with a demonic figure between a lion and an antelope, probably is as late as the cylinder from Enkomi just cited. In both pieces the engraving and the spacing of the figures are comparable. Moreover, the cylinder from Bamboula can be related to a cylinder in the Ashmolean Museum,[17] which forms a link between the Bamboula and Enkomi cylinders here discussed. The stratigraphic context for B 1627 is LC IIIA. In view of the association of B 1627 with the cylinder from Enkomi, however, the date in the late thirteenth or early twelfth century B.C. suggested by the place of discovery probably marks the date when the cylinder was buried rather than when it was made.

In contrast with the assured engraving of B 1627, the carving of another cylinder from Bamboula, B 1628, is poor and apparently uncertain. The forked object held by the male figure between two horned animals, for example, cannot be clearly recognized. This unsightly steatite cylinder was covered with gold foil. Traces of gold foil on two crudely made faience cylinder seals found at Thebes in Boeotia[18] suggest that such enhancement with the valuable, shiny gold foil was practiced repeatedly on the

10. E.g. *AJA* 52 (1948) Pl. VIII:10–13.
11. P. Dikaios, *Enkomi*, vol. IIIa (Mainz, 1969) (E. 780) Pls. 179:1, 180:1, and 185:11C.
12. *AJA* 52 (1948) Pl. X:33 associated with *ibid.*, Pl. X:32 (our B 1626) and with Pl. IX:21. All were included in Group III.
13. W. F. M. Petrie, *Ancient Gaza IV* (British School of Archaeology in Egypt, Egypt. Res. Account, Publ. 56 London, 1934) Pl. XII:3; also in *Iraq* (1949) Pl. XXI:143.
14. The only other stand on a cylinder seal from Cyprus is seen on a faience cylinder from Enkomi, *SCE* I, 474:67 and Pl. CL:11 (E. 2.67).
15. Dikaios, *Enkomi* IIIa. Pls. 179:6, 180:6, 185:6 (E. 1261).
16. For comment on this development, cf. E. Vermeule, *Greece in the Bronze Age* (Chicago, 1964) 208.
17. B. Buchanan, *Catalogue of Ancient Near Eastern Seals in the Ashmolean Museum* I. *Cylinder Seals* (Oxford, 1966) Pl. 59:960.
18. Thebes, Nos. 184 and 209 (unpublished).

Aegean periphery of the area where engraved cylinder seals were in use, and where clarity of impression may not have been the principal concern of makers and wearers of cylinder seals. The gold-covered cylinder from Bamboula, which was found in an LC IIA context, and the frequent presence of gold caps at the ends of cylinders of Cypriote style[19] indicate the wealth accumulated by some of the inhabitants of the island in the early fourteenth century B.C., the period in which the excavator's date for B 1628 falls.

Even cruder than the engraving of B 1628 is that of B 1629, in which a man and animals are deeply scratched with a thin tool into the soft steatite of the cylinder. Perhaps this piece is the work of an amateur seal cutter since the man in the seal design seems to float in the air instead of walking on a ground line, a convention usually retained in Cypriote cylinders. Moreover, the animals are placed helter-skelter in the field; for example, a bird upside down, a horned animal parallel to the man and at right angles to the ground line, if such a line had been shown at the base of the cylinder. Yet the rendering of animals almost follows the conventions observed in some of the crude cylinders of Cyprus, e.g. AJA 52 (1948) Pl. XI:43, 44. These crude cylinders, however, are engraved in a manner that is far more assured and professional than the design of B 1629. It is possible that the unskilled and perhaps secondary engraving of that cylinder was made in the LC IIIA period, the date of the stratum in which the burial containing the cylinder B 1629 was found.

The ninth cylinder from Bamboula, B 1630, with a king or hero shooting arrows at a bull and a bird, derives its linear style from that of Egyptian scarabs, as C. F. A. Schaeffer has noted. He assembled the extant examples of this group[20] and placed them in his Iron I period (corresponding to the LC IIIA context in which B 1630 was found). In this easily recognizable style of design, cylinders as well as stamp seals were engraved with hunting and ritual scenes which differ from the repertory of deities, demons, and monsters of the Elaborate-style seals of the Late Bronze Age, and which foreshadow the dominant themes of the Iron Age in much of the art of the Levant.

B 1622 (S 103; 49-12-150) T. 12:21 (D) LC IIA. *Pl. 38a.* C-surface unevenly worn. Ivory colored steatite. Sacred tree flanked by two rampant lions, small human figure between lions' tails and hindlegs; numerous small drillings in field. L: 2.8. D: 1.1. AJA 52 (1948) Pl. IX:23. **B 1623** (S 104; 49-12-152) T.12:23 (D) LC IIA. *Pl. 38b.* C—surface worn. Dk.

gray steatite. Long-robed figure with three short oblique lines behind head, facing right, standing with one hand raised behind small sacred tree and large griffin seated on hindlegs. Human figure wears long flaring skirt marked by vert. lines and held to waist by belt; covering of upper body indefinable. L: 2.33. D: 0.78. AJA 52 (1948) Pl. X:28. **B 1624** (S 81) C-C:2 LC IIC. *Pl. 38c.* C-i. Dk. gray steatite. Long-robed figure touching rump of ibex to left with one hand, raising other behind griffin. Bull's head in field. L: 2.8. D: 1. AJA 52 (1948) Pl. X:29. **B 1625** (S 82:K 70) A-D:2 (St. 2b) LC IIIA. *Pl. 38d.* C-i. Dk. gray steatite. Griffin standing on all four feet before sacred tree, at left of which is small recumbent ibex with head turned backwards. One rosette over back of ibex, second in upper field beside bull's head, at left of which is large drilling. Cross crudely cut over ibex and rosette in secondary engraving. L: 2.2. D: 0.9. AJA 52 (1948) Pl. X:30. **B 1626** (Mi 195; 49-12-298) T.19:30 (C) LC IIIA. *Pl. 38e.* C-i. Much worn. Blue-gray fine-grained sl. ls. stone. Human or divine figure seated with raised hand before stand or altar supporting indefinable object. Horned animal before altar. Bull's head and bird(?) with spread wings in upper field. Two unconnected rows of drillings in field. L: 2.0. D: 0.8. AJA 52 (1948) Pl. X:32. **B 1627** (S 6) A-D:2 (VII, 2) LC IIIA. *Pl. 38f.* C-i. Dk. steatite. Man or demon with belt or short skirt grasping horned animal with ribbed body, sitting on hindlegs. Lion sitting on hindlegs behind man or demon; between latter and horned animal, lion's(?) head; three drillings behind lion. Terminal: sacred tree. AJA 42 (1938) 268, Fig. 10:c; AJA 52 (1948) Pl. XI:56. **B 1628** (Mi 169) T.36:4 LC IIA. *Pl. 38g.* Gray steatite covered with gold leaf; gold ring(s) at ends. One ring missing. Gold sheath about ⅔ pres. Man walking to right grasping one prong of forked object (branch or staff) beside which is small horned animal which faces right toward sacred tree; second animal on other side of tree; star(?) in upper field. L: 1.8. D (of ring): 0.67. D (of seal): 0.62. AJA 52 (1948) Pl. XI:57. **B 1629** (Mi 194; 49-12-294) T.19:26 (C) LC IIIA. *Pl. 38h.* C-i. Much worn. Dk. gray-blue steatite. Nude male figure holding dagger(?), facing ibex turned at right angles to ground line with head facing upward and turned back; dog in reverse direction; bull(?) back to back with dog; smaller, indefinable animal in reverse direction in lower field. L: 2. D: 0.9. AJA 52 (1948) Pl. XI:46. **B 1630** (S 5) A-2:2(VII,2) LC IIIA. *Pl. 38i.* C-i. Gray steatite. Man with Egyptian (horizontally hatched) robe and ovoid headdress—with pendent ribbons visible below shoulder—shooting with bow and arrow at bird over bull. L: 2.62. D: 1.18. AJA 42 (1938) 268, Fig. 10b; AJA 52 (1948) Pl. XI:55; *Enkomi-Alasia*, 94, Fig. 35.

19. E.g. *Corpus of Ancient Near Eastern Seals in North American Collections* I (henceforth *Corpus* I) (New York, 1948) No. 1072.

20. C. F. A. Schaeffer, *Enkomi-Alasia* (Paris, 1952) 88 ff. and Pls. VI–VIII.

Stamp Seals

At the end of the Bronze Age in Cyprus, in the LC IIIA period, to be precise, stamp seals began to replace cylinders on the island. The domed shape of these Cypriote stamps, which have an oval base and a large perforation through the narrow side and are usually of greenish gray or black steatite, is distinctive of Cyprus and not precisely paralleled elsewhere, although domical seals of a different shape appeared at about the same time at Palestinian sites.[21] Tabloid and truncated pyramidal forms had occurred earlier in Cyprus; one pyramidal seal stone was found in a tomb in Akaki in which nothing was later than 1300 B.C.[22] Perhaps B 1637, a small, truncated flattened pyramid, found on the surface and interpreted by the excavator as a piece of steatite cut for a dome-shaped seal, should be considered another pyramidal example. Pyramidal and tabloid seals, however, are very small in number and never approximated the popularity of the domed stamps of the LC III period. A few of the latter were made by the same engravers who had carved cylinder seals, but in the majority a new spirit made itself felt. Some are done with a care and naturalism in motif and execution not seen earlier,[23] others have a new and linear stylization of single figures like birds, still others have motifs for which few if any parallels can be found in cylinder seal designs; the last-mentioned type is usually very crudely executed.

An example of a domed stamp seal engraved in the style of cylinder seals is B 1631. The Egyptianizing figure of an archer flanked by two plants is placed vertically within the oval surface of the seal. Obviously the motif is an abbreviation of the entire scene of the cylinder B 1630, which must have been carved by the same engraver. Occasionally, this seal cutter, whose products Schaeffer assembled in a group (see above, note 20), seems to have also made stamp seals.[24]

Three domed stamps, B 1632 to B 1634, manifest a distinctive style in which a single figure, griffin, bird, or animal is placed horizontally within the oval sealing surface. The form of the figure is deeply hollowed out in the seal, and details are indicated by parallel linear hatching, often in different directions as in B 1633. The head of the griffin in B 1632 no longer has the circular shape distinguishing renderings of such monsters in Late Bronze Age cylinders like B 1623 to B 1625. Instead, the griffin has a head indicated by two lines which form an open

beak, and the eye is a pointed oval. The head could be easily thought of as an abbreviated rendering of the head of the griffin on the ivory mirror handle from Enkomi[25] to which the monster of the seal also corresponds in the heavy proportions, rather than to the lithe griffins with closed beaks of Late Bronze Age cylinders. The stylization of the wings, a roughly triangular shape marked with oblique hatching, differs from the typically Cypriote wing in Late Bronze Age cylinders which has the bones, corresponding to the humerus plus ulna of the arm, clearly divided off from the radial bars that indicate the feathers. Again, the shape of the wing (though not its interior marking) is comparable to the ivory from Enkomi. The stratigraphic date for B 1632 is LC IIIB; one hesitates, however, to place this stamp later than B 1633 and B 1634, the two stamp seals which seem to belong to the same group and which will now be discussed.

The first, B 1633, shows a bird with raised wing

21. M. Schaeffer presented a useful survey of conical seal types of Syria and Palestine in *Enkomi Alasia*, 79 ff. from which it follows that the domed Syrian examples preceding those of the Late Bronze Age of Cyprus are separated from the latter by more than one and a half millennia, since they date from about 3000 B.C. and earlier (cf. the seals *op. cit.*, 79, Fig. 29), except Nos. 4 and 8 (D. G. Hogarth, *Hittite Seals*, Oxford, 1920, Nos. 284 and 280) which are Iron Age and later than the Cypriote ones under consideration. Moreover, the Syrian seals are usually larger and not so strongly arched as the Cypriote pieces.
The Palestinian examples of domical shape are taller than those of Cyprus, have a circular base and a narrow perforation (see Schaeffer's examples, *op. cit.*, 82, Fig. 30).
It is conceivable that the special form of the domical stamp seals of Cyprus had been inspired by 'rock anchors', so called by H. Frost, "From Rope to Chain: On the Development of Anchors in the Mediterranean," *The Mariner's Mirror* 49/1 (Feb. 1963) 1 ff., especially pp. 8–9. Some such anchors appear to have been found at Enkomi, P. Dikaios, *Enkomi* IIIa, Pl. 150:1 (E.4039/1). Such a form might have been considered appropriate and propitious by seafaring Cypriotes.
22. Information kindly supplied by V. Karageorghis.
23. The finest example is the domed seal engraved with the head of a helmeted warrior perhaps found at Enkomi, cf. P. Dikaios in *RDAC*, 1937–1939, 202 s.v. Domed seal of black stone, Pl. XLIII, 1, also reproduced in Dikaios, *Enkomi* IIIb Pl. xxx.
24. A black steatite prism or tabloid found at Idalion, *SCE* II, Pl. CLXXXV:1323, in the same general style, is more cursorily engraved, as is a cylinder in the Ashmolean Collection, Buchanan, *op. cit.* in note 17 above, No. 986. Even in Schaeffer's group there are striking differences among the cylinders in the amount of care and detail accorded the figures. It is likely therefore that more than one seal cutter worked in this style on the island.
25. *ExC* Pl. II, 872[4].

145

and fan tail with interior horizontal, vertical, and oblique filling lines. Such a design is unknown in earlier seal carving, and it seems justifiable therefore to look elsewhere for its possible inspiration. The closest parallel seems to be furnished by a bird on a Late Minoan III alabastron from Phaistos.[26] It is interesting to note in this connection that Benson considered the possibility that his Long Beak Painter of several kraters from Enkomi, in what was formerly called by Furumark and others Rude Style, was a "transplanted Aegean, possibly a Minoan rather than a Mycenaean, who reflects in his work in a somewhat distant milieu the transition from LH IIIB to LH IIIC."[27] The stratigraphic date of LC IIIA for the stamp B 1633 would fit such a relation with the pottery very well.

Together with B 1633 was found a second seal of the same shape and gray paste, B 1634. Here the lines which appear on the neck and foreparts of the animal are more irregular than in B 1633 and do not cover the entire body; instead, they look like the naturalistic rendering of the long hair of a mountain sheep or goat. Were these two different seal designs made by the same man who experimented with different styles? This seems more likely than to assume that two seals which are so similar in shape and material were made by two different engravers.

The tendency toward naturalism noted in B 1634 is also found in B 1635, a domed seal of rock crystal engraved with two recumbent bulls. The motif of the seal closely resembles that of the gold seal ring with a vitreous paste bezel found in the Bronze Age cemetery of Kouklia, near Old Paphos.[28] Variation consists in the fact that the bulls of B 1635 have their heads turned toward each other—which is not the case in the seal ring—where, furthermore, a sign in the Cypriote script appears between the heads of the animals instead of a plant as in the Bamboula seal.

More striking is the difference in execution, which shows careful modeling in the ring but more schematic rendering with use of a fine drill in B 1635. It is possible that some of the schematic appearance was caused by the difficulty offered by the rock crystal of the Bamboula seal to the rendering of subtle linear and modeled detail.[29]

A close parallel for the motif of two seals from Bamboula and Kouklia is furnished by the panel of the two recumbent bulls on the gaming board from Enkomi,[30] dated in the LC III period and thus comtemporary with the seal from Bamboula. The repeated indication of relation between different crafts in Cyprus—seal engraving, ivory carving, and pottery painting—suggests that different craftsmen were concentrated in the same artisans' quarter. To this should be added the fact that stamp seal engravers were apparently creating a new repertory and were thus open to influences from other works of art. It is, of course, also possible that the gaming board and the stamp seals derived their inspiration from a large fresco or relief in one of the contemporary palaces or sanctuaries of Cyprus.

In contrast to the stamps just discussed, B 1636 has a design consisting merely of lines which may have been meant to represent a bull turned to the right, though a different creature may have been intended and even the direction in which it turns is uncertain. In the linear character of the design the seal manifests some Egyptian tendencies reminiscent of the cylinder and stamp seals B 1630 and B 1631, although the absence of linear markings in the body and the crudeness of the design makes such an assumption less likely.

Definitely Egyptian in inspiration are two scarabs, B 1638 and B 1639, each of which shows on the base a falcon-headed figure grasping a scepter or standard beyond which a *uraeus* snake rears up. In B 1639, a falcon-headed figure, standard, and *uraeus* seem to have merged into a continuous design, a stage probably datable in the Ramesside period on the basis of parallels in tombs of the XX Dynasty at Tell Fara (Beth-Pelet) in Palestine.[31]

The falcon-headed figure, Ra or Horus Harakhti' in Egypt, might have been easily acceptable to

---

26. *AJA* 42 (1938) Pl. XXVI:5.

27. *AJA* 65 (1961) 343.

28. *JHS* (1953) 133 and Pl. IV:b; also *ILN* (May 2, 1953) 711, Fig. 6. An article by V. E. G. Kenna, "The Kouklia Ring from Evreti," *BCH* 92 (1968) 157–167 seems to have been written in ignorance of the archaeological context and previous publications of the seal ring. Kenna's photographs appear to be the same as those published in *ILN*, a drawing added by him is imprecise.

29. Cylinder seals and gems of rock crystals have more schematic designs than seals carved in other material. E. g. a few examples from *Corpus I*: Nos. 201, 272, 278–281, 415, 522, 827, 836. These cylinders range from the Akkad to the Achaemenid periods. Only cylinders of the Early Kassite and Mitannian styles show little if any differentiation between cylinders of rock crystal and other hard stones favored by the craftsmen working in these two styles, in which the designs are usually schematic with a strong tendency toward geometric abstraction. For Mycenaean gems of rock crystal cf. A. Sakellariou, *Corpus der minoischen und mykenischen Siegel* I (Berlin, 1964) numbers cited on p. XXI s.v. Bergkristall.

30. *ExC* Pl. I.

31. Cf. O. Tufnell, *Lachish IV*, 109, 4th paragraph, No. 367, for comments on the stage of design in which the figure's limbs merge into a cobra. For references to the motif of falcon-headed gods cf. *ibid*. 103–104, for parallels from Beth-Pelet to which Miss Tufnell refers, cf. W. M. F. Petrie, *Beth-Pelet* I, Pl. XXXIII:362–366; P. Dikaios, *Enkomi IIIa* (E. 1437, E. 1591, E. 1261) Pl. 179:4–6, 180:4–6, 185:4–6.

Cypriotes, who seem to have considered a griffin-headed demon or a priest in griffin's mask carved on their cylinder seals[32] to be an effective deterrent to evil powers. A snake likewise seems to have played an important role in the religion and iconography of Cyprus.[33] The popularity of the motif of the scarabs B 1638 and B 1639 may therefore have been partly due to its association with specifically Cypriote concepts. At the same time, the appearance of these scarabs marks the increasing influence of Egyptian glyptic designs (already noted in the case of B 1630 and B 1631), which was to continue into the early first millennium B.C.

Differing radically from these Egyptianizing objects is the large terracotta stamp with a griffin, B 1640 (not reproduced in this volume), from an LC IIIA context. The only comparable object excavated on the island was a large stone seal with a bucranium and a sign in the Cypro-Minoan script, discovered in Late Bronze Age context in the Apliki miners' settlement and probably used for stamping copper ingots.[34] The Apliki stamp, however, is much larger than the Bamboula piece. A few seals of the latter shape and size, however, not obtained from regular excavations, are in the collection of the Cyprus Museum in Nicosia. Two of these could be of Late Bronze Age style, though, like B 1640, they are much larger than the usual seals of that period. According to V. Karageorghis, objects shaped like those under consideration are still used today by some of the women in the villages of Cyprus to decorate their cakes. The deep-cut carving of "seal" stones would indeed leave a better impression on dough than on all but the moistest clay. We may therefore provisionally consider B 1640 a stamp for cakes, presumably with some ritual significance, since the representation of the griffin stepping onto an object which suggests a sign in the Cypro-Minoan script[35] doubtless had some religious significance.

B 1631 (Mi 204; 49-12-297) T.19:29(C) LC IIIA. *Pl. 38k.* C-i. Domed with oval base; perforation through n. side. Gray-green steatite. Man with ovoid headdress and pendent ribbons, wearing hor. striped robe, pulling bow. Two plants on either side in lower field. H: 1.4. L (of base): 1.7. W: 1.5. **B 1632** (Mi 193; 19-12-276) T.19:4(F) LC IIIB. *Pl. 38l.* C-i. Shape and material like B 1631. Griffin standing before plant. H: 1.5. L (of base): 1.6. W: 1.5. **B 1633** (S 8) A-D:2(VII,2) LC IIIA. *Pl. 38m.* C-i. Shape like B 1631. Pale mottled gray paste. Bird with raised wing and fan tail before branch. Body of bird decorated by hatching in various directions. H: 1.6. L (of base): 2. W: 1.7. *AJA* 42 (1938) 268, Fig. 10:d. **B 1634** (S 9) A-D:2(VII,2) LC IIIA. *Pl. 38n.* C-i. Shape like B 1631. Gray paste. Horned animal standing before plant(?). Foreparts of animal decorated with lines suggesting mane. H: 1.5. L (of base): 1.3. W: 1.2. *AJA* 42 (1938) 268, Fig. 10:e. **B 1635** (Mi 118) T.16. *Pl. 38o.* C-i. Shape like B 1631. Clear rock crystal. Recumbent bull turning its head toward second bull whose head is turned toward first bull while foreparts point in opposite direction. Between them two leaf-like objects perhaps representing a tree. *UPMB* 8 No. 1 (1940) 14. **B 1636** (Mi 203; 49-12-296) T.19:28(C) LC IIIA. *Pl. 38p.* C-i. Shape like B 1631. Dk. gray-blue steatite. Linear design suggesting bull(?). H: 1.5. L (of base): 1.5. W: 1.1. **B 1637** (S 88) B-Surface. *Pl. 37.* C-i. Truncated flattish pyramid. Lt. gray-blue steatite. Neither pierced nor engraved. H: 1.7. L (of base): 1.8. W: 1.2. **B 1638** (Mi 116) T.16:4. *Pl. 38j.* Complete. Scarab. Sky-blue powdery paste reinforced with gelatine solution. Falcon-headed figure grasping standard beyond which is *uraeus.* H: 0.7. L (of base): 1.2. W: 0.8. **B 1639** (Mi 117) T.16:5. *Pl. 38q.* C-i. Scarab. Material like B 1638 but sl. darker. Falcon-headed figure grasping standard beyond which is *uraeus;* solid disk in sky. H: 0.8. L (of base): 1.2. W: 1. **B 1640** (S 3) A-D:2(VII,2) LC IIIA. Handle broken off. Stamp with square base and pierced lug handle. C: red-brown to brown, sl. bur. Winged griffin. PH: 3. (Square) base: 5. *AJA* 42 (1938) 268, Fig. 10:a; *ANE,* Pl. VIII:14 and Fig. 15.

32. E.g. *AJA* 52 (1948) Pl. IX:14, 22; L. Delaporte, *Catalogue des cylindres . . . de la Bibliothèque Nationale* (Paris, 1910) No. 477, L. Delaporte, *Catalogue des cylindres orientaux . . . Musée du Louvre* II (Paris, 1923) Pl. 106:20 (A. 1193); M. Ohnefalsch-Richter, *Kypros* (London, 1893) Pl. LXXXVII:9.

33. Cf. E. Sjöqvist, "Die Kultgeschichte eines cyprischen Temenos," *ArchRW* 30 (1933) 309–359, especially pp. 331 ff. Cf. also the Cypriote cylinder seal in the Louvre published by V. E. G. Kenna, *Syria* 44 (1967) p. 112, Fig. 1 (AO. 11992).

34. *AJ* 32 (1952) Pl. XXVI b, discussed by Miss J. duPlat Taylor on p. 163, s.v. seal. She noted the similarity to the piece from Bamboula and also mentioned related finds from Sinda. The latter have not been published with photographs.

35. Cf. J. F. Daniel, "Prolegomena to the Cypro-Minoan Script," *AJA* 45 (1941) 282:16 (S.2), a sign resembling a Latin F placed on the seal with the long bar parallel to the ground line and two short bars pointing upwards.

LATE BRONZE AGE CYPRIOTES FROM BAMBOULA: THE SKELETAL REMAINS[1]

by J. Lawrence Angel

In March (and early May) 1949 I studied remains of 61 people excavated from Late Bronze Age (mainly LC III) tombs numbers 2–21 in the Bamboula cemetery at Episkopi (ancient Kourion) by the late J. F. Daniel. In 1956 and 1958 I studied human bones from Tomb 40 (LC IIIa) excavated in 1956 by J. L. Benson, representing 20 people. Tomb E 1, outside the circuit wall in Trench 2, is Early Bronze Age but contained only unusable fragments of an adult female skeleton. Tomb 25 at Kaloriziki is Submycenaean in date and contained fragments of the skull of a child 6–7 years old. Tomb 4 dated 500–450 b.c. at Bamboula provided occipital regions, and other fragments, of two males about 28–35 years old as judged by the lambdoid suture. Two incomplete skeletons of people killed in an earthquake of about 370 b.c. represent a 23-year-old female perhaps type C or E with marked parietal bosses, small teeth (M_1 crown 10.0 x 10.4, M_2 9.0 x 10.1), a big nasal spine and slight alveolar prognathism; and a more fragmentary youth.

I studied also remains of eight adults and three children from Hellenistic tombs at Ayios Ermoyenis (Hagios Hermogenes) on the other side of Episkopi, near the sea, excavated by the late George H. McFadden; the most complete of these I describe briefly in Angel, 1955, p. 70. Bamboula Tomb 34, uncertain in date, contains a 25-year-old woman.

The present report centers on the Late Bronze Age material, part of which Hjortsjö and Axmacher published in 1959. Probably because of the death of the excavator in charge (Daniel), Hjortsjö makes mistakes. He describes his 17 skulls as being of *Middle* and Late Bronze Age date, excavated by *George McFadden* (not the excavator) at Kourion Bamboula on the *west* (correctly southwest) coast of Cyprus. Hjortsjö also overlooks the mending of the skulls and in fact describes each one as broken; it is possible that they were re-broken in shipping to Sweden, since four useful skulls are omitted and parts of others missing which I had used in 1949. The total material was in a very poor state to start with because of the destructive effect of chemical soil changes, as well as mechanical stirring of tombs by recurrent flooding and by repeated family funerals (cf. Fürst, 1933, pp. 6–11). The 21 skulls in restorable condition (Table 2) therefore often lack faces, and the lower jaw accompanies the skull only in one case.

Tombs 2–21 include 36 adult males, 19 adult females, 2 adolescents, 2 children, 2 infants; whereas tomb 40, dug by Benson, includes 4 male and 2 female adults, 2 adolescents and 9 children, with 3 infants. This lack of youngsters in the tombs dug in the 1940's may well reflect poor preservation, since the top numbers assigned to graves show that 100 skeletons were numbered: plausibly many of those not boxed for study were children. It is also probable that in the Bronze Age stillborn infants were often thrown away outside the tombs, since the Caskeys' very completely excavated Middle Bronze Age Lerna sample (N=230) from the Argolid (Angel, 1958) shows 35% infants and 21% children (plus adolescents). But Benson's carefully excavated Tomb 40 at Bamboula has more children than adults! Though this may be a sampling accident we will consider later another explanation.

The mean age at death of adults is 34.7 for 34 males and 30.9 for 16 females. This is one to four years younger than the Late Bronze Age means for Greece (39.3 for 164 males and 32.1 for 101 females) and suggests slightly less healthy living conditions in Kourion than in Attica, Argolis, and Pylos (Angel,

1. For the opportunity to stay at Episkopi and to study these and other anthropological data I am grateful to the University Museum and to its Director, Dr. Froelich Rainey, and owe particular thanks to the late Drs. Bert Hodge Hill, John Franklin Daniel, and George H. McFadden who were in charge of the Museum's expedition to Cyprus. I would also like to thank Dr. Porphyrios Dikaios, Director of the Cyprus Museum, and A. H. S. Megaw, then Director of Antiquities for Cyprus, for their interest. The trip was made possible by Fellowships from the John S. Guggenheim Foundation and from the Wenner-Gren Foundation; I express my deep thanks to these institutions and to the Jefferson Medical College and the late Dean George A. Bennett for leave of absence. The study of this material is facilitated by N. I. H. Grant A-224 and continuations.

1960). Dental health, however, is quite good: lesions average 2 per palate or jaw (1.7 loss, 0.3 abscesses, 0.1 caries, but with 14— instead of 16 alveolar spaces, and 6.8 teeth dropped out in the tomb and hence only 5.5 teeth remaining per jaw, causing underestimate of caries). Omitting 2 palates with only 3 and 5 spaces each (see Table 1) the sample is 14 adult palates and 3 jaws. Doubling the number of lesions to equate with the whole mouth gives 4 lesions for 28— spaces compared with 6.4 lesions for Late Bronze Age Greece (N=130) with 27+ spaces preserved.

Table 1, listing all the Late Bronze Age material, fragmentary and complete, gives data on cranial deformation, presence or absence of metopic suture, size of browridges and supramastoid crest, and morphological type for comparison with other series.

ARTIFICIAL DEFORMATION

This cultural trait, the practice of binding the head in infancy to change its shape, takes several forms. Over 30% of the Bamboula skulls are affected, without apparent restriction to any particular tomb group or family. And though two skulls (19:50, 19:31) tend toward occipital flattening, the typical Bamboula deformation is of the "Cypriote" type: pressure on the vertex behind bregma by a pad held by a bandage down to the nape of the neck (cf. Fürst, 1933, p. 49) affects the obelion arch of the parietals and slightly widens and lengthens the head. Fürst (1933) and Hjortsjö (1947) record this in 18 of 49 adult skulls from contemporary Enkomi in East Cyprus, but not at Melia (Ayios Jakovos) directly to the north in the coastal range, nor at Lapithos on the north coast until the transition to the Iron Age (Buxton, 1931). Buxton and Fürst state that this type of deformation occurs in one of six unpublished Late Minoan skulls of Hawes, and I note it in incipient form in *80 Myc.*, one of 13 skeletons from the fill above and in a well in the south room of the North Megaron of the Cyclopean Terrace Building at Mycenae excavated by Wace in 1952–53; all three restorable skulls (females) from this group would fit into our samples from Bamboula, Enkomi, or Melia. This type of deformation is plausibly a hallmark of Cypriote immigrants into Crete and Argolis. Fürst (1933, pp. 92–93) argues that this is not only Cypriote but probably invented at Enkomi as a local version of the "classical" annular binding to elongate a longish head. This latter occurs in two Enkomi skulls from a particular tomb (= family), Grave 10, in which occur several skulls of Basic White and Iranian type (conceivably foreigners). Head elon-

gation is well-known in Egypt in Nefertiti and her children and imitators, and earlier in Chalcolithic Byblos (Vallois, 1937).

A single massive male skull from latest Neolithic Erimi (Angel, 1953, 1962), just east of Kourion-Bamboula shows extensive obelion flattening (combined with postmortem parietal warping); so Cypriote type deformation may date from the fourth millennium. In any case, deforming the head with some type of flat surface and bandages is a striking custom of the pre-pottery Neolithic people at Khirokitia in the south-central hills, where artificial occipital flattening is extreme in some families (Rix and Buxton, 1938, Angel, 1953); its absence is striking in Neolithic Sotira (Angel, 1962) just north of Kourion, and in Neolithic to Middle Bronze Age skulls on the north coast (Buxton, 1920, Hjortsjö, 1947): apparently it was not attempted except in a short-headed group. Some occipital flattening recurs in 36 FCM at Melia among 31 skulls and in 36 FCE from Enkomi, among 49 skulls. Short heads are common here. Iron Age, Classical, and Roman skulls (Angel, 1955) show no deformation; but some living Cypriotes show occipital flattening: the custom must have survived. Thus the idea of deformation as a selective, family-choice, custom is five thousand years old in Cyprus. We cannot say with certainty, however, if the Cypriote type of deformation was invented at Enkomi, at Bamboula in the Late Bronze Age, or earlier.

One possible origin of these types of cranial deformation might be an exaggeration of attempts to correct manually the skull-moulding produced at birth by passage through the mother's pelvis. The nonuniformity of the custom, more striking at Enkomi than at Bamboula, certainly suggests differences in local tradition within the populations.

METOPIC SUTURE

This is one of the group of heritable traits found in excess at Neolithic Khirokitia, where it affects 17% of the sample of 71 (Angel, 1953). Retention of the metopic suture dividing the frontal bone occurs in 11% of 73 Late Bronze Age Cypriotes from Melia and Enkomi (Fürst, 1933, and Hjortsjö, 1947). This is normal for Europeans. But it is absent in 28 adult skulls from Bamboula.

BROWRIDGE SIZE

This also is a trait in which Neolithic Khirokitians, males, are peculiar, with 10% weak, 40% +, 50% ++, and 0 +++. Corresponding values for Bamboula are 15% weak, 35% +, 45% ++, 5% +++, not differing significantly from Khirokitia and apparently slightly below the usual European strength.

In this trait Neolithic Khirokitian males show 40% + and 60% ++; a sharp flange is typical, reflecting strength of lower posterior temporal muscle fibres in adjusting to the rather steep angle of chewing of this group. Figures for Bamboula are 55% +, 41% ++, 4% +++.

Although types give a misleading order to the relatively random association of genetic traits, they do express diverse directions of growth pattern and give a preliminary picture of a population's diversity.

Based on material from Greece (Angel, 1946, 1960) the following six type groupings fit the surrounding areas approximately. Type A (Basic White) is the tendency toward a long, rugged skull vault, gabled, sometimes angular, with strong browridges and a robust face of average height (sometimes low) with low orbits and thick nose; it predominates early in Mesopotamia, Palestine, Sicily, Sardinia, and the Atlantic coasts of Europe. Type B (Mediterranean) has a small, gracile, linear skull, paedomorphic, with small straight forehead and projecting occiput; the narrow, almost triangular face has high smooth-browed orbits, nose with weak spine, and slightly prognathous pinched mouth; it predominates in ancient Libya, later Sicily, and less strongly in Spain and Egypt and the Near East. Type C (Alpine) is short-headed, oval or sphenoid in shape, with bulging side walls and forehead and low, rather flat face of rounded hexagonal shape, small nose, strong chin; versions of this are typical in Cyprus (Neolithic to modern) and throughout Central Europe. Type D (Nordic-Iranian) has a long and high muscular but well-filled vault with deep occiput and high sloping forehead above a long rectangular-shaped face with deep chin and sloping mouth, salient nose, sloping orbits; this is a dominant trend in early Iran (cf. Hissar especially) and in Hallstatt, Reihengräber, and Anglo-Saxon cemeteries. Type E (Mixed Alpine) is a paedomorphic mesocrane type, massive, with flat lambda, inflated frontal region, and strongly orthognathous, low-mouthed, trapezoid face, with big nose root; it is characteristic among Romano-Etruscans, Franks, South Illyrians, Scyths, etc. Type F (Dinaric-Mediterranean) combines an almost short-headed byrsoid skull vault, short at the back, with pinched and sloping forehead above a big and high hexagonal face whose long thin nose continues the forehead profile and deep chin matches the sloping jaw; this occurs in Lower Egypt, marks Roman-Byzantine samples in the Levant, and especially in the Balkans; an exaggerated version of this tendency, *usually* artificially deformed, occurs in Armenia, later North Iran (cf. Sialk), and Anatolia as the Armenoid type.

Individual Descriptions: Undeformed Males

5-1 *CCB*, a male of about 25, is a broad and low-vaulted skull lacking the central base and lower face. It is ovoid rather than sphenoid in form, fairly small, rounded except for almost vertical medium lambdoid flattening and marked cerebellar fullness. The low forehead is slightly pinched, above low rectangular orbits and anteriorly projecting cheekbones. The face was not prognathous, and the alveolar fragment shows no teeth loss, but a single preserved incisor, with medium wear. This fits type C 5, the low-headed Eastern Alpine tendency of Cyprus and the central Aegean islands. *Pl. 68.*

5-2 *CCB* is a notably long ovoid and lowish skull, also without basi-occiput and most of the face, male, about 37 years old. The narrow, robust vault, *hausform* from the rear, has a projecting occiput and strong mastoids 29 mm. long. The forehead is pinched in above the strong browridges, deeply recessed nasion, and low, rectangular orbits. The face was not prognathous and the two teeth on the right maxilla are markedly worn; three teeth were lost in life with an abscess active at pm 2. The skull as a whole is closer to the typical Basic White (A 3) than to classic Mediterranean in tendency. *Pl. 69.*

19-3 *CCB* is a short and broken skull vault, male, about 28. The vault rises from a low and almost vertical forehead to a vertex placed far back and descends in a short occiput. Because of bulging parietal bosses and narrow base (bi-mastoid 121) and forehead, the skull is hayrick-shaped from behind and sphenoid-rhomboid from above. Around square orbits the forehead is pinched, cheek bones strong, and average nose root only slightly recessed. This is a high-skulled C 4 Eastern Alpine, having slight Dinaroid tendencies. *Pl. 68.*

19-27 *CCB*, a 27-year-old, small male skull lacking the lower jaw, is narrow ovoid in top view, angular in profile, with sloping forehead and prominent and deep occiput whose full cerebellar region and flat temporals make the rear view ellipsoid. The mastoids are strong (28 mm.). Strong but compressed cheekbones bound low rectangular orbits and suggest a rectangular face. The straight nose is thick-bridged and wide and the maxilla slightly prognathous. The relatively spacious palate shows 3 teeth lost and 10 others lost in life, with marked wear on the remaining one. This tends toward the long-faced version of Mediterranean (B 4) with Iranian (occiput, nose) and negroid (palate, nose) tendencies. The right jugular foramen is unusually large. *Pl. 67.*

19-30 *CCB* is the partial vault (right side) of a 24-year-old apparently male skull, narrow ovoid, not high, with almost vertical forehead, projecting occiput, and a few lambdoid Wormian bones: Mediterranean (B 4) tendency. *Pl. 67.*

19-34 *CCB* is a 33-year-old male skull lacking jaw and left temporal, relatively well-filled ovoid and with a round vault in rear view. Above strong browridges a capacious forehead leads to a long parietal region but rather short and blunt occiput. There are 6-7 lambdoid Wormian bones. The rather small, perhaps square face has ellipsoid orbits, a quite thick-bridged and wide nose, and a rather prognathous mouth with definite subnasal grooves. Three remaining teeth show marked wear; one is carious, and 7 teeth were lost in life from the 11 preserved alveolae. Basic White (A 4) and Eastern Alpine (C 5) tendencies combine in Mixed Alpine (E 3) intermediacy with negroid mouth traits. *Pl. 68.*

19-35 *CCB* is the complete skull of a 33-year-old male. The ovoid vault is smoothly curved throughout, high, with vertical forehead, almost flat temporals and a projecting and deep occiput which creates an ellipsoid rear view. Mastoids are long (32 mm.) with large retromastoid foramina for emissary veins on the left. The wide forehead dominates a small but rectangular face, compressed and light in mid-section, orthognathous, with projecting and bilateral chin. The ellipsoid orbits droop only slightly (8 degrees) on each side of a small nose. The small palate is parabolic with a small ridge-torus. The dentition has escaped disease except for traces of pyorrhea; excellent teeth show medium wear, with a 4-4-4 upper and 5-4-5 lower molar pattern, and an edge bite. This is a typical Mediterranean skull (B 4) with suggestion of Iranian tendencies in occiput and jaw ramus. *Pl. 67.*

19-42 *CCB* is a broad male skull of about 38, lacking jaw and central skull base. The byrsoid vault, rounded in rear view, is marked by strong browridges of continuous form (bi-orbital 94) on an extremely pinched and low sloping forehead, a high vertex placed far back, and a sharply curved occiput. Flaring out from the narrow forehead the face is either squat hexagonal or trapezoid (depending on the missing jowls) with high-rooted but broad nose, and orthognathous mouth region. The broad palate has two teeth, with marked wear, one abscessed, and eight spaces for lost teeth with one of these abscessed too. In consonance with the deteriorating dentition, both articular eminences show arthritic erosion. This approximates the European Alpine (C 1) type, but with Basic White (A 3) traits. *Pl. 68.*

19-43 *CCB* is a linear skull, male, about 30, lacking only the lower jaw. The byrsoid-pentagonoid vault, with pinched forehead, long and low parietals with fairly flat sides, has a projecting and sharply curved occiput and long mastoids (34 mm.). The rather small and prognathous, probably rectangular face, has rectangular orbits, a small and projecting nose, projecting mouth and tilted (10 degrees) and long elliptical palate. Teeth are perfect, with slight wear, a wrinkled 4-3+-3 molar cusp pattern, and probably a slight over-bite. This typical Mediterranean (B 2) skull has slight linear Basic White (A 1) and possible negroid features. *Pl. 67.*

Undeformed Females

19-41 *CCB* is a 42-year-old female skull with broken lower face. The long vault is angular (pentagonoid) in top and side view and a rounded hayrick from behind, with prominent and very sharply curved occiput. There are at least two lambdoid Wormian bones. The pharyngeal tubercle and angular spine of sphenoid are large, and articular eminence slope slight. Below browridges of medium strength the low nose root blends directly out of the forehead and separates notably high square orbits. The nose was probably thick and the face medium in height and orthognathous. Seven out of the 10 spaces preserved (left side) showed teeth lost in life; the two remaining teeth have medium wear. This combination of traits tends more in the direction of Basic White (A 3) than of other linear types (B 2 or D 3). *Pl. 69.*

21-1 *CCB* is a 20-year-old female skull with wisdom teeth still erupting. The high vault is angular (pentagonoid) in top and side view, and has a peculiarly deep occiput and ellipsoid rear view, with marked projection of occipital condyles and central skull base. Square orbits and thin nose mark the orthognathous, probably rectangular face. A perfect dentition shows a 4-3-3 molar cusp pattern. This fits Mediterranean (B 4) a little more closely than Iranian (D 4) or A 3. *Pl. 69.*

21-1a *CCB* is a female mandible, broken, with median chin, perhaps older than 21-1, and *apparently* belonging to another individual more lateral in form. The third molars are suppressed, no teeth are carious or lost in life, molar cusp numbers are 5-4-0, and wear is medium (slight on m 2s).

21-3 *CCB* lacks the right temporal region and mandible, and is a female about 27 years old. The high and long vault is rather angular (pentagonoid) in top and side view and has a hayrick shaped rear view with almost flat sides and deep and well-curved occiput. The face is orthognathous, possibly square, with rhomboid orbits and a projecting but very wide nose plus some alveolar prognathism. The relatively wide and high palate has perfect dentition and slight wear on the 4 remaining teeth (12 were lost in the ground). This skull tends in a Basic White (A 3) direction a little more than Iranian (D 3) with a trace of negroid appearance. *Pl. 69.*

DEFORMED SKULLS

5-3 *CCB* is a 29-year-old male with + degree of artificial deformation of Cypriote type—enough so that bregma is over 3 mm. higher than vertex at the usual point behind the ear holes when the skull is in the Frankfort (eye-ear) plane. The well-filled vault, almost ellipsoid with its wide forehead, has a projecting occiput exaggerated by the deformation: it would have been a little higher, narrower and shorter if undeformed. The short face has rhomboid orbits and a concave and unimpressive nose with wide root and narrow bridge. The horizontal palate (+ 2 degrees plane angle) has perfect dentition (4-3-3 molar cusps) with average wear except that the canines erupted too far lingually. The combination of traits suits the Mixed Alpine type (E 1). *Pl. 70.*

6-1 *CCB*, a 33-year-old male, has extreme Cypriote type deformation pushing the forehead forward as well as pinching the occiput. The vault probably would have been relatively angular and broad. Browridges are smallish but continuous (like Khirokitia). The wide and hyperorthognathous face has ellipsoid orbits, a wide nose with little depression at nasion, and a strongly tilted chewing plane (25 degrees), perhaps resulting from the deformation. The dentition appears perfect, though all but 3 teeth were lost post mortem in the ground. The femora, tibiae, radius and 4th and 5th lumbar vertebrae indicate a short-medium rather stocky man with sharp lumbar curve. The skull probably fits the Mixed Alpine type (E 3) trend better than Alpine (C 1). *Pl. 71.*

6-2 *CCB* is a huge and long skull with only slight deformation, lacking only the palate and central base, a male about 35. The long ellipsoid vault is well-filled, robust, with broad forehead, strong browridges and mastoids (36 mm.). The face, deep-chinned and perhaps square, has ellipsoid orbits and nose with high root. The dentition (lower jaw) is perfect but only 4 teeth remain (cusps 4-4-?, average in wear) after loss in the ground. Stature (167) is above average for the Bronze Age, the femur relatively slender and lumbar vertebrae arthritic. Feet are not large and show no "squatting" facets. The skull fits Basic White type A 3, tending in a Mixed Alpine (E 2) direction. *Pl. 70.*

18-1 *CCB* is the partial vault (right lower portion missing) of a 45-year-old male, large, long, ellipsoid, robust and only slightly deformed. The front two-thirds of the palate (10 spaces) shows loss of pm 2s and right i 2 in life, and + pyorrhea. Teeth wear (3 teeth) seems not great. This is Basic White (A 3) with E 1 tendencies.

18-5 *CCB* is a similar vault (incomplete on the lower left) of a 34-year-old male, large, fairly broad, apparently rhomboid and hayrick-like (rear view), quite robust, with high nose, and clear-cut deformation. This is Mixed Alpine (E 1) with A 5 tendencies. *Pl. 70.*

19-47 *CCB* is a wide skull lacking lower jaw, male, 37, with just above average deformation. The rounded vault was not high and had bulging sidewalls and very sharp supramastoid crests. The squat hexagonal face had low ellipsoid orbits and thin nose. It is very orthognathous with a tilted palate perhaps because of the deformation. Four teeth were lost in life and 6 after death (one abscessed) with 3 alveolar spaces also broken away. One of the 3 remaining teeth is carious and another abscessed; wear is marked. This is an Eastern Alpine skull, allowing for effects of deformation probably type C 5. *Pl. 71.*

19-50 *CCB*, a small male skull 33 years old, shows slight deformation, occipital as well as Cypriote. The short ovoid vault has rather small but continuous type browridges and strong supramastoid crests. The lower face had square orbits and a short nose. No teeth were

lost from the 5 alveolar spaces preserved. This fits an Alpine (C 2) classification. *Pl. 71.*

19-48 *CCB* is the skull of a young adult (*ca.* 25) apparently female, with pronounced Cypriote deformation, affecting middle parietals and bulging frontal especially. The vault was rounded with relatively long mastoids (26 mm.) and continuous type (small) browridges. The very orthognathous face was apparently long, with square orbits. The dentition (14 spaces left) is perfect with only slight teeth wear. The skull approximates the Dinaric-Mediterranean (F 2) tendency. The frontal bone is thickened. *Pl. 71.*

19-31 *CCB* from an adolescent, 15 or 16, probably male, has only slight deformation. The face is missing. The spheno-occipital synchondrosis shows no signs of fusing. The ovoid, high, and rather capacious vault has a full cerebellar region and projecting condyles. The vault fits Mixed Alpine type (E 3). *Pl. 70.*

40-1 *CCB* includes a tibia fragment and the incomplete and osteoporotic right side of the skull of a child four to five years old, since the mastoid is very small but the crowns of permanent upper incisors and first molar are fully formed. The skull seems to have been relatively long, with rather sloping and open-angled jaw—perhaps Basic White (A 3) or Iranian (D 4)—and slight Cypriote type deformation. The molar crowns, 10.1 x 11.1 mm. long and wide, show incipient Carabelli cusps. The tympanic plate is perforated. But the striking note (*Pl. 73*, top left) is the marked porotic hyperostosis (Hooton, 1930, pp. 316–319; Angel, 1964, 1966) and cribra orbitalia (Welcker, 1888). The hyperostosis of the diploë affects the parietals, above the left asterion and over the right parietal boss area where thickness is 3 to 5 mm. in contrast to 1 mm. general vault thickness; hyperostosis also affects the frontal bone on the orbit roofs (cribra orbitalia).

40-1a *CCB* is noteworthy only for the marked grooves extending radially out from the parietal bosses on *both* tables of an infant skull.

40-1b *CCB* includes unmeasurable fragments of robust femur, tibia, humerus and clavicle of an adult male (*Pl. 73*, lower left), left metatarsal I (59 mm. long; basal facet 16 x 28; shaft 12 a.-p. x 11 tr.), right metacarpals II and III (63 and 60 mm. long; with basal phalanx 39 mm.), and the body of the third cervical vertebra showing medium arthritic exostoses and measuring 16 x 27 mm. a.-p. and transverse, and 11 and 12 mm. for anterior and posterior heights. The petro-mastoid region of the right temporal bone shows a marked crest and suggests a short skull. The right cheek bone is rather slender, with very small marginal process and several foramina for the zygomatiofacial branch of the maxillary division of the trigeminal nerve: possibly the face was linear rather than broad with the skull approximating the Dinaric-Mediterranean (F 1). Probably the man was short and stocky.

40-1c *CCB* includes femur shaft and frontal bone of an older infant, the frontal showing deep markings for blood vessels.

40-2 *CCB* (*Pl. 73*, upper center) includes a left glabellar area and orbit rim showing flat forehead-nose transition and absent browridge; a right temporal bone with perforation of the tympanic plate and fairly small mastoid process (19 mm. high), and supramostoid crest below medium; a right occipital squama which is thin, rather weakly marked internally by the tentorium and right lateral venous dural sinus, and strikingly flat. The lambdoid suture is wide open. All together these pieces suggest female sex, late adolescent age, and a short skull, possibly Eastern Alpine (C 4) in tendency.

40-2a *CCB* is the right occipital squama of a male adult, with just enough of the lambdoid suture preserved to show ++ closure (*Pl. 73*, right side of uppermost center picture). The occipital crest is pronounced, and the squama rather flat transversely though with an average curvature in the sagittal plane, suggesting a wide skull without occipital protrusion. The lateral sinus marking is wide.

40-3 *CCB* (*Pls. 73*, right, and *74*, left) is the broken left skull and right skeleton of a child about 5 years old. The clavicle measures 74 mm. and is flatter than usual. The ulna is about 90-100 mm. long. The femur measures 156? without epiphyses; subtrochanteric a.-p. and tr. 12 x 16 and midshaft 13 x 12, hence normal platymeric and pilastric indices of 75.0 and 108.3; the gluteal crest and fossa are very slight, bowing is average, and there is a suggestion (*Pl. 73*, lower right) of the neck erosion area, produced by the zona orbicularis crossing in full extension, which is a feature of young prehistoric Greeks (Angel, 1959, 1964a). The tibial shaft has an oblique prism section and a.-p. and transverse diameters of 14 x 12: cnemic index 85.7. There are 3 or 4 significant lines of arrested growth at the ends of the shafts of tibia (*Pl. 74*, left middle) and femur at the knee, a region of rapid bone growth. These show repeated illness. The ribs are thickened. The long bones tend to show inner shells, almost like sequestra, underneath the outer compact shaft; this is clearest in the ulna shown in *Pl. 74*, left middle.

The skull fragments (*Pl. 74*, upper left) include a temporal bone with perforated tympanic plate and small mastoid (12 mm.), an occipital with relatively flat, wide squama and foramen magnum 23 x (30) mm., a wide frontal with almost flat browridges, parietal fragments, and an open-angled jaw; suggesting a fairly capacious Alpine type skull (perhaps C 3). Porotic hyperostosis on frontals and orbits (*Pl. 74*) is as striking as in 40-1 *CCB*, and in addition the greater wing of the sphenoid is greatly thickened: the frontal region is 8 mm. thick in contrast to 2–3 mm. for the rest of the vault.

Although childhood skull porosity alone might suggest Barlow's disease or infantile scurvy (Harris, 1933; Mellanby, 1950) from nutritional deficiency, the lack of remodelling of marrow cavities of long bones (persisting inner shells), inflation of skull diploë, and development of holes presumably from pressure of vascular tissue against the outer table of the skull vault are evidence of strikingly increased activity of bone marrow and suggest one of the hemolytic anemias (Caffey, 1937; Wintrobe, 1951, pp. 563-688; Moseley, 1965). Among these thalassemia and sicklemia are the obvious choices.

40-3a *CCB* comprises a strongly curved tibia and temporal and frontal fragments of a young child just beyond the age of metopic suture fusion.

40-3b *CCB* includes the incomplete and ununited left innominate bone of a male (?) just below the age of puberty (*Pl. 74*, center), and a left femur measuring 296 mm. without epiphyses. Subtrochanteric a.-p. and transverse diameters are 17 x 22, midshaft diameters 17 x 16 and lower breadth 54; platymeric and pilastric indices thus are 77.3 and 106.2, typical at this period; bowing is slight and muscle markings slight though with porosity at the areas of gastrocnemius origin (*Pl. 74*). The ischium and pubis respectively measure 60 and 50 mm. and the sciatic notch is medium in width, suggesting male sex perhaps. The auricular surface of the fragmentary ilium measures 24 x 36 mm. The right calcaneus measures 57 x 31 x 34 mm. in length x breadth x height and has separated facets on the sustentaculum tali and a strong lateral process at the heel (*Pl. 74*, bottom center).

40-3c *CCB* is a newborn infant skeleton shown in *Pl. 74*, upper right. The right femur is 73 mm. long and measures 8 x 8 and 6 x 6 in subtrochanteric and midshaft thicknesses; the right radius is 50 and the right ischium 20, quite comparable with Bronze Age newborn infants from Greece.

40-3d *CCB* is a right 5th metatarsal 65 mm. long (*Pl. 74*, upper extreme right).

40-4 *CCB* includes the occipital and fragmentary left side of a child of about 3. The occipital's condylar (exoccipital) and basal portions are unfused; the squama is sharply curved with constriction between cerebral and cerebellar portions: lambda-inion arc and chord are 64 and 57, with an 11 mm. arc height. Type B is suggested (*Pl. 74*, right) by this occiput.

40-5 *CCB* includes 195 mm. of a right femoral shaft with a.-p. and transverse diameters of 33 and 26 giving pilastric index of 126.9 suiting the big pilaster and + bowing. Left metatarsals 2-5 (shafts) and tibia fragments likewise suggest a robust (stocky?) adult male.

40-5a *CCB* is the left temporal bone (*Pl. 74*, right middle) and thin and non-muscular vault fragments of an adult, apparently female, of about 40. The average mastoid process projects 24 mm. below a very weak supramastoid crest and fairly high (?) squama (40 x 82 mm.) with little fullness. The articular eminence, low, projects only 4 mm. below the glenoid fossa and is 11 mm. long; there is a strong postglenoid process guarding the tympanic plate and elliptical meatus. The occiput shows only a trace of curve or crest and gives the impression of a short skull, perhaps Eastern Alpine.

40-6, 7, and 8 *CCB* are normal skull fragments of children respectively 4, 3, and 8 years old (*Pl. 74*, right lower). The left temporal (6) does show a definite tympanic plate perforation. The left maxilla shows milk teeth all in use and permanent M_1 erupted but lost *post mortem*.

40-9 *CCB* consists in parts of the right side of the skull vault of a young child with complete metopism. Browridges are absent. An occipital fragment with 10 belongs here.

40-10 *CCB* is the broken right lower extremity of an adolescent (girl?) in whom the middle and basal phalanges have epiphyses just ready to fuse with shafts. The femur shaft only measures 285 (suggesting bone length of 340 with neck and epiphyses): the girl was short. Subtrochanteric a.-p. and transverse 19 x 24 give a platymeric index of 79.2 and midshaft diameters 20 x 17 give high pilastric index of 117.65, with medium bowing and above average gluteal fossa. The tibia shaft (diameters 23 x 18 and cnemic index 78.3) is Type IV, rhomboid in section, with marked popliteal fossa for soleus origin: a fairly muscular extremity.

40-11 CCB includes right extremity bones (humerus, ulna, femur, tibia) and a left femur of a middle-aged male, fairly tall. 245 mm. of the humeral shaft (295 if complete??) show 22 x 16 diameters (72.7 index, rather flat), plano-convex section and very strong insertion for the deltoid muscle. The ulna fragment likewise has a strong crest for the interosseous membrane. Femora lacking lower ends and heads are 415 long (perhaps 450-460 complete?). Subtrochanteric a.-p. and transverse of 25 and 31 on both sides give platymeric indices of 80.6, and midshaft a.-p. and transverse left and right of 27+ x 27 and 29 x 26 give pilastric indices of 100 and 111.5. Bowing is average and the gluteal crest medium. There is little torsion. The right tibia is 364 mm. long (*Pl. 74*, lower right) allowing for breakage of the malleolus, suggesting 170 cm. as the upper limit of stature. The plateau measures about 73 mm. across and tilts at about 14°, a strong retroversion. The a.-p. and transverse of 35 x 26⁻ give a normal 74.3 cnemic index. Shaft shape is a laterally concave prism (II) and the popliteal crest is average. The long bones tend to be sinuous, with a lateral flange on the femur, but no excessive flattening. Body build was probably not slender.

Discussion

In terms of surrounding populations in time and space Tables 3 and 4 separate the Bamboula people as sharply from other Cypriotes as from contemporary mainland Greeks. Already late Neolithic Sotira and Erimi (in the Kourion area) differ sharply from Khirokitia (Angel, 1953, and 1961) in being more linear and in general more Mediterranean. Likewise the Neolithic through Middle Bronze populations near Lapithos on the north mountain-coast strip (Hjortsjö, 1947, Buxton, 1920) are Mediterranean with some Iranian traits, in contrast to the south-central (and central?) mountain region where the very early colonists at Khirokitia (Angel, 1953) are dominantly Eastern Alpine in type, and not especially small.

Transitional to the late Bronze Age, the northeastern site of Melia (Fürst, 1933) continues this south-central tradition except that with some reduction in skull and face breadths and increase in face linearity there is increased Dinaric-Mediterranean (F) frequency; Fürst (1933, pp. 65, 82) notes that Melia is dominated by material from one tomb (8) and relatively uniform. He errs, however, in using the specific term "Armenoid" to describe the central tendency here since the general face size and nasality of Eastern Alpine Cypriotes are much smaller than those specified by Bunak, von Eickstedt, Vallois and others for Armenoids. Enkomi (Fürst, 1933, pp. 28, 84–89) on the other hand, as a flourishing seaport had a quite heterogeneous population, only in part derived from a stock like that at Khirokitia; in particular, Grave 11 shows a family with Basic White and Iranian traits which Fürst correctly parallels with early Mesopotamian and Syrian long-heads; these could also be paralleled in Greece, especially in the pre-Greek stratum of population.

Bamboula at Kourion largely continues the Sotira-Erimi trend of linear dominance over a strong Alpine minority and differs significantly from Melia and Enkomi in four ways: the Bamboula skulls are narrower and lower, but also smaller and much widernosed. The obvious region to search for ethnic connections is Mycenaean Greece, partly because of the extension of the Arcadian dialect of Greek to Cyprus. Tables 3 and 4 show much similarity in form but a sharp difference in size and nose width. The obvious source for a gracile Mediterranean element with wide nose and some prognathism is Egypt and Libya. Perhaps such a link is involved also in the evolution at Enkomi and Bamboula of the "Cypriote" type of deformation. At the same time the Greek (Argolid?) similarities are not negligible. Plate 72 shows in 40 *Myc*, a male excavated by Tsountas, possible Egyptian-like linearity (narrow-nosed). In the three skulls excavated by Wace from the well in the south room of the North Megaron of the Cyclopean terrace building and shown here in Pl. 72 one can see similarity with Eastern Alpines from Melia and Enkomi and, as noted before, traces of "Cypriote" and occipital deformation; these are females and their presence suggests the possibility that the Mycenaeans used Cypriote slaves, perhaps in family groups (78 and 81 *Myc* are *very* similar). Bamboula may reflect both Greek and Egyptian mixture.

The porotic hyperostosis in tomb 40 is far more important than these questions of population mixture. Almost certainly two out of the nine children (and three infants) in this tomb died from thalassemia. This is an inherited anemia caused by an excessive fragility of red blood-cells, often with an excess of slightly abnormal hemoglobin A2 and excess of foetal (F) hemoglobin (Dacie, 1960, pp. 200–242; Kunkel & Wallenius, 1955). It depends on a recessive gene (or genes). A person inheriting two thalassemia genes, homozygous, therefore, has thalassemia major and will show a full-blown anemia, with splenic enlargement (Dacie, 1960; Neel, 1951, 1953), massive hypertrophy of bone marrow with osteoporotic and thin cortex (Caffey, 1937), recurrent crises and death usually in childhood. Inheritance of a single thalassemia gene, or thalassemia minor, usually produces no visible effect but is often recognizable from presence of abnormal hemoglobins. Heterozygotes occur in 5–50% of different populations in Italy, Greece, Cyprus, the eastern Mediterranean and in a fairly continuous belt via India to the Far East (Dacie, 1960; Neel, 1951, 1959). Sicklemia (hemoglobin S) is less damaging to the homozygote than is thalassemia usually, and to the heterozygote child offers equally good protection against falciparum malaria. It is a possible explanation for porotic hyperostosis in the Eastern Mediterranean since it does occur there today as well as in Western and Central Africa and eastward to Indonesia.

The puzzle is to explain these variable but high frequencies of a deleterious and semi-lethal gene. The usual explanation is that thalassemia, like sicklemia, in single dose gives the heterozygote (or "carrier") relative immunity from the malarial parasite (Carcassi, Cepellini and Pitzus, 1957; Cepellini, 1959; Lehmann, 1959). Hence in a region of endemic malaria the carriers of these harmful genes for hemoglobin defects have enough selective advantage over normal people so that the gene frequency (of thalassemia or sicklemia) may rise to 20%: more normal children die of malaria and more normal women lose infants than thalassemic carrier children or women. The exact frequency depends, however, on the balance of this advantage with the vital disadvantage of the lethal anemia from the gene in homozygous form (double dose). We describe such an evolutionary equilibrium as balanced polymorphism (Allison, 1955; Neel, 1958).

So far all our data on occurrence of thalassemia and much of our data on malaria are from contemporary observation: there is little historical depth, although Motulsky (1960), Haldane, and others have pointed out that a number of infectious diseases, including especially falciparum malaria, have pro-

duced evolutionary effects first through differential mortality and fertility and then through occurrence of balanced polymorphism. Bruce-Chwatt (1965) and Dunn (1965) have each developed further the hypothesis of P. C. C. Garnham and others that the protozoan parasites producing quartan (*Plasmodium malariae*) and tertian (*P. vivax*) malarias, and also *P. ovale*, developed in our Primate ancestors probably at the end of Eocene times, but after the splitting off of the Platyrrhine group of monkeys which got this malaria from African slaves only three centuries ago. There was then a long period, about fifty million years, for these three parasites to adjust to their Primate hosts so that they produce relatively mild symptoms. This is in striking contrast to *Plasmodium falciparum*, which is a new form, maladjusted like many fresh mutants, different enough so that some parasitologists make for it a new subgenus, *Laverania*. Its main new feature is that it attacks human red blood-cells in all developmental stages and almost immediately (without the other Plasmodia's sojourn in the liver), often kills, and is only checked strikingly when abnormal hemoglobin (such as S) makes the red-cell protein so viscous that the amoeboid plasmodium cannot engulf it. My observation (Angel, 1966) that almost half of the skulls from Early Neolithic Çatal Hüyük and Nea Nikomedeia have some degree of porotic hyperostosis, with 3–5 mm. extra thickness of marrow-filled diploë in many of them, has led me to the hypothesis that after the first appearance of the falciparum mutation in late Paleolithic times the Neolithic revolution set the real battle between man and *Plasmodium falciparum*. The immense increases in population, over 100-fold in the Near East, together with the ecological disturbances of farming (cf. Jones, 1909, Livingstone, 1958) would have promoted increases in local *Anopheles* populations wherever standing water was introduced or marshiness extended, and thus would have promoted the disease parasites which these vectors carried. Wiesenfeld (1967) has analyzed this interaction with mathematical models which suggest that sicklemia or thalassemia could reach high frequency in as short a time as 20 generations, and I think that a rapid increase of this sort is what explains the observed frequencies of porotic hyperostosis (though other anemias may have contributed to this also). Likewise this protection for children, allowing them to have time to develop an immunity to falciparum malaria, seems to have been what allowed the advances of later Neolithic and the Bronze Age. Then with improvement in farming and drainage of marshes and ponds there was a steady decrease in frequency of porotic hyperostosis and presumably of falciparum malaria (Angel, 1967), with sharp rise in Hellenistic times and later when malaria was reintroduced into Greece and the Aegean (Jones, 1909). Porotic hyperostosis is rare at Khirokitia (9% slight degree) probably because the immediate area is too rocky and steep to support anophelines.

The Bamboula porotic hyperostosis, therefore, has a double importance: it is highly probable that thalassemia and malaria have coexisted in several areas of Cyprus from Neolithic to modern times (cf. Banton, 1951), and it is equally probable that in Cyprus, as well as most of the Mediterranean, malaria has had a marked selective effect. The relative persistence of local types may depend to some extent on such selective pressures (cf. Angel, 1948) though the marked changes in frequency of porotic hyperostosis in Greece (Angel, 1960, 1966) as well as changes in population size and migration show that the evolutionary effect of malaria and other diseases, such as plague or amebiasis, is no constant one (Motulsky, 1960) because of the complex interrelations between the evolution and ecology of human and bacterial or viral populations.

SUMMARY

(1) The Late Bronze Age population of Kourion-Episkopi, excavated from the Bamboula chamber tombs by Daniel and by Benson, provides a much broken sample of 81, with average age at death of adults at 33 years rather than 36 found for mainland Greeks, and, in tomb 40, 12 children and infants out of 20 people represented.

(2) The occurrence of fully developed porotic hyperostosis, a symptom of thalassemia major, in at least two of the nine children from this tomb suggests that thalassemia was frequent in the Bronze Age, as in modern Cyprus, as a response to endemic malaria; in ancient as in recent times endemic disease put pressure on the population and the death rate of children was correspondingly high.

(3) In contrast with the original pre-ceramic Neolithic people of Khirokitia (very short-headed), the Bamboula population continues the later Neolithic pattern of Mediterranean dominance over Eastern Alpine in S. W. Cyprus (and North Cyprus) in significant contrast to the Eastern Alpine dominance at isolated Melia and cosmopolitan Enkomi in east Cyprus. There are indications in nose breadth, prognathism, and small size of African (Egyptian?)

links. Similarities with Mycenaean Greeks also occur; and certain skulls from a well in the citadel at Mycenae are plausibly those of a Cypriote family group, perhaps slaves. This is speculation.

(4) Data on body build are inadequate. Possibly the modal trend was muscular and stocky, without extreme flattening of long bone shafts.

(5) The Cypriote type of cranial deformation occurs at Bamboula in some families (about 25%) as also at Enkomi; a Neolithic origin for this form is possible; a link with annular deformation of Egypt is plausible. The still older (Khirokitia) custom of fronto-occipital deformation is very rare in the Late Bronze Age but recurs in 19th century Cyprus. Both types occur in the Mycenaean skulls of possible Cypriote origin.

(6) These data suggest that the movements of people and of family customs within and beyond Late Bronze Age Cypriote communities are complex, and cosmopolitan.

BIBLIOGRAPHY

Allison, A. C. 1955 Aspects of polymorphism in man. Cold Spring Harbor Symp. on Quant. Biol. *20:* 239–252.

Angel, J. Lawrence 1946 Social biology of Greek culture growth. Am. Anthropol. *48:* 493–533.

———— 1948 A Macedonian refuge area and stability of type. Am. J. Phys. Anthr. n.s. *6:* 242.

———— 1951 Troy, the human remains. Suppl. Monogr. 1, in C. W. Blegen, Troy. Excavations conducted by the University of Cincinnati 1932–1938. Princeton University Press, Princeton, N.J.

———— 1953 The human remains from Khirokitia. Appendix pp. 416–430 in P. Dikaios, Khirokitia. Oxford University Press, London.

———— 1954 Social biology in a Cypriote village. Am. J. Phys. Anthr. n.s. *12:* 298.

———— 1955 Roman tombs at Vasa: the skulls. Appendix III pp. 68–76 in J. DuP. Taylor, Roman tombs at Vasa. Report of the Dept. of Antiquities, Cyprus, 1940–48, Nicosia.

———— 1958 Human biological changes in ancient Greece, with special reference to Lerna. Yearbook Am. Phil. Soc. 1957: 266–270.

———— 1959 Early Helladic skulls from Aghios Kosmas. Appendix pp. 167–169 in George E. Mylonas, Aghios Kosmas. Princeton University Press, Princeton, N.J.

———— 1960 Physical and psychological factors in culture growth. Selected papers of the Fifth Internat. Congr. of Anthr. and Ethnol. Sciences, Philadelphia, Sept. 1–9, 1956: 666–670. ed. A. F. C. Wallace, University of Pennsylvania Press, Philadelphia.

———— 1961 Neolithic crania from Sotira. Appendix 1 pp. 223–229 in P. Dikaics, Sotira. The University Museum, Philadelphia, Pa.

———— 1964 Osteoporosis: thalassemia? Am. J. Phys. Anthr. n.s. 22: 369–374.

———— 1964a The reaction area of the femoral neck. Clinical Orthopaedics 32: 130–142.

———— 1966 Porotic hyperostosis, anemias, malarias and marshes in the prehistoric Eastern Mediterranean. Science 153: 760–763 (August 12).

———— 1967 Porotic hyperostosis or osteoporosis symmetrica. Ch. 29 pp. 378–389 in Don Brothwell and A. T. Sandison, eds., Diseases in antiquity. C. C Thomas, Springfield, Ill.

———— 1968 Ecological aspects of palaeodemography. pp. 263–270 in Don R. Brothwell, ed. The skeletal biology of earlier human populations. Symp. for the study of human biology VIII. Pergamon Press, Oxford, England.

Axmacher, B. and C.-H. Hjortsjö 1959 Examen anthropologique des crânes constituant le matériel protohistorique exhumé à Bamboula, Kourion, Chypre. Lunds Universitets Arsskrift N.F. Avd. 2, Bd. 55, Nr. 2.

Baker, J. R. 1965 The evolution of parasitic Protozoa. pp. 1–27 in A. E. R. Taylor, ed., Evolution of Parasites. 3rd symp. Prit. Soc. for Parasitology. Blackwell.

Banton, Arnold H. 1951 A genetic study of Mediterranean anemia in Cyprus. Am. J. of Human Genetics 3: 47–64.

Bruce-Chwatt, L. J. 1965 Paleogenesis and paleoepidemiology of Primate malaria. Bull. World Health Org. 32: 363–387.

Buxton, L. H. D. 1920 The anthropology of Cyprus. J. Roy. Anthr. Inst. 50: 183–285.

———— 1931 Künstlich deformierte Schädel von Cypern. Anthr. Anzeiger 7: 236–240.

Caffey, John 1937 The skeletal changes in the chronic hemolytic anemias. Am. J. Roentgenol. and Radium Therapy 37: 293–324.

Carcassi, V., R. Cepellini, and F. Pitzus 1958 Frequenza della talassemia in quatre popolazioni Sarde e suoi rapporti con la distribuzione dei gruppi sanguigni e della malaria. Boll. Inst. Sieroter, Milan 38: 206–218.

Cepellini, R. 1959 Blood groups and haematological data as a source of ethnic information. pp. 177–188 in C. E. W. Wolstenholme and C. M. O'Connor, eds., Medical Biology and Etruscan origins. Ciba Foundtn. Symp. Little Brown & Co., Boston.

Chini, V., and C. M. Valeri 1949 Mediterranean hemopathic syndromes. Blood 4: 989–1013.

Dacie, J. V. 1960 The hemolytic anemias. Part I. The congenital anemias. 2nd ed. Grune & Stratton, New York.

Dikaios, P. 1947 A guide to the Cyprus Museum. Dept. of Antiquities Govt. Printing Office, Nicosia, Cyprus.

———— 1953 Khirokitia. Final report on the excavation of a Neolithic settlement in Cyprus on behalf of the department of Antiquities, 1936–46. Oxford University Press, London.

Dunn, Frederick L. 1965 On the antiquity of malaria in the western hemisphere. Human Biol. 37: 385–393.

Fürst, Carl M. 1933 Zur Kenntnis der Anthropologie der prähistorischen Bevölkerung der Insel Cypern. Lunds Univ. Arsskrift N.F. Avd. 2, Bd. 29, Nr. 6:

Guest, E. M. 1938 The human remains. pp. 58–62 in P. Dikaios, The excavations of Erimi, 1933–1935. Report of the Dept. of Antiquities, Cyprus, Part I, Nicosia.

Harris, H. A. 1933 Bone growth in health and disease. Oxford University Press, London.

Hjortsjö, Carl-Herman 1947 To the knowledge of the prehistoric craniology of Cyprus. Särtryck ur Kungl. Hum. Vetenskapssamfundet i Lund, Arsberattelse 1946–47, Lund.

Jones, W. H. S. 1909 Malaria and Greek history. Univ. Manchester Publ. XLIII, University Press, Manchester, England.

Kunkel, H. C., and G. Wallenius 1955 New hemoglobins in normal adult blood. Science 122: 288.

Lehmann, H. 1959 The maintenance of the hemoglobinopathies at high frequency. In J. H. P. Jonxis and J. F. Delafresnaye, eds., Abnormal hemoglobins. Blackwell, Oxford.

Livingstone, Frank B. 1958 Anthropological implications of sickle cell gene distribution in West Africa. Am. Anthropologist 60: 533–562.

Mellanby, Sir Edward 1950 A story of nutritional research. The effects of some dietary factors on bones and the nervous system. Abraham Flexner Lectures No. 9. Williams & Wilkins, Baltimore, Md.

Moseley, John E. 1965 The paleopathologic riddle of "symmetrical osteoporosis." Am. J. Roentgenol., Radium Therapy & Nuclear Med. 95: 135–142.

Motulsky, Arno G. 1960 Metabolic polymorphisms and the role of infectious diseases in human evolution. Human Biology 32: 28–62.

Moulder, James W. 1962 The biochemistry of intracellular parasitism. University of Chicago Press, Chicago, Ill.

Neel, James V. 1953 Haemopoietic system. Ch. 24, pp. 446–475, in Arnold Sorsby, ed., Clinical genetics. Butterworth, London.

———— 1951 The population genetics of two inherited blood dyscrasias in man. Cold Spring Harbor Symp. on Quant. Biol. 15: 141–158.

———— 1958 The study of natural selection in primitive and civilized human populations. Human Biology 30: 43–72.

———— 1959 Genetic aspects of abnormal hemoglobins. In J. H. P. Jonxis and J. F. Delafresnaye, eds., Abnormal hemoglobins. Blackwell, Oxford.

Rix, M. M., and L. H. D. Buxton 1938 The anthropology of prehistoric Cyprus. Man 38: 91–92.

Rix, Michael M. 1950 Cranial measurements. Appendix 6 in Stewart, Eleanor and James, Vounous 1937–38. Skrifter utgivna av Svenska Inst. i. Rom, XIV. Gleerup, Lund.

Vallois, Henri V. 1939 Les ossements humains de Sialk. pp. 113–142 in R. Ghirshman, Fouilles de Sialk 1933, 1934, 1937. II (Louvre, Dept. Antiqu. Orient. Serie Arch. V), Paris.

Welcker, Hermann. 1888 Cribra Orbitalia. Ein ethnologisch-diagnostisches Merkmal am Schädel mehrerer Menschenrassen. Archiv für Anthrop. *17:* 1–18.

Wiesenfeld, Stephen L. 1967 Sickle-cell trait in human biological and cultural evolution. Science *157:* 1134–1140 (Sept. 8).

Wintrobe, M. W. 1951 Clinical hematology, 3rd ed. Lea & Febiger, Philadelphia.

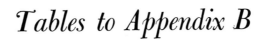

Tables to Appendix B

TABLE 1. Late Bronze Age—Bamboula

Tomb: Skull	Parts Preserved (lower jaw absent unless noted)	Estimated Age	Sex	Type	"Cypriote" Deformation	Metopism	Brow-ridges	Supra-mastoid Crest	Pathology and/or Remarks
2:1	Skeleton fragments	37??	F.	?	Abs?	?	?	?	Unrestorable
2:3	Face & occiput frag.	40?	M??	F?	Abs?	?	?	++	Long-faced? (delicate)
2:4	Frontal & frags. skeleton	30?	F??	?	?	?	+	?	Long-bones appeared Male
2:5	Fragments	Adult	P?F?	?	?	?	?	?	No skull
2:6	Skeletal fragments	Adult	M.	?	?	?	?	?	No skull
3:1	Partial skullcap	40?	M?	C?	Abs.	Abs.	?	+	
3:3	Occiput, parietals	25?	F.	?	?	?	?	?	
3:4	Frontal, broken	45?	M.	C?	Abs.	Abs.	+	?	
3:5	Broken skullcap	30?	M?	C?	Abs.	Abs.	?	?	Broad forehead
5:1	Skull; incompl. face	25	M.	C5	Abs.	Abs.	+	+	Male pelvis; narrow tibia: 52.8; stature 162.4
5:1a	Tibia	Adult	M.						Stature 167.3
5:2	Skull; broken face	37	M.	A3	Abs.	Abs.	++	++	3 of 8 teeth lost; 1 abscess
5:3	Skull; face	29	M.	E1	+	Abs.	++	++	0 dental lesions; Cs lingual in position
6:1a	Leg, forearm, clavicle	Adult	M.						Narrow tibia: 63.4; stature (170.9)
6:1	Skull; face	33	M?	E3	++	Abs.	sm.	+	0 dental lesions; stature (162.6)
6:1b	Tibia & forearm	Adult	F.	?					Stature (158.6)
6:2	Skull; jaw, broken face	35	M.	A3	Sl.	Abs.	++	++	0 dental lesions (jaw only); arthritis = +; stature 166.8
6:2a	Arm	Adult	F.						Stature (155.4)
12:3	Frontal & fragments	30?	M.	?	?	Abs.	+++	??	
12:5	Broken skullcap	30?	F.	?	Abs.	?	?	?	
12:6	Broken skullcap	30??	M?	C?	Abs.	Abs.	?	?	
12:9	Maxilla	45?	M.						
12:10	Occiput & temporal	25	F.						
12:11	Occiput & temporal	36??	M.					++	
12:12	Temporal	Adult	M.					++	
12:15	Fragments	Adults(?)	M. and F.						
16:1	Fragments	30?	F?	E??	?	Abs.	++-	+?	
16:2	Rt. side skull, broken	40	M.	E??	?	Abs.	++	++	
16:3	Fragments	Adult	P?F?	?	Sl.	?	?	sl.	
16:4	Fragments	Adult	M?	?	?	?	+	+	
18:1	Skull, fragmentary face	45	M.	A3	Sl.	Abs.	++	++	3 of 10 teeth lost
18:2	Skull, fragmentary	30??	F.	?	?	?	?	sl.	
18:3	Occiput fragments	40?	M.	?	?	?	?	+	
18:4	Fragments	12	?	?	?	?	?	?	Older child
18:5	Skull, lacking face	34	M.	E1	+	Abs.	++	++	
18:6	Occiput & temporal	34	M.	C?	Abs.	?	?	++	
18:7	Occiput	30	M.	?	+??	Abs.	?	?	
19:1	Broken skullcap	33	F.	?	Abs.	Abs.	+	+	
19:3	Skull, lacking face	28	M.	C4	Abs.	Abs.	?	?	
19:6	Skeleton, fragments	0	?	?	?	?	?	?	Newborn? infant
19:7	Skull fragments	2½	?	?	?	?	?	?	Young child
19:8	Fragments	3½	?	?	?	?	?	?	Young child

No.	Specimen	Age	Sex						Remarks
19:18	Skull, broken	1–	?	?	(++)	?	?	?	10-month infant
19:27	Skull	27	M.	B4	Abs.	Abs.	++	++	3 of 14 teeth lost; large rt. jugular foramen
19:30	Skullcap, right	24	M.	B4	Abs.	Abs.	++	++	
19:31	Skull, lacking face	ca. 15	M??	E3	Sl.	Abs.	sm.	+–	Adolescent; spheno-occ. syn. open
19:32	Occiput & parietal	38	F.	C	Abs.	Abs.	sm–	?	
19:34	Skull	33	M.	E3	Abs.	Abs.	++	+	1 lost, 1 carious of 11 spaces
19:35	Skull with jaw	33	M.	B4	Abs.	Abs.	++	++	0 dental lesions of 32 spaces
19:41	Skull, face broken	42	F.	A3	Abs.	Abs.	++	++	7 lost of 10 tooth-spaces
19:42	Skull	38	M.	C1	Abs.	Abs.	++	+++	8 lost, 2 abscesses (9 lesions), 15 spaces; + arthr. of artic. eminences
19:43	Skull	30–	M.	B2	Abs.	Abs.	++	++	0 lesions of 16 spaces
19:47	Skull	37	M.	C5	++	++	++	+++	(7 lesions of 13 spaces); 4 lost, 1 carious, 2 abscesses
19:48	Skull	25	F?	F2	++–	sm.	sm.	++	0 lesions of 14 spaces; frontal thickening
19:50	Skull	33	M.	C2	sl–	sm.	sm.	+	0 lesions of 5 spaces
21:1	Skull	20	F.	B4	Abs.	sm.	sm.	+–	0 lesions of 16 spaces
21:1a	Jaw	25??	F?	(C or E?)	Abs??	?	?	++–	0 lesions of 14 spaces; M3s suppressed
21:2	Occiput, broken	28	M.	B?	Abs?	?	Abs.	+–	
21:3	Skull, lacks rt. temp.	27	F?	A3	Abs?	?	sm+	+–	
21:4	Skull base, face, broken	36?	M.	C?	Abs??	?	?	sm.	0 lesions of 16 spaces
40:1	Rt. temporal, frontal, face, parietals, tibia	4+	(M)	A3	?	?	sl–	sm.	++ porotic hyperostosis; tymp. pl. perforated; Carabelli cusp trace
40:1a	Skull fragts.	< 6 mos.	?		?	?			+ raying around par. boss, inside & out
40:1b	Ft. malar—skel. fragts., 3 metacarps, 3rd cerv. vert.							++	Rel. powerful, robust; sl. arthr.
40:1c	Frontal bone, femur	40+	M.	C??	?	?	?		Deep vessel markings
40:2	Rt. temporal, l. orbit rim	1 yr?	?	C4	?		?	+	Tymp. pl. perforated; occ. rel. flat
40:2a	Rt. occipital	14+	F.	C4?	Abs?	Abs?	Abs.	+	Occ. crest = ++; temp. of 1b does not connect; no proof if same person
40:3	L. side skull, broken, rt. clavicle, ulna, femur, tibia, ribs	5	M.	C3	Abs.	Abs?	Trace	sl.	++ porotic hyperostosis; arrested growth lines; long bones have inner shells
40:3a	Temporal, frontal frag, curved tibia	3–	M?				Abs.		Tibia curved
40:3b	L. femur & hip, rt. calcaneus	11	F??						Normal
40:3c	Rt. side skeleton & jaw	birth	M?						Normal
40:3d	Rt. metatarsal V. lgth. = 65	0	F??						No proof if part of 5a
40:4	Frags. of parietal, occip., temporal	ca. 30	F??	B			sm.		Occip. condyles not fused (exoccipital); occ. curve = ++
40:5	Rt. femur 420?? tibia fragts., L. metatarsals 2–5	ca. 3	F???						Stocky? stature (161); + bowing; ++ pilaster
40:5a	Vault frgts. = Thin, temporal	ca. 33	M.	C4	Abs.		Abs.	v. sm.	Occ. curve trace; tymp. plate intact; normal
40:6	L. temporal, rt. brow ridge	40?	F.		Abs.	Abs.		Trace	Tymp. plate perforated; normal
40:7	Skull fragts.	4–	F???						
40:8	Frags. L. maxilla	3+	?						Milk teeth erupted; normal
40:9	Frags. of vault, esp. rt. frontal	8	M.		Compl. Abs.				
40:10a	Occip. fragt.	2–	?				Abs.		
40:10	Rt. femur, tibia, phalanges	14+	F?						Guess stature 138; normal
40:11	Rt. humerus & tibia, pair femora	45	M.						Long bones "sinuous," stocky, muscular; stature 168; normal

TABLE 2. Individual measurements and indices

Skull	UNDEFORMED MALES									UNDEFORMED FEMALES AND CHILDREN					
Number	CCB 5-1	CCB 5-2	CCB 19-3	CCB 19-27	CCB 19-30	CCB 19-34	CCB 19-35	CCB 19-42	CCB 19-43	CCB 19-41	CCB 21-1	CCB 21-1a*	CCB 21-3	CCB 40-1	CCB 40-3
Sex	M.	M.	M.	M.	M.	M.	M.	M.	M.	F.	F.	F.	F.	M.?	M.?
Age	25	37	28	27	24	33	33	38	30	42	20	(25)	27	4+	5–
Horizontal Circumference	501??	510	502	494	(516)	507	512	513	502	491	492	—	508	—	—
Sagittal arc	363	368	(370)	360	(380)	371	377	358	365	346	353?	—	368	—	—
Frontal arc	128	129	114	120	(130)	122	130	117	120	122	117	—	127	—	(110)
Parietal arc	127	126	126	129	(138)	130	134	123	125	118	119	—	126	—	—
Skull lgth. (glab.-occ.)	174	185	172	179	183?	180	182	183	185	174	173	—	182	—	—
Height (basion-bregma)	(125)	(125)	(127)	133	(135)	131??	140	(133)	130	122	137	—	138	—	—
Height (auric.-vertex)	105	112?	114?	116	(111)	106+?	118	119	110	106	110	—	119	—	—
Base lgth. (bas.-nas.)	(86)	(102)	(98)	104	95	94	105	(110)	101	93	101–?	—	103	—	—
Skull breadth	142	126	146	133	136??	141?	137	146	134	132	130	—	137	—	—
Minimum frontal br.	94	91	(92)	94	97??	96	102	86	86+	94	92	—	95	23	24
Cheek br. (bizygomatic)	121??	(124)	(128)	126	—	128??	124+??	132+?	121+?	124	125+?	(90)	(122)	—	14—
Jowl br. (bigonial)	—	—	—	—	—	—	96	—	—	—	—	—	—	—	—
Jaw br. (bicondylar)	—	—	—	—	—	—	109	—	—	—	—	(118)	—	—	—
Face height (nas.-menton)	—	—	—	—	—	—	111	—	—	(50)	(108)*	—	—	—	—
Upper face ht.	(69)	(67)	—	72?	—	66	65	65??	66??	(69)	65	—	64+	21 corp	20 corpus
Chin height	—	—	—	—	—	—	32	—	—	—	—	30	—	21 corp	20 corpus
Jaw lgth. (condyle-chin)	—	—	—	—	—	—	102	—	—	—	—	—	—	—	—
Minimus ramus breadth	—	—	—	—	—	—	34	—	—	—	—	—	—	23	24
Jaw corpus thickness (M1)	—	—	—	—	—	—	15	—	—	24	14	14	—	14	14—
Nose height	(49)	—	—	53	—	48	48	53	44	(50)	46	—	45+	—	—
Nose breadth	(21)	—	—	32	—	36	23+	29	22	(25)	20	—	28	—	—
Interorbital br. (dacr.)	21	(22)	(22)	23	—	(25)	23	21	19	24	19	—	23?	—	—
Orbit breadth (left)	36	41??	37r	37	—	40r	37	39	38	35	39	—	40?	—	—
Orbit height (left)	29	31	31r	31	—	30r	31	33	31	35	34+	—	33	—	—
Alveolar lgth. (ext. palate)	—	—	—	58?	—	(58)	54	54	58??	(47)	52?	—	51	—	—
Alveolar breadth	—	—	—	66	—	(62)	58	63??	62	(60)	59	—	68	—	—
Parietal thickness	5	4	4+	6	4	6	6	5+	5–	5+	4	—	3+	1-5*	2-8*
Face profile angle	—	—	—	84?	—	74??	86	89	79??	—	81	—	83	—	—
Jaw angle	—	—	—	—	—	—	127	—	—	—	—	14	—	140	142
Cranial (lgth.-br.) index	81.61	68.11	84.88	74.30	74.32?	78.33	75.27	79.78	72.43	75.86	75.14	—	75.29	—	(over 80??)
Mean auric. ht. index	66.45	72.02	71.70	74.36	—	66.04	74.61	72.34	69.59	69.28	72.61	—	74.60	—	—
Fronto-parietal index	66.20	72.22	—	70.68	71.32?	68.08	74.45	58.90	64.18	71.21	70.77	—	69.34	—	—
Cranio-facial index	85.21	—	—	94.74	—	90.78	90.51	90.41	90.30	93.94	96.15	(89.05)	—	—	—
Upper facial index	(57.02)	—	—	57.14	—	51.56?	52.42	49.24	54.54	(55.64)	52.00	52.46	—	—	—
Nasal index	(42.86)	—	—	60.38	—	54.17	47.92	54.72	50.50	(50.00)	43.48	62.22	—	—	—
Type	C5	A3	F2	B4	B4	E3	B4	C1	B1	A-3	B4	(C or E?)	A-3	—	(C-3)
Numbers used by Axmacher and Hjortsjö (1959)	II	I	V	VI	VII	IX	omitted	XI	XV	X	XIV	—	omitted	—	—

Deformed Males, Females, and Adolescents

Skull	CCB 5-3	CCB 6-1	CCB 6-2	CCB 18-1	CCB 18-5	CCB 19-47	CCB 19-50	CCB 19-48	CCB 19-31	Martin	Biometric
Sex	M.	MP	M.	M.	M.	M.	M.	F.	M?P		
Age	29	33	35	45	34	37	33	25	15?		
Horizontal Circumference	533	512	555	535?P	535?P	532	499	503	519	23a	U
Sagittal arc	(369)	(356)	388	(378)	365	350—	352	342	(377)	25	S
Frontal arc	118	130	128	127	119	116	118	124	136	26	S_1
Parietal arc	130	106	133	125	115	119+	120	113	127	27	S_2
Skull lgth. (glab-occ.)	184	176	195	189	184	184	170	171	185?P	1	L
Height (basion-bregma)	126+	137	136?P	(129)	(134)	134	128?P	(129)	140	17	H'
Height (auric.-vertex)	110	113	120	(119)	(117)	110	110	114	119	(21)	(OH)
Base lgth. (bas.-nas.)	97	97	(103)	—	(104)	103	83?P	(101)	(102)	5	LB
Skull breadth	148	148	150	142?P	146?P	153	146	147	144	8	B
Minimum frontal br.	99	97	106	96?P	(97)	99	94	98	98	9	B'
Cheek br. (bizygomatic)	132	126	130?	—	—	139	135+?P	121?P	(124)?P	45	J
Jowl br. (bigonial)	—	—	(100)	—	—	—	—	—	—	66	w_2
Jaw br. (bicondylar)	—	—	—	—	—	—	—	—	—	65	w_2
Face height (nas.-menton)	64	—	—	—	—	—	—	—	—	47	GH
Upper face ht.	—	69	—	—	—	67	67	69	—	48	G'H
Chin height	—	—	37	—	—	—	—	—	—	69	h'
Jaw lgth. (condyle-chin)	—	—	—	—	—	—	—	—	—	68(1)	ml
Minimus ramus breadth	—	—	—	—	—	—	—	—	—	71a	rb'
Jaw corpus thickness (M1)	—	—	16	—	—	—	—	—	—	—	—
Nose height	48	49	48	—	—	50	45	50	—	55	NH
Nose breadth	26	27	(25)?	—	—	22	(23)	24	—	54	NB
Interorbital br. (dacr.)	23	(21)	25?P	(24)	23	19—	24	(21)	—	49a	DC
Orbit breadth (left)	41	38	38	—	—	38?P	37	35?	(35)r	51a	O₁'L
Orbit height (left)	29	34	33	—	—	29	34	32	(34)r	52	O₂'L
Alveolar lgth. (ext. palate)	54	54?P	—	—	—	47?P	(49)	(54)	—	60	G'ₗ
Alveolar breadth	63	61	—	—	—	60?P	(56)	(60)	—	61	EB
Parietal thickness	7—	6	5+	5	—	6—	5—	7—	5—	—	—
Face profile angle	85	95?P	—	—	—	(91)	(85)	89	—	72	PL
Jaw angle	—	—	—	—	—	—	—	—	—	79	mL
Cranial (lgth.-br.) index	80.43	84.09	76.92	75.13?	79.35?P	83.15	85.88	85.96	77.84	B/L	8 × 100/1
Mean auric. ht. index	66.26	69.75	69.56	(71.90)	—	65.28	69.62	71.70	72.34	2OH/L + B	(21) × 200/1 + 8
Fronto-parietal index	66.89	65.54	70.67	67.60?P	—	64.70	64.38	66.67	68.06	B'/B	9 × 100/8
Cranio-facial index	89.19	85.13	86.67	—	—	90.85	92.46?	82.31?P	86.11?P	J/B	45 × 100/8
Upper facial index	48.48	54.76	—	—	—	48.20	49.63	57.02?P	—	G'H/J	48 × 100/45
Nasal index	54.17	55.10	—	—	—	44.00	(51.11)	48.00	—	NB/NH	54 × 100/55
Type	E-1	E-3	A-3	A-3	E-1	C-5	C-2	F-2	E-3?		
Numbers used by Axmacher & Hjortsjö (1959)	XVII	?	XVI.	IV	III	XII	omitted	XIII	VIII		

TABLE 3. Mean measurements of undeformed male skulls from prehistoric sites in Cyprus and from Mycenaean Greece. Means in parentheses (face and auricular height in Lapithos sample) include some careful estimates from photographs. Significant divergences (t-test) of Bamboula sample from other Bronze Age samples are italicized.

Periods	Prepottery Neolithic		Late Neolithic		Early and Middle Bronze		Late Bronze Age							
Sites	Khirokitia		Sotira and Erimi		Lapithos and Vounous		Melia at Ayios Yakovos		Enkomi		Bamboula at Kourion		Attica, Argolis, Messenia, etc.	
Area in Cyprus	S.C.		S.W.		N.		N.E.		E.		S.W.		Greece	
Authorities	Angel, 1953		Angel, 1961 and 1953		Buxton, 1920, Fürst, 1933, Hjortsjö, 1947, Rix, 1950		Fürst, 1933		Fürst, 1933, Hjortsjö, 1947		Angel		Angel, 1946, 1953, and unpublished data	
	M	N	M	N	M	N	M	N	M	N	M	N	M	N
H. circumf.	518.5	15	513.0	4	511.8?	9	511.1	18	511.3	22	*505.1*	8	522.0	93
Parietal arc	122.8	15	128.5	6	131.2	12	127.2	22	127.8	21	*127.5*	8	130.0	84
Length	174.4	15	184.8	6	181.2	24	175.0	21	174.8	22	*180.3*	9	186.6	104
Auricular ht.	117.7	11	117.3	6	(118.0)	10)	119.2	16	117.6	21	*112.8*	8	115.7	96
Bas.-nas. lgth.	97.3?	14	101	1	(106.8)	4)	98.3	17	97.6	21	*99.8*	5	99.5	60
Breadth	151.9	16	141.8	6	141.5	24	144.3	22	143.3	22	*137.9*	9	141.2	106
Min. frontal	101.7	15	99.0	3	95.9	18	98.5	21	96.4	22	*93.2*	8	96.6	96
Bizygomatic	134.9	10	128.3	3	(124.7)	3)	129.2	13	130.1	12	*125.3*	6	129.6	60
Upper face ht.	66.7	9	69.3	3	(68.3)	6)	67.9	17	68.2	17	*66.8*	5	67.8	46
Chin ht.	33.0	16	35.8	5	(32)	1)	32.0	8	31.7	6	*32*	1	33.6	57
Nose ht.	50.6	9	53.0	2	(48.0)	5)	49.6	17	50.6	19	*49.2*	5	49.1	45
Nose br.	24.3	11	24.7	3	(24.2)	4)	23.4	17	24.7	19	*26.4*	5	24.1	48
Cranial Index	87.6	15	77.0	6	78.1	24	82.4	21	82.1	22	*76.6*	9	76.2	100
L.-aur. ht. I.	67.9	11	63.5	6	(65.1)	4)	68.1	16	67.5	21	*62.7*	8	62.0	*
Br.-aur. ht. I.	77.6	11	82.7	6	(83.4)	*)	82.7	16	82.2	21	*81.8*	8	81.9	*
Fronto-par. I.	67.1	15	68.3	3	68.1	18	65.3	20	67.2	21	*68.2*	8	68.1	89
U. facial I.	49.5	8	54.1	3	(54.8)	*)	52.3	13	53.2	12	*53.0*	5	52.7	41
Nasal I.	47.5	8	48.1	2	(50.0)	4)	47.1	17	48.8	19	*53.4*	5	49.1	44

TABLE 4. Mean percentage occurrence of morphological types in total adult samples (including deformed skulls) in prehistoric Cyprus and Mycenaean Greece.

PERIODS	Prepottery Neolithic	Late Neolithic	Neolithic, Early and Middle Bronze	Late Bronze Age			
SITES	Khirokitia	Sotira and Erimi	Karavas, Lapithos and Vounous	Melia at Ayios Yakovos	Enkomi	Bamboula at Kourion	Attica, Argolis, Messenia, etc.
AREA IN CYPRUS	S.C.	S.W.	N.	N.E.	E.	S.W.	Greece
AUTHORITIES	Angel, 1953	Angel, 1961 and 1953	Buxton, 1920, Fürst, 1933, Hjortsjö, 1947, Rix, 1950	Fürst, 1933	Fürst, 1933, Hjortsjö, 1947	Angel	Angel, 1946, 1953 and unpublished data
TYPES							
A	4.1	20	23.1	11.4	3.6	18.9	33.1
B	2.7	20	12.8	2.9	9.1	19.0	18.6
D	0*	10	5.1	0*	10.9	0*	14.5
F	8.2	10	10.3	20.0	20.0	8.1	8.2
E	11.0	5	18.0	22.8	12.7	18.9	9.3
C 1-3	32.9	15	17.9	8.6	27.3	13.5	9.3
C 4-5	41.1	10	12.8	34.3	16.4	21.6	7.0
N	73	10	39	35	55	35	172

NOTE: * Iranian *traits* appear in several skulls.

APPENDIX C

CONVERSION LIST OF FINDS

Key to abbreviations:

B	= Bamboula	L	= Lamp	S	= Seal
F	= Figurine	M	= Metal	SH	= Stamped Handle
G	= Graffito	Mi	= Miscellaneous	Sh	= Sherd
Gl	= Glass	P	= Pot	St	= Stone

Field No.	Publication No.	Field No.	Publication No.	Field No.	Publication No.	Field No.	Publication No.
P 725	B 404	P 777	B 926	P 943	B 450	P 995	B 1013
726	405	778	948	944	451	996	1008
727	526	779	849	945	452	997	294
728	551	780	850	946	901	998	530
729	573	781	851	947	410	999	458
730	527	782	971	948	411	1201	902
731	1004	783	814	949	412	1202	617
732	846	784	933	950	528	1203	1209
733	899	785	439	951	529	1204	874
734	602	786	1575	952	499	1205	585
735	1574	787	569	953	555	1206	693
736	865	788	498	954	574	1207	875
737	847	789	852	955	127	1208	771
738	928	790	622	956	128	1209	1014
739	929	791	407	957	1003	1210	1015
740	620	792	440	958	701	1211	1100
741	621	793	853	959	856	1212	1101
742	406	794	913	960	897	1213	783
743	1012	795	408	961	261	1214	99
744	900	796	934	962	262	1215	100
745	697	797	927	963	263	1216	130
746	497	798	935	964	264	1217	131
747	819	799	872	965	265	1218	132
748	123	800	975	966	302	1219	133
749	124	802	914	967	227	1220	134
750	230	803	820	968	129	1221	135
751	376	804	949	969	980	1222	136
752	812	805	409	970	994	1223	137
753	773	806	854	971	196	1224	138
754	669	807	1326	972	1062	1225	139
755	700	808	855	973	608	1226	140
756	811	809	815	974	453	1227	165
757	552	810	964	975	565	1228	96
758	553	811	965	976	523	1229	98
759	1121	812	915	977	524	1230	72
760	767	813	916	978	454	1231	73
761	125	814	863	979	455	1232	74
762	348	815	628	980	456	1233	75
763	126	816	554	981	457	1234	76
764	663	930	1213	982	413	1235	77
765	848	931	584	983	434	1236	78
766	930	932	46	984	414	1237	81
767	947	933	47	985	575	1238	82
768	946	934	441	986	401	1239	83
769	931	935	442	987	1170	1240	233
770	813	936	443	988	231	1241	173
771	932	937	444	989	177	1242	174
772	963	938	445	990	178	1243	175
773	940	939	446	991	202	1244	176
774	941	940	447	992	1092	1245	197
775	942	941	448	993	232	1246	1226
776	943	942	449	994	1063	1247	199

Field No.	Publication No.	Field No.	Publication No.	Field No.	Publication No.	Field No.	Publication No.
P 1248	B 198	P 1317	B 1180	P 1386	B 85	P 2654	B 534
1249	208	1318	1181	1387	86	2655	830
1250	209	1319	823	1388	87	2656	917
1251	210	1320	774	1389	255	2657	587
1252	211	1321	781	1390	179	2658	471
1253	212	1322	787	1391	187	2659	472
1254	213	1323	788	1392	188	2660	1158
1255	214	1324	1016	1393	186	2661	973
1256	215	1325	1156	1394	228	2662	247
1257	203	1326	1157	1395	245	2663	331
1258	314	1327	1093	1396	1224	2664	109
1259	287	1328	1094	1397	257	2665	110
1260	288	1329	580	1398	206	2666	1159
1261	289	1330	268	1399	204	2667	1177
1262	291	1331	269	1400	217	2668	784
1263	372	1332	258	1401	189	2669	205
1264	303	1333	235	1402	702	2670	200
1265	306	1334	236	1403	531	2671	1182
1266	304	1335	237	1404	469	2672	1108
1267	371	1336	238	1405	532	2674	768
1268	373	1337	239	1406	556	2675	473
1269	374	1338	240	1407	586	2676	588
1270	370	1339	241	1408	436	2677	859
1271	1154	1340	242	1409	836	2678	868
1272	1155	1341	243	1410	470	2679	979
1273	996	1342	244	1411	866	2680	738
1274	986	1343	461	1412	867	2681	715
1275	987	1344	462	1413	283	2682	712
1276	772	1345	463	1414	105	2683	721
1277	375	1346	464	1415	106	2684	728
1278	780	1347	465	1416	107	2685	1210
1279	758	1348	466	1417	108	2686	713
1280	680	1349	467	1418	246	2687	718
1281	681	1350	468	1419	1107	2688	282
1282	686	1351	416	1420	789	2689	420
1283	687	1352	1017	1421	280	2690	906
1284	679	1353	417	1422	281	2691	474
1285	688	1354	418	1423	1129	2692	674
1286	654	1355	419	1424	1130	2693	824
1287	655	1356	903	1425	1040	2694	475
1288	651	1357	904	1426	1044	2695	581
1289	642	1358	905	1427	1045	2696	775
1290	643	1359	503	1429	525	2697	785
1291	644	1360	504	1430	279	2698	607
1292	645	1361	1047	1431	988	2699	293
1293	435	1362	1018	1432	312	2702	937
1294	925	1363	1103	1712	221	2704	860
1295	873	1364	1104	1713	222	2705	618
1296	857	1365	1105	1739	757	2706	589
1297	858	1366	253	1841	976	2707	535
1298	821	1367	254	1842	936	2708	864
1299	822	1368	193	2635	533	2709	816
1300	609	1369	216	2636	164	2710	223
1301	694	1370	79	2637	146	2711	939
1302	459	1371	332	2638	229	2712	725
1303	460	1372	1106	2639	739	2713	726
1304	477	1373	981	2640	720	2714	727
1305	500	1374	982	2641	722	2715	201
1306	501	1375	333	2642	724	2716	260
1307	502	1376	396	2643	740	2717	194
1308	344	1377	377	2644	723	2718	995
1309	835	1378	141	2645	714	2719	190
1310	101	1379	142	2646	716	2720	334
1311	102	1380	143	2647	972	2721	1227
1312	103	1381	144	2648	717	2722	977
1313	104	1382	145	2649	218	2723	80
1314	234	1383	159	2650	88	2724	89
1315	1102	1384	169	2651	266	2725	111
1316	1179	1385	84	2653	147	2726	160

Field No.	Publication No.	Field No.	Publication No.	Field No.	Publication No.	Field No.	Publication No.
P 2727	B 877	P 2822	B 1091	P 2907	B 786	Sh 115	B 676
2728	878	2823	1161	2908	831	116	611
2731	352	2824	308	2909	284	117	11
2732	1184	2825	309	2910	918	118	92
2733	148	2826	299	2911	919	119	335
2734	90	2827	1064	2912	920	120	349
2735	983	2828	1117	2913	782	121	35
2736	984	2829	966	2914	827	123	647
2737	1211	2831	838	2915	828	124	1042
2739	397	2832	839	2916	832	126	682
2740	1327	2833	967	2917	840	127	677
2741	48	2834	817	2918	841	128	1193
2742	695	2835	945	2919	879	129	1065
2743	1175	2836	762	2920	833	130	1214
2744	1176	2837	818	2921	834	131	667
2745	296	2839	950	2922	869	132	908
2746	307	2840	861	2923	870	133	558
2747	760	2841	49	2924	871	134	559
2748	112	2842	154	2925	610	135	924
2749	113	2843	698	2926	842	136	911
2750	114	2844	117	2927	843	137	560
2751	115	2845	992	2928	844	138	625
2752	149	2846	479	2929	845	139	629
2753	150	2847	769	2930	295	140	561
2754	151	2849	480	2931	732	141	543
2755	267	2850	360	2932	664	142	1237
2765	195	2851	826	2933	285	143	317
2766	248	2852	862	2934	220	144	51
2767	761	2866	603	2937	167	145	1052
2768	1212	2867	590	2938	1169	146	1141
2769	978	2868	591	Sh 63	B 59	147	327
2770	1116	2869	592	64	346	148	398
2771	729	2870	582	65	706	149	657
2779	1185	2871	583	66	707	150	36
2780	1186	2872	593	67	505	151	1051
2781	161	2873	594	68	1122	152	1
2782	152	2874	595	69	1048	153	492
2783	162	2875	596	70	623	154	425
2785	180	2876	922	71	646	155	426
2786	163	2877	923	72	316	156	1109
2788	116	2878	276	73	638	160	641
2789	153	2879	619	74	666	161	1023
2790	249	2880	278	76	50	163	703
2791	476	2881	481	77	378	164	1131
2792	421	2882	482	78	649	165	506
2793	422	2883	424	79	708	166	1220
2794	423	2884	483	81	639	167	2
2795	837	2885	484	82	1049	168	3
2796	825	2886	485	83	185	169	37
2800	741	2887	486	85	1229	170	366
2801	764	2888	487	86	1050	171	379
2803	776	2889	912	87	490	172	347
2804	777	2890	488	88	1236	173	181
2805	1228	2891	489	89	272	174	12
2806	745	2892	91	93	1191	178	65
2807	731	2893	536	94	64	180	1215
2808	974	2894	537	95	1567	183	321
2809	730	2895	538	96	1020	184	753
2811	733	2896	539	97	1009	185	689
2812	345	2897	540	98	1192	186	626
2813	938	2898	541	99	1021	187	636
2814	944	2899	542	101	61	188	685
2815	765	2900	557	105	1041	190	670
2816	1019	2901	907	106	1022	191	630
2817	898	2902	118	107	624	192	675
2818	478	2903	250	108	1199	193	671
2819	1046	2904	251	111	491	194	747
2820	1160	2905	361	112	709	195	4
2821	1183	2906	310	113	710	196	754

Field No.	Publication No.	Field No.	Publication No.	Field No.	Publication No.	Field No.	Publication No.
Sh 197	B 631	Sh 286	B 26	Sh 393	B 659	Sh 493	B 513
198	690	287	1238	394	430	494	286
199	1142	288	493	395	41	495	576
200	711	289	27	398	364	496	1125
202	13	290	494	399	31	497	1070
203	14	291	155	400	660	498	1133
204	1143	292	1201	402	1217	499	1007
205	1144	294	755	403	53	500	63
206	1123	300	683	404	322	501	1196
207	15	305	704	405	320	502	1197
208	1200	306	604	411	634	503	668
209	652	307	226	414	1241	505	1119
210	16	310	1075	415	330	506	1174
211	653	311	508	416	45	507	1202
212	55	312	62	420	744	508	259
213	17	313	876	421	742	509	616
214	566	314	545	422	743	510	985
215	544	315	383	426	1086	511	1005
216	38	317	495	427	1132	512	386
217	18	318	1110	428	54	513	433
218	648	319	363	430	1027	514	1053
219	5	320	751	436	353	515	571
220	350	321	605	438	323	518	691
221	56	322	1163	439	328	519	1030
242	633	323	60	440	326	520	1054
243	672	324	705	441	329	521	692
246	1187	325	1081	442	354	522	577
249	368	326	989	443	32	523	910
250	402	327	427	444	33	524	696
251	1172	328	614	445	1124	525	297
252	613	329	66	448	598	526	514
253	382	330	909	449	511	527	1031
254	1095	331	1025	450	385	528	359
255	21	332	658	451	1230	529	93
256	7	333	358	452	68	531	515
257	507	334	665	454	997	532	437
222	19	335	428	459	627	533	606
223	1145	336	1085	460	661	534	1084
224	6	337	1026	461	119	535	256
225	1162	338	1069	462	1028	536	1178
226	20	339	67	463	1147	537	578
227	399	341	509	464	512	538	684
228	612	344	510	465	9	539	678
229	632	345	367	466	431	540	656
230	601	351	318	467	432	542	564
231	1171	352	319	468	734	543	1328
232	1146	353	324	469	549	545	1432
238	637	364	1194	471	1082	546	1071
240	650	370	1010	472	1148	547	1134
260	22	371	1218	473	10	548	270
262	699	372	69	474	369	549	1231
263	315	373	362	475	1149	550	999
264	39	374	597	476	70	551	579
265	23	375	1216	477	570	552	662
266	8	376	40	478	748	553	516
267	24	377	52	479	1029	554	1550
268	634	378	28	480	156	556	517
269	1024	379	43	481	120	557	518
270	1074	381	29	482	182	558	1619
271	25	382	30	483	336	559	1551
272	57	383	429	484	1164	560	520
273	1068	384	546	485	1165	561a-b	1595
274	58	385	1195	486	1083	562	1188
276	562	386	547	487	640	563	1552
280	563	387	548	488	34	565	1596
281	380	388	384	489	71	566	1553
282	381	389	880	490	1150	567	337
283	1173	390	615	491	365	570	1055
284	1240	391	325	492	550	571	1056

Field No.	Publication No.	Field No.	Publication No.	Field No.	Publication No.	Field No.	Publication No.
Sh 572	B 1057	Sh 665	B 1558	745	1120	G 30	B 390
573	1076	666	1097	746	1207	31	391
574	1077	667	921	747	342	32	800
575	1066	669	1011	748	1208	33	392
576	635	670	340	749	1234	34	801
577	1087	672	1232	750	1080	35	802
578	1072	673	1233	752	1002	36	393
579	1433	674	1151	753	343	37	1112
580	1434	675	1189	754	357	38	1113
581	277	676	496	755	1576	39	803
582	1088	677	1032	756	572	40	804
583	44	678	1033	757	1600	41	959
584	519	679	1034	758	998	42	1594
602	750	680	1035	759	568	43	1138
603	1554	681	1036	760	95	44	805
604	968	682	1037	761	122	45	890
606	1316	683	1038	762	737	46	1073
607	1555	684	1039	763	97	47	1168
608	1556	685	1221	764a	172	48	1114
609	1557	686	1098	764b	252	49	778
610	1597	687	1058	765	158	50	438
611	1598	688	1059	766	415	51	1139
612	746	689	1060	767	1089	52	960
613	719	690	1061	768	305	53	394
614	1599	691	599	F 41	B 1560	54	806
615	1435	692	1190	57	1568	55	961
616	969	693	1078	58	1561	56	891
617	1006	694	1079	59	1569	57	395
620	273	695	1127	60	1562	58	1140
621	735	696	1099	61	1570	59	807
622	736	697	1118	62	224	60	991
623	219	698	1128	63	1563	61	892
624	191	699	403	64	1564	62	808
625	207	700	1166	65	1571	63	809
626	183	701	1167	66	225	64	893
627	171	702	300	67	1565	65	271
628	184	703	301	68	1566	66	894
629	157	704	298	69	1572	67	895
630	292	705	1001	70	1573	68	1458
631	192	706	1203	71	1617	69	763
632	274	707	1204	G 1	B 954	70	1115
633	1043	708	1205	2	884	71	779
634	42	709	1222	3	1223	72	896
635	749	710	355	4	885	73	810
636	951	711	313	5	388	74	962
637	1067	712	166	6	792	75	311
638	168	713	94	7	886	Gl 90	B 1330
640	351	714	1225	8	793	91	1331
641	387	715	1135	9	794	92	1332
643	1126	716	1206	10	887	93	1333
644	290	717	953	11	770	94	1320
645	338	718	1198	12	600	95	1334
647	756	719	970	13	955	96	1347
647a	790	720	1436	14	795	97	1335
648	881	721	1559	15	888	98	1321
649	1000	723	1188	16	389	99	1329
650	1111	725	356	17	796	181	1348
651	993	726	1152	18	1219	182	1336
652	275	727	1239	19	956	183	1337
653	1096	729	521	20	957	184	1338
656	759	730	522	21	797	185	1339
657	882	731	567	22	889	186	1340
658	170	732	1153	23	766	187	1341
659	339	736	791	24	1137	188	1350
660	952	738	1242	25	400	189	1352
661	990	739	673	26	829	190	1342
662	121	740	1090	27	798	334	1343
663	752	741	341	28	958	M 10	B 1620
664	883	742	1136	29	799	11	1621

Field No.	Publication No.	Field No.	Publication No.	Field No.	Publication No.	Field No.	Publication No.
M 12	B 1318	M 1037	B 1293	Mi 157	B 1369	S 1	B 1592
13	1274	1038	1304	158	1370	2	1614
15	1382	1039	1302	159	1371	3	1640
15a	1383	1040	1309	160	1372	4	1444
16	1428	1041	1250	161	1373	5	1630
18	1429	1042	1301	162	1374	6	1627
19	1303	1043	1315	163	1375	7	1445
20	1305	1044	1288	164	1357	8	1633
21	1299	1045	1273	165	1344	9	1634
22	1275	1046	1259	166	1368	10	1605
23	1306	1048	1289	167	1378	11	1527
24	1263	1049	1256	168	1358	12	1528
25	1252	1050	1387	169	1628	13	1446
26	1276	1051	1251	170	1359	14	1578
27	1425	1052	1380	171	1360	15	1579
29	1430	1054	1290	172	1379	16	1580
30	1264	1055	1257	173	1397	17	1581
32	1390	1056	1389	174	1420	18	1606
33	1312	1079	1281	175	1398	19	1616
34	1391	Mi 100	B 1615	176	1522	20	1582
35	1284	101	1509	177	1523	21	1583
36	1291	103	1510	178	1247	22	1584
37	1277	104	1531	179	1361	26	1607
207	1384	105	1506	181	1376	27	1542
210	1272	106	1532	182	1345	28	1585
211	1319	107	1407	183	1363	29	1447
212	1381	108	1419	184	1524	45	1437
213	1294	109	1408	185	1346	46	1438
214	1295	110	1393	186	1590	47	1440
215	1260	111	1410	189	1248	48	1504
216	1261	112	1411	190	1536	49	1608
217	1265	113	1392	191	1243	76	1549
218	1266	114	1394	192	1399	77	1349
219	1385	115	1395	193	1632	78	1448
220	1258	116	1638	194	1629	79	1424
221	1296	117	1639	195	1626	80	1418
222	1267	118	1635	196	1421	81	1624
223	1253	119	1354	197	1400	82	1625
224	1254	120	1353	198a	1323	83	1529
225	1268	121	1612	198b	1351	84	1586
226	1292	122	1548	198c	1439	85	1530
227	1300	123	1511	199	1412	86	1593
229	1386	124	1512	200	1401	88	1637
230	1282	125	1513	201	1402	89	1409
233	1278	126	1514	202	1356	90	1609
234	1313	127	1515	203	1636	91	1610
235	1314	128	1516	204	1631	92	1611
237	1307	129	1517	205	1403	94	1543
239	1249	130	1518	205a	1591	95	1544
240	1310	131	1519	206	1537	96	1545
241	1279	132	1520	206a	1618	99	1587
244	1426	133	1521	207	1404	100	1588
245	1427	136	1533	207a-b	1577	101	1589
246	1311	138	1534	208	1413	102	1431
250	1280	139	1535	209	1414	103	1622
892	1317	141	1601	210	1415	104	1623
893a-c	1271	142	1602	211	1405	SH 222	B 1235
894	1441	143	1603	212	1406	St 25	B 1469
1024	1269	145	1613	213	1422	26	1459
1025	1262	146	1604	214	1423	28	1488
1026	1285	148	1355	552	1442	29	1496
1027	1308	149	1322	553	1388	30	1491
1028	1283	150	1396	554	1443	31	1478
1030	1255	151	1364	555	1507	32	1470
1031	1270	152	1362	556a	1416	33	1497
1032	1297	153	1377	556b	1417	34	1546
1033	1298	154	1365	557a	1324	36	1494
1034	1286	155	1366	557b	1325	37	1460
1035	1287	156	1367	559	1508	38	1461

CONVERSION LIST

Field No.	Publication No.	Field No.	Publication No.	Field No.	Publication No.	Field No.	Publication No.
St 39	B 1479	St 55	B 1492	St 72	B 1246	St 522	B 1476
40	1498	56	1483	73	1473	524	1456
41	1499	57	1465	74	1450	539	1477
42	1500	58	1484	75	1451	540	1468
43	1501	60	1502	76	1452	541	1486
44	1449	61	1503	77	1474	542	1487
45	1489	62	1495	79	1505	543	1490
47	1471	63	1472	85	1538	544	1540
49	1462	64	1485	86	1539	545	1525
50	1463	65	1244	90	1493	546	1526
51	1464	67	1466	519	1453	547	1541
52	1480	68	1467	520	1454	899	1457
53	1481	70	1547	521	1475	952	1455
54	1482	71	1245				

INDEX

Pottery fabrics treated in the Catalogue are here omitted.

PLATE 1

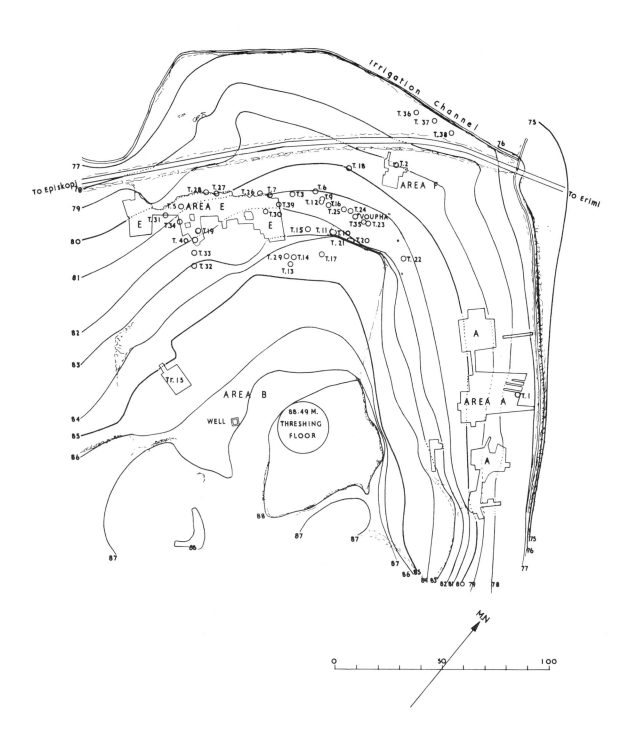

TOMBS

PLATE 2

Tomb 1 and Circuit Wall

"Street of Tombs" with Tomb 5 in foreground

Tomb 6, upper level

Tomb 12 at level of Skeletons I and II

Tomb 17a

Tomb 19—1.8 m.

PLATE 3

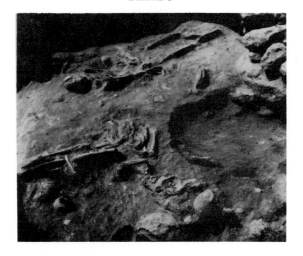

Tomb 2

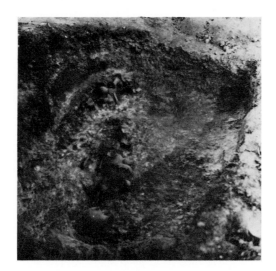

Tomb 11

Tomb 19

PLATE 4

Tomb 29

Tomb 30

Tomb 32: dromos

Tomb 33

Tomb 37 before removing slabs

Tomb 40

PLATE 5

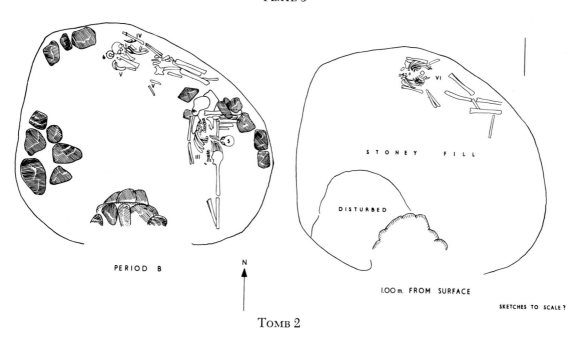

PERIOD B

N

1.00 m. FROM SURFACE

STONEY FILL

DISTURBED

SKETCHES TO SCALE ?

TOMB 2

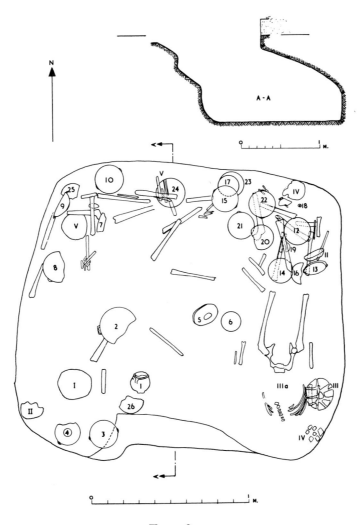

N

A - A

0 _____ M.

0 _____ M.

TOMB 3

PLATE 6

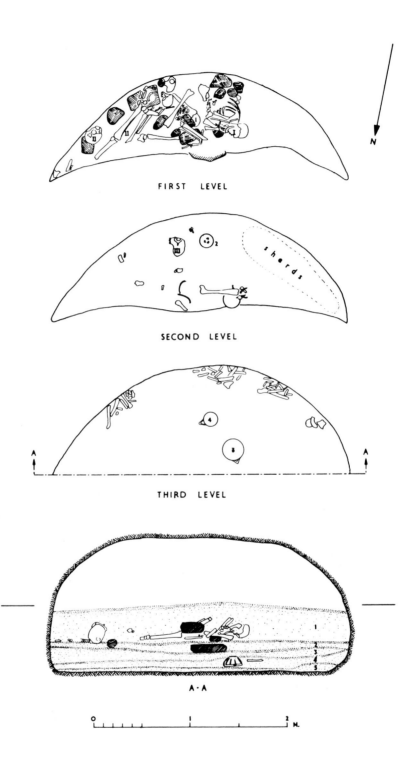

FIRST LEVEL

SECOND LEVEL

THIRD LEVEL

A·A

0   1   2 M.

TOMB 5

PLATE 7

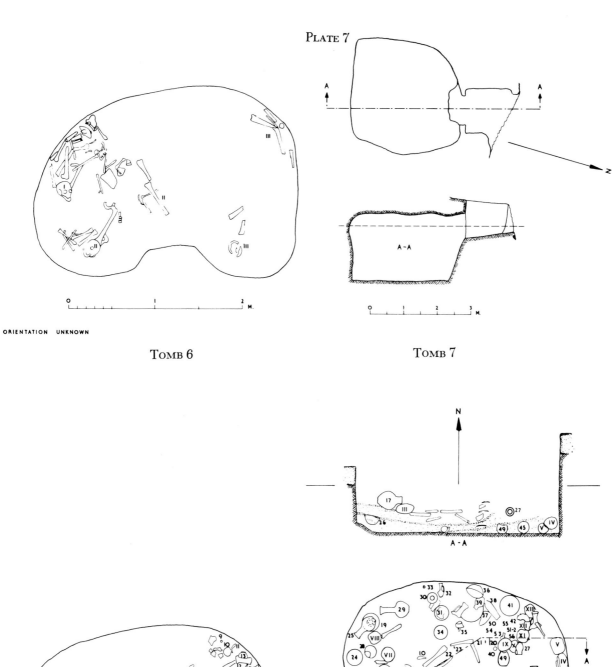

ORIENTATION UNKNOWN

Tomb 6

Tomb 7

Tomb 11

Tomb 12

Plate 8

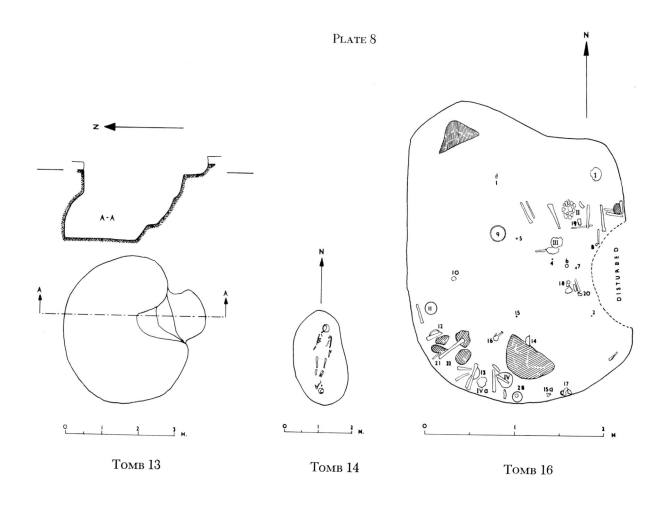

Томв 13

Томв 14

Томв 16

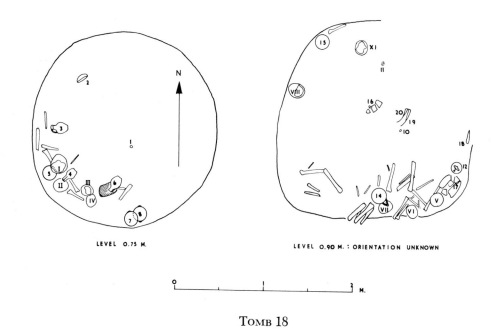

LEVEL 0.75 M.

LEVEL 0.90 M. : ORIENTATION UNKNOWN

Томв 18

PLATE 9

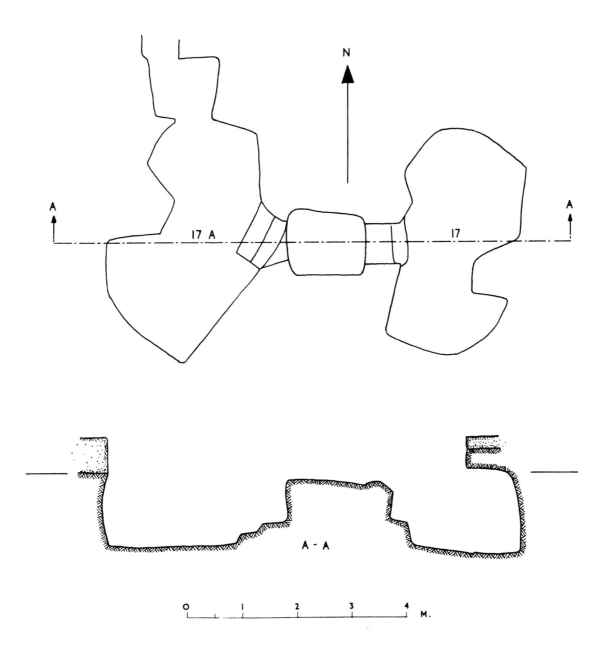

TOMBS 17 AND 17A

PLATE 10

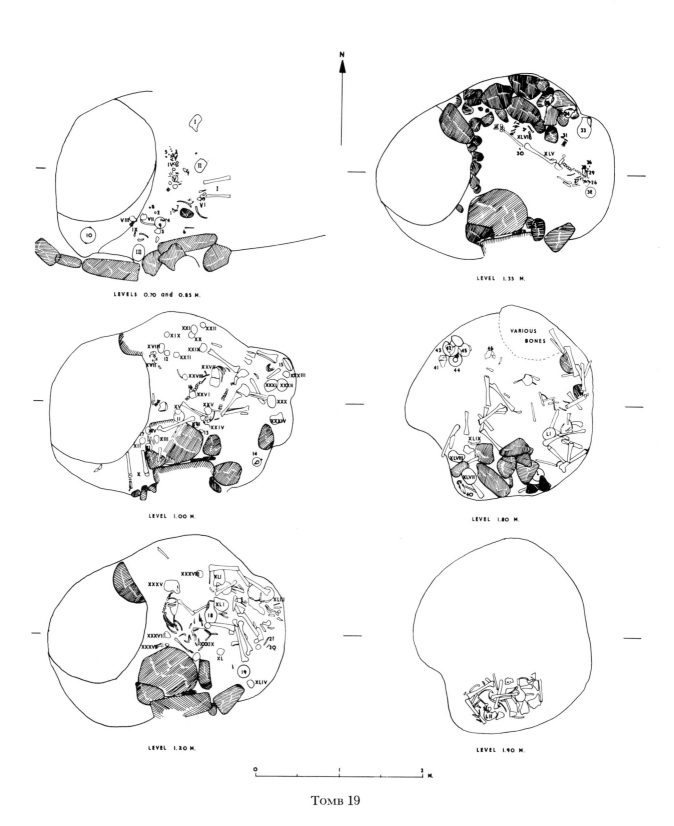

LEVELS 0.70 and 0.85 M.

LEVEL 1.35 M.

LEVEL 1.00 M.

LEVEL 1.80 M.

VARIOUS BONES

LEVEL 1.20 M.

LEVEL 1.90 M.

0 1 2 M.

TOMB 19

PLATE 11

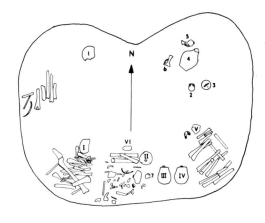

SKETCH TO SCALE?

TOMB 21

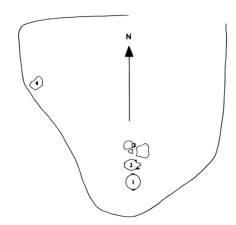

SKETCH TO SCALE?

TOMB 23

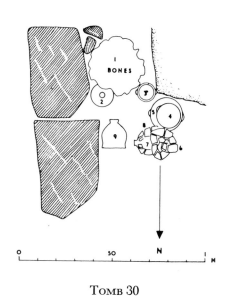

TOMB 30

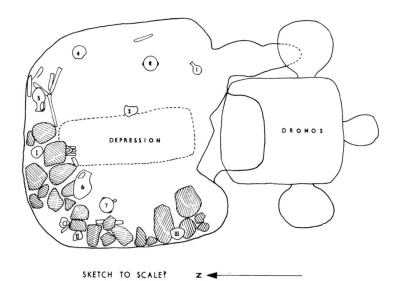

SKETCH TO SCALE?

TOMB 32

PLATE 12

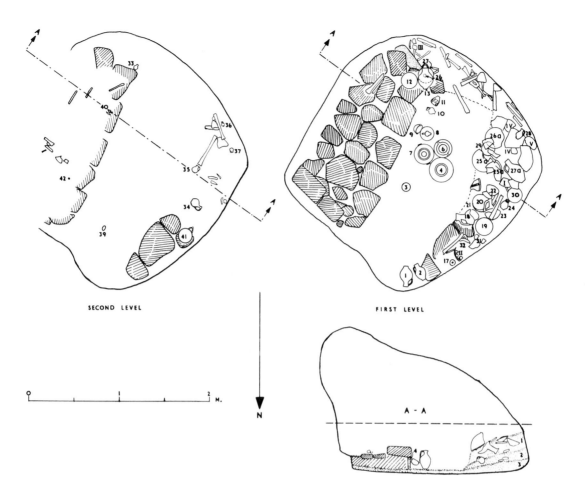

SECOND LEVEL

FIRST LEVEL

N

A - A

TOMB 33

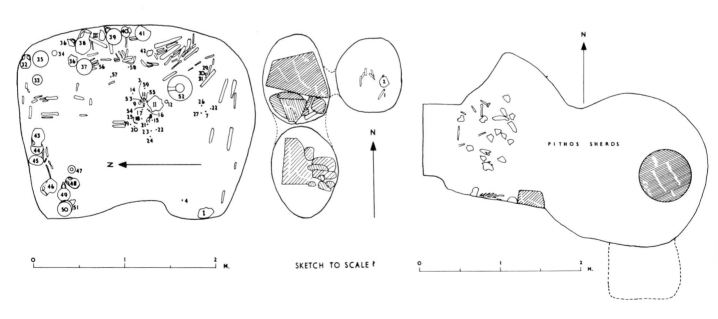

TOMB 36

SKETCH TO SCALE?

N

PITHOS SHERDS

N

TOMB 37

TOMB 38

PLATE 13

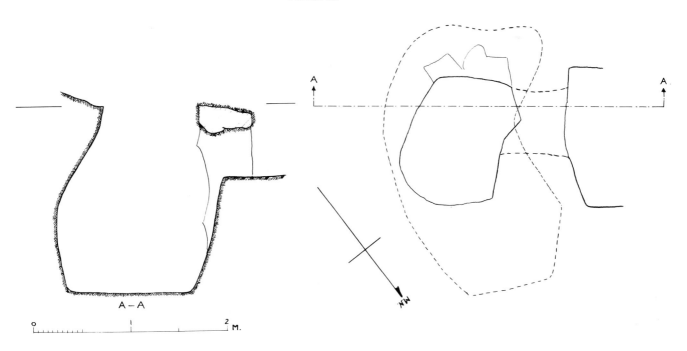

A – A

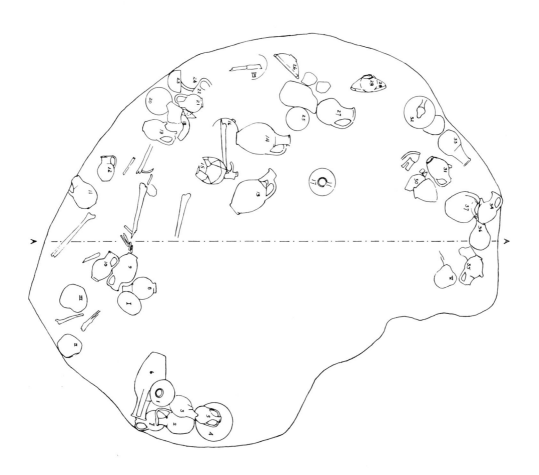

TOMB 40

PLATE 14

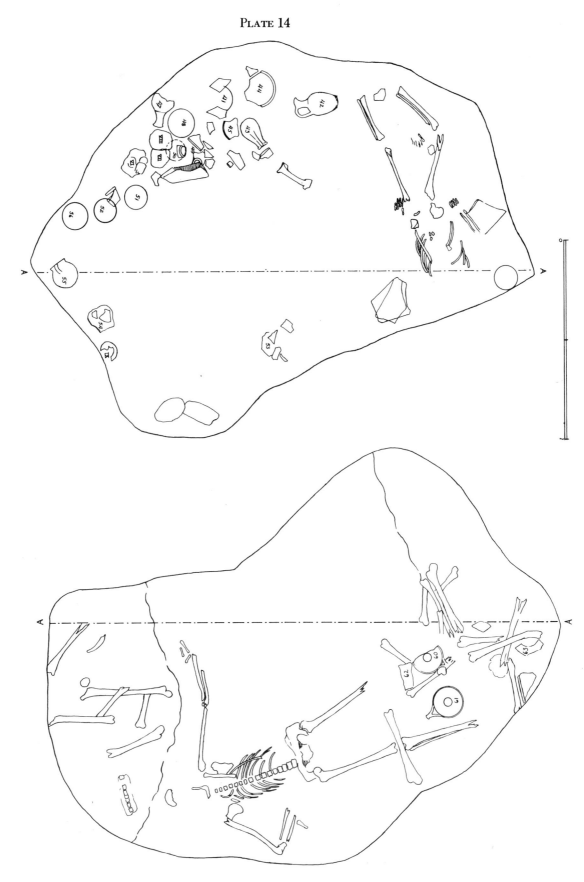

TOMB 40

PLATE 15

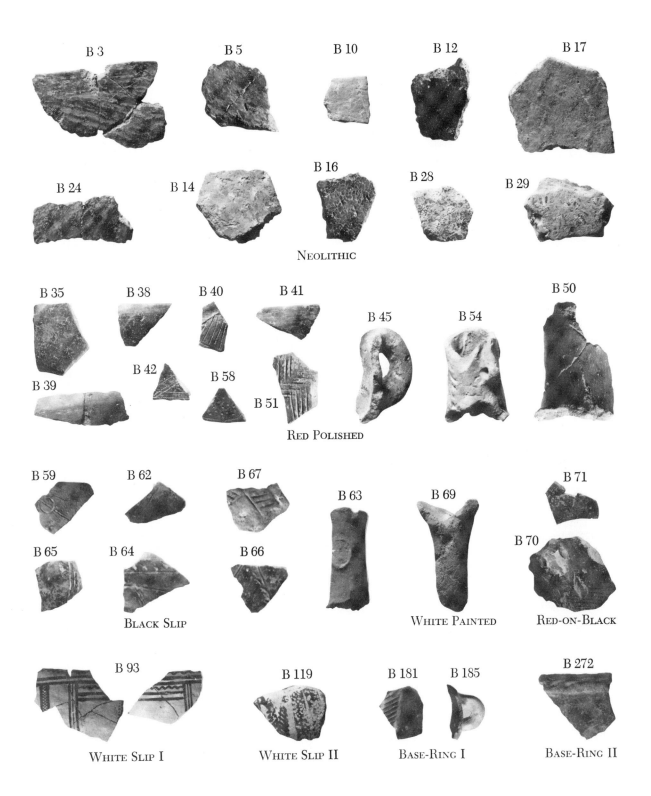

B 3　B 5　B 10　B 12　B 17

B 24　B 14　B 16　B 28　B 29

NEOLITHIC

B 35　B 38　B 40　B 41　B 50

B 39　B 42　B 58　B 45　B 54

B 51

RED POLISHED

B 59　B 62　B 67　B 63　B 69　B 71

B 65　B 64　B 66　B 70

BLACK SLIP　WHITE PAINTED　RED-ON-BLACK

B 93　B 119　B 181　B 185　B 272

WHITE SLIP I　WHITE SLIP II　BASE-RING I　BASE-RING II

PLATE 16

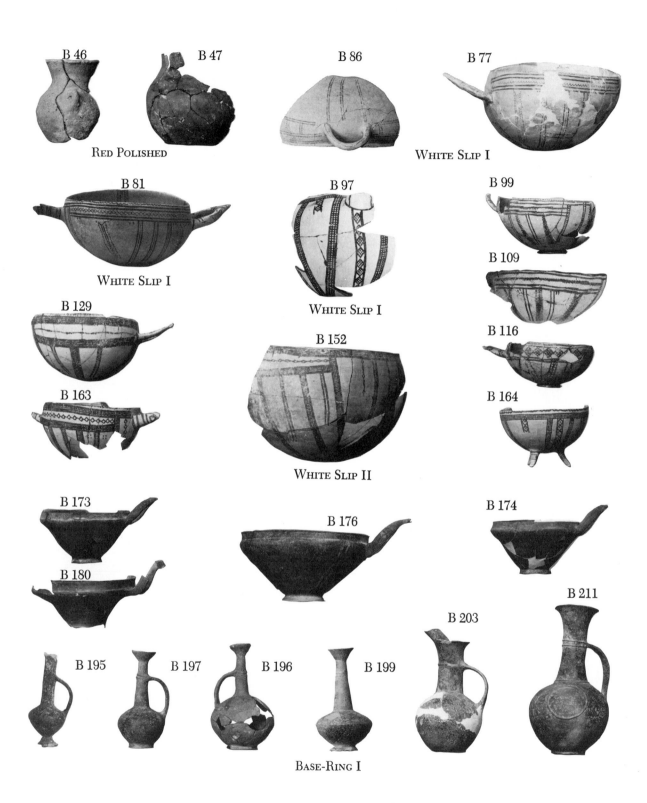

B 46   B 47   B 86   B 77

RED POLISHED   WHITE SLIP I

B 81   B 97   B 99

WHITE SLIP I   B 109

B 129   WHITE SLIP I   B 116

B 163   B 152   B 164

WHITE SLIP II

B 173   B 176   B 174

B 180   B 211

B 203

B 195   B 197   B 196   B 199

BASE-RING I

PLATE 17

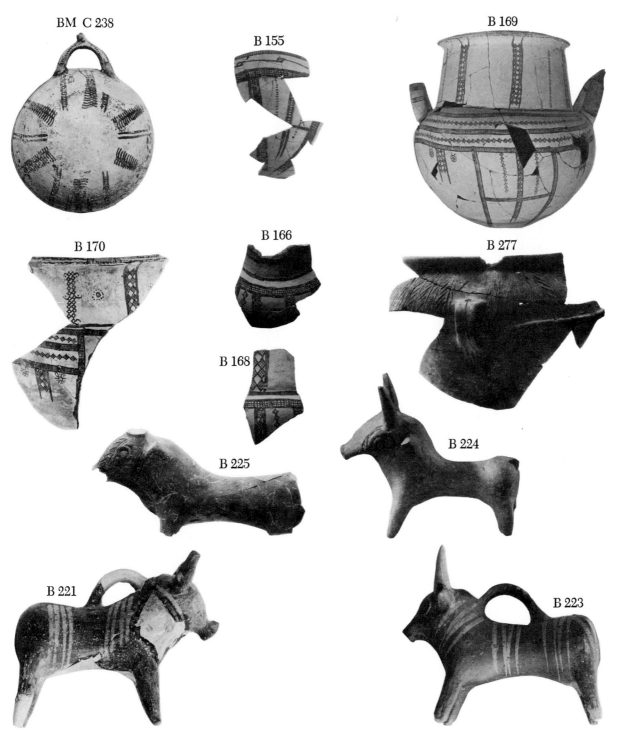

BM C 238

B 155

B 169

B 170

B 166

B 277

B 168

B 225

B 224

B 221

B 223

WHITE SLIP II AND BASE-RING II

PLATE 18

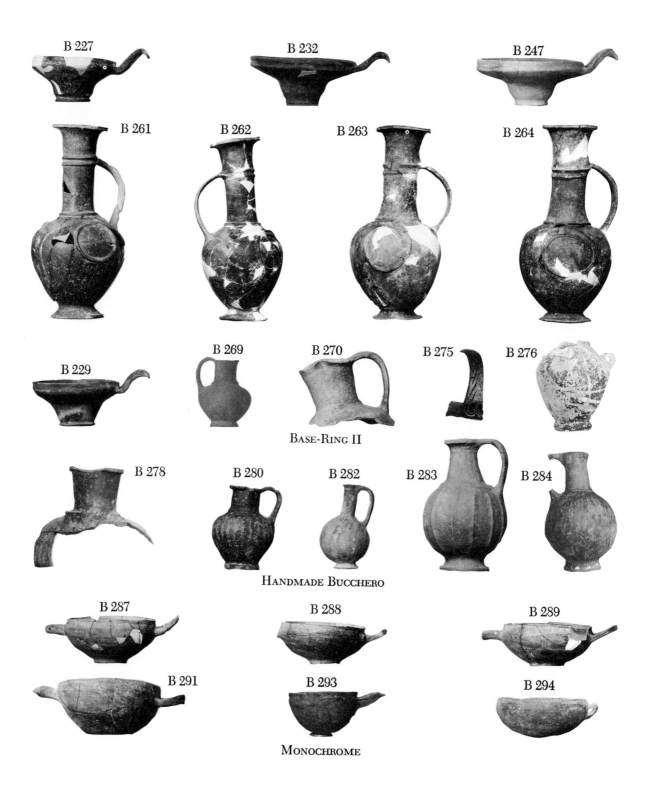

B 227   B 232   B 247

B 261   B 262   B 263   B 264

B 269   B 270   B 275   B 276

B 229

BASE-RING II

B 278   B 280   B 282   B 283   B 284

HANDMADE BUCCHERO

B 287   B 288   B 289

B 291   B 293   B 294

MONOCHROME

PLATE 19

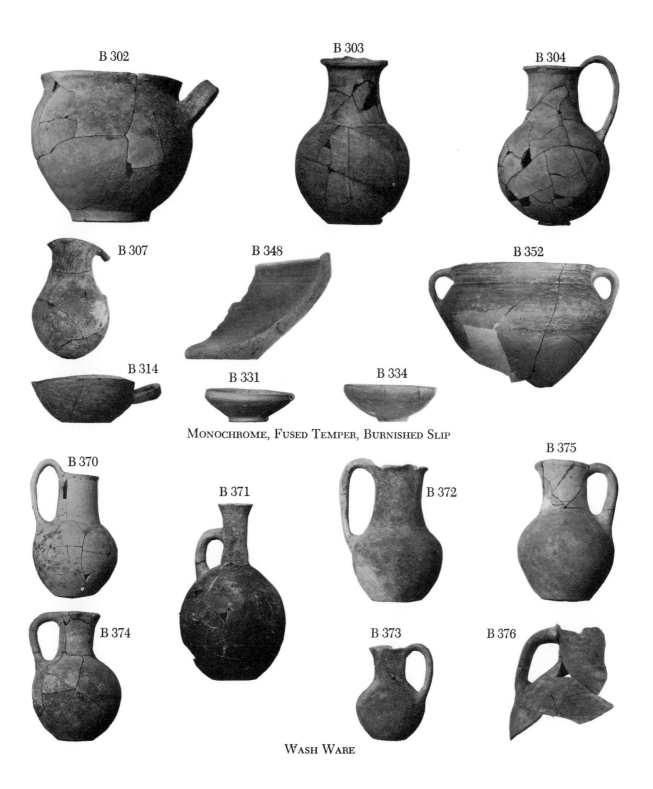

B 302

B 303

B 304

B 307

B 348

B 352

B 314

B 331

B 334

MONOCHROME, FUSED TEMPER, BURNISHED SLIP

B 375

B 370

B 371

B 372

B 373

B 374

B 376

WASH WARE

PLATE 20

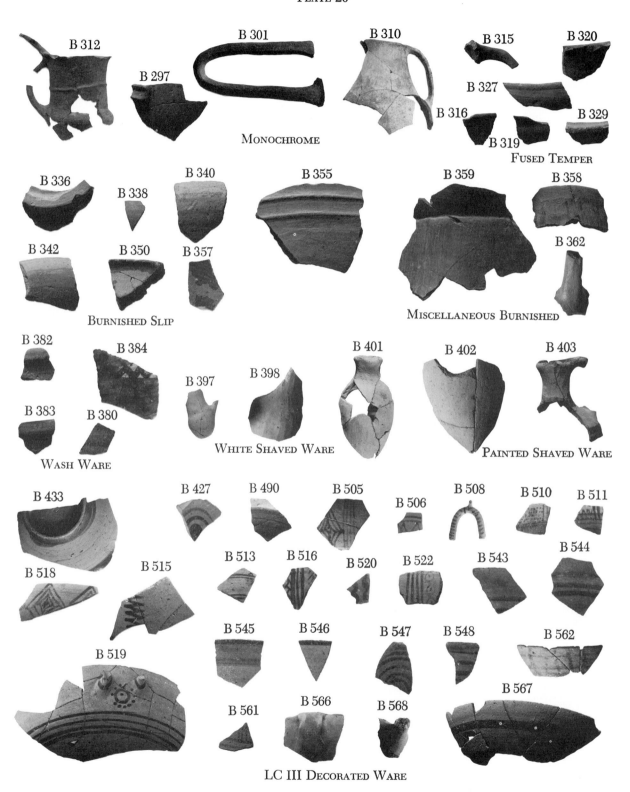

B 312
B 297
B 301
B 310
B 315
B 320
B 327
B 316
B 319
B 329

MONOCHROME

FUSED TEMPER

B 336
B 338
B 340
B 355
B 359
B 358
B 342
B 350
B 357
B 362

BURNISHED SLIP

MISCELLANEOUS BURNISHED

B 382
B 384
B 401
B 402
B 403
B 397
B 398
B 383
B 380

WHITE SHAVED WARE

PAINTED SHAVED WARE

WASH WARE

B 433
B 427
B 490
B 505
B 508
B 510
B 511
B 506
B 518
B 515
B 513
B 516
B 520
B 522
B 543
B 544

B 545
B 546
B 547
B 548
B 562
B 519
B 567
B 561
B 566
B 568

LC III DECORATED WARE

PLATE 21

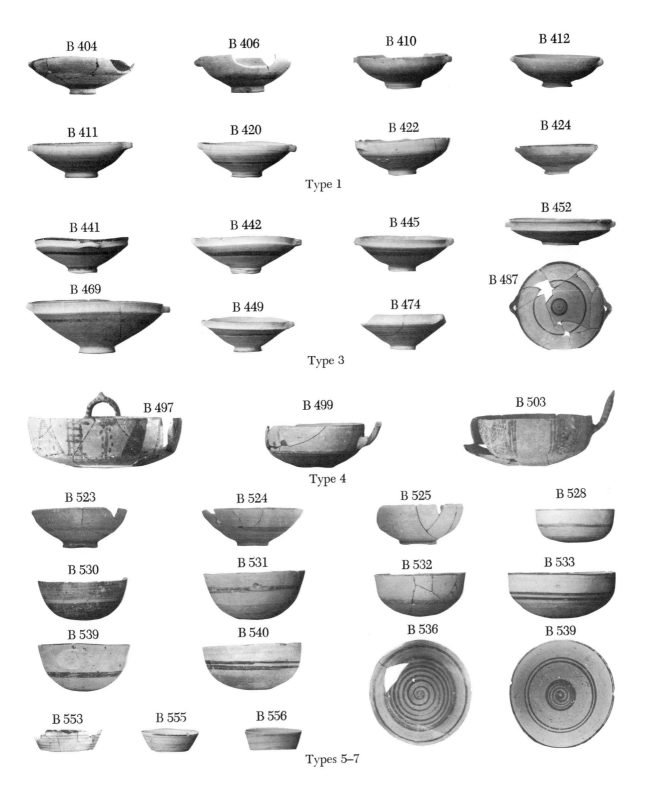

B 404

B 406

B 410

B 412

B 411

B 420

B 422

B 424

Type 1

B 441

B 442

B 445

B 452

B 469

B 449

B 474

B 487

Type 3

B 497

B 499

B 503

Type 4

B 523

B 524

B 525

B 528

B 530

B 531

B 532

B 533

B 539

B 540

B 536

B 539

B 553

B 555

B 556

Types 5–7

LC III DECORATED BOWLS

PLATE 22

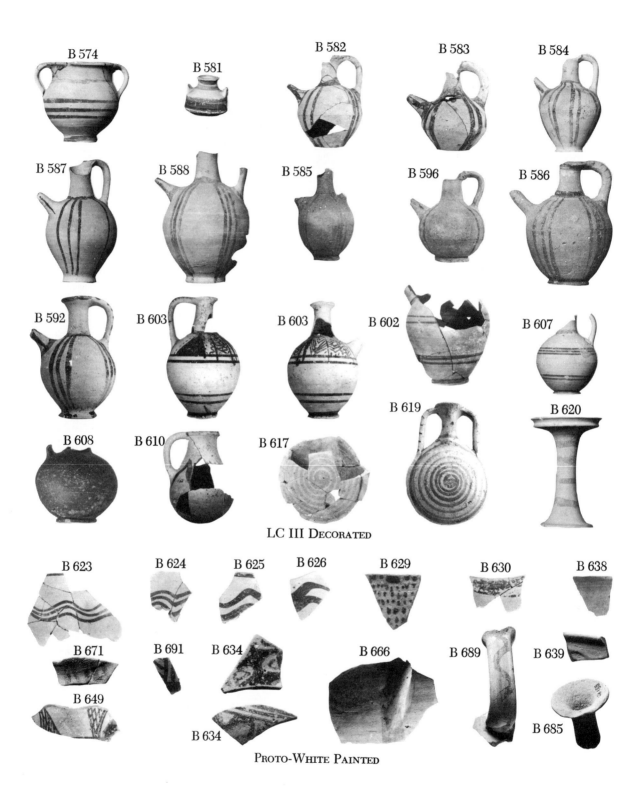

B 574 B 581 B 582 B 583 B 584

B 587 B 588 B 585 B 596 B 586

B 592 B 603 B 603 B 602 B 607

B 619 B 620

B 608 B 610 B 617

LC III DECORATED

B 623 B 624 B 625 B 626 B 629 B 630 B 638

B 671 B 691 B 634 B 666 B 689 B 639

B 649 B 634 B 685

PROTO-WHITE PAINTED

PLATE 23

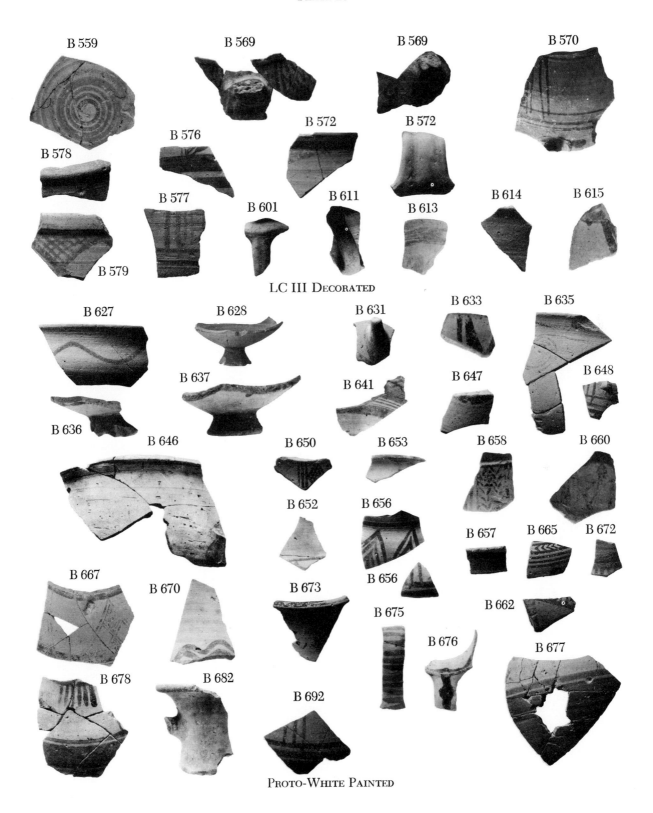

B 559

B 569

B 569

B 570

B 576

B 572

B 572

B 578

B 601

B 611

B 613

B 614

B 615

B 577

B 579

LC III DECORATED

B 627

B 628

B 631

B 633

B 635

B 637

B 641

B 647

B 648

B 636

B 646

B 650

B 653

B 658

B 660

B 652

B 656

B 657

B 665

B 672

B 667

B 670

B 673

B 656

B 675

B 662

B 676

B 677

B 678

B 682

B 692

PROTO-WHITE PAINTED

Plate 24

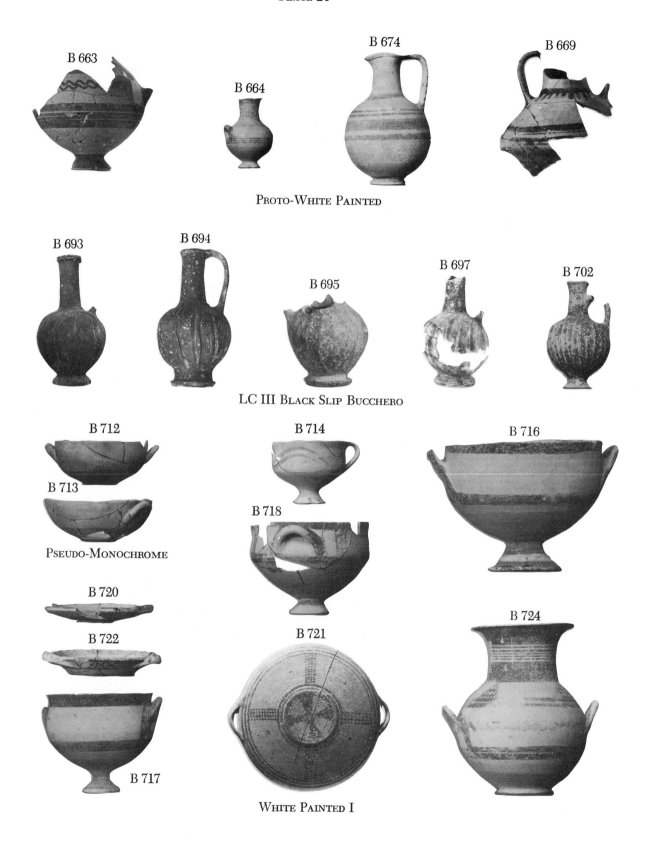

B 663

B 664

B 674

B 669

Proto-White Painted

B 693

B 694

B 695

B 697

B 702

LC III Black Slip Bucchero

B 712

B 714

B 716

B 713

B 718

Pseudo-Monochrome

B 720

B 722

B 721

B 724

B 717

White Painted I

PLATE 25

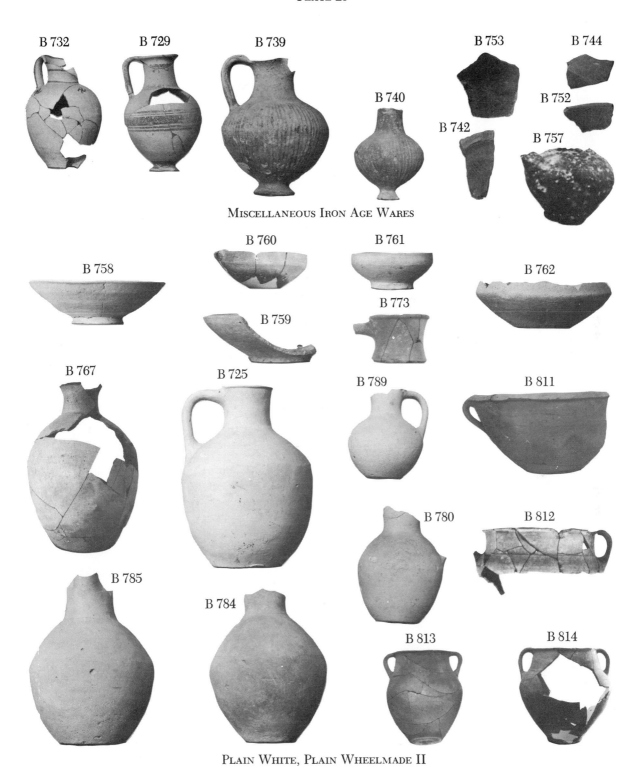

B 732   B 729   B 739   B 753   B 744

B 740   B 752

B 742   B 757

MISCELLANEOUS IRON AGE WARES

B 760   B 761

B 758   B 762

B 773

B 759

B 767   B 725   B 789   B 811

B 780   B 812

B 785

B 784   B 813   B 814

PLAIN WHITE, PLAIN WHEELMADE II

PLATE 26

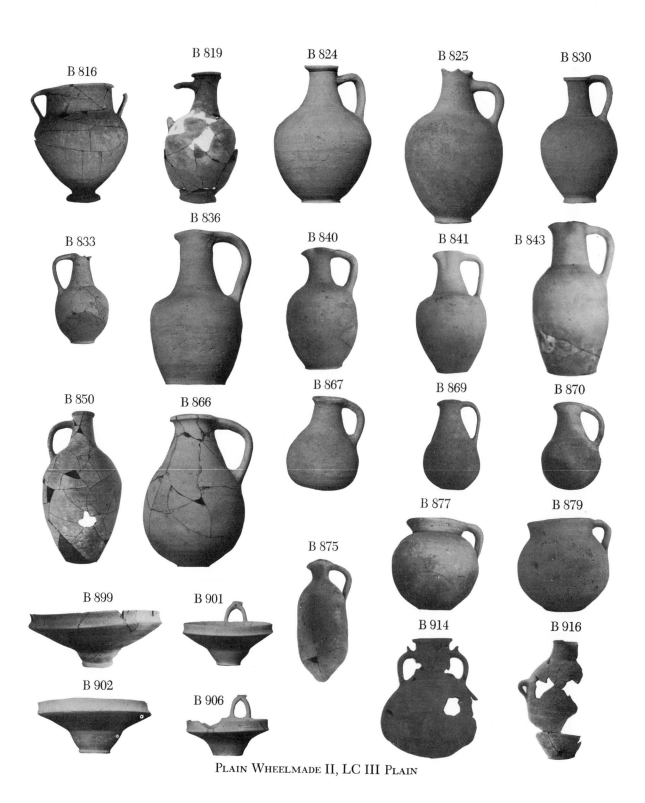

B 816 B 819 B 824 B 825 B 830

B 833 B 836 B 840 B 841 B 843

B 850 B 866 B 867 B 869 B 870

B 875 B 877 B 879

B 899 B 901 B 914 B 916

B 902 B 906

PLAIN WHEELMADE II, LC III PLAIN

PLATE 27

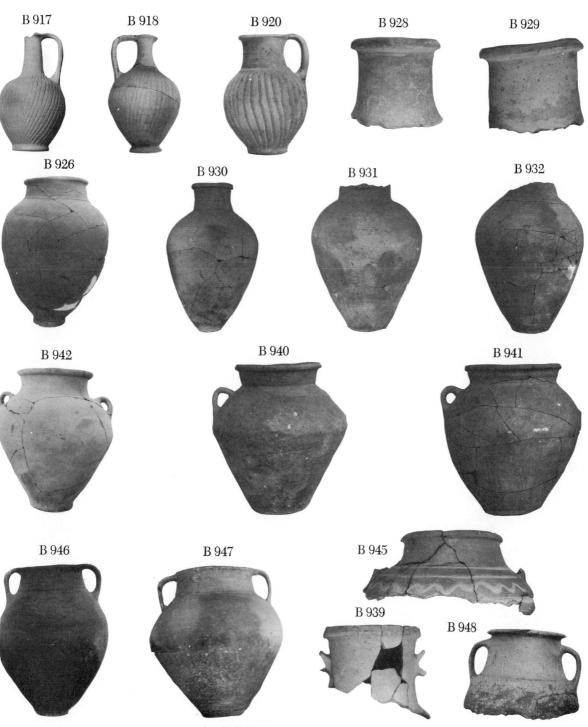

B 917   B 918   B 920   B 928   B 929

B 926   B 930   B 931   B 932

B 942   B 940   B 941

B 946   B 947   B 945

B 939   B 948

LC III PLAIN, PITHOS WARE

PLATE 28

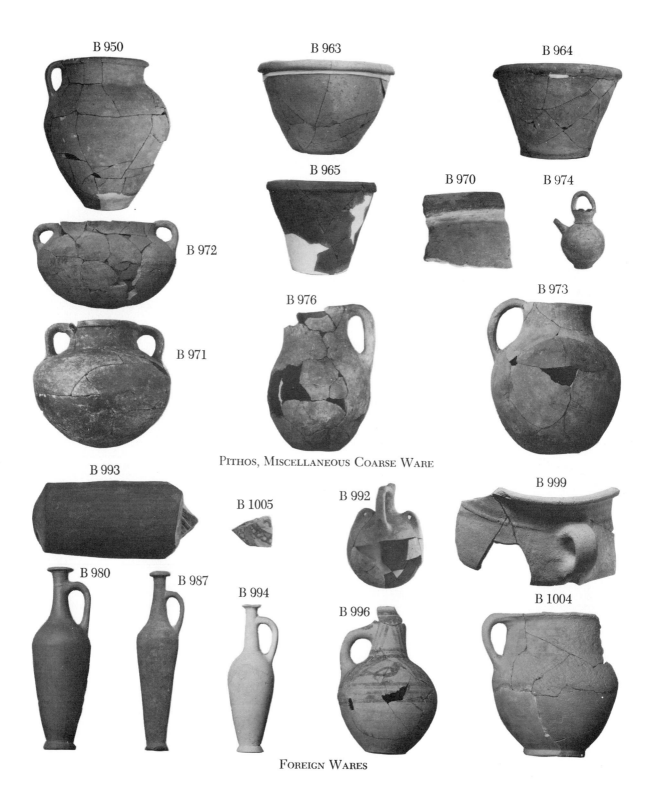

B 950

B 963

B 964

B 965

B 970

B 974

B 972

B 976

B 973

B 971

PITHOS, MISCELLANEOUS COARSE WARE

B 993

B 999

B 1005

B 992

B 980

B 987

B 994

B 996

B 1004

FOREIGN WARES

PLATE 29

B 700

B 701

B 708

B 709

B 737

B 737

B 747

B 738

B 737

B 707

B 748

B 756

B 750

B 749

B 924

B 880

B 865

B 741

B 851

B 768

B 978

B 952

B 911

MISCELLANEOUS CYPRIOTE WARES

B 997

B 998

B 1000

B 1001

B 1002

B 1011

B 1020

B 1032

B 1033

B 1038

B 1028

B 1030

B 1031

B 1035

B 1048

B 1042

B 1058

B 1055

B 1065

B 1057

B 1057

B 1057

MYCENAEAN

PLATE 30

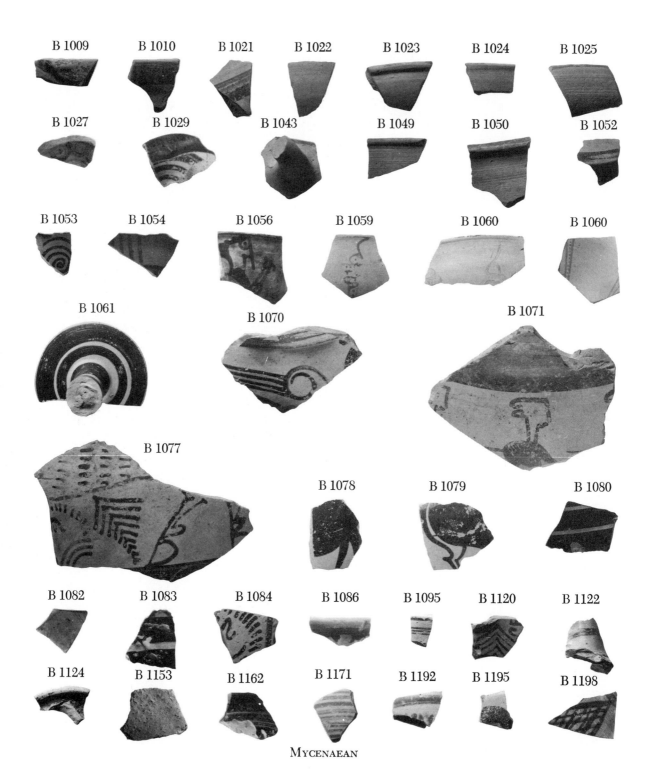

B 1009   B 1010   B 1021   B 1022   B 1023   B 1024   B 1025

B 1027   B 1029   B 1043   B 1049   B 1050   B 1052

B 1053   B 1054   B 1056   B 1059   B 1060   B 1060

B 1061   B 1070   B 1071

B 1077   B 1078   B 1079   B 1080

B 1082   B 1083   B 1084   B 1086   B 1095   B 1120   B 1122

B 1124   B 1153   B 1162   B 1171   B 1192   B 1195   B 1198

MYCENAEAN

Plate 31

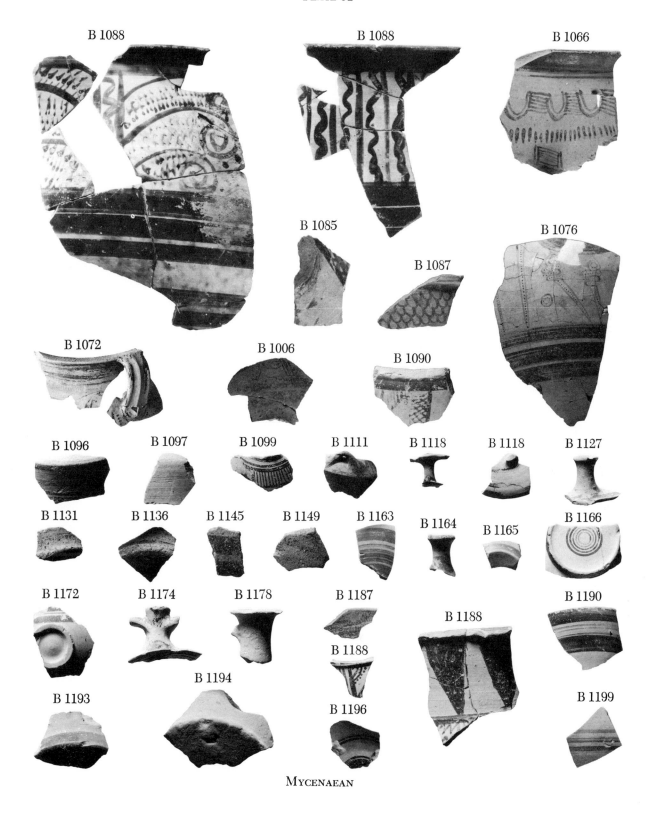

B 1088   B 1088   B 1066

B 1085

B 1087

B 1076

B 1072   B 1006   B 1090

B 1096   B 1097   B 1099   B 1111   B 1118   B 1118   B 1127

B 1131   B 1136   B 1145   B 1149   B 1163   B 1164   B 1165   B 1166

B 1172   B 1174   B 1178   B 1187   B 1188   B 1190

B 1188

B 1194

B 1193   B 1196   B 1199

MYCENAEAN

PLATE 32

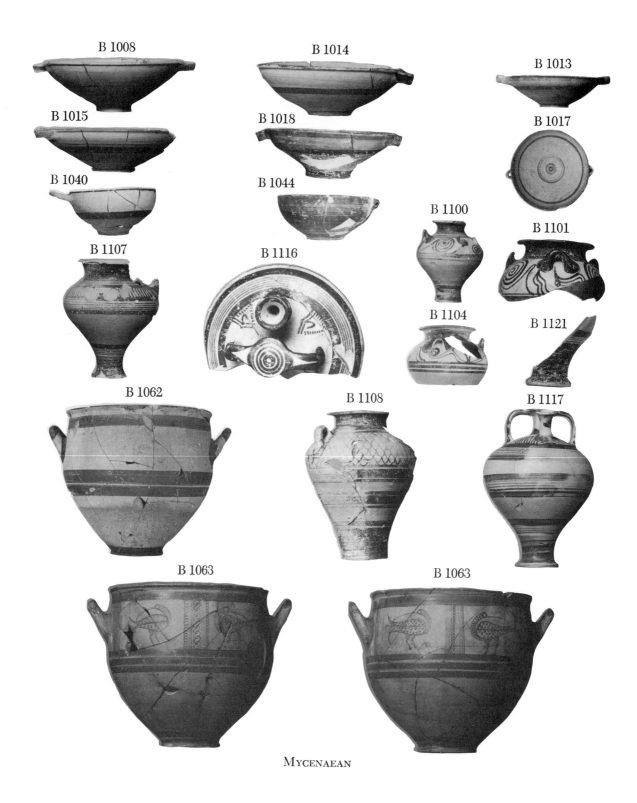

B 1008

B 1014

B 1013

B 1015

B 1018

B 1017

B 1040

B 1044

B 1100

B 1101

B 1107

B 1116

B 1104

B 1121

B 1062

B 1108

B 1117

B 1063

B 1063

MYCENAEAN

Plate 33

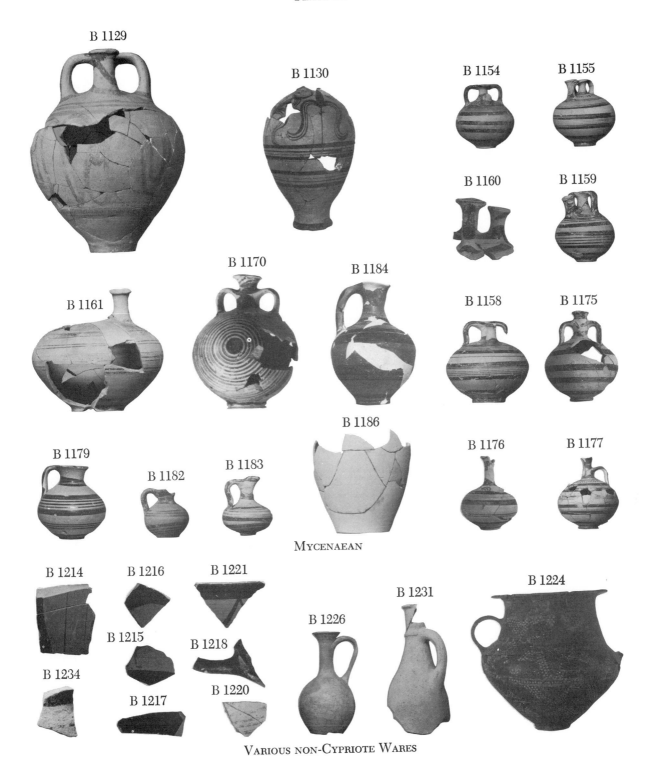

B 1129

B 1130

B 1154

B 1155

B 1160

B 1159

B 1161

B 1170

B 1184

B 1158

B 1175

B 1179

B 1182

B 1183

B 1186

B 1176

B 1177

Mycenaean

B 1214

B 1216

B 1221

B 1231

B 1224

B 1226

B 1215

B 1218

B 1234

B 1217

B 1220

Various non-Cypriote Wares

PLATE 34

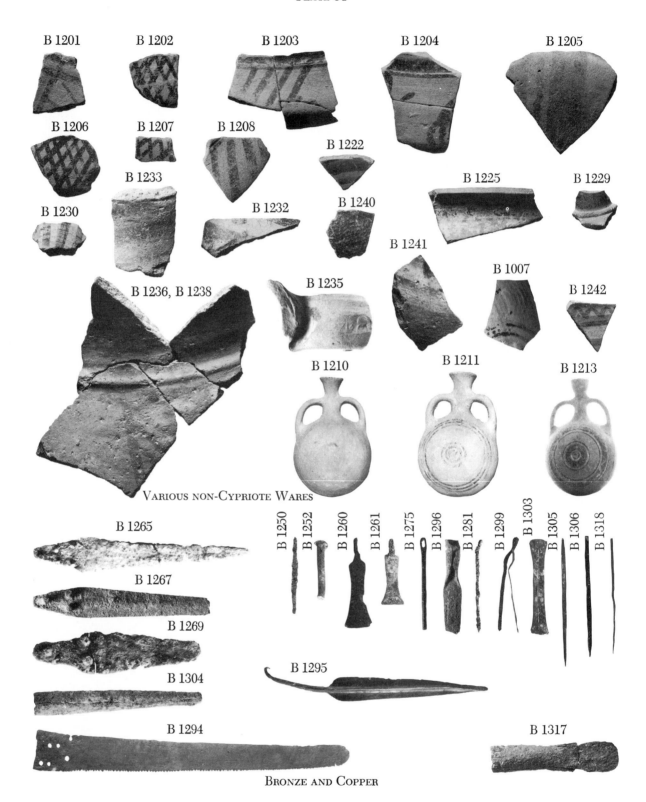

B 1201　　B 1202　　B 1203　　B 1204　　B 1205

B 1206　　B 1207　　B 1208

B 1222

B 1233

B 1230　　B 1232　　B 1240

B 1225　　B 1229

B 1241

B 1236, B 1238　　B 1235　　B 1007

B 1242

B 1210　　B 1211　　B 1213

VARIOUS NON-CYPRIOTE WARES

B 1265

B 1267

B 1269

B 1304

B 1295

B 1294

B 1250　B 1252　B 1260　B 1261　B 1275　B 1296　B 1281　B 1299　B 1303　B 1305　B 1306　B 1318

B 1317

BRONZE AND COPPER

PLATE 35

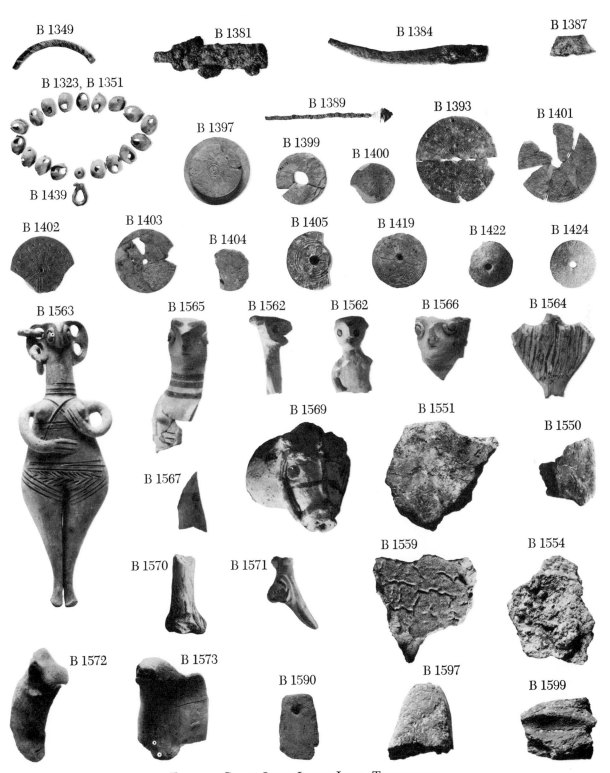

B 1349

B 1381

B 1384

B 1387

B 1323, B 1351

B 1389

B 1393

B 1401

B 1439

B 1397

B 1399

B 1400

B 1402

B 1403

B 1404

B 1405

B 1419

B 1422

B 1424

B 1563

B 1565

B 1562

B 1562

B 1566

B 1564

B 1569

B 1551

B 1550

B 1567

B 1559

B 1554

B 1570

B 1571

B 1572

B 1573

B 1590

B 1597

B 1599

FAIENCE, GLASS, IRON, IVORY, LEAD, TERRACOTTA

PLATE 36

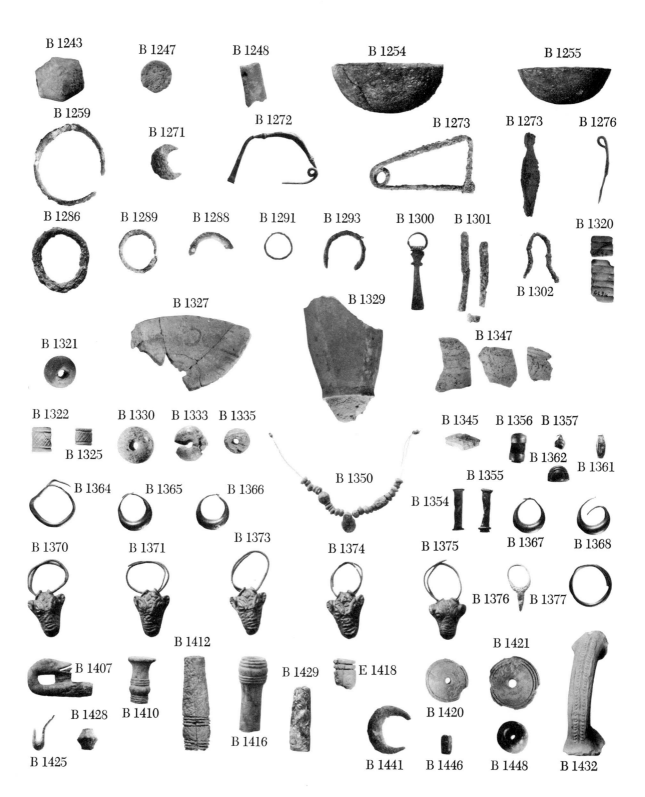

B 1243 B 1247 B 1248 B 1254 B 1255
B 1259 B 1271 B 1272 B 1273 B 1273 B 1276
B 1286 B 1289 B 1288 B 1291 B 1293 B 1300 B 1301 B 1320
B 1302
B 1327 B 1329 B 1347
B 1321
B 1322 B 1330 B 1333 B 1335 B 1345 B 1356 B 1357
B 1325 B 1362 B 1361
B 1355
B 1364 B 1365 B 1366 B 1350 B 1354 B 1367 B 1368
B 1375
B 1370 B 1371 B 1373 B 1374 B 1376 B 1377
B 1412 B 1421
B 1407 B 1429 E 1418
B 1428 B 1410 B 1420
B 1425 B 1416 B 1441 B 1446 B 1448 B 1432

ALABASTER, BONE, BRONZE, FAIENCE, GLASS, GOLD, IVORY, LEAD, SEAL IMPRESSION, SILVER, STONE

PLATE 37

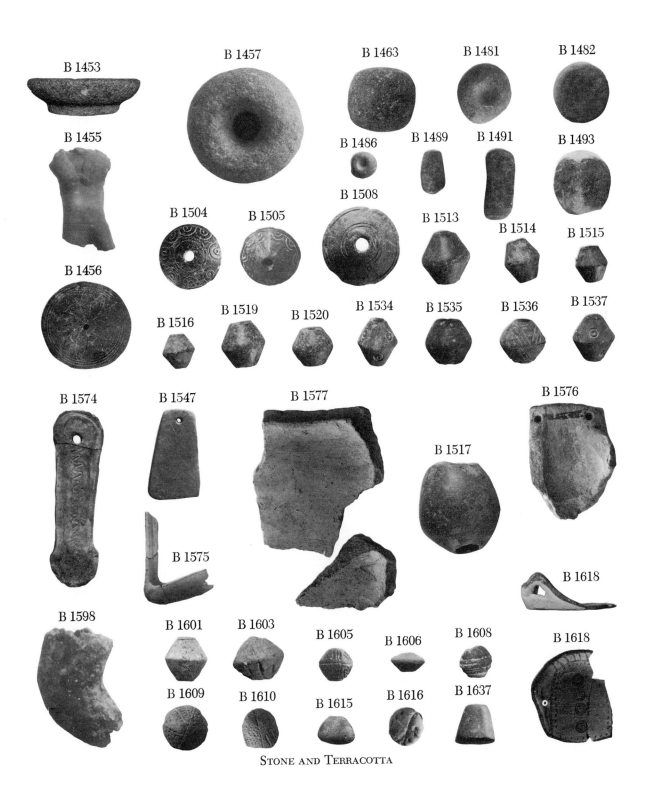

B 1453

B 1457

B 1463

B 1481

B 1482

B 1455

B 1486

B 1489

B 1491

B 1493

B 1456

B 1504

B 1505

B 1508

B 1513

B 1514

B 1515

B 1516

B 1519

B 1520

B 1534

B 1535

B 1536

B 1537

B 1574

B 1547

B 1577

B 1576

B 1517

B 1575

B 1618

B 1598

B 1601

B 1603

B 1605

B 1606

B 1608

B 1618

B 1609

B 1610

B 1615

B 1616

B 1637

STONE AND TERRACOTTA

PLATE 38

B 1622

B 1623

B 1624

B 1625

B 1626

B 1627

B 1628

B 1629

B 1630

B 1638

B 1631   B 1632

B 1636

B 1639

B 1633   B 1634

B 1635

GLYPTICS

PLATE 39

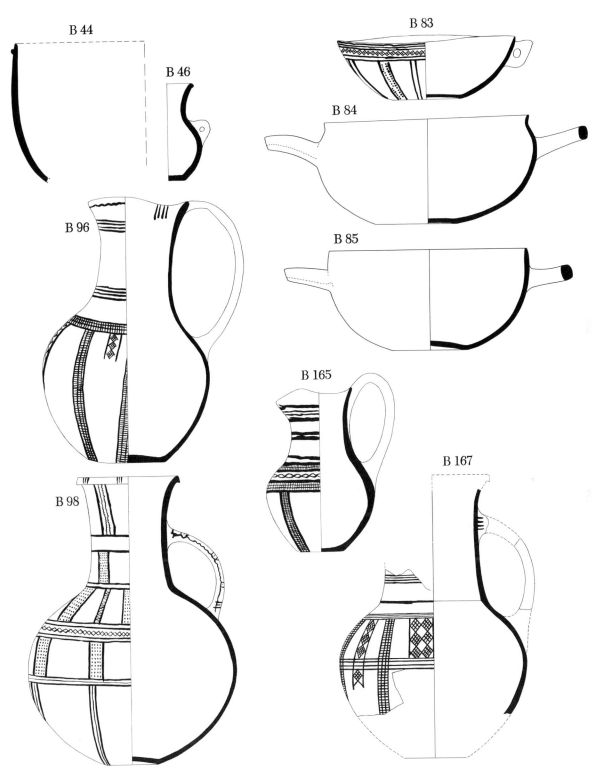

B 44

B 46

B 83

B 84

B 85

B 96

B 165

B 167

B 98

RED POLISHED, WHITE SLIP I AND II

Plate 40

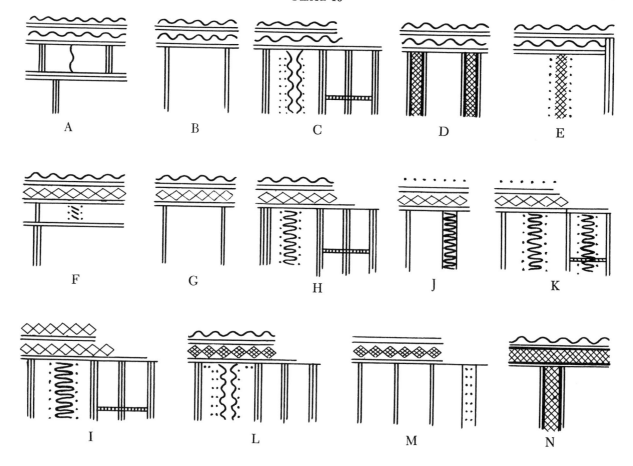

White Slip I

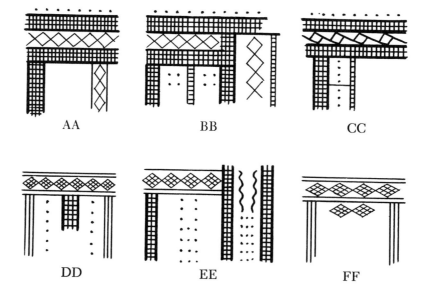

White Slip II

PLATE 41

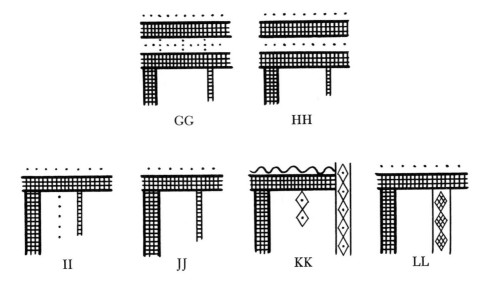

GG HH

II JJ KK LL

MM

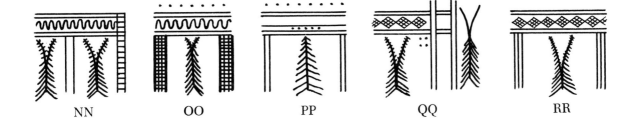

NN OO PP QQ RR

WHITE SLIP II

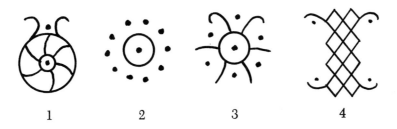

1 2 3 4

FILL ORNAMENTS

PLATE 42

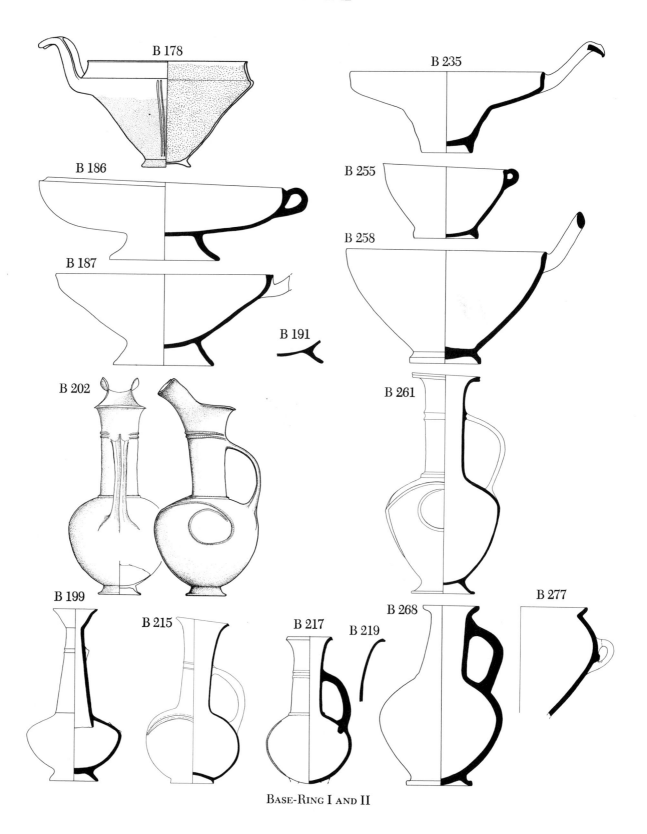

B 178

B 235

B 186

B 255

B 187

B 258

B 191

B 202

B 261

B 199

B 215

B 217

B 219

B 268

B 277

BASE-RING I AND II

PLATE 43

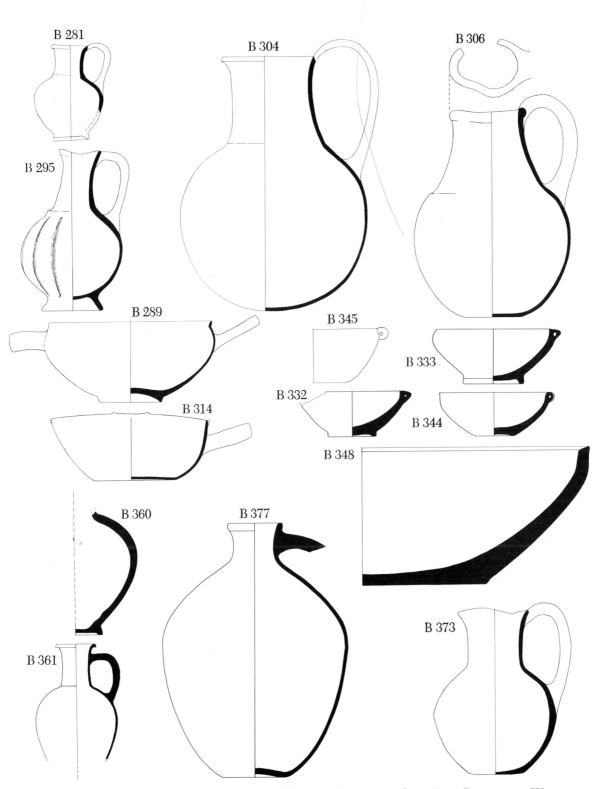

B 281

B 304

B 306

B 295

B 289

B 345

B 333

B 332

B 344

B 314

B 348

B 360

B 377

B 373

B 361

HANDMADE BUCCHERO, MONOCHROME, FUSED TEMPER, BURNISHED SLIP, PINK BURNISHED, WASH

PLATE 44

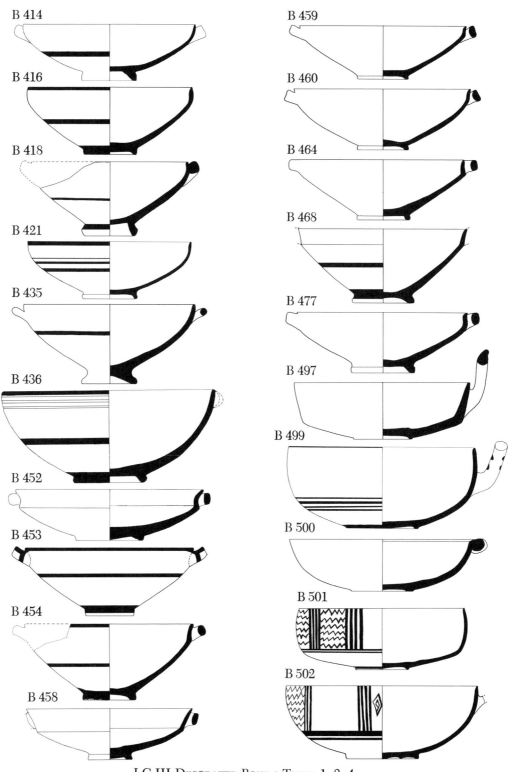

B 414
B 416
B 418
B 421
B 435
B 436
B 452
B 453
B 454
B 458

B 459
B 460
B 464
B 468
B 477
B 497
B 499
B 500
B 501
B 502

LC III DECORATED BOWLS TYPES 1, 3, 4

PLATE 45

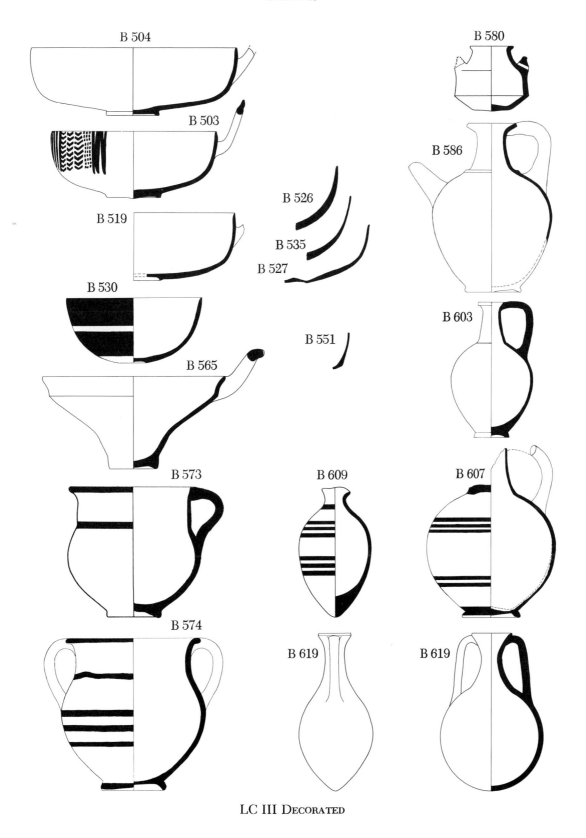

B 504

B 503

B 519

B 526

B 535

B 527

B 530

B 565

B 551

B 573

B 609

B 607

B 574

B 619

B 619

B 580

B 586

B 603

LC III DECORATED

Plate 46

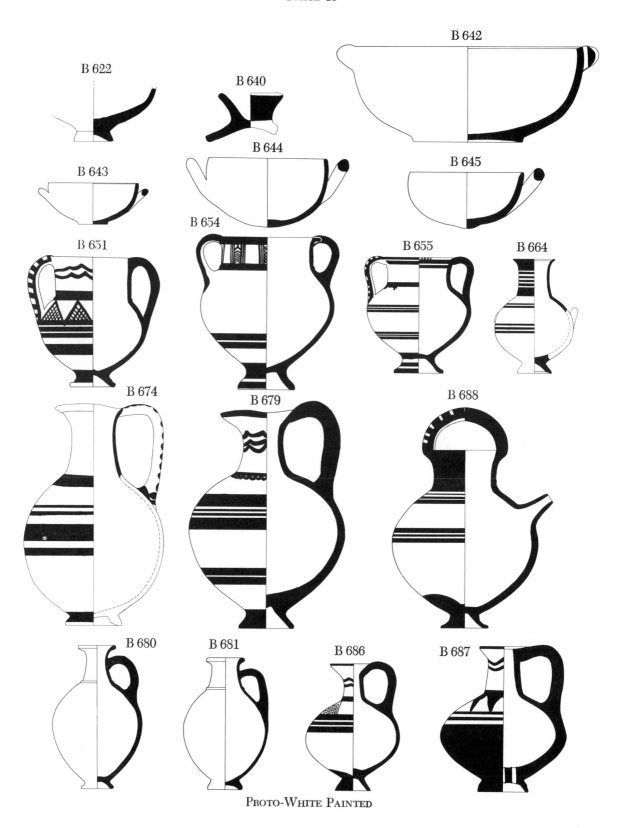

B 642

B 622

B 640

B 643

B 644

B 645

B 651

B 654

B 655

B 664

B 674

B 679

B 688

B 680

B 681

B 686

B 687

Proto-White Painted

PLATE 47

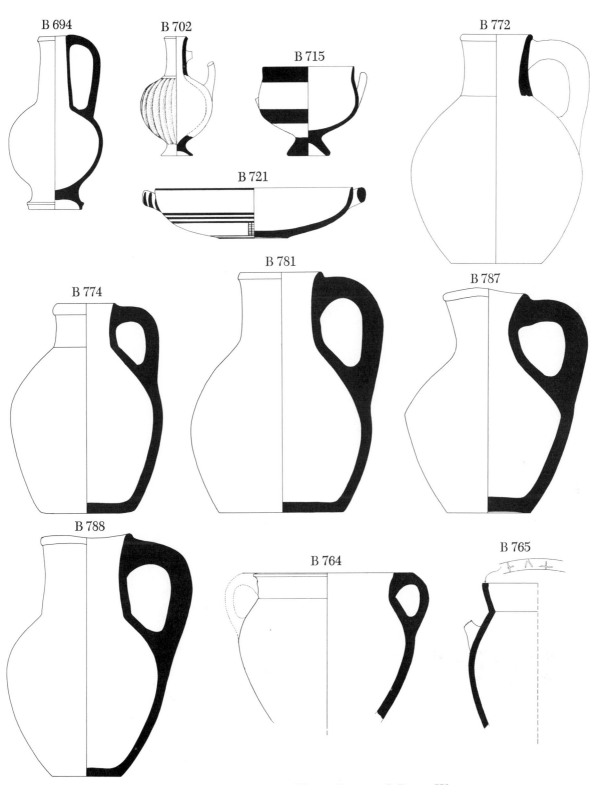

B 694

B 702

B 715

B 721

B 772

B 774

B 781

B 787

B 788

B 764

B 765

LC III BLACK SLIP BUCCHERO, WHITE PAINTED I, PLAIN WHITE

PLATE 48

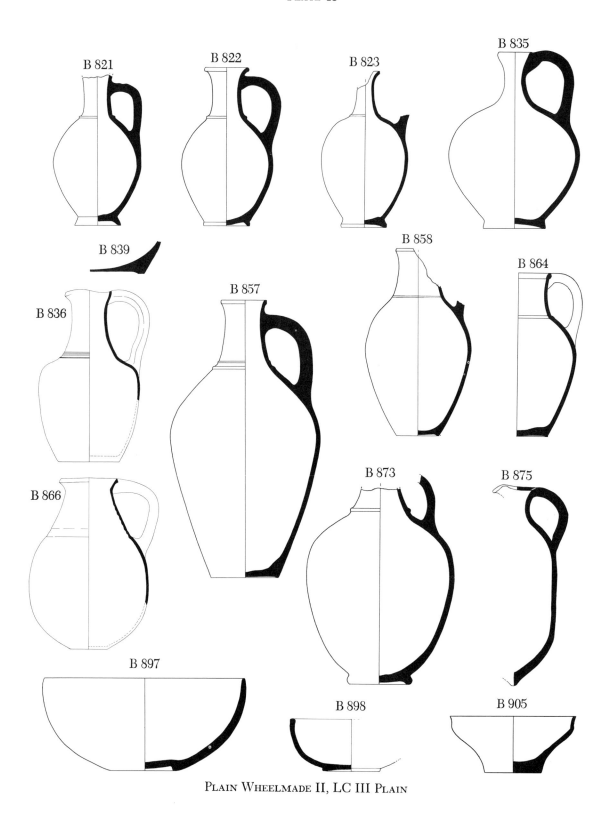

B 821

B 822

B 823

B 835

B 839

B 858

B 864

B 836

B 857

B 866

B 873

B 875

B 897

B 898

B 905

PLAIN WHEELMADE II, LC III PLAIN

Plate 49

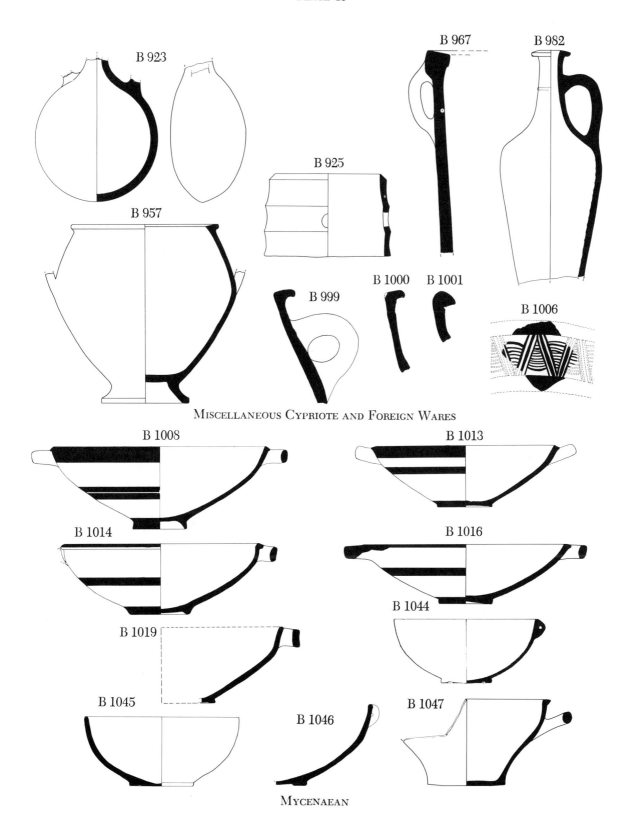

B 923

B 967   B 982

B 925

B 957

B 999   B 1000   B 1001

B 1006

Miscellaneous Cypriote and Foreign Wares

B 1008   B 1013

B 1014   B 1016

B 1019   B 1044

B 1045   B 1046   B 1047

Mycenaean

Plate 50

B 1092

B 1093

B 1094

B 1062

B 1102

B 1103

B 1105

B 1106

B 1108

B 1156

B 1177

B 1179

B 1180

B 1181

B 1188

B 1189

Mycenaean

PLATE 51

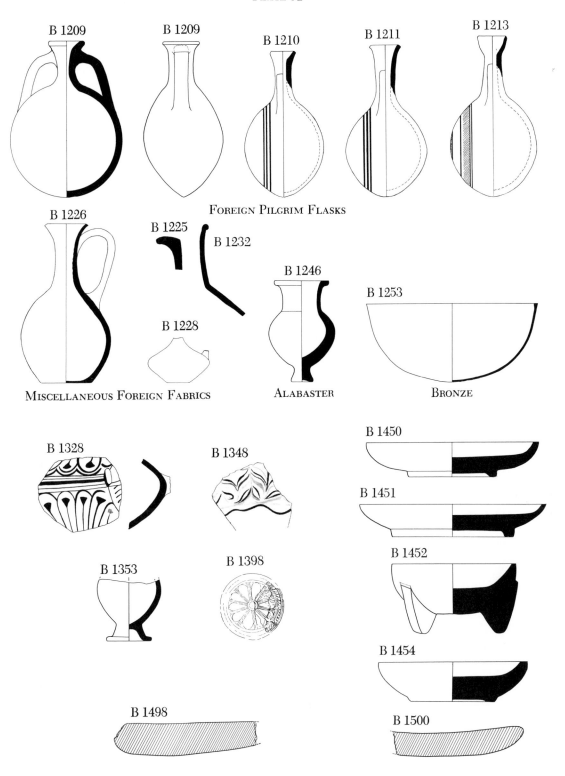

B 1209   B 1209   B 1210   B 1211   B 1213

FOREIGN PILGRIM FLASKS

B 1226   B 1225   B 1232   B 1246   B 1253

B 1228

MISCELLANEOUS FOREIGN FABRICS   ALABASTER   BRONZE

B 1450

B 1328   B 1348   B 1451

B 1452

B 1353   B 1398   B 1454

B 1498   B 1500

FAIENCE, GLASS, IVORY, STONE

PLATE 52

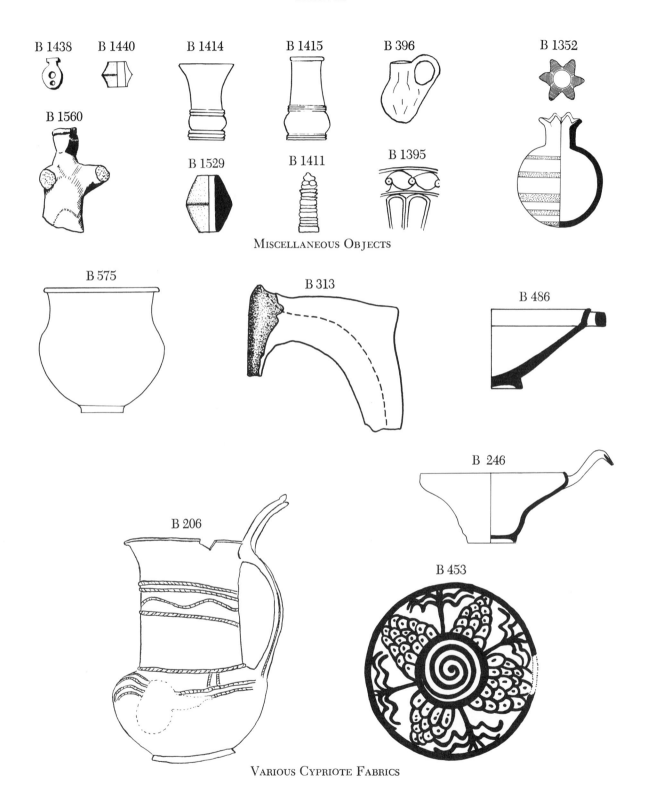

B 1438   B 1440   B 1414   B 1415   B 396   B 1352

B 1560

            B 1529   B 1411   B 1395

MISCELLANEOUS OBJECTS

B 575   B 313   B 486

                                                                    B 246

B 206

                                                              B 453

VARIOUS CYPRIOTE FABRICS

PLATE 53

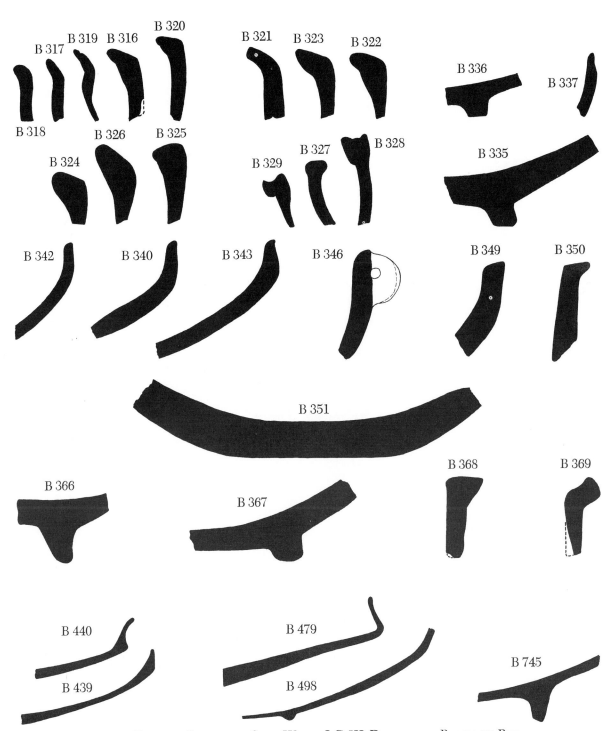

B 317 B 319 B 316 B 320 B 321 B 323 B 322 B 336 B 337 B 318 B 326 B 325 B 324 B 329 B 327 B 328 B 335 B 342 B 340 B 343 B 346 B 349 B 350 B 351 B 366 B 367 B 368 B 369 B 440 B 479 B 439 B 498 B 745

FUSED TEMPER, BURNISHED SLIP, WASH, LC III DECORATED, BLACK-ON-RED

PLATE 54

B 996

B 1117

B 1104

B 1184

B 1005

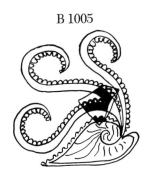

B 1326

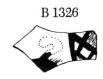

B 1047

Piraeus Museum Mycenaean bowl from Boula

British Museum C 722 Cypriote imitation of
Mycenaean bowl

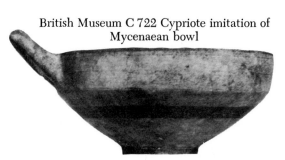

VARIOUS NON-CYPRIOTE WARES

PLATE 55

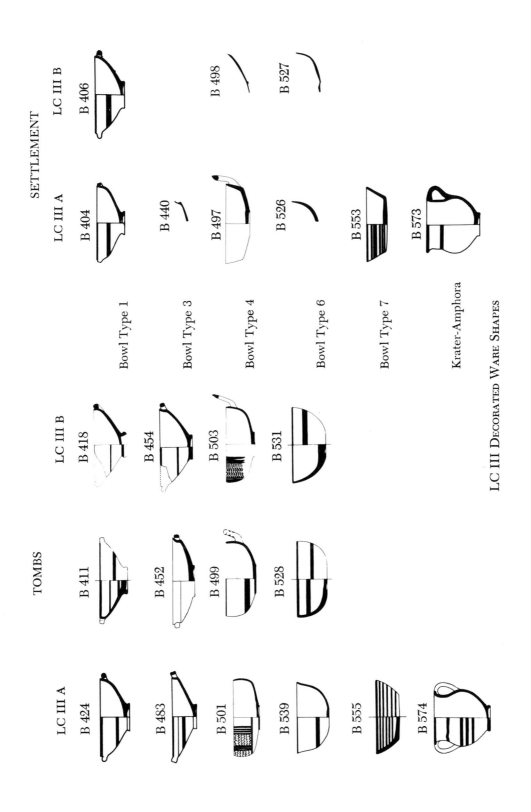

SETTLEMENT

LC III B

B 406

B 498

B 527

LC III A

B 404

B 440

B 497

B 526

B 553

B 573

Bowl Type 1

Bowl Type 3

Bowl Type 4

Bowl Type 6

Bowl Type 7

Krater-Amphora

LC III DECORATED WARE SHAPES

LC III B

B 418

B 454

B 503

B 531

TOMBS

B 411

B 452

B 499

B 528

LC III A

B 424

B 483

B 501

B 539

B 555

B 574

PLATE 56

LC III Decorated Ware Shapes

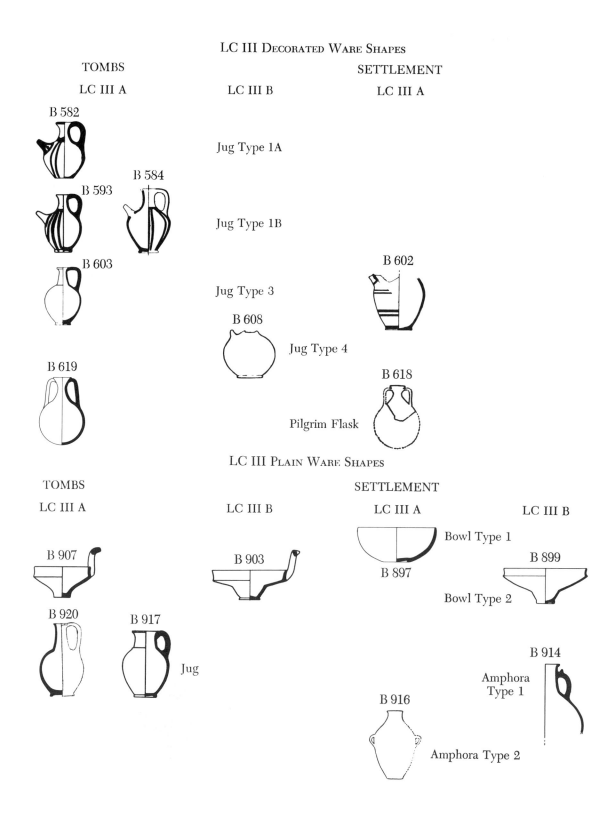

TOMBS

SETTLEMENT

LC III A

LC III B

LC III A

B 582

Jug Type 1A

B 593

B 584

Jug Type 1B

B 603

B 602

Jug Type 3

B 608

Jug Type 4

B 619

B 618

Pilgrim Flask

LC III Plain Ware Shapes

TOMBS

SETTLEMENT

LC III A

LC III B

LC III A

LC III B

Bowl Type 1

B 907

B 903

B 897

B 899

Bowl Type 2

B 920

B 917

B 914

Jug

Amphora
Type 1

B 916

Amphora Type 2

PLATE 57

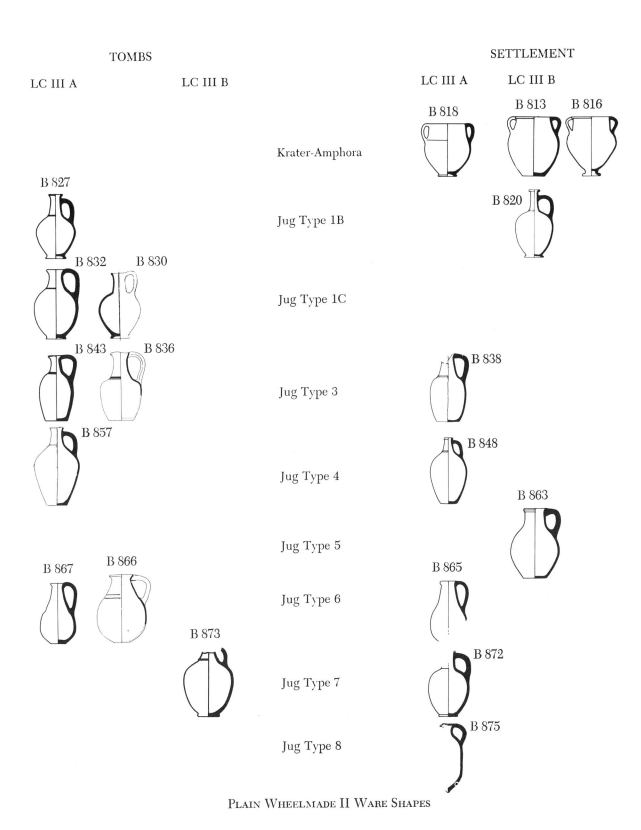

TOMBS

SETTLEMENT

LC III A

LC III B

LC III A

LC III B

B 818

B 813

B 816

Krater-Amphora

B 827

Jug Type 1B

B 820

B 832

B 830

Jug Type 1C

B 843

B 836

Jug Type 3

B 838

B 857

Jug Type 4

B 848

Jug Type 5

B 863

B 867

B 866

Jug Type 6

B 865

B 873

Jug Type 7

B 872

Jug Type 8

B 875

PLAIN WHEELMADE II WARE SHAPES

PLATE 58

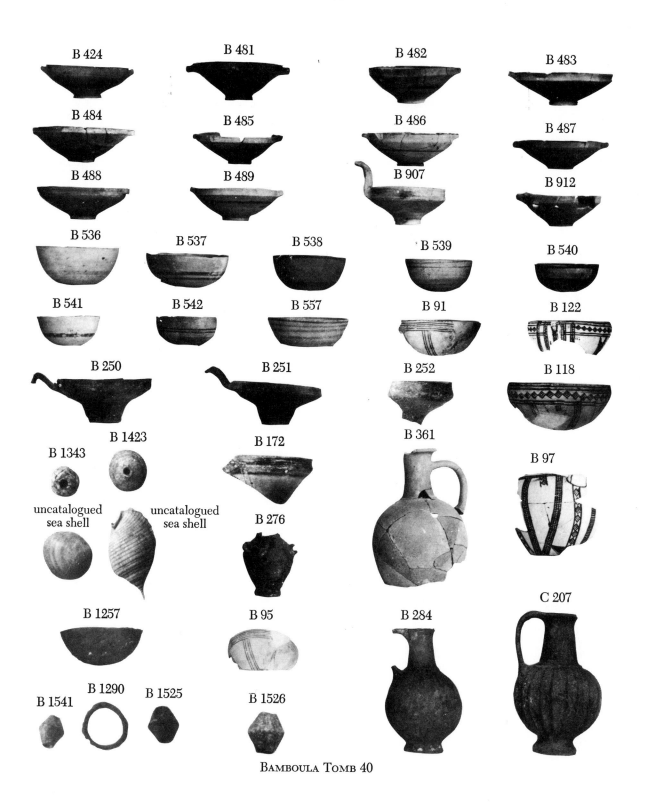

B 424   B 481   B 482   B 483

B 484   B 485   B 486   B 487

B 488   B 489   B 907   B 912

B 536   B 537   B 538   B 539   B 540

B 541   B 542   B 557   B 91   B 122

B 250   B 251   B 252   B 118

B 1343   B 1423   B 172   B 361   B 97

uncatalogued sea shell   uncatalogued sea shell   B 276

C 207

B 1257   B 95   B 284

B 1541   B 1290   B 1525   B 1526

BAMBOULA TOMB 40

PLATE 59

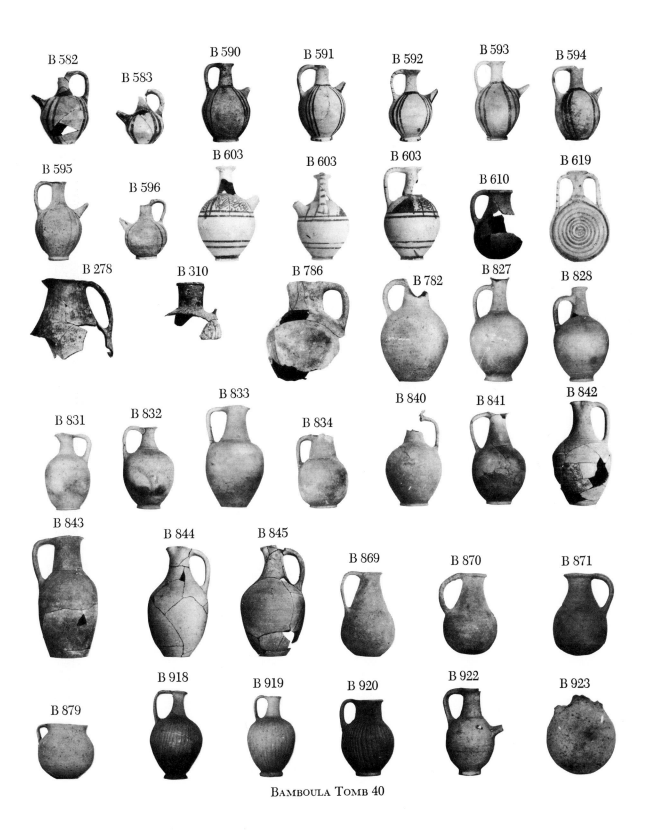

B 582

B 583

B 590

B 591

B 592

B 593

B 594

B 595

B 596

B 603

B 603

B 603

B 610

B 619

B 278

B 310

B 786

B 782

B 827

B 828

B 831

B 832

B 833

B 834

B 840

B 841

B 842

B 843

B 844

B 845

B 869

B 870

B 871

B 879

B 918

B 919

B 920

B 922

B 923

BAMBOULA TOMB 40

PLATE 60

BAMBOULA TOMB 33

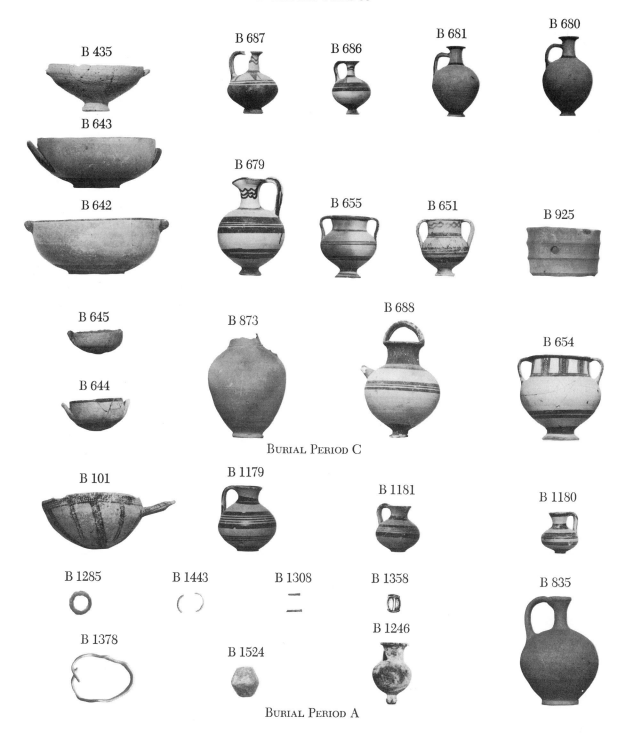

B 435

B 687

B 686

B 681

B 680

B 643

B 642

B 679

B 655

B 651

B 925

B 645

B 873

B 688

B 654

B 644

BURIAL PERIOD C

B 101

B 1179

B 1181

B 1180

B 1285

B 1443

B 1308

B 1358

B 835

B 1246

B 1378

B 1524

BURIAL PERIOD A

PLATE 61

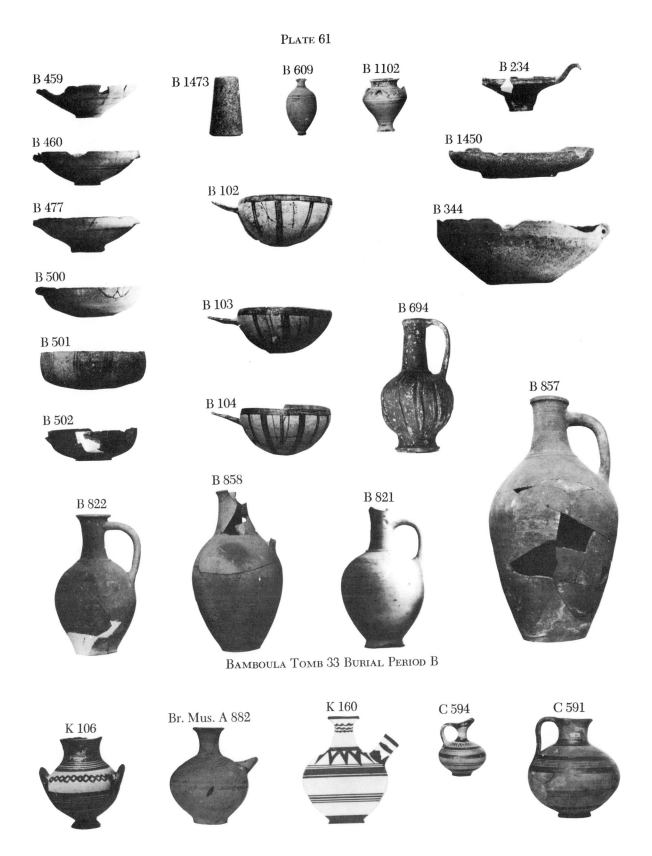

B 459
B 1473
B 609
B 1102
B 234
B 460
B 1450
B 477
B 102
B 344
B 500
B 103
B 694
B 501
B 857
B 502
B 104
B 858
B 821
B 822

BAMBOULA TOMB 33 BURIAL PERIOD B

K 106
Br. Mus. A 882
K 160
C 594
C 591

MATERIALS PERTINENT TO THE STUDY OF LC III POTTERY

PLATE 62

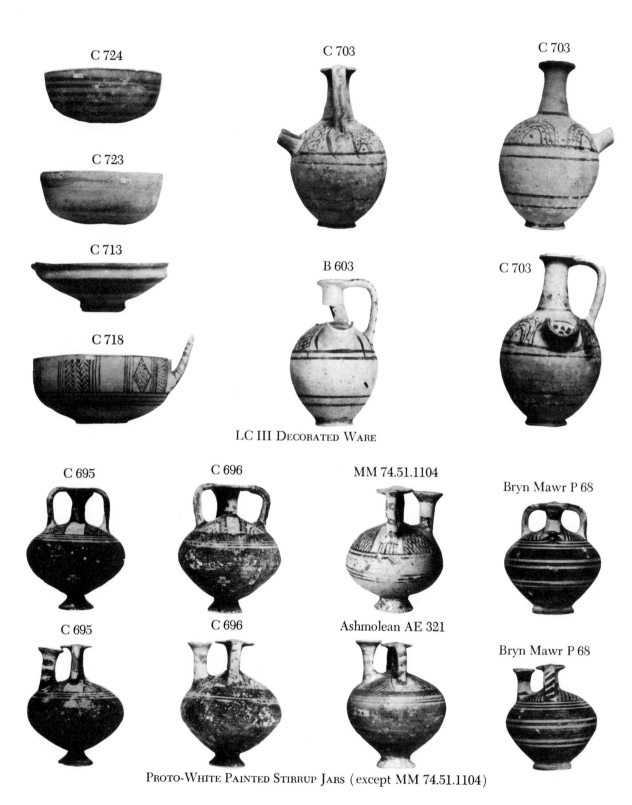

C 724

C 723

C 713

C 718

C 703

C 703

B 603

C 703

LC III DECORATED WARE

C 695

C 696

MM 74.51.1104

Bryn Mawr P 68

C 695

C 696

Ashmolean AE 321

Bryn Mawr P 68

PROTO-WHITE PAINTED STIRRUP JARS (except MM 74.51.1104)

PLATE 63

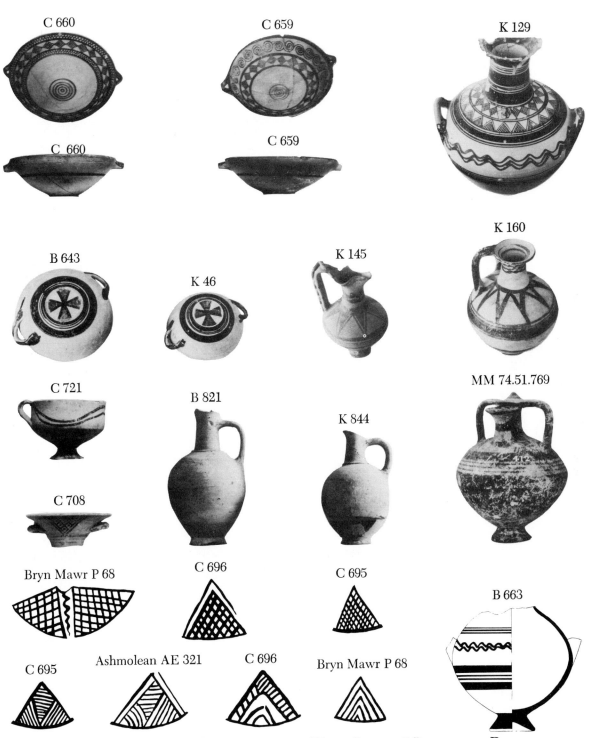

C 660

C 659

K 129

C 660

C 659

B 643

K 46

K 145

K 160

C 721

B 821

K 844

MM 74.51.769

C 708

Bryn Mawr P 68

C 696

C 695

B 663

C 695

Ashmolean AE 321

C 696

Bryn Mawr P 68

LC III Decorated, Proto-White Painted and White Painted I Pottery and Decoration

PLATE 64

LC III Decorated Bowl Patterns

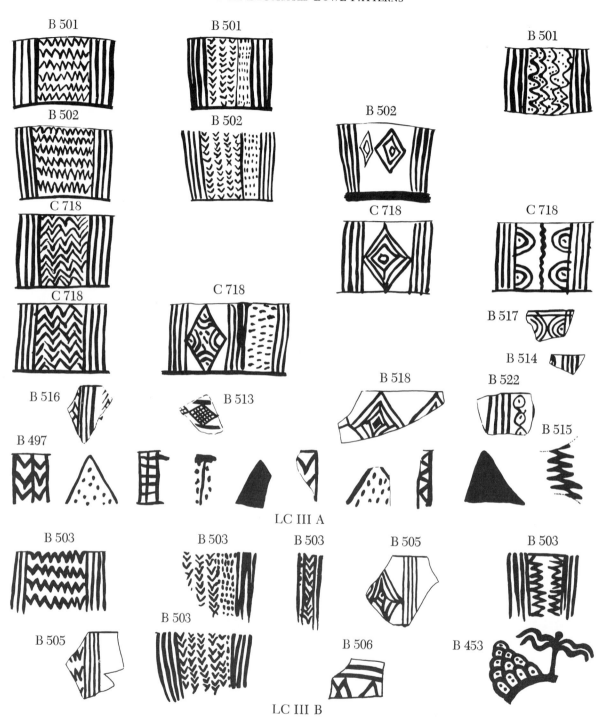

B 501   B 501   B 501
B 502   B 502   B 502
C 718   C 718   C 718
C 718   C 718   B 517
                B 514
B 516   B 513   B 518   B 522
B 497   B 515

LC III A

B 503   B 503   B 503   B 505   B 503
B 505   B 503   B 506   B 453

LC III B

PLATE 65

B 603

C 703

C 703

B 579

B 579

B 610

B 569

B 569

B 578

B 569

Jugs and Kraters

B 511   B 509   B 562   B 520   B 519   B 510

Bowls, mostly unstratified

LC III DECORATED WARE DESIGNS

PLATE 66

B 624 B 623 B 626 B 625
B 658 B 670 B 691 B 656 B 656
B 662 B 634 B 635 B 629 B 665
B 648 B 634 B 650 B 649 B 671
B 654 B 654 B 654 B 681
B 644
B 667 B 666

PROTO-WHITE PAINTED PATTERNS: BOWLS ABOVE; OTHER SHAPES LOWER HALF

PLATE 67

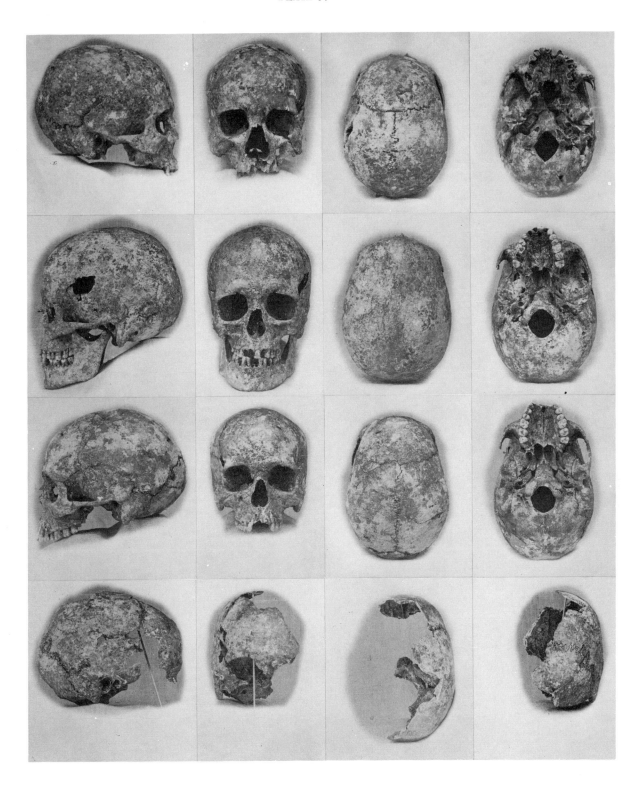

Undeformed male skulls of relatively linear form. From above down: 19-27, 19-35, 19-43, and 19-30 CCB

PLATE 68

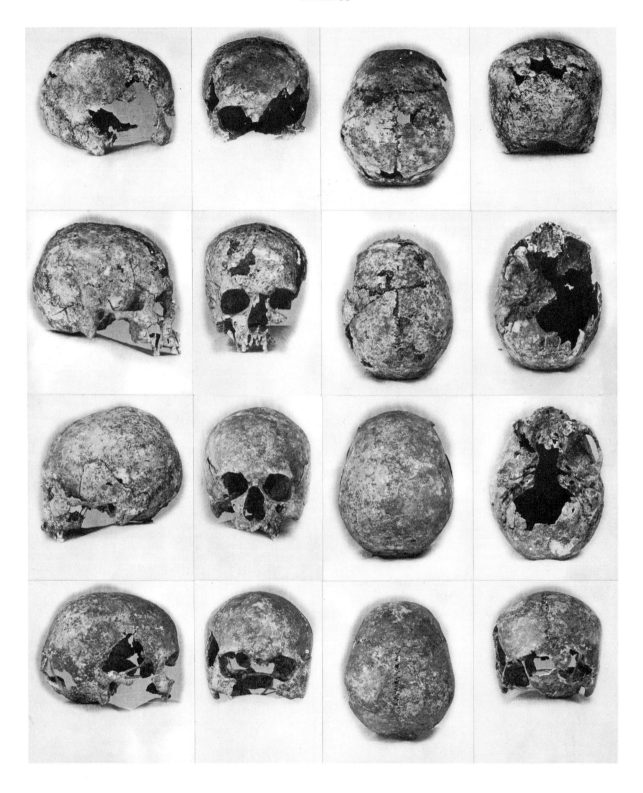

Undeformed male skulls of relatively lateral form. From above down: 19-3, 19-34, 19-42, and 5-1 CCB

PLATE 69

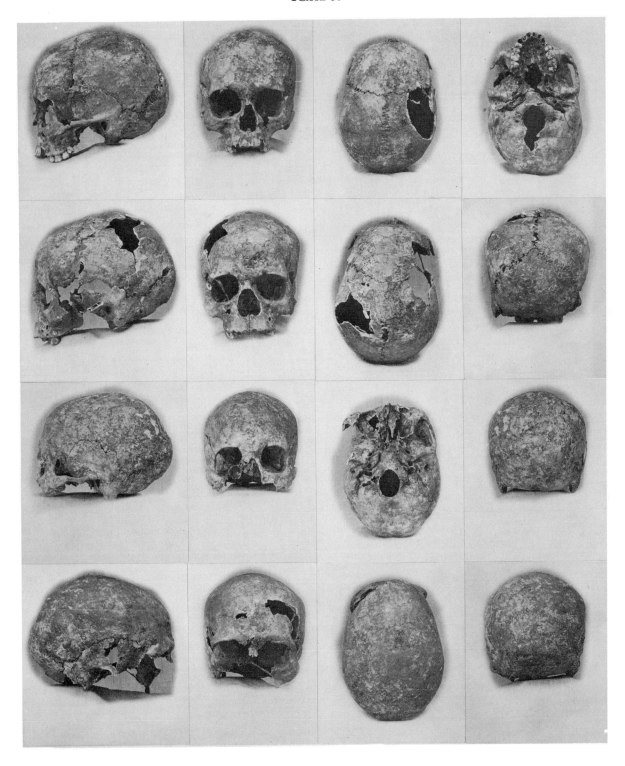

Undeformed female skulls and a male, bottom, of Basic White type, all relatively linear. From top to bottom: 21-1, 21-3, 19-41, and 5-2 CCB

PLATE 70

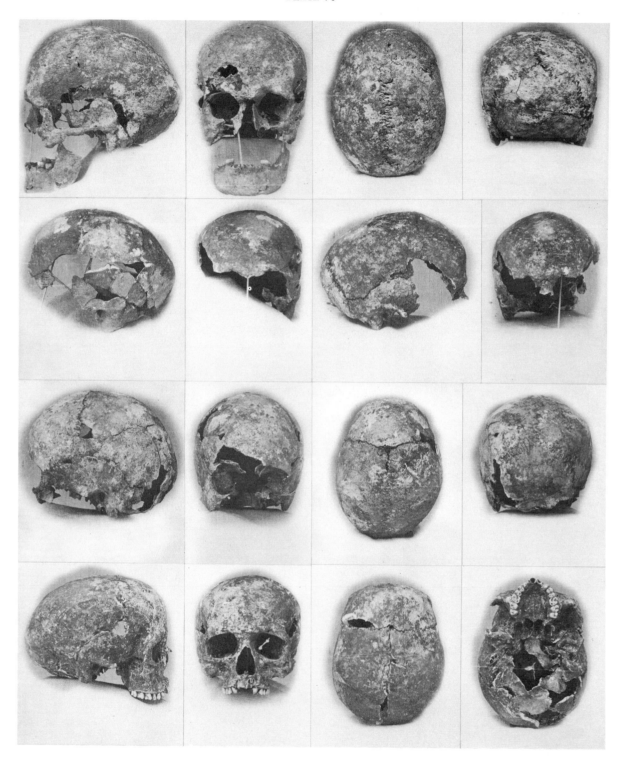

Deformed male skulls of types A and E. From top to bottom: 6-2, 18-1 (left), 18-5 (right), 19-31 (adolescent), and 5-3 CCB

PLATE 71

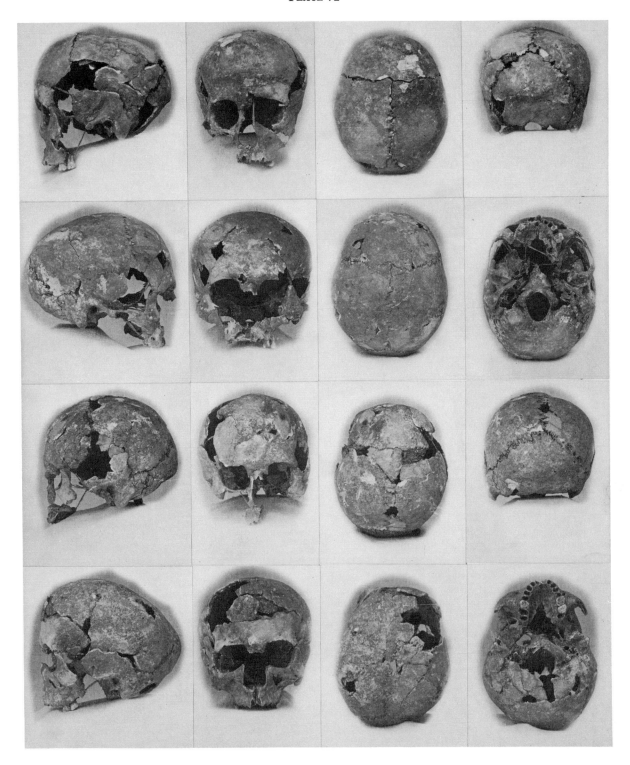

Deformed skulls of types F, C, and E, relatively lateral in form, male except for the top one. From top to bottom: 19-48 (female), 19-47, 19-50, 6-1 CCB

PLATE 72

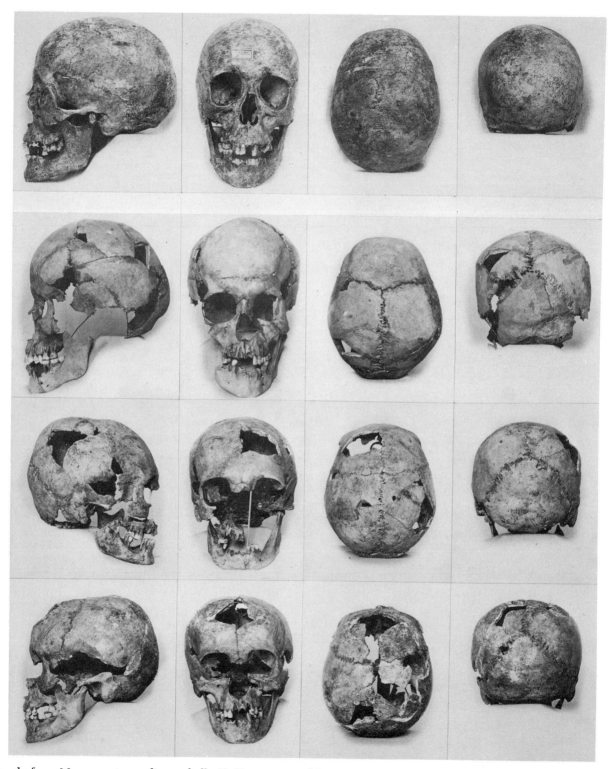

People from Mycenae: top, a linear skull, 40 *Myc*, excavated by Tsountas in 1899, comparable with Bamboula skulls in Pl. 67. 80, 78, and 81 *Myc* from above down, excavated by A. J. B. Wace in 1953 from a well in the Cyclopean Terrace Building; 80 *Myc* is comparable with 19-48 *CCB*, and Melia (Ayios Yakovos).

PLATE 73

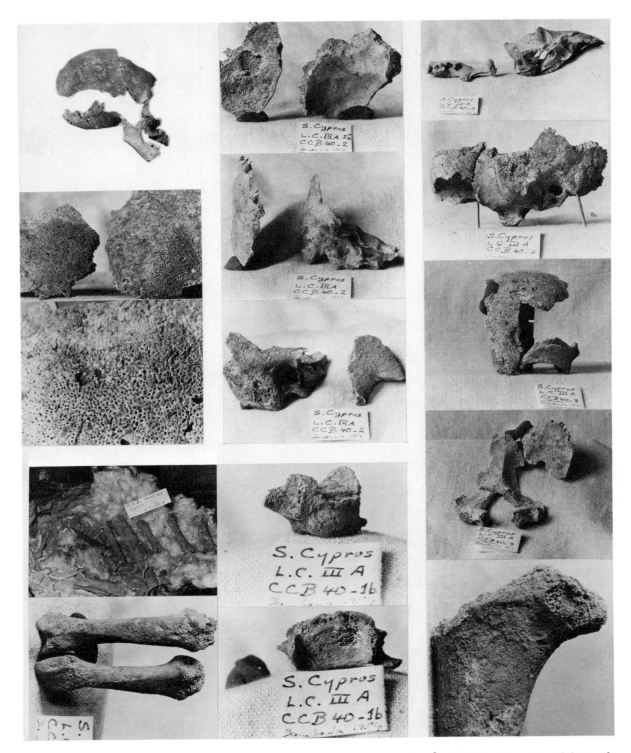

Tomb 40: top left No. 1, to show probably linear skull and osteoporosis; bottom left No. 1b, male adult, to show metacarpals and cervical vertebra with slight arthritis; top center, occipitals, temporal and smooth glabella region of 2a and 2; and right, left half of base, frontal and occipital of No. 3 to show thickening, and tympanic plate perforation, and upper end of femur to show area of slight neck erosion and growth zones for head and great trochanter.

PLATE 74

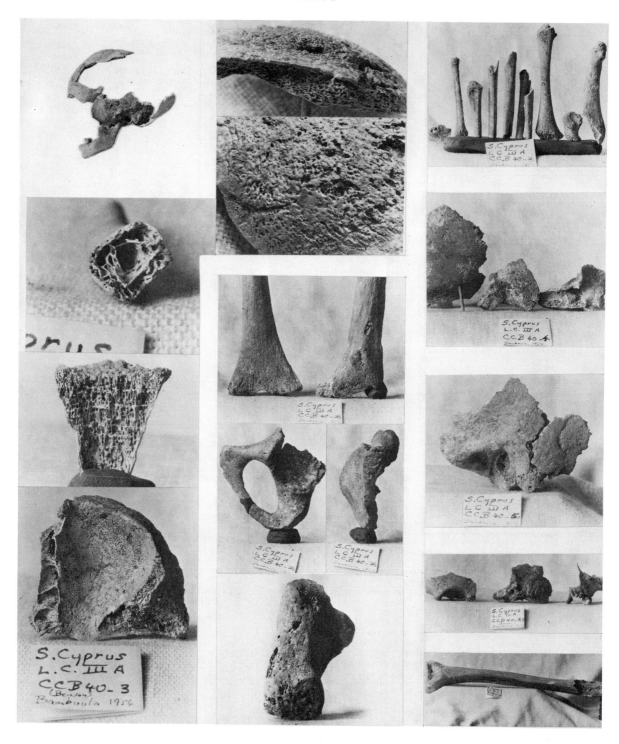

Tomb 40: left side No. 3, continued, showing cranial osteoporosis, "double" shaft of ulna from bone-forming imbalance in any hemolytic anemia, upper end of tibia with lines of arrested growth, reflecting illness each year or so. Center, No. 3b. Right, 3c, d, 4, 5a, 6, 8, 11.